PELAGIUS

LIFE AND LETTERS

PELAGIUS

LIFE AND LETTERS

B. R. Rees

THE BOYDELL PRESS

First published in two separate volumes

Pelagius: A Reluctant Heretic
First published 1988
Reprinted in hardback and paperback 1991

The Letters of Pelagius and His Followers
First published 1991

The Boydell Press, Woodbridge

Reprinted in one volume 1998

Transferred to digital printing

ISBN 978-0-85115-714-6

The Boydell Press is an imprint of Boydell & Brewer Ltd
PO Box 9, Woodbridge, Suffolk IP12 3DF, UK
and of Boydell & Brewer Inc.
668 Mt Hope Avenue, Rochester, NY 14620, USA
website: www.boydellandbrewer.com

A CiP catalogue record for this book is available
from the British Library

This publication is printed on acid-free paper

Contents

Preface to the 1998 Edition

The more one reads about the 'monk' Pelagius and the so-called 'Pelagian Controversy' the more conscious one becomes of the urgent need for an up-to-date account of what actually happened between Pelagius and his opponents. Students of history and church doctrine as well as the general reader need to be alerted to the results of scholarly research over the last four or five decades. Pelagius has been given a bad press over the centuries, of this there can be no doubt.

In the course of writing *Pelagius: a Reluctant Heretic* (the volume which forms the first part of this book) I became increasingly aware that very few of the Pelagian texts to which I was referring were available in an English translation. I hope that the second part of this book will make good that deficiency. Readers will find in it versions of all the letters and homilies in letter form which can be attributed with reasonable certainty to Pelagius and his followers; one or two sometimes included in Pelagian bibliographies are excluded only because I do not consider them eligible and one or two which are included are marginal cases. I have rendered the texts as simply and clearly as possible; the footnotes are not intended to do more than give internal cross-references.

I wish to thank my friend Gerald Bonner for encouraging me to write these books; my publishers for undertaking this venture and maintaining their usual high standards of production; Jean Walcot for her patience in turning my script into first-class copy; and, last but by no means least, my loving wife for her unfailing and uncomplaining support.

Volume I

Pelagius: A Reluctant Heretic

For my dear wife, Zena

Introit

'I have become a great theologian in a short time,
and you are going to see the evidence of it.'

BLAISE PASCAL[1]

Pascal made this claim, no doubt with tongue in cheek, soon after beginning
his Socratic cross-examination of the learned doctors of the Sorbonne in order
to establish the precise difference between them on the subject of divine grace
and its relation to free will; but it was not long before he found himself totally
disillusioned with their sophistry and decided to abandon the reasons of the
mind for those of the heart.[2] I make no such claim even in jest; indeed, I have
to confess that there have been times when my own modest attempt to
comprehend the issues and ramifications of the first great debate on the same
subject has left me feeling just as nonplussed as Pascal and rather like poor
old Kaspar must have felt when asked to explain the causes of the Battle of
Blenheim. Small wonder! Confusion has surrounded both Pelagius and
Pelagianism ever since, and even before, the heresiarch's condemnation. For
centuries now the adjective 'Pelagian' has been a convenient term of abuse in
the Christian Church and Pelagius himself a bogyman for upright clerics to
evoke when wanting to frighten wayward members of their flock. John
Cassian, Vincent of Lérins and Faustus of Riez in the fifth century, Erigena in
the ninth, Alexander of Hales, Peter Abelard, Duns Scotus and Thomas
Aquinas in the twelfth and thirteenth, William of Ockham in the fourteenth,
Melanchthon and Arminius in the sixteenth, John Wesley in the eighteenth,
Teilhard de Chardin in the twentieth – all in turn have been dubbed
'Pelagian', 'Semi-Pelagian' or 'Synergist', treated as victims of the same
disease and consigned to ecclesiastical quarantine, and even that 'battered
liberal' Erasmus did not enjoy complete immunity from it. Christians in the
West seem to have been peculiarly susceptible to attacks of the virus: in
fourteenth-century England Archbishop Thomas Bradwardine detected a
Pelagian hiding beneath every academic gown, just as Reinhold Niebuhr in
twentieth-century America saw Pelagians in every pew: Pelagianism has often
been described as 'the English disease', and we are told that by the early years
of the present century the United States had 'gradually made its way, from

---

[1] *Les Provinciales*, ed. L. Cognet, *Garnier Frères*, 1965, i. 8.
[2] Unamuno, 23, comments that Kant too 'reconstructed with the heart that which with the
head he had overthrown'.

being the most Calvinist, to being the most Pelagian of Christian nations.'[3]

Pelagianism is indeed an ever-recurring temptation and has survived all the onslaughts of its adversaries to challenge Arianism for the dubious honour of having been the most persistent of Christian heresies. How many members of the average congregation today realise that not a few elements of the services which they attend are still being criticised as 'Pelagian'? Anglicans, for example, if challenged on the subject, might well reply, 'Oh no! we are using the *ASB*!' But it is precisely the *Alternative Service Book 1980* which came under fire a few years ago from a Professor of Ecclesiastical History on the grounds that much, too much, of its liturgy is Pelagian.[4] Prayers, it is claimed, asking God for some moral of spiritual improvement are in fact calculated to urge the worshipper only to *self*-improvement, and even in the *ASB* version of the famous Franciscan prayer 'Pelagius prevails'. The author of the article referred to, summarised in *The Times* under the heading 'Old Heresy clouds New Liturgy', is clearly not only against the *ASB* but also against Pelagius, and for the traditional, Augustinian reason that no good human action is possible without the grace of God to inspire and sustain it. One is reminded of the comment of a writer already quoted that, in the modern Church, 'the hymns may assume predestination, but the sermons are Pelagian'. The same writer, concluding his sketch of the influence of Pelagianism on the Church and the Church's resistance to it, sums up with the statement that 'any movement towards Pelagianism is bound in the end, so long as Christianity survives, to be resisted'.

But even Passmore feels obliged to admit that 'not a few modern readers will sympathise with Pelagius in this debate, seeing in him the blunt Englishman [*sic*] cutting through the tortuosities of North African sensuality and sensibility.'[5] It is an incontrovertible fact that many good Christians over the intervening centuries have suspected that, despite the bad press which Pelagius has received, there may have been more than a grain of truth in his teaching. 'Pelagius', writes R. F. Evans, who has done as much as anyone in recent years to dispel the clouds of misunderstanding, 'is one of the most maligned figures in the history of Christianity. It has been the common sport of the theologian and the historian of theology to set him up as a symbolic bad man and heap upon him accusations which often tell us more about the theological perspective of the accuser than Pelagius.' Giants like Harnack and Karl Barth have sometimes passed hasty and misleading judgements on him for advancing views which were not his at all, the former dismissing him as '*im tiefsten Grunde gottlos*', and others have followed suit by crediting – or,

---

[3] Passmore, 115. More recently an Anglican clergyman has remarked: 'Pelagius lives on, not in official formularies or in academic theology. British Christians tend to a theology of self-help and morality' (M. Jackson, 244). Reinhold Niebuhr once described F. R. Tennant's *The Concept of Sin* as 'the most elaborate of modern Pelagian treatises' but Passmore regarded it as 'not a particularly original book' (109).

[4] Hall, 2ff. For a broadly similar view of liturgical translations used in the Roman Catholic Church cf. Cooper, 43, 50, a reference which I owe to a former student, Tom Dawkes.

[5] Passmore, 95, 100, 114.

rather, debiting – him with all the tenets of Pelagianism *per saturam*.[6]

Small wonder then that this kind of radical misunderstanding has spread to lesser mortals deriving their knowledge from secondary sources and concerned to draw analogies with fields far removed from theology, like a reviewer of a book entitled *The Benn Heresy*, who has commented that 'Benn himself refers approvingly to Pelagius, that ancient Briton who thought that good works were sufficient for entry to heaven without necessarily believing in God.' Now it may well be that Mr Tony Benn sees himself as a latter-day Pelagius in the field of politics and Pelagius as a kindred spirit in that of theology, both of them pursued and persecuted by the misguided and often malicious mouth-pieces of the establishment whose personal prejudices inhibit them from penetrating to the essential truth underlying the arguments of their opponents. But one doubts if he would be so naïve and ill-informed as to think that Pelagius held that belief in God was not essential in a Christian: Pelagius lived in the Roman Empire of the fourth and fifth centuries, not in the Britain or America of the twentieth century whose theological climate nurtures rumours of God dead and myths of God incarnate.

No, Pelagius was not *gottlos*; he was 'fundamentally a Christian moralist', and he wanted, above all else, 'to be an orthodox theologian of the Christian Church and to be known as such'.[7] As for Pelagianism, Gerald Bonner has rightly emphasised that recent research – to which, incidentally, he has made a significant contribution – has demolished the monolithic view of it: the Pelagians were not 'a party with a rigidly defined doctrinal system; they were a mixed group, united by certain theological principles which nevertheless left the individual free to develop his own opinions upon particular topics'.[8] What was to become a notorious heresy began as an ascetic movement but, since Jerome and Augustine in the fifth century, theologians have lumped both heresy and movement under the same name and treated Pelagius as the eponymous founder of both. From the early fifth to the late twentieth century he has fallen a victim to over-simplification and culpable misinterpretation of the evidence offered by his writings and used against him by his opponents, and, as a result, the very real and profound differences separating him from Augustine and the Church have been obscured. The two protagonists have been seen as black and white, the one a symbol of heresy and the other of orthodoxy, the one condemned and degraded, the other canonised and exalted. But the question which both sought to answer is perennial: 'at stake is a much more basic conception of what the very nature of human existence is according to Christianity. Set in the context of human freedom, the Pelagian controversy asked the perennially radical question of the quality of human behaviour, and the sources of good and evil in this world.'[9] It is a question which is as important today as it was when it became the subject of debate between Christians for the first time and Pelagius and Augustine

[6] R. F. Evans, 1968(a), 66f.; on Pelagius' 'poor press' in modern times see Phipps, 131f.
[7] Ibid., 42, 92.
[8] Bonner, 1970, 31.
[9] Haight, 32.

clashed with each other in a battle which was to end in tragedy for Pelagius.

But what of the man himself, his life and personality? 'A cultivated and sensitive layman . . . an elusive and gracious figure, beloved and respected wherever he goes, . . . silent, smiling, reserved':[10] these vivid phrases of R. G. Collingwood suggest a rich store of information and anecdote of the kind we associate with the *Lives* of many VIPs of the ancient world. The reality is very different: there is no *Life* of Pelagius, and hard facts about his life are at a premium. We possess seven works which have survived more or less intact and are generally agreed to have come from his own pen – a commentary on the Pauline Epistles, a confession of faith and five letters which are, in fact, minor treatises[11] – as well as several more attributed to him at one time or another, a number of isolated fragments and Augustine's numerous quotations from his two major treatises now lost. In none of these is there even a trace of autobiographical detail, which well accords with our general impression of a modest, retiring man who would have shrunk in distaste from the degree of publicity, not to say notoriety, thrust upon him by posterity. The pen-pictures contributed by his contemporaries, who can hardly claim to be objective, leave us with little more than an indication that he must have had a distinct tendency to obesity. He is said to have possessed 'the torso and strength of a wrestler and a fine, corpulent figure', 'the shoulders of a Milo', 'broad shoulders and a stout neck'; 'he displays his fat even upon his forehead'; and, not surprisingly, 'he moves along at the stately pace of a tortoise'.[12] Due allowance must obviously be made for the extravagance of theological polemic.

What do we know about his birth and death? In short, precious little. We know the date and place of neither; but it is reasonably certain that he was born not long after 350 in Britain and died not long after 418 somewhere in the countries adjoining the Eastern Mediterranean, just possibly in Egypt.[13]

[10] Collingwood and Myres, 308.

[11] R. F. Evans, 1968(b), argues that only four of the letters attributed to Pelagius by Plinval, 1943, 1947, were actually works of Pelagius: *On the Christian Life* (PL 40, 1031–46); *On Virginity* (PL 30, 162–8) (CSEL 1, 225–50); *To Celantia* (PL 22, 1204–29) (CSEL 56, 329–56); *On the Divine Law* (PL 30, 105–16). The *Letter to Demetrias* (PL 30, 15–45; 33, 1099–1120), though attributed to various authors at various times, is now accepted as an authentic work of Pelagius. It has sometimes been suggested that the quality of the Latin text, which is higher than that of his other works, may imply that Pelagius was assisted by someone else, the most obvious candidate being his faithful *amanuensis*, Annianus of Celeda, described by Orosius as his 'armour-bearer' and by Jerome as his 'voice' and 'shadow'. Annianus also translated the sermons of John Chrysostom, adding two Epistles of his own, one of which, prefixed to Matthew, shows some resemblances in its phraseology to the *Letter to Demetrias* (see Garnier in PL 48, 626–30).

[12] Jerome, *Letters* 50, 4 (PL 22, 515) (CSEL 54, 392); *Dialogue against the Pelagians* I, 28 (PL 23, 522); Orosius, *Book in Defence against the Pelagians: On the Freedom of the Will*, 31 (PL 31, 1200) (CSEL 5, 657); Jerome, *Dialogue* III, 16 (PL 23, 586).

[13] While I cannot find any firm evidence to prove that he spent his last years in Egypt, I agree with J. Ferguson, 1956, 114, and 1980, 117, and Wermelinger, 210, that the traditional assumption that he went to Egypt from Palestine is preferable to any other, since Cyril of Alexandria did not at first assent to his condemnation and he may have joined Melania and Pinianus on their second journey to Egypt (Wermelinger, 251). Syria would have been the obvious place of asylum after John's successor in Jerusalem, Praylius, had withdrawn support for his cause there; but if he did go there, it is strange that Marius Mercator did not mention it.

Augustine, Paul Orosius, Prosper Tiro of Aquitaine and Marius Mercator, all contemporaries, and Gennadius of Marseilles, a near-contemporary, refer to him as *Brito, Britto, Britannicus* or *Britannus*,[14] and only Jerome as *Scotus* or *Scottus*, that is to say, 'Irish',[15] but this may have been no more than a current term of abuse. J. B. Bury, however, took Jerome's reference seriously and combined it with his additional phrase 'from the locality of the Britons' to produce a compromise to the effect that he was an Irishman who came from a family which had settled in western Britain,[16] and Heinrich Zimmer attributed the very high regard in which the Irish came to hold him later to his having been born in Ireland.[17] But Britain is by far the strongest candidate for the honour, if such it be, of having provided him with his birthplace, even if all efforts to pinpoint its precise location have been characterised by ingenuity rather than conviction. It remains as uncertain as that of Homer and almost as keenly competed for: at different times the main contenders have emerged as the south-west, south-east and north of England and, of course, Wales, that traditional stronghold of dissent.[18] As for speculations that his name was a hellenised form of Muirchu (Irish) or Morgan (Welsh), they deserve only to be buried along with many other 'pure fantasies about his background'.[19]

It is reasonably certain then that he hailed originally from Britain but we can only guess why he left it for Rome; Souter once made the interesting suggestion that he did so because of a difference of opinion with his father[20] but he may have done so simply to further his career, as did many other young men of his time, including Augustine, who left Africa for the same reason. It is probable that he came of good family and had been given a sound education, *pace* Jerome and Orosius, in classical literature and philosophy, which he was to extend by wide reading in the Church Fathers after his arrival in Rome in the early eighties of the fourth century. There have been speculations that he spent some time in Gaul or Palestine before moving on to Rome but these are unsupported by factual evidence,[21] and the idea that the law was his first choice of career, though attractive and promoted by Plinval and R. F. Evans as helping to explain the legalistic tone of much of his

[14] Augustine, *L*, 186, 1 (PL 33, 816) (CSEL 57, 45); Orosius, *Book in Defence*, 12 (PL 31, 1182) (CSEL 5, 620); Prosper, *Chronicle*, year 413 (PL 51, 591), *Poem on the Graceless*, i. 13 (PL 51, 94); Marius Mercator, *Footnotes to Words of Julian* (PL 48, 111A); Gennadius, *On Famous Men*, 43 (PL 58, 1083 – *v.l.* in *codice Corbeiensi*).

[15] *Commentary on Jeremiah* III, pref. (PL 24, 758) (CSEL 59, 151).

[16] Bury, 1904, 26ff.; 1905, 296.

[17] In his *Pelagius in Irland*; see 122, n. 100.

[18] For discussions of Pelagius' origin see H. Williams, 1912, 200ff.; Souter, 1922–31, 1ff.; Plinval, 1943, 57ff.; J. Ferguson, 1956, 39ff.

[19] Bonner, 1972, 32. Ferguson, 1956, 40, 1980, 115, is reluctant to accept the argument advanced by Souter, 1922–31, 2, that the not infrequent appearance of the names Pelagius and Pelagia before Pelagius' time rules out the need to invent a Latin name to represent his Celtic one. For earlier examples of the names Pelagius and Pelagia in Greek see Pape-Benseler II, 1159, and for Libanius' fellow-pupil Pelagius, who became consular governor of Syria in the second half of the fourth century, *Der Kleine Pauly* IV, 593; there was also a martyr-saint Pelagia in the late third/early fourth century (Livingstone, 389f.).

[20] Souter, 1907, 423ff.; 1915, 180; 1922–31, 3.

[21] H. Williams, 1912, 199f.

teaching, is based solely on Jerome's remark that the 'monk' who had criticised his attack on Jovinian in 393 or 394 'had abandoned the law and turned his attention to the Church'.[22] Jerome is not the only contemporary to describe him as a 'monk'[23] but it is a description which he himself does not recommend to his supporters.[24] 'This apparently simple and insignificant question has sharply divided scholars' with Bury, N. K. Chadwick and Hugh Williams, for example, in the Ayes lobby and Plinval and Grosjean in the Noes.[25] Certainly he never belonged to a religious community in the formal sense, and perhaps we should dub him 'honorary monk' in view of his undoubted adoption of an ascetic way of life. Both Orosius and Pope Zosimus were later to speak of him as a layman,[26] and he was never ordained, as was his friend Celestius – by the Church in the East after his condemnation by that of the West – nor does he ever seem to have sought ordination, thus revealing an apparent lack of total commitment which was hardly likely to endear him to professionals like Jerome and Augustine.

In sum, all we are able to say with any conviction about his origins and early life is that he was a Briton, was born sometime in the early part of the second half of the fourth century, emigrated to Rome in the early eighties and was neither a monk nor a priest. The rest is buried in the quicksands covering his 'prehistory', and we can now struggle out of these on to rather firmer ground. Having arrived there, we shall first give a blow-by-blow account of the origins and course of the Pelagian controversy, then examine in greater detail the case for and against Pelagius, and end by tracing the aftermath of his condemnation as the first major heresiarch of the Western Church and its confirmation by the Church in the East. This happened at the Council of Ephesus in 431, which included in its canons one which placed under threat of arbitrary excommunication anyone who failed to dissociate himself from

[22] *Letters* 50, 2. Plinval, 1943, 63ff., and R. F. Evans, 1968(a), 31, both accept this view but Ferguson, J., 1956, 43f., has reservations, pointing out that 'though his skill in controversy may indicate some legal training, he is not referred to as a lawyer like his associate Celestius'. The question whether Pelagius was really the target of Jerome's letter will be discussed in c. I.

[23] Augustine refers to him as a monk in *PP*, xx. 36 (PL 44, 342) (CSEL 42, 92) and in *H*, 88 (PL 42, 47); Mercator in his *Footnotes to Words of Julian*, pref. 2 (PL 48, 111).

[24] *On the Divine Law*, 9 (PL 30, 115), assuming with R. F. Evans that Pelagius was the author of this tract, which he cites as *On the Law*.

[25] Hanson, 1968, 144, n. 2.

[26] Orosius, *Book in Defence*, 4 (PL 31, 1177) (CSEL 5, 607), 5 (PL 31, 1117) (CSEL 5, 609); Zosimus, *Letter on the Case of Pelagius*, 3 (PL 20, 657; 45, 1721) (CSEL 35, 104). Passmore, 121, describes him as 'that indomitable layman', and Ferguson, 1956, 144ff., discusses his concern for the vocation of a layman and for the importance of the laity in the Church. Celestius, on the other hand, 'is said to have reached the priesthood in Asia' (*L* 175, 1; 176, 4) (PL 33, 760, 764) (CSEL 44, 654, 667). Mercator, *Memorandum on the Name of Celestius* i. 2, records that this happened at Ephesus 'by fraudulent means' but Garnier denies that he was ever a monk (PL 48, 72f., 282). Orosius' *Book in Defence*, described by Plinval, 1943, 283, as '*un pamphlet assez mince, mais le plus amusant des pamphlets religieux*', is certainly 'no theological masterpiece and like the writings of Marius Mercator oversteps the bounds of the tolerable but it is carefully composed throughout and is no mere hotch-potch of quotations' (Wermelinger, 67). The same writer (ibid.) questions whether Augustine ever read his *Book in Defence* and suggests that his 'independent stance' on the delicate matter of the doctrine of grace at a time when it was not yet settled excited general displeasure in Africa.

'the opinions of Celestius', that is, Pelagianism. In a sense it was no more than a *quid pro quo* for the action of Pope Celestine in declaring Nestorius a heretic in 430 in response to a dossier on him received from Cyril of Alexandria and accompanied by a request that the Western Church should give its opinion on Nestorianism. Thus, as a matter of courtesy rather than a result of reasoned debate, the Eastern Church overruled the earlier decision of the Synod of Diospolis, which came under its jurisdiction, in favour of Pelagius.

It may be useful at this point to add a note of explanation on the relationship between the Eastern and Western Churches at the time of the Pelagian controversy. By the end of the fourth century the tetrarchy formally established by Diocletian in 293, by which the western and eastern parts of the Roman Empire were each given their own Augustus and Caesar but with the intention that they should maintain unity of government throughout the Empire, remained in existence only in theory, since the two sons of Theodosius I in practice ruled East and West with equal rights. This *de facto* political division resulted in a corresponding separation of the Catholic Church into two components in East and West. Though the Church in the West, which included North Africa, and that in the East, which included Egypt, remained in communion with each other, their theological interests reveal a marked difference for historical and cultural reasons. Whereas in the late fourth and early fifth centuries the Eastern Church continued to grapple with metaphysical problems such as the nature of God and the relation of the Son to the Father, the Western Church became more concerned with the practical questions of the relationship of Rome to the other provinces and the formulation of a doctrine of salvation which would be wholly consistent with traditional teaching. The importance of the Pelagian controversy in both of these connections cannot be overestimated.

I

A FAMOUS VICTORY

'What they fought each other for
I could not well make out.
But everybody said, quoth he,
That 'twas a famous victory.'

ROBERT SOUTHEY[1]

Augustine tells us that, possibly around 405, Pelagius had heard a bishop in
Rome, believed by some to have been Paulinus of Nola, quoting the famous
sentence from the tenth book of the *Confessions*, 'Give me what you command,
and command what you will' – *da mihi quod iubes, et iube quod vis*. 'This', he
comments somewhat ruefully, 'was more than he could stomach and, contradicting it with some show of anger, he almost went to law with the man who
had referred to it.'[2] But the doctor of grace knew nothing of this at the time
and, in any case, had other fish to fry then; and so Pelagius continued
unimpeded with his vigorous campaign to reform the moral standards of
Christians in Rome. Indeed, we are tempted to wonder if we would ever have
heard of Pelagianism without the rude intervention of Alaric the Visigoth,
who unwittingly sealed the fate of it. For it was the imminence of Alaric's
attack on the capital city which drove Pelagius in 409 to join the general
exodus from Italy and make his way, perhaps via Sicily, to Africa, where
Augustine saw him but did not converse with him,[3] and thence to Palestine.
But before he left Rome, he had completed his commentary on the Pauline
Epistles and had made known in it his views on grace and free will and

---

[1] 'After Blenheim', *The Golden Treasury*, ed. F. T. Palgrave, Oxford 1929, 214.
[2] *GP* xx. 53 (PL 45, 1026); the offending sentence is in *C*, X, xxix. 40 (PL 32, 796) (CSEL 33,
256). Courcelle, 1947, 270ff., 1963, 580, suggested that the bishop concerned may have been
Paulinus of Nola, who was a friend of Pelagius during the latter's stay in Rome as well as a
correspondent of Augustine but was 'not a fighter' (Frend, 1984, 678) and did not get involved in
the controversy between the two men. Martinetto, 83ff., argued that Pelagius' first reactions to
Augustine's doctrine of grace appear in his Pauline commentary and his treatise *On the Hardening
of Pharaoh's Heart*. This is almost certainly true of the commentary, though Wermelinger, 22,
reminds us that Pelagius does no more than mention many interpretations with which he does
not himself agree; but the date and authorship of the treatise, held by Plinval to have been
written by Pelagius c. 397–8 and published by him on behalf of G. Morin in 1947, 137ff. (PLS 1,
1506–39), are still uncertain.
[3] *PP* xxii. 46 (PL 44, 346) (CSEL 42, 100).

1

baptism as well as many other topics around which the Pelagian controversy was to centre.[4]

In Palestine he was confronted first by Jerome and, a little later, by the Spanish priest Paul Orosius, himself a refugee from the barbarians, who had escaped from his native country, as he was later to claim, 'with the help of a cloud which suddenly enwrapped me'.[5] He was 'the man who gave to the Mediterranean world the remains of the first Christian martyr, St Stephen',[6] presented to him by Avitus, a fellow-presbyter from Bracar, to take back there on his return, though, in the event, he had to leave them at Minorca on his return journey. At this time, however, on his arrival in Palestine, it was he who brought Pelagianism into the open and first linked the names of Pelagius and Celestius as 'joint sowers of the heresy in Africa',[7] though Pelagius had played no part in the controversy there. After some initial skirmishing Pelagius was charged with heresy before Bishop John of Jerusalem at the Synod of Diospolis in 415, only to be acquitted after dissociating himself from the more extreme views of Celestius. Thus encouraged, he wrote his two major treatises, now lost, On Nature and On Free Will to clarify his own views and, he hoped, to justify them. But his real troubles were only beginning: both Jerome in Palestine and Augustine in Africa remained unconvinced of his innocence and identified him as the teacher of Celestius, using his pupil merely as a front man to conceal his own responsibility for the new heresy.

Dissatisfied with the outcome of the Synod of Diospolis and egged on by Augustine, whose case had been strengthened by synods held at Carthage and Milevis, the African bishops now appealed to a higher authority, that of Pope Innocent I. After some delay, not unreasonable if, as he claimed, he knew of no Pelagians in Rome at the time, he ruled that Pelagius and Celestius be excommunicated unless they renounced their heretical opinions. 'The case is closed', cried Augustine in triumph – causa finita est;[8] but his elation was premature, since both men appealed against the decision. The exact sequence of events which followed is somewhat blurred but the events themselves stand out clearly. Innocent's successor, Zosimus – the former had died in the meantime – re-opened the case, only to pronounce an ambiguous

---

[4] Souter at one point (1922–31, 4f.) claims that internal evidence establishes that it was not written before 'about 405' and recalls that, according to Marius Mercator (*Memorandum on Celestius* ii. 1 in PL 48, 83), it was in circulation before 410, the year when Alaric finally entered Rome; but elsewhere (ibid. 188ff.) he suggests a dating between 404 and 409, and Duval, 1980, 526, prefers one between 406 and 410. The date generally accepted for Rufinus of Aquileia's translation of Origen's commentary on Romans, on which Pelagius drew extensively, is 405–6 (Murphy, 192ff.; Hammond, 403ff.). So, since Pelagius may well have left Rome in 409, it is safest to date his commentary between 405/6 and 409.

[5] *History against the Pagans* iii. 20, 194 (PL 31, 839) (CSEL 5, 183).

[6] Hunt, 211; cf. H. Chadwick, 1976, 190; Wermelinger, 89.

[7] Bonner, 1972, 45.

[8] *S* 131, x. 10 (PL 38, 734); Bonner, 1963, 343, n. 1, warns that this famous phrase has often been misquoted and that too much should not be made of it in the present context, since it was clearly one of which Augustine was very fond.

verdict, which could have been regarded as something of a 'climb-down'[9] and was certainly little to the taste of the African bishops. They returned to the attack, and the Emperor Honorius now intervened from his retreat in Ravenna, mainly in the interests of public order, which he saw as threatened by riots in the city of Rome allegedly activated by the Pelagians remaining there and a physical attack on a retired official, Constantius, who had openly opposed the views of Celestius as being without scriptural support – *sine scriptura*.[10] He issued an imperial rescript banishing Pelagius, Celestius and all their adherents, though it is doubtful if the two leaders were still in Rome at the time. Almost simultaneously, over two hundred African bishops in council passed a series of canons against what had by now become known as Pelagianism, and Zosimus in his *Epistula Tractoria* of 418 finally condemned both Pelagius and Celestius of heresy and excommunicated them. Celestius continued to contest this decision in Rome and Constantinople without success but Pelagius, after an unsuccessful appeal at Jerusalem, was forced to leave Palestine and 'vanishes from history, his face set eastward, elusive to the last'[11] – though some romantics have seen him marching westwards to die in Britain. The heresy which bore his name was again condemned, somewhat summarily, as 'the opinions of Celestius' at the Council of Ephesus in 431 along with Nestorianism, the Church in the East at last setting its seal of approval on the earlier decision of that in the West.

From the tangled web of charge and counter-charge which led to this outcome and which may never be completely unravelled, one fact at least stands out: to the end, Pelagius never saw himself as a heretic, much less as a heresiarch. He was at heart a moral reformer who, as he became familiar with Christian society in Rome at the turn of the fourth century, became also more and more critical of its moral standards and responded to the general laxity and extravagance he saw around him by preaching the need for simple and virtuous living based on man's freedom to choose for himself what he would, and would not, do. By his teaching, writing and example he attracted to himself, like Jerome before him, a circle of Christians of like beliefs, many of them rich and influential. He and they naturally sought to express themselves by formulating the principles on which their beliefs were founded, and it is to this period of his life that some of his extant letters and his Pauline commentary, 'the earliest extant work of a British author',[12] belong. Other members of the movement expressed themselves in different ways and with differing emphases, so that it became increasingly difficult for their opponents to disentangle the views of Pelagius from those of his associates. But, at the time of his arrival in Palestine, there was one stalwart of the Church awaiting

[9] J. Ferguson, 1956, 110; Wermelinger, 127ff., discusses possible reasons for Innocent's reluctance to condemn Pelagius and Celestius outright at this stage.

[10] Prosper, *Chronicle*, year 418 (PL 51, 592).

[11] Collingwood and Myres, 309.

[12] M. R. James, *The Cambridge History of English Literature* I, 1908, 65, cited in Souter, 1922–31, ix.

3

him there who was never in any doubt as to the extent of his responsibility for this new heresy which had reared its ugly head.

In a letter to an old friend, Domnio, living in Rome, Jerome had referred as long ago as 393 or 394 to a certain monk who had been publicly attacking him for his treatise *Against Jovinian*.[13] The identification of this 'monk' as Pelagius was first made by Plinval in 1943[14] and, thereafter, generally accepted by scholars.[15] But it was R. F. Evans who first made a comprehensive review of the evidence for it, citing twelve heads under which Pelagius could be compared with the unnamed monk of the letter written by Jerome.[16] More recently, he has been strongly challenged by Yves-Marie Duval on the grounds that (a) most of the points of the comparison used by him could be shared by Pelagius with others on Jerome's black list and are no more than '*clichés de polémique*'; (b) there is no sound evidence for connecting the 'jealousy' of Pelagius attributed to Jerome by Augustine and Julian with a time earlier than around 414 and 415; and (c) Jerome's own statements on 'jealousy' similarly cannot be referred to the earlier period in the later part of the fourth century when the correspondence between Domnio and Jerome took place. In sum, it is not a pen-picture of Pelagius which is contained in Jerome's letter; it is a '*portrait-robot de l'hérétique*', an identikit picture of the typical heretic as Jerome saw him.[17]

Duval is justified in claiming that the references which have been cited from Augustine, Julian and Jerome himself, in order to establish a clash between Pelagius and Jerome in, say, 394 and to identify it as the cause of the ill will which existed between them later, must be subjected to a much closer examination than anyone before his paper has seen fit to give to them. But his case for disputing the identification of Pelagius with the monk referred to in Jerome's letter on the grounds of the contents of the letter itself is much less convincing, however ingenious and carefully argued. The pen-picture which it gives us just does not read like an identikit picture of a typical heretic: it reads – and *feels* – like a portrait of an actual, living individual whom Jerome knew personally and had been able to identify from Domnio's letter. Domnio may well have named Pelagius in his letter, which has not survived, and the fact that Jerome does not repeat the name proves nothing: it was accepted practice, as Duval admits, for those engaged in theological controversy at that time not to name names, and Jerome himself names Pelagius only once in the course of all his attacks upon him, and that in a letter written probably in 418 not long before his own death and at a time when the battle was as good as

[13] *Letters* 50 (PL 22, 512–16) (CSEL 54, 388–95).

[14] Plinval, 1943, 50ff.

[15] E.g. J. Ferguson, 1956, 44f., 77f.; Myres, 1960, 22, nn. 10, 11; 24, nn. 15, 16; Hammond, 426, n. 1; Kelly, 1978, 187ff.; Wermelinger, 46f., 49f. Brown, 1972, 221, n. 4, on the other hand, is less confident, though he accepts that R. F. Evans has made 'a somewhat stronger case' than Plinval.

[16] R. F. Evans, 1968(a), 31ff.

[17] Duval, 1980, 530ff.

over.[18] Nor is his previous acquaintance with Pelagius in dispute: he refers to their former relationship in his *Commentary on Jeremiah* as something which he realises that he must take care not to appear to be damaging.[19] And there does not appear to be a single instance elsewhere in the ample repertory of his invective where he employed the tactical device which Duval attributes to him on this occasion.

If the identification of Pelagius with the unnamed monk of the letter to Domnio is correct, as is probable, *pace* Duval, then it has the considerable advantage of helping to explain Jerome's attitude to Pelagius on the latter's arrival in Palestine, because there would be an old score to settle between them, and they would have crossed swords on a previous occasion. The main issue then had been the supreme merit of celibacy: 'Jerome condemns marriage' was how he summed up the burden of Pelagius' criticism. What exactly had Pelagius said, and done, to give offence? In the letter there is more abuse than argument, and we learn little from it about the real issues. Pelagius is referred to as 'a certain gossipy monk, a wanderer around the streets, the cross-roads and the highways, a pettifogger, a sly detractor, who with a beam in his own eye strives to remove the mote from another's.' 'He delivers harangues against me', complains the aggrieved Jerome, 'and gnawing at the books I wrote against Jovinian, tears them and pulls them apart.' This scoundrel, ignorant as he is of the works of Aristotle and Cicero, dares to criticise one who is well versed in philosophy, the Christian Fathers and the scriptures; he is one who acknowledges no teacher but claims to be inspired and instructed by God himself. Jerome goes on to cast aspersions on such a man's sense of vocation, his constant association with women, his habit of instructing them in the privacy of their bedchambers instead of coming out into the open and conducting a debate by correspondence with views set out in writing and supported by argument. If he would but venture to do this, he would soon find out his mistake in attacking such an adversary; he would hear in reply across the many seas, lands and peoples which separated them the echo of Jerome's cry: 'I do *not* condemn wedlock, I do *not* condemn marriage.'[20]

At the same time Jerome proceeded to clarify his views on marriage in more moderate terms in a letter to his friend Pammachius at Rome, insisting that his earlier remarks on the subject should not be taken to indicate that he condemned it for those who chose it because they felt unable to pursue the higher course of celibacy.[21] There was nothing unusual in such a position, and many other Christians, including Pelagius, would have agreed with it; it was the intemperate, indeed vitriolic, tone of his treatise *Against Jovinian* which had excited criticism. In it his polemic had been sustained and reinforced by

---

[18] *Letters* 152 (*RB* 27, 1910, 1–11) (CSEL 56, 364) – a letter to Riparius, in which Jerome more than made up for any previous reticence on his part occasioned by his preference for correcting the Pelagians rather than dishonouring them (*Commentary on Jeremiah* IV, 1, 3).

[19] *Commentary on Jeremiah* IV, pref. (PL 24, 785) (CSEL 59, 222).

[20] *Letters* 50, 5 (PL 22, 516) (CSEL 54, 394).

[21] *Letters* 49, 5 (PL 22, 511f.) (CSEL 54, 357).

personal abuse, libel and misrepresentation of the kind once described by N. H. Baynes as 'ecclesiastical Billingsgate':[22] for example, he refers to Jovinian as 'a debauched preacher', 'an old serpent' and 'a dog returned to his vomit', fastening on him the nickname 'Christian Epicurus' which many others were to adopt later. His language was so virulent that even his old friends reacted in the opposite way to which he had intended, and Pelagius was only one of many who rose to defend Jovinian, though not accepting his extreme views. Jerome had good cause to be sorely disappointed with the outcome of this controversy: it had been a thoroughly unpleasant episode in his battle-scarred career as a defender of the faith and one which he would doubtless have preferred to be forgotten.

We can well imagine his annoyance when, nearly twenty years later, this same Pelagius turned up in Palestine to disturb the relative peace of his retreat like Banquo's ghost at the feast, and when he began to curry favour and join forces with another old antagonist of his, Bishop John of Jerusalem. Pelagius and Jerome were soon at odds with each other again in 413, when both were invited to send letters of advice to a young girl named Demetrias, who came from a rich and influential Roman family with which both men had been closely associated in Rome. To Demetrias, who had recently decided to take the vow of virginity and become a nun at the age of fourteen, each wrote after his own fashion, Jerome taking the opportunity to warn her not to bother her head too much with theological problems raised by adherents of Origen, a snide reference to Pelagius,[23] and Pelagius to stress the importance of the part played by the human will in enabling individuals to choose and perform right actions and so to win salvation, and of the existence in human beings of 'a kind of natural sanctity'.[24]

The reference to Origen reveals that there was another old controversy from his past which Jerome suspected Pelagius of trying to revive to his discredit. He had certainly been an admirer of Origen in his earlier days; but he had insisted in his *Defence against Rufinus* written in 401 that his admiration for Origen was confined to the latter's work as an exegete of the scriptures and

---

[22] I owe this quotation to Bonner, 1972, 82, n. 176.

[23] *Letters* 130 (PL 22, 1107–24) (CSEL 56, 175–201).

[24] *Letter to Demetrias*, 4, 25ff. (PL 30, 19; 33, 1101); this 'natural sanctity' is often linked by Pelagius to *conscientia*, to which, however, he gives 'a wider connotation than our own "conscience" ' (Ferguson, 1956, 142). The letter also made a great stir among Augustine's circle. He had written to congratulate Proba and Juliana on Demetrias' vocation as soon as they had told him of it (*L* 150 in PL 33, 645) and had also, in 414, addressed to Juliana his treatise *On the Good of Widowhood* (PL 40, 429–50) (CSEL 41, 303–43), the latter part of which contained a warning against listening to the 'tittle-tattle of certain men, enemies of the grace of God, who are trying to defend freedom of the human will' (xvii. 21). Juliana does not seem to have been altogether happy with the suggestion that a family like hers could ever be tainted with heresy, and so, after receiving a copy of the *Letter to Demetrias*, he and his friend Alypius write to her again in 417 to explain the grounds for their earlier anxiety, urging her to avoid all 'teachings contrary to grace' and identifying Pelagius as the author of the letter on the evidence of another letter of Pelagius, though he had earlier asked *her* to identify him. Juliana did distance herself from Pelagius after his condemnation, and the *Letter to Demetrias* was one of the documents used against him by the African Councils: as Wermelinger points out, 205, n. 353, Augustine's refutation of *Letter to Demetrias*, c. 11, in his own letter to Juliana (*L* 188, in PL 33, 849ff.) (CSEL 57, 120ff.) (ii. 4) was wholly in the spirit of the fifth canon of the Council of Carthage in 418.

did not extend to his dogmas.[25] As a result of the recriminations which followed this debate, he had forfeited the friendship not only of Rufinus but also of John of Jerusalem. So, without too great a concern for theological niceties, he now launched into a vigorous attack on Pelagius in his *Dialogue against the Pelagians*, in his letters to friends and even in his *Commentary on Jeremiah*, on which he was currently engaged and in which he attacked Pelagianism twenty-two times, apart from making several references in his preface to its founders, including, of course, Pelagius. This man is a 'huge, bloated, Alpine dog, weighed down with Scottish oats, . . . able to rage more effectively with his heels than with his teeth'.[26] Had he, Jerome, not long ago pulverised the arguments of Rufinus just as he had demolished those of Jovinian? It was intolerable that an upstart monk, semi-educated and himself under the shadow of heresy, should now try to disinter the bones of old adversaries and use them to embarrass him. He must be quashed once and for all – 'battered with the club of the spirit', as he typically put it,[27] and along with him all those whose discredited causes he was espousing – John of Jerusalem, still a thorn in his flesh, Rufinus Tyrannius of Aquileia, who had died in Sicily in 410,[28] and the last fading traces of the ghost of Origen, 'that insane allegorist',[29] whose works had been rejected and condemned by the Church at Rome in the person of Pope Anastasius in 400 acting under pressure from Theophilus, Patriarch of Alexandria.[30]

Thus it was Jerome who first took up the cudgels and openly challenged Pelagius to combat, just as he had done in about 394, but at that time without success: by accusing him of fostering Origenism through his own misunderstanding of Jerome's *Commentary on Ephesians* as a work packed with borrowings from Origen, Pelagius was impugning his authority as an orthodox teacher of the Church, especially now that Origenism had been formally condemned not only in Alexandria, Syria and Palestine but also by Rome. As always, attack was Jerome's best method of defence, and he concentrated his attack on pinning the label of Origenist on Pelagius in turn on the grounds that, by teaching that a baptised Christian was able to live without sin, if he so willed, he was simply preaching Origenism. It was this doctrine of *impeccantia*, 'sinlessness', that Pelagius was called upon to renounce at a diocesan synod called by John of Jerusalem in 415. He acknowledged that this was what he taught but, when asked how he could reconcile it with divine grace, cleverly skated over the thin ice by quoting the scriptures on the necessity of grace and anathematising anyone who denied that grace was essential.[31] His accuser, Orosius, was thrown out of his stride but the same charge appeared as one of

---

[25] *Defence against Rufinus* I, 11–17 (PL 23, 397–492); cf. *Letters* 84. 2 (PL 22, 744f.) (CSEL 55, 121f.).

[26] *Commentary on Jeremiah* III, pref. (PL 24, 758) (CSEL 59, 151).

[27] Ibid.

[28] *Life of Tyrannius Rufinus* II, 20 (PL 21, 191); cf. the *Notitia* of Schoennemann (PL 21, 15) and Hammond, 372ff.

[29] Kelly, 1975, 316, with the relevant passages in n. 43.

[30] *Life* II, 19 (PL 21, 277–85); Schoennemann's *Notitia* (PL 21, 14).

[31] *PP* vi. 16; xiv. 37; xv. 38; xxx. 54 (PL 44, 329f.; 342f.; 350f.) (CSEL 42, 68f.; 93f.; 106ff.).

the seven items in a *libellus* drawn up against Pelagius by two exiled Gallican bishops, Heros and Lazarus, at the Synod of Diospolis in December of 415.[32] Here again he reiterated his defence and qualified his teaching on *impeccantia* by adding that it was only possible if a man's efforts were combined with the help of divine grace.

The Synod was satisfied with this explanation but not Jerome: he continued to equate Pelagius' 'sinlessness' with Stoic *apatheia*, that is, the ability of man to rise above the passions, and to repeat his charge that here was conclusive proof that Pelagius was an Origenist, since it was Origen who had tried to adapt such pagan ideas to Christian thought. But Origen was no Stoic: 'although there is much knowledge of Stoicism and an evident debt to the Stoic theodicy, it is a mistake to overestimate this Stoic element in his mental furniture and to label him a Stoic'.[33] For example, in his treatise in eight books *Against Celsus*, 'the only large-scale work by Origen that survives intact in Greek',[34] he makes great use of Stoic arguments to refute Celsus' attack on Christianity, mainly because he first assumed him to be an Epicurean; but he insisted that reason by itself was not enough if one wanted to attain to a true knowledge of God. 'Human nature', he wrote, 'is not sufficient to find God unless it is helped by God who is the object of the search; and he is found by those who, after doing all they can, admit that they need him.'[35] Pelagius would have agreed with this statement but, try though he did, he was unable to dislodge his opponent from his entrenched position by arguing that his doctrine was not the equivalent of Stoic *apatheia* and that he was not harking back to Stoic teaching on the equality of sins either. The cunning old man knew that in Origenism he had as good a stick with which to beat Pelagius as any other; by this time there were few theologians who could not be accused of revealing at one time or another one of the countless heads of this 'hydra of heresies'.[36] So, for Jerome, Pelagianism was, in his own words, nothing but 'a new heresy springing out of an old'.[37]

[32] Ibid. i. 2; iii. 5, 9; iv. 12; v. 13; vi. 16; xii. 27 (PL 44, 320f.; 322f.; 325; 326f.; 329f.; 336) (CSEL 42, 52f.; 56f.; 63f.; 64; 68f.; 80f.). Neither of the two accusers seems to have appeared in person before the Synod, one being ill and the other excused attendance, and it is uncertain to what extent they were involved in the composition of the indictment. Their absence perhaps indicates that they were no more than front-men for Jerome and Orosius, and they were clearly right out of their theological depth; in addition, they had already been discredited by the circumstances of their expulsion from Gaul, a factor which must have had some effect on the attitude of the judges to their prosecution of a man of high standing like Pelagius. The indictment, which had to be translated into Greek sentence by sentence for the benefit of the Synod, is discussed in detail by Wermelinger, 71ff.; see my Appendix II.

[33] H. Chadwick, 1966, 107.

[34] J. W. Trigg, 215.

[35] I owe this quotation to H. Chadwick, 1966, 82f.

[36] Theophilus' phrase in his Festal Letter of 402, quoted in Cross, 993, s.v. *Origenism*.

[37] *Commentary on Jeremiah* V, xxv. 3 (PL 24, 834) (CSEL 59, 301); cf. II, x. 23, IV, 24ff. (PL 24, 751, 817) (CSEL 59, 139, 268). But, as R. F. Evans, 1968(a), 6, points out, 'Jerome's attacks are never wholly deficient in truth'; in his *Commentary on Jeremiah* II, x. 23 and *Dialogue against the Pelagians* I, 32 (PL 24, 751; 23, 525) (CSEL 59, 110, 127) he cites two sentences from Pelagius' *Book of Testimonies*, known to Augustine under the title of *Book of Chapters* and to Gennadius under that of *Book of Selections*, to the effect that 'all men are governed by their own free will' and 'man can be without sin' (PL 48, 594ff., *Tituli* LXXII and C).

Now, as he struggled to free himself from the clutches of his Scylla, Pelagius found himself being dragged down into the bubbling cauldron of his Charybdis. His treatises *On Nature* and *On Free Will*, written to defend his position on sin and 'sinlessness', attracted the adverse attention of Augustine, since in them he had too little to say about divine grace and too much about the human will. Thus his Odyssey had taken him from Rome to Africa and from Africa to Palestine, and events that took place in all three combined to bring about his downfall. But it was in Rome that the course of his future had been mapped out: it was there that he had first fallen foul of Jerome, it was there that he had first clashed with Augustine's doctrine of grace and had written his commentary on the Pauline Epistles, it was there that he had made friends with Celestius, already branded as a heretic by the Council of Carthage in 411. There too he had made the acquaintance of another associate who was to play just as important a rôle in his personal drama, though himself dead by the time the controversy got under way; this was Rufinus the Syrian, 'that mysterious and somewhat sinister figure',[38] the third of the Pelagian musketeers, held by some to have been the real founder of the heresy.

For Rufinus of Syria's involvement in the heresy we have two pieces of evidence. In his *Book of Footnotes on Words of Julian*[39] Marius Mercator, a friend and disciple of Augustine, wrote: 'This most stupid but none the less hostile criticism of the orthodox faith was first introduced into Rome in the papacy of Anastasius of sacred memory (that is, between 399 and 402) by a certain Rufinus, a Syrian by race, who, not daring to promote it on his own, was clever enough to hoodwink a British monk named Pelagius into doing so, having given him a thorough grounding in the aforesaid unholy and foolish doctrine.' Rufinus of Syria was the man referred to by Celestius when defending himself at Carthage as 'the holy priest Rufinus . . ., whom he had heard deny the transmission of sin',[40] and also the author of a *Liber de Fide* written probably between 399 and 402.[41] Is there sufficient evidence in its contents to prove that it had a strong influence on Pelagius?

The scribe who contributed the following gloss to the Leningrad manuscript of the *Liber de Fide*, probably in the sixth century, had no doubt that Rufinus was a Pelagian: 'The book is Pelagian and full of the blasphemies of the Pelagians, for, under the pretext of conducting a debate with the Arians,

---

[38] Bonner, 1972, 19. Wermelinger delivers the *coup de grâce* to those who have attempted to identify this Rufinus with Rufinus of Aquileia and to Marrou's invention of a third Rufinus (1969, 465ff.) on the grounds that Rufinus of Syria could not have been the priest who travelled to Rome from Palestine c. 399/40 at the behest of his master Jerome, because it was unthinkable that one of Jerome's pupils could have held Pelagian ideas. Rufinus of Bethlehem is without doubt the Rufinus of Syria who wrote the *Liber de Fide*.

[39] Pref., 2 (PL 48, 111).

[40] *OS* iii. 3 (PL 44, 387) (CSEL 42, 168).

[41] Bonner, 1970, 36ff., sets out the arguments in favour of this dating: M. W. Miller, 8ff., dated the *Liber de Fide* to 413–28 but had been misled by the arguments of Altaner, refuted by Refoulé, 1963(a) (cf. de Blic, 518f.). The *Liber de Fide* is in PL 48, 451–88.

he has injected into it the poisons of his own heresy.'[42] This is the judgement of a man writing with hindsight long after the event, and it is evident from the book itself that its author's main targets were the trinitarian heresies of Arianism, Eunomianism and Sabellianism: 'in a work of sixty-one chapters only cc. 29–41 and 48 can be regarded as indubitably Pelagian, and not all the doctrine there expressed can be called unorthodox.'[43] The villain of the piece is Origen, who is subjected to virulent attacks again and again. It is only after firing a salvo at Origen's theory of the pre-existence of souls that the author turns aside, as it were, to direct a volley at the traducianists, whom he then dismisses as stupid and mad for asserting that 'Christ destines unbaptised children to the punishment of everlasting fire'.[44] Of grace and predestination Rufinus has nothing to say, and his views on Adam and the Fall were to be subsequently modified or rejected by Pelagius and even Celestius.

On the other hand, on the subjects of original sin and infant baptism he provides 'a manual of Pelagianism'.[45] When he writes that 'infants receive baptism not on account of their sins but in order that they may through baptism be, as it were, created in Christ and become partners in his heavenly kingdom', that 'infants who are not born in sin yet merit the grace of baptism that they may be co-heirs of Christ's kingdom', and that 'if infants are baptised because of Adam's sin, then those born of Christian parents ought not to be baptised at all',[46] Rufinus is anticipating some of the commonplaces of Pelagian teaching which Augustine was to reject again and again in his arguments against Pelagius and his associates. But it must be pointed out that Pelagius himself never explicitly denies that infants needed baptism for the remission of their sins; on the contrary, he will re-affirm his acceptance of such a need in his *Liber de Fide* submitted to Pope Innocent in 417, and, elsewhere he will ask, 'Who can be so impious as to deny to an infant of any age the common redemption of the human race?.'[47] It was Celestius, not Pelagius, who was to continue to maintain to the very end – in *his Liber de Fide* submitted to the Pope at the same time as that of Pelagius – Rufinus' central thesis that infants were baptised not on account of inherited sins but in order that they might gain entry into the kingdom of heaven.[48] This does not make Rufinus *ipso facto* the founder of Pelagianism; but it was to this topic that Augustine devoted much of his second sermon delivered at Carthage in 413,[49] just as he had directed most of the earlier part of his *On the Merits and Forgiveness of Sins and Infant Baptism* in 411/12 to a refutation of Rufinus' *Liber de Fide.*[50]

Whatever we may think of the claim that Rufinus was the real founder of

---

[42] PLS 1, 1099; Miller, 36, n. 4.
[43] Bonner, 1970, 37.
[44] *Liber de Fide* 41 (PL 48, 477f.).
[45] Bonner, 1970, 43; see also his comments in 1972, 25, 30, 36.
[46] *Liber de Fide* 40, 48 (PL 48, 477, 482).
[47] *OS* xix. 21 (PL 44, 395) (CSEL 42, 181).
[48] *Liber de Fide* 19 (PL 48, 503).
[49] *S* 294 (PL 38, 1335–48); *PP* xi. 25 (PL 44, 335) (CSEL 42, 79).
[50] This suggestion was first made by de Blic, 518f., and later taken up by Refoulé, 1963(a), 47.

Pelagianism – a subject to which we shall return later – it was certainly Rufinus and Celestius, not Pelagius, who were the first targets of Augustine's anti-Pelagian campaign. He did not openly attack Pelagius until 415, when he wrote his treatise *On Nature and Grace* as a riposte to Pelagius' *On Nature*. Earlier, in *On the Merits and Forgiveness of Sins and Infant Baptism*, Pelagius is not mentioned until the third book, in which Augustine argues against the views expressed in his commentary on the Pauline Epistles, only just received and described as 'containing very brief expository comments': but he is still reluctant to believe that the views on original sin which he has found there are those of Pelagius himself, whom he refers to as 'a holy man, as I am told, who has made no small progress in the Christian life'.[51] Nor is there any reference by name to Pelagius in the second anti-Pelagian treatise, *On the Spirit and the Letter*, also written in 412 and aimed at 'a not very troublesome group of men',[52] though this work too is in part an answer to Pelagius' commentary. In 413 he addresses a letter to Pelagius as 'My lord greatly beloved and brother greatly longed for', and the letter is couched in the most friendly terms, even if we allow for the extravagant phraseology of contemporary epistolography.[53] In 414, writing to a Sicilian lawyer, Hilarius, to enlighten him on matters on which a debate had already begun among Sicilian Christians, such as the possibility of sinlessness and the fate of infants dying without baptism,[54] he still makes no explicit connection between those who were causing his correspondent such deep anxiety – among them, no doubt, the man known as the 'Sicilian Briton' or 'Sicilian Anonymous'[55] – and Pelagius himself, now far away in Palestine.

Yet, only three years later, in his treatise *On the Proceedings of Pelagius*, he was trying to convince his readers that he had identified Pelagius as a heretic as long ago as 412, and that his cordial letter of 413 contained many hidden meanings, including a warning that he must amend his ways or else: 'lord', he claims, was no more than a conventional form of address for one Christian to use in writing to another, 'brother' meant that this was how he was bound to regard a fellow-Christian, and 'greatly longed for' indicated only that he had wanted to see Pelagius in person to discuss his opinions and statements with him.[56] These explanations may well be justified; but, as Augustine goes on to argue, the sting of his letter comes in the tail, and the one remark which can be fairly described as 'coded', if we accept his explanation for it, is concealed in the final sentence: 'At the same time, I must warn you rather to pray for me that *the Lord may make me* the kind of man you already suppose me to be.' This, he maintains, is a clear hint of the absolute

---

[51] *MFS* I, i. 1 (PL 44, 185) (CSEL 60, 3). Wermelinger, 23, remarks that the emphasis on infant baptism in this work has often led to its being cited by the second half of its full title – *On Infant Baptism*.

[52] *SL* ii. 3 (PL 44, 202) (CSEL 60, 156).

[53] *L* 146 (PL 33, 596) (CSEL 44, 273f.).

[54] *L* 157 (PL 33, 674–93) (CSEL 44, 449–88).

[55] Morris, 1965, 37ff., argues that he was a Briton but Bonner, 1972, 5f., does not accept this view, preferring to call him 'the Sicilian Anonymous'.

[56] *PP* xxvi. 51; xxvii. 52; xxix. 53 (PL 44, 349f.) (CSEL 42, 104ff.).

necessity of divine grace. If such it indeed was, then Pelagius certainly missed the hidden meaning intended; otherwise, would he have produced this very letter at the Synod of Diospolis as a testimonial from Augustine to his good standing?

Opinions will always differ as to the intention of Augustine's letter to Pelagius in 413 and as to his attitude to Pelagius prior to 415; probably his initial hesitation was prompted partly by the fact that he saw in Pelagius an ally against the Manichees, partly by the high reputation which Pelagius had won among his many influential supporters in Rome. But by the time he came to write his *Retractations* in 426–7 Augustine himself was in no doubt at all. In the relevant passage he explains that he had not mentioned Pelagius or others by name in his first anti-Pelagian treatise simply because he still hoped at that time that this would be the best way to correct them without alienating them further; again, he had mentioned Pelagius by name in the third book of that treatise 'with considerable commendation because his life and conduct were praised by many'.[57] At this stage he had been concerned only to refute certain statements made by Pelagius in order to show him the error of his ways and had been reluctant to attack him personally; but when he continued to defend his views 'with persistent animosity' and after his 'disciple' Celestius had been condemned for holding similar opinions, a more direct line of attack was called for and from now on no holds were barred.

There had been a similar hardening of Augustine's heart against the Donatists, who had by no means been finally disposed of when the real dangers of Pelagianism became fully apparent to him. Thus, at the very time when he was able to justify his *volte-face* in accepting the necessity to exercise *disciplina* in dealing with one obdurate group of dissidents, the man now acknowledged as leader of the African Church found himself being confronted by another – indeed he might well have quoted the great Roman poet whom he had once so admired: *primo avulso non deficit alter!*[58] Is it surprising if he lost his patience with this new coterie, which went so far as to question the importance of infant baptism by insisting that infants were not baptised for the remission of sins? They were now getting perilously close to the central issue of the Donatist controversy, though it had been the re-baptism of adults which had been the main bone of contention for them. In the eyes of Pelagius adult baptism and the grace which it bestowed upon the repentant sinner stood at the very heart of Christian belief; but he too placed no more emphasis on infant baptism than had the Donatists. It was not relevant to his teaching

---

[57] *R* II, 33, ed. Bogan, II, 60 (PL 32, 644) (CSEL 36, 171), supported by *L* 157 (PL 33, 674–93) (CSEL 44, 449–88), probably written in 413; cf. *L* 186 (PL 33, 815–32) (CSEL 57, 45–80), addressed to Paulinus of Nola in 417. In case the word *Retractations* may mislead the reader, it should be explained that it comes from the Latin *retracto*, not *retraho*, and means 're-examinations'. Wermelinger, 270f., maintains that the predominance of the Pelagian controversy in the work suggests that it could be regarded as a book of vindication against Pelagian ideas.

[58] Vergil, *Aeneid* VI, 143 – omitting, of course, the adjective *aureus*, 'golden', hardly appropriate in this case.

on man, and he was content to declare himself an agnostic as to the fate of those who died unbaptised: 'I know where they do not go but where they do go I do not know.'[59]

Augustine too had once dismissed this problem almost in despair and was to agonise about it to the end of his life. But he had set himself to carry out an exhaustive examination of all the available evidence, had resolved the question to his own satisfaction at least and had made his definitive judgement available in his seven books *On Baptism against the Donatists*, begun around 400 and completed probably some years later. The purpose of baptism, as he saw it, was to counteract a specific effect of original sin, and it was therefore imperative that it be administered as soon as possible after birth, since 'except by becoming a member of the Body of Christ there is no hope of salvation.'[60] He had been startled in 411 to learn that the Pelagians were claiming that by baptism children gained sanctification, not remission of sins.[61] It had thus become clear to him that the gravamen of the charges against Celestius lay in his denial of the need for infant baptism as an antidote for the transmission of original sin, and he believed Celestius to be a pupil of Pelagius. We have seen that there is no evidence that Pelagius held precisely the same views on infant baptism as had been advanced by his associate, who had displayed a strange lack of tactical finesse in pressing such views in Africa, where the subject of infant baptism was one of special importance to Christians. But it seemed to Augustine that, when cornered, Pelagius either would or could not give a straight answer and that his arguments against original sin in his book *On Nature* would have the effect of undermining one of the most cherished practices of the Church. Augustine had been made painfully aware at Carthage in 413 that his own views were still in danger of being misunderstood when, in order to pacify his congregation, he had found it necessary to fall back on Cyprian, the martyred bishop of that city, as his authority. This priceless jewel still needed protection from careless handling by men who did not appreciate its value. The plain fact is that, where infant baptism was concerned, Pelagius and Augustine were on entirely different wavelengths: what was of little significance to the one was absolutely crucial for the other.

Around 415 then, Augustine's attitude to Pelagius altered. But the reason he gives for it, namely, his reading of Pelagius' *On Nature*, has been called into question,[62] since it contains nothing new when compared with his commentary on the Epistles of Paul. In other words, *On Nature* was not so much a sudden shock as the last piece in a jig-saw with which he had been wrestling for three years, the final proof that Pelagius' unorthodox position on a number of matters fundamental to the Christian faith, like grace, original sin and

[59] *OS* xxi. 23 (PL 44, 395f.) (CSEL 42, 182). Contrary to the view expressed by Augustine, Pelagius did not teach that there was a middle place for infants dying unbaptised between heaven and hell, nor did he attempt to distinguish between the kingdom of God and eternal life; see Refoulé, 1963(b), especially 248f.

[60] *S* 294, x. 10 (PL 38, 1341).

[61] *MFS* III, vi. 12 (PL 44, 192f.) (CSEL 60, 139).

[62] R. F. Evans, 1968(a), 82ff.

baptism, must now be subjected to a frontal assault and no longer by oblique hints and warnings. Nor was it only the orthodox faith which was being threatened; it was the personal authority of Augustine himself as a spokesman of the Church. In this book Pelagius was using quotations from respected Catholic writers, including Augustine, and, in particular, seemed to be employing as ammunition against him statements from his early work *On Free Choice*, written against the Manichees in the years between 388 and 395.[63] In fact, the citations were used because Pelagius agreed with them but, always on the alert for the smallest signs of a Manichean revival, he also thought that he had found some in Augustine's teaching on original sin and predestination elsewhere in this book, since the former he saw as restoring to evil its Manichean status and the latter as the virtual equivalent of Manichean fatalism.

It has often been suggested that Augustine never entirely freed himself from the influence of some aspects of the Manicheism of his youth, and he may well have been conscious of being open to suspicion on that score even now, when he was at the zenith of his career. We can imagine his annoyance when he found that Pelagius was not above encouraging such a suspicion and charging him, the erstwhile hammer of the Manichees, with crypto-Manicheism. Had he to prove again that he had broken with this devilish creed years ago? Already, on at least one occasion, that of his consecration as bishop in 395, the old charge had sparked off a scandal, when the senior bishop of Numidia had refused for a time to preside at the ceremony and the Donatists had not been slow to use this refusal against him.[64] Towards the end of his life Julian of Eclanum, the last of his Pelagian adversaries and in many ways the most hostile and the most able, was to torment him with this same charge, and he was forced to clarify his position *vis-à-vis* both Pelagianism and Manicheism.[65] Now this trouble-maker Pelagius was accusing both Jerome and himself of neo-Manicheism, just as they in turn were doing the same to him.

Why was Manicheism still so important? What was there about this strange, Gnostic heresy that made it so popular as a smear-word in the early fifth century? 'For a sensitive man of the fifth century', writes Peter Brown, 'Manicheism, Pelagianism and the views of Augustine were not as widely separated as we would now see them: they would have appeared as points along the same great circle of problems raised by the Christian religion.'[66] And Gerald Bonner describes Augustine's earlier polemic against the Manichees as 'a highly important preparation for theological discussions which were not envisaged at the time when he wrote'.[67] Problems were then

[63] *NG* lxi. 71 – lxx. 84 (PL 44, 282–90) (CSEL 60, 286–99).

[64] *LPet* III, xvi. 19 (PL 43, 366f.); *CD* IV, lxiv. 79; III, lxxx. 92 (PL 43, 545f., 591f.) (CSEL 52, 557ff., 495).

[65] *TLP* II, ii. 2ff. (PL 44, 572f.) (CSEL 60, 461ff.) lists the similarities and differences between Manichees, Pelagians and Catholics. It is ironical that at the outset of the controversy the only common ground between Augustine and Pelagius was their opposition to Manicheism as defenders of free will.

[66] Brown, 1967, 370.

[67] Bonner, 1963, 194.

14

raised and argued about which were to develop into major issues in the debate with the Pelagians and, in the course of this debate, Augustine 'defined Pelagius' terms for him', just as Pelagius 'made him (Augustine) re-think his assumptions as no-one else could have done . . . and presented him with a new perspective on evil'.[68] Ever since his youth Augustine had been preoccupied, almost obsessed, with the problem of evil: 'Where then is evil, and whence has it come, and by what path has it crept in hither? What is its root, and what its seed?', he asks in his *Confessions*, reiterating the same questions again and again.[69] In his account of his own spiritual and intellectual pilgrimage he traces the slow and often painful steps by which he arrived at his final solution, one of them being his temporary attachment to Manicheism. No doubt it had first appealed to him because of its dualism of good and evil, which corresponded to his experience as a young man, tugged this way and that by bodily desires and repugnance to the actions to which they led him. Evil seemed to him at that time, as it did to the Manichees, to be a powerful force dragging him down into the depths of degradation, in other words, to be the root of all sin. But further examination revealed that this could not be the right answer: 'like many other simple explanations, it raises as many problems as it resolves.'[70] The idea of a god whose powers were limited in the struggle against evil was not to Augustine's taste, and he abandoned it after nearly nine years of adherence for his own interpretation of Neoplatonism. Evil, he now came to see, could not be substance but must be privation of good, a corruption of God's creation, permitted by him to exist for his own good but inscrutable purposes. Augustine's debate with the Manichees had all-important consequences for his concept of man, since it made him realise that, whereas Adam had been created good, he had also been created with free will, thus making him liable to sin through the wrong exercise of that free will; Adam fell because he turned away from good and from God *by his own choice*, and his sin was a voluntary act of evil.

Here we reach the main battleground on which Augustine and Pelagius were to fight. The very arguments for man's responsibility, exercised by use of his free will, which Augustine had deployed against the Manichees, were now being adapted by Pelagius to suit his own case that man had the power to save himself, always provided that he had accepted the saving grace of baptism *of his own choice*. Augustine's reply was to insist upon the sole power of grace to act upon man: the Pelagians, he wrote, are a new brand of heretics, 'certain pseudo-monks who, under the pretence of defending the freedom of the will, dispute the grace of God and endeavour to overthrow the foundation of the Christian faith'.[71] So the controversy came to centre around two different interpretations of free will and grace, with each party to it accusing the other of over-emphasising one of these at the expense of the other. 'The

[68] G. R. Evans, 1982, 148.
[69] *C* VII, v. 7 (PL 32, 736) (CSEL 33, 147).
[70] Bonner, 1963, 197.
[71] *PP* xxxv. 61 (PL 44, 355) (CSEL 42, 116).

two men disagreed radically on an issue that is still relevant, and where the basic lines of division have remained the same: on the nature and sources of a fully good, creative action.'[72] And so a debate which began almost coincidentally between a dedicated defender of Christian orthodoxy and an equally single-minded reformer of Christian morals will lead to a public examination of some of the most profound issues affecting the faith which both sincerely professed.

By 415 Augustine had finally realised that the time had come to direct his artillery at Pelagius across the no man's land which separated them. His 'pupil' Celestius had been condemned but he himself had escaped to Palestine and was there carrying the fight to Jerome; a letter from Sicily warned that Pelagianism was rife there,[73] an appeal had come from Spain for help in resisting new doctrinal errors which had spread to that region and were joining forces with Priscillianism,[74] and the Spanish priest Orosius had arrived in Africa, seeking advice on the same subject, possibly with the encouragement of the African bishops.[75] When Orosius moved on to Palestine, he went armed with two letters from Augustine to Jerome. These letters,[76] each of them virtually a minor treatise, are of the highest importance, not least because they show Augustine's deep concern for the human implications of issues raised in his debate with Pelagius, though the latter is not referred to by name. The first issue is that of infants dying unbaptised and condemned to eternal punishment through no fault of their own, if Augustine's theory of predestination were correct, an issue which was to trouble him to the end of his days; he was no *tortor infantium*. He now sought Jerome's help with this problem and, in order to justify his own position, set it in the context of his views on the origin of the soul, which he rightly perceived to be the starting-point of any doctrine of transmitted sin. What if Jerome still adhered to his earlier view, that is, of separate creation by God of each soul on conception?[77] If so, it was imperative that he and Jerome should be seen to be in agreement on a subject which was fundamental to his whole case against the Pelagians and that no trace should remain of the rift which had grown between the two great doctors of the contemporary Church since their

[72] Brown, 1967, 371.
[73] *L* 156, replied to in 157 (PL 33, 673–93) (CSEL 44, 448–88).
[74] Orosius, *Enquiry or Memorandum to Augustine on the Error of the Priscillianists and Origenists* (PL 42, 665–70) (CSEL 18, 151–71); see *R*, II, 44, ed. Bogan, II, 70 (PL 32, 648f.) (CSEL 36, 183). In reply Augustine wrote his treatise *Against the Priscillianists and Origenists* in 415 (PL 42, 669–78) but in it he reveals little knowledge of the Spanish heresy, and his principal account of it was not to appear until he addressed his book *On the Heresies* to the deacon Quodvultdeus in 429.
[75] Avitus, *Letter to Palchonius* (PL 41, 805f.); see Davids, 23f.
[76] *L* 166, 167 (PL 33, 720–41) (CSEL 44, 545–609); the letters were entitled *On the Origin of the Soul of Man* and *On the Opinion of the Apostle James* respectively.
[77] Jerome, *Defence against Rufinus* II, 4 (PL 23, 389). The main alternative to creationism in Augustine's day was traducianism, the belief that a child's soul was transmitted to it by its parents along with its body, and we shall have occasion later to observe how difficult Augustine found it to choose between these two theories of the soul's origin. As an orthodox Christian the third possibility was not open to him, namely pre-existence or reincarnation, since it was mainly associated with Gnosticism and Origen, both of them anathematised by the Church.

disagreement of many years earlier. But if he had any fears that the old man had to be alerted to the need for the strongest possible, concerted action against Pelagius, now that he had passed into his sector of the battlefield, he had misread Jerome's attitude to Pelagianism, which, as we have seen, had already led him into a bitter war of attrition by 415. In fact, Jerome's reply did not arrive until 416 and was very brief, merely explaining his failure to reply earlier.[78]

Thus it was that the two most articulate and influential personalities in the Western Church joined forces against Pelagius and that both saw not only the Church but also their own reputations to be at stake. The exasperated Jerome had never been one to pull his punches when in the ring with his opponents or even, for that matter, with his friends when they offended him. All the eloquence and violence of his invective were now aimed at these pestilential Pelagians and especially at the man whom he believed to be their leader. By 417 Pelagianism had become for him 'an unceasing, obsessional pre-occupation',[79] no doubt aggravated by an attack upon his monastery at Bethlehem in 416, commonly held to have been instigated by Pelagians. For his part, Augustine must have found this heresy not only dangerous but also a tiresome distraction from the manifold tasks of a bishop, already quite enough to tax him in weakened health. Nor should it be forgotten that though, unlike Jerome, kindly and patient by nature, he too was a man who never failed to push his views to their logical conclusion. In pressing his case on the need for salvation even if it meant applying coercion, on the eternal damnation of infants dying unbaptised, on the absolute necessity for regeneration through baptism within the Church, on the exclusive power of divine grace to save or destroy, on a form of predestination which limited the number of the saved right from the moment of creation – in all the multifarious aspects of the Christian faith on which his brilliant and comprehensive mind touched and fastened through his long career, he was impelled to adopt extreme positions in order to buttress his own arguments and demolish those of his opponents.[80] The fundamentals of his life's work were now being challenged by one who lacked his practical experience and his unrivalled knowledge and under-standing of Christian scriptures and doctrine.

Pelagius, as the main target of Augustine's last and greatest counter-attack on the enemies of the faith, was out-manoeuvred and out-gunned from the start and, at the last, driven from the field with ignominy and branded as a heretic and an outcast. In the words of George Orwell, taken from the original preface to *Animal Farm* which was suppressed at the time when he wrote it: 'Anyone who challenges the prevailing orthodoxy finds himself silenced with surprising effectiveness.'[81] In the words of Augustine himself, pronounced against the Donatists, '*Securus iudicat orbis terrarum*': 'the verdict of the world is

---

[78] *Letters* 134 (PL 22, 1161f.) (CSEL 56, 261ff.).
[79] Kelly, 1975, 324.
[80] Cf. Bentley-Taylor, 232f.
[81] I owe this reference to Thorpe, 6.

conclusive.'[82] These 'palmary words of St Augustine' became 'the shadow of a hand upon the wall' for Cardinal Newman, when he took his final step towards Rome, and were later recast and expanded in his own uncompromising terms: 'the deliberate judgement, in which the whole Church at length rests and acquiesces, is an infallible prescription and a final sentence against such portions of it as protest and secede.'[83]

It was indeed 'a famous victory'; but if we are to begin to appreciate its significance for the Western Church at this point in its history, we must try to set it in its historical context – the process of Christianisation of the Roman Empire which had begun with Constantine's adoption of Christianity as the official religion of that Empire and had gained a slow but steady momentum in the course of the fourth century. The old pagan order, though now deprived of imperial patronage, had not been completely swept away but still 'survived in an uneasy synthesis with the new: people and institutions and much of cultural life were still rooted in the pagan past'.[84] Yet this 'façade of continuity', as Peter Brown has explained, 'only masks an important change' in that 'the secular traditions of the senatorial class, traditions which one might have assumed to be intimately bound up with the fate of their pagan beliefs, came to be continued by a Christian aristocracy'.[85] The Christianisation of the Roman Empire must be seen not simply as a result of imperial pressure or a change of taste and attitude but rather as part of a prolonged and complex process of development.

In dealing with such a complex and, in terms of documentation, elusive process it is not easy to trace the precise steps by which it took place or to evaluate the relative importance of the many factors which contributed to it. But it is generally agreed that the legislative measures introduced by the Emperors in order to repress paganism, though often necessary and at least partially and temporarily effective, were much less influential in the long term than the less obvious pressures exerted by the need for social conformity. Among these was the practice of mixed marriages between pagan and Christian, which the Church had long ceased to discourage because it usually seemed to work out in its favour; but while giving full weight to the influence upon their husbands of the growing number of educated women converted to Christianity, we must not overemphasise this factor, since, as Brown has rightly warned us, 'we do not know when they became Christian', and it would be unwise to ignore 'the immense *esprit de corps* of a Roman *gens*'.[86] The appeal of the more extreme forms of asceticism emanating from the East and increasing in popularity in the West also needs to be taken into account, as do the effect of miraculous cures, the emotional appeal of stories of martyrdom and, not least, the tendency to syncretism which had for so long been one of

[82] *LParm* III, 24 (PL 43, 101) (CSEL 51, 131).

[83] *Apologia pro Vita Sua*, Everyman's Library 1949, 120f.

[84] Frend, 1984, 554; I am greatly indebted to him for his excellent account of the process of Christianisation in Pt. III, c. 16.

[85] Brown, 1972, 168.

[86] Ibid. 174.

the most prominent features of Roman religion. But perhaps most important of all was the classical culture of the age, shared by pagan and Christian alike, which provided a common ground enabling them to live together and, in the end, to accept Christianity as the only available means of ensuring that the Roman state could supply the religious foundation demanded both by its past traditions and by its present circumstances. Thus, in late-fourth-century Rome, 'the conventional good man of pagan Rome had imperceptibly become the conventional good Christian "believer" ';[87] but there were many who began to be concerned with the problem of deciding what exactly was the kind of behaviour and way of life and what were the moral standards which should distinguish the true Christian from the conforming pagan.[88] Sincere and thoughtful Christians in Rome were anxiously seeking for an answer to this question, and many derived fresh inspiration from the pilgrimages which they undertook and which brought them under the influence of practices and ideals that recalled the spirit of total dedication characteristic of their predecessors when faced with persecution and martyrdom. To lead them in their search and point them in the right direction they needed gurus, spiritual mentors of high moral standing and steeped in the scriptures, and among those who answered their call were Jerome and Pelagius, both of whom found their way to Rome by different routes before the end of the fourth century. Jerome's last stay in Rome was a brief one – from 382 to 385 – and he left under a cloud; but Pelagius stayed longer and became the leader of a large and influential circle of loyal adherents comprising not only educated aristo-crats, many of them women, but also clerics who were later to form the nucleus of the opposition to his final condemnation in 418.

As we have seen, Pelagius' central message, though at first addressed to a comparatively limited audience, had profound implications for the Church as a whole: it was 'firmly based on a distinctive idea of the Church'[89] as a perfect religious institution consisting of perfect Christians wholly dedicated to the observance of the strict code of behaviour enjoined by its founder and followed by his apostles. In a treatise *On the Christian Life*, now generally accepted to have been written by Pelagius himself, he insists that 'God wanted his people to be holy',[90] an injunction spelt out by one of his followers in terms whose meaning is unmistakable: 'Surely it is not true that the Law of Christian behaviour has not been given to everyone who is called a Christian? . . . There can be no double-standard in one and the same people.'[91] The members of Pelagius' Church were to be *integri*, 'perfect, authentic, without moral blemish';[92] there was no place in it for nominal Christians, camp-

---

[87] Ibid. 193.
[88] Markus, 1974, 123, reminds us that Eusebius had long before deplored 'the hypocrisy of those who had crept into the Church' (*Life of Constantine*, iv. 54) and that Augustine himself 'around 400 . . . was worried about the influx of half-converted, "feigned" Christians, as he called them'.
[89] Brown, 1972, 194.
[90] *On the Christian Life*, 9 (PL 40, 1038; 50, 392).
[91] *On Riches*, vi. 3 (PLS 1, 1387).
[92] *Letter to a Young Man* (*Humanae referunt litterae*), 3 (PLS 1, 1378).

followers who had crept into its shelter under pressure from the need for political or social conformity. Their baptism had presented them with the unique opportunity to become 'authentic Christians' once and for all by abandoning their old pagan ways and leading a new life: it had 'placed a glass wall between the past and the present'.[93] This unique opportunity they had squandered by lapsing into their old, comfortable habits of self-indulgence and careless pursuit of Mammon.

But the blame for this lapse was not theirs alone: their established leaders in the Church were at least as culpable, since it was they who had misled their flock by encouraging them to accept standards of Christian behaviour which were no more than second-rate. It was at this point that Pelagius clashed with Augustine and other leaders of the Church, and we have noted his indignation when he heard the tenth book of the *Confessions* read out in Rome. What he heard convinced him that its author had betrayed a great tradition of Western Christianity. 'It is Pelagius', maintains Brown in a memorable sentence, 'who had seized the logical conclusions of this tradition: he is the last, the most radical, and the most paradoxical exponent of the ancient Christianity – the Christianity of discontinuity.'[94] Brown goes on to argue that it was still possible to find a place in late-fourth-century Italy for a Christianity of discontinuity, and it was Augustine's great hero Ambrose who had pointed the way ahead. But the Church which set out to put such a Christianity into practice would be a minority Church, a Church of the *élite* and for the *élite*, a leaven in the lump. And the emergence and survival of such a minority Church was a possibility that neither the leaders of the established Church nor the representatives of the imperial government could afford to countenance. They were bound to see it as a fresh source of division at a time when what Rome needed most of all, especially after its shattering experience at the hands of the Goth, was security and solidarity. The established Church was to be the main agency of those who sought to supply this need, and any challenge to its integrity must be resisted and crushed. Thus the final defeat of Pelagius and his followers was not only a rejection of what the Church judged to be a heresy in theological terms but an elimination of what was identified as a potentially dangerous source of schism in the body social and politic.

[93] Brown, 1972, 195.
[94] Ibid. 200. Not the least of the debts owed to Brown by students of Pelagius and Pelagianism are his three seminal papers on the Christianisation of the aristocracy and the patrons and other supporters of Pelagius. The extent of my personal indebtedness to Peter Brown's publications both in this chapter and elsewhere in my book is indicated by the number of times I have quoted from them, realising that their elegance and succinctness defy any attempt at paraphrase.

II

THE 'TRUE' SPOKESMAN

'Religious history, like all history, is written by the victors, who naturally present their own favourites as the "true spokesmen for the founding revelation".'
PETER L. BERGER[1]

So it was in the aftermath of the battle between Pelagius and his opponents, when the noise of conflict began to die down and the protagonists had sheathed their swords. Both Jerome and Augustine left behind them a great corpus of their works, among them the latter's fifteen anti-Pelagian treatises, all intact and only one unfinished; we have also at our disposal writings by Prosper of Aquitaine, Paul Orosius and Marius Mercator, all contemporaries of Pelagius who were opposed to his teachings and exerted a considerable influence on the later historians of the Church. Of his own works only a handful have survived, along with a number of quotations embedded in Augustine's treatises, sermons and letters and selected by him solely in order to refute them. But enough remains to ensure that he has not lacked supporters over the intervening centuries, many of whom have denied that he was a heretic. Are they any better placed to judge a heresy of the early fifth century than we are to adjudicate on the resounding controversy which followed the publication of *Essays and Reviews* in the middle of the nineteenth?

A heresy is a product of a particular period of history, and to try to detach it from its historical context is a very risky business. The word itself, derived from the Greek noun *haeresis*, which had the primary meaning of 'choice', came to be applied to philosophical schools as having chosen a certain 'way of thought'.[2] In the New Testament it is found in the Acts of the Apostles describing the Sadducees and Pharisees as parties or divisions within the Jewish religion, and Josephus uses it in the same sense.[3] But already – in Acts, Corinthians and Galatians – it is also being used *in malam partem* of the Nazarenes as a religious sect whose ringleader is identified as Paul,[4] and from Ignatius onwards it is used more and more to describe theological error. In Christian terminology of the second century a *haeresis* is no longer a 'choice' but a *'wrong* choice', and a heretic is one who has followed a *'wrong* way of

---

[1] Berger, 146.

[2] Dionysius of Halicarnassus, *On Literary Composition*, 2; he is referring to Stoicism in this instance.

[3] Of Sadducees: Acts 5, 17; Josephus, *Jewish Antiquities* 13, 171. Of Pharisees: Acts 15, 5; 26, 5; Josephus, *Life*, 10, 12, 171 and elsewhere.

[4] Acts 24, 5; cf. 24, 14 and 28, 22; 1 Cor. 11, 19; Gal. 5, 20.

thought', thus encouraging a division in the ranks of the Church. Pelagius was deemed to be a heretic because he had made a wrong choice in the considered view of the ecclesiastical establishment of his day, and no amount of retrospective judgement, short of formal rehabilitation, can ever alter that verdict. 'Not to say what the Church says' is 'the real criterion of heresy'.[5]

Strictly then, Pelagius was, and is, a heretic in the eyes of the Catholic Church, and his condemnation as such is an unquestionable datum of history, whatever we in the more permissive atmosphere of the late twentieth century may think, or argue, to the contrary. But whether his condemnation was justified is another matter and one which we are entitled to subject to the closest examination – even if we accept the warning that contemporary scholarship is tending to become so enamoured of ancient heretics for various reasons, not all of them theological, as to be capable of turning 'into an article of interpretive faith' the words of the American poet, 'Truth forever on the scaffold, Wrong forever on the throne.'[6] 'Heresy', the *Concise Oxford Dictionary of the Christian Church* tells us, 'is the formal denial or doubt of any defined doctrine of the Catholic faith.'[7] Can it be with justice applied to Pelagius? If so, it is the duty of those who hold that view to justify it by establishing beyond reasonable contradiction that there was such a defined doctrine and that he either denied or doubted it.

In these times it is not sufficient to repeat Augustine's claim that 'the verdict of the world is conclusive'; too often history has shown that verdict to be wrong and to represent no more than the last gasp of a corrupt and effete establishment. Just recently we have celebrated the five-hundredth anniversary of the birth of Martin Luther. How many of his contemporaries would have credited the possibility that the time would come when Church and State would vie with each other in claiming him as their own 'true spokesman'? Perhaps only one, Erasmus. Living as he did in the very centre of a maelstrom of charges and counter-charges of heresy, he could still maintain: 'We are not obliged to believe everything in the writings of the Christian fathers, and if we are in error, we are not necessarily heretics: not every error is heresy';[8] and in defending his own sturdiest opponent, Luther himself, 'They simply cry heresy, but no author is free from heresy, whether ancient or modern.' Again, in his controversial interpretation of the parable of the wheat and the tares, he concludes: 'Let them grow together until the harvest', identifying the tares with the heretics whom others wanted to root out altogether.[9] Pelagius, of course, was a heretic in the eyes of Erasmus, who 'did take seriously the consensus and avowed that save for its authority he might

[5] Robinson, 28.

[6] James Russell Lowell, 'The Present Crisis' in *Complete Poetical Works*, Boston 1925; I owe this reference to Henry, 126.

[7] Livingstone, ed., 237.

[8] The Leiden edition of Erasmus, ed. Leclerc, 1703, repr. 1963, V, 1172F–1173A; cf. 1172A and Bainton, 1977, 322.

[9] *Erasmi Epistolae*, ed. P. S. and Mrs Allen, 1906–58, III, 939; Leiden ed. IX, 1015–94; see Bainton, 1977, 193, 253f.

easily have been a Pelagian or an Arian' but 'adhered to it only on theological matters which he considered insoluble or inconsequential'.[10] Can we, endowed with the hindsight of the fifteen centuries which separate us from Pelagius, hope to determine whether the questions which he raised are for us insoluble or inconsequential? We can at least take our cue from a Christian as wise and humane as Erasmus and beware of condemning Pelagius out of hand merely because the 'true' spokesmen so condemned him at the height of the Pelagian controversy, even if it was they who won the overwhelming approval of the Councils of the Church. 'What councils?' Erasmus once asked; 'there were Greek Councils which did not know Latin at all.' 'Don't listen to the Greeks', rejoined a friend; 'they were heretics too.'[11] Yes, there are heretics and heretics, and a man can even be a 'heretic in the truth': 'because his pastor says so, or the assembly so determines, without knowing other reason, though his belief be true yet the very truth he holds becomes his heresy.'[12]

We do not lack modern theologians of considerable distinction to reinforce the need for caution in differentiating between heretics, pseudo-heretics and 'heretics in the truth'. 'All exploration, whether in the theological or socio-logical field', said John Robinson, 'involves the risk, indeed the certainty, of mistakes. But it is at least arguable, from the study of church history, that more damage has almost always been done *in the long run* by the suppression of opinion than by any error given rein by freedom',[13] *Experto credite*. He goes on to illustrate his point by summarising the notorious cases of John Macleod Campbell, found guilty of heresy by the Church of Scotland in 1831, and of Bishop Pike, accused of heresy in 1966. And John Macquarrie has pointed out that Campbell's book *The Nature of the Atonement*, which appeared twenty-five years after his deposition from the ministry of his Church, is now recognised as 'one of the classics of Scottish theology'.[14] The lesson which he proceeds to draw from this unhappy episode and its ironical outcome is that it is not enough to detect and expose in an alleged heresy a contradiction of some particular formulation but that it is also necessary to show that it is in conflict with 'the reality of faith that this dogmatic formulation sought to express' and is 'excluded as a possible reinterpretation or re-expression of the faith.'[15] If heresy *is* suspected, then the best way to combat it is by a clear and affirmative statement of the true position of the Church, thus correcting bad

[10] Bainton, 1977, 239f. Erasmus agreed with Luther that salvation is by faith alone and that man cannot be perfect but he disagreed in wishing to give man credit for good deeds done.

[11] *Epistolae* II, 465; cf. Leiden ed. IX, 752f. and Bainton, 1977, 167.

[12] John Milton, *Areopagitica* in *Complete Prose Works* II, Yale and Oxford 1959. T. H. Huxley, *Science and Culture* xii, in his essay 'The Coming of Age of the *Origin of Species*' says much the same in different words: 'Irrationally held truths may be more harmful than reasoned errors.'

[13] Robinson, 29, quoting from the evidence which he gave to the committee appointed to examine the case against Bishop Pike and which was incorporated in its report. It is interesting to note in the context of Pelagianism that it was Reinhold Niebuhr, one of the most severe critics of its appearance in modern theology, who wrote of 'residual awareness of the possibility of error in the truth in which we believe, and of the possibility of truth in the error against which we contend', a quotation which I owe to Professor David Greenwood.

[14] Macquarrie, 1975, 45.

[15] Ibid., 46.

theology with good. Schleiermacher, he reminds us, held that 'there are in fact only a few basic heresies, and what makes any one of these a heresy is that when the implications of the position are followed out, the whole Christian faith collapses.'[16]

In all fairness, it must be added that Macquarrie is careful to distinguish in his discussion of heresy and the criteria which may be properly employed in identifying it between the situation today and that which faced the Church in its first five centuries. Thus it may be that in the case of some great heresies of the past the issues have never since been 'wrought out so clearly and argued with such amplitude for stakes that were incalculably high.'[17] Yet it would not be irrelevant to comment that Campbell's 'error' was in teaching 'that God's reconciling grace is offered to all men and not just to a predestined few',[18] and that this, as we shall see, was something on which Pelagius rightly insisted and which Augustine wrongly rejected as a result of his misinterpretation of scripture. But it was only one of the issues of principle about which they were in fundamental disagreement. The questions which we must endeavour to answer are: Was the teaching of Pelagius such that, if its implications were followed out, it would have caused the collapse of the whole Christian faith? Was it in conflict with 'the reality of faith' and so 'excluded as a possible reinterpretation or re-expression' of it? Was a serious attempt made to 'correct bad theology with good'? Was Pelagius, to use a definition of heresy in the twelfth century, 'a heretic who not only fell into error but, on being shown his error, persisted in it'?[19] It may help us to try to establish how Pelagianism was seen by the Church of the early fifth century against the background of earlier heresies.

The main preoccupation of the early Fathers was to resist the attacks of paganism and the insidious teachings of Gnosticism in its many forms, and the identification of heresy was at this stage a concomitant of the process of formulating Christian doctrine, indeed was often indispensable to such a formulation. Controversy revolved around two focal and related issues – the nature of the Godhead and the interrelation of the three persons of the Trinity: Monarchianism and its variations (Adoptionism, Modalism, Sabellianism and Patripassianism), Docetism and Montanism were all, in a sense, no more than skirmishes leading up to the all-out battle with Arianism, the principal heresy denying the divinity of Jesus, which was to rage throughout the fourth century and to threaten to tear the Church from limb to limb, leaving its scars unhealed until the seventh century, when the Lombards were finally converted to orthodoxy. As for Apollinarianism, the first great christological heresy, denying the full manhood of Jesus, it was eventually forbidden as a form of public worship in 381, by which time heresy had become a crime against the state.

By the time of Pelagius then, there were two accepted doctrines which had

[16] Schleiermacher, 95f., quoted in Macquarrie, 47.
[17] Murray, 44, quoted in Macquarrie, 44.
[18] Macquarrie, 45.
[19] Moore, 3.

been hammered out against the heretics and laid down by the Church in black and white, those of the Incarnation and the Trinity. No one could, or did, accuse Pelagius of denying these two fundamental doctrines; on the contrary, his teachings show that he lost no opportunity of attacking any who had done so, and not even Augustine claimed that his christology was other that orthodox.[20] As for Origenism, we have seen that Jerome's attempt to cast its dark shadow over him was either sincere but misguided or a deliberate, tactical riposte to the revival of insinuations that he himself was tarred with the same brush. Manicheism too was a blunt stick which could be used to beat Jerome and Augustine with as much, or as little, justification as Pelagius. By now 'Manichee' had become 'an imprecise term of general abuse',[21] and Jerome admits that 'any grave and pale ascetic' was likely to be so labelled.[22] But it was still a force to be reckoned with in the later fourth century and, despite the increasing severity of the laws directed against it and particularly of the Edict of Theodosius in 382, it could still command considerable support in Africa and some even in Rome – 'for Rome hides several of them', in Augustine's words.[23] When Orosius was sent by bishops in Spain to consult Augustine on how best to combat the threat of Priscillianism, this Spanish heresy was closely linked with Manicheism by them because they saw it as a fresh manifestation of the Manichean menace.

Priscillianism has the doubtful distinction of being the first heresy of the West, preceding Pelagianism by a few decades. 'In the seventies of the fourth century', writes Henry Chadwick in his definitive study of it, 'the Spanish churches were stirred by a new voice: a devout cultivated layman named Priscillianus began to ask his fellow Christians to take their baptismal renunciation more seriously and to give more time to special spiritual study.'[24] 'Priscillian's call is strongly ascetic', he comments, 'addressed not merely to isolated individuals, but to the faithful willing to give an unreserved dedication to Christ their God.' Priscillian, in other words, like Pelagius, wanted reform within the Church, not apart from it, and the response was encouraging, quickly spreading to Galicia and from there across the Pyrenees to Aquitaine; it has 'something of that contagion characteristic of a revival Awakening', and 'its effect came to be passionately divisive'. But at the council of Saragossa in 380 and at Priscillian's trial in 386 at Trier, though Patripassianism was added to the other charges against him, the main charge was that of Manicheism, which he disavowed with great vehemence, adjudged by Chadwick to have been 'passionate and surely sincere'.[25] But neither passion nor sincerity proved to be of any help to him, and a combination of ecclesiastical pressure and political connivance succeeded in engineering his

---

[20] J. McW. Dewart, 1982, 1221, 1227 sums up the position in 412; but in 1231ff. she goes on to describe Augustine's later attacks on the soteriology of Pelagius and his associates.

[21] H. Chadwick, 1976, 146; for references see n. 2.

[22] *Letters* 22, 13; *Against Jovinian* i. 3 (PL 22, 402) (CSEL 54, 161) (PL 23, 212f.)

[23] *C* V, x. 19 (PL 32, 715) (CSEL 33, 106).

[24] H. Chadwick, 1976, 8.

[25] Ibid., 97.

conviction on a primary charge of sorcery and his execution by order of the Emperor Maximus soon afterwards. And 'it was the taint of Manichean heresy that made the graver charge easy to believe.'[26]

This judicial murder is of great significance for anyone who tries to recreate the ecclesiastical climate of the period, highlighting as it does the dangers facing nonconformists of being accused *per saturam* of any heretical beliefs that the establishment could discover even the slightest justification for attributing to them. Like Pelagius, Priscillian had started out with a programme for moral reform of the Church; he ended by being convicted and executed on charges of holding opinions and encouraging practices condemned not only by the Church but also by the civil power. Heresy was now a crime against the State as well as a sin against the Church, and a heretic was now liable to suffer drastic punishment at the hands of the secular authorities, if his case were brought to their attention. We are witnessing the unforeseen consequences of the alliance between Constantine and the Church in the early fourth century, foreshadowing the Caesaropapism of the East and the secular authority of the papacy in the West. By the close of the fourth century, reinforced by imperial edicts against Arians, Manichees, Photinians, Eunomians and Apollinarians, the Church had won for itself such an unassailable position that it could refuse to tolerate any form of Christianity not sanctioned by itself. It might dare to challenge and modify the wishes of the imperial house, as Ambrose succeeded in doing on more than one occasion; but it could also demand its support when such a strategy seemed to be the only one likely to achieve its purposes. All it had to do was to throw the book at its opponents.

At the same time, and through the efforts of Augustine more than anyone else, the Western Church was becoming increasingly conscious of its new rôle as an integrated body outside the boundaries of which there was no hope of salvation – *extra ecclesiam nulla salus*[27] – and within which there was a necessity for united action to eliminate emerging heresy. It was to mobilise such action that Orosius sought the help of Augustine in Africa and Jerome in Palestine in 415, and Augustine's comparative ignorance of Priscillianism at that stage did not inhibit him from writing his treatise against it and Origenism in the same year. Jerome too had displayed little interest in the Spanish heresy and, for him, showed himself 'remarkably neutral';[28] his main interest, when alerted to the danger by Orosius – and that thirty years after the execution of the heresiarch –, was in its connections with Manicheism and so, in his view, with Pelagianism, and he recognised the need to close ranks in defence of the Church. Of Pelagianism, however, he had already made his own diagnosis: had he not already sized up Pelagius and the kind of delinquents with whom he was associated – men like Jovinian, Rufinus of Aquileia and John of Jerusalem? Origenism, Manicheism, Priscillianism, Pelagianism – what did it

[26] Ibid., 143f.
[27] *B* IV, xvii. 24 (PL 43, 170) (CSEL 51, 250); the actual order of the words as quoted from Cyprian is *salus extra ecclesiam non est.*
[28] H. Chadwick, 1976, 152.

matter how one classified them, when all were but symptoms of the same malignant disease threatening the body of Mother Church? What did matter was firmness of purpose enabling one to seize the knife and cut the cancer out before its poison could spread any further. His response to Pelagianism was like that of the Spanish bishops to Priscillianism; it was founded on the need for immediate and positive action without bothering too much about theological niceties.

Augustine was more clinical in his approach; it was his practice to examine the symptoms of theological error with the utmost care and to try to coax them away before resorting to radical surgery. But once his patient was on the operating table, he could be as bold as the next man in his incisions. As he saw the situation, the activities of Pelagius could have been left to Rome to deal with, so long as their effects were limited to that area; but once they had spread to Spain, which Priscillianism had shown to be vulnerable to schism and heresy, quite possibly to Sicily, and thence to Africa and Palestine, the very heart of Christianity, it was time not merely to scotch the snake but to kill it. Unlike Jerome, whose primary interest was in biblical exegesis, Augustine had both the knowledge and the experience to perceive that Pelagianism raised issues so profound that, to use Schleiermacher's dictum, if their implications were followed out, the result would be the collapse of the traditional faith as he understood it. It was not enough to accuse Pelagius of trying to resurrect old heresies: the real quarrel with him was over new issues much more fundamental and urgent, namely, his reductionist interpretations of original sin and divine grace resulting from an excessive emphasis on the freedom of the human will.

Now, however closely Augustine's doctrine of original sin might be bound up with that of grace, there was as yet no agreed view of it which could command universal support, as Celestius had astutely pointed out to the Council of Carthage. In the event, it was Pelagius' neglect of divine grace that led to his condemnation, and it was this which demanded Augustine's immediate attention. Pelagius' doctrine of grace was not only totally inadequate in his eyes, but also threatened the sacrament of baptism by its denial of original sin. It was his bounden duty as a bishop of the Church and its acknowledged leader in Africa to search out and destroy anyone who was rash enough to reveal deviationist tendencies in dealing with such vital matters: 'such a man', he affirmed, 'must be removed from the public ear and anathematised by every mouth.'[29] A threat to baptism was a threat to grace.

'The Christian doctrine of God's grace is a complicated and confusing subject, more so than is always realised', wrote Leonard Hodgson in his characteristically lucid analysis of the problems associated with its traditional formulation.[30] Ambiguities and uncertainties, he went on, increase rapidly when one climbs over the fences surrounding one's own denomination and ventures into the territory next door. He asks three questions about grace:

[29] *PMR* xxi. 44 (PL 44, 318) (CSEL 42, 47).
[30] Hodgson, 1968, II, 138; cf. 1936, 34.

'How can the same word mean such different things to different traditions of Christian theology, is it merely a disagreement on the meaning of terminology, or is there a deeper issue at stake?' His conclusion is that there *is* such an issue and that it is the problem of 'reconciling the ethical and personal character of the Christian religion with man's utter dependence on God's free gift of salvation'. This was also the conclusion of a report of a theological committee of the Faith and Order Movement in 1929: the recognition both of divine sovereignty and of human freedom is 'the fundamental conviction of religious life'.[31] But in his introduction to this report William Temple had to admit that, although the committee had been able to demonstrate that, in many instances, the same truth was being asserted in different forms, there were still very real differences remaining.

Indeed there were, and some of them were such as to challenge the very assumptions on which the committee had been established and the procedures which it had followed. Only a year after the report was published, a theologian of the Roman Catholic Church, which had elected not to send a representative to join the committee in its deliberations, published a work criticising in the strongest possible terms not only this attempt but any attempt to reconcile differing views on the subject of divine grace as 'a betrayal of the true faith'.[32] In its final statement the committee itself confessed that 'while from the point of view of philosophy the two points of view are irreconcilable, they represent the only basis on which the religious life can be built up'; 'our religious convictions demand dependence on God, our ethical convictions demand human freedom. The mistake that has been made has been that theologians have aimed at philosophical consistency.'[33] If this is a mistake, then both Augustine and Pelagius were guilty of it, since the problem of reconciling divine sovereignty with human freedom lay at the heart of their controversy, each maintaining that he, and not the other, was correctly interpreting key statements and ideas found in the scriptures and especially the Pauline Epistles, as well as in the writings of the early fathers. This was to be their bone of contention, at which they were to tug relentlessly from either end.

By the first century A.D. the Greek word *charis* already bore several senses. In classical and Hellenistic Greek it was used in three main ways: objectively, subjectively and concretely. Objectively, it could mean 'outward grace, charm, beauty', as it does as early as Homer and Hesiod; subjectively, 'grace

---

[31] Whitley, ed., 20.

[32] Hodgson, 1936, 2; the book referred to there and discussed in detail in 35ff. – A. Nygren, *Agape and Eros* – appeared in English as translated by A. G. Hebert in 1932 but had been written two years before; it cannot therefore be regarded as a reply to the committee of the Faith and Order Movement.

[33] Whitley, ed., 20. H. Chadwick, writing of the 'orthodoxy' of Origen, uses even stronger terms: 'Orthodoxy is a word that suggests clear-cut and absolute lines of division. It begins to look different if we ask whether some theologians may be more orthodox than others, whether there are degrees of understanding, whether, if we all see through a glass darkly, some may be more able to see a little clearly than others . . . absolute confidence is possible only for two classes of people, saints and idiots' (1966, 122f.).

or favour felt by the doer or receiver of a kindness', both being found in Aeschylus and Sophocles; concretely, 'a favour or boon granted or returned', a sense extended in early papyri and inscriptions, for example, as 'a grant from the Emperor'. In view of the steady growth of the imperial cult in the first century A.D. it is not surprising to find examples of a subjective sense of 'imperial favour' in inscriptions from that period. In fact, the sense which we find in them is not far removed from the generalised sense of 'divine grace' in Paul: Nero refers to his conferment of freedom on the Greeks as a gift of his *charis*, Gaius Caligula speaks of the 'abundance of the grace which is immortal' and of promotion 'by the grace of Gaius Caesar'. T. W. Manson may well have been right in seeing such a sense as 'supplying the linguistic starting-point' for its Christian use, especially when its use in the Septuagint appears to be normally confined to rendering the Hebrew word meaning 'favourable inclination or regard', the mercy and loving kindness of God being expressed by the Greek word *eleos* meaning 'mercy'. In the Psalms the word *charis* occurs only twice, both times in the objective sense of 'outward grace', as it does on three occasions when it is used in Proverbs; in Zechariah it occurs twice as the 'spirit of grace', and in Isaiah and Jeremiah not at all. Philo too limits his use of *charis*, normally in the plural, to the natural gifts of God, and in other Jewish religious writers 'the word plays no distinctive part'.[34]

In the New Testament *charis* is to be found on numerous occasions but not in Matthew or Mark and only eight times in Luke and three in John, and none of the occurrences in Luke or John, the latter all in the first chapter, point to the emergence of a new, specifically Christian sense. As Manson put it, 'While therefore Jesus in his own person is the source of the grace of which the New Testament speaks, he is not the source of the language used for describing it. This source was most probably Paul.'[35] It was his intense experience accompanying and following his conversion that impelled Paul to abandon the Jewish system of law and merit in which he had previously placed his whole trust. He determined to build his new life on the secure basis of God's grace and, to describe it, he employed the Greek word which he found ready to hand and already currently in use to denote the gracious favour of the Roman Emperor. This grace, unlike the Jewish idea of mercy, which was no more than an aid to righteousness, offered the possibility of salvation to all by giving them the chance to create a new life and acquire a new status. It was 'a quality manifested in operation', calling and 'justifying', that is, accounting righteous, those whom God had foreknown and selected from the beginning.[36] It was both premundane and temporal, a grace of election and justification but not of sanctification. And, with occasional differences in language and emphasis, the same generalised concept of grace is found in the other New Testament writings.

[34] Manson, in Whitley, ed., 33ff.
[35] Ibid., 42.
[36] N. P. Williams, 1930, 11.

The early Christians were so deeply convinced of their absolute dependence on God's grace and of the validity of their day-to-day experience of its operation that they saw no reason to differentiate between its manifold aspects or the means by which it was bestowed upon them – beyond, that is, the redemption won for them by Jesus through his crucifixion. The early Greek Fathers give 'only particular descriptions of grace and do not offer formal definitions, for which indeed no necessity arose in the Christian East'.[37] Creation, providence and redemption all fell within the province of 'original' grace, and man shared in these according to his capacity to do so; for his eternal salvation he also needed the 'specific' grace conferred only by baptism, which was a prerequisite for spiritual growth. The early Latin Fathers, living as they did in an age of romantic heroism, shared his belief in the saving grace of baptism and were strengthened in it by the bitter exigencies of persecution. Grace, now rendered by the Latin word *gratia*, was offered unconditionally and universally but could be appropriated only through baptism in faith. Thereafter, the Christian would be confirmed by God in the power to do good by his obedience (Tertullian) or his loyalty (Cyprian), which would be properly rewarded by the ability to withstand the trials and temptations of life.[38]

So much for the prehistory of grace, grace before Augustine, who was to be the first to construct a comprehensive doctrine: henceforth, 'the part of God and man in salvation and the harmony between grace and liberty indisputably form the central core of the teaching of the Bishop of Hippo'.[39] By 397, two years after his consecration as bishop, the foundations of his great doctrine of grace had been laid. But it was with his conversion in 386 that his absorbing interest in it may be said to have begun. Like Paul, he underwent a 'cataclysmic experience of instantaneous conversion from sin to God',[40] and, from that moment, his moment of truth, when the veil of uncertainty was torn aside, he was at last able to see the whole of his earlier life as a preliminary to the direct intervention of God. As a young man he had known temptation and

[37] Gloubokowsky, in Whitley, ed., 105.
[38] Watson, in Whitley, ed., 106ff.; N. P. Williams, 1930, 16ff.
[39] Portalié, 177.
[40] N. P. Williams, 1930, 19; the 'authenticity' of Augustine's conversion is discussed in Rees, 5ff. But though adhering to his defence of the 'authenticity' of Augustine's conversion experience, the author of this article now readily acknowledges that his interpretation of that experience was simplistic: it fails to give due weight to the fact that Augustine's account of it was written after he had devoted a decade of serious study to Paul's *Epistles* and to the account of Paul's conversion in *Acts* 9 and, as a result, had come to interpret his own experience in the light of his understanding of Paul's. Frederiksen, 1986, has convincingly argued that 'As Augustine's theological opinions changed, so did his views of Paul – and, correspondingly, of himself' (22), and that 'Augustine's account of his conversion in the *Confessions* . . . is a theological reinterpretation of a past event, an attempt to render his past coherent to his present self. It is, in fact, a disguised description of where he stands in the present as much as an ostensible description of what occurred in the past. And he constructs his description from his reading of Acts 9 as well as from his new theological convictions' (24). In general terms, 'the convert thus sees the subsequent events of his life in light of his conversion; but, à l'inverse, his description of his conversion should be read in light of these subsequent events' (33). We shall see that, in relation to Augustine's restatement of his doctrine of grace, the crucial turning-point was his reading of the *Epistles* at the time of his replies to his friend Simplicianus in 396–7.

been tortured by doubt, he had searched for a solution to the problem of evil in the philosophers, in the scriptures and in Manicheism, he had listened intently to the sermons of Ambrose, and still he had waited in vain for some light that would guide his feet with certainty, still he remained in 'a state of wavering uncertainty'. His intensive reading of Paul had brought him to the point where he could exclaim in an agony of self-realisation: 'What shall wretched man do? Who shall deliver him from the body of this death but your grace through our Lord Jesus Christ? All this sank down into the heart of my being by some wonderful means, when I read "the least of your Apostles".'[41]

Yet he was still unready to take the leap of faith: his will was still divided, his mind knew at last what it ought to will but was unable to will it, because his will resisted his efforts, and, in despair, he cried out with Paul, 'The good that I would I do not, the evil I would not that I do.' And then, at the right moment of psychological crisis, came the words of a child heard in a garden,[42] 'Take up and read, take up and read!', and they set his will free. The verse which he read gave him an unequivocal answer to the dilemma which he had thought to be intractable. Begging God to give him chastity, he had added 'But not yet!' Now at last he realised that his intellect and his unaided will could take him no further, that he *must* respond to the moral imperative specifically addressed to him. What he had failed all along to do by the exercise of his own will he could only do by surrendering that will to the will of God, revealed to him by an act of grace. 'By grace', he repeated, 'by grace are we saved through faith.' From that moment he was never again to doubt that the evil with which he had been plagued came from within himself and the only cure for it was the divine grace. 'Late', he cries out, 'late have I learned to love you. You were within me, and I was outside in the world; and it was there that I was searching for you. You were with me but I was not with you. Yet it was you who called to me and cried to me and broke down the barrier of my deafness. Now there can be no hope for me except in your great mercy. Give me the grace to do what you command and command me to do what you will.'[43] The verse which he had read spoke to his own condition, pointing to the very sins of which he was most conscious: 'I had no wish to read any further nor any need to do so. For immediately, at the end of this sentence, as if by the illumination of certainty poured into my heart, all the shadows of doubt were dispersed.'

But he did read further – in that same Epistle which he had been commanded to take up and read. And there he was to find most of the raw ingredients for his doctrine of grace and his theory of original sin. Hitherto these two ideas had developed quite independently, insofar as they could be said to have developed at all; now he was to elaborate and combine them in one great intellectual system, identifying the origin and true nature of sin and indicating the only remedy for it, that *amplior medicina*, that grace which was

---

[41] *C* VII, xxi. 27 (PL 32, 748) (CSEL 33, 167f.).
[42] Ibid., VIII, xii. 29 (PL 32, 762) (CSEL 33, 194).
[43] Ibid., X, xxvii. 38, xxix. 40 (PL 32, 795f.) (CSEL 33, 255f.).

infinitely more potent than the evil with which man had been infected. His doctrine of grace would be 'solemnly adopted' by the Church, and the second Council of Orange would borrow its canons 'word for word from his writings'.[44] True, some aspects of it would later be rejected because of misinterpretation and misuse, and others, like original sin and predestination, would be hotly debated over the centuries. But 'it is Augustine who must be reckoned as the real artificer of the ecclesiastical concept of grace in the sense of divine power, as of the companion concept of original sin.'[45] Together they formed the 'reality of faith' with which Pelagius was held to be in conflict, the 'good theology' with which Augustine now attempted to correct the bad.

On a first reading of Pelagius' book *On Nature* it had seemed to Augustine that the writer might be innocent of the charge of denying the grace of God; but, as he read on, his worst suspicions were confirmed, since the grace described there turned out to be quite different from the true doctrine of the Church: Pelagius had too much to say about free will enabling man to choose good but nothing about the grace which is able to prevent the wrong use of free will leading man to sin; indeed, he seemed to be replacing grace by free will as the means of salvation. Thus Augustine had diagnosed what he saw to be the root cause of the Pelagian disease: 'the opinion hitherto kept in concealment is now out in the open, that the possibility of not sinning is attributed to the grace of God because God is the author of that human nature in which it is inseparably implanted'.[46] So, Pelagius *is* denying that God's help must be sought whenever we have to resist temptation and that this help is made available to us in Jesus, 'the medicine of the mediator',[47] which alone has the power to heal our corrupt nature inherited from Adam. The grace which Pelagius teaches turns out in the end to be no more than nature created with free will, 'a poisonous perversion endangering salvation',[48] and his clumsy attempt at Diospolis to combine this 'natural grace' with the help given by God to man in the moral law and the teaching of Jesus may have succeeded in pulling the wool over the eyes of his judges but will never succeed in convincing Augustine that he is not reducing the grace of God to the inferior status of a mere adjunct to the will of man. In his *Letter to Demetrias* Pelagius may speak of men as 'deserving the grace of God and, by the help of the Holy Spirit, more easily resisting the evil spirit', and in his treatise *On Free Will* he may suggest that 'men may more easily accomplish by grace that which they are commanded to do by free will'. 'But why', asks Augustine,

---

[44] Portalié, 177; of the nine canons only three are concerned with the question of grace – 4–6, discussed in Wermelinger, 197ff. and 194. Elsewhere too (224) Portalié claims that 'propositions taken verbatim from Augustine . . . were sanctioned by the Council of Orange'; but, as Küng, 1964, 168 has warned, 'the dogmatic value of II Orange is disputed', and it would be unwise to assume, as Portalié appears to have done, that the second Council of Orange set the seal on 'Augustinian' orthodoxy, since there is some doubt as to whether all the canons, and if all or only the first eight, were approved by Pope Boniface II.
[45] N. P. Williams, 1930, 19.
[46] *NG*, li. 59 (PL 44, 275) (CSEL 60, 276).
[47] Ibid., lxvii. 80 (PL 44, 286) (CSEL 60, 293f.).
[48] *PP* xxiii. 47 (PL 44, 347) (CSEL 42, 101).

'why does he insert the phrase "more easily"? Expunge it, and you leave not only a full but also a sound sense.'[49]

Pelagius gives every indication that he understands the burden of the charge made against him but without on any occasion accepting its validity. 'Very ignorant persons', he complains, no doubt including Augustine among them without mentioning him, 'consider that in this respect we are doing an injury to the divine grace, because we say that it in no way perfects our sanctity without the exercise of our own free will – as if God would have imposed any command on his grace without also supplying its help to those whom he has commanded.'[50] He goes on to add: 'This grace we do not, as you suppose, allow to consist only in the law but also in the help of God. God helps us through his teaching and revelation by opening the eyes of our heart, by pointing out to us the future so that we may not be preoccupied with the present, by uncovering the snares of the devil, by enlightening us with the manifold and ineffable gift of heavenly grace. Does the man who says all this appear to you to be denying grace? Is he not admitting both the free will of man and the grace of God?' 'No', replies Augustine, 'most certainly, no, he does not, because he is making the grace of God consist in the law and teaching.'

This charge is repeated again and again in Augustine's anti-Pelagian treatises: Pelagius is restricting divine grace to the response of the human will to the law as set out in the scriptures and to the teaching of Jesus. He may do his best to conceal this by affirming that 'God works in us to will what is good, to will what is holy, when he rouses us from our devotion to earthly desires and our love of the present only after the manner of dumb animals, by the magnitude of our future glory and the promise of its rewards, when, by revealing wisdom to us, he awakens our sluggish will to longing for him, when he urges upon us all that is good.' 'He means by grace,' Augustine repeats, 'nothing else but law and teaching.'[51] And, 'although he makes that grace of God whereby Christ came into the world to save sinners to consist simply in remission of sins, he can still accommodate his words to this meaning by alleging that the necessity of such grace for every hour, moment and action of our lives comes to this, that while we recollect and keep in mind the forgiveness of past sins, we sin no more, aided not by any supply of power but by the strength of our own free will as it recalls to our minds in our every action the advantage conferred on us by remission of sins'.[52] Thus his theology of grace continues to be built around the very opinion which he condemned at Diospolis, namely, that 'God's grace and assistance are not given for single acts but consist in free will or law and teaching'.[53] 'Let them therefore read and understand, observe and acknowledge that it is not by the voice of law and teaching resounding outside but by a secret, wonderful and

[49] *GC* xxvii. 28, xxix. 30 (PL 44, 374f.) (CSEL 42, 148f.).
[50] Ibid., vii. 8 (PL 44, 364) (CSEL 42, 130f.).
[51] Ibid., x. 11 (PL 44, 365f.) (CSEL 42, 133ff.).
[52] Ibid., ii. 2 (PL 44, 361) (CSEL 42, 125f.).
[53] Ibid., iii. 3 (PL 44, 361) (CSEL 42, 126f.); *PP* xiv. 30 (PL 44, 337) (CSEL 42, 84).

ineffable power from within that God works in men's hearts to produce not only revelations of the truth but also good dispositions of the will'.[54]

Pelagius was thus impaled on the horns of a dilemma of his own making. When he maintained that divine grace had been bestowed on man at his creation by the gift of free will, he laid himself open to a charge of neglecting the possibility of 'any supply of power' thereafter by an infusion of divine grace enabling man to answer God's call. As R. F. Evans, by no means unsympathetic to Pelagius, rightly emphasises: 'It would be unfaithful to the man himself to save his "orthodoxy" by reading in some doctrine of infused grace which is not there.'[55] On the other hand, when Pelagius tried to counter this by anathematising those who denied that God's grace was needed for every action and by affirming that it was made available as a form of assistance to the baptised in the recollection of remission of sins, reinforced by law and teaching and by the example of Jesus, he found himself accused of having no doctrine of *internal* grace, because he could not bring himself to make an unambiguous declaration of the way in which it operated. Even when he attempted to safeguard his position by adding that God helps man by 'the manifold and ineffable gift of heavenly grace', he seemed to his opponents to be thinking in terms of intellectual enlightenment rather than spiritual assistance. His whole teaching of grace was constructed around the central premise of the absolute freedom of man's will when faced with a choice between good and evil, a freedom given to man by God but, once given, not subject to God's interference.

Again and again in the course of the controversy Augustine found it necessary to correct this wrong emphasis on the freedom of the human will and to assert the absolute sovereignty of divine grace and the omnipotence of God. He returned to the subject in one of his last treatises, *On Rebuke and Grace*, in which he replied to the queries of Valentinus and his monks at Hadrumetum in 426/7 and included a brief but definitive summary of the Catholic teaching on relationship between God and man and between divine grace and human conduct: 'It is impossible', he writes, 'to doubt that the wills of men are incapable of resisting the will of God and preventing him from doing what he himself wishes', 'He has the wills of men under his control more than they themselves have', and 'To will or not to will is in the power of one who wills or does not will but only to such an extent that he cannot impede the divine will or overcome its power.' For 'God, without doubt, has most absolute power to incline men's hearts in whatever direction he pleases'.[56]

Augustine and Pelagius were as far apart as the average employer and trade union in a modern industrial dispute – and just about as likely to reach agreement on a mutually satisfactory compromise by what are known as 'conciliation processes'. They had a common interest, namely, the welfare and preservation of the institution to which they both belonged, but they

[54] *GC* xxiv. 25 (PL 44, 373) (CSEL 42, 145).

[55] R. F. Evans, 1968(a), 111.

[56] *RG* xiv. 43, 45 (PL 44, 942ff.).

started out from opposite extremes: Augustine began with God, Pelagius with man. His view of man was not of one created perfect only to be corrupted by the sin of Adam passed on from generation to generation but of one who began to sin from that moment when he became consciously able as a child to imitate the sins of others, not because his own flawed nature forced him to do so but because he was ignorant of its true essence and potential. His will had been corrupted not by the sin of Adam but by bad example and habit, and it was this 'long habit of doing wrong'[57] which had been incorrectly identified with, and located in, human nature by those who adhered to the doctrine of original sin. To enable man to correct his faults, God had first provided 'the file of the law';[58] but, in the event, not even this aid could enable man to overcome the overwhelming force of bad habit, though it remained strong enough to enable him to recognise the error of his ways and to become conscious of his sins. Man was still in possession of the capacity to live without sin but was prevented from doing so by his inability to draw upon 'the treasure within his soul',[59] that free will with which God had endowed him at his creation. In order to make full use of this gift, he must develop a right understanding of his nature.

Pelagius begins his *Letter to Demetrias* with an analysis of the human will. 'Whenever', he writes, 'I have to speak about moral instruction and the way to live a blameless life, it is my practice first to demonstrate the power and nature of the human will and to show what it is able to achieve. By a more careful examination of the human will it becomes possible to see that the status of man is better and higher for that very reason for which it is thought to be inferior: it is on the choice of which of two paths to follow, on this freedom to choose either alternative, that the dignity of the rational mind is based . . . and it is from this finally that all the best men win praise, from this their reward; nor would there be any virtue at all in the good of one who perseveres if he had not been able to cross over to the path of evil.'[60]

To enable man to make the right choices, he has been endowed with three faculties or capacities – *posse, velle* and *esse*, 'natural ability or potential', 'will' and 'action'.[61] The first of these is the capacity to be righteous and not to sin, which is part of man's nature, given to him at his creation; the second is the capacity to make his own free choice of right action; the third is the capacity to translate that choice into right action and to live according to the nature given to him by God, that is, without sin. The first cannot be taken away from him, and he never loses the ability to do good; but if he is to exercise it properly, he must employ the second and third, which are both under his control. But what has actually happened is that the first capacity, though

---

[57] *Letter to Demetrias* 8 (PL 30, 23; 33, 1104); cf. 17 and 24 (PL 30, 31f., 38f.; 33, 1111, 1115), and Augustine, *GC* xxxix. 43 (PL 44, 380) (CSEL 42, 156f.) and *OS* xxvi. 30 (PL 44, 400) (CSEL 42, 190).

[58] *Letter to Demetrias*, loc. cit.; cf. *OS* xxvi. 30 (PL 44, 400) (CSEL 42, 190).

[59] *Letter to Demetrias* 6 (PL 30, 22; 33, 1103f.)

[60] Ibid., 2, 3 (PL 30, 16f.; 33, 1100).

[61] *GC* iii. 4, iv. 5 (PL 44. 361ff.) (CSEL 42, 127f.).

reinforced by the law as embodied in the scriptures, has atrophied because of man's failure to make the right use of the second, and in order to bring it into play again, he has been offered the opportunity of redemption by the saving death of Jesus, who forgives his sins, restores his will and sustains it by his own teaching and example.

So Pelagius would argue that he has not neglected grace, since his doctrine provides for a grace of creation, a grace of revelation and a grace of redemption. But he would be anxious to stress the rôle of God not only in these but also in the operation of the will: 'For certainly it is of God alone that man is able to do and carry through a good action, and this capacity can exist alone without the other two but they cannot exist without it.'[62] And, elsewhere, 'How can that possibly be understood to be without the grace of God which is considered to belong specially to him?'[63] Yet, insist though he may again and again that it is God who, in the first place, has given man the possibility of doing good as his original endowment of grace and has confirmed and strengthened it by revelation and by redemption through Jesus, his dialectic compels him to balance this insistence with another, even stronger, that 'when we really do a good thing or speak a good word or think a good thought, it proceeds from ourselves'.[64]

Pelagius' God has been compared to Paley's watchmaker: he built the machine and put its parts in sound working order, stood back to admire his work and, when it proved to be operating inefficiently, intervened dramatically to correct its faults and enable it to function more efficiently in the future. But he stopped short of replacing the part which had been most responsible for the technical breakdown, and he remained outside all the time. For Augustine, on the other hand, the religious life was centred around the realisation that God lives within the human soul while remaining distinct from it, immanent and yet transcendent. 'Soul, self-knowledge and knowledge of God became interdependent: to know oneself properly involves an awareness of the indwelling presence of God, and this awareness can grow only by the power of grace and its consequent redirected love, from dim sensation to surer awareness to eventual vision.'[65] Thus God worked from within, had been there from the beginning and could exercise his power whenever he saw that the right moment to do so had arrived. God is nearer to us, claimed Augustine, than we are to ourselves; he is no remote mechanic, no absentee landlord, but an ever-present force working in us to correct the will which has made the wrong choices and to guide it gently back to the way of salvation.

In one of his anthologies which became so popular in the fifties and sixties Victor Gollancz quoted a definition of grace from the Oxford Dictionary as 'the divine influence which operates in men to regenerate and sanctify, and to impart strength to endure trial and resist temptation'. 'The definition', he

---

[62] Ibid., iv. 5 (PL 44, 362) (CSEL 42, 128).
[63] NG xlv. 53 (PL 44, 272) (CSEL 60, 271f.); cf. xliv. 52, li. 59 (PL 44, 272, 275) (CSEL 60, 271, 276).
[64] GC xvi. 17 (PL 44, 369) (CSEL 42, 139).
[65] I have been unable to trace the source of this quotation.

comments, 'is as good as any: but no one who has not experienced Grace can really understand it. Most people do experience it sooner or later.'[66] Augustine knew that he had experienced it himself; but he was also convinced that the teaching of Pelagius was not true to his own experience. Pelagius was making the same mistake that he had once made himself, and he must be taught the truth. But he found him to be a most reluctant pupil, one who could never resist the temptation to try to teach his grandmother to suck eggs!

[66] *The New Year of Grace*, ed. V. Gollancz, London 1961, 104.

III

THIS VEXED MATTER

> 'But that which God's foreknowledge can foresee
> Must needs occur, as certain men of learning
> Have said. Ask any scholar of discerning;
> He'll say the Schools are filled with altercation
> On this vexed matter of predestination
> Long, bandied by a hundred thousand men.'
>
> GEOFFREY CHAUCER[1]

Augustine, as the 'true' spokesman, cannot be faulted for not doing his utmost to 'correct bad theology with good' in his efforts to convince Pelagius that his own interpretation of the grace which he had experienced was the only correct and legitimate one, a task to which he applied all the zeal of a convert and the dedication of a 'twice-born' Christian. But it was all of no avail, for Pelagius refused to abandon his own conviction of the validity of free will and continued to argue his case for giving it a countervailing rôle in the drama of man's salvation. It is true that, when pressed, he yielded to the extent of modifying his view by admitting that human will needed divine assistance, only to be dismissed as a time-server and sophist for his pains. Both men were so engrossed in their debate that they would have turned a deaf ear to the pragmatic advice of a modern novelist, delivered presumably without benefit of theology, that 'freewill has to be experienced, not debated, like colour or the taste of potatoes.'[2] Both instead, like 'the hundred thousand men' of Chaucer's Schools, preferred the verbal gymnastics of a *cause célèbre* which was to reverberate down the centuries. And, without doubt, it was Augustine who proved to be holding the stronger brief of the two, by his adroit handling of it satisfying the judges of his day that Pelagius' 'grace of creation' was far from being, as he claimed, an inner force, implanted in man by God to enable him to avoid sin and win salvation. It was no more than a capacity, always present and available perhaps but not always in employment and, even when employed, inadequate by itself. It worked in man only when he willed the

---

[1] *Canterbury Tales: the Nun's Priest's Tale*, ed. N. Coghill, Harmondsworth 1951, 294.

[2] W. Golding, *Free Fall*, London 1959, 5. Hodgson, 1936, 177f., notes that 'the question whether the distinction between those who do and those who do not respond to the redeeming activity of God is to be ascribed to divine predestination or human free will' was 'judged by Temple (*Nature, Man and God*, London 1934, 400ff.) to be insoluble on the knowledge at our disposal', and he adds that 'mysteries remain which we cannot solve but must accept in faith our own ignorance, not trying to make dogmatic assertions about them which are regarded as *articuli stantis aut cadentis ecclesiae*' – 'articles on which the Church stands or falls'.

good but not when he exercised his notional freedom *in alteram partem*, that is, to choose evil. But how, in that case, does God help the will when it chooses good? In the absence of any clear and firm statement to the contrary from Pelagius, it must be concluded that God does so, as Augustine maintains, only through the moral law and the teaching and example of Jesus. With Pelagius it was the human will that prevailed.

Augustine's belief in the inner working of God's grace triumphed over 'the strongly ethical and non-mystical type of religion favoured by Pelagius'.[3] For Augustine, grace was primarily an internal force, an ever-present, ever-available invitation to accept God's help through the exercise of a more profound kind of freedom which modified and directed the operation of the will, and only those who had been given the inner strength to respond to that call could hope to be saved. 'No one prior to Augustine had really asserted anything like this need for an inner working of God within human freedom',[4] and his conviction of this need sprang from his reflection on his own experience of conversion, prompting the only significant amendment of his earlier views on grace as expressed in his treatise *On Free Will*, written between 388 and 395 to defend the freedom of the will against Manichean determinism. Then he had maintained that man's progress depended on his response to a divine call freely made by God and freely accepted by man in faith. But, by 397, when he replied to the questions put to him by his friend Simplicianus, a change of emphasis had taken place, since the definitive solution had been revealed to him. 'Previously', he wrote later, 'I had tried to solve the question by upholding the freedom of the will; but it was the grace of God that prevailed.'[5] By then he had reached the conclusion, which he was to reinforce and defend resolutely and inflexibly ever after, that election to grace must precede any mere human decision to accept it.

The sticking-point for Pelagius was precisely this insistence on the part of Augustine that man receives from God 'both the act of willing and the power to do what is willed',[6] a doctrine of grace which, in his view, undermined the freedom of the human will. But, of course, Augustine did not agree. 'There are some who suppose', he complains towards the end of his life, 'that the freedom of the will is denied whenever God's grace is maintained.'[7] But that is only because they fail to comprehend the true nature of will, which is not a faculty – 'he had no faculty psychology'[8] – but the human psyche in its rôle as moral agent; it is not the will that wills but the man who uses it, the *whole* man employing his will as one of the functions of his soul. Nor is it possible for a man to be forced to will, since every man must be able to decide for himself in accordance with the workings of his own nature. A firm distinction must

[3] N. P. Williams, 1927, 333.
[4] Haight, 36.
[5] *R* II, 1 (PL 32, 629) (CSEL 36, 132), ed. Bogan, II, 27. Like Winston Smith in Orwell's *1984* 'he had won the victory over himself. He loved Big Brother.'
[6] *GC* xxv. 26 (PL 44, 373) (CSEL 42, 146).
[7] *R* II, 66 (PL 32, 656) (CSEL 36, 203), ed. Bogan, II, 92.
[8] Bourke, ed., 68.

therefore be drawn between *voluntas* as 'the man willing' and *liberum arbitrium* as 'freedom of choice'.

When we make our 'free' choice of action, Augustine tells us, we do so by using our *liberum arbitrium* but this, by itself, is not sufficient to enable us to choose good without the aid of the Good which is all powerful; 'it suffices (only) for evil', and so we often fail to put into effect the good choices we have 'freely' made.[9] All good acts require divine aid – *adiutorium Dei* – and it is this divine aid which alone gives us true *libertas*, because it sets us free to do good. This is true freedom of will, infinitely superior to a purely human freedom of choice such as Adam possessed before his Fall. At that time Adam was able *not* to sin but we, his descendants, if we are in a state of grace and if we persevere to the end, are *unable* to sin; *non posse peccare*, 'to be unable to sin' – that is the essence of our true freedom, which we can only realise by God's grace. It is only by God's grace that we are 'set free from sin', whereas those who are not given that grace remain in enslavement to sin through their exercise of *liberum arbitrium* unaided. In order to become truly free, man must become 'a servant of God', in whose service is the only perfect freedom.

It is generally agreed that Augustine's explanation of free will is both more sophisticated than that of Pelagius and truer to Christian experience. But it does raise problems by introducing a theory of predestination which is, to say the least, controversial. 'The totality of mankind' as seen by Augustine has been compared, for instance,[10] to a figure consisting of three concentric circles: the outermost contains 'the vessels of wrath', whose place in the 'damnèd mass' is irredeemable because their subjection to original sin leaves them beyond the reach of God's mercy; the next circle contains those whom the grace of 'justification' – a term used by Augustine not in the Pauline sense of 'accounting righteous' but to mean 'making righteous' – temporarily rescues from the mass but only for them to sink back again into it through lack of the grace of 'perseverance'; the innermost circle is reserved for 'the vessels of mercy', elected from the beginning to salvation, justified by grace and endowed with grace to persevere to the end.

Of the three groups only the last is predestined in the absolute sense, being 'the few chosen' as against 'the many called' but not 'prepared' to answer the call, who differ from the elect in not having 'efficacious' grace as well as the 'sufficient' grace given to all – 'sufficient', it would seem, to be in their case insufficient! The elect have *adiutorium quo*, 'the aid by which they are enabled to be saved', in addition to *adiutorium sine quo non*, 'the aid without which it would be theoretically impossible to be saved'.[11] Thus, while God's grace is in

[9] *RG* xi. 31 (PL 44, 935), reading *parum*, 'insufficient for', not *nihil* 'of no avail'; cf. *GFC* xv. 31 (PL 44, 899f.), *E* xxx–xxxii, 9 (PL 40, 246ff.).

[10] N. P. Williams, 1930, 24f.

[11] Ibid., 36; for the distinction between *adiutorium quo* and *adiutorium sine quo non* see especially *RG* xii. 34 (PL 44, 936f.); for the distinction between *posse non peccare* and *non posse peccare RG* xii. 33 (PL 44, 936). There are several passages in Augustine's works which indicate that, while he is not prepared to deny that *non posse peccare*, 'not to be able to sin', is a theoretical possibility, his own experience and his knowledge of human frailty lead him to conclude that no man is able not to sin *in this world* except by the grace of perseverance, the *adiutorium sine quo non*, nor can any man be sure that he has been given that grace.

theory available to all, in practice only those who have been 'prepared' will accept it when it is offered to them. The non-elect have not been so 'prepared', and we are left with the harsh but seemingly inescapable conclusion that they are not recipients of God's mercy and so are condemned to eternal damnation for a sin which they did not themselves commit but of which, nevertheless, they are held to be guilty, a conclusion which Augustine's remorseless logic does not permit him to mitigate even for children dying unbaptised; their fate can only be referred to the 'occult justice' of God, whose judgements are inscrutable – an echo of the Pauline plea, *O altitudo*: 'O the depth of the riches both of the wisdom and knowledge of God! How unsearchable are his judgements, and his ways past finding out!'[12] All men stand condemned by God's justice because of the sin of Adam, and it is to his mercy alone that the elect owe their remission of sentence; the first we must accept, for the second we must be duly thankful.

This depressing cameo of human destiny would have been classified by Aristotle as a plot with a 'double' ending, leading to a happy outcome for the one set of participants and quite the opposite for the other.[13] To the elected minority it offers a hope of eternal salvation through the intervention of divine benevolence; for the great majority, shut out for ever from the *numerus clausus neque augendus neque minuendus* or 'fixed quota' imposed by divine providence, it means a sentence of condemnation without prospect of remission. In attempting to explain how faith can be man's own act and yet be called forth by God, Augustine for the first time advances a doctrine which was later to be termed 'effective calling' by Calvinists and 'efficacious grace' by Roman Catholicism. It is this *effective* calling, this *efficacious* grace which produces the right response from 'the few chosen', because it is 'congruous' with their condition: their response is held by Augustine to be in perfect harmony with their call, which is made in such a way and at such a time that they, as God alone foreknows, will be unable to reject it.

But if 'that which God's foreknowledge can foresee must needs occur', what place is there for man's exercise of his free will? The paradox had been presented to Origen by his friend and 'taskmaster' two centuries before: 'If God knows the future beforehand and it must come to pass', wrote Ambrose of Alexandria, 'prayer is vain.'[14] More than that, not only prayer but all human action is vain, for what is the point of playing the game, if the dice are loaded? Augustine was to insist in his treatise *On the Predestination of the Saints*, written in 428/9, that predestination and foreknowledge were not the same: 'Predestination cannot exist without foreknowledge, but foreknowledge may exist without predestination.'[15] 'There are things which God foresees, but

[12] Romans 11, 33.

[13] *Poetics*, c. 13, 1453a 30–3.

[14] Origen, *De Oratione* V, 6 – a reference I owe to Lucas, 1970, 71. Origen's reply (VI, 3) was: 'The foreknowledge of God is not the cause of all future events and of the actions which will be performed by us of our own impulse'. Cf. Boethius, *De Consolatione Philosophiae* V, iv, ·13ff.: 'reason, which because it does not consider foreknowledge to be the necessary cause of future events thinks that the freedom of the will is in no way hindered by foreknowledge.'

[15] *PS* x. 19 (PL 44, 975).

which he himself does not intend to bring about' is how he puts it. But for Pelagius, like 'any scholar of discerning', the theory of election outlined above involved a form of predestination which he could not endorse, because it contained implications of what appeared to him to be theological determinism. Was Augustine's doctrine of election really a form of predestination which abolished the freedom of the human will, and ruled out all possibility of reconciling it with divine grace? If so, had there been a change of emphasis, as we have suggested, in Augustine's understanding of the *modus operandi* of election around 396 or 397, when he answered the questions of Simplicianus? And did this in turn, reinforced by his reading of contemporary theologians and his battle with the Donatists, lead around 406 to his adoption of a theory of original sin which marked 'a decisive change in his career as a theologian'?[16]

These are the sort of questions around which the battle-lines of the future were to be drawn up. 'At all times', wrote Eugène Portalié, 'adversaries of freedom of will – predestinarians, Wycliffites, Calvinists, and Jansenists – have availed themselves of the authority of Augustine. Catholic theologians, it is true, have generally recognised that Augustine safeguarded the rights of freedom of will, but they are strangely divided concerning the nature of this freedom and the explanation of the divine action in Augustine's writings.'[17] After citing three weighty dissentients among the Catholic ranks and noting that contemporary Protestants, including even the most sincere admirers of Augustine, are unmerciful in their criticism of him on this score, he goes on to insist that 'Augustine never retracted his principal ideas on freedom of choice; he never modified his thoughts on the factor which is its essential condition, that is its complete power of choosing or determining itself.'[18] He then proceeds to construct the strongest possible defence of Augustine's position, proving at least to his own satisfaction that it enabled him to reconcile divine grace with human freedom. Such a defence, coming from one so highly regarded as an Augustinian scholar, deserves to be treated with the utmost respect, even if to many other scholars it has seemed to be less than objective.

Portalié's case may be summarised under three headings. First, the will, in making any decision, is influenced by certain motives and, in deciding which, if any, of these to follow, it is free to choose for itself: 'nothing attracts the will to action unless it is seen; what each one decides to take or leave is in his power.'[19] *But* it is God who, by virtue of his omnipotence, is able to choose those motives which he will present to man. Secondly, 'man is not the master of his first thoughts': no one has power over what chances to come into his mind but to give consent or withold it is in the power of his own will.'[20] *But* it is God, not chance, who determines what these first thoughts will be. Thirdly, God, by virtue of his omniscience, knows what answer man will give to each of the motives and thoughts presented to him: 'A man does not sin because

[16] TeSelle, 1970, 266.
[17] Portalié, 177f.
[18] Ibid., 197.
[19] *FC* III, xxv. 74 (PL 32, 1307) (CSEL 74, 151).
[20] *SL* xxxiv. 60 (PL 44, 240) (CSEL 60, 220).

42

God, whose knowledge is infallible, foreknew that fortune or fate or something else would sin but that man himself would sin, who, if he wills not, sins not. *But* if he wills to sin, that God also foreknew.'[21] The grace of God thus works not by compulsion but 'by way of infallible attraction', gently guiding and persuading his elect to make their own right choices by presenting them with those thoughts and motives which he foreknows to be congruous with their needs and circumstances, and these, of course, will vary from one man to another.

'The chief theological argument for determinism', comments John Lucas in his discussion of free will,[22] 'is the argument from omniscience, although other arguments from omnipotence and grace are also invoked.' Portalié employs all of these arguments but denies that the result is 'theological determinism'. Furthermore, he does not doubt 'first, that Augustine has formed a true and perfectly logical system without contradictions, the basis of which did not vary since the time he became a bishop if we are to judge by his later works; second, that in this system human liberty was affirmed until the day of his death so accurately that no trace of an irresistible and necessitating impulsion ever appears in it.'[23] A similar conclusion has been reached by another Roman Catholic theologian of a later generation, Mother Mary Clark, in her exhaustive examination of Augustine's teaching on free will, and another Roman Catholic, the philosopher A. H. Armstrong, accepts her conclusion 'that Augustine really tried to maintain in his anti-Pelagian period his admirable earlier teaching on human free will and was to a great extent successful in reconciling it with his belief in predestination'.[24] But he then goes on to amplify his rider 'to a great extent' by explaining that one of the reasons for Pelagian opposition to Augustine – apart, that is, from their conviction of the reality of free will – was 'that the Augustinian account of God's dealings with mankind makes God so intolerably unfair': 'he seems to have lost sight of, or at any rate, to have failed to maintain, that simple belief in God's universal and equitable goodness which is the foundation of the faith of pagan Platonists and Pelagians, and very many orthodox Christians.'[25] In other words, 'the examiner not only knows how many are to pass but has already determined *who* is to pass. All the same, if people fail, it is entirely their own fault. Not everybody finds this reasoning satisfactory.'[26]

Ay, there's the rub! Many, like Pelagius, would see the operation of divine grace on the human will as described by Augustine and defended by Portalié as 'an irresistible cogency of grace', among them the Protestant von Harnack and the great Lutheran Augustinian scholar Loofs.[27] And N. P. Williams

[21] *CG* V, 10 (PL 41, 152f.) (CSEL 40, i. 230).
[22] Lucas, 1970, 71.
[23] Portalié, 179.
[24] A. H. Armstrong, 1972, 22.
[25] Ibid., 23.
[26] Passmore, 99n., paraphrasing 'in the language of John Barth's novel *Giles Goat-Boy*' 'the orthodox Roman Catholic view that although the number of the elect is predetermined, no man is predestined to be damned'.
[27] Portalié, 178f.

agrees with the last two at least on this subject: 'There is no struggling against a force which represents all the might of omnipotence, directed by all the intellectual resources of omniscience.' 'God', he continues, 'is in the position of a chess-player, gifted with telepathic and hypnotic power of an infinitely high degree, who not only foresees all the other player's moves, but actually makes them, acting through the other's mind and brain, and consequently has won the game before it has even begun.'[28]

Among the faulty weapons in Augustine's armoury are two of his favourite proof-texts. The first is Proverbs 8, 35, which he quotes more than fifty times – *voluntas praeparatur a Deo*, 'the will (of man) is prepared by God'.[29] But this is not how the text appears in the Vulgate, which reads *hauriet salutem a Deo*, 'he shall obtain favour of the Lord' (AV and RV). Augustine is using a pre-Vulgate, possibly an African Old Latin version, itself a literal rendering of the Greek Septuagint; this gives him 'wish', which he renders by the more positive Latin word for 'will', *voluntas*, instead of the original Hebrew word translated as 'favour', and 'is prepared', *praeparatur*, instead of 'shall obtain'. The first proof-text, 'a consecrated formula to which he returns tirelessly',[30] is thus too insecure to bear the weight which he puts upon it. Even if we were to accept it in the form in which Augustine uses it, what, we would be bound to ask, does *praeparatur* mean in his vocabulary? The question has been hotly debated; for example, 'does *praeparatur* imply that God enables us to will, or that he so arranges that we should in fact will (freely)?',[31] that is, in accordance with his will and through his grace?

If the second, then it could be and has often been argued that all man's powers of self-determination are in that case ruled out, and Augustine is advancing a form of moral determinism. Another of his proof-texts turns out to be just as unsatisfactory: 'For God wishes that all men should be saved . . . not, however, so as to take from them their free will, by the good or bad use of which they will be most righteously judged.'[32] When Augustine goes on to add that 'unbelievers indeed act contrary to the will of God when they do not believe . . . Thus God's will is for ever invincible', he shows that he has again misinterpreted his proof-text, having been misled into a non-universalist perversion of the true meaning of 1 Timothy 2, 4, so that 'who will have all men to be saved' (AV and RV) and 'whose will it is that all men should find salvation' (NEB) become 'all men who are saved are saved by God's will'; in other words, salvation follows of necessity if God so wills, '*quia necesse est fieri si voluerit*'.[33] Elsewhere he seeks to evade the issue – or appears to – by

<hr>

[28] N. P. Williams, 1930, 28; cf. 30, where he adds: 'The human chess-player . . . invariably does what the Divine player wishes him to do: but he does it of his own accord.'

[29] Sage, 1964, 19f., collects the references to Augustine's fifty-three quotations of this verse.

[30] Portalié, 203; Sage, 1964, 1, describes it as acting as a '*fil d'Ariane*' through the undergrowth of the controversy on Augustine's doctrine of grace, and quotes La Bonnardière as emphasising it as 'the *leitmotiv* of the anti-Pelagian polemic' in her article in *REA* IX, 1963, 78.

[31] Rist, 235f.

[32] *SL* xxxiii. 58 (PL 44, 238) (CSEL 60, 216).

[33] *E* ciii. 27 (PL 40, 280).

suggesting that 'all men' is the same as 'all the elect' or 'men of every kind'.[34] Methinks the good saint doth protest too much!

Is Augustine's grace then 'irresistible to those to whom it is offered'?[35] The Abbé Portalié, Mother Mary Clark and many others continue to affirm that at least Augustine did not think so and that he was justified. But Pelagius and many other ministers of grace over the centuries would not agree. Despite Augustine's denials to the contrary, which began as early as 412, when he wrote in his treatise *On the Spirit and the Letter*, 'Do we then by grace nullify free will? God forbid! No, rather we establish free will, since it is grace that cures the will whereby righteousness is freely loved',[36] and for all his ingenuity in attempting to distinguish between 'will' and 'free choice', he has laid himself open to a charge of ambiguity of the kind he himself brought against Pelagius' defence of free will. N. P. Williams has summed up the matter with his usual clarity and objectivity: 'If Christianity had accepted Pelagius' account of human nature as its presupposition, it would have ceased to be a "religion" in any intelligible sense of the term.'[37] But he proceeds to describe Augustine's conception of freedom as 'very abstruse and difficult' and concludes that 'it is clear that Augustine, whether consciously or not, is really trying to run with the hare and hunt with the hounds'.[38] And Leonard Hodgson is no less critical of Pelagianism: for instance, 'there is no form of Christianity which cannot be perverted and debased if Pelagianism is not checked', and 'Pelagianism is bad philosophy as well as bad religion.'[39] But, while detecting a reflection of the Augustinian distinction between 'free choice' and 'freedom' in his own differentiation of two types of freedom, the one imperfect because human and the other perfect because divine, he is fully aware of the danger of preaching determinism, even 'double determinism', to which both he and Augustine could be exposed, and of linking his second type of freedom with a quasi-scientific theory of causation which, in Augustine's case, makes insufficient allowance for the workings of the love of God.[40]

Williams's book on grace was written in the thirties, and Hodgson's Gifford Lectures were delivered in the sixties; both were theologians of high standing in their day, and there is no reason to suspect the soundness of their judgement on an issue which they both considered to be of the greatest importance. But what of the present generation of Protestant theologians writing in English? It could be argued that any selection which we make is bound to be unsatisfactory and that the views expressed will reveal more of the cast of thought of those selected, as well as the predilections of the present writer, than of the merits and demerits of Augustine's theory of predestination.

[34] *RG* xv. 44 (PL 44, 943); *CG* XXII, i. 2 (PL 41, 751f.) (CSEL 40, 2, 582f.); *J* IV, viii. 44 (PL 44, 760). But Thonnard, 1963, 284, 1964, 122, insists that in their context these refinements fit harmoniously into the pattern of Augustine's explanation of predestination.
[35] Rist, 228.
[36] *SL* xxx. 52 (PL 44, 233) (CSEL 60, 208).
[37] N. P. Williams, 1927, 357.
[38] Ibid., 369f.
[39] Hodgson, 1936, 29, 142.
[40] Hodgson, 1968, II, 142.

Still, it should not be too difficult to take a small sample representing different points along the broad spectrum of contemporary theology. Maurice Wiles, for example, in discussing 'the work of the Holy Spirit at the level of personal experience', writes that 'the fundamental problem is that of doing justice both to the integrity of personal being and to the all-pervasive nature of that grace which we are trying to describe.'[41] And, when he turns to the controversy between Pelagius and Augustine as the classic expression of 'the clash of contrasting approaches' to this topic, he agrees with Williams and Hodgson that Augustine won the approval not only of the contemporary Church but also of the majority of later historians of doctrine because of 'his far more profound apprehension of the issues involved', including the nature of human sin. But he concludes that 'it is when he attempts to turn this descriptive insight into a causal account of the origin and transmission of man's sin that the trouble begins', since 'there is no escape, as Augustine himself unwittingly demonstrates, from a doctrine of predestination which strikes at the roots of morality, of true humanity and of belief in a loving God.'[42]

In the course of a discussion of the incarnational theology of some contemporary scholars, including Wiles, R. P. Hanson criticises their view that the doctrine of the incarnation held by the Fathers of the Church 'stands or falls' by their belief in the historicity of the Creation and the Fall, citing the case of Augustine's doctrine of grace against Wiles in particular. 'The historicity of the story of Adam and Eve', he argues, 'was precisely not an integral part of Augustine's doctrine of grace. On the contrary, it was by insisting upon tying his acute and penetrating observations about the human will and the human personality to this story, taken as a scientific account of the origin of the human race, that Augustine ruined his doctrine of grace.'[43] Thus, setting aside the problematical question whether or not Augustine did believe in that Fall as a historical event, we find that Wiles and Hanson, though disagreeing on certain fundamental aspects of the Christian faith, have nevertheless arrived at a not very different position on the Augustinian theory of predestination. Hanson would presumably have accepted Wiles's statement that the results of this attempt to combine a doctrine of grace with a causal, quasi-scientific account of the origin and transmission of sin have been 'disastrous'.

There is then a consensus of opinion among all four Protestant theologians so far quoted that Augustine was at least misguided in persisting in his efforts to protect his doctrine of grace by grappling it with hoops of steel to the myth of Adam and Eve and their Fall as if it were a fact of history, when he had no real need to do so, and that, by so doing, he weakened, rather than strengthened, his own case. What is more, he has left us with an impression of God which makes the Creator appear to be less loving than his creatures are commanded to be. Other contemporary theologians have seized upon this

[41] Wiles, 1974, 94.
[42] Ibid., 95; cf. Wiles, 1982, 129.
[43] Hanson, 1976, 89.

point and have commented upon the paradox that Augustine, surely one of the most loving of men and well-loved by others, should have become so obsessed with the idea of God's power that he left little room for his love, the love of 'a God whose power lives only and wholly in his love'.[44] He thus fell a victim to his own logic when faced with 'the ancient conundrum of a God who is both all-powerful and all-loving'[45] which even today often leaves orthodox Christians at a loss for an answer.

Yet 'most of us today', comments another modern theologian, 'have travelled far enough from Augustine and Calvin to believe that the heavenly Father of Jesus' teaching *wants* to save all men. We can no longer accept the dark doctrine of double predestination with its negation of the central Christian message of the love of God.'[46] Of course, John Hick is not referring specifically here to the Pelagian controversy but is making his comment in the context of a summary of evidence supporting universalism. Nevertheless, his comment is still valid, as is the particular reference to Augustine. Norman Pittenger too, remarking on the failure of early theologians properly to understand the movement of Hebrew religion away from 'primitive Yahwism' to a vision of God as 'the power that makes for righteousness' and its consequent stress on the divine *chesed* or 'faithful loving-mercy', describes the conventional model of God (with Whitehead) as 'ruthless moralism'.[47] He notes also how often some of the greatest theologians in the history of the Church seem to have a dual personality – the one side of it revealing deep faith in God and insistence on his loving care and gracious concern for creation, the other a totally different theological aspect insisting on 'absoluteness, unrelatedness, unchangeableness, and impassibility or inability to share in the world's anguish'. 'Of course', he adds, 'the assertion of God's love is never denied, but it is given a secondary (or adjectival) place.' And his prime example of this dichotomy is none other than Augustine, 'the doctor of the divine love'.[48]

There are also modern philosophers writing about theology who are just as suspicious of the (mainly Catholic) view that Augustine's theory of predestination was never in danger of abolishing the freedom of the human will. In his discussion of theological determinism John Lucas notes that 'theologians are insufficiently reluctant to contradict themselves, and have often taken unwholesome delight in invoking human freedom to explain away evil, and denying it in order to attribute all good to God.'[49] After describing Augustine as 'the most theocentric of all the fathers', he contrasts his explicit statement that man does have free will, for example, in his treatise *On Free Will*, with his later attitude in his controversy with Pelagius, when 'he came to

[44] Pittenger, 15f.
[45] Toynbee, 79. As L. Dewart, 191, comments: 'An omnipotent God would differ from Zeus only in that his bolts had an infinite voltage.'
[46] Hick, 1976, 250.
[47] Pittenger, 13f.
[48] Ibid., 15.
[49] Lucas, 1970, 76.

hold a position in which human freedom has no part to play', because 'the whole tendency of his mind was to attribute everything to God'. Elsewhere he approves of Augustine's insistence that 'not unto him should be ascribed the glory, but unto God' but also of Pelagius' protest that the language used by Augustine, 'if taken literally, denied the manhood of God's children and, in allowing them no mind of their own, put them on a par with sticks and stones'.[50] In other words, 'in forcing man into his kingdom God would have turned the human thou into an it.'[51]

Perhaps the hypothetical objection to quoting from a selection of contemporary students of theology which was made earlier may appear to have been sustained and justified, now that the citations have been paraded for inspection, and we may be reminded of Wittgenstein's advice: 'Whereof one cannot speak thereof one must be silent.'[52] However, our last witness, also a contemporary philosopher, John Rist, cannot possibly be accused of having approached this problem without the necessary degree of objectivity. His contribution to a collection of critical essays on Augustine's philosophy immediately follows a logical analysis by William L. Rowe of Augustine's answer to the character given the name Evodius in the treatise *On Free Will*: 'Since God knew that man would sin, that which God foreknew must necessarily come to pass. How then is the will free when there is apparently this unavoidable necessity?'[53] We are thus brought back by the circling wheel to the question which worried Chaucer, and Rowe formulates it as follows: 'how it is possible both that we voluntarily (freely) will to perform certain actions and that God foreknows that we shall will to perform these actions.'[54] By a process of logic Rowe concludes that Augustine did not succeed in solving the problem of how God's foreknowledge is compatible with free will, the problem, that is to say, which Augustine has made Evodius pose. The subject to which Rist addresses himself is related to this and he attacks it not by means of logic alone but through an exhaustive examination of Augustine's statements on predestination and its relation to free will. He stresses at the outset the danger of pulling contrary opinions out of such a large corpus of writings and of hiding behind the ambiguity of a word like 'freedom', 'now almost a meaningless term' – though not meaningless for Augustine even if 'it did not carry the same emotional overtones as those with which we are familiar'.[55]

No brief summary can do justice to the incisiveness of Rist's argument but we can at least try to indicate the main lines which it takes. After explaining Augustine's doctrine of the nature of the human will upon which his theory of free choice is based, Rist reaches the crucial question whether Augustine's

[50] Lucas, 1976, 1.
[51] Hick, 1976, 243.
[52] Or, in another, less poetic version: 'What can be said at all can be said clearly, and what we cannot talk about we must pass over in silence' (*Tractatus Logico-Philosophicus* 2, Pref., translated by D. F. Pears and B. F. McGuinness, London 1971).
[53] *FC* III, ii. 4 (PL 32, 1272) (CSEL 74, 92f.).
[54] Rowe, 209f.
[55] Rist, 219f.

predestination is twofold, some being predestined to salvation, others to damnation. He quotes the definition of predestination given in the treatise *On the Gift of Perseverance* as a foreknowledge and 'preparation' by God of those acts of kindness by which those who are to be saved are saved, which suggests that, though all those who are saved are saved by God's acts of kindness, it does not follow that all those who are offered such acts of kindness are in fact saved: 'the distinction between positively willing something and being willing to let something happen' is thus one of which Augustine is conscious. But there are passages in which this formal definition 'does not seem to cover his position',[56] since elsewhere he refers to 'predestination to death',[57] 'the hardening of men's hearts' so that they are able to commit sin,[58] and 'predestination to punishment'.[59] Such references do not by themselves provide proof positive that double determination is intended, only perhaps that God *may* allow sin and damnation to take place. Even the notorious sentence taken up by the Jansenists as their trump card against Molinism is open to different interpretations: when Augustine writes that 'assistance is given to the weakness of the human will so that by divine grace it might be *unchangeably and invincibly* influenced in its action',[60] he would appear to be indicating that such grace cannot be resisted. But it has been argued – for example, by Mother Mary Clark – that the true meaning is that it is the will which, through grace, is irresistible, and she, like Rist, points out that Augustine never uses the adjective *irresistibilis* or *insuperabilis* to describe grace itself – does he use these adjectives at all?[61] Nevertheless, Rist concludes that 'such an interpretation is almost certainly incorrect': in this passage as in all of Augustine's works written after 396/7 'man is not even able to accept or reject whatever graces may or may not be offered to him'.[62] Although Augustine could have used material which was to hand so as to develop a theory establishing the priority of grace and the 'preparation' of man's will without denying him the ability to use that will to accept or reject the divine call, he deliberately chose not to do so; 'all men are thus "free", the elect from serious sins, the damned from virtue.'[63]

At this point we might well sympathise with Pelagius and be willing to forgive him if, from his place in heaven or hell or limbo or chained for all eternity to a rock in the Caucasus like that earlier 'heretic' Prometheus, he were to throw back at his old adversary the gibe that the latter once hurled at him: 'Either I do not understand what he means or he does not himself.'[64] We might also go farther and, with some justification, claim that the responsibility for the length and bitterness of the Pelagian controversy can be attributed as

[56] Ibid., 227.
[57] *SO* IV, xi. 16 (PL 44. 533) (CSEL 60. 395f.).
[58] *GFC* xxiii. 45 (PL 44. 910f.).
[59] *E* xxvi. 100 (PL 40. 244f.).
[60] *RG* xii. 38 (PL 44. 940).
[61] Clark, 108ff.
[62] Rist, 239.
[63] Ibid., 241.
[64] *NG* xlvi. 55 (PL 44. 273) (CSEL 60. 273).

much to Augustine's change of front in his understanding of predestination and election as to Pelagius' obduracy in pressing his case for the human will. Having decided that it was not enough to maintain that man could win salvation by freely accepting God's freely given grace, Augustine proceeded to evolve a theory of predestination which ultimately depended on a causal connection between man's sin and Adam's fall – between 'man's first disobedience' and 'the fruit'. As early as the Second Council of Orange the Church found it necessary to tone down his more extreme view of predestination, even while accepting the general principle of original sin. And that principle, in turn, was to be re-examined and considerably modified, if not altered out of all recognition, in the Middle Ages.

It has been suggested that if Augustine had been able to jettison his views on infant damnation and if he had not misinterpreted the biblical text that 'God wishes all men to be saved', he might have found it possible to 'develop an understanding of grace and predestination quite different from that usually associated with him'; he would then have been doing 'what many Christian thinkers of all persuasions have done in recent times'.[65] But his theology was a seamless robe, woven closely together in the course of a long life of reflection and controversy, and to suppose that this piece or that could be removed from the whole without damage to the remainder would be to misunderstand the nature of the man himself and of his involvement in the Church of his day. No less than Pelagius, he was a child of his own times, and it was his historical rôle to take ideas which had already been aired and were still being debated by others and to mould them into a comprehensive system acceptable to the African Church as he knew it and to the Christian Church as he wanted it to be, making them 'correlative members of a vast intellectual scheme' and thus adding 'a whole area to the domain of systematic theology'.[66] Within this system his concept of original sin was a close companion of his doctrine of grace, and both were, in his firmly held view, inseparable from his theory of predestination. But such a system, as even one of his most sympathetic interpreters among contemporary Augustinian scholars admits, 'is too legalistic and lacking in charity to reconcile with the continual emphasis laid by Augustine himself on the supernatural virtue of charity, from which the God of his predestinarian writings seems to be wonderfully immune'.[67] And the same scholar goes on to point out that 'Augustinian

[65] TeSelle, 1970, 330.
[66] N. P. Williams, 1930, 19.
[67] Bonner, 1963, 390. But, notwithstanding his reservations as to Augustine's views on predestination, Bonner, 1986(a), 385, in his conclusion to a discussion of Augustine's conception of deification has rightly reminded us that 'predestination is, however, too fundamental to Augustine's mature theology, and too much a part of the heritage of Western Christian theology, to be ignored in serious ecumenical debate. If East and West are to come to a common theological mind, as opposed to publishing agreed statements of doctrine, the issues raised by the doctrines of deification and predestination have alike to be faced, and are not lightly to be dismissed as being, in the one case, unchristian, and in the other as being the rationalisation of the mystery of human freedom and divine grace.' See also his n. 64 on the danger involved in attempting to rationalise the differences between Pelagius and Augustine, which 'fails to do justice to Pelagius, still less to Augustine'.

predestination is not the doctrine of the Church but only the opinion of a distinguished Catholic theologian'.[68] But let us allow N. P. Williams the last word on the subject: 'The conception of Grace as Power, with its logically necessary context of an apparently arbitrary predestinarianism, seems to dissolve away the moral character of God and sublimates Him into a non-moral Absolute, to Whom, or Which, it is useless to cry for mercy or help.'[69] As it turned out, Augustine's obsession with predestination was just as open to criticism as Pelagius' obduracy in defending the freedom of the will, and Pelagius had every justification for resisting it.

[68] Ibid., 392. As Wermelinger, 196, points out, none of the canons of the Council of Carthage in 418 goes into the matter of Augustine's doctrine of predestination, and we shall observe in c. 6 the disturbing effect which its extreme expression in his letter to Sixtus, written in the same year (L 194) (PL 33, 874–91) (CSEL 57, 176–214), had upon the monks of Hadrumetum and the objections raised by the Semi-Pelagians when they too found that this novel doctrine threatened to depreciate the proper exercise of free will. By the time he came to formulate his charges against the Pelagians for the last time in 428 in his treatise On the Heresies addressed to Quodvultdeus his formulation employs the same material as earlier versions but the perspective has entirely altered: in H 88 (PL 33, 47–50) predestination as the logical basis for the absolute gratuity of grace directs his entire presentation of Pelagian ideas. Wermelinger, 282, rightly describes this abbreviated version of the Pelagian heresy as unhistorical and capable of being correctly grasped only if we compare it with earlier abbreviated versions in TLP IV, vii. 19 (PL 44, 622f.) (CSEL 60, 542), in J III, i. 2 (PL 44, 702f.) and in GP ii. 4 (PL 45, 996). Augustine's last word on predestination as an item in his indictment of the Pelagians is to be found in his letter to Vitalis, Bishop of Carthage, written around 427 (PL 33, 984f.) (CSEL 57, 414–16), 'an excellent resumé of his struggle against the Semi-Pelagians' (Portalié, 191), in which he once again emphasises that grace is not given to all but to those to whom God wills to give it, that is, the elect. His opponents might well have reacted by quoting, if they had been able to do so, Spurgeon's perhaps somewhat irreverent 'prayer': 'Lord, hasten to bring in thine elect and then elect some more'!

[69] N. P. Williams, 1930, 6.

51

IV

PECULIAR GRACE

'It was through one man that sin entered the world, and through sin death, and thus death pervaded the whole human race, inasmuch as all men have sinned.'

Romans 5, 12[1]

'God bless us all, this was peculiar grace.'

EDMUND BLUNDEN[2]

In his frank and deeply moving autobiography Harry Williams recounts a nightmare which, though he did not grasp its significance at the time, turned out to be of 'fundamental importance' and pointed the way to his understanding of the spiritual problem which tormented him and to his entry into the Community of the Resurrection at the age of fifty. He dreamt that he was watching a play in a theatre when something prompted him to turn round and look behind him towards the back of the auditorium; there he saw a human monster, unseen by the players and the rest of the audience, engaged in hypnotising the players so that their every word and action resulted from his dictation and they 'were in fact no more than the servile creatures of the monstrous all-powerful hypnotist'.[3] Regardless of their doom, the little victims played!

The monster was human, and Williams does not suggest that his nightmare is an allegory applicable to the general situation of humanity. But one is immediately reminded in the present context of Passmore's examiner, who sets the papers and 'not only knows how many are to pass but has already determined *who* is to pass' and yet punishes the rest for their failure, and of N. P. Williams's telepathic chess-player, 'who not merely foresees all the other player's moves, but actually himself makes them . . . and consequently has won the game before it has even begun'.[4] Is one not reminded too of the God of Augustine's theory of predestination? No, its defenders will reply: Augustine's God is no malevolent hypnotist, no Svengali, but the playwright himself in disguise, employing a benign and appropriate form of therapy which gently induces his actors to play the rôles assigned to them as they

---

[1] *NEB*, Harmondsworth 1964, *The New Testament*, 251f.

[2] *Poems 1914–30*, London 1930, 'Report on Experience', 284.

[3] H. A. Williams, 1984, 147. An earlier version of this story appeared in his contribution to a series of lectures delivered in the University of Cambridge in 1963 and edited by A. R. Vidler (H. A. Williams, 1963, 52ff.). But there the man who had the dream is described as 'a person of some academic intelligence . . . a devout and rather high Anglican', and the monster as 'the god he was really worshipping', which makes the citation even more relevant to the present context.

[4] See c. III, 44, n. 28.

should be played and so not to ruin a performance which would be perfect if it were not for their blunders, while at the same time enabling them fully to realise their own potential. But what if they fail to come up to scratch? Well, that is their fault, not the playwright's, and they should be grateful to him for having given them the chance to show what they can do. Unfair to Augustine? Possibly, but was he 'fair' to Pelagius, and was his God 'fair' to his creatures?

In this connection it may be of use to recall the judgement which Jung once passed on Freud: 'He was a great man and, what is more, a man in the grip of his daimon.'[5] Augustine too could be said to have been in the grip of his daimon, a daimon residing in his lifelong preoccupation with evil as revealed in human sinfulness, and it survived him to cast its shadow over the subsequent history of the Christian Church in the West through the immense influence of his writings. To quote Harry Williams's recollection of the view of Christian thinkers held by a much-loved colleague: 'St Augustine took the worst of St Paul, and Calvin the worst of St Augustine.'[6] It was Paul's teaching on grace that provided Augustine with the foundation of his own much more comprehensive and sophisticated doctrine; but he carried his interpretation of that teaching to limits which left him with a theory of predestination unacceptable to the majority of later theologians – though not to Calvin, who proceeded to carry it even farther. Augustine must bear a major part of the blame for the kind of absurd situations in which Christians get involved when they try to reconcile the goodness of God with the evil of his creation, leaving us often with a picture of 'a God who is half Genghiz Khan and half St Francis'.[7] For example, in the wake of the disaster to York Minster a leader in *The Times* bore the heading 'Act of God', while on another page the Archbishop of Canterbury was reported to have repeated the words of a fire officer, 'The Lord was on our side as we battled against the flames'![8] Evidence of a split personality? Not at all: just a classic illustration of the Augustinian God's practice of tempering justice with mercy.

Yet readers of Jung will know that his judgement of Freud was not intended to be wholly adverse,[9] and our judgement of Augustine would be totally lacking in balance if we were to concentrate solely on his unhappy theory of predestination, neglecting the positive, countervailing merits of his doctrine of grace. The great strength of this doctrine lay in his realisation through personal experience and subsequent reflection of the power of God's love working in us for good; its great weakness resulted from his determination to objectify, even hypostatise, that power and to direct it towards the quasi-juridical correction and vicarious punishment of mankind for a mythical

[5] Jung, 176.
[6] H. A. Williams, 1984, 156.
[7] Toynbee, 79.
[8] 11 July 1984; needless to say, the leader and report provoked a long and revealing correspondence in later issues and were to be linked later with 'theological' discussions of the famine in Ethiopia.
[9] Elsewhere (389) he describes himself as also 'in the grip of a daimon', and this is apparently a characteristic of 'a creative person . . . captive and driven by his daimon'.

crime of which it was innocent, thus making man responsible for the fallibility of God's world. Whether or not we are prepared to accept such a damaging criticism of one of the greatest of the Christian Fathers will depend to a great extent on our own theological stance. Some will remain so convinced of the validity of his definition of true freedom, his *libertas* or *libertas maior*, 'the glorious liberty of the sons of God', that they will be prepared to overlook, even justify, the patent defects of his theory of predestination and their consequences for his doctrine of grace; others will find his theory of predestination so flawed that they begin to suspect his doctrine of grace, indeed his entire theodicy, as well. But one thing is certain: the relationship of human freedom to divine grace was the crucial issue on which Augustine and Pelagius differed. Never in the history of philosophical and theological controversy can two protagonists have argued with greater sincerity and conviction about an issue of such fundamental importance not only to the theoretical discussions of philosophers and theologians but also to the religious life of the mass of ordinary men and women. Yet Augustine claimed all along to be as passionate a defender of human freedom as Pelagius, refusing to admit that the debate was between freedom and determinism. Pelagius, on the other hand, was just as adamant in insisting that it was.

If we were able to employ a time-machine to transport them to the late twentieth century, where would Pelagius and Augustine take up their stand in the perennial debate between free will and determinism? Given time to familiarise themselves with the nuances of contemporary terminology, they might well be inclined to apply to each other respectively the labels of 'existentialist' and 'theological determinist'. Pelagius might well add to his eclectic repertoire of citations from his authorities one from John Macquarrie summarising Sartre's view that 'if God has already laid down what humanity is to become, then freedom is an illusion'.[10] Augustine, for his part, might well rejoin by adapting a sentence from the same paragraph to support his claim that human freedom, as defined by Pelagius, was incompatible with the existence of God, because it made insufficient allowance for the operation of his grace. And Pelagius would not be slow to counter the label of 'existentialist' pinned upon him by his adversary with another quotation from the same author: 'But it is with St Augustine that we come to the most powerfully existentialist presentation of Christianity since St Paul, and one that has been of such enduring significance that even today existentialists, Christian and non-Christians alike, acknowledge an affinity with the great North African scholar.'[11]

But if they were to continue to play Augustine's game of answering every quotation made by Pelagius with one of his own, the former would certainly come out best in finding support for his basic tenet that all human exercise of free will is subject to restrictions. Even in Macquarrie, whose reference to his

[10] Macquarrie, 1982, 15.
[11] Macquarrie, 1973, 47.

alleged influence on existentialists he would regard as less than complimentary, he could turn up the statement that 'Even if we accept that there is a genuine human freedom, this freedom occurs within a setting that is already determined',[12] and following his normal practice of extending the range of his authorities to those whom he might consider to be more 'orthodox', he might supplement this by a quotation from Pannenberg: 'The principle of individual freedom is not a self-evident fact of human nature.'[13] And, finally and with a gesture of triumph, he would pounce upon another pronouncement by the same theologian in a different work: 'Man's freedom requires a religious basis. Freedom only grows from participation in absolute truth, from the human being's bond with the divine mystery of his life.'[14]

Fortunately for them perhaps, Augustine and Pelagius were not in a position to foresee that their main bone of contention would be gnawed at by their epigoni for centuries to come and from angles and directions so numerous that it would be in danger of being obscured altogether. It would be kinder at this point to reverse the action of our time-machine and return our combatants, not a little bewildered at the way in which the term 'freedom' has been turned into an indispensable weasel-word of the twentieth century, to the age to which they belonged and a theological milieu which they understood. Augustine's theory of predestination, however important and however relevant to his interpretation of human freedom, is only one of a package of related issues during the course of the Pelagian controversy. We must now turn to two others, which he considered to be of equal importance in his controversy with Pelagius – original sin and baptism, both of them issues over which there had already been no lack of disagreement among the Fathers of the Church and between East and West, both of them essential ingredients of the Augustinian doctrine of grace and of the teaching of the Church on salvation and redemption.

When Augustine set about the task of constructing his theory of original sin, there was a substantial store of materials to hand. For scriptural foundation he turned, as ever, to Paul and, in particular, to Romans 5, 12–21. But Paul did not work in a theological vacuum; from popular Jewish thought he would have inherited two different accounts of the Fall of Man in Genesis 3 and 6. The first of these was not the historical source of the doctrine of the Fall, which had emerged in the post-exilic thought of the Jews as they reflected on the actual sin which they experienced within and around them and, seeking to find an explanation of its existence in a world originally created good, fastened upon the narrative contained in Genesis 6. This account had been ousted in time by the alternative version in Genesis 3 with its hint of a link between sin and sexual awareness, 'the first emergence of a *motif* which runs through much of Christian Fall-speculation'.[15] The story of

---

[12] Macquarrie, 1982, 18.
[13] Pannenberg, 1977(b), 18.
[14] Pannenberg, 1977(a), 47, summarising Hegel's conception of freedom.
[15] N. P. Williams, 1927, xii; cf. 34, 45, 58.

Adam and Eve in Genesis 3, however, does not contain a reference to original sin as such nor does it depict them as 'originally righteous' in the sense in which this has come to be understood. Both of these ideas may well have germinated and developed in the popular religious thought of the pre-Christian period and, combined with Genesis 3, could have produced, in the view of Williams, a doctrine of the Fall showing Adam's fall as resulting not only in human mortality but also in an inherited tendency to do evil (original sin) and an imputed responsibility for it (original guilt). Paul might have seen this possibility, and he may also have known of the idea found in Rabbinical teaching and variously described as 'the evil impulse, inclination, disposition or imagination'.[16] If so, then he chose to use the idea in such a way as to alter its original meaning by making it the effect, and not the cause, of Adam's sin and locating it not in the 'heart' but in the 'flesh' as unreservedly evil.

In fact, however, it is the story in Genesis 3 which forms the main basis of Paul's teaching on original sin, and he has nothing to say about original guilt or original righteousness. In 1 Corinthians 15, 21 and 22 he is concerned solely with the origin of physical death in Adam's sin and does not discuss the question of hereditary sinfulness. But in Romans 5, 12–21 he sees Adam's sin not only as the origin of physical death but also as the origin of sin, and Adam's descendants as infected with sinfulness by some mysterious means which he does not attempt to explain. This crucial passage is notoriously difficult to follow, let alone to interpret, but its main concern is surely not to elucidate the origin of human death and sin in Adam – Paul takes these as axiomatic – but to emphasise that the law has proved to be counter-productive as an antidote to them and that the only remedy is the redemption of man through baptism and membership of Christ. 'Here, at last, we have in fully developed shape, albeit stated without scholastic preciseness of definition, that momentous doctrine of the Fall and the Redemption as correlative conceptions, as twin pillars bearing up the fabric of Christian soteriology.'[17]

Thus Paul identifies the source of death and sin as the Fall of Adam and insists that the inbred disease in man which resulted resided in his 'flesh' or 'members' as an impulse to evil curable only by the grace offered to man by the redemptive act of Jesus. But, of course, he left many questions unanswered, since he was not engaged in writing theological monographs but in addressing letters of rebuke, advice or encouragement to different congregations as the need arose. And so the early Fathers did not inherit from him an unambiguous doctrine of original sin, and the evidence shows that they did not give it serious consideration: according to one authority, 'In all the writings of the Apostolic Fathers the name of Adam occurs but once, and the Earthly Paradise and the fatal tree are not mentioned at all.'[18] Nor did the Greek

---

[16] Cohen, 496ff., discusses a medieval attempt to identify the 'evil inclination' with original sin in the Thomist sense, and K. Armstrong, 61, comments: 'In Judaism sin is a regrettable fact of life, but not a matter for desperation. Everybody sins but God will forgive.' She also reminds us that the 'evil impulse' is a source of much that is good and creative.

[17] N. P. Williams, 1927, 131.

[18] G. Boas, *Essays on Primitivism and Related Ideas in the Middle Ages*, Baltimore 1948, 15 – a reference I owe to Passmore, 87 and 341, n. 43.

Fathers give it a high priority in their debate and speculations, though generally accepting Pauline teaching on the subject in a vague manner and without closer re-examination. Indeed, neither the Fall nor original sin appears to be mentioned in local baptismal creeds or even in the Nicene creed; for a genuinely Catholic doctrine of both we must apparently go back to the New Testament and Paul.[19]

It was Irenaeus in the second century who first produced a systematic explanation of these subjects in the course of his counter-attack on Gnosticism but his theodicy, far from being a deliberate attempt to develop Paul's teaching, encouraged a much more optimistic view of man. For him, man's rôle is not that of one created perfect only to fall into sin but of one brought into being with all the imperfections endemic in human nature but with the prospect of development as a part of God's creative plan into the divine 'likeness' revealed to him in Jesus. The emphasis here is not on a Fall in the past but upon a growth in the future, and the Irenaean theodicy was later to find many supporters from Nemesius of Emesa and Theodore of Mopsuestia in the fourth and early fifth centuries to Schleiermacher in the eighteenth and nineteenth. There are many echoes of it in modern theology too but, vis-à-vis Augustinianism, it was never more than 'a minority report'.[20]

In his massive Bampton Lectures N. P. Williams distinguishes between the two classical versions of the Fall-doctrine which appear in the first four centuries of the Church by categorising them as the 'Hellenic, once-born or minimising' and the 'African, twice-born or maximising', and he traces the first clear sign of a bifurcation to Origen and Tertullian, when they reacted in different ways to the Gnostic threat in the late second and early third centuries. In his first, more optimistic interpretation, which he specifically declares to be no more than speculation and certainly not intended as dogmatic, Origen dismisses the story of Adam and Eve as 'a pictorial façade'[21] and the Fall-doctrine as an inference from Christian reflection on the phenomenon of evil. But in his later writings he tends to juxtapose with this another, more sombre version after being introduced to the practice of infant baptism at Caesarea, rightly perceiving, as many others signally failed to do after him, that the rite preceded the doctrine at least in fact, if not in thought: children were not baptised because of original sin, rather original sin explained why infant baptism was so important. And, in his later view, 'the conception

---

[19] Kelly, 1978, 351, however, finds that there was in the Greek Fathers 'the outline of a real theory of original sin', though it fell short of Augustinianism. 'The Fathers', he goes on, 'might well have filled it in and given it greater sharpness of definition had the subject been directly canvassed in their day.'

[20] Hick, 1983, 97. Beatrice, 1978, 206f., 306 (summary), links Melito with Irenaeus as a supporter of this 'more moderate opinion'. But de Simone, 209, recalls the statement of Daniélou, 1973, II, 404f., that Irenaeus does retain the idea of original sin as the cause of the bondage in which men find themselves as a result of Adam's first sin but presents the latter as 'in the highest degree excusable'; in technical terms, this is the distinction between *peccatum originale originatum*, on the one hand, and *peccatum originale originans*, on the other.

[21] N. P. Williams, 1927, 215.

of original guilt creeps in by the side of original sin'.[22] From being regarded as a weakness, not a disease, or, in more technical terms, as a *privatio*, not a *depravatio*, original sin becomes a more positive kind of pollution having physical consequences with guilt attached to them. But, while emphasising the importance of infant baptism, Origen still sees it as only one step in the process of salvation and assigns a higher priority to the baptism of the Spirit.

N. P. Williams maintains that it was Tertullian who first laid the foundation of an African doctrine of original sin as a form of positive corruption, derived from Adam and transmitted thereafter from parent to child, a hereditary handicap for which he coined the phrase *originis vitium*:[23] he was thus the founder of the theory of traducianism through the physical act of procreation, based on his materialistic view of the soul and on the idea of 'seminal identity'; but he did not go so far as to evolve an explicit doctrine of original guilt, and he held firmly to the view that infant baptism was an unnecessary, possibly even an objectionable, practice in view of the danger of post-baptismal sin. Cyprian, the second of the great African Fathers, took the doctrine a stage further by combining the hereditary infection by sin with redemption from that sin through baptism and therefore stressed the utmost importance of baptism as early as possible, suggesting that original sin might be linked with original guilt. But, fifty years after the appearance of Williams's Bampton Lectures, we have learned to be wary of being tempted to follow him too far in his search for an 'African' origin of the definitive Augustinian statement of the doctrine of original sin and hereditary guilt. It is true that, in appealing to tradition for support in his defence of the essential orthodoxy of his own views on the subject in his treatise *On the Merits and Forgiveness of Sins and Infant Baptism* in 412, Augustine cites Cyprian as his main authority; but he also relies heavily on Jerome and the scriptures in pressing his point that Pelagius is wrong in arguing that original sin is not an article of the true Christian faith.

Had he chosen to do so, he could also have found support in the Greek Fathers for at least some of his tenets: there were brave men before Agamemnon, and there were defenders of original sin before Augustine, Jerome and even Cyprian. In his book *Tradux Peccati* the Italian theologian Beatrice traces the source of the doctrine to territories unexplored by Augustine or, for that matter, N. P. Williams – 'Encratite circles, which were widespread in Egypt in the second half of the second century, and of which Julius Cassianus was an authoritative exponent'. He claims that the doctrine then spread to African and Latin Christianity and that Tertullian, Cyprian,

---

[22] Ibid., 220ff. More recently, J. W. Trigg, 111, describes Origen's theodicy as 'a vision of extraordinary moral grandeur and perhaps as satisfactory a solution, from the perspective of faith, to the problem of theodicy as has ever been suggested'. In 272, n. 31, he finds it 'curious that Hick, 1966, does not deal with Origen, who exemplifies far better than Irenaeus himself the "Irenaean" theodicy'.

[23] *On the Soul*, 41 (PL I, 2, 764). Augustine does not use the phrase *originale peccatum* in his earlier anti-Pelagian works, e.g. *MFS* and *SL*; there he prefers *delictum*. But by the second Council of Carthage *originale peccatum* has become firmly established in Africa and appears in its second canon.

Hilarius, Ambrosiaster and Ambrose all tried to reconcile it with the need to safeguard traditional teachings on creation, marriage and free will. Their successors were left with 'an unresolved antinomy', which Augustine and Pelagius set about trying to resolve in their different ways with the result that both sides in the controversy were forced to adopt extreme positions and 'it was only by dint of extremely refined conceptual acrobatics, with very fine distinctions, did Augustine succeed in proclaiming his allegiance to orthodoxy'.

The present writer lacks the qualifications to assess the evidence presented by Beatrice with the thoroughness which it merits, and Beatrice himself admits that he advances his novel theory with caution in view of the fragmentary nature of the texts employed, which are frequently difficult to decipher. But, notwithstanding this frank admission and the severe drubbing to which Beatrice has been subjected by some scholars, notably R. J. De Simone, if he were right, then the seeds of the doctrine of original sin would have been sown in the East as early as the end of the second century and transplanted from there to Africa and the West by the early third.

For the next development we must look to the writer whose commentary on the Pauline Epistles – omitting Hebrews, still regarded as non-Pauline by the West – is 'generally acknowledged to be the most impressive literary and historical study of those writings prior to the Renaissance'.[24] His precise identity remains uncertain: the name by which we know him, 'Ambrosiaster', was coined by Erasmus and reminds us that his works were long ascribed to Ambrose; but Augustine, who was greatly influenced by his reading of them, referred to him as 'sanctus Hilarius',[25] and many today prefer to describe him as 'Hilarius', though Augustine almost certainly confused this 'Hilarius' with Hilary of Poitiers. In his commentary on the Epistles Augustine found, *inter alia*, a convenient mistranslation of Romans 5, 12 which gave him a scriptural proof-text for 'original guilt': the Greek text meaning 'for that all men sinned' (AV and RV) or 'inasmuch as all men have sinned' (NEB) was incorrectly rendered as 'in whom, i.e. Adam, all men sinned'.[26] 'The fatal legacy was received only too gladly'[27] but it is doubtful if 'Ambrosiaster' had the slightest intention of using his mistranslation in this way, since he, like the Greek Fathers, took it to mean that, while Adam's sin brought physical death to men, it was their own sins that condemned them to a second 'death' in Hell. This is clearly not a doctrine of original guilt or even of original sin, but by his error in translation 'Ambrosiaster' made a significant, if unwitting, contribu-

[24] TeSelle, 1970, 157.

[25] *TLP* IV, iv. 7 (PL 44, 614) (CSEL 60, 528); on Augustine and Ambrosiaster see Beatrice, 159–73.

[26] The Vulgate also gives us *in quo omnes peccaverunt*, a literal rendering of the Septuagint leading to the erroneous interpretation in the first place; but the relative *quo* is too far from its supposed antecedent *unum hominem* to justify such an interpretation – except in the eyes of one who was searching for support in the scriptures for a theory of original sin, as Augustine was. At first, he had taken *quo* as referring to Adam or to sin but then realised that the Greek word for 'sin' was feminine: thus his alternative explanation in *MFS* I, x. 11 (PL 44, 115f.) came to be superseded by his definitive version in *TLP* IV, iv. 7 (PL 44, 614).

[27] N. P. Williams, 1927, 309.

tion to the ongoing debate. Ambrose was the first of the Latin Fathers to give unequivocal expression to a doctrine of original righteousness, and at the same time as Gregory of Nyssa, an admirer both of Plotinus and of Origen and 'the first Christian philosopher',[28] was propagating it in the East. For Ambrose, however, this original righteousness did not entirely disappear with the fall of Adam; rather it weakened with each succeeding generation until it died out altogether. Yet, notwithstanding his opposition to traducianism, which he shared with 'Ambrosiaster', he holds the view that the human race *was* identified with Adam, and he makes several references to original sin as an inherited bias to evil and, at least once, to original guilt; but for him, like 'Ambrosiaster', our punishment is the result of our own sins, for which the only remedy is baptism.

All these ideas were in circulation and under discussion at the time when Augustine set himself to produce his own blueprint for a doctrine of original sin. He had already been 'moving steadily away from the metaphysical aspects of the problem of evil, and the academic questions they raised, towards a preoccupation with practical and pastoral aspects which became far more important for him in the last decades of his life'.[29] He was now satisfied that evil was not a substance, a negative force engaged in perennial conflict with the power of positive good, but the privation of that good, to which all the evil in the world was attributable. At the human level sin, suffering and unhappiness were all products of the privation of good in the soul, a malfunction of the personality manifested in the failure of the human will as revealed in Adam's first sin. But the will was non-corporeal, and so Adam's sin must have been transmitted not through the body but the soul; any attempt to argue that 'original sin, lodged by inheritance in the body, moves, as it were, sideways, from the body into the soul' when the latter is created, would remove sin from the province of the will.[30] Such ideas were both erroneous and dangerous; but so was the Pelagian idea that man could avoid sin by the proper exercise of his own free will. There was an urgent need to correct this error by restating the catastrophic effect of Adam's fall on human nature. In the course of this restatement Augustine found it necessary to clarify and refine some of his own earlier ideas on original sin in the light of the intensive study which he had devoted to the story of Adam's fall in his *Literal Commentary on Genesis* during the years 401 to 414.

So, like Paul and many others after him, he returned to the Adam story in Genesis. Adam, he maintained, had sinned through pride, which led him to love himself more than his creator and, as a result, to misuse the free will which God had given him by allowing Eve to tempt him to disobey the divine command not to eat of the tree of the knowledge of good and evil despite a clear and unequivocal warning of the dire consequences. He then again succumbed to pride when he tried to place the whole blame on Eve instead of

[28] Sheldon-Williams, 456.
[29] G. R. Evans, 118f.
[30] Ibid., 125; Augustine is here refuting the errors of Vincentius Victor in *SO* I, vi. 6 (PL 44, 477f.) (CSEL 60, 307).

admitting his own guilt and begging for God's mercy. For his sin he was condemned to banishment from Eden, physical death and eternal punishment and his descendants to suffer the same punishment ever after by inheriting both the fatal flaw resulting from his sin and the guilt attached to it. This flaw, *vitium originis* or the sin of origin, was *concupiscentia carnis*, the sexual desire leading to intercourse, which by his sin he had lost the power to control through exercise of his will. Adam's sin thus brought disaster not only upon Adam himself but upon the whole human race, since the deterioration in his nature resulting from his fall was to be passed on to his descendants, who passed it on in their turn to theirs, so that all children are 'born in sin', except Jesus alone, who, not having been begotten and conceived 'after the flesh', was free from sin.[31] Furthermore, although baptism frees Christians from the guilt, *reatus*, attached to the original sin, even they continue to produce children infected with concupiscence by the act of procreation at the moment of conception:[32] the *reatus*, the guilt is counteracted by baptism but not the *actus* of that concupiscence, which remains inherent in human nature. Thus all men and women are born with a double inheritance, the concupiscence inherited from Adam's sin and the guilt which is remitted in baptism but which returns when the act is again committed.[33] By this clever distinction between the act and the guilt of sin Augustine was able to parry the Pelagians' claim that a baptised man freed from original sin by baptism ought to be able to beget children also free from original sin and so not in need of baptism to free them from it.[34]

Any brief summary of the Augustinian doctrine of original sin is bound to appear over-simplified and to run the risk of misleading the reader, and anyone who makes so bold as to essay such a summary is entitled to point out some of the difficulties involved in his self-imposed task. One of these is that he has to deal with a doctrine which, like many other Augustinian doctrines, was subjected to constant revision under pressure from critics demanding clarification of aspects of it which they seemed incapable of understanding. Another is that Augustine unfortunately left us no explicit definition of original sin: as he himself admits as early as 388 in a treatise written against the Manichees, 'nothing is more a matter of common knowledge as a subject to preach upon, nothing of a mystery to comprehend, than that old sin, *antiquum peccatum*[35] – and in all the years of controversy which followed and during which he struggled to unravel the mystery he found it either unnecessary or impossible to make good that deficiency. But enough has been said so far to enable us to identify the two components which are fundamental: they are concupiscence and seminal identity.

In Augustinian thought generally concupiscence is the human tendency to

---

[31] *J* V, xv. 52 (PL 44, 813). Thus for Augustine 'the only cure [for *concupiscentia*] is through Jesus', because he was born and lived without sin (Bonner, 1962, 310, citing *E* xli. 13) (PL 40, 252f.).

[32] *MC* I, xviii. 20, xix. 21 (PL 44, 425f.) (CSEL 42, 232f.).

[33] Ibid., I, xxvi. 29 (PL 44, 430) (CSEL 42, 241f.).

[34] *MFS* II, ix. 11, xxv. 39 (PL 44, 158, 175) (CSEL 60, 82f.).

[35] *MBC* I, xxii. 40 (PL 32, 1328).

turn away from the supreme good to the lesser goods of creation; it was the first sin, of which Adam was guilty by his disobedience, but it also contained within it the seeds of many other sins. Augustine lists the sins of concupiscence as pride, sacrilege, homicide, spiritual fornication, avarice and theft[36] but, in this connection, its chief manifestation is sexual desire, fed and watered by man's instinct to reproduce his species, in itself necessary, of course, but nevertheless of all forms of concupiscence 'the most violent and the least amenable to the commands of reason and of God'.[37] Adam's first sin was a sin of pride, attributable to concupiscence in its broadest sense of self-love or self-centredness; but it was to the concupiscence which resulted, *concupiscentia carnis* or sexual concupiscence, that his descendants were to be in thrall ever after: they formed the *massa damnati*, 'the lump of sin', and were condemned to remain there by God's judgement, unless they were released by his mercy. Concupiscence as sexual desire is both the original sin, the *peccatum* to which all are heirs, and the reciprocal penalty which it incurs, the *poena peccati*.[38]

Of these two Augustinian notions the first is easier to assimilate today, when we are accustomed to the idea of inherited defects in the human personality and may well be willing to accept that the defect inherent in original sin might qualify as one of them, since it is not an acquired characteristic or adaptive change in the Lamarckian, physical sense. But if, in these times of so-called enlightenment, we are no longer prepared to believe that a person named Adam ever existed, it would follow that there was no fall of Adam and that any defect of personality to which humanity may be prone is therefore the result not of a sin committed by 'the first man' but, along with other human tendencies, capacities and propensities, of our genetic inheritance: the story of the fall is 'not about Adam but about Man'.[39] As for the second notion – that all men are by inheritance liable to reciprocal punishment as a result of Adam's fall – this too is *a priori* untenable on grounds already given for rejecting the first. But, in fairness to Augustine, we are obliged to examine his reasons for holding this notion and not to dismiss it out of hand on grounds which he can hardly be blamed for not anticipating.

We find that his main justification was the mistranslated verse Romans 5, 12, supported by the reference to Levi in Hebrews 7, 9–10. From these two proof-texts he deduced that all men are 'in their fathers' loins' before conception and that all who have ever lived or will live in the future are 'infinitesimally minute portions of the Adam who sinned',[40] and so they participate prenatally in the primeval sin. He is thus able to find them guilty on two counts – of having 'sinned in Adam' and of possessing concupiscence as a result by seminal identity with Adam, an idea which he found, for example, in Ambrose but which had been hinted at earlier by Irenaeus, Origen and Tertullian. He also appeals to other scriptural passages, but we

[36] *E* xiii. 45 (PL 40, 254).
[37] N. P. Williams, 1927, 366.
[38] *MFS* II, xxii. 36 (PL 44, 173) (CSEL 60, 107f.).
[39] Lucas, 1976, 42.
[40] N. P. Williams, 1927, 372.

find that three of these are also mistranslations;[41] to tradition, but his triumphant demonstration of it to Julian somehow manages to omit reference to those of the Fathers who held views contrary to his own;[42] to established practices which featured in the rite of baptism and would be inexplicable if there were no original sin, such as insufflation, exorcism and renunciation of the devil, but this we can dismiss as a blatant *petitio principii*; and, finally, to the actual state of the contemporary world, which we might well prefer to explain in other ways more acceptable to the twentieth century.

Much has been written in recent years on the subject of Augustine's theory of sexuality and, in particular, the radical change which it underwent as he laboured to defend himself against the criticisms of the Pelagians and especially of Julian of Eclanum. Brown, for example, has drawn our attention to an important addition to the evidence for such a change contained in a letter, recently discovered and published by Divjak and written by Augustine around 420–1.[43] This letter is a part of his campaign to protect himself against the claim made by Julian and his supporters that he had condemned the urge to marry, *concupiscentia nuptiarum*, and to prove that his critics were themselves guilty of failing to make the vital distinction between this urge to marry and the urge of the flesh, *concupiscentia carnis*. The urge to marry had been blessed by God and was a human response to the need for social cohesion as supplied by the legitimate union of man and woman for the purpose of begetting children; *concupiscentia carnis*, on the other hand, the sexuality which all men had inherited in consequence of Adam's first sin, was asocial, and not even the Christian institution of marriage could entirely eradicate it. The institution of marriage was thus linked to the creation, the present nature of sexuality to the fall of Adam. The letter to Atticus reveals Augustine's anxiety to establish once and for all that his critics had misunderstood his teaching on sexuality and were totally mistaken in attributing to him a suggestion that it had originated with Adam's fall or had been inspired by the devil.

Adam's first sin was not a result of his sexuality: it was a capacity with which God had endowed him but which, as a result of his sin, he lost the power to control by use of his free will. Adam and Eve had not been created as asexual beings in an 'angelic' state only to slip from it into a more 'material' condition. Such an explanation of the fall of man had satisfied Christians for many generations and, at the time of his conversion, had seemed to Augustine too to be entirely acceptable; in 386 it had appealed to him, as it had to Ambrose and others, as a satisfactory model for the ascetic way of life. How

[41] His favourite texts are: Psalms 51, 5; Job 14, 4, 5 (Septuagint version); John 3, 5; Ephesians 2, 3; and, of course, Romans 5, 12.

[42] *J* I, vii. 30 (PL 44, 661): 'You are convicted of error from all sides; the great testimonies of the Saints are clearer than the light of day.' In I, vii. 34 (PL 44, 665) he appeals to the authority of Jerome, whose extensive knowledge of the scriptures and the Fathers he acknowledges, and in *MC* II, xii. 25 (PL 44, 450f.) he insists that 'it was not I who invented the theory of original sin, which the catholic faith has believed from ancient times'.

[43] No. 6 in Divjak's collection; see also H. Chadwick, 1983, 429. In trying to summarise the effect of this change on Augustine's theory of sexuality I have been greatly helped by Brown, 1983(a) and (b), and by Bonner, 1986(b), a very recent article of which he sent me an offprint with his customary kindness.

then had he come to reject it thirty years later on the grounds that it was an inadequate, even mistaken, explanation of human sexuality? The answer is to be found in the thorough re-examination to which he had subjected the evidence for Adam's fall in the course of writing the twelve books of his *Literal Commentary on Genesis*: this is the watershed in the history of his intellectual progress towards a definitive view of sexuality and its relation to marriage. His intensive study of the earlier chapters of Genesis led him to change his understanding of God's command to Adam and Eve to increase and multiply and replenish the earth, which he now interpreted literally, not allegorically as hitherto, and to advance a fresh view of Adam's sexuality in paradise. This new interpretation, adumbrated in his commentary on Genesis, was later to be expounded in full in the fourteenth book of his *City of God* as his considered view of the human condition and to be maintained and repeated until his death. Augustine had come to see human sexuality, *concupiscentia carnis*, no longer as a sin *tout court* but as a symptom of the malaise resulting from Adam's sin which had infected the human condition thereafter, rendering the whole of humanity subject to a reciprocal punishment from which it could gain remission only through the mercy and by the grace of God. Adam's sin was thus a paradigm of the sinfulness of mankind and its estrangement from the will of God, and human sexuality, *concupiscentia carnis*, the most revealing, though not the only, manifestation of its fallen state.

In constructing his doctrine of original sin over a period of years Augustine, as we have seen, did not begin with a *tabula rasa*: Cyprian, Ambrose and 'Ambrosiaster' can all be said to have at least suggested the idea of original guilt, the idea of concupiscence is found in Tertullian and that of seminal identity in Ambrose and others – and it may well be that the source of the doctrine is to be located in second-century Egypt. Augustine did not pluck his doctrine out of the air nor did he proceed to force a doctrine of his own invention on the African Church. His colleagues there had certainly by this time come to regard him as '*le grand porte-parole de la théologie africaine*'[44] but there was nothing to prevent them from opposing his views if they considered them to be extreme or even 'unorthodox'; instead, they gave him their unqualified support throughout the Pelagian controversy. As Bonner has pointed out, not only was Aurelius, Bishop of Carthage, enunciating an Augustinian doctrine of original sin as early as 411 at the Council of Carthage which condemned Celestius but more than two hundred African bishops reaffirmed it in the canons of the Council held in 418, the first two of which are '*un sommaire satisfiant des quatres premières thèses de 411*'.[45] There is thus an

---

[44] Bonner, 1967, 99.

[45] Ibid., 103. In his detailed analysis of the canons of 418 Wermelinger, 168, notes that the emphasis of the theological discussion underlying them has shifted since 411, only the first three now treating the connection between Adam's sin and inherited guilt. He also maintains (174) that the canons of 418 do not *sanction* the Augustinian theory of inherited sin as such (my emphasis) but, rather, provide no more than an answer to objections made to it by its opponents, omitting any reference to essential features of Augustine's thought on the subject such as the idea of 'corporative personality' and the connection between sin and *concupiscentia* and giving only a hint of Augustinian *reatus* or guilt (175).

element of continuity in their decisions which gives the lie to anyone trying to suggest that there had been a sudden change of front on the subject of original sin brought about by Augustine. Even if, as it has been argued,[46] Pope Zosimus in his *Epistola Tractoria* of 418 did see fit to water down the second canon of Carthage referring to the original guilt of unbaptised children, there is good reason to believe that the question of the damnation of infants dying unbaptised was a *theologoumenon*, a topic for theological discussion, not only in Africa but also in Italy and, possibly, in Gaul and Spain also before the Pelagian controversy had begun.[47]

The voices which gave assent to the nine canons of the Council of Carthage in 418 were those of the African bishops but the spirit which informed them was that of Augustine, and it is inconceivable that he would not have played a major rôle in formulating them or at least the last seven,[48] so closely do they correspond to the views which he had been expressing over and over again in the course of his debate with Pelagius. Nor is this surprising if we recall that the major points in his doctrine of original sin had already been aired as long ago as 396/7 in his reply to questions on the faith addressed to him by his old friend and adviser Simplicianus. It was to this treatise that he was to refer frequently in later years to support his contention that his teaching on grace and related topics had remained substantially consistent ever since the beginning of his episcopate. There we find his first use of the terms *originale peccatum, originalis reatus* and, taken from 'Ambrosiaster', *massa peccati*;[49] there too the ideas of concupiscence and original righteousness are adumbrated. Of course he will refine or elaborate upon the meaning of all these terms in the intervening years before the start of the Pelagian controversy. In those years he will go on to grapple afresh with his conception of the nature of man, to work out in detail his theory of predestination and to integrate them and weave them into the fabric of his definitive doctrine of grace.

In his analysis of Augustine's line of thought at this time, TeSelle takes up Sage's point that the term *originale peccatum* as used in the treatise *To Simplicianus* does not yet bear the full sense of '*péché originel*' as 'original sin' but signifies no more than '*péché d'origine*' or 'sin from the beginning', that is, of each individual life.[50] And he accepts that 'there is not yet a doctrine of

---

[46] Floëri, 1954, 755ff. Wermelinger's book *Rom und Pelagius* is essentially an attempt to answer the question raised by Floëri: to what extent does Zosimus in his *Tractoria* identify himself with the African doctrine of *tradux peccati*? His final conclusion (283ff.) is that there is no absolute certainty as to how far he (Zosimus) has moved towards it but considerable doubt as to whether he has accepted it in its full sense. In other words, his stance on the subject was, possibly deliberately, ambiguous; and on the subject of infant baptism the fragments of his *Tractoria* which have been preserved (PL 20, 693f.) leave open the question whether the sin which must be expiated in baptism is inherited. It goes without saying that, in the circumstances, his position was differently interpreted by the opposing sides in the subsequent debate about the correctness of the decision taken by Carthage and by Honorius, though it must be observed that neither ever appealed to Zosimus as an authority when recalling the decisive factors leading to the condemnation of Pelagius and Celestius.

[47] Refoulé, 1963(a), 49.

[48] Bonner, 1967, 103.

[49] *VQS* I, q. 1, 10; q. 2, 16, 20 (PL 40, 106, 121, 125).

[50] Sage, 1967, 212.

original sin' at least in the sense given to it in Augustine's later and final formulation, since the meaning of *originalis reatus* in the reply to the second question posed by Simplicianus has been misinterpreted. 'But now', he goes on, 'Augustine begins to think of man as captured by his first sin and becoming increasingly accustomed and addicted to them.'[51] Various shifts of emphasis are detected in this period and attributed to such factors as the influence of the Donatist controversy and, possibly, of the *Book of Rules* of the Donatist theologian Tyconius,[52] his extensive study of the works of Cyprian and the ever-present reminder of the teachings of his hero Ambrose provided by Paulinus of Milan, who had come to Carthage about 405 to write his biography of Ambrose and remained there to lead the attack on Celestius in 411. TeSelle even goes so far as to suggest that the 'decisive change' leading to Augustine's formulation of his definitive doctrine of original sin may be located in or around the year 406 not long after Paulinus' arrival in Africa.[53]

Niceties of this kind can safely be left to the professional theologians to discuss, even if it is unlikely that they will ever be resolved to everyone's satisfaction. But the general question of the credibility of the Augustinian doctrine of original sin is far too important to be entrusted to professionals alone, since many of them, while rejecting Augustine's mistaken attempt to base his arguments on the historicity of the myth of the Fall and Adam's first sin, still tend to defend the ultimate validity of the theory which resulted as a true description of the human condition and show great anxiety to save the baby when disposing of the bath-water. Hence, they still do their best to uncover the universal truth which they believe to be enshrined in it, its 'symbolic' meaning, its 'religious significance', its 'essential' as opposed to its 'accidental' element,[54] the wine in the bottle which is worth preserving even if the label may be out-of-date. For example, N. P. Williams concludes that 'Augustine's picture of a "Golden Age" and of an earthly Paradise tenanted by a saintly couple belongs to the realm of mythology'. Yet, when he comes to evaluate Augustine's doctrine of original sin, his resolution fails him, and he tails off into the face-saving statement that 'in the sense of the *vitium* or inbred disease of human nature, it would seem to be marked by psychological acuteness and truth'.[55]

What then is this symbolic meaning, so valuable that it must be preserved at all costs? That man has a radical propensity to evil?[56] But may he not also

[51] TeSelle, 1970, 180.

[52] On the possible influence of Tyconius see TeSelle, 1970, 180ff., where he discusses Pincherle's case, and for a possible similarity to the views of Tyconius Babcock, 1982, 1212ff.

[53] TeSelle, 1970, 266.

[54] Webb, 75.

[55] N. P. Williams, 382. Bonner, 1962, 311ff., finds Augustine's 'theological doctrine of the Fall' 'scientifically untenable' but his teaching on *concupiscentia* 'surprisingly modern' and suggests that Augustine is 'nowhere more relevant than in the field of psychology'.

[56] Webb, 116ff., suggests that Kant, though rejecting the doctrine of grace, reveals in his own teaching of a radical evil in the will a doctrine very close to that of original sin or, as he terms it, *peccatum originarium*, eschewing the German word for it, *Erbsünde*, because he does not accept that it was a hereditary disease.

have a radical propensity to good, being capable, as Pelagius argued, of turning *in utramque partem*, 'in either direction'? 'Is there, in human nature, as theology has often taught and as the not unpopular neo-Calvinism appears to teach, an ingrained bias to evil?'[57] If so, how are we to reconcile it with evolutionary theory and the DNA code of modern genetics? Knowing, as we have done since the discoveries of Mendel, that our genes, passed on from one generation to another in the germ cells, 'from time to time undergo sudden, spontaneous and apparently random changes in their form, technically termed mutations',[58] are we to see original sin as a product of one such mutation, 'some morally lethal gene, which arose as a result of a single mutation at a past moment of time'?[59] Do we then go on to attribute it not to a combination of random chance and iron necessity, as the molecular biologist Jacques Monod has done,[60] but as a part of God's programming of his eternal design for man?[61] Or try another tack and explain the fallen state of man as a residual effect of his 'animal past'? But such an interpretation would be 'profoundly unfair to animals'.[62]

Many prefer to resist the temptation to indulge in such exercises in mental acrobatics in order to explain *obscurum per obscurius* and to concentrate on extracting the 'essential' element in original sin as the key to its symbolic meaning, and the majority nowadays see pride as the front runner. 'Pride', we are told, 'is the movement whereby a creature . . . tried to set up on its own, to exist for itself',[63] 'that unwanted but unavoidable self-centredness, that sense of alienation and tension and moral failure which we experience and observe within ourselves and others as an empirically encountered phenomenon';[64] it is 'perhaps the oldest of human temptations. . . . Many theologians, from Augustine to Niebuhr, have believed that pride is the ultimate sin'.[65] And Geoffrey Lampe, in a posthumous paper in which he accepted as 'still meaningful' the interpretation of salvation as deliverance from sin itself, understood as 'alienation from God through the choice of self-centredness', went on to refer to 'Augustine's disastrous notion that sexual desire and activity is a primary expression of irrational and ungodly selfishness (*con-cupiscentia*)'.[66] All this, of course, is true in relation to human experience, and we have had occasion to note that pride or self-centredness was included in Augustine's list of sins inherent in Adam's first sin. But it is essential for the

[57] Bezzant, 97.
[58] Hardy, 1975, 30.
[59] Lucas, 1976, 42.
[60] Bartholomew, 16ff., provides a comprehensive review of Monod's case and of responses to it by theologians, scientists and philosophers.
[61] See, for example, Thorpe and, more recently, Montefiore.
[62] Badham, 57 and 136, n. 33.
[63] C. S. Lewis, as quoted in Joad, 338.
[64] Hanson, 1976, 42.
[65] Macquarrie, 1982, 240; before Augustine Ambrose did the same, and Augustine regarded him as his most weighty authority in the controversy over grace, though as Wermelinger, 273, rightly points out, in his register of witnesses against the Pelagians in *TLP* IV, viii. 20 – xii. 32 (PL 44, 623ff.) he gives far greater space to Cyprian.
[66] Lampe, 1981, 20.

sake of clarity to distinguish between that first sin of Adam and original sin as the flaw to which Augustine was to attribute all subsequent sins. The 'ultimate sin' may well be pride but the original sin resulting from it, the flaw, was in Augustine's view concupiscence in the sense of 'carnal desire'. If it were not so, it would seem very strange that Augustine should have written a whole treatise devoted to an examination of the relationship between marriage and concupiscence, in which he explicitly defines concupiscence as 'carnal desire', at once the cause of the first act of procreation and the stigma attached to it and to all such acts thereafter, the very root of man's propensity to evil.

It was precisely this propensity that the Fall-doctrine was pressed into service to explain in the first place, and, on an evolutionary view of man's origin and development, that doctrine, along with Adam and Eve and the Serpent and the Garden and all its other paraphernalia, simply disappears from history and reverts to its proper place in the creation-myths of other religions. If the Adam-story were to continue to fulfil its traditional Augustinian rôle as a form of theodicy, it would need 'to be understood in a historical and not merely symbolic way':[67] it would be seen in parallel with the historical event of the death of Jesus, as Paul unquestionably was the first to see it. His teaching on the Fall and original sin was solidly based on the historicity of both events; but what happens if the historicity of the second event succeeds, as it has done, in surviving the intensive criticism to which the biblical evidence has been subjected since the beginning of the nineteenth century, whereas the first has long lost any claim to be deemed historical? The blunt answer is that the first 'event' is an event no longer and has been deprived *ipso facto* of its traditional *raison d'être*, which was to buttress a theory of substitutionary atonement.

But even when this *raison d'être* still escaped without challenge, the Augustinian doctrine of original sin never fully satisfied the Vincentian triad of criteria for acceptance as a dogma of the Christian Church – that is, of having been believed *ubique, semper et ab omnibus*, 'in all places, at all times and by all Christians'. After the Council of Ephesus in 431, when the 'opinions of Celestius' were formally condemned but in the vaguest and most general of terms by the East, down to the 'Great Schism' of 1054, only a modified Augustinian doctrine survived in the West and the East showed practically no interest in the subject. In the late twentieth century its survival is as tenuous as the fading smile on the face of the Cheshire Cat, and it could be argued that all that is left behind of the symbolic truth which it once contained is the self-evident statement that there are in our personalities certain inherited, as distinct from environmental, features which lead us to want to put Number One first and, not infrequently, to harm other people in doing so.

Against the backcloth of modern biology, physiology and psychology perhaps it would be more honest to stop paying lip-service to this morbid

---

[67] Wiles, 1974, 67f.

doctrine of 'sin . . . accumulating at compound interest'[68] and to consign it to that region of limbo which is reserved for such failed theories as alchemy and phrenology, phlogiston and Piltdown man. This suggestion is not as frivolous as it might appear to be nor is it prompted only by the naïve attitude of those who 'reject the doctrine of original sin because the law-abiding citizen will rightly refuse to be held responsible for the crimes committed by his ancestors'.[69] Rather it springs from a strongly held conviction that it is a doctrine which has done the Christian Church far more harm than good. By preaching the absolute necessity to purge man of his inherited sin in order to save his soul, it has provided countless 'well-meaning' individuals with a ready-made pretext for pursuing their diligent campaign for souls without any thought for the mere lives of their victims – witness the heresy trials of the Middle Ages, the ruthlessness of the Crusades, the sadistic horrors of the Inquisition and so on *ad nauseam*. It has also fostered that obsessive antipathy to the sexual act which marred the thought of the Church from Paul onwards until it was elevated into doctrine by Augustine's stigma on the act of procreation. Even the Mariological doctrines of the Virgin Birth and the 'immaculate conception' often confused with it, though both derive most of their authority from a scatter of dubious texts, 'have something to do with the negative valuation of the sexual act on the part of the Fathers of the Church', as Hans Küng has put it with his usual frankness.[70] Both of them, and especially the second, he continues, 'have become largely pointless as a result of increasing criticism of the Augustinian view'. From this standpoint Augustine has a lot to answer for. What, if anything, can we find to say in his favour in the light of modern theology and science?

When he makes his final assessment of the value of Augustine's doctrine of the Fall and original sin, N. P. Williams comes to the conclusion that two of his 'great conceptions', those of original righteousness and original guilt, 'in their strict Augustinian form, are worthless from the point of view of modern thought'; as for the third, original sin itself, 'the common underlying element' in Christian teaching over the centuries goes back to Paul, the authority 'unquestionably claimed by all who have handled the subject from Justin Martyr to Baius and Quesnel'. He summarises this common underlying element as 'the inherent infirmity' in human nature, consisting in the discord between 'flesh' and 'spirit', 'which may be described in modern terms as weakness of will-power, defective control over the emotional impulses, or imperfect power of inhibiting the spontaneous flow of psychic energy along the channels of the primary instincts'. This, he maintains, is the only conception of the inherent infirmity misnamed 'original sin' which can be said to be truly 'Catholic' in the Vincentian sense, and it is already present in the Pauline idea of 'inherent weakness of will': 'tradition and dogmatic development, broadly interpreted, have added absolutely nothing to the language of Scripture'. As for the Fall, he maintains that 'Catholic Christianity as such is

[68] Hanson, 1976, 41.
[69] Webb, 75; cf. 72.
[70] Küng, 1977, 454.

69

committed to no more than the bare assertion that there *was* a Fall, a primal rebellion of a created will', 'a pre-cosmic vitiation of the whole Life-Force at the very beginning of cosmic evolution', resulting in an 'inbred disease of human nature'.[71]

Such an evaluation contains many echoes of the intellectual milieu or *episteme*[72] of the period in which Williams wrote and published his Bampton Lectures and of its limitations. But, over sixty years later, in his exciting clarification of biblical faith in the light of current evolutionary theory Gerd Theissen also returns to Paul and, in particular, to the contrast which he draws in Galatians 5, 19ff., between the fruits of the 'spirit' and the works of the flesh, forms of behaviour with a biological orientation and involving sexuality, aggression and greed. 'The biological conditioning of sins in the sphere of sexuality and the consumption of food is obvious. In the major group of aggressive forms of behaviour – enmity, dispute, jealousy, anger, intrigues, discord, partisan behaviour and envy – it is probable.' Paul, he continues, 'goes directly against the modern approach which by contrast sees the origin of anti-social behaviour in the "suppression" of biological needs', and he 'rather than our all-too-superficial modern awareness is right in seeing an antagonism in principle between flesh and Spirit, i.e. between tendencies towards behaviour with a biological foundation, on the one hand, and human culture, *even if Spirit is more than human culture* (my emphasis), on the other'. Tendencies in the opposite direction, that is, towards altruism – 'original goodness' – derive their strongest support from a religious faith capable of offering symbols of fellowship and community, brotherhood and sisterhood that discourage genetic rivalry and enable human beings 'to take that small (*sic*) step beyond previous evolution which allows them to have inklings of a freedom from the power of genetic and social egoism'. In support of this view he quotes Dawkins' book *The Selfish Gene* with 'its impressive confession of the human capacity to transcend natural and social "egoism"': 'we alone can rebel', affirms Dawkins, 'against the tyranny of the selfish replicators.'[73]

Theissen's main argument is drawn in part from two papers by the psychologist and evolutionary scientist D. T. Campbell, written as a plea for 'effective social curbs on human selfishness in the society of the future' and a protest against the hostility of 'present-day psychology and psychiatry in all their major forms to the inhibitory messages of traditional religious moralising'.[74] And his conclusion is in line with these two statements of Campbell: 'the truth could be what liberal theologians love to deny, that we have preprogrammed tendencies of behaviour which are held in check by strong cultural control in the opposite direction and that when the cultural systems of restraints collapse they unleash a terrifying "proneness to degeneration

[71] N. P. Williams, 1927, 380, 459f.

[72] I first came across this Greek word used in the sense of 'the system of thought characteristic of a particular historical epoch' in Cupitt, 1985, 4; Cupitt tells us that it was introduced by Foucault in his book *Les Mots et les Choses*.

[73] Theissen, 134ff., 140ff., 188, n. 14; Dawkins, 1976, 215.

[74] Campbell, 1975, 253; 1976, 167.

among human beings". We experience the tension within us between biological and cultural evolution as "guilt". We are aware that we need not automatically follow predisposed tendencies to behave. We can direct them. But all too often we are defeated by them. We are predisposed to sin.' In the conflict between this biological disposition to sin and the social and cultural demands for altruism our only help comes from the operations of the Holy Spirit.[75] Campbell, writing from a scientific and non-religious standpoint, expresses the same opinion differently: 'human urban social complexity is a product of social evolution and has had to counter with inhibitory moral terms the biological selfishness which genetic competition selects continually.'[76]

What would Augustine have to say about all this? We can imagine him grunting at this point, 'He means nothing more than the law and teaching.' True, he might find in Campbell's papers some support for his own view of 'seminal identity'; but he would obviously deplore the disappearance from the scene of divine grace and the absence of any mention of the Fall, as well as the fact that the actual term 'original sin' appears only in the title of the first paper. What of Theissen? He too makes no mention of the Fall and, as Augustine would be quick to perceive, describes 'original sin' at one point as 'certainly not a very good term'. But while the scientist defines altruism in purely genetic terms, the theologian does at least acknowledge a 'proneness to degeneration in human beings' and, what is more, identifies the Holy Spirit as the sole cure for the disease. Thus Augustine might be able to hear faint echoes of his *concupiscentia* and his *medicina* for it in Theissen: after all, he has at least advanced one step beyond Pelagius by discounting the possibility that mankind can raise itself by its own bootstraps,[77] even if his statement that 'the central reality offers its unconditional support to their imperfect trial and error' might send off a dangerous whiff of Pelagianism. It is in this respect that the theologian takes a leap of faith over the boundaries of the scientist's definition of culture in purely human terms, and he is able to do so because he believes that God the creator has not entirely abandoned men to their own feeble resources and that they still retain 'the possibility of experiencing, now, already – within a transitory and often unsuccessful life – the intrinsic goal of the whole of evolution: harmony with God'.[78]

I am aware that I may be criticised for concentrating on Campbell's thesis, on his own admission heterodox, when there are others much more truly representative of current orthodoxy in the fields of psychology and evolutionary theory. But I have selected it precisely because it seems to me to be more

---

[75] Theissen, 146ff.

[76] Campbell, 1976, 202; cf. D. Young, 1974(a), 403: '. . . during evolution it may be expected that the genetic programming of the behaviour of the species will tend increasingly to be influenced by the social behaviour of that species'.

[77] This is the 'falsely consoling thought' involved in 'that very English disease, Pelagianism' according to an Anglican clergyman Peter Mullen, attacking the 'psychological or spiritual teachings of Jenkins and Cupitt' (*The Times*, 25 May 1985): 'historically considered', such teachings are 'a recrudescence of Pelagianism'. On reading that they are 'Pelagians', Jenkins and Cupitt may well have felt rather like Monsieur Jourdain in *Le Bourgeois Gentilhomme* when he learnt that he had been using prose all his life without knowing it!

[78] Theissen, 174.

favourable to Augustine than any other variation on the theme of natural selection – be it Darwinist, neo-Darwinist or anti-Darwinist – that I have so far met: by his development of it Theissen is enabled to reconcile it with biblical faith and with the Christian belief in God as the creator and preserver of all mankind. But does modern evolutionary theory permit such a divine rôle within the parameters of genetic research? Has it not been entirely undermined by those who hold that the universe is no more than a product of a combination of 'chance and necessity', to use the title of a book which its author Monod believed to be 'a virtual disproof of almost (sic) all that religion stands for', 'biological proof of the absence of a master-plan', establishing once and for all that 'belief in a universe in which man is destined to appear is contrary to modern biology'?[79] Monod's case is founded on the discovery of the DNA code and the unpredictable mutations which occur in the process of molecular replication, and as yet it has not been 'seriously challenged, though it is claimed to be incomplete at a number of points'.[80] But what Monod has actually done is to state a case for the non-existence of God in its most extreme form; he has not succeeded in *proving* the non-existence of God or of a divine plan or that human beings are not an integral part of such a plan. When he asserts that 'our number came up in the Monte Carlo game' and that 'man at last knows he is alone in the unfeeling immensity of the universe, out of which he emerged only by chance', he is making a deduction which owes more to his own attitudes as a self-confessed atheist than to his acknowledged expertise in molecular biology.[81] There are many others who have examined the same kind of evidence as Monod, as well as other kinds of evidence which he did not take into account, and have reached a different conclusion.

For example, a professor of statistics who, like myself, admits to being only an amateur theologian, after a thorough examination of the views of those who have taken up the challenge made by Monod, concludes that 'the reality of chance is not merely compatible with the doctrine of creation but is required by it' and proceeds to formulate 'a doctrine of providence which, while allowing that God is ultimately responsible for everything that happens', does not postulate 'his intimate involvement in all things'. And, in the present context, it is worth taking note of his claim 'that only in a world of real uncertainty can people grow into free responsible children of their heavenly father'.[82] Nor is Bartholomew a voice crying in the wilderness: the Quaker

[79] Bartholomew, 2, 16; the second quotation is taken from a BBC interview with Peter Medawar at the time when Monod's book first appeared.

[80] Ibid., 19; the author suggests that 'Monod has set up what might be called a "natural anti-theology" '.

[81] Monod, 137, 167. But Gunton, 526, in his discussion of the theological conclusions emerging from Young's articles in the same number of *Theology*, rightly comments that 'theologians, at least in principle, are not bound to be terrified by discoveries in the biological sciences; yet these discoveries, he adds (528), provide 'an essential backdrop for any contemporary theology of man', quoting from D. Young, 1974(b), 477. Young also emphasises (471) that 'it is particularly easy to overlook the limitations of the biological approach and *to slide from biology into philosophical discussion*' (my emphasis).

[82] Bartholomew, 145.

animal ethologist Thorpe, while agreeing with Monod that 'to attempt to understand the natural world in the way in which science attempts the task is inherently worth doing', maintains that science can also 'yield some understanding, however dim, of the enduring reality underlying the transient natural world'.[83] Neither Bartholomew nor Thorpe denies the rôle of chance in evolution, as the titles of their books – *God of Chance* and *Purpose in a World of Chance* – abundantly show; but both reject the idea that the element of chance rules out the possibility of a divine purpose. And they have the support of the Anglican Bishop of Birmingham in a former book in which he is concerned to explain 'how God could be conceived of as acting purposefully in a world where the driving force appears to be chance – the very antithesis of purpose' and finds the most probable explanation to be that 'matter orders itself in a way that is optimal for life by the personal will of an omniscient and infinite God'.[84] All three, approaching the problem from different angles, are able, like Theissen, to develop a doctrine of the Spirit based on natural religion and to affirm God's immanence without contradicting the findings of modern science. But, it may be argued, just as Monod is an atheist, these three are convinced Christians and every bit as likely to be lacking in objectivity. Was Koestler then also a Christian? It was he who wrote the memorable sentence: 'Man is neither a plaything of the gods nor a marionette suspended on its chromosomes.'[85]

'If the hand of God is to be recognised in this continuous creation, it must be found not in isolated intrusions, not in any gaps, but in the very process itself.'[86] This conclusion broadly summarises the common denominator in the arguments of the statistician, ethologist and theologian from whom we have just quoted. But not one of them, as far as I have been able to discover, finds it necessary to discuss Augustine's doctrine of original sin in the light of contemporary science and philosophy, although presumably all three would agree that we have a 'natural' inclination to do evil, a 'proneness to degeneration'. This apart, what is left of the Augustinian synthesis? The plain truth is that modern evolutionary theory, warts and all, has just about completed the work of demolishing it, begun by the Pelagians and Semi-Pelagians and continued by Aquinas, Duns Scotus, the Franciscans and others in the Middle Ages, as well as the Reformers. Augustine's extrapolation of Paul's insight into the true nature of the human and cosmic struggle with evil was flawed from the outset by his insistence on tying it firmly to the story of the Fall. Whether or not he really believed that the story contained in the early chapters of Genesis was the literal truth is open to debate;[87] but he certainly behaved as if he did, and when as a result he proceeded to base his doctrine of original sin upon it, he was building on sand, and his elegant

---

[83] Thorpe, 1f.

[84] Montefiore, 171.

[85] Thorpe, 115, cites Koestler's sentence but without giving the reference.

[86] Taylor, 28.

[87] On occasions Augustine suggests that he had at least an inkling of what we now know as evolution, when he is discussing creation and related topics; a brief selection of relevant passages from *CG, T* and *LCG* will be found in Bourke, ed., 100ff.

structure now lies shattered like a child's sand-castle in the ebbing tide. It was biology that gave it the final push, and even the Christian myth of original sin makes sense in the late twentieth century only if it is expressed in terms that are not inconsistent with the discoveries of modern biology and is treated as a symbolic description of man's inbuilt tendency to place his own selfish interests before those of his fellow-creatures, be they human or animal, vegetable or mineral.

As for the term 'original sin', it is 'certainly not a good one', especially when it has been stripped of almost all its Augustinian associations and has been reduced, if not to a cliché, at most to serving as a convenient synonym for man's tendency to evil or as a useful antidote to modern notions of perfectibility. If we wish to employ it to express this tendency to evil, we must remember to allow for another, opposing tendency which man has developed in response to the civilising influence of human culture. Man's tendency to do evil is not the result of a sin committed by his first ancestor but of his genetic inheritance, which stretches back to that moment in time when molecules first merged to form DNA and pairs of cells joined and multiplied in the primeval soup. In the course of human evolution this tendency has been to some extent counteracted by a tendency to altruism, stimulated and encouraged by ethical constraints and religious experience; both of these tendencies have reacted and continue to react to man's physical and social environment *in utramque partem*, leaving him as a pig-in-the-middle, caught in the perennial encounter between the forces of good and evil. The Christian's choice between these opposed forces stems not from a divine election made once and for all in the remote past, but from the way in which he or she responds or fails to respond to the message and example of Jesus and to the subconscious pressures of the Spirit, deftly applied.[88]

All this, of course, is anathema to the Roman Catholic Church – not least because of the possible implications for its theology of infant baptism. Writing his *Apologia pro Vita Sua* only five years after the appearance of Darwin's *The Origin of Species*, Newman set the scene: he could see no reason to change his mind on the subject of the doctrine of original sin, maintaining that for him it was 'almost as certain as that the world exists, and as the existence of God'. This is not at all surprising when we take into account his view of dogma as

[88] This view of the interaction between genetic selfishness and cultural altruism approximates to that of Theissen; while accepting that 'there is a continuity between biological and cultural evolution' (9), he rejects the idea that the latter is simply the continuation of the former. He also notes (184, n. 38) that Wilson's conclusion in his book *Sociobiology: the New Synthesis* that 'religions develop to the degree that they further the survival and influence of their adherents' is criticised by Austin's article in *Zygon*. The question to what extent, if at all, altruism is able to counteract the 'selfish gene' has been the subject of a sharp, though so far inconclusive, debate. For example, Wilson's book and Dawkins' *The Selfish Gene*, as well as Mackie's article in *Philosophy*, have come under fire from Mary Midgeley, 1979, which provoked replies from Dawkins and Mackie two years later in the same journal. Unrepentant, Midgeley has carried on her attack in her most recent book (1985); Singer and Trigg have also made important contributions to the ongoing debate, as have Lumsden and Wilson, but the latter appears to have modified his earlier, more extreme thesis to some extent. I am indebted to my friend Robin Attfield for his help with the bibliography on which this note is based.

expressed earlier in the same work: 'From the age of fifteen, dogma has been the fundamental principle of my religion; I know no other religion; I cannot enter into the idea of any other sort of religion.'[89] It is hardly more surprising, even if it is not a little daunting, to find Pope Pius XII insisting a hundred years later that the first eleven chapters of Genesis 'do pertain to history in the true sense and must not be considered on a par with myths'.[90] What, in that case, is truth, and what is myth, and what is the distinction between them, we may well ask? Dogma has never really changed; it has only become more complex, and its history reveals no more than a negative struggle to avoid 'the hateful charge of novelty'.[91] As for the Anglican Church, original sin and predestination are still enshrined in its Thirty-Nine Articles, to which its clergy have to give a general assent, and any attempt to remove or even amend them would drive its Anglo-Catholic minority into doctrinal schism.

Further West in recent years we have observed the emergence and growing influence in America of a movement among conservative, evangelical Christians to turn back the clock by arguing that evolution is not a fact but either a philosophical theory or a scientific myth and that the Genesis version of creation and the Garden of Eden demands a literal interpretation.[92] Certainly we have no right to assume that biology has spoken its last word on the subject of evolution nor must we fall into the trap of allowing it to usurp the functions of sociology and ethics. But this does not entitle the 'creationists', or anyone else for that matter, to attempt to expose scientists to ridicule merely because they have the honesty to admit that natural selection can no longer be regarded as the only significant factor in the process of evolution and engage in open debate on the origins of life and of the universe. Theologians too who bravely endeavour to explain contemporary theories of creation and evolution in terms which make sense to ordinary Christians 'in the pew' deserve better treatment than to be pilloried by some of their colleagues and thrown to the wolves lurking in the sensation-seeking media. When will the Church wake up to the fact that it must stop dusting paper flowers and begin cultivating roses?[93] Not so long as it refuses to acknowledge 'the possibility of profiting by encouraging exploration along divergent paths', not so long as it continues to confuse myth with history, not so long as it 'dreams of things that never were'.[94]

Alas, poor Pelagius, where rode he the while? Certainly not on the back of a horse named Original Sin, which he had crossed off his list of potential starters before the race had even begun: *non est dogma* was his dismissive

[89] Newman, 218, 67.

[90] *Humani Generis*[2], trans. A. C. Cotter, Weston, Mass., 1952, a reference which I owe to Cupitt, 1979, 77.

[91] The heading of c. 5 in Wilken, taken from a paraphrase of Matthias Flacius, *Catalogus testium veritatis*, Frankfurt 1666, Pref., 1f., cited on p. 109.

[92] The 'creationists' seem to have had the support of no less an authority than the President of the United States of America, who, 'during his campaign for the Presidency, referred to evolution as "only a theory"' (Angela Tilby, *The Times*, 15 August 1981).

[93] Küng, 1977, 121; I am grateful to Marion Eames for giving me the precise reference.

[94] L. Dewart, 150; Wilken, 193.

comment at Diospolis.[95] Out of the package of goodies offered to him under the label of original sin by Augustine all he was prepared to accept was that Adam's sin resulted not only in his own death but also in that of the whole of mankind, and he, like Augustine but with a different interpretation, accepted the current Latin mistranslation of Romans 5, 12 as 'in whom (that is, Adam) all men sinned', since he knew even less Greek than his more distinguished opponent.[96] More than that he defiantly refused to swallow. The main authority for his views he, like Augustine, found in Paul, and he saw no reason to question the statements contained in 1 Corinthians 15, 22 and in Romans 5, 12 to 19. But his interpretation of these was very different from that of Augustine, as he had made abundantly clear in his commentary on the Pauline Epistles written in 405–9, where he had explained Romans 5, 12, 15 and 19 as referring to man's sin as the result not of an inheritance from Adam but of imitation of his *example*.[97] As we have noted, it was such a denial of original sin which first attracted the adverse attention of Augustine to the Pelagians in 411, although it was Rufinus of Syria and Celestius who were then his main targets. This denial had implied a thoughtless but none the less dangerous threat to the rite of infant baptism, and his subsequent reading of Pelagius' commentary and of his works *On Nature* and *On Free Will* confirmed his suspicions that Pelagius was just as culpable in this respect as his associates, indeed largely responsible for the wrong views that they held.

On baptism Augustine and Pelagius were separated from each other by an apparently impassable gulf, covered with 'thick-ribbèd ice'. For Augustine baptism made available to man a means of grace by which he could be set free from the penalty attached to original sin as well as the sins which he had actually committed. It did not, however, take away the urge to sin, which required the constant application of grace to resist it and reinforce the right exercise of 'free' choice, nor did it make man perfect: 'it merely cleans the

[95] 'I anathematise them as fools but not as heretics, for there is no dogma' – referring to those who held the opinions attributed to him under the sixth item in the charge-sheet.

[96] Scholars have differed on the question whether Pelagius knew Greek. For example, R. F. Evans, 1964, 21, n. 5, states that 'he cannot understand the assertion of Hedde and Amann, 392, that Pelagius made his replies to the council [of Diospolis] in Greek' and quotes *PP* i. 2 in support of this statement. But he has misunderstood the passage quoted, which refers not to a verbal response made by Pelagius but to a reading in Latin from one of his works, which, like the charges against him, was translated by an interpreter. *Contra*, Wermelinger, 58, n. 81, claims that Pelagius spoke Greek at Diospolis on the authority of Augustus' statement in *PP* ii. 4; but he too has misread his text: all that it tells us is that Pelagius' response to one of the questions put to him by his judges was *Graeco eloquio prolatum*, that is, '*expressed* in Greek' – again by the official interpreter. What we do know is that Pelagius read the works of Origen and the *Sentences of Sextus* in Rufinus' Latin translation of them (R. F. Evans, 1968(a), 47, 65; H. Chadwick, 1959, 120). If he knew any Greek at all, it would not have been, as Hugh Williams, 1912, mistakenly believed, because he was 'one of many Latin Christians of the West to begin to visit sacred sites in the East c. 380', but simply because some of the Greek of his *amanuensis*, Annianus of Celeda, may have rubbed off onto him through their constant association. Pelagius interpreted Romans 5, 12 as meaning that all men sin by following the *example* of Adam and not through inheriting his sin by transmission (PLS 1, 1136; Souter, 1922/31, 41).

[97] PLS 1, 1136ff.; Beatrice, 41–63, has a good summary of the Pelagian criticisms of the doctrine of original sin.

slate for him.'[98] What of Pelagius' teaching? His commentary on Paul contains many references to the sacrament of baptism as applied to adults: briefly, it is 'the sacrament of justification by faith *alone*'[99] – and this addition of the word 'alone' encouraged the great Augustinian scholar Loofs to comment that the *sola fide* had no more energetic defender before Luther than Pelagius! Those who seek baptism, said Pelagius, show that they possess 'trust from the whole heart', 'faith in the promises of God',[100] and by baptism they are cleansed of their sins, that is, those which they have committed, and made righteous by the grace of God. Thereafter, freed from their previous sins by the 'word' speaking to them in baptism, they need the help of that word again in the form of *doctrina*, 'teaching', in order to remain righteous by obeying the law of God. Baptism is thus needed to cancel actual sins committed, and no more. And Pelagius, following 'Ambrosiaster', identifies predestination with foreknowledge:[101] God foreknows those who will accept faith and seek to be baptised but he does not compel them to accept baptism nor does he compel them to persevere in their search for righteousness. Rather, he provides them in Jesus with the teaching which will enable them to do so.[102] We are again reminded of Augustine's wry and oft-repeated comment: 'he means nothing but the law and teaching.'

And what of the baptism of infants as opposed to that of adults? Here Pelagius was presented with a problem with which he never succeeded in coming to terms. 'Nowhere', comments R. F. Evans in summing up Pelagius' theology of baptism, 'does Pelagius show that he was able to refine his theological language in such a way as to offer an intelligible rationalisation for speaking of redemption and the remission of sins as applied to infants.'[103] Thus we arrive at a question which is of vital importance for anyone trying to understand Pelagius' attitude to the charge of heresy which was brought against him and, to use a modern phrase, made to stick. Why was he not as explicit on the subject of infant baptism in his *Liber de Fide* as Celestius was in his? Both statements of belief were presented to the Pope at the same time and were couched in language which is almost verbally identical, except that Celestius added certain phrases and sentences to his version which are not present in that of Pelagius, among them an amplification of his views on baptism.[104] Although we have no evidence that the two men sat down together to work out their affirmations in close collaboration, thus presenting

[98] G. R. Evans, 131.

[99] R. F. Evans, 1968(a), 113; for examples of Pelagius' use of the phrase *sola fide* see his expository notes on Romans 3, 28; 4, 5,; 5, 1; Galatians 3, 11 and 26; Ephesians 2.8; 3.11; (PLS I, 1129, 1131, 1133f., 1149, 1277, 1279, 1293, 1296).

[100] On 1 Timothy 6, 10 (PLS I, 1357); on Galatians 3, 11 (PLS 1, 1277); *On the Divine Law*, 2 (PL 30, 107).

[101] On Romans 8, 29, 30 (PLS I, 1149f.).

[102] On Galatians 3, 24 (PLS I, 1279).

[103] R. F. Evans, 1968(a), 118f.; on the relation between infant baptism and original sin see Beatrice, 105–19.

[104] Garnier printed the two confessions of faith side by side for easier comparison in his fifth dissertation on the first part of Marius Mercator's works (PL 48, 498ff.).

a united front to their accusers, it is difficult to explain such a degree of unanimity if they did not do so. If they did, it is understandable that Celestius, as a trained lawyer, would insist on qualifying the terms employed in the statement so as to make their precise meaning more precise. But it is just as possible that Pelagius deliberately chose not to be as explicit as his friend on some subjects. He, unlike Celestius, confined himself to affirming that 'we' – and he is here speaking for himself – 'hold likewise one baptism, which we maintain ought to be administered with the same sacramental formula to infants as to adults.'[105]

Augustine had no difficulty in showing up the blatant inconsistency of this statement and describing it as simply 'a heresy struggling to conceal itself under ambiguous words',[106] and it is hard to believe that Pelagius himself was unaware of this basic inconsistency.[107] He must have known that only Tertullian of the Latin Fathers had opposed the practice of infant baptism and that Cyprian, on the other hand, had affirmed that it was needed for remission not only of sins but of original sin as well. He must also have realised that, though theories of original sin and original guilt were being used to safeguard and justify infant baptism – or so it must have seemed to him –, in fact they were historically preceded by it as a traditional institution of the Church, and he never questioned the scriptural evidence on which it was originally based. Either he did not understand what was involved in his denial of original sin or he was trying to protect himself against a charge which had proved to be successful when brought against Celestius. The second of these possibilities, the one which Jerome and Augustine strenuously maintained, is the only tenable answer but it calls for some qualification. Plinval suggested that 'anything touching on the rites and practices of the Church was very much more serious than that which affected controversial and still not defined points of pure theory: search for the precise nature of Adam's sin and evaluation of its subsequent repercussions could offer only a speculative interest, but considerable importance was at once attached to what directly affected the practice and real efficacy of the sacrament.'[108] Bonner too seems to be moving in the same direction when he writes that 'perhaps, indeed, the clue to Pelagius' orthodoxy or unorthodoxy lies not so much in his concept of grace as in that other, vehemently debated topic, the baptism of infants *in remissionem peccatorum*, "for the remission of their sins".'[109] It is always dangerous to attempt to project into the distant past an interpretation which appears convincing many centuries later; but, in this case, Pelagius' seemingly conscious decision to avoid the issue in his *Liber de Fide* would seem to justify us in concluding that he *was* fully aware that to deny the efficacy of baptism for infants would be to forfeit any residual claim to orthodoxy on his part. The picture that others had built up of one whose

[105] PL 48, 502.
[106] *OS* xxi. 23 (PL 44, 396) (CSEL 42, 182).
[107] Augustine exposes it in *MFS* I, xxxiv. 63 (PL 44, 146f.) (CSEL 60, 63f.).
[108] Plinval, 1943, 257.
[109] Bonner, 1966, 358.

orthodoxy was already undermined by his heretical views on grace would be completed if he could also be shown by his own confession to be casting doubt on a practice which was essential to the Christian Church.

But it would not be sufficient or equitable to attribute Pelagius' affirmation of baptism merely to a conscious attempt to deceive: of course he must have realised that, if he wanted, as he certainly did want, to be known as an *integer Christianus*, 'a complete Christian', he *had* to accept baptism as an essential tenet of the faith. Nor is there reason to doubt that he accepted it in all sincerity, for was it not also essential to his own teaching on the need for regeneration? The only significant difference between Augustine and himself was that he wanted to limit its efficacy to the remission of sins already committed, whereas Augustine was determined to maintain its validity as a means to the remission of original sin as well. Thus Pelagius finished up by adopting an ambiguous position, affirming his belief in baptism and his acceptance of the rite by which it was traditionally administered in one article of his confession of faith, while continuing in another to maintain the freedom of the human will to make its own choices, though 'always', he was careful to add, 'with divine assistance'.[110] But one of these choices was presumably to seek and accept baptism, and this infants were unable to do because, as he argued elsewhere, 'they do not yet make use of the rational will'.[111] On his own premises and the conclusions which he had built upon them he was in this way shown to be in favour of admitting infants to a sacrament for which he could offer no theoretical support; as Augustine was quick to point out, he was making a mockery of baptism.[112] His only justification of this paradox was to ask, 'Who is so impious as to forbid the common redemption of the human race to an infant of any age?'[113] 'What redemption does he mean?', asked his opponent scornfully: 'Is it from evil to good, or from good to better?' If the former, from what source could the evil have come other than the original sin of Adam? If the latter, then Pelagius would be falling back on the opinion of Celestius that infants at birth were in the same state as Adam before his fall, an opinion which, along with others attributed to his friend, he had anathematised at Diospolis. He was thus confronted with 'Hobson's choice' or, to use a contemporary metaphor, a 'catch 22 situation': if he renounced infant baptism, he would be declared a heretic; if he affirmed it, his whole theology became a nonsense.

It was left to the last and most acute of Augustine's Pelagian adversaries, Julian of Eclanum, to spell out in full what his predecessors had either adumbrated (Rufinus of Syria and Celestius) or glossed over (Pelagius), that infants, though untainted by Adam's sin were still capable of receiving through baptism 'spiritual illumination, adoption into the sons of God, membership of the heavenly city of Jerusalem, sanctification and transfer into

---

[110] PL 48, 491, 504.
[111] *OS* xv. 16 (PL 44, 393) (CSEL 42, 177f.).
[112] *MFS* I, xxxiv. 63 (PL 44, 146) (CSEL 60, 64); cf. *J* III, v. 11 (PL 44, 708).
[113] *OS* xix. 21 (PL 44, 395) (CSEL 42, 181).

the members of Christ with possession of the kingdom of heaven'.[114] Julian's terminology reminds us of Garnier's observation that the writings of the Pelagians reveal here and there a kind of anticipation of medieval views on sanctifying grace, and de Blic also refers to the statement of Celestius that infants 'because they have no natural strength, must have baptism conferred on them by the generosity of grace' as being of remarkable modernity'.[115] The last phrase tempts us to reflect whether the Church is any further forward today in its search for a solution to the age-old problem of infant baptism than it was in the fifth century. To judge by a recent report commissioned by the World Council of Churches, it is still wrestling with the same problem of reconciling opposing views on the subject, and its difficulties seem even more intractable in the light of the proliferation of its internal divisions since the Reformation. The report submitted by theologians of all shades of opinion and entitled 'Baptism, Eucharist and Ministry' – the order of the words is not without significance – makes it clear that if Church unity is to be visibly achieved, one of the essential prerequisites is a basic agreement on baptism, and denominations are urged to prepare the way for such an agreement by reconsidering their own position on baptism – and, where applicable, confirmation – and re-examining their theology of baptism before turning to their actual practice of it. The question that they must face fairly and squarely is 'whether infant baptism can bear the full weight of the theology of baptism and the consequent nature of the baptismal commitment'. The report does not claim that it has been able to resolve the question of infant baptism *vis-à-vis* the baptism of believers, but it does conclude that 'while infant baptism may have been practised in the apostolic church, baptism on profession of faith is the most clearly attested pattern'. To be baptised, it maintains, means to be admitted to share in the life, death and resurrection of Jesus after confession of sin and conversion of heart and to undergo an ethical orientation through the Holy Spirit.[116]

Plus ça change, plus c'est la même chose? Pelagius at least might have thought so; he would certainly not have hesitated to accept the substance of the last three sentences, after mastering the terminology in which they are expressed. He would have thoroughly approved of the statement of the meaning of baptism and, in particular, of the query placed against infant baptism, and he would have been delighted with the reference to a fresh 'ethical orientation through the Holy Spirit'. He was unfortunate in being long before his time. Today, with the deck swept almost clean of the last traces of his two pet aversions,

[114] In his letter to Florus, a great part of which Augustine has preserved in his replies to the points raised in it in *IWJ* I, 53 (PL 45, 1076) (CSEL 85/1, 50).

[115] *Dissertation* VII (PL 48, 658). Cf. Brown, 1967, 387, where specific reference is made to Thomas Aquinas, 'whose humane synthesis Julian had anticipated on many points'. I shall say something about different views of Julian in c. VI.

[116] For this summary I am indebted to an article by John Pilkington which appeared under the heading 'Muddle over Christian Initiation' in *The Times*, 9 June 1984. The quotations are from *Baptism, Eucharist and Ministry*, usually referred to as the Lima Document and published by the World Council of Churches, Geneva 1982, Commentary 6, p. 3, and IV, C, 16. See also the Seven Studies with the same title by John Matthews, published by The British Council of Churches, 3ff.

Augustinian predestination and original sin, and the ship's officers under orders to rethink the aims and methods of one of their favourite drills, infant baptism, he might have had to suffer no worse a fate than to face a campaign mounted by them so as to prevent him from gaining promotion to their own ranks – like the bishop who has recently found himself in the centre of an unwelcome controversy but, if he had had the misfortune to serve under the command of the Bishop of Hippo, might have been forced to walk the plank in the steps of John McLeod Campbell, F. D. Maurice, Edward King and Rowland Williams in the nineteenth century and Bishops Barnes and Pike, Teilhard de Chardin and Hans Küng, John Robinson and Don Cupitt and many others in living memory![117] *Autres temps, autres moeurs*: as it turned out, the fate which Pelagius suffered was one which he shared with many other radical teachers of the past, that of not being understood, let alone appreciated, by his contemporaries. And, like Origen and unlike John Chrysostom, who, though little influenced by Origen, fell an unlikely victim to the fourth-century campaign against Origenism and to whom Julian of Eclanum frequently refers as one of his authorities, Pelagius was never to be rehabilitated. To adapt an oft-quoted line of a Latin poet: *Victrix causa deis placuit sed victa Britanno*, 'the gods backed the winning cause, the Briton the one that lost'.[118] Yet, as we have tried to demonstrate, the cause of Augustine in the matter of original sin and infant baptism was far from being well founded, as in that other 'vexed matter' of predestination. Though 'no Christian thinker in his senses will maintain that Augustinianism is a heresy' – except, perhaps, a 'heresy in the truth' – 'a theological opinion may be profoundly erroneous without being either formally or materially heretical'.[119] Augustine, unlike Pelagius, backed a winning cause but, in so doing, he betrayed the fact that his was indeed a 'peculiar grace'.

---

[117] The least well-known of these, Rowland Williams, Vice-Principal of St David's College, Lampeter from 1850 to 1862, provides us with an interesting case in point. One of the seven Anglican contributors to *Essays and Reviews* (1860), he was suspended from his benefice as Vicar of Broad Chalke for a year by the Dean of Arches as a result, though the judgement was reversed by the Judicial Committee on the Privy Council in 1864. His first book, *Rational Godliness* (1855), had provoked a reviewer in the Welsh theological journal *Yr Haul* to proclaim: 'Parents, it is no longer safe for you to send your sons to Lampeter College while the German principles of *Rational Godliness* are taught there.' His contribution to *Essays and Reviews* was regarded as a fierce challenge, 'as if the author were determined to throw into the orthodox camp a bomb which should not fail to explode'. But his opinions 'seem very unexciting today' (see O. W. Jones, iv–v; Price, 97ff.). In an article in which he considers *Essays and Reviews* in the light of more recent theology Ieuan Ellis comments that 'on the face of it now (and this was already true by the 1890s) it is hard to see what all the controversy was about', and 'it inevitably lost its novel features by the end of the century' (396f.).

[118] Lucan, *The Civil War* I, 128 – reading *Britanno* for *Catoni*, which incidentally does not alter the metrical scansion of the line.

[119] N. P. Williams, 1927, 382. Anyone who has read his Bampton Lectures will recognise the extent to which I am indebted to him for his patient research and illuminating comments on the history of the doctrines of the Fall and Original Sin – though I am not unaware that his considered views on both subjects have not found favour with everyone and that some aspects of them require revision.

V

A DIFFERENT DRUMMER?

'If a man does not keep pace with his companions, perhaps it is because he hears a different drummer – let him step to the music he hears however measured or far away.'

H. D. THOREAU[1]

Reflecting on the great storm of controversy which followed the appearance of the second, revised edition of his commentary on the Pauline Epistles, Karl Barth is said to have remarked: 'It was like a man climbing inside a church steeple in the dark: stumbling up the steps, he clutches for support, only to discover that he has taken hold of the bell-rope – and, before he realises what is happening, he has caused the bell to ring out with an almighty boom.'[2] Perhaps Pelagius felt much the same when he became aware of the angry reactions to his writings among the church leaders of his day. He might fairly be described as one who had adversarial theology thrust upon him, one who would have been content if he had been able to go on just writing his letters and treatises for the benefit of his Roman circle of friends sympathetic to his campaign for the moral reform of the Church.

Certainly he gives little impression of having realised what a hornets' nest he was stirring up about his ears when he set up his standard again in Palestine and began preaching his crusade there. It was a time when the Holy Land was becoming a place of refuge for 'a new breed of enforced pilgrims'[3] – 'latter-day Lazaruses in flight from the west and packing the holy places', as Jerome typically described them while struggling to find time to complete his commentary on Ezekiel.[4] There Pelagius was confronted first by his old antagonist Jerome, then by Paul Orosius, 'a young man set upon me by my enemies',[5] and, finally, by the two Gallican bishops, Heros of Arles and Lazarus of Aix, expelled for supporting Constantine III and excommunicated by the Pope as trouble-makers. The warm support of old associates

---

[1] *Walden*, London 1968, 287.

[2] Berger, 72; Bainton, 1950, 64, applied the same passage to Luther's experience after the appearance of *Ninety-Five Theses*.

[3] Hunt, 204.

[4] Apart from numerous references to them in the Prefaces to his *Commentary on Ezekiel* he also complains of the disturbances to 'the peace and quiet which he longed for' in the Prefaces to his *Commentary on Jeremiah* (PL 24, 758) (CSEL 59, 221) and to his *Dialogue against the Pelagians* (PL 23, 517). By this time he must have been approaching his eightieth year.

[5] In his letter to Pope Innocent; the surviving fragments come from *GC* and *OS* and were assembled by Garnier in his *Dissertation* VI (PL 48, 610f.), this reference being to 610B.

from Rome now also in exile and of Bishop John, the arch-enemy of Jerome, and his acquittal at Diospolis lulled him into a false sense of security; up to the very end he seems to have laboured under the misapprehension that, once his theological position had been made perfectly clear to his critics, reason would prevail and he would be left to live out his life in peace. In the event, he was as much to blame as any other member of that 'amazing group of *emigrés*' which had settled in Palestine for turning the Holy Land into 'a theological bear-garden'.[6] His haven of rest became a fiery furnace, through which he passed without ever seeming to grasp just how he had come to be in it in the first place.

It is tempting to allow our sympathy for Pelagius' plight to run away with our capacity for objective judgement and to see him as the innocent victim of the machinations of powerful opponents. Such an impression would not be true to the facts of the case: even the polemic of Jerome, often distasteful and misdirected though it was, did not lack a certain foundation of truth, and Augustine, as we have seen, expended much time and effort which he could ill afford in exposing the errors of Pelagian teaching on free will and grace. Yet even Pelagius' *Liber de Fide*, his final attempt to convince the established Church of his essential orthodoxy, while it contained twenty-six articles of faith, most of them quite impeccable by any standard, was largely irrelevant to the main charges brought against him and only showed him to be as stubborn as ever in his defence of free will and its controlling part in the operation of the divine grace. In the twenty-fifth article he can still affirm his own formula for reconciling free will and grace as if all Augustine's Olympian thunder had fallen on deaf ears: 'We confess the freedom of the will in such a way that we always need the grace of God.'[7] He was indeed marching to the beat of a different drummer, firmly resolved to keep to his own pace regardless of that set by others.

Is it conceivable then that 'he rather missed the point of the attack'?[8] Opinions will always differ on this question but one thing is certain: his own out-and-out refusal to admit that his critics had some basis for their charges itself supplied them with ammunition of which they were happy to take advantage. The two treatises which he wrote in Palestine to explain and defend his case were to be skilfully mined and exploited by his more experienced opponents, using judiciously selected quotations from them in order to set him up as an Aunt Sally for their own missiles. It is true that these quotations are all that remain of the two original works and that we must allow for the risks attendant on a procedure which takes discrete passages from an author's writings out of their context; but nothing we can find in them can fairly be said to have been out of keeping with the opinions expressed in Pelagius' surviving letters and in his commentary on the Pauline

[6] Brown, 1967, 356, where he compares this 'amazing group of Latin *émigrés* settled in Jerusalem' to 'the white Russians in Paris in the 1920s'.

[7] PL 48, 491, 504; the term *Libellus Fidei* is often used as an alternative to *Liber de Fide* in describing such confessions of faith.

[8] Bonner, 1966, 356.

Epistles. His own sheer cussedness contributed as much to his eventual downfall as the superior tactics and ecclesiastical clout of his adversaries. Battles are lost more often than they are won – in the theological arena as on the military front.

There is another temptation to which many have succumbed, and that is to try to transplant to the contemporary scene the Pelagius revealed to us in the course of his controversy with Jerome and Augustine, a lot which he shares with many other, more renowned personalities of antiquity. Some see him as primarily a humanist, striving to fight his way out of the dim shadows of revealed religion into the purer air of rationalistic humanism. But he was no humanist or rationalist, and, as for those whose enlightened twentieth-century liberalism leads them to envisage him as a bluff, rather jolly, Dickensian figure vainly pitting his puny strength in defence of human freedom against obscurantist theories of divine omnipotence – why, they would run miles to get out of his sight if confronted with the real Pelagius in person! Here was a man who would have turned the whole Christian Church into a reform school if he had had his way and, this accomplished to his own satisfaction, would have had not the slightest compunction in consigning to Hell all who remained outside of their own choice: 'In the day of judgement', he solemnly pronounced, 'no forbearance will be shown to the ungodly and the sinners but they will be consumed in eternal fires.'[9] He was a moral perfectionist for whom even the most venial sin brought with it the danger of everlasting punishment, and his personal opposition to Augustine's concept of a *massa damnata* stemmed not so much from humanitarian feelings as from his uncompromising denial of the latter's teaching on original sin and predestination on *a priori* grounds. The identification of Pelagius with the 'once-born' and Augustine with the 'twice-born' Christian, though not without some superficial attraction, is simplistic and seriously distorts our picture of both men.[10]

Another rich source of misunderstanding in connection with Pelagius has been the perennial attempt by scholars to determine the extent to which his theology can be claimed to have been original, playing their favourite game of *Quellensforschung* and combing his extant works for echoes of previous writers. Jerome was the first in the field as soon as he detected Pelagius' indebtedness to the *Sentences of Sextus*, a second-century collection of moral and religous aphorisms attributed to the third-century martyr Pope Xystus or Sixtus II by Rufinus of Aquileia in his preface to his Latin translation. This ascription was accepted by Pelagius without question and, at first, by Augustine too but he

[9] *PP* iii. 9 (PL 44, 325) (CSEL 42, 60).

[10] N. P. Williams, 1927, 331f., and elsewhere overstresses this identification: in some respects Pelagius was more like what we now know as the 'twice-born' or 'born-again' Christians than was Augustine. Little is gained, and perhaps much lost, by trying to categorise the personalities of the past in terms of present ideas. And Pelagius seems to have suffered from misrepresentation at the hands of both his critics and his admirers: I have read of his 'cheerful liberalism' and of his 'theology . . . closely akin to modern humanism', and I have seen him described as 'the herald of Love' and most odd of all, as 'a British cleric who stressed the idea of grace'. But I shall refrain from naming the scholars concerned in order to spare their blushes.

was later to be 'corrected' by Jerome, who held that the true author of the work was none other than 'the heathen philosopher Sextus', identified by him as a Pythagorean.[11] Augustine was naturally very happy to accept this identification, since he, like Jerome, thereby found another way to discredit Pelagius for claiming the support of a greatly venerated Christian for his teaching – and Jerome, of course, was never slow to grasp another cudgel with which to batter the ghost of his old antagonist Rufinus at the same time. But, as Henry Chadwick has demonstrated in his authoritative study of the *Sentences*, Rufinus did no more than state that there was a tradition – *tradunt*[12] – to the effect that Xystus was the author, and this was undoubtedly true in the fourth and early fifth centuries. Since then many attempts have been made to identify the author but all alike have foundered on the reefs of inadequate or misinterpreted evidence: 'All we know', concludes Chadwick, 'is that the author was Sextus, that Origen thought that the book was Christian, that some Christians in the fourth century came to identify him with Xystus II.'[13] Pelagius, though wrong in accepting on the seeming authority of Rufinus of Aquileia that Xystus II was the compiler of the *Sentences*, was right in thinking that it was written by a Christian, 'whose ecclesiastical principles and spiritual ideals determined his choice of material'.[14]

Chadwick is interested not in the question 'Where did he (Sextus) find this?' but in another, much more important and more likely to meet with a satisfactory answer – 'What did he do when he found it?' The same question could be applied to Pelagius' use of Sextus. What he found in him was a summary of teaching on the theme of how to achieve moral and spiritual perfection which was wholly consistent with his own ethical approach to Christianity. As to his use of what he found one example speaks volumes. When he maintained the God-given sovereignty of the human will, he could point to the thirty-sixth *Sentence*: 'God has granted to men the freedom of their own choice with the undoubted end in view that by living purely and without sin they might become like God.' In his treatise *On Nature and Grace* Augustine, at that time under the impression that the quotation came from a work by a Christian bishop and martyr, dismissed it as a misunderstanding of true doctrine, using Romans 5, 4 to support his contention. What would he have said if he had known at the time of writing, as he came to know later, that Xystus was not the author of the *Sentences* and that Pelagius' proof-text was no more reliable than some of his own? R. F. Evans has shown that Rufinus had imported into his Latin version of this *Sentence* views not in the Greek version of Origen, which reads: 'God has given to the believing man a freedom which is divine and therefore pure and without sin.'[15] Reading the *Sentences* in

[11] *Commentary on Ezekiel* VI, 18 (PL 25, 173); *Commentary on Jeremiah* IV, 22, 24ff. (PL 24, 817) (CSEL 59, 267); *Letters* 133, 3 (PL 22, 1152) (CSEL 56, 246); *NG* lxiv. 77 (PL 44, 285) (CSEL 60, 291); *R* II, 42 (PL 32, 647) (CSEL 36, 180) (Bogan, ed., II, 68).
[12] In his Preface to the *Sentences*, 7f.; H. Chadwick, 1959, 9.
[13] Ibid., 135.
[14] Ibid., 137.
[15] R. F. Evans, 1968(a), 64 – the printing errors in the Greek of n. 148 are of no importance as far as the meaning is concerned.

Rufinus' Latin version, Pelagius was 'encouraged to suppose that he had found, in a precise maxim of the bishop Xystus, authority for one of his most cherished teachings' – to which we might add, 'and one that was absolutely fundamental to his whole theology'.[16] The answer to our question, 'What did he do when he found it?', as applied to Pelagius, is that he used it to enhance his own claim to orthodoxy in defending his views on the freedom of the human will as God's gift to man.

But Jerome, like Augustine, was not to know of Pelagius' error in following Rufinus' text, and his charge against him in this connection was therefore misguided when he accused him not of having misused his source but of having relied on Stoic teaching transmitted by Origen in order to propagate and strengthen his own. Here Jerome was on less firm ground: Pelagius was not heavily indebted to Stoicism despite what has been described as his 'Stoic-like severity of judgement',[17] and Jerome's attempt to characterise him as more Stoic than Christian at heart does not stand up to closer examination, being largely based on the great scholar's own incorrect identification of the author of the *Sentences* as a pagan philosopher, coupled with his equation of Pelagius' 'sinlessness' with Stoic *apatheia*. The same initial prejudice led him to go even farther in trying to blacken Pelagius' name by association. In a letter written around 414 to his friend Ctesiphon he names as Pelagius' precursors in the heresy not only Origen, Jovinian and Rufinus of Aquileia but also Evagrius of Pontus, Palladius, Priscillian, the Manichees, the Euchites, a fourth-century Mesopotamian sect otherwise known as 'the Messalians', and other 'heralds of sinlessness' unnamed – for good measure![18] All of these were equally disreputable characters in Jerome's eyes, and he gleefully summoned them up from the past to discredit Pelagius. And another contemporary of Augustine and Pelagius, Marius Mercator, as well-disposed to the former as he was hostile to the latter, addressed two of his works to an attack upon the Pelagians. He saw Rufinus of Syria as the founder of the heresy and the main villain of the piece, using Pelagius and Celestius as his mouthpieces; but he also suggested that its origins were to be found in Theodore of Mopsuestia,[19] and his seventeenth-century editor, the Jesuit Jean Garnier, after an eloquent comparison of heresies with great rivers whose sources can be traced far back to small, remote streams, added Paul of Samosata to Theodore as another of these tributaries.[20]

But if we are to throw away Occam's razor altogether and include in the list of Pelagius' precursors Paul of Samosata, 'a convenient whipping-boy to take the blame for doctrinal aberrations with which he had little connection',[21] and

---

[16] Ibid., 65; H. Chadwick, 1959, 120 also comments that Pelagius certainly found Rufinus' translation 'highly congenial reading'.

[17] Passmore, 95.

[18] *Letters* 133 (PL 22, 1150ff.) (CSEL 56, 241ff.); see Garnier, *Dissertation* I (PL 48, 257).

[19] PL 48, 258ff.

[20] Ibid., 257f., where Theodore is said to have received the 'poison' from Paul and then transmitted it to both Nestorius and the Pelagians.

[21] Wallace-Hadrill, 70.

Theodore of Mopsuestia, who is 'neither a Pelagian nor an Augustinian',[22] why not go even farther and add Nemesius of Emesa as well, since he too 'has been accused (slightly anachronistically) of Pelagianism',[23] though he seems rather to have been a Synergist before his time? Obviously, if we were left only with the 'evidence' relied on by these self-appointed detectives, we might wonder whether Pelagius had a mind of his own at all and, if so, whether there was a single original thought in it. But, fortunately, the researches of the present century have pointed us towards a safer way through the 'wand'ring mazes'. In particular, Torgny Bohlin's exhaustive examination of the sources of Pelagius' theology, based on Souter's monumental edition of his commentary on the Epistles, 'has provided a new point of departure for Pelagian studies'.[24] His conclusion is that no single line of Pelagius' thought can be traced back to an earlier tradition but that his main achievement – his *Meisterstück* – was rather to have built upon what he found in both western and eastern theology and to have drawn together from them a synthesis of two distinct and contrasting emphases, the one on creation and the other on atonement. This new unity he employed as a powerful weapon against the Arians and his *bêtes noires*, the Manichees, quoting chapter and verse from his authorities as he went along. He found the idea of will as a gift from God in Rufinus of Aquileia's version of Origen's commentary on Romans, as he did that of the freedom of the human will; this he developed into a form of grace, blending the western and eastern traditions to produce a grace of creation and a grace of redemption, ideas which he would also have met in his reading of 'Ambrosiaster'. His objection to the idea of the inevitability of sin, as taught by the Manichees, would have been reinforced by his reading of Rufinus the Syrian's *Liber de Fide*, where too he found confirmation of his own views on original sin and infant baptism.

Plinval's comment is, at least to a certain extent, a just one when he refers to Pelagius' 'disposition to assimilate from an author only what agreed with his own ideas'.[25] And Augustine would certainly have supported this judgement: for example, towards the end of his treatise *On Nature and Grace* he gives several illustrations of Pelagius' habit of employing to his own advantage passages which could be understood in a neutral sense, taken from Lactantius, 'the blessed Hilary', Ambrose, John Chrysostom and, the supreme act of lese-majesty, from Augustine's own works written at an earlier date.[26] But that does not necessarily mean that Pelagius was some kind of intellectual magpie, scavenging industriously amongst the débris left by others for items which were to his own taste. If it did, then which one of us could claim to be entirely immune to the same charge? The practice followed by Pelagius is one which is common to all writers who enter into debate with opponents, and

---

[22] Ibid., 163; Norris, 184ff., and Appendix I, 240ff., has surely disposed for the last time of the charge that Theodore was a 'Pelagian'.

[23] F. M. Young, 1983, 168.

[24] Bonner, 1966, 352.

[25] Plinval, 1943, 81.

[26] *NG* lxi. 71–lxvii. 81 (PL 44, 282ff.) (CSEL 60, 286ff.).

that not only in the theological field. Many – possibly too many – quotations have been made in this book by the present writer but what does that tell the reader about him? Only that he has read certain works and used them to support or illuminate his arguments, not necessarily that he has met the ideas expressed in them for the first time; he may, on the contrary, have reached at least some of them under his own steam and then rejoiced to find that others have advanced similar ideas independently and with greater authority and clarity of expression. Pelagius does not always name the sources of his quotations but he is not thereby convicted of plagiarism – or should we coin a word 'Pelagiarism'? The writers of antiquity were never as critical of plagiarism as we are, and, in the period when Pelagius was writing, it was common practice among theologians not to name their authorities, unless they were scriptural, and no disgrace was attached to it.

Bonner is right when he warns us that 'no final judgement upon the personal views of Pelagius seems possible at the present state of our knowledge.'[27] *O si sic omnes!* There would then be some hope of a reduction in the number of misleading judgements which are still being made by contemporary writers. As it is, we are not in a position to slip back into those early years in the fifth century and to discover by that means exactly how Pelagius' mind worked when he wrote his treatises after his arrival in Palestine. But it would not be unreasonable to suggest, however tentatively, that his views on infant baptism, sinlessness, predestination and original sin – all of which his critics claim to have identified as borrowings from others – followed logically from his own *idée fixe* of the freedom of the human will and were used to provide a theological framework within which to defend it. It was this concept which formed the corner-stone of all his teaching and to which he returned with monotonous regularity, refusing to abandon it even when he submitted his confession of faith to the Pope. It was his fear that Augustine, the very man who had so vigorously and successfully defended free will against the Manichees, might now be weakening it by his teaching on grace, which aroused his first protest in Rome in the early years of the century. From it the rest of his theology followed 'as the night the day'; around it centred not only the great controversy which was to plague Augustine to the very end of his days but also the continuing debate which has niggled the established Church from time to time ever since. Nor was Pelagius the only Christian theologian to be concerned in the defence of free will: Origen had insisted on it, John Chrysostom was still preaching it at the time when Pelagius was launching his movement for moral reform at Rome, lesser mortals like Nemesius and Theodore also proclaimed it, Nestorius compounded his difficulties by making man's capacity to make a free response to the divine call an essential part of his doctrine – and, centuries later, Erasmus was to leap to its defence against Luther.

No, it does not inevitably follow from Pelagius' practice of quoting Catholic authorities that he was merely appropriating their ideas for his own use; what

[27] Bonner, 1966, 375.

it does indicate is that his main motive was to employ them to protect his own claim to orthodoxy. This was what infuriated Augustine most of all, especially when some of the works cited were his own, written before he had achieved his reputation as 'the Doctor of Grace' and his maturity as a theologian. But the plain truth is that he was no better placed than we are to single out individual items in the teaching of Pelagius and to state categorically, 'This is borrowed from X and that from Y'. In fact, he gives no indication of having tried to do so. At the time it was virtually impossible to make such judgements in the midst of the confusion which had begun to surround the Pelagians from the moment when they first appeared on the theological stage. There is no recognised body of doctrine which can fairly be described *tout court* as 'Pelagianism' in the sense that it can be attributed to Pelagius alone; rather there are opinions of Rufinus the Syrian, of Celestius, of the Sicilian Anonymous, of Julian of Eclanum, and of Pelagius himself, some of which but by no means all they can be said to have held in common, others on which they disagreed, and yet others which are more strongly emphasised in the teaching of each one in turn. But, in the eyes of Jerome and Augustine and their supporters, all were tarred with the same brush: *ab uno disce omnes* was the considered verdict of the early-fifth-century Church.

We are reminded of the ambiguous situation facing Darwin and Wallace in the nineteenth century when the latter 'put forward his views as early as 1864, only five years after Darwin's *Origin of Species* and seven years *before* Darwin's *The Descent of Man*'.[28] Who then was the true founder of Darwinism? A similar question faces us in connection with Pelagius and Pelagianism: it is the most difficult question of all, the sixty-four or, allowing for inflation, sixty-four thousand dollar question – was Pelagius justifiably regarded and designated as the true heresiarch by his contemporaries and so by posterity? Not, surely, if that means that he was the 'only begetter' of the heresy which bears his name. In fact, it does not seem to have needed one: like little Topsy, 'it just growed and growed' in the minds of its opponents. But there can be no doubt that Pelagius was regarded as the leading figure amongst the group around which it was seen to have developed, and the name *Pelagiani* appears for the first time to describe them in 415, when Jerome wrote his treatise against them.[29] In his works directed against them before 415 Augustine had scrupulously avoided naming names partly in order to give an opportunity to these embryonic heretics to amend their ways, as he himself claimed, and partly,

[28] Hardy, 1975, 62; cf. 1965, 64ff. and 1966, 35f.: 'it was a good thing that he [Darwin] let Lyall and Hooker know [of his own theory of natural selection]. Otherwise perhaps we might not be talking of Darwinism today but of Wallacism.'
[29] *Dialogue against the Pelagians* (PL 23, 495–590). Plinval, 1943, 216, n. 3, suggests that the name *Pelagiani* may have originated among Pelagius' friends, quoting Jerome's sardonic remark in *Letters* 133, 12 (PL 22, 1160): 'You laugh and rejoice that some are called by your name, others by that of Christ.' He also claims that Augustine once refers to the Pelagians as *Pelagianistae* in *S* 183, viii. 12 (PL 38, 992) but that word is used in the vocative *singular* in the passage cited. It is also found in Cassian, *On the Incarnation of Christ* I, 3 (PL 50, 23), in Possidius' *Life of Saint of Augustine*, 18 (PL 32, 48) and in Gennadius, *Prolegomena on the Writers of the Church*, 86 (PL 58, 1052); Praedestinatus, *Heresies*, 88 (PL 53, 618) refers to 'Pelagians or Celestians'.

also, in accordance with the convention of the time. Now he adopted the name with the greatest alacrity and, one must in fairness to him add, with every justification. By virtue of his reputation and his writings Pelagius stood out above Rufinus the Syrian and Celestius and the others, and above Celestius by seniority as well. Rufinus had died at the end of the first decade and took no part in the actual controversy, though his *Liber de Fide* left significant marks upon it; Celestius had been condemned in 411, and his excommunication relegated him to the rôle of cheer-leader from the touchline.

But Pelagius remained on the field, Pelagius was continuing to write, Pelagius had gathered a fresh band of supporters in Palestine. What other name could have been given to the heresy, since heresies must have a name – otherwise how can one attack them? Aristophanes the Greek comedian, if he had been alive, might have coined a new, portmanteau word 'Rufino-Celestio-Pelagianism', and even Garnier in the seventeenth century sometimes referred to 'the Celestian heresy', which is not surprising, since he, perhaps more than anyone before the twentieth century, realised and tried to grapple with the complexity of its origins and the issues involved in the controversy. But, at the time, Augustine and his supporters, not to speak of Jerome, were not concerned with such minutiae: for them 'Pelagianism' was the only possible name to give to the heresy. Thus Pelagius became, *faute de mieux*, the eponymous founder of a heresy for which he was both then and for ever after to be held responsible. Once he had written his two treatises *On Free Will* and *On Nature* the die was cast: it was only a matter of time before the mills of the Church would grind him out of existence.

'How Pelagian was Pelagius?' Pelagianism has had a long and varied history in one form or another, in the course of which it has been used as an appropriate whipping-post to which to tie anyone who has been suspected of challenging the Augustinian doctrine of grace, and as a result, many mis-understandings of the original teaching of Pelagius have arisen. But, after the condemnation of Pelagius and Celestius and the entry into the fray of the last of the Pelagians proper, Augustine did his best to set the record straight in his treatise addressed to Pope Boniface in 421 and directed against two letters from Julian and eighteen other bishops who refused to subscribe to Zosimus' *Epistula Tractoria* condemning Pelagius and Celestius. Smarting from their personal attacks upon him as a kind of recidivist Manichee, he conceived the brilliant idea of demonstrating that, far from being neo-Manichean, the Catholic Church, of which he was the spokesman, stood firmly, like an Aristotelian mean, between the extremes of Manicheism and Pelagianism. He summed up the main issues on which the Pelagians were at variance with the teaching of the Church under three headings: denying original sin, denying that God's grace is essential to salvation and preaching that, by the right use of his free will, a baptised Christian is able to remain without sin.[30] Of course, there are subsidiary charges of a minor nature but these three are at the heart

---

[30] *TLP* III, viii. 24 (PL 44, 606f.) (CSEL 60, 516).

of the matter, and he repeats the same summary of Pelagian errors in *On the Gift of Perseverance*, written in 428–9.[31] This then is what it means to be a Pelagian.

Was Pelagius a Pelagian in the sense that he could fairly be found guilty on all three main counts? Certainly, he would have to plead guilty on the first: like the other Pelagians, he strongly denied the existence of original sin. Augustine quotes him as saying in his book *On Free Will*, 'Evil is not born with us, and we are procreated without fault',[32] a statement frequently reiterated in different words elsewhere in his writings. So much for the first charge. The second is, however, more complex, and the case against the accused less clear-cut than the prosecutor – one is tempted to say 'the inquisitor' – ever succeeded in realising. Like many brilliant and dynamic personalities, Augustine tends sometimes to assume too readily that terminology can bear only the interpretation which he himself put on it and, as with his misguided attempt to establish that Pelagians equated 'the kingdom of God' with 'eternal life',[33] an equation more acceptable to theologians of the twentieth century than to those of the early fifth, that everyone else must have started out from the same premises as himself. Yet, at an early stage in the controversy, even he is forced to admit that he has been encouraged by Pelagius' words to believe that he is not denying the grace of God – only to discover as he reads further, that he is mistaken in this assumption. And, in his defence, the accused is able to refer to passages in his works as cited by the prosecutor in which he insists that man needs God's help to be good and be saved: for example, 'God helps us by his teaching and revelation, opening the eyes of our heart, pointing us to the future so that we may not be absorbed in the present, discovering to us the snares of the devil, enlightening us with the manifold and ineffable gift of heavenly grace.'[34] This very quotation was one which J. B. Mozley used to support his contention that Pelagius includes in his idea of grace 'those divine impulses and spiritual assistance commonly denoted by the word'.[35]

But one swallow does not make a summer, and even this statement of Pelagius can be attacked by the prosecution on the grounds that it is only a little less disingenuous than many others from his works. Why then did he 'never make an unambiguous declaration of true internal assisting grace'?[36] Why did he always couch his description of it in terms which made it appear to his opponents to be no more than a form of divine *assistance* to human free will? Surely because he, like the other Pelagians, was bound to give his loyalty first and foremost to the idea of free will as implanted in man by God, the 'grace of creation', which, along with the 'grace of atonement', that is, of

---

[31] *GP* ii. 4 (PL 45, 996). Wermelinger, 278ff., traces the various changes of emphasis in the formulations of the charges against Pelagius.
[32] *OS* xiii. 14 (PL 44, 392) (CSEL 42, 175f.).
[33] Refoulé, 1963(b), especially 253f.
[34] *GC* vii. 8 (PL 44, 364) (CSEL 42, 131).
[35] Mozley, 1855, 54, 1878, 50; see Bonner, 1966, 351, n. 4.
[36] Bonner, 1966, 356.

forgiveness through baptism, gave him the twin pillars of his doctrine. For example, 'That we are able to do, say, think any good comes from him who has endowed us with this ability and who also *assists* it . . . but that we really do a good thing or speak a good word or think a good thought proceeds from our own selves.'[37] And again, 'The man who hastens to the Lord and desires to be directed by him, that is, who makes his own will depend upon God's . . . does all this by nothing else than by his freedom of will.'[38] A third statement, in his *Letter to Demetrias*, brings Pelagius even closer to the brink when he says: 'It is by doing his will that we may *merit* his divine grace.'[39]

Augustine takes pains to spell this out in his summary of the second main charge against the Pelagians: they refuse to deny the charge of claiming that 'the grace of God whereby we are justified is not given freely but according to our merits'.[40] And so, despite his frequent assertions in his commentary on the Epistles that baptism is the sacrament of justification *by faith alone*, on which we have already remarked, Pelagius seems to understand this faith not as something inspired by God but as something which proceeds naturally from the right use of free will, which is no more than a faculty, albeit God-given, and, still worse, as something which 'merits' the divine gift of grace.[41] How can Pelagius insist that baptism is the sacrament of justification *by faith alone*, while still maintaining that faith 'merits' the grace of God? As R. F. Evans has shown in his admirable account of Pelagius' theology of baptism, it is a matter not so much of inconsistency as of the misleading use of language and particularly, of the words 'faith' and 'merit'.[42] By faith Pelagius means the trust in Jesus with which the convert approaches God when he seeks 'justification' through baptism and by which alone he can be said to 'merit' grace to absolve his past sins and so 'justify' him, that is, make him righteous. He then 'has the same status as one who has fulfilled the whole law';[43] 'water has cleansed his body, the 'word' has cleansed his soul'.[44] Man's faith is thus securely based on the act of Jesus in intervening to redeem man through baptism by his death and to strengthen him thereafter by his teaching and example. Yet man is a sinner who has no merit by virtue of which he may claim this grace of atonement and revelation: 'faith merits grace only in the sense that it is the indispensable and freely chosen condition of the effectual working of grace.'[45] Thus Pelagius could argue that his 'merit by faith' is not to be equated with merit by works, since it is not merit by works which makes the sinner righteous but faith alone, rewarded by forgiveness of sins through baptism: faith alone 'absolves him as to the past,

---

[37] *GC* xvi. 17 (PL 44, 369) (CSEL 42, 139).
[38] Ibid., xxii. 24 (PL 44, 371f.) (CSEL 42, 143).
[39] *Letter to Demetrias* 25 (PL 30, 40; 33, 1117).
[40] *TLP* III, viii. 24 (PL 44, 606) (CSEL 60, 516f.); cf. *GP* ii. 4 (PL 44, 996).
[41] *GC* xxxi. 34 (PL 44, 376) (CSEL 42, 152); cf. *On the Divine Law* 2 (PL 30, 107).
[42] R. F. Evans, 1968(a), 117ff.
[43] On Romans 10, 4 (PLS 1, 1157).
[44] On Ephesians 5, 26 (PLS 1, 1304).
[45] R. F. Evans, 1968(a), 118.

justifies him as to the present and prepares him for future works of faith'.[46] It is vital to observe the precise sequence of events – faith first, then righteousness of faith, then righteousness of works, bringing the whole process to its proper fulfilment.

'Righteousness of works'? This phrase at once revives the old doubt in the minds of the jury, and it is confirmed when they hear the third charge, that of preaching 'sinlessness', which almost overlaps the second and had been brought against Pelagius in the first and sixth items of the case made out by his accusers at the Synod of Diospolis. Under the first item he had been confronted with his statement that 'a man cannot be without sin unless he has acquired a knowledge of the law'.[47] To this he had replied that he had used these words but not in the sense in which they were understood by others: 'I did not say that a man cannot sin if he has acquired a knowledge of the law but that by knowledge of the law he is helped not to sin, as it is written, "He hath given them a law for help"'. This reply had been accepted by the Synod but Augustine attributed that to their inability to understand the contents of Pelagius' book, which was in Latin, and to their being misled by his reply, which was also in Latin and was translated into Greek for their benefit and was understood by them in their own terms. Under the sixth item his accusers had cited another statement from the same book: 'A man can be without sin if he wishes'.[48] Augustine quotes his reply to this in full: 'I did indeed say that a man can be without sin and keep the commandments of God, if he wishes; for this ability has been given to him by God. However, I did not say that any man can be found who has never sinned from his infancy to his old age but that, having been converted from his sins, he can be without sin by his own efforts and God's grace, yet not even by this means is he incapable of change in future.' Again the Synod expressed itself satisfied with his reply, which they took in the sense that 'a man is able to be without sin with God's help and God's grace.' Augustine, on the other hand, pointed to the vagueness of Pelagius' affirmation of grace, which his judges generously interpreted as being consistent with Paul's teaching, not realising that elsewhere in his writings Pelagius had explicitly stated that this 'grace' depended on the capacity of not sinning which man had received from God at creation through the gift of free will. And, again, Augustine maintained that the Synod had wrongly acquitted Pelagius because they misunderstood his statements.

It was Jerome, of course, who had first drawn attention to Pelagius' teaching of 'sinlessness' and accused him of lifting this idea bodily from Rufinus of Aquileia's version of the *Sentences of Sextus*. In a letter written around 414[49] and in his *Dialogue against the Pelagians* he concentrated his attack upon this idea as a reiteration of Origen's teaching that it is possible for a man

---

[46] On Romans 4, 6 (PLS 1, 1131).
[47] *PP* i. 2 (PL 44, 321) (CSEL 42, 52).
[48] Ibid., vi. 16 (PL 44, 329) (CSEL 42, 68f.).
[49] *Letters* 133 (PL 22, 1147ff.) (CSEL 56, 241ff.).

to attain God's perfection – it is a *ramusculus Origenis*, 'a little twig of Origen'[50] – and the Stoic doctrine of *apatheia*. He linked this with Pelagius' insistence that all commandments of God were equally binding on Christians, which he saw as the equivalent of the Stoic teaching of the equality of sins. To this secondary charge Pelagius replied that he did not teach that all sins were equal in gravity but that, once a man has fallen into the habit of committing minor sins, he is in danger of going on to commit major sins as well; God's punishment, however, is graded according to the gravity of the sins committed.[51] To the main charge of preaching 'sinlessness' he replied that he was referring to the standard by which a *man* can be judged to be 'sinless', not that which would be applicable to *God*: God, he maintained, would not ask man to match that divine standard but one appropriate to man's status and condition, nor would he ask man to match even that standard by obeying his commands, if it were impossible for him to do so.[52] But it was not impossible, at least in theory, for a man to attain perfection in this life, though it could not be claimed with any certainty that anyone had, in practice, succeeded in doing so and in remaining sinless to the end.[53] Pelagius' proof-text is from the Sermon on the Mount: 'Be ye therefore perfect, even as your Father which is in heaven is perfect',[54] the very same text which has become a *locus classicus* – one might say *tritus* – in all subsequent debate on the subject of Christian perfectibility, as theologians have striven to reconcile it with the Hellenic concept of God as 'simple, absolute being', on the one hand, and with Augustinian teaching on man's inevitable sinfulness, on the other.[55] The *NEB*, for example, renders it: 'You must therefore be all goodness, just as your heavenly Father is all good.'

However many new facets of the problem have been revealed in later discussion of it, there can be little doubt that the majority of Christians have found Pelagius' teaching on sinlessness to be unacceptable. In the present context and not for the first time, Pelagius found himself driven into a tight

[50] *Dialogue against the Pelagians*, Pref., 1 (PL 23, 495ff.); *Letters* 133, 3 (PL 22, 1152) (CSEL 56, 247). The word *impeccantia* does not occur in classical Latin, though the adjective *impeccabilis*, meaning 'faultless', appears in Aulus Gellius once in the second century A.D. It may well have been a neologism coined by Jerome to express the sense of the Greek *apatheia*; if so, perhaps he should have taken note of Seneca's warning in *Letters* 9, 2 that even the literal translation of *apatheia*, that is, *impatientia*, is inadequate: 'we are bound to fall into ambiguity, if we want to express *apatheia* summarily by a single word and render it by *impatientia*, since this may be understood in the opposite sense to that which we wish it to bear.' The word *impeccantia* is no less ambiguous, and I have been unable to find a single instance of its use in Augustine. In any case, although the charge of preaching 'sinlessness' was brought against Pelagius at the Synod of Diospolis, it was declared to be orthodox as long as it did not involve a renunciation of divine grace, and its importance decreased as Augustine laid more and more stress on his doctrine of grace with its corollaries, original sin and predestination (Wermelinger, 82, 281).

[51] *Liber de Fide* 16 (PL 48, 490, 502); *Letter to Celantia* 6 (PL 22, 1207); *On Virginity* 7 (PL 30, 167ff.).

[52] *Dialogue against the Pelagians* I, 16, 21 (PL 23, 509, 514).

[53] Souter, 1907, 437 (PLS I, 1541f., fr. 2).

[54] Matthew 5, 48.

[55] Passmore, 69, describes the first concept as 'metaphysical' and the second as 'moral or anthropological', that is, relating to man.

corner from which he had his work cut out in trying to extricate himself. Jerome had awakened a suspicion which was to attach itself to Pelagius ever after, so that, whenever Christians have to oppose the idea of human perfectibility, they always see in it 'a latent Pelagianism or "angelism", the idea that man can attain perfection by some heroic endeavour',[56] and when they describe an individual or his doctrine or his prayer as 'Pelagian', it is that idea which is foremost in their minds and not his denial of original sin, or, much less, his defence of free will. He might be prepared to admit that his citation of long list of patriarchs, prophets and others from the scriptures as examples of righteous men and women 'did not necessarily involve him maintaining that any individual had in fact achieved such sinless living',[57] and he could hardly fail to do so when his prosecutor pointed out to him that righteousness and sinlessness were not synonymous terms.[58] But it would have been contrary to his moral theology and his teaching on man if he had been willing to abandon the possibility of sinlessness altogether, and, above all else, it would have been a betrayal of his emphasis on the freedom of the will to choose for itself: free will is necessary to the man who wishes not to sin, and that free will has been given to him by the same God who wishes him to be without sin. For him, free will and sinlessness walked hand in hand.

Such an emphasis on free will was, as we have seen again and again, anathema to Pelagius' chief prosecutor, because it led, in his view, to the neglect of the paramount need for indwelling grace. At first, it was not the idea of sinlessness by itself which attracted Augustine's main criticism, and, in 412, when writing his treatise *On the Spirit and the Letter*, though he draws attention to it as a Pelagian tenet, he does not bother to press home his attack on those who maintain that a sinless life is possible in this world; they are not, he says, 'not a cause for great concern on that account'.[59] It is when they go farther and argue that such sinlessness is made possible by the use of free will, not the grace of God as he understands it, that he takes serious issue with it. It was in vain that Pelagius continued to protest that the will itself was a form of grace given to man at his creation; nor were his accusers able to comprehend his argument that the God who had created man would be an unjust God if he punished him for committing sins which, by his very nature, he was incapable of avoiding. In his *Liber de Fide* he tried for the last time to defend himself against the charge of preaching sinlessness by summarising his true position: 'Those who say with the Manichee that man cannot avoid sin are as much in error as those who assert with Jovinian that a man is unable to sin.'[60] Taken by itself, this statement is unexceptionable, making the point that Pelagius is both anti-Manichee and anti-Jovinian; but he then went on to destroy the effect of it by adding: 'Both of these are wrong because they remove the freedom of the will, whereas we always maintain that a man is always able to

[56] See E. J. Tinsley in Richardson, ed., 255.
[57] *PP* vi. 16 (PL 44, 329f.) (CSEL 42, 69).
[58] *NG* xxxviii. 45 (PL 44, 268f.) (CSEL 60, 267).
[59] *SL* ii. 3 (PL 44, 202) (CSEL 60, 156); the actual words used are *multum molesti*.
[60] *Liber de Fide* 25(PL 48, 491, 504).

sin and not to sin, so that we always confess that we are endowed with free choice.' In this instance his statement is verbally identical with that of Celestius, and, as his prosecutor immediately perceived, it was only another reiteration of his idea of a free will which could work *in utramque partem*, 'in either direction'.

Of the three main charges then it could be fairly said that all three were proven – proven, that is to say, in that Pelagius' denial of original sin, his theology of grace and his perfectionism all conflicted with the teaching of the contemporary Western Church and of Augustine, in particular, which was to mean for centuries much the same thing. Yet the fear that Pelagius expressed that Augustine's teaching on grace in the *Confessions* at first and then in his anti-Pelagian treatises and elsewhere could be interpreted by misguided Christians as an open invitation to forget their own rôle in their own salvation was to re-echo down the centuries. Even Luther, who would have no truck with Pelagius and regarded Augustine, along with Paul, as his most reliable guide to a true Christian faith, was to lament the apathy and abuse arising from misunderstanding of Augustinian doctrine and endemic in his own day. A millennium earlier John Cassian had foreseen this danger and had given voice to his concern that the views of Augustine on grace might, if accepted in their extreme form and without modification, deprive the members of his community of the motivation needed to keep them on the path of righteousness: 'Cassian knew his own monks.'[61] Thus, in the lifetime of Augustine and possibly even before Pelagius was at rest in his grave, a respected Christian described by some as the father of Semi-Pelagianism and by others as the father of Semi-Augustinianism pointed to a *media via* between the two main protagonists in the Pelagian controversy. Semi-Pelagianism would meet with the same fate as Pelagianism and would be condemned along with it at the Council of Orange; but it remained on the agenda, a thorn in the flesh of the establishment for all that, and it would be revived in the sixteenth century by Philip Melanchthon in the form of Synergism, a name which was an invention of his opponents and not himself.

The misgivings of Pelagius were never to be completely stifled: he was destined to become 'a Phoenix too frequent', and perhaps this is the most impressive vindication of the countervailing misgivings of Jerome and Augustine when they foresaw the very real danger to the unity of the Church – 'the wild thickets of this heresy, which we are sorry to see shooting out buds, nay, growing into trees, day by day'.[62] Day by day? No, century by century, and perhaps for as long as the foundations of Christian belief are still debated,

---

[61] Passmore, 98. Elsewhere (114) he quotes Karl Barth as asking in a lecture on 'The Humanity of God', delivered in 1956, 'What if the result of the new hymn to the majesty of God should be a new confirmation of the hopelessness of all human activity?', and (115) refers to Perry Miller's description of how Pelagianism developed in a New England community as it came to find itself incapable of 'disciplining those who sat back and waited for God's grace to fall, or not to fall, upon them': 'if God can, if he chooses, lift a saint from a dunghill, why not be warm and cosy in the dunghill, awaiting his grace?'.

[62] *PP* xxxv. 65 (PL 44, 357) (CSEL 42, 120).

the buds continue to grow into trees and those trees to flourish! There will always be those who, like Leslie Dewart, will find themselves compelled in all honesty and even at the risk of giving offence to conclude: 'It is possible that the maintenance of bare orthodoxy is no criterion of the sufficiency and adequacy of the authoritative (and other) teaching of the Church.'[63] 'Amen to that!' could have been Pelagius' last *cri de coeur*.

---

[63] L. Dewart, 71f., n. 17; cf. 128, n. 6. As H. Chadwick comments in his discussi n of the orthodoxy of Origen, 'Orthodoxy is a word that suggests clear-cut and absolute lines of division. It begins to look different if we ask whether some theologians may be more orthodox than others, whether there are degrees of understanding, whether, if we all see through a glass darkly, some may be able to see a little more clearly than others'; and 'If he [Origen] remains a perennially enigmatic and embarrassing figure in the history of Christian thought, this is perhaps most due to the fact that we tend to begin the study of Origen by asking whether or not he is orthodox, and find that in the process we are continually driven back to the prior question: what is the essence of orthodoxy?' (1966, 122f.).

VI

MARCHING ON

'John Brown's body lies a mould'ring in the grave,
His soul is marching on.'

CHARLES S. HALL[1]

In 418 Pelagius was condemned by the Pope and excommunicated by the
Church which he had set out to reform; in 431 the 'opinions of Celestius' and
all who were associated with him were again condemned, this time by the
third ecumenical council at Ephesus. But in the years between, the establishment's battle with Pelagianism had continued to rage furiously while Julian of
Eclanum, 'a natural dialectician, with a bent for speculative thought that
Pelagius did not possess',[2] vigorously probed the weaknesses of Augustine's
position, and Augustine responded with 'the cold competence of an old, tired
man, who knew only too well how to set about the harsh business of
ecclesiastical controversy'.[3] Julian, who came of noble stock and whose father
was a bishop, had won for himself a high reputation in the best circles as a
young man for his many talents and for his attachment to the simple life: he
had even sold his estates to relieve the poor at a time of great famine, and
Paulinus of Nola, a friend of his father, had composed a poem in his honour to
celebrate his marriage to the daughter of another bishop.[4] Had it not been for
his enthusiasm in the cause of Pelagius and Celestius he 'might have ended

---

[1] *John Brown's Body*, attributed to Charles Sprague Hall in the edition of the *Oxford Dictionary of Quotations* which I possess, though it seems to have been removed from the latest edition. Perhaps this is because it has been attributed also to Thomas Brigham Young and Frank E. Jerome amongst others, and no one appears to be quite certain who its author was. In some versions 'is' is found in place of 'lies' in the first line.

[2] G. R. Evans, 143.

[3] Brown, 1967, 384; Burnaby, 1938, 231, writes in a similar vein of the later Augustine: 'a man whose energy has burned out, whose love has gone cold'. But though he did not complete his last reply to Julian, *IWJ*, he managed to find enough energy to write six books of it and, in his last three years, also wrote *PS* and *GP* as well as *H* and two other works.

[4] Gennadius, *On Famous Men*, 45 (PL 58, 1084), in his continuation of Jerome's work with the same title; Paulinus, *Poems* 25 (PL 61, 633f.). Frend, 1984, 802, refers to Gennadius as a 'Semi-Pelagian' – he was a friend of Faustus of Riez – and notes that he was one of the few Westerners of his day who knew Greek, and it is interesting to observe that it is he who tells us that Julian also had a thorough knowledge of Greek (op. cit. 46). Wermelinger, 228, suggests that his knowledge of eastern theologians may have been overestimated, since he cites only two of them in his treatise *To Turbantius*, John Chrysostom and Basil of Caesarea, according to Augustine, *J* I, v. 16–17, vi. 21 (PL 44, 650f., 654f.), and the same two with Theodore of Mopsuestia added in *To Florus*, III, 111 (PL 45, 1295) (CSEL 85/1, 432). But Augustine is notoriously selective in his citations of the works of his opponents.

his days as an honoured figure in the Church'.[5] But instead, in 418, along with eighteen other Italian bishops, he was deposed from his see and banished for refusing to subscribe to Zosimus' *Epistula Tractoria*, and in 419 he retired to the Near East, whence he launched a spate of letters and treatises against Augustine and his supporters.[6]

The strength of Augustine's reaction to these criticisms may be gauged by the fact that no fewer than ten of his fifteen anti-Pelagian works date from the period following the condemnation of Pelagius and Celestius in 418, all of them written as rejoinders either to Julian or to those of his own friends and correspondents who raised questions on issues involved in his debate with Pelagius. The first of these, entitled *On the Grace of Christ and Original Sin*, was written soon after 'the conviction and condemnation of the Pelagian heresy along with its authors by the bishops of the Church at Rome – first Innocent and then Zosimus – with the co-operation of letters from African councils',[7] and was addressed to Pinianus, his wife Melania and her mother Albina, who had been befriended by him at Thagaste and were now in Palestine. His intention in writing it was to reassure them by providing them with a definitive summary of his case against the Pelagians and an answer to the defence made by Pelagius in a letter which he had written to them after his condemnation, protesting his orthodoxy and knowing them to have been sympathetic to his cause at the time when they had all been together in Rome.

Not long after this Augustine addressed two books *On Marriage and Concupiscence* to Count Valerius, a long-established supporter of his views who has been described as '*plus catholique que le pape*',[8] the second of them being a reply to criticisms of the first contained in the four books of Julian's treatise *To*

---

[5] Bonner, 1963, 347. His earlier career had been unexceptionable: a *lector* in his father's church at the time of his marriage (Paulinus, *Poems* 25, 143f.) (PL 61, 633f.) and a deacon *c.* 408, when Augustine asked his bishop, Memorius, to pass on to him a copy of the sixth book of his treatise *On Music*, referring to him in the most complimentary and affectionate terms and inviting him to Hippo (*L* 101, 4) (PL 33, 369) (CSEL 34, 543), he was made Bishop of Eclanum by Pope Innocent I *c.* 416, when he was about thirty years old. It is difficult to reconcile the aspersions cast on his morality by Augustine in *J* V, vi. 24 (PL 44, 799) with his high reputation as a young man and the esteem in which Augustine himself professes to hold him in *L* 101; and Mercator's assertion (*Book of Notes on Words of Julian* iv. 5) (PL 48, 132) that he had corrupted one of his sisters after his adoption of them on the death of their parents must be taken to refer to indoctrination and not to immoral behaviour on his part. As for the eighteen bishops who supported him originally by refusing to subscribe to the condemnation of Pelagius and Celestius on the grounds that they had not been given a fair trial, not all of them can be proved to have persisted in their loyalty to him by joining him in exile; for example, Augustine makes much of the defection of Turbantius in *IWJ* I, 1, II, 11, IV, 30 and V, 6 (PL 45, 1051, 1146, 1353, 1436f.) (CSEL 85/1, 5, 170).

[6] A complete list of fragments attributed to Julian as well as other writings on which there is no general agreement as to his authorship of them may be found in PLS 1, 1571; see also *CC* 88, 335–98 and Duval, 1979, 162–70.

[7] *R* II, 50 (PL 32, 650) (CSEL 36, 187) (Bogan, ed. II, 76); the attentive reader will have noticed that Bogan has numbered the entries in *R* continuously from the beginning of Book I to the end of Book II. CCSL 57, 1984, ed. A. Mutzenbecher, is an up-to-date edition and commentary to which I have been unable to refer.

[8] Brown, 1967, 362.

Turbantius, now lost.[9] The revived controversy was continued by Julian's eight books *To Florus*, also lost, and three treatises of Augustine written between 420 and 429.[10] Since Julian's works have not survived, we have to judge him on the many quotations which Augustine made from them, setting them out in dialogue form along with his own replies. It is therefore difficult, if not impossible, to reconstruct a coherent picture of Julian's theology, and it comes as no surprise to find that scholars have differed considerably in their assessment of his personality and his contribution to the ongoing debate. Bonner, for example, detects in Julian's character 'an arrogance of a most unattractive nature' and criticises him both for his lack of respect for Augustine, whom he dismisses on different occasions as the 'Punic Aristotle', a 'Punic philosophiser' and 'defender of the donkeys', and for being 'well nigh obsessed' with the idea of concupiscence.[11] Brown, on the other hand, though he too finds Julian to be 'not a sympathetic person', is a little more kindly disposed towards him and believes that 'we have only begun to appreciate the extent of his learning and originality'.[12] The actual debate between the two protagonists, as it is recorded by Augustine, seems to have done little more than grind out the old, well-worn issues all over again – free will, infant baptism, original sin, predestination and, of course, Augustine's alleged neo-Manicheism, a topic with which he became more and more exasperated under the provocation of his new opponent's bitter and often damaging attacks. Despite Julian's attempts to open up new lines of criticism, the controversy between the two men resembles one of those bare-fisted fights which took place before the Queensberry Rules were introduced to 'civilise' boxing and offers a most unedifying example of the combination of jaw-jaw with war-war. The record of it provided by Augustine reflects small credit on either of the two participants and can hardly be recommended to budding

[9] *MC* (PL 44, 413–74) (CSEL 42, 211–319); *R* II, 53 (PL 32, 651) (CSEL 36, 189f.) (Bogan, ed. II, 79).
[10] *TLP* (PL 44, 549–638) (CSEL 60, 423–570), addressed to Pope Boniface; *J* (PL 44, 641–874); *IWJ* (PL 45, 1049–608) (CSEL 85/1, 3–506).
[11] Bonner, 1963, 347; 1962, 303; see also Brown, 1967, 383. Brown, 1983(a), has more recently demonstrated that Julian's most important contribution to the Pelagian controversy may well have been his success in provoking Augustine to undertake an intensive re-examination of his views on marriage and *concupiscentia* and, as a result, to formulate a theory of sexuality which was in direct conflict with current medical opinion but was to exert a profound influence on the moral and social climate of Latin Christianity. Brown, 63ff., summarises the essential differences between Augustine and Julian on this subject 'by setting Augustine's attitude against the inherited conglomerate of late classical notions with which it tacitly parted company' – and led Julian to describe him, not altogether inaptly, as a *novus iste physicus* (*IWJ* V, 11; PL 45, 1142).
[12] Brown, 1967, 383, 387. Wermelinger, 228, points out that there is no evidence for any direct pupil-teacher relationship between Julian and Pelagius, though they may have met in Rome, and describes the former as an unusually independent thinker: he mentions Pelagius by name only once according to Wermelinger, 228, n. 54, in *IWJ* IV, 112 (PL 45, 1405) but even there the names of Pelagius and Celestius do not seem to occur in a direct quotation. Wermelinger, 264ff., examines the changes which have taken place in the modern evaluation of Julian's thought since Bruckner's study as a result of the work of Refoulé and Bouwman and concludes that the Bishop of Eclanum can no longer be labelled as a 'faithless rationalist', even if Bouwman still maintains that he was a 'radical rationalist' in his polemical works (265, n. 262).

theologians as good bedside reading: in all this 'there's no musick, no harmony, no peace'.

In 423 Julian had sought refuge with Theodore of Mopsuestia, mistakenly supposing that he would find him sympathetic to the Pelagian cause. We have no reason to suppose that he was treated with anything but courtesy and kindness by Theodore but his admiration for the learned bishop was not reciprocated, and Marius Mercator, who had no great love for either, records that, after Julian's departure for Constantinople to try his luck there, the Cilician bishop was persuaded by his colleagues to concur in the decision of a local synod which anathematised Julian and his doctrine.[13] After his condemnation in 431, along with Celestius and other Pelagians, by the Council of Ephesus, Julian made his way back to Italy, where he failed to obtain reinstatement as bishop, and eventually died in Sicily after a life of which almost half had been spent in exile. And so the last of the Pelagians also bit the dust, and a life which had started with promise of great things finished in dishonourable exile, and the man who had made Augustine's last years so uncomfortable that he was described as 'the Cain of our times', passed his own in teaching Latin to the children of a Pelagian family.[14]

By then Augustine had gone to his long rest; but he had done so in the sure knowledge that, although the Vandals were already encamped around the walls of his beloved Hippo, the bastion which he had constructed to defend his own reputation and the teaching on which it was founded had been seen to be impregnable against all the assaults of the Pelagians. Was there not in his library a copy of the imperial rescript of Honorius and Theodosius II which empowered bishops to depose and banish from any part of the Empire all those who might still cling to the last vestiges of Pelagianism, and had not a later edict, issued to the propraetor of Gaul by Theodosius II and Valentinian III and instructing him to summon to a court of enquiry Gallican bishops who were still recalcitrant, demonstrated to the Church that the imperial policy with regard to Pelagianism was being conscientiously pursued by the secular authorities?[15] Yet all was not quiet on the western front or even in that African sector in which Augustine was established as the chief spokesman of the Church, Not all the documents relating to the controversy had penetrated to the monasteries, and not all of the monks had digested those which had. Around 426 a bombshell shattered the peace of the monastery at Hadrumetum on the south-eastern coast of Tunisia, when a monk named Florus, visiting his home at Uzalis near Carthage, came across a copy of Augustine's letter to the Roman presbyter Sixtus, later to become Pope Sixtus III, written about 419 and setting out his doctrine of predestination in its severest form.[16] Florus, who appears to have been an admirer of Augustine, was obviously delighted with his find and made a copy to the dictation of his companion Felix, with

---

[13] PL 48, 297, 360; for the last years of his life see Vignier in PL 45, 1040ff.

[14] PL 48, 297.

[15] PL 45, 1726f.; L 201 (PL 33, 927) (CSEL 57, 296ff.); PL 45, 1751.

[16] L 194 (PL 33, 874ff.) (CSEL 57, 176ff.); 216, 2, 3 (PL 33, 975; 44, 914) (CSEL 57, 397ff.).

whom he sent it back to Hadrumetum, while he himself stopped off at Carthage on the return journey.

Felix returned in due course to his monastery at Hadrumetum with the copy of the letter to Sixtus and, unbeknown to his abbot Valentinus, circulated it among the brethren. It immediately set the cat among the pigeons; it had been 'a manifesto of unconditional surrender written in the heat of controversy'[17] and at once became the subject of intense disagreement among the monks, some of them favouring a doctrine of grace which denied the freedom of the will, others maintaining that the free will is assisted by grace so as to enable men to know and to do what is right. Augustine was made aware of this disagreement by two of the monks, Cresconius and Felix, when they visited him at Hippo, and he at once wrote to the abbot explaining the true meaning of his letter to Sixtus to the best of his ability in the space available in a letter and, at the same time, asking him to send to him at Hippo the man by whom they said the disturbance had been caused, meaning Florus.[18] Florus did make the journey to Hippo himself but found Augustine prevented by poor health from discussing the matter as fully as he would have liked to do.[19] But meanwhile Augustine kept with him under instruction Cresconius and Felix as well as another Felix, who may well have been the monk who had brought the copy of the letter to Sixtus back to the monastery. Doubtless he set about his self-imposed task of assuaging their fears with 'the serene intransigence of a man who was sure of the heart of his message';[20] but he also sent another letter to Valentinus and his monks as well as a whole treatise addressed to the abbot and his brethren,[21] and, for good measure, a batch of documents relevant to the Pelagian controversy from the authorities of the Church at Rome, at Carthage and in Numidia, including the canons of the Council of Carthage and letters written by himself. This, he thought, would settle the matter once and for all; but, as often happened to him in the course of his many battles for the faith, he overestimated the power of his arguments to dispel the doubts of those who did not fully appreciate their strength and essential reasonableness.

In the event one word only led to another, and, faced with the objection made by the monks that his statements meant that we ought not to rebuke a man for failing to keep God's commandments but only to pray that he be given the grace which would alone enable him to keep them, he found himself constrained to compose yet another treatise, in which he contended that we are justified in rebuking a fellow Christian who sins but that such a rebuke would be effective only if he were one of God's elect.[22] The abbot Valentinus had written in the meantime to explain how the incident at Hadrumetum had arisen and how he had tried to deal with it and to exonerate Florus from any

[17] Brown, 1967, 399.
[18] *L* 214 (PL 33, 968ff.) (CSEL 57, 380ff.).
[19] Morin, *RB* 18, 1901, 243; cf. 1896, 481ff.
[20] Brown, 1967, 403.
[21] *L* 215 (PL 33, 971–4; 44, 875–80) (CSEL 57, 387–96); *GFC* (PL 44, 881–912).
[22] *RG* (PL 44, 915–46).

blame attached to his part in it. In his letter he described how he had sought the advice and support of his neighbours, Evodius of Uzalis, an old friend and supporter of Augustine, and a presbyter named Sabinus, as soon as he had learned of the trouble which the letter to Sixtus was causing among his monks, only to find that even their replies had failed to convince the dissidents. What a fascinating picture! Of an abbot sitting on a theological volcano without being aware of its existence, of monks trekking to and fro across north Africa to sit at the feet of Augustine and receive instruction from him, and of the great man himself, whose polemic had restored order in the African Church and whose teaching was to shape the development of Christian theology for centuries, finding the time and the patience to allay the fears of a handful of worried individuals. And this, as Brown reminds us, 'was the vehement opponent of Julian of Eclanum'.[23] It was but the smile on the face of the tiger, and the abbot and his monks could count themselves lucky that Augustine does not seem to have been troubled thereafter by the disturbances at their monastery. It had arisen in the first place because the majority of the monks were simple men, dedicated to the pursuit of the ascetic life and holding uncomplicated Christian beliefs, so that much of the great battle which had been waged in the more subtle atmosphere of the theologians had passed over their heads almost unnoticed. What the Hadrumetum incident gives us is 'an exceptional opportunity of watching the immediate reaction of the humbler religious of St. Augustine's time to some of the more difficult of his writings'.[24]

We may assume therefore that peace returned to Hadrumetum as a result of Augustine's efforts and that he could dismiss the incident as no more than a storm in a teacup. But his treatise *On Rebuke and Grace*, like that *Against Julian*, did not escape the notice of others elsewhere, and a more serious debate was soon to begin in southern Gaul which was to lead to the rise of Semi-Pelagianism and to compete with Augustine's debate with Julian for his attention as a polemicist until the end of his life in 430. In 427/8 an old friend and correspondent, Prosper Tiro of Aquitaine, wrote to him warning him of unrest among the monks at Marseilles: 'many of the servants of Christ who live in the city of Marseilles', he wrote, 'believe that the part of your writings against the Pelagian heretics which argues for the calling of the elect in accordance with divine intervention is contrary to the opinion of the Fathers and to the common feeling of the Church.' In other words, they held that Jesus came into the world to bring salvation to all men alike and rejected the notion that only some are predestined to salvation, the others to damnation. The bone of contention is thus the same as it had been in the case of the monks of Hadrumetum: it was Augustine's extreme doctrine of predestination. The monks, it seems, made a firm distinction between predestination and foreknowledge, and Prosper further warns that they were not without the backing of influential spokesmen, mentioning one in particular who was an

[23] Brown, 1967, 402.
[24] N. K. Chadwick, 1955, 179.

admirer and adherent of Augustine's doctrine in all respects except this one of predestination, Helladius or Euladius, Bishop of Arles, who had long expressed an intention of writing to him for an explanation.[25] A letter couched in similar terms from a distinguished layman Hilary must have reached Hippo about the same time, referring to the same difference of opinion in the region of southern Provence.[26]

Augustine's response to these two warning letters came with the usual promptness and took the form of another dose of prescribed reading in a treatise in two books *On the Predestination of the Saints* and *On the Gift of Perseverance*, the second of which is traditionally published as a separate work; both are dated in 428/9 and neither reveals the slightest hint of compromise.[27] The monks, Augustine maintains, are in error if they suppose that his doctrine of predestination is a novel one and contrary to the teaching of the Church, since it has always been proclaimed and is a logical development of the teaching of Paul. What greater authority can they, or anyone, ask for? If they are concerned about the possible effect of the doctrine on their fellow-monks and their congregations, then the correct tactic is not to disturb them by over-emphasising predestination to damnation but, rather, to adapt their message to the needs and understanding of their hearers, stressing that all who try sincerely to obey the will of God will be given the strength to follow his commandments and the perseverance to maintain their faith to the very end. Haunted as he was by the spectre of advancing barbarism and its threat to the very existence of the Church, he was convinced that perseverance was the only answer for Christians concerned for their own salvation as well as the survival of their religion. But such a message, 'a doctrine for fighting men', 'a hard message for a hard age', 'a doctrine for survival, a fierce insistence that God alone could provide men with an irreducible core', was too strong for Christians for whom the bell had not yet tolled and whose main concern was for the preservation of their own chosen way of life and the quest for their own salvation sustained by the simple belief that 'God wishes all men to be saved' – a text which Augustine continued to misinterpret and even Prosper could dismiss as 'a trite objection'.[28]

The monks of southern Gaul were part of the great monastic movement which had sprung up in Egypt in the third century and had spread to the west in the fourth, and they were by nature and training more attuned to the theology of the eastern Church than to that of the west. They had come to regard themselves as the true custodians of the faith and of its ancient

[25] L 225 (PL 33, 1002–7; 44, 947–54) (CSEL 57, 454–68). In para. 9 all but one of the MSS give us *Hilarium* but O. Chadwick, 1945, and 1968, 128, puts forward a convincing argument for accepting that the sole MS which reads *elladium* provides a more intelligible chronology for the Bishops of Arles from 426 to 430 as well as for Augustine's last three years, if we take it to refer to Euladius or, possibly, Helladius. It seems to be generally accepted now that Euladius was the bishop in question.

[26] L 226 (PL 33, 1007–12; 44, 954–60) (CSEL 57, 468–81).

[27] PS (PL 44, 959–92); GP (PL 45, 914–1034).

[28] Brown, 1967, 403ff., 401; Prosper, *Letter to Rufinus* xiii. 14 (PL 51, 85A) – literally, 'an objection made by men of no understanding'.

traditions, and the niceties of recent controversy elsewhere seem to have escaped their notice. Now they realised that their whole way of life was being challenged and the partnership between divine grace and human will which they had always hitherto taken for granted was in danger of being undermined. They found a worthy champion in John Cassian, to whom Prosper and Hilary had not referred by name in their letters but who was to become the central figure in the ensuing debate. A former disciple of John Chrysostom, he had fled to the west in 405, a victim no doubt, like his master, of the Origenist witch-hunt in the east. It was he who had founded the two monasteries, one for men and the other for women, at Marseilles around 415, and his reputation stood high in the western Church, so high that he was invited in 429/30 by Leo, archdeacon and later Pope of Rome, to act as its spokesman against Nestorius. He was certainly no Pelagian; on the contrary, he would connect Pelagianism with Nestorianism as Marius Mercator did and might well have agreed that 'the Nestorian God is the father of the Pelagian man'. He faithfully performed the task imposed upon him by Leo the Great, with whom he had formed a friendship in Rome many years earlier, by composing his treatise *On the Incarnation of Christ* in seven books in 430 or soon after.[29] Thus his credentials as priest, abbot and theologian were impeccable.

Cassian accepted the 'full Augustinian meaning of grace as an interior working of God within the soul'; likewise he rejected the Pelagian idea of 'perfect liberty to choose between right and wrong' as a definition of free will.[30] But his experience of teaching novices, for whom he had already written his *Institutes* setting out the rules for a monastic life,[31] showed him that, within the operation of divine grace, room had to be left for the will to exercise responsibility for a man's choice of action. Again and again in this work he emphasises the imperative need to strive by daily effort and constant prayer to employ the will rightly and to the limits of its capacity, while never forgetting that the grace of God is necessary in order to achieve this end. 'No absurdity is to be seen in the retention of these two propositions within one man', comments Owen Chadwick, but he goes on to add that they 'appear incompatible in Cassian' and that 'Cassian is not the only writer in whom they have looked incompatible'.[32] It was his theological training in the east and his experience of the monastic life that led him to overlook this incompatibility. He came to favour a successive theory of will and grace: 'first the will acts, then the grace is given. The eastern monks had said, "Grace springs from the desire for it." Cassian followed them.'[33] Thus he was not an Augustinian in the strict sense of the word since he could not share Augustine's view of the Fall or of concupiscence. All this he was to explain in his thirteenth *Conference*, which he devoted to a study of grace and in which,

[29] PL 50, 9–376.
[30] O. Chadwick, 1968, 113f.
[31] PL 49, 53–476.
[32] O. Chadwick, 1968, 116.
[33] Ibid., 114.

though reiterating the absolute dependence of man upon God, he advanced an alternative view of predestination in an attempt to rescue the Augustinian doctrine from the charge of fatalism.[34] He was soon to be supported by other leaders of the monks in southern Gaul, Vincent of Lérins, and, a little later, Faustus, abbot of Lérins and later Bishop of Riez, both of whom were more outspoken in their attack on Augustinian predestination.[35]

And so the group described by Prosper in his letter to Augustine as 'the remnants of the Pelagian heresy' and by their contemporaries in Provence as 'the Massilians' came to gain the name of 'Semi-Pelagians' in the seventeenth century, when the relationship between predestination and grace again became one of the principal items on the agenda of theological controversy. This traditional description of the Massilians has often been criticised as misleading on the grounds that they were much closer to Augustine than Pelagius: Harnack, for example, dismissed it as 'a malicious heretical term' and identified Semi-Pelagianism as 'popular Catholicism made more definite and profound by Augustine's doctrine'.[36] Some, like Loofs, preferred the term 'Semi-Augustinians', and others have settled for 'Anti-Augustinians', though this may well be regarded as even more misleading. But it was certainly as opponents of Augustine that Prosper saw them when he leapt to the latter's defence and took on the rôle of custodian of Augustinianism in southern Gaul – 'le chevalier d'une grande cause'.[37]

At first, in his Letter to Rufinus and poem On the Graceless,[38] he limited himself to an indirect attack on Cassian and his supporters in the manner of Augustine in his earliest anti-Pelagian period; but when this provoked others to reply, he appealed to Pope Celestine for a decree against Pelagianism. In 431 he and his friend Hilary journeyed to Rome to put their case in person but Cassian's high reputation protected him, and the papal decree which resulted in 431, entitled Apostolici Verba and addressed to the bishops of Gaul and especially Cassian's bishop, Venerius of Marseilles, failed to express either approval of Augustinianism or open condemnation of the Massilians, so that both sides felt justified in interpreting it in their own favour. Prosper was forced to moderate his attack on Cassian and change his ground to a criticism of his teaching on the source and operation of the will: his treatise Against the Collator, written around 432 and examining twelve propositions from Cassian's thirteenth Conference, simply cited texts of his own choosing in refutation of those quoted by Cassian but without mentioning him by name, another echo of Augustine's tactics in his first reactions to Pelagius' teaching, and it was as

[34] PL 49, 898–954.

[35] Faustus is described as a Briton, ortu Britannum, in Avitus, Letter to Gundobadus, MGH vi. 2, p. 30, which may have led N. K. Chadwick, 1959, 26ff., 254ff., to develop her 'curious theory' that he was of aristocratic birth, the son of Vortigern by the daughter of Magnus Maximus, dismissed by Hanson, 1968, 64, as 'so unlikely as to be impossible'. He may just as well have been a Breton.

[36] Harnack, 321, n. 2. The term 'Semi-Pelagian' was first applied to the Molinists in the polemic of their opponents but it could have been used just as appropriately to describe medieval theologians such as William of Ockham; see Adams, 370ff., Pelikan, I, 319.

[37] Jacquin, 300.

[38] PL 51, 77–90; 91–148.

much a parody of Cassian's theology as the writings of his opponents were held to be a caricature of Augustine's.[39] Its contribution to the debate was minimal, and a second appeal to Rome, this time addressed to Celestine's successor, Sixtus III, met with as little success as the earlier one. 'In one sense', comments Owen Chadwick, 'the *Contra Collatorem* marked the beginning of the end of the controversy. It is probably the earliest document in which Prosper abandoned the attempt to preach predestination and irresistible grace.'[40] No doubt he had by now realised that the Massilians had displayed considerable shrewdness in concentrating their attack on these two, linked aspects of Augustine's teaching as his Achilles' heel, and Faustus of Riez continued to exploit their weakness, bringing about their condemnation by local synods around 475. But he was really no more a Pelagian in the strict sense of the word than his master Cassian had been; indeed, he had demonstrated this fact by writing a treatise *On Grace and Free Choice*, which was specifically directed against Pelagianism and in which Pelagius himself was described as a 'pestilential doctor'.[41]

As for Cassian, despite his monumental influence on the spirituality of western Europe through his teaching on the ascetic life – 'the first theologian of the religious orders' and 'in the high Middle Ages the chief "doctor" of the monks'[42] – his criticism of Augustine was never to be forgotten, let alone forgiven. Though the Council of Orange in 529, summoned and presided over by Caesarius of Arles, who was himself strongly opposed to the Semi-Pelagians and had written a treatise to refute Faustus' *On the Grace of God and Free Choice*,[43] condemned the doctrine that some are predestined to evil as anathema, it also reaffirmed the Augustinian teaching on grace and free will and rejected Cassian's theory of the successive operation of will and grace. And its canons or, at least, the first eight of them on justification, mainly taken from Augustine's works and supported by a statement of the bishops' own creed, were confirmed by Pope Boniface II. Furthermore, the so-called Gelasian decree, listing Cassian among those whose writings lacked the approval of the Church, was later to be incorporated in the Church law of the high medieval period. 'Such was the penalty for opposing Augustine's doctrine of grace.'[44]

Yet this was the man who could write: 'We may first show to our brethren true humility from the very bottom of our heart, assenting to nothing which will sadden or hurt them. . . . Then, next after this, we must maintain with

[39] *Against the Collator* (PL 51, 213–76); *Responses* (PL 51, 155–74, 177–86) – these were replies to Augustine's critics, especially the author of the so-called *Vincentian Objections*, though we cannot be quite certain that Vincent was the author. Wermelinger comments that Prosper's booklist is an almost complete list of Augustine's anti-Pelagian works with the exception of the controversial works written for the monks of Hadrumetum and for Hilarius and Prosper – *GFC, RG, PS* and *GP* (248 and n. 158).

[40] O. Chadwick, 1968, 134.

[41] PL 58, 783–836.

[42] O. Chadwick, 1968, 158.

[43] *The opinions of the lord Caesarius against those who explain why God gives grace to some but not to others* (Morin, ed.).

[44] O. Chadwick, 1968, 152.

the utmost firmness this same humility towards God. And this will be fulfilled by us in such a way as not only to acknowledge that we are powerless to accomplish anything relating to the perfecting of virtue without his assistance and grace, but also to believe honestly that our being worthy to comprehend this is in fact a gift from him.' And again: 'Experience proves that all the good in everyone is the work of the God of the universe. . . . The God of all must be held to be working all goodness in everyone, stirring up, protecting, strengthening; but not in such a way as to destroy the free will which is in our gift.'[45] His writings show him to have been one of the most attractive of the Western Fathers, a humble Christian and a dedicated teacher of his monks, and he deserved better treatment at the hands of posterity – perhaps 'a little generous prudence, a little forbearance and some grain of charity', qualities which John Milton once commended for those who sought 'to join and unite into one general and brotherly search for truth'.[46] Like Pelagius, who might justifiably have hoped for a better fate than excommunication from the Church which he loved, he too fell a victim to the same 'prelatical tradition of crowding free consciences and christian liberties into canons and precepts of men' that Milton so deplored. Such was the temper of the fifth-century Church and of Augustine, the man who impressed his individual stamp upon it and upon western theology for centuries to come.

Meanwhile, before Cassian's death and while Prosper was still pursuing his campaign against Semi-Pelagianism, ominous signs began to appear of the spread of the dreaded virus even farther afield. As early as 432 Prosper commends Pope Celestine's diligence in 'freeing Britain from this same disease by shutting off from that remote corner of the ocean certain enemies of grace who were occupying the soil of their native land'. And, in his *Chronicle* written many years later in Rome, he names Agricola, son of Bishop Severian, as one of those enemies of grace who had 'corrupted the churches of Britain by introducing his own dogma into them'.[47] At the suit of the deacon Palladius, Celestine sent Germanus of Auxerre to Britain as his representative, and he 'dislodged the heretics from their stronghold and guided the Britons back to the catholic faith'. Now it is important to note that these two references, brief and terse as they are, represent in fact the only first-hand evidence for Pelagianism in fifth-century Britain which we possess and the only evidence in which we can place any confidence. The rest is intelligent or not so intelligent guesswork, based on secondary sources, most prominent among them being Constantius' *Life of Germanus*, written about 480. In it Constantius, who was 'a hagiographer, not an historian' and whose sole purpose in writing was not to give a report on contemporary Britain but 'to glorify Germanus',[48] includes a vivid but almost wholly unreliable account of the visit of 429, adding that the saint was accompanied by another, Lupus of

---

[45] *Institutes* XII, 32f. (PL 49, 474ff.), as translated by N. K. Chadwick, 1955, 223.
[46] *Areopagitica*, 554 (Complete Prose Works II, 1643–8, Oxford, 1959).
[47] *Against the Collator* 21, 2 (PL 51, 271); *Chronicle*, year 429 (PL 51, 594f.) (Stevenson, 351). On Agricola see now Markus, 1986, 201ff.
[48] Thompson, 1984, 85f.

Troyes. He attributes the visit not to a decision of the Pope, as does Prosper, but to one taken by a Gallican Synod of which we have no mention elsewhere, and he also recounts a second visit made by Germanus between 441 and 448, this time accompanied by Severus of Trier, to which Prosper does not refer at all.[49] Not everyone has been willing to accept the historicity of this second visit: Nora Chadwick, for example, suggested that 'the second journey looks suspiciously like a duplication of the first, possibly incorporating a variant tradition'.[50] The two accounts could well be different versions of the same story, later used and embellished by Nennius and others in order to enhance the reputation of legendary heroes like Germanus and Lupus as a part of 'their strategy of bringing the Welsh Church at the turn of the eighth and ninth centuries under the newly introduced Roman order'.[51] If the account of the second visit has an historical basis, as most historians seem ready to accept, then it is hard to reconcile the apparently overwhelming success credited to the first visit with a need for Germanus to make a second for the same purpose less than twenty years later. Whether the second visit did take place and, if so, at what date is a question which will continue to be debated; in the present context it is important only as a possible indication of the strength of British Pelagianism in the fifth century and of the duration of its survival.

As to the first visit, much could be and indeed has already been said about the omissions from Constantius' admittedly colourful description of it – about the absence of any mention of British bishops at the debate with the Pelagians, about the lack of any reference to Roman officials except 'a man with tribunician authority', whatever that may be taken to mean, and about the writer's failure to tell his readers when or where the debate took place or the great battle against the Picts and Saxons which was fought after it and in which Germanus led the Britons to a glorious 'Alleluia Victory' on Easter Day.[52] Such omissions are attributable only to Constantius' almost complete

---

[49] Constantius, *Life of Germanus*, 12ff., 25ff. (Krusch and Levison VII, 247ff.). Thompson, op. cit., 55ff., after noting that there is general agreement with a date in the 440s and that most place it between 444 and 448, suggests 437 for the second visit, 'a possible, even a probable date' and withdraws his earlier preference (1957, 135ff.) for 444 with the wry comment – *horresco referens*!

[50] N. K. Chadwick, 1955, 255ff.; 1958, 23; 1963, 142; cf. J. Evans, 177. But Thompson, 1984, 4, thinks that Chadwick 'goes too far' and that Hanson, 1968, 50 is nearer the mark when he concludes that Constantius may have known only that a second visit took place but almost no details of what happened in the course of it.

[51] Hanson, 1968, 52; see also N. K. Chadwick, 1955, 268ff., Loyer, 24, Hardinge, xiii and G. Williams, 1f.

[52] Thompson, 1984, 50ff., tentatively suggests the London area as a possible site for the debate but with the caveat that this is 'only make-believe'. As for the battle, Welsh tradition locates it at Maes Garmon, 'Garmon's Field', in Mold, and Morris, 1965, 162ff., in the Vale of Llangollen on the Dee, provoking Alcock, 102, to remark that it could just as well have been 'a valley in the Chilterns'! And he, Kirby, 49f., and Dumville, 1977, 186, rightly warn that it is impossible to reconcile Germanus of Auxerre with the Welsh Garmon, who is 'the dynastic or territorial saint of Powys' (Dumville) or 'a Welsh ecclesiastic of that name' (Alcock). No wonder that Saunders Lewis in his play *Buchedd Garmon* (Aberystwyth 1937) abandons historical 'fact' for poetic licence by bringing two Welsh saints Paulinus and Illtud to Auxerre to supplicate for Germanus' help and Germanus himself first to Caerleon on the Usk and finally to Maes Garmon to confront and defeat his British opponents on Easter Day! But at least he never claimed to be a historian.

ignorance of events in Britain at the time and of its religious state some fifty years before he wrote his *Life*, whereas his picture of events in Gaul is rich in detail and clearly drawn from personal knowledge. His account of the visits of Germanus to Britain, on the other hand, contains 'practically no details . . . because he knew none'.[53] All he appears to have known was that such visits took place, and the only detail which most of our authorities accept as historical is the visit of Germanus and Lupus to the shrine of Alban at Verulamium. But even this, it has recently been suggested, may have been no more than an attempt to associate the cult of the British martyr with continental orthodoxy: Constantius' *Life* must be used with caution as an historical source and should be regarded as 'primarily an allegory'.[54]

Trying to ascertain the true facts about fifth-century Pelagianism in Britain is like trying to make bricks without straw or at least almost without straw, if we accept, as we surely must, that at least Prosper's references to it are reliable. From those references we might conclude that the movement which Germanus was commissioned to extirpate was a religious one, probably activated by Pelagian exiles in flight from the continent after the condemnation of their leaders and the subsequent persecution of the remnant, among them Agricola, who need not necessarily have been a cleric himself. On the same premises the phenomenon would not have been of long duration – about ten years or, if the second visit is accepted, about thirty: Prosper believed that one visit was sufficient to bring it to an end, Constantius that a second was needed to do so, adding that the Pelagians were then sent into exile.[55] Thompson maintains that, by the time when Gildas was writing around the middle of the sixth century, 'Pelagianism was dead, buried and forgotten':[56] certainly Gildas makes no mention of it, although he laments that British Christians of his time were plagued by Arianism. But it has often been pointed out that Gildas' silences are notorious and may mean nothing, and it has also been suggested that 'perhaps some lingering Pelagian influences, may be detected in Gildas himself'.[57] But, as Thompson has observed, the passages quoted do not bear out this opinion: the brief sentence from the Pelagian tract *On Virginity* which Gildas repeats and which is found also with a slight change of wording in another Pelagian work from the same period had already been cited by others and could well have become an ethical commonplace by then. Gildas attributes it to *quidam nostrum*, 'one of ours', which is open to many

[53] Thompson, op. cit., 13. Others have been less cautious: for example, G. A. Williams, 22, goes so far as to state that 'Germanus debated with their (*sc.* the Pelagians') spokesman, the son of a bishop', presumably Agricola, not mentioned by Constantius, and that Aetius 'sent Germanus with the Bishop of Troyes to Britain', referring to Vortigern as 'another opponent of Germanus'.

[54] Wood, 14; but he, 8, may have misunderstood Prosper's reference to Agricola, attributing the British heresy not to the latter, as does Prosper, but to his father.

[55] Thompson, 1984, 28ff., comments that it is odd they should have been sent into exile by the congregation and finds the description of their destination – *ad mediterranea* – as hard to explain as others before him.

[56] Thompson, 1979, 211; cf. 1985, 54f.

[57] W. H. Davies, 140 and 149, n. 105; Myres, 1951, 227f., takes a similar view.

interpretations, and he would not have used it if he had been aware that it was unorthodox.[58] Thompson concludes that extracts from Pelagian writings may well have been circulating in the sixth century without being recognised as heretical. More recently, a contributor to a collection of essays on Gildas has cited other passages in his *On the Ruin of Britain* which might be explained as echoes of Pelagianism but has suggested that they reveal only that Pelagian texts and ideas were still in circulation in Britain at the time when Gildas was writing, 'nothing more'.[59] And if Pelagianism was still remembered in the middle of the sixth century, though no longer a force to be reckoned with, it is just possible that its roots in Britain were stronger then either Prosper or Constantius realised.

Such a possibility provided the basis for a novel theory, advanced by Myres and developed by Morris, that the outbreak of Pelagianism which Germanus was sent to quell was much more than simply an offshoot of the heresy.[60] Myres used the popular meaning of *gratia* in the Theodosian Code, that is, of 'judicial corruption in the courts, official hanky-panky of all kinds in public life' as the starting-point for his argument that 'Pelagius and his friends may have been attempting, however confusedly, an attack upon the social corruption inherent in a totalitarian regime, rather than initiating, as Augustine insisted, a barefaced assault on the fundamentals of the Christian faith', going on to link this attack with the political situation in early fifth-century Britain. Morris, following another path but in the same general direction, re-examined a batch of Pelagian documents from the same period and concluded that Britain was the home not only of Pelagius himself but also of a group of young radicals, one of whom, 'the Sicilian Briton' now in exile, was the author of the documents concerned. Britain had thus provided the soil in which Pelagianism first took root as early as the mid-nineties of the fourth century, when Victricius of Rouen was summoned to Britain to settle differences which had arisen between the British bishops. 'Poor Victricius', comments Charles Thomas, 'continually, if marginally, found, interred in speculative footnotes'.[61]

Myres's thesis was that early British Pelagianism represented a conscious effort to shake off the last shackles of imperial rule and revive older Roman virtues by men who resented the intrusion of Augustinian orthodoxy as the alien doctrine of a foreign government, and this was taken on board by Morris

[58] Thompson, 1979, 212f. The reference to *On Virginity*, 6 (PL 30, 167) is in Gildas, *On the Ruin (and Conquest) of Britain* II, 38, 2: *non agitur de qualitate peccati sed de transgressione mandati*, 'it is not a question of the nature of the sin but of the fact of having disobeyed an order', a quotation repeated in *On Works*, 13, 1 (PLS 1, 1438f.) with the minor change of *agitur* to *actum est*. The same sentiment appears also in the Pelagian letter *Honorificentiae tuae*, 1 (PLS 1, 1689).

[59] Wood, 8. O'Sullivan, 180, dates *On the Ruin of Britain c.* 515–20 but 'with a real possibility remaining that it was written within a decade before the earlier or after the later date'; Dumville, 1984, 84, prefers the second quarter of the sixth century or possibly the third.

[60] Myres, 1960, 21ff.; Morris, 1965, 26ff.; see also Myres, 1968, 6, and Morris, 1968, 61ff.

[61] A. C. Thomas, 1981, 51. Victricius' visit to Britain at the request of his fellow-bishops there is recorded in his *On the Praise of the Saints*, 1 (PL 20, 443), and Pope Innocent's letter to him in the Peterborough text of the *Anglo-Saxon Chronicle* is 'a Latin interpolation under the year 403' often linked with this visit but without any implication 'that it had anything to do with Pelagianism in Britain' (Thomas, op. cit., 55).

as an early example of a British tendency towards political radicalism and social egalitarianism. The common basis which they shared was a conviction that there was much more to British Pelagianism than had hitherto been realised and that, far from being a relatively brief and insignificant offshoot of a continental heresy, it was a factor of considerable importance in the social and political history of Britain in the early decades of the fifth century, especially around the 'time of troubles' in 409/10 and probably even earlier in the nineties of the preceding century. But there are several differences in detail, as there are in the sources employed by the two scholars, and it is difficult to reconcile Myres's well-to-do landowners, the 'well-dressed and well-heeled' audience of Constantius' account,[62] with Morris's young radical thinkers: 'by any textbook definition', the latter argues, 'the crisp argumentation' of the Pelagian treatise *On Riches* is socialism, 'socialism of a coherence and urgency that was hardly to be met again before the nineteenth century, or at earliest the end of the eighteenth'. In support of his case he presents a number of quotations from his 'Sicilian Briton', including this striking passage: 'They do not understand that the reason why the poor exist is that the rich own too much. Abolish the rich and you will not be able to find the poor. If no one possesses more than he needs, all will have as much as they need. For it is those who are rich that are the reason for the many who are poor.'[63]

But despite the patent enthusiasm with which Myres and Morris propounded their theses and the unquestionable skill with which they deployed their arguments they were to find very few supporters,[64] and they soon came under attack from all sides, as theologians, archaeologists and historians of Roman Britain began to discover weaknesses in the evidence employed to build up this new and exciting scenario for Romano-British politics in the early fifth century. In the first place, Pelagius never saw himself as heading a movement for social reform nor is there a shred of evidence that he and his immediate circle sought to exploit the popular sense of the word *gratia* as 'graft' in order to boost their own theological opinions. On the contrary, Pelagius' main defence of his orthodoxy was the claim that he was *not* an 'enemy of grace': Pelagianism, as we have emphasised, was an ascetic movement in origin, and its appeal was for better Christians and not for a more democratic form of government. Nor do the Pelagian tracts and letters from the early fifth century which gave Morris the evidence for his thesis show any noticeable trace of the catastrophical events taking place in Britain at the time when they were written, and Morris's attempt to link the Pelagian letter

---

[62] Johnson, 116.

[63] *On Riches*, 12, 2 (PLS 1, 1401); Morris, 1965, 50f. The six Pelagian documents first published by Caspari consisted of two letters and four tracts, three of these also in letter form: *Honorificentiae tuae, Humanae referunt litterae, On Riches, On Evil Doctors and Works of Faith and Future Judgement,* usually cited as *On Works, On the Possibility of Not Sinning,* and *On Chastity* (PLS 1, 1687–94, 1375–80, 1380–1418, 1418–57, 1457–64 and 1464–1504 respectively). Plinval attributed all six to Pelagius but Caspari to Agricola and Morris to his 'Sicilian Briton'.

[64] For example, Salway, 443, 727; Frere, 376; Ward, 284f.; D. S. Evans, 1971, 3, n. 10.

Humanae referunt litterae with the unrest of 409 and 410 has been shown to depend on an incorrect interpretation of the phrase 'perpetual consulate' in the last sentence of the letter. As for the authorship of the tracts *On the Christian Life* and *On Virginity*, attributed by Morris to 'Fastidius' and his 'Sicilian Briton' respectively, they are far more likely to have been the work of Pelagius himself. Moreover, even if we are prepared to accept that all the Caspari documents were written by the same man, there is good reason to doubt whether he was a Briton at all. And the attempt to cast Vortigern in the rôle of arch-Pelagian and leading opponent of Germanus has absolutely no evidence to support it.[65]

After a judicious summary of the pros and cons of the Myres–Morris theses, Thomas concludes that it is doubtful if heresies like Pelagianism '*were* ever applied socially to the extent where they governed or modified history'.[66] He aptly reminds us of the warning given by A. H. M. Jones that nationalist and socialist theories applied to heresies seem to be based 'on a radical misapprehension of the mentality of the Later Roman Empire': modern historians who so apply them are 'retrojecting into the past the sentiments of the present age'.[67] Jones was referring, of course, to Arianism, Donatism and Monophysitism but his salutary warning might equally have been addressed to Myres and Morris and their interpretation of Pelagianism in Britain. This tendency to explain the past by analogies with the present, though already visible in nineteenth-century historians of the ancient world, was perhaps never more prevalent than in those heady decades immediately following the Second World War, when many historians appeared to have forgotten that they were dealing with periods of history during which political ideology still hovered back in the wings, awaiting the opportunity to make its entrance on-stage several centuries later.

Nevertheless it would be a great mistake – and it would also be unjust – to dismiss the investigations of Myres and Morris as entirely without merit: Myres deserves credit for having forced others to re-examine the evidence for the rise of Pelagianism in Britain in the early fifth century against the backcloth of the political situation at the time, and Morris for having made a significant contribution to the problem of the authorship of the Pelagian tracts and letters written in that period. Whereas the founders of Pelagianism produced works wholly free from political undertones, much of the literature first brought to our attention by Caspari was written by individuals deeply conscious and strongly critical of the social and political inequalities of

[65] I have culled these criticisms from Liebeschuetz, 1963, 237, 1967, 446; Thompson, 1977, 314 and n. 42; Cameron, 215; R. F. Evans, 1968(a), 37ff.; Bonner, 1972, 5f.; Hanson, 1968, 19. They have been aptly summed up by Jarrett, 1983, 25: 'the evidence justifies, and perhaps compels, agnosticism'. Brown, 1972, 184, n. 1, also comments: 'It is impossible to veil my disagreement with these two scholars'; but, in fairness to them, he goes on to add: 'It would be ungrateful not to record how much my own interest in the Pelagian controversy owes to their erudition and freshness of approach.'

[66] A. C. Thomas, 1981, 59.

[67] A. H. M. Jones, 1959, 295, in an article which should be compulsory reading for historians writing about the heresies of the early Christian Church.

contemporary society and utilising Pelagian theology in order to highlight the need for social justice. But that does not entitle us to claim that these Pelagian converts were the force behind the appearance of the heresy in Britain in the second quarter of the fifth century, much less that they represented a radical party in Romano-British politics as early as 409, or even earlier in the last decade of the fourth century. When the 'evidence' adduced by Myres and Morris is subjected to closer examination, Victricius, 'Fastidius', that *fantôme indécis*,[68] the Sicilian 'Briton' and all the other extras in 'this insubstantial pageant faded' melt into thin air and leave not a rack behind! We are left with what we started – Prosper's references to Agricola as instigator of the Pelagian unrest and to the first visit of Germanus in 429: Germanus came to Britain at the request of the Pope to nip Pelagianism in the bud. He fulfilled this task, and, if we are prepared to place any confidence at all in Constantius' farrago of folklore, legend and allegory, he *may* have become involved in a minor skirmish with Picts and Saxons. But his activities were confined to the south-eastern corner of the island and, if he did make a second visit, he certainly did not travel via Brittany to the western regions or venture as far as North Wales or northern Britain.[69]

But we are not yet out of the wood: even if Germanus did not extend his second mission to the western regions, we cannot rule out the possibility that the ghost of Pelagius, well and truly laid in the south-eastern corner of Britain, was still haunting the Celtic fringe and, in particular, that part of it which many in the past have held to be his homeland – Wales, if it is 'meaningful to talk of Wales before England exists'.[70] In his *magnum opus*, his *Life of St. David*, the eleventh-century Welsh scholar Rhigyfarch (Ricemarch) refers to Germanus' second visit to Britain and records that, even after this visit, 'the Pelagian heresy was recovering its vigour and obstinacy, implanting the poison of a deadly serpent in the innermost regions of our country'.[71] To combat this threat to true belief a synod of 'all the bishops of Britain' assembled at Brefi, now Llanddewi Brefi in Dyfed, and was attended by 'one

[68] Plinval, 1943, 46, applying the same description to Agricola as well.

[69] J. Evans, 185, with whom Thompson, 1984, 47f., now agrees, withdrawing his earlier suggestion (1979, 215) that Germanus went 'to a more westerly point' on his second visit. Plinval, 146, sent him to the borders of Scotland and Candida Casa, and Meissner I, 84, to the north of Britain. But they, unlike Saunders Lewis, lacked the benefit of poetic licence.

[70] Jarrett, 1983, 35.

[71] Rhigyfarch, *Life of St. David*, 49 (J. W. James, 21, 43). He uses the same metaphor to describe Pelagianism, 'the serpent's poison', as Gildas, *On the Ruin of Britain* I, 12, 3 (Winterbottom, 20, 93), does in writing of Arianism; this metaphor was, of course, a traditional one to apply to any heresy in the early Christian Church but its occurrence in both contexts does prompt the rather naughty thought that neither Rhigyfarch nor Gildas knew the difference between Pelagianism and Arianism. In a lecture which is eminently sane and judicious, yet not without its touches of quiet humour, my former colleague Simon Evans describes the situation facing anyone who tries to uncover the facts of David's life as one in which 'it is not easy to distinguish between saga and history' (10f.), and the tremendous literary activity of the period in which Rhigyfarch wrote as 'works that are full of the marvellous, the miraculous and the incredible' (12). Particularly relevant to the present context is his conclusion that Rhigyfarch's *Life* was intended to contribute to his father Bishop Sulien's diplomacy (14) by establishing the priority of the church of Dewi over those of Bangor and Llandaff and of Dewi himself over Patrick, Gildas, Teilo, Daniel and Dyfrig, as well as his ascendancy over the Irish and the Cornish (15ff.).

hundred and eighteen bishops and an innumerable multitude of priests, abbots, clergy of other ranks, kings, princes and lay men and women'. So vast was the assembled throng that none of the bishops was able to make himself heard, and, on the advice of Paulinus, David was summoned from somewhere nearby and preached from a hill which rose miraculously beneath his feet. Such was his eloquence that the heresy was at once overcome and the true faith restored; later, a second synod, the 'Synod of Victory', was summoned and reaffirmed the decisions of the first. If Rhigyfarch is recording an historical event, then surely, it is argued, no better location could have been chosen for the holding of a synod to suppress a recrudescence of Pelagianism than Brefi, 'situated in what would have been a focal area of some importance in the days of St. David, at a convergence of minor routes among the hills'.[72]

As one reads the narrative of the Synod of Brefi, one has a strong feeling of *déjà lu*, evoked by the many reminiscences in it of Constantius' account of Germanus' missions to Britain: the totally one-sided debate with the Pelagians in which no Pelagian either spoke or is even named, the vast multitude present, the accompanying miracles, the overwhelming success of the defender of orthodoxy, the second occasion needed to confirm the result of the first, and even the name given to it, recalling the 'Alleluia Victory'. Is it inconceivable that Rhigyfarch adapted Constantius' account to the greater glory of David, in order to demonstrate that a Celtic saint could be just as effective in uprooting heresy as any imported saint from Gaul, however prestigious? He was writing in the eleventh century, when Lanfranc and Anselm pursued their campaign to extend the jurisdiction of their Church and when, despite the general acceptance of catholic views in Wales by 768, it might still be of some tactical importance for the Welsh to establish that the Celtic Church had a tradition founded on sound orthodoxy, even before that other Augustine came to Britain to convert the Angli and made his abortive attempt to persuade the representatives of Celtic Christianity to accept Roman practices and discipline.

Some will find it incredible that Rhigyfarch, a highly respected scholar with family connections in Llanbadarn Fawr in Dyfed through his father Sulien, twice Bishop of St. David's, could have invented this revival of Pelagianism and adapted Constantius to suit his own purposes, even supplying Paulinus, traditionally a fellow-student of David and a friend of Germanus, with a major rôle in his narrative of the synod of Brefi. But we do have to take account on the other side of the balance sheet of three countervailing items: Prosper's assertion that Germanus eliminated the heresy in 429, Constantius' that he finally did so in the middle of the fifth century, and Gildas' failure to mention Pelagianism in the middle of the sixth. One would certainly have expected Prosper not to miss an opportunity of referring to his *bête noire* if it still existed in Britain in the mid-fifth century, bearing in mind that his

[72] Bowen, 1983, 59; elsewhere (1982, 31) he describes it as 'a veritable Piccadilly Circus in Early Christian Times', and G. A. Williams, 5, as 'a veritable Crewe Junction of the sea-routes which laced the Irish Sea and the Western Approaches'.

Chronicle extended to 455. But Prosper, it will be countered, is not infallible and, in any case, was far away in Rome by that time, Constantius is *capable de tout*, and Gildas' silences are no more than signs of his ignorance. Might not Rhigyfarch have been resurrecting a folk-memory of an earlier recurrence of the heresy in an area with which he was thoroughly familiar? Is it quite unthinkable that it could have infiltrated into south-west Wales in the fifth century and exerted a continuing influence in popular religious thought there until the sixth? After all, a heresy does not need to be fully articulated in precise theological terms in order to survive and retain its grasp on the imagination of the unlearned.

In fact, there is archaeological evidence which may be interpreted as suggesting that there *were* Pelagians in that same area of Wales around the same period and that they had come there not from south-eastern Britain but from Ireland, thus linking the synod of Brefi with the Irish settlements in south-west Wales between the late fourth and early sixth centuries.[73] Much has been written about these settlements and, in particular, about a batch of ogham and ogham/Latin inscriptions attributed to their influence and found on tombstones and other memorials in the fifth and sixth centuries.[74] These inscriptions have been discovered in Dumnonia, Brycheiniog, Gwynedd and even in north Scotland, as it now is, but the heaviest concentration is in Dyfed. Most of them include a filiation-formula using the word *maqqi* or its Latin equivalent *filius* or both, unlike the Latin inscriptions predominating in Gwynedd during the same period, which employed the same formula as the bulk of Romano-Christian inscriptions on the continent and omitted the patronymic in deference, it has been suggested, to the Gospel injunction to 'call no man your father on earth'.[75] But in the case of the Dyfed memorials, it has been argued, the inclusion of the filiation-formula is rather an indication of Pelagianism and of a conscious rejection of the doctrine of original sin. In North Wales in the same period, on the other hand, there is a markedly lower proportion of inscriptions which include a filiation-formula, most of them in Latin and very few in ogham, and the predominance of the formula *hic iacit (iacet)* there may be due to a closer relationship with the continent – though one must add that it could equally well be attributed to the fact that, unlike the Déisi, who came to south-west Wales from southern Ireland, the Féni, who came from central Ireland to north Wales, never succeeded in establishing themselves to anything like the same extent, 'their memorial being little more than the survival of their name in its British form'.[76] However that may be, David, we are told, 'bore a traditional hostility to the Irish invaders' of his

[73] Bowen, 1982, 23ff., 1983, 61ff.

[74] Nash-Williams, 3ff. A revised edition of this work is currently being prepared, and I am indebted to one of the joint editors, W. Gwyn Thomas, for the advance information that, though Nash-Williams suggested that some of the relevant inscriptions may be early fifth century, it does not now seem likely for any with the filiation formula.

[75] Nash-Williams, 6, quoting Le Blant, *Inscriptions de la Gaule* I, 126, a quotation repeated by many others since.

[76] Powell, 173.

own area and would have had no truck with any perverse practices or unorthodox views with which they were associated.[77] As for Gildas, who seems to have known nothing of the outbreak of Pelagianism in south-eastern Britain, he is just as unlikely to have heard of a recurrence in south-western Wales, since the synod of Brefi was no more than a tribal gathering, not even remotely resembling the grand ecclesiastical convention of British Christians recorded by Rhigyfarch half a millennium later.

From this standpoint there is nothing inherently impossible in the idea of a Pelagian influence which was still a force to be reckoned with in south-west Wales a century after its elimination from south-eastern Britain; and if there was such an influence, then we should look for its source not on the continent but in Ireland, since there had long been a two-way traffic between Wales and Ireland. The ogham script, now generally accepted to have been 'based on a fourth-century classification of the Roman alphabet, as used by grammarians in the late empire', was invented either in Ireland itself or 'in south Wales by an Irish immigrant exposed to Roman schooling'.[78] And the *maqqi*-formula too is found in Ireland: after an exhaustive analysis of all the instances of its occurrence which he was able to discover in Ireland, Kenneth Jackson counted over three hundred, the great majority from Kerry, Cork and Waterford, and it was from these very areas that the Irish settlers came to south Wales from the late fourth to the early sixth centuries, members of the Déisi and Uí Líathain tribes of southern Ireland who presumably brought their filiation-formula with them.[79]

But are we justified in assuming that the use of such a formula is an indication of Pelagian influence, or is it rather no more than a relic of an earlier pagan practice long discarded by Christians elsewhere? As Jackson reminds us, the practice of 'defining a man's name by adding his father's' is 'absolutely typical of all Celtic languages at all periods': such a formula is 'distinctive of the lands bordering on the Irish Sea' and 'rightly at home in a pagan tribal society, where descent was a major factor in a person's status'.[80] A similar formula in Latin has also been found on some continental memorials up to the middle of the fifth century, pagan as well as Christian. But many of the memorials in ogham or ogham/Latin in south-west Wales contain words or terms with a specifically Christian flavour and some of them are marked with an early form of the cross; not all of them can be proved to be Christian

---

[77] Bowen, 1982, 25; 1983, 65f.

[78] A. C. Thomas, 1981, 299. In his article contributed to *Hermathena* in 1943 my old friend L. J. D. Richardson recalled the theory of R. A. S. Macalister that ogham writing was derived from an early form of the Greek alphabet and argued a strong case for accepting it and for holding that the word Ogham itself was also Greek in origin and derived from the forgotten Greek letter *agma*. Lacking Richardson's great knowledge of comparative philology and being no longer, regrettably, able to consult him, I record this divergence from the conventional view as a matter of interest and *honoris causa*.

[79] Jackson, 1953, 152; more recently Coplestone-Crow, 1ff., has suggested that there were two distinct waves of settlers, the first in the late fourth and early fifth century and the second in the late fifth and early sixth.

[80] Jackson, 1953, 168; Alcock, 241f.

but most of them are, certainly the later ones.[81] Nevertheless, even if the literacy which they imply can have come only from association with a Romano-Christian society, the filiation-formula itself may still have been an echo of an earlier pagan background.

Were the Irish immigrants Christians when they arrived in Wales? If so, by whom had they been converted in Ireland? And could they have been Pelagians on arrival? The simple, straightforward answer to the first two questions would be that they were Christians on arrival and that they had been converted by Patrick or his successors. But such an answer would beg many questions: as Nora Chadwick once commented somewhat ruefully, 'Every question connected with St. Patrick bristles with difficulties.'[82] For example, 'Patrick seems to write as if all the Irish were heathens on his arrival';[83] but Prosper, though he describes Ireland as 'the barbarous island' as opposed to Britain, 'the Christian island', also tells us that in 431 Pope Celestine gave it its 'first bishop', Palladius.[84] This was certainly the same Palladius who had persuaded the Pope to send Germanus on his first mission to Britain, and the decision to appoint him 'first bishop of the Irish' may have been taken after consultation with him on his return to Auxerre, if, as has been suggested, he had accompanied Germanus to Britain.[85] But Prosper categorically states that he was sent to 'the Irish who believed in Christ', and this statement would be consistent with the practice of the Church at Rome at this time not to despatch missionaries to pagan areas.[86]

And that is Prosper's last word on the subject of Palladius' mission to Ireland: he has nothing to say about its duration, its success or its failure. Later Irish writers, however, were not short of ideas as to what happened to him: he was forced to leave Ireland prematurely by the antagonism of the Irish bishops, whoever they may have been at this time, or because he was

[81] A. C. Thomas, 1981, 299, 1971, 106; cf. Jackson, 168, Alcock, 241f. I am grateful to W. Gwyn Thomas for the following comment based on his revision of the section in Nash-Williams which is concerned with these memorials: 'Leaving aside those inscriptions referring to *presbyter*, *sacerdos*, *in pace* or with early forms of a cross (and even some of the undatable Irish ogam-inscribed stones include *bendacht*, *ab* (for 'abbot'), *aspog* and *isgob*, *grimitir* (= *cruimther*, *presbyter*) as well as many with *anm* (name) which is reckoned to be specifically Christian), the basic question would be whether British or Irish inscriptions would have been made without a Christian context. I would have thought the implied literacy could have come only from an ecclesiastical source.' This, he emphasises, is a 'subjective view'. Cf. Jackson, 1953, 176, n. 1: 'There is no reason to suppose that there was anything about the Ogam script essentially repugnant to Christianity and that an Ogam inscription means that the man commemorated must have been a pagan.' Richards, 151f., also observes that many of them 'had distinguishing Christian symbols'.

[82] N. K. Chadwick, 1961, 19. D. S. Evans, 1984, 10f., makes a similar remark about David: 'When we go back as far as Saint David, we find that every corner is dark.'

[83] Hughes, 1966, 31.

[84] *Against the Collator* 21, 2 (PL 51, 271); *Chronicle*, under the year 431 (PL 51, 595); Stevenson, 351.

[85] O'Rahilly, 1942. 19; see Hanson, 1968, 54, n. 2.

[86] In a letter addressed to 'all the bishops of the provinces of Vienne and Narbo' (*Letters* 4, V, 7 in PL 50, 434) Pope Celestine himself declares: 'Let no bishop be given to those who are unwilling [to receive him]; let the agreement of the clergy, common people and men of standing be required.' As Thompson, 1985, puts it: 'The idea of a Catholic missionary bishop did not yet exist in the early fifth century.'

homesick, or that he was martyred by the Irish, or that he did not reach Ireland at all but died 'in the extremities of Britain' or 'in the land of the Picts'; 'the variety of these stories', comments Hanson, 'shows the ignorance of their authors'.[87] It is probable that 'Palladius left very little impression on folk-memory in Ireland',[88] and that his mission was of no long duration and became confused by some elements of later Irish tradition with that of Patrick, perhaps for lack of evidence, perhaps deliberately in order to enhance the latter's reputation as the *bona fide* founder of Irish Christianity, 'the Apostle of the Irish', while other elements of the same tradition may have been just as anxious to preserve at least the memory of Palladius as evidence of an historical link with the Church at Rome – though it is not impossible that they believed Patrick to have been sent by the Pope also.[89] Incidentally, Patrick does not mention Palladius; but neither Prosper nor Bede mention Patrick, although Bede twice refers to Palladius' mission, presumably on Prosper's authority.[90]

The only tenable explanation of Prosper's failure to record Patrick's mission to Ireland is that he knew nothing of it, since it was authorised and promoted not by the Pope but by the bishops of Britain. On the subject of his appointment Patrick too is silent: his own version of the reason for his return to Ireland is that he was summoned in a dream by a man called Victoricus, who came 'as it were, from Ireland with countless letters', including one entitled 'The Voice of the Irish', pleading with him to return to them.[91] Even the date of that return is based only on the conjectures of later Irish writers, who may well have plumped for the first year available after Prosper's date for the mission of Palladius on the assumption that, after its failure or abandonment, Patrick was sent his successor. But the question of the date of Patrick's return as bishop to Ireland is one of those which 'bristles with difficulties': some have argued for a considerably later date in the middle of the century, and there is even a theory of 'two Patricks', the one earlier, the

[87] Hanson, 1968, 182ff.; cf. Thompson, 1985, 173.

[88] Binchy, 143.

[89] As in the letter of Columbanus to Pope Boniface IV in 613 (Sancti Columbani Opera, ed. Walker), quoted by Binchy: 'The catholic faith, as it was first delivered *by you* (my emphasis), is maintained unbroken.'

[90] Bede, *Ecclesiastical History* i. 13, 24 (Everyman's Library, London 1970, 20, 281); Bede uses the same phrase as Prosper, 'to the Scots (*sc.* Irish) that believed in Christ'. 'Patrick', comments Binchy, 168f., 'was buried in a mysterious silence for the century and a half which followed his death' – a silence for which ample compensation has since been made! Thompson, 1985, adds: 'Patrick was almost completely unknown on the Continent in his lifetime and for centuries after it.'

[91] *Confession*, 23 (Stevenson, 352). Patrick concludes his account of this dream with the words: 'Thanks be to God that after very many years the Lord granted to them according to their cry.' If his return to Ireland as bishop was an answer to the appeal, then it would have been long delayed. But Thompson, 1985, maintains that Patrick may well have responded much earlier by returning to Ireland as a deacon in 431 'or even earlier' and suggests that he may have served as a deacon under Palladius (39, 175). The only direct reference which Patrick himself makes to his appointment as bishop is in his *Letter to the Soldiers of Coroticus*, 1 (Stevenson, 356): 'I, Patrick, a sinner and unlearned, declare that I am indeed a bishop, resident in Ireland.'

other later and also called 'Patricius'.[92] There is indeed confusion in the little isle! 'Of the origin of Irish Christianity we know absolutely nothing', commented Charles Plummer writing in 1896, and a more recent writer, quoting him, adds the question: 'Are we really much wiser now than then?'[93] On the basis of linguistic evidence revealing a number of loanwords borrowed into Irish from Latin and mainly religious or ecclesiastical Jackson concluded that 'the early development of Irish Christianity was fostered mainly from Britain' and that 'small communities of Christians may have existed in parts of Ireland already by the beginning of the fifth century, presumably founded by British missionaries'; but he then went on to add that 'if so, they were of little importance in a nation whose religion was still overwhelmingly pagan' and that 'the real conversion of Ireland began with the mission of St. Patrick in 432'.[94]

Whatever the date of Patrick's return may have been, the regions in which he operated were the north and north-east, not those from which Irish settlers started out for south-west Wales, and, in any case, despite attempts to unearth traces of anti-Pelagianism in his writings or to argue that his emphasis on the need to obey the call of the free will was Pelagian in origin,[95] there is no good reason to believe that he was consciously either Pelagian or anti-Pelagian: he was a fisher of human souls, not a spinner of theological webs. As for Palladius, whose mission is traditionally located in the south or central-east regions from which the settlers came, he was too closely associated with Germanus to have been a Pelagian or crypto-Pelagian and would hardly

[92] O'Rahilly, 1942, 8 and 48, n. 5; Carney, 1961, 1ff., 26ff., 114ff.; Binchy, 114, 129ff. After examining the 'evidence', Hanson, 1968, 191, concludes that 'all strictly dichotomous two – Patrick theories must be abandoned'. Thompson, 1985, 166–75, devotes an Appendix to Patrick's chronology, in which he dates his appointment as bishop 'some years, let us say, after 434'; in his Introduction, xiii, he dismisses 'the value of the *Lives* and the Irish annals and other later documents': 'It cannot be stressed too often that Patrick's own writings contain *all* the valid evidence about his life and thought which we possess.' This seems to me to be a fair comment on the 'small mountain of guesswork, mythology and political and ecclesiastical propaganda . . . which grew up about his name'.

[93] Plummer, II, 26, cited by Harrison, 307, who makes the apt comment. Thompson, 60, also remarks: 'If we ask, then, how Christianity had reached Ireland before 431, the answer is very obscure', and he does well to remind us (61, n. 10) that 'there is no direct evidence for Christianity in Ireland in the fourth century'.

[94] Jackson, 1953, 122; Thompson, on the other hand, adheres to the statement of Prosper and maintains that 'the bulk of the Christians in Ireland in 431 were Irish, not immigrants from Britain' (1985, 56, 64f.). He further suggests the possibility that it was in Patrick's earlier period as a deacon in Ireland that he began his work as a missionary and that this was with the permission or even encouragement of Palladius, whom 'it is not easy to visualise as a great missionary' (174f.). Nor does he see Patrick as Palladius' immediate successor: he may well have been 'at best the *third* Catholic bishop to go to Ireland', having succeeded the man who was appointed bishop on the occasion when he himself was rejected by his 'seniors' in Britain (170, 68ff.).

[95] Traces of anti-Pelagianism and Pelagianism in Patrick have been found by Nerney, 97f., 106ff., and criticised by Hanson, 1968, 173ff., and Hardinge, 29ff., respectively. I am glad to find that Thompson, 1985, 36, agrees with me: 'Although four popes had thundered against it, it seems to have passed Patrick by' – referring, of course, to Pelagianism. And, elsewhere, 54, n. 4, he reminds us that 'Patrick was not familiar with Augustine's *Confessions*', citing O'Meara, 1956, 190ff., and 1976, 44ff. In that case it is hardly likely that he had become familiar with the fifteen anti-Pelagian treatises.

have been sent to Ireland by the Pope as its 'first bishop' if he had been. Thus, if it was Pelagian influence which motivated the use of the filiation-formula found in memorials from Pembrokeshire and the neighbouring areas, neither Patrick nor Palladius could have been responsible for it. No doubt there were Christians in Ireland at the time of Palladius' mission, as Prosper tells us and as the busy two-way traffic between Wales and Ireland would lead us to expect, the descendants or successors of fourth-century traders or British slaves snatched from their homeland by raids like that of which Patrick himself was a victim but probably not, *pace* Jackson, the converts of British missionaries. The Irish settlers who came to south-west Wales or, at least, some of them may well have been members of these small Christian communities; but there is no evidence to prove that they were Pelagians. At the end of a characteristically animated exposition of his views on the subject Emrys Bowen once dismissed my mild reservations with the Parthian shot: 'The trouble with you historians is that you simply won't listen to what the archaeologists have to tell you!' Well, we have listened to them and re-examined the archaeological data, and we have found that the evidence is far from conclusive.

Bowen's thesis would have been much more sympathetically received at the turn of the century, when modern research into Pelagianism was only just burgeoning, when a writer on the Celtic Church could confidently assert that Pelagius was 'a Goidelic Celt educated at the monastery of Bangor Iscoed' and that 'the faith of the Goidelic Celts . . . is usually called, from its great exponent, Pelagianism', and when a great historian was propounding his theory that Pelagius 'descended from Irish settlers in Somerset, Devonshire or the south-west coast of Wales'.[96] It was also the time when Zimmer's *Pelagius in Irland* appeared and was rightly applauded by Souter and others for its seminal contribution to the establishment of a reliable text of Pelagius' commentary on the Pauline Epistles. Zimmer reminded his readers that the Irish Church was being blamed for a resurgence of Pelagianism as early as 640 in a letter from Pope John IV and that an Irish collection of canons dated around 700 twice cites Pelagius as an authority.[97] The *Book of Armagh*, a codex

[96] Willis Bund, 108; Bury, 1904, 26ff., 1905, 43, 296.

[97] The papal letter, written to the clergy of northern Ireland by John as Pope-elect and three other members of the Roman *curia*, has long been something of a puzzle, not least to me. But Cróinín, 505ff., has demonstrated that Bede's repetition of it in *Ecclesiastical History*, 2, 19 is based on a misunderstanding of the true reason for the letter, which was to censure the Irish for celebrating Easter, as Rome supposed, on the fourteenth day of the moon *contra orthodoxam fidem*; by doing this, the letter continues, they were 'trying to revive a new heresy from an old'. This old heresy was, of course, Pelagianism! But, as Cróinín rightly remarks, 'even the Romans realised that a Pelagian revival in Ireland would be a curious development, for they pointed out themselves *non solum per istos CC annos abolita est, sed et cotidie a nobis perpetua (sic) anathemate sepulta damnatur*' – 'Pelagianism has not only been dead for these two hundred years but also buried, being daily condemned by us under perpetual anathema'. John and his colleagues were replying to a letter sent from Ireland to Pope Severinus and attributed the error of the northern Irish to Pelagian denial of grace, since the celebration of Easter on the fourteenth day of the moon 'preempted the pasch and, by the same token, denied the efficacy of the Resurrection as the true instrument of man's redemption'. Bede, citing only excerpts from the letter, fell into the same trap and, as Cróinín points out, again links the same two errors in his *De temporum ratione*, 6. I am

dating from the late eighth or early ninth century, also contains several references to Pilagius (*sic*) as the author of a commentary on the Pauline Epistles, and, on the eve of completing his book, Zimmer had the great personal satisfaction of discovering the St Gall MS of that commentary, catalogued before 900.[98] The later Irish Church certainly reveals a considerable respect for the Pelagian commentary, which 'was popular in Irish circles for a long period when it was unknown (under that name) elsewhere'; but even Zimmer was forced to admit that the St Gall MS was composite in character and apparently the work of some Irish medieval scholar.[99] But he allowed his enthusiasm to carry him too far – 'his historical sense failed him'[100] – when he tried to retroject Pelagius' later popularity with the Irish into the period of his lifetime by arguing that he was an Irishman himself and began to formulate his teaching before leaving his native land – as did Esposito a little later with his 'curious theory' that Pelagius was not only Irish but may have converted Patrick before his departure from Ireland.[101]

'When the tide set from Ireland to the continent, the Irish missionaries took their Pelagius with them.'[102] Very true: there is evidence of the existence of manuscripts of the Pelagian commentary in three libraries on the continent, all of them connected with the Irish mission and one of them being St Gallen.[103] But that was a long time after the Irish immigrants set out for Wales and, according to Bowen's theory, brought *their* Pelagius with them. No one would be more pleased than the present writer if it were possible to establish that Pelagius' journey started in Ireland, that his Pelagianism began there and that its influence outlived him both there and in Wales into the sixth century. On the evidence at present available, however, such a conclusion would be pure fantasy, best left in the Celtic twilight to which it properly belongs.

not qualified to assess Croínín's case that the northern Irish were using the table of Victorius of Aquitaine and not the eighty-four-year cycle, as scholars have hitherto held; but his general conclusion may well be correct. If so, J. F. Kelly's remark, cited by Croínín, that 'Bede's intriguing and puzzling reference must remain just that' is no longer true, and yet another of Zimmer's bubbles has at last been pricked. The papal letter is not evidence for a seventh-century revival of Pelagianism in northern Ireland.

[98] Turner, 1902–3, 137. The first leaf of *Codex Sangallensis* 73, containing the author's name and prologue, was lost between the ninth and nineteenth centuries.

[99] Souter, 1907, 431. Turner, 1902–3, 138f., comments that the MS reveals a considerable degree of contamination and 'is not a faithful reproduction of the original Pelagius'. But, as Loyer, 79, reminds us, the choice of commentaries at this date must have been very limited; cf. Croínín, 505, n. 2.

[100] E. James, 362, recalling Kenney, 77: 'Heinrich Zimmer, the Ishmael of Celtic Studies, whose hand was against every man's'. Turner, 132, describes *Pelagius in Irland* as 'not so much about Pelagius as about his Commentary on St. Paul's Epistles, and not so much about Ireland as about Irish scholars and manuscripts on the continent'. Poor Zimmer seems to have been the cause of much wit in others; but it was he and Souter who laid the foundations for our present text of the commentary, and Souter generously acknowledged his debt to the pioneer work of his predecessor.

[101] Esposito, 134f.; Hanson, 1968, 38, n. 3.

[102] Turner, 1902–3, 137, citing *inter alia* Sedulius Scotus' reference to Pelagius' exposition of Romans 1, 17.

[103] Souter, 1922–31, 418.

A more plausible explanation of the persistence of Pelagianism in Britain has been recently advanced by Markus.[104] 'Is there any reason', he asks, 'why the British Church should not have been as inhospitable to the newly forged Augustinian orthodoxy as was Italy, or as indifferent as, apparently, that part of the Greek Church which was not positively sympathetic to Pelagius? The British Church might, for all we know, have been more hostile.' He suggests that there may have been 'a pre-Pelagian tradition' in Britain, 'perhaps containing a range of views similar to that found in Italy, perhaps even more drawn towards the Pelagian end of the spectrum'. The appeal for help against the British 'Pelagians' may have come from a new, 'orthodox' group – 'orthodox' in the new, African and Continental sense – opposed by Agricola on his return from the Continent to defend the faith of his father, Bishop Severianus, because it represented 'new-fangled ideas' imported from that quarter perhaps very recently. Markus stresses the conjectural nature of his suggestion; but it would tie in well with the opposition of Julian and his supporters in Italy, the hostility of some of the monks at Hadrumetum to Augustine's extreme views on free will and predestination, and the similar reaction of Cassian and the Semi-Pelagians. It might also explain the 'total disappearance from the subsequent record of a "heresy" which only an isolated and probably small group had ever recognised as a "heresy" in Britain'. This pre-Pelagian tradition, of course, could not be described as 'Pelagian' before the Pelagian controversy made explicit those elements in it which thereafter became known as 'Pelagian'.

What then have we gained by our long, hesitant trek across the Roman Empire from the eastern shores of the Mediterranean to the western isles in our pursuit of the last, lingering manifestations of Pelagianism in the years immediately following the condemnation of its eponymous 'founder'? Precious little, it must be admitted, in terms of hard, historical fact. But our journey will not have been in vain if we have at least succeeded in demonstrating that the heresy, 'the proudest heresy of all', continued to exercise a strong appeal far beyond the small circle of discredited ascetics with whom it originated. In the monasteries of southern Gaul it spoke to the condition of men of the stature of John Cassian, Vincent and Faustus, and it still speaks to all those who, like them, find themselves unable to endorse the doctrines of Augustine in their most uncompromising form; and, though driven out of Africa, Palestine, Italy, Asia Minor and Gaul and stifled almost at birth in Britain, it lived on to fight another day.

In the monasteries of the continent the old controversy went on simmering and disturbing the peace of the monks many centuries later, as in the debate between Henry of Lausanne and William of St. Thierry from 1133 to 1135, when Henry's rejection of 'the medieval rôle of the clergy as dispensers of God's grace in favour of the responsibility of the individual' was 'carried to extreme lengths involving Pelagianism: original sin was rejected . . . [and]

[104] Markus, 1986, 199ff.

baptism could not be conferred on infants without understanding'.[105] But the next great battle in England was to come in the fourteenth century, when that 'Doctor Profundus', Archbishop Thomas Bradwardine, wrote his *De Causa Dei* 'in revulsion against emphasis on free will and disregard of divine grace as preached in the schools' with William of Ockham as his main target.[106] 'The word Pelagian once again became common currency', and 'it is hard to know what the outcome would have been had not the Black Death of 1348–50 supervened, carrying off the greater part of the participants, Bradwardine included'.[107] It has been argued that even Langland's theological outlook in *Piers Plowman* is in fact Semi-Pelagian and that, in adopting it, he was merely accepting 'the standard solution to the problem of justification in his day' as advanced by Ockham and his followers.[108] But though the main issues around which controversy centred in the fourteenth century were still grace, free will and predestination, the original boundaries between Augustinianism and Pelagianism had by then become hopelessly blurred as scholars searched for a more contemporary statement of definitions, and names of existing heresies, such as Pelagianism, Donatism and Manicheism, were used almost indiscriminately to brand ideas which appeared to be unorthodox.[109] And thereby hangs another tale – for others to tell.

---

[105] Lambert, 50; for the full text of this debate see, for example, Moore, 46ff.

[106] Leff, 1957, 13.

[107] Leff, 1967, I, 302.

[108] Adams, 369, 374ff., and, for passages in the *Pardon* which are suggestive of Semi-Pelagianism, 377, 385, 390f., 393, 394f., 401.

[109] As, for example, in Albert the Great's *Compilatio de novo spiritu* (Leff, 1967, I, 311).

Recessional

'It is not easy to feel any deep emotion when Tweedledum defeats Tweedledee.'

E. A. THOMPSON[1]

'Oh, will it boote thee
To say a Philip or a Gregory,
A Harry, or a Martin taught thee thus?
Is not this excuse for mere contraries,
Equally strong? Cannot both sides say so?'

JOHN DONNE[2]

'What if Pelagius after all were more right than his detractors?'

H. D. LEWIS[3]

It is quite understandable that Edward Thompson, reflecting on the controversy between Augustine and Pelagius and accustomed to marshalling and analysing historical data, should find himself out of sympathy with the manner in which such theological debate tends to be conducted, with the apparent unreality of the issues involved and with the ambivalence of the conclusions reached. 'The mountains will go into labour, and there will be born – an absurd little mouse', he might well exclaim with the Roman poet or repeat the famous question with which the African Church Father began his attack on the 'stupidities of the philosophers': 'What has Athens to do with Jerusalem, the Academy with the Church?'[4] It is inevitable that, to a twentieth-century observer, Augustine and Pelagius must often seem to be as irrelevant and as unreasonable as Lewis Carroll's ineffectual siblings, when they hurl chunks of scripture at each other in turn, following these up with

---

[1] Thompson, 1984, 25. The eighteenth-century minor poet John Byrom seems to have felt much the same when he wrote his *Epigram on the Feuds between Handel and Bononcini*:

'Strange that such high dispute shou'd be
'Twixt Tweedledum and Tweedledee.'

But this is not the time or place to discuss the origins of these two gentlemen and their history before Alice met them!

[2] *Satyres* III, 95–9, in *The Poems*, ed. H. J. C. Grierson, Oxford 1933, 139f. It may be of interest to note that, in the same century, the Quaker George Fox addressed a similar question to an Anglican congregation at Ulverstone: 'You will say, Christ saith this and the apostles say this, but what canst thou say?' (*Journal*, ii. 512).

[3] *Morals and the New Theology*, London 1947, 138; I am indebted to the author for locating the precise reference for me. Its context is a defence of Tennant and 'other liberal thinkers' at the end of a discussion of Tennant's book *The Concept of Sin*, referred to in n. 3 to my *Introit*. 'To dismiss their books with contempt as "Pelagian treatises"', comments Lewis, 'is sheer evasion.'

[4] Horace, *Ars Poetica*, 139; Tertullian, *De Praescriptione Haereticorum* vii. 9 (PL 2, i. 23).

lengthy and tedious exegeses which prove only that their chosen citations, far from being conclusive, are capable of being interpreted in at least two different ways. Unable to perceive that 'arguments about scripture achieve nothing but a stomach-ache or headache',[5] they generally end up by dismissing each other's arguments with 'Nohow' or 'Contrariwise'. Their *modus pugnandi* reminds one of Stephen Leacock's two embattled knights, who believed that the best way to settle their differences was to lie down in turn and allow their adversary to jump upon them in full battle-order, until the demands of honour were satisfied and they themselves resembled a pair of flattened sardine-tins!

My second quotation suggests that Thompson is in very good company, that of the 'metaphysical' poet who became Dean of St. Paul's. Other poets too, relying on their imagination rather than reasoned argument or intellectual speculation, have shown irritation with theological debate and its consequences. We have already had occasion to note how, in the same century as Donne, John Milton expressed his irritation at 'the prelatical tradition of crowding free consciences and Christian liberties into canons of men'; elsewhere in the same work he complains of 'troublers and dividers of unity, who neglect and permit not others to unite those dissever'd pieces which are wanting to the body of Truth'.[6] A little earlier, Edmund Spenser was just as critical of the 'deep learning' which led to 'doubts among Divines and difference of texts' and so to a 'diversitie of sects and hateful heresies'.[7] Pascal, as I have commented before, though no poet, as far as I am aware, found the intellectual antics of the learned theologians of the Sorbonne so distasteful that he abandoned analytical reasoning for intuitive faith. Modern theologians too sometimes display impatience with the controversies of their forerunners and even their peers: Rahner, one of the foremost theologians of the present century, once warned of 'the danger of wild and empty conceptual acrobatics',[8] and Richard Hanson describes the behaviour of Jerome over Pelagius and of Theophilus over Chrysostom as an example of 'the magnifying of fairly trivial faults' as 'part of the stock-in-trade of ecclesiastical warefare in the fifth century'.[9] Theology, for all its uses, is not an exact science, and trying to treat it as if it were leads only to confusion and exposes it to derision; nowhere is this more likely to happen than in that grey area where saints and heretics have fought their battles to win the prize of orthodoxy.[10]

Orthodoxy was the prize for which Augustine and Pelagius fought their

---

[5] Wilken, 42, citing Tertullian, op. cit., xvi. 2 (PL 2, i. 35).

[6] *Areopagitica*, 550f.; see my n. 12 to c. II.

[7] *Prosopopoia or Mother Hubberds Tale*, 385, Globe ed., London/New York 1893, 516.

[8] Lampe, 1977, 228, quoting K. Rahner, *The Trinity*, London 1970, 48.

[9] Hanson, 1968, 136, n. 1.

[10] This is not a cheap gibe at theologians, many of whom are among my best friends; but not all of them seem to be aware of the risks involved in trying to draw fine distinctions between heretics and saints. 'The conflict between heresy and orthodoxy is not one between an established and generally accepted doctrinal tradition and attempts to subvert, change or modify it by innovations but between elements crystallised out of a pre-existing, undifferentiated range of acceptable doctrinal opinions' (Markus, 1986, 198).

battle in the fifth century, but the issues which they debated were by no means as trivial as they may now appear to have been: in their eyes such issues were, on the contrary, of paramount importance to the Christian Church. Modern theologians have a wide range of contemporary problems from which to pick and choose as possible subjects for their discussions – creation and the 'Big Bang', evolution and 'creationism', liberation theology and racism, sexism and feminism and homosexuality, abortion and artificial insemination, ecology and the state of the inner cities and so on, quite apart from more traditional topics in the fields of doctrine, Church history and biblical scholarship. Augustine and Pelagius, on the other hand, did not debate appropriate issues of their own choice; yet those which they did debate were every bit as real, as crucial and as relevant in the fifth century as those of present-day theology are in the late twentieth, and some of them were being given a thorough airing for the first time in the history of the Church. In handling these issues they were able to draw upon a legacy of doctrine which was common to both of them, and consequently, there were many basic assumptions which they shared and never thought it necessary to question. For example, both argued on the basis that the scriptures were infallible as long as they were correctly interpreted; both adhered to the classical idea of divine and human nature as static and unchanging; both were natural ascetics, so obsessed with the problem of sin that, whichever of them won the day, their debate would leave the Church in the West dominated by sin for centuries to come; both were so preoccupied with the salvation of the individual that they neglected to explore that healthier and saner dimension of corporate salvation which is a recurrent theme in both Old and New Testaments. But both remained convinced that the issues which united them were far less in need of discussion than those which kept them apart, and, once their battle-lines had been joined, neither was prepared to give an inch to his opponent, neither was able to conceive it possible that he was mistaken.

And so Tweedledum went on complaining that Tweedledee had 'spoiled his nice, new rattle', and Tweedledee was just as adamant in maintaining that he had done no such thing. Augustine's 'nice, new rattle' was, of course, his doctrine of grace, which he believed Pelagius to be deliberately spoiling by his excessive emphasis on the freedom of the will; Pelagius, on the other hand, held it to be an 'overvalent idea',[11] because it threatened to restrict or even destroy that freedom. The other issues which they debated were all peripheral

---

[11] I noted this phrase in the course of my reading but have been unable to track down its provenance; nor have I been able to find the word 'overvalent' in the dictionaries which I have consulted. But its meaning is clear, and it can be applied to Augustine's doctrine of grace in two ways: more obviously, of course, to the extreme positions which it led him to adopt but also to one of the more unhappy results of this doctrine over the centuries in the Western Church, namely, its neglect of the doctrine of the Holy Spirit. It is ironical that the man whose treatise *On the Trinity* is held by many to have been his greatest doctrinal work should have contributed to much to this neglect by failing to give the Holy Spirit its proper place in his doctrine of grace and thus, albeit unintentionally, causing it to become the Cinderella of Western theology. Fortunately, much has been done to redress the damage in recent years, especially by Charles Raven and Geoffrey Lampe in this country.

to the central issue at stake, and, in their treatment of the relationship of divine grace to human freedom, both made the same mistake, that of attempting to define the undefinable. Grace is not something that we can define: it is something that we can only experience. Human freedom too is 'just a fact of experience', and nothing that we can learn from physics or psychology will ever prevent us from using it as a working hypothesis in our daily lives. In the last of his Reith Lectures John Searle, from whom I have just quoted, after satisfying himself that he had been able to keep both his commonplace conceptions and his scientific belief in his discussions of the relationship between mind and body, had to admit that he was unable to reconcile the two sides of the 'characteristic philosophical conundrum' presented by the perennial question of freedom and determinism: He concludes that 'neither this discussion nor any other will ever convince us that our behaviour is unfree'.[12] If Searle, a Professor of Philosophy with a vast range of modern knowledge at his disposal, has in the end to confess himself unable to solve this conundrum, what chance had Augustine and Pelagius of solving it with their much more limited resources?

It might be interjected that they had at least at their disposal a weapon which the Reith Lecturer of 1984 seems to have discarded; they could invoke the Christian doctrine of grace. But it was precisely this doctrine which was the nub of the matter for them, and both Pelagius and, later, the Semi-Pelagians maintained that Augustine had distorted it by arguing for a form of predestination, even double predestination, which was contrary to the teaching of the Church. His justifiable insistence on the absolute priority of the divine initiative in the work of human salvation appeared to them to have led him to adopt an extreme position which threatened to undermine the whole foundation of the Christian life as an active and loving co-operation between God and man. All that he had succeeded in doing, albeit unwittingly and 'in the grip of his daimon', was to replace the Christian God with the Nature of the Stoics, endowed with the superhuman faculties of omnipotence, omniscience and omnipresence but robbed of the infinite power of love. Whether by Nature or God, man was programmed from the beginning of the world to find his freedom only by sacrificing it to the laws of the one or to the will of the other. Pelagius argued that Augustine had deprived man of his freedom to respond to God, Augustine that it was only by surrendering his apparent freedom that man could be truly free. By winning the argument in the end, Augustine left God to play 'the ancient rôles of Clotho the spinner of life-threads or Lachesis the dispenser of lots'[13] – to which I venture to add 'or Atropos the irresistible or all three working together in harmony'.[14]

But if this was how the Doctor of Grace may have appeared to his critics, Pelagius left himself just as open to the charge of having pushed his argument

---

[12] My quotations are taken from Searle's final lecture, 'The Freedom of the Will', as published in *The Listener* of 13 December 1984, 10ff.

[13] L. Dewart, 212, n. 35.

[14] The idea of the *Fates* or *Moirai* as a group of three daughters of Zeus appears as early as Hesiod, *Theogony*, 904–6, and reappears in Plato, *Republic* X, 614b–21d and especially in 617c.

to unacceptable extremes in the view of his opponents, who happened to include the leaders of the Western Church at that time. In his anxiety to stress the human rôle in the pursuit of righteousness he failed to give the divine rôle what they considered to be its proper place; instead, by his over-emphasis on the freedom of the human will and on its ability to cope with the problems presented by human weakness when faced by day-to-day pressures, he gave the appearance of having lapsed into a kind of naturalism. He believed in divine grace, however inadequately he may have defined it; he believed in it as a means of redemption and as a means of salvation available to all men and women alike; but either he had no doctrine of infused grace or he was unable to make it explicit. He was 'not a notably adroit theologian in the midst of controversy',[15] and his argument that the human will was itself a form of interior grace was totally rejected by his critics. It may be true that, as Frend suggests, 'in circumstances other than those of the first decades of the fifth century, his teaching might have provided a basis for a Christian ethic which would have set the seal on the conversion of the empire; medieval Europe might possibly have been built on different and more optimistic foundations.'[16] It may also be true that, even if he would not have been willing to admit it openly, he at least offered just a hint of a possible compromise by the care which he took to qualify his own emphasis on the ability of men to choose good by adding the phrase 'with the assistance of God' both at Diospolis and in his confession of faith presented to the Pope. But he was faced by an adversary who could not admit the possibility of any compromise on a matter which he believed to be of vital importance for the survival of the Christian Church, one whose 'worst enemy was his pursuit of controversy to the bitter end and his inability to concede the least right to an opponent'.[17] In his dealings with Pelagius, Augustine followed his normal practice of identifying his opponent's main weakness and of concentrating his attention upon it. The protagonists in the Pelagian controversy had stumbled upon one of the 'bundle of paradoxes' comprising our understanding of providence, 'which Christians also know as grace', 'religious truth which may be stated only as antinomy'.[18] 'If either of the symbolic positions espoused in Pelagianism and Augustinianism is taken by itself without the modifications that the other demands, if they are simply pitted against each other in an either/or fashion with no attempt at integration, one will inevitably be led to the untenable extremes that each position implies.'[19] This is a salutary warning, which John Cassian in the fifth century acknowledged at great personal cost, and we, in the late twentieth century, when the Christian Church is again at the

[15] R. F. Evans, 1968(a), 106.
[16] Frend, 1984, 675. More recently (1985, 139f.), Frend sums up the controversy between Augustine and Pelagius as follows: 'So, Augustine in arguing for the solidarity of mankind and making that bond of association sin was asserting a lasting truth. But this is not the whole truth about humanity. Pelagius was equally right in asserting the dignity and responsibility of man.'
[17] Frend, 1984, 676.
[18] I am quoting here from a most interesting article by J. S. Whale in *The Times* of 9 March 1985, entitled 'Paradoxes of Providence'.
[19] Haight, 42.

crossroads, ignore only at our own peril. We might also agree with the same writer's conclusion that 'because Christianity has unanimously judged that Augustine's is *essentially* the Christian doctrine, his view must provide the key to how this integration is to be effected, how the two poles will relate to one another.'[20] But Augustine and Pelagius were born into a world not yet ready to perceive and accept the truth of such a conclusion and the need for such an integration, and neither, engaged as he was in a heated debate, would have regarded it as anything other than a betrayal of his most cherished and fundamental beliefs.

For them it was a fight to a finish, and at the end of the day it was Augustine's high standing as an acknowledged leader of the Church and his proven skill as a controversialist that won the battle. After the Synod of Diospolis had announced its verdict in favour of Pelagius, Augustine's determination to destroy his opponent and all that he stood for hardened into an obsession. It was he who revived the subject of Pelagius' orthodoxy as soon as the records of Diospolis were made available for examination; it was he who masterminded the all-out campaign of the African Church to enlist the support of the Emperor and the Pope of Rome and to overcome the latter's reluctance to endorse an unambiguous condemnation of Pelagius and Celestius;[21] it was he who, indefatigable as ever, picked off Pelagius' main supporters one by one and reduced them to silence;[22] and it was he who continued the witch-hunt into the far corners of the Empire by ensuring that there would be no area of the Church in which Pelagius and his friends might be able to find asylum.[23]

Hans Küng, who has also experienced what it means to be submitted to treatment almost amounting to persecution at the hands of the leaders of his Church, though without, in his case, having to undergo the ultimate penalty for internal dissent, once made the pertinent comment that 'any heresy involves both a strengthening and a weakening of the Church': what is gained in certainty by a more precise formulation of doctrine is lost in vitality by trying to make this formulation too dogmatic.[24] It is a matter of opinion whether or not Augustine's treatment of Pelagius was, to say the least, uncharitable; it was certainly not in keeping with his usually kindly and sympathetic behaviour when dealing with fellow-Christians and may be excused as a justifiable reaction to provocation. But it was in keeping with the spirit and temper of theological debate in the fifth century, when white was white and black was black, when theologians had yet to learn and admit that there is more than one path leading to truth, that 'doctrine is not an end but a

[20] Ibid.; the emphasis is mine. The chapter from which I have quoted, entitled 'Augustine: grace and autonomy', is an admirable summary of the main issues in the Pelagian controversy as they relate to contemporary society.

[21] Patout Burns, 1979(b), analyses the part played by Augustine in this phase of controversy.

[22] Wermelinger, 210.

[23] H. Chadwick, 1983, 428ff. and 440, summarises and discusses the relevant letters – 4, 6 and 10 – in Divjak's collection.

[24] Küng, 1964, 99.

beginning'.[25] It would have been naïve of Pelagius to expect any better treatment than, for example, Priscillian of Avila and Rufinus of Aquileia had received before him. But it can be argued that, when the Church in its wisdom decided in the last resort to excommunicate him, it lost a potential source of vitality: it was depriving itself of the services of a committed Christian who had much to offer through his teaching and example to ordinary folk like the monks of Hadrumetum and Southern Gaul, incapable of fully appreciating a doctrine of grace which seemed to them to endanger the freedom of choice essential to their Christian way of life.

Oh, what a fall was there! Yes, and some of us must feel 'the dint of pity' for Pelagius.[26] For myself, I have to admit that, in trying to recount the vicissitudes of his star-crossed career, I may have shown more sympathy for him than the strict demands of historical objectivity permit. My thoughts have often strayed to his last days in Egypt – or wherever he may have been forced to spend them – and I have dared to hope that at the end there was someone who was not afraid to grant him that communion of which his Church had deprived him and the loss of which must have been for him 'the most unkindest cut of all'. He wanted above all else to be a good Christian, working for the reform of the Christian Church from within, he sincerely believed that his teaching was orthodox and consistent with that Church's tradition, and it was in order to prove this to his critics that he allowed himself to become involved in an arduous and prolonged controversy for which he was by ethos and training quite unsuited. And I have been reminded of how, in the midst of a time of even greater turmoil for the Church, Erasmus wrote to Jodocus Jonas of Erfurt to discourage him from too close an association with Martin Luther and to urge him to work instead for reform from within the Church. In his second letter he draws Jonas' attention to the shining example of two such reformers, whom he considered to have been true and sincere Christians. The first of these was Johan Vitrier, whom he had met in 1501 at the Franciscan house of St Omer in Artois, and after commenting that his 'jewel of a Vitrier' had indicated to him in the course of their conversation that he had found no theologian whose genius he admired more than Origen, he remarked that, when he had teased Vitrier by expressing some surprise that he should take pleasure in the writings of a heretic, he had received this prompt reply: 'The mind that produced so many learned works written with such fervour could not but have been the dwelling-place of the Holy Spirit.'[27]

[25] Haight, 42.

[26] Frend, 1985, 11, for example, confesses to 'an instinctive sympathy for history's runners-up', numbering Pelagius among them.

[27] *Erasmi Epistulae* IV, 1211, 508; Allen, 1918, 89ff. Bainton, 1977, 85, claims that 'he [Vitrier] was for Erasmus the perfect exemplification of the *philosophia Christi*' and also points out that 'Vitrier passed into oblivion' unlike the second of Erasmus' two reformers, John Colet. He may not have suffered that fate but 'he constantly inveighed against ecclesiastical abuses and, though he never challenged the doctrines of the Christian Church, was often accused of heresy' (Livingstone, 117). I am indebted to my friend Ceri Davies for reminding me of this passage in Erasmus.

This is true of Origen, whom Jerome himself once described as 'the greatest teacher of the Church since the apostles',[28] and of whom Henry Chadwick writes: 'If the meaning of orthodoxy is to wish to believe as the Church believes, then there can be virtually no hesitation in pronouncing Origen as orthodox. . . . The model of Christ himself is always before his eyes.'[29] It is true of Luther, of whom Erasmus may well have been reminded by Vitrier's judgement of Origen. And although his works fall short of those of Origen and Luther both in number and in quality, it is surely true also of Pelagius. 'What if Pelagius after all were more right than his detractors?' It is possible that our re-examination of the strengths and weaknesses of both sides in the Pelagian controversy may have persuaded some that he was or, at least, that his theology of grace could be adjudged no less 'orthodox' than that of Augustine. But in trying to arrive at an objective decision when both sides are in some respects right and, in others, wrong it would be more prudent to keep an open mind. The principal significance of the Pelagian controversy lies, after all, not in the personalities who were involved in it nor even in the arguments which they advanced but in the issues which were raised and which are as important today as they were in the fifth century of the Christian era, 'the very mainspring of the Christian religion and life'.[30] But 'now we have talked enough about this problem to satisfy a sensible man.'[31]

[28] H. Chadwick, 1966, 97; Jerome, pref. to *Onomasticon* or *Liber de nominibus Hebraicis* (PL 23, 772): *post apostolos ecclesiarum magistrum*.

[29] H. Chadwick, 1966, 122. Chadwick comments that Origen 'wanted to be a Christian, not a Platonist'; Pelagius wanted to be known as a Christian, not a Stoic, and saw himself as a traditionalist, defending the true faith against the innovations of Augustine. Wilken, 178ff., maintains that Arius too could be said to have been the traditionalist in the Nicene controversy and Athanasius and his supporters the innovators, adding that 'all heresies are backward-looking'.

[30] Sell, 143.

[31] William of St Thierry; the translation is that of Moore, 51.

Appendix I

Works attributable to Pelagius

At first glance this list may seem to be an impressive one but closer inspection will reveal that only seven works listed have survived intact; the remainder are either lost or represented only by fragments. Many others have been attributed to Pelagius at various times in the past but must now be declared to be either *adespota* or attributable to other writers of the Pelagian persuasion; they have not been included in my list nor have the statements made by Pelagius at the Synod of Diospolis, which will be found in full in Appendix II.

Uncertainty as to Pelagian authorship was an inevitable result of the excommunication of the Pelagians and the general attempt to suppress their opinions in the aftermath of the controversy. As a result works of Pelagius in circulation in the fifth century and those immediately following it tended to be attributed *faute de mieux* to more reputable authors. The earlier editors of Migne's *Patrologia Latina* had therefore to be content with tacking them on to the works of Hilary, Athanasius, Ambrose, Jerome, Paulinus of Nola, Sulpicius Severus and, save the mark!, even Augustine. But when interest in Pelagius began to revive and scholars to react to the patent hostility with which he seemed to have been treated by their predecessors, some of them took this as the signal for a free-for-all: Plinval, for example, published a list which contained almost every work which could be attributed to Pelagius on any conceivable ground, though he later found it necessary to recant and remove a number of them after more careful consideration.

In this list readers will find only the basic references which will enable them to locate Pelagius' works in the main collections of the writings of the Fathers of the Church. For more detailed information as to their provenance and exegetical history they are referred to the bibliographies contained in PLS 1, 1101–9 and the most recent volume of the *Dictionnaire de spiritualité, ascetique, mystique, doctrine et histoire* (Vol. 12B, 2889–942), which is more up-to-date and also more comprehensive and reliable.

A. Extant works

1.   *Commentary on the Epistles of Paul* (*Expositiones XIII Epistularum Pauli Apostoli*): PLS 1, 1110–374; CPL 728.

2.   *Letter to Demetrias* (*Epistula ad sacram Christi virginem Demetriadem*): PL 30, 15–45; 33, 1099–120; CPL 737 = 633, 1.

3. *Confession of Faith* (*Libellus fidei ad Innocentium papam*): PL 45, 1716, 18; 48, 488–91; CPL 731 = 368, 236 = 633, 16.

4. *On the Christian Life* (*Liber de vita christiana*): PL 40, 1031–46; 50, 383–402; CPL 730.

5. *Letter to Celantia* (*Epistula ad Celantiam*): PL 22, 1204–29; 61, 723–36; CSEL 29, 436–59; 56, 329–56; CPL 745.

6. *On the Divine Law* (*Epistula ad Thesiphontem de scientia divinae legis*: PL 30, 105–16; CPL 740.

7. *On Virginity* (*Epistula ad Claudiam de virginitate* or *Ad Mauritii filiam laus virginitatis*): PL 18, 77–90; 20, 227–42; 30, 163–75; 56, 329–56; 103, 671–84; CSEL 1, 225–50; CPL 741.

B. Fragments

8. *On the Trinity* (*Libri tres de fide Trinitatis*): PL 39, 2198–200; PLS 1, 1544–60; CPL 748a–f.

9. *Extracts from the Divine Scriptures* (*Eclogarum ex divinis scripturis Liber*): PL 23, 519–26; 48, 594–6; CSEL 42, 52–107; 60, 547; CPL 750.

10. *To the Widow Livania* (*Libellus exhortatorius ad quandam Livaniam viduam*): PL 48, 598; CPL 754.

11. *On Nature* (*Liber de natura*): PL 48, 599–606; CSEL 42, 190–200; 60, 231–99, 456f.; CPL 753.

12. *Letter (II) to Augustine* (*Epistula ad Augustinum episcopum* or *Chartula defensionis suae*): PL 48, 608; CSEL 42, 111–13.

13. *Letter to a Friend* (*Epistula ad amicum suum quendam presbyterum*): PL 48, 609; CPL 749b.

14. *In Defence of Free Will* (*Pro libero arbitrio libri IV*): PL 48, 611–13; PLS 1, 1539–43; CSEL 42, *passim*; CPL 749.

15. *Letter to Pope Innocent* (*Epistula purgationis ad Innocentium papam*): PL 20, 608–11; 48, 610–11; CSEL, 42, 150–81; CPL 749a.

16. *Fragments from the Collection of Sedulius Scotus* (*Fragmenta e collectione Sedulii Scoti*): PLS 1, 1570; CPL 756.

17–18. *Pelagian Fragments of Vienna* (*Fragmenta pelagiana Vindobonensia*): PLS 1, 1561–70; CPL 755.

19. *To a Widow* (*Liber primus ad viduam*): PL 23, 586; 44, 329; CSEL 42, 68.

C. Lost Works

20. *Letter to Paulinus* (*Epistula ad sanctum virum Paulinum episcopum*): v. PL 44, 378; CSEL 42, 154.

21. *Letter to Constantius* (*Epistula ad sanctum Constantium episcopum*: ibid.

22. *Letter (I) to Augustine* (*Epistula ad Augustinum episcopum*): v. PL 48, 606; CSEL 42, 104.

The Synod of Diospolis

At the Synod of Diospolis in A.D. 415 Pelagius was confronted with a number of statements which he was alleged to have made in his writings as well as others attributed to Celestius. These are given below together with his replies and the comments of the Synod. The Latin text will be found in *PP* i. 2–xx. 44 (PL 44, 320–46) (CSEL 42, 51–99), and the translation is my own, as elsewhere in this book except where otherwise indicated.

1. A man cannot be without sin, unless he has acquired a knowledge of the Law.
   Pelagius: I did indeed say this but not in the sense in which they understand it. I did not say that a man who has acquired a knowledge of the Law cannot sin, but that by knowledge of the Law he is helped not to sin, as it is written: 'He hath given them a law for help.'
   Synod: What Pelagius has said is not inconsistent with [the teaching of] the Church.

2. All men are governed by their own will.
   P.: This I stated on account of free will, which God helps when it chooses good; man, however, when he sins, is himself to blame as of free will.
   S.: Nor is this inconsistent with the teaching of the Church.

3. In the day of judgement the unrighteous and sinners are not to be spared but to be consumed in eternal fires.
   P.: I stated this in accordance with the Gospel, in which it is said of sinners: 'These shall go away into eternal punishment but the righteous to life eternal.' And if anyone believes differently, he is an Origenist.
   S.: This too is not inconsistent with [the teaching of] the Church.

4. Evil does not enter our thoughts.
   P.: This I did not state in this way. What I did state was that the Christian ought to take pains not to think evil thoughts.
   S.: [This, as was proper, the Bishops approved.]

5. The kingdom was promised even in the Old Testament.
   P.: This can be proved by the Scriptures but heretics deny it in disparagement of the Old Testament. I, however, said this following the authority of the Scriptures, since it is written in the prophet Daniel: 'The

135

saints shall receive the kingdom of the Most High.'

S.: Nor is this inconsistent with the faith of the Church.

6. A man can be without sin, if he wishes.

P.: I did indeed say that a man can be without sin and keep the commandments of God, if he wishes, for this ability has been given to him by God. However, I did not say that any man can be found who has never sinned from his infancy up to his old age, but that, having been converted from his sins, he can be without sin by his own efforts and God's grace, yet not even by this means is he incapable of change for the future.

[Other statements alleged to have been made by Pelagius in a letter and another work addressed to a widow were also cited against him.]

P.: The rest of the statements cited are not in my works nor have I ever said such things.

S.: Since you deny having written such things, would you anathematise those who hold them?

P.: I anathematise them as fools but not as heretics, since there is no dogma [respecting these opinions].

S.: Since Pelagius has now anathematised with his own utterance this foolish talk which has been introduced, rightly replying that a man can be without sin with the help and grace of God, let him now reply to the other points in the accusation.

7. [Statements were then cited which were said to have been found in the teachings of Celestius:]

(a) Adam was created mortal and would have died whether he sinned or not.

(b) Adam's sin injured only himself and not the human race.

(c) The Law sends us to the kingdom no less than the Gospel.

(d) There were men without sin before Christ's coming.

(e) New-born infants are in the same state as Adam was before his transgression.

(f) The whole human race neither dies through Adam's death or transgression nor rises again through the resurrection of Christ.

[Further points were next introduced in connection with a mention of Augustine's name, having been transmitted to him by Catholic brethren in Sicily:]

(g) A man can be without sin, if he wishes.

(h) Infants have eternal life, even if unbaptised.

(i) Rich men who have been baptised, unless they renounce everything, are not credited with any good that they may seem to have done nor can they possess the kingdom of God.

P.: On the statement that man can be without sin I have spoken earlier; however, on the statement that there were men without sin before the Lord's coming I also say that before Christ's coming some men lived holy and righteous lives according to the teaching of the Holy Scriptures. As for the rest of the statements, even by their own testimony they were not made by me, and I am not obliged to satisfy them on these counts; yet, for the satisfaction of the Holy Synod, I anathematise those who hold or have ever held such opinions.

S.: To these points aforesaid Pelagius, who is present, has given us adequate and proper satisfaction by anathematising those which were not his.

8. The Church here is without spot or wrinkle.

P.: I have said this but in the sense that the Church is cleansed by the laver from every spot and wrinkle and that the Lord wishes it to remain so.

9. [Statements were then cited from a book by Celestius chapter by chapter but rather according to the sense than the actual words, since the accusers had been unable to adduce all the words:]

(a) We do more than is commanded in the Law and the Gospel.

P.: This they have set down as my statement; what I said, however, was consistent with what Paul states on the subject of virginity: 'I have no commandment of the Lord.'

S.: This too the Church accepts.

(b) God's grace and help are not given for single actions but consist in free will or in the Law and teaching.

(c) God's grace is given according to our merits, since he seems to be unjust if he gives it to sinners.

[By these words, according to Augustine, he implied: For that reason grace itself has been located in my will according as I have been worthy or unworthy of it. For if we do all things by grace, it is not we who are overcome by sin when we are overcome by sin but the grace of God, which wished to help us by all means and was not able to do so.

(d) If it is the grace of God when we overcome sin, then He Himself is at fault when we are overcome by sin, because He has been either unable or unwilling entirely to protect us.

P.: It is for those who say that these are the opinions of Celestius to look to it whether they really are his. I, however, have never held such views and I anathematise the man who does hold them.

S.: The Holy Synod accepts this condemnation of yours of these false statements.

(e) Every man is able to possess all virtues and graces [and this implies the removal of the diversity of graces which the Apostle teaches].

P.: I have said it but they have made an accusation which is both malicious and inept; for I do not remove the diversity of graces but I say that God gives all graces to him who has been worthy to receive them, even as He bestowed them on Paul.

S.: Your interpretation of the gift of graces, which are concentrated in the Holy Apostle, conforms to the interpretation of the Church.

(f) Men cannot be called sons of God, unless they have been made completely free from sin.

(g) Forgetfulness and ignorance are not subject to sin, since they occur not according to the will but according to necessity.

(h) Will is not free if it stands in need of God's help, since everyone has it in his own will either to do or not to do something.

(i) Our victory comes not from God's help but from free will. [Augustine adds that he, that is, Celestius, was said to have made this inference in the following words: 'The victory is ours, since we took up arms of our own will, just as the fault is ours when we are overcome, since we neglected to arm ourselves of our will.' And, Augustine goes on to say, he cited as evidence from the Apostle Peter 'we are partakers of the divine nature', from which he formed this conclusion: 'for if our soul is not without sin, therefore God too is subject to sin, since part of him, that is, our soul, is beholden to sin.']

(j) Pardon is not given to the repentant according to the grace and mercy of God but according to the merit and efforts of those who have become worthy of mercy through repentance.

S.: What does the monk Pelagius say in reply to these points which have been read out? For the Holy Synod and God's Holy Catholic Church condemn them.

P.: I say again that these opinions are not mine by their own testimony, and I am not obliged to give satisfaction for them. Those statements, however, which I have admitted to be mine I maintain to be correct; but those which I have said not to be mine I condemn according to the judgement of the Holy Church, pronouncing anathema on everyone who opposes and contradicts the teachings of the Holy Catholic Church. For I believe in the Trinity of the one substance and in all things in accordance with the teaching of the Holy Catholic Church. If anyone has opinions, however, which are different from hers, let him be anathema.

S.: Now since we have received satisfaction in respect of the charges brought against the monk Pelagius in his presence and since he gives his assent to sound doctrines but condemns and anathematises those contrary to the faith of the Church, we adjudge him to belong to the communion of the Catholic Church.

Pelagius was thus acquitted on the basis of his replies to the charges concerned with statements which he admitted to have been his own and of his condemnation of those which he denied ever having made. But to complete the picture and to explain why it was that Augustine was so dissatisfied with the outcome of the Synod we need to read the latter's comment at the end of his account of the proceedings as recorded in *PP* xxi. 45 (PL 44, 346) (CSEL 42, 99):

They judged him as one of whom they knew nothing, especially in the absence of those who had drawn up the indictment against him, a man whom they were thus quite unable to judge with greater care; yet, in spite of this, they utterly destroyed the heresy itself. Those, however, who know what Pelagius has been in the habit of teaching or who have

138

resisted his arguments or who congratulate themselves on having been set free of his error, how can they possibly not regard him as suspect, when they read his disingenuous confession condemning his past errors but so expressed as to imply that he never held opinions different from those to which approval was given by his judges on the basis of his replies?

In other words, Pelagius went scot-free; but his heresy stands condemned!

Appendix III

The Pelagian controversy: a summary

c. 380   Pelagius arrives in Rome and gains a high reputation as an ascetic, spiritual mentor and moral reformer.

390–9   He meets Celestius and, towards the end of the decade, Rufinus the Syrian.

c. 402–5   He expresses strong dissent from the view of grace revealed in Book X of Augustine's *Confessions* and writes his *On the Trinity* and *Extracts*.

406–9   He writes his *Commentary on the Pauline Epistles*.

c. 409   He leaves Italy and arrives in Palestine via Carthage.

411/12   Celestius, who stays in Carthage, is condemned by the Council there for his heretical opinions; he leaves soon after for the East. Augustine attacks the teachings of Celestius and Rufinus the Syrian on original sin and infant baptism in his *On the Merits and Forgiveness of Sins and Infant Baptism*.

412   He follows this up with his *On the Spirit and the Letter*.

413   Pelagius comes under attack from Jerome in Palestine. He writes his *Letter to Demetrias* but Jerome also writes to her, taking the opportunity to warn her against adherents of Origenism, among whom he now counts Pelagius.

c. 414   Pelagius defends himself in his treatise *On Nature*.

415   Augustine writes his *On Nature and Grace* in reply. He also sends Orosius to Jerome, armed with two important letters and an anti-Pelagian dossier to alert Jerome against the Pelagians. Jerome refers to them unfavourably in his *Commentary on Jeremiah* and redoubles his efforts to discredit them in his *Letter to Ctesiphon* and, later, his *Dialogue against the Pelagians*, begun about this time.

    Orosius' charges against Pelagius and Celestius are dismissed as not proven by the Synod of Jerusalem, and he responds with his *Book in Defence against the Pelagians*. Pelagius is accused of heresy by Heros and Lazarus but is acquitted by the Synod of Diospolis. Celestius is ordained priest at Ephesus but Augustine renews his attack with his *On the Perfection of Man's Righteousness*.

c. 416	Pelagius writes his treatise *In Defence of Free Will* in response to the attacks of Orosius, Jerome and Augustine.

| 416 | Pelagius and Celestius are condemned by Councils at Milevis and Carthage. Pope Innocent responds to three letters from the African bishops and the news of an attack on Jerome's monastery allegedly by Pelagians by excommunicating Pelagius and Celestius, while giving Pelagius an opportunity to justify himself either by appearing before him in Rome or by letter. Pelagius sends him a *Letter in Justification* and *Confession of Faith*, supported by a letter of commendation from Praylius, John's successor as Bishop of Jerusalem. Innocent dies early in 417, and the documents are received by Zosimus, his successor. |

| 417 | Augustine gives wide circulation to his work *On the Proceedings of Pelagius*. Expelled from Constantinople by the Patriarch Atticus, Celestius now appeals to Pope Zosimus, submits his *Confession of Faith* to him and appears before a tribunal at Rome. Zosimus reserves judgement for two months pending the appearance before him of Celestius' accusers but informs the African bishops that he is acquitting Pelagius for lack of firm evidence against him and asks them to recognise that Pelagius and Celestius have not yet been finally cut off from the Church. |

| 418 | Augustine responds with his treatise *On the Grace of Christ and Original Sin*, and the African bishops by again writing to Zosimus, respectfully asking him to confirm the decision of his predecessor. The Emperor Honorius now intervenes from Ravenna, alarmed by the news of an assault by Pelagians on a retired official in Rome and reports of unrest there. He issues an imperial rescript in which he condemns all those who deny the Fall and orders the banishment of Pelagius and Celestius from Rome, assuming them to be still there. The Council of Carthage passes a series of nine canons against Pelagianism, and Zosimus, now under great pressure from the African bishops as well as the opponents of the Pelagians in Rome, publishes and circulates an *Epistula Tractoria* condemning Pelagius and Celestius and excommunicating them. After further intervention by Augustine, Pelagius is expelled from Jerusalem and then from Palestine and, possibly after a brief stay in Antioch, seeks refuge in Egypt with a small number of his remaining supporters, who are already there. In the meantime eighteen Italian bishops, led by Julian of Eclanum, refuse to subscribe to Zosimus' *Epistula*, their appeal is rejected, and they are condemned, deposed from office, and, after a final refusal to subscribe, excommunicated and banished from the towns of Italy. |

| 419 | Julian at once begins to attack Augustine's 'neo-Manicheism', and Augustine responds with Book I of his *On Marriage and Concupiscence* |

and *On the Soul and its Origin*. Julian replies to the former with his four books *To Turbantius*.

420–1   On receipt of Julian's *To Turbantius*, *Letter to Rufus* and *Letter to the Romans* Augustine publishes the second book of his *On Marriage and Concupiscence* and his work *Against Two Letters of the Pelagians*. Julian replies with his *To Florus* in eight books, written in Cilicia while he is under the protection of Theodore of Mopsuestia.

421–2   Augustine writes six books *Against Julian* to refute the charges made in *To Turbantius*.

426–7   Augustine sends his treatises *On Grace and Free Will* and *On Rebuke and Grace* to allay the doubts of the monks at Hadrumetum.

c. 428   Julian, forced to leave Cilicia, arrives with three other Italian bishops in Constantinople and appeals to the Emperor there and the Patriarch Nestorius; the latter writes to Pope Celestine at Rome for confirmation of the condemnation of the Italian bishops and is asked by the Pope to condemn them and confirm the sentence passed on them by the Church in Rome. His response is pre-empted by an imperial degree expelling Julian and his supporters from the city and mainly brought about by the submission by Marius Mercator of a *Memorandum on the Name of Celestius*.

428–9   Augustine responds to Prosper's and Hilary's anxiety about the monks of Provence with his treatises *On the Predestination of the Saints* and *On the Gift of Perseverance*.

430   Augustine dies, leaving his reply to Julian's treatise *To Florus* unfinished.

431   The Council of Ephesus condemns 'the opinions of Celestius' and confirms the deposition of Julian and his supporters. Julian again flees and returns to Italy, where he is refused permission to receive communion by Pope Sixtus III.

c. 443–5 Julian dies in Sicily.

The Drinking Song of Pelagius

Pelagius lived in Kardanoel
And taught a doctrine there,
How whether you went to Heaven or Hell,
It was your own affair;
How whether you found eternal joy
Or sank forever to burn,
It has nothing to do with the Church, my boy,
But was your own concern.
Oh, he didn't believe
In Adam and Eve,
He put no faith therein!
His doubts began with the fall of man,
And he laughed at original sin!
With my row-ti-tow, ti-oodly-ow,
He laughed at original sin!

Whereat the Bishop of old Auxerre
(Germanus was his name),
He tore great handfuls out of his hair,
And he called Pelagius Shame:
And then with his stout Episcopal staff
So thoroughly thwacked and banged
The heretics all, both short and tall,
They rather had been hanged.
Oh, he thwacked them hard, and he banged them long,
Upon each and all occasions,
Till they bellowed in chorus, loud and strong,
Their orthodox persuasions.
With my row-ti-tow, ti-oodly-ow,
Their orthodox persuasions.

Now the Faith is old and the devil is bold,
Exceedingly bold indeed;
And the masses of doubt that are floating about
Would smother a mortal creed.
But we that sit in a sturdy youth

And still can drink strong ale,
Oh – let us put it away to unfallible truth,
Which always shall prevail!
And thank the Lord
For the temporal sword,
And howling heretics too,
And whatever good things
Our Christendom brings,
But especially barley brew!
With my row-ti-tow, ti-oodly-ow,
Especially barley brew!

After subjecting my readers to many *longueurs* in the course of this little book, I feel obliged to offer them by way of compensation this ditty from the pen of one who could find humour in any person or subject, Hilaire Belloc. It comes from his *farrago* entitled *The Four Men* and is elsewhere found under a different title: 'Song of the Pelagian Heresy for the Strengthening of Men's Backs and the very Robust Outthrusting of Doubtful Doctrine and the Uncertain Intellectual'. I am indebted to my friends Lisbeth David and Lou Matthews for drawing my attention to it and subsequently unearthing it along with the music to which it can be sung. Even Pelagius has his funny side.

Short Reading List

The books listed below will give readers who may wish to extend their knowledge of the various aspects of the Pelagian controversy a reasonably comprehensive introduction. They are listed in order of publication but the bibliography must be consulted for the full details.

J. Burnaby, *Amor Dei*
G. de Plinval, *Pélage: ses écrits, sa vie et sa réforme*
J. J. O'Meara, *The Young Augustine*, p/b
J. Ferguson, *Pelagius*
H. I. Marrou, *St Augustine and His Influence through the Ages*
E. Gilson, *The Christian Philosophy of St Augustine*
F. van der Meer, *Augustine the Bishop*
G. Bonner, *Augustine: Life and Controversies*
P. R. L. Brown, *Augustine of Hippo: a Biography*, p/b
R. F. Evans, *Pelagius: Inquiries and Reappraisals*
E. TeSelle, *Augustine the Theologian*
G. Bonner, *Augustine and Modern Research on Pelagianism*
R. A. Markus, ed., *Augustine: a Collection of Critical Essays*, p/b
P. R. L. Brown, *Religion and Society in the Age of St Augustine*
J. N. D. Kelly, *Jerome: His Life, Writings and Controversies*
E. Portalié, *A Guide to the Thought of St Augustine*
O. Wermelinger, *Rom und Pelagius*
D. Bentley-Taylor, *Augustine: Wayward Genius*
H. I. Marrou (with A.-M. La Bonnardière), *St Augustin et l'augustinisme*, p/b
W. T. Smith, *Augustine: His Life and Thought*, p/b
G. R. Evans, *Augustine on Evil*
W. H. C. Frend, *Saints and Sinners in the Early Christian Church*, p/b
H. Chadwick, *Augustine*, p/b

Translations

A Select Library of the Nicene and Post-Nicene Fathers, Michigan, 1974
The Works of Aurelius Augustinus, Edinburgh, 1871–6
Ancient Christian Writers, Westminster, Maryland/London, 1946–
Fathers of the Church, New York/Washington, 1948ff., 1960ff.
Library of the Christian Classics, Philadelphia, 1953, 1955

The Essential Augustine, ed. V. J. Bourke, Indianopolis, Indiana, 1964

Confessions, City of God, Harmondsworth, 1961, 1964 (Penguin Classics)

Confessions, City of God, Select Letters, London/Cambridge, Mass., 1957ff. (Loeb Classical Library)

Walking in the Light: The Confessions of St Augustine, D. Winter, London/ Wheaton, Illinois, 1986 (paraphrased selection)

Abbreviations

(a) Works of Augustine cited:

B	On Baptism, VII (De baptismo contra Donatistas)
C	Confessions, XIII (Confessiones)
CD	Against Cresconius the Donatist, IV (Contra Cresconium grammaticum partis Donati)
CG	On the City of God, XXII (De civitate Dei)
E	Enchiridion on Faith, Hope and Charity (Enchiridion ad Laurentium de fide, spe, caritate)
FC	On Free Choice, III (De libero arbitrio)
GC	On the Grace of Christ (De gratia Christi)[1]
GFC	On Grace and Free Choice (De gratia et libero arbitrio ad Valentinum)
GP	On the Gift of Perseverance (De dono perseverantiae)
H	On Heresies (De haeresibus ad Quodvultdeum)
IWJ	Incomplete Work against Julian, VI (Opus imperfectum contra Iulianum)
J	Against Julian, VI (Contra Iulianum haeresis Pelagianae defensorem)
L	Letters (Epistolae)
LCG	Literal Commentary on Genesis, XII (De Genesi ad litteram)
LParm	Against the Letter of Parmenian, III (Contra epistolam Parmeniani)
LPet	Against the Letters of Petilian, III (Contra epistolas Petiliani Donatistae)
MBC	On the Moral Behaviour of the Catholic Church and of the Manichees, II (De moribus Ecclesiae Catholicae et de moribus Manichaeorum)
MC	On Marriage and Concupiscence, II (De nuptiis et concupiscentia)
MFS	On Merits and Forgiveness of Sins and Infant Baptism, III (De peccatorum meritis et remissione et de baptismo parvulorum)
NG	On Nature and Grace against Pelagius (De natura et gratia contra Pelagium)
OS	On Original Sin (De peccato originali)[1]
PMR	On the Perfection of Man's Righteousness (De perfectione iustitiae hominis)
PO	Against the Priscillianists and Origenists (Contra Priscillianistas et Origenistas ad Orosium)

[1] I have listed the two volumes of the treatise On the Grace of Christ and on Original Sin separately for convenience.

PP	*On the Proceedings of Pelagius* (*De gestis Pelagii*)[2]
PS	*On the Predestination of the Saints* (*De praedestinatione Sanctorum*)
R	*Retractations*, II (*Retractationes*)
RG	*On Rebuke and Grace* (*De correptione et gratia*)
S	*Sermons* (*Sermones*)
SL	*On the Spirit and the Letter* (*De spiritu et littera*)
SO	*On the Soul and its Origin*, IV (*De anima et eius origine*)
T	*On the Trinity*, XV (*De Trinitate*)
TLP	*Against Two Letters of the Pelagians*, IV (*Contra duas epistolas Pelagianorum ad Bonifacium Papam*)
VQS	*On Various Questions for Simplicianus* (*De diversis quaestionibus VII ad Simplicianum*)

---

[2] The title of the treatise *De Gestis Pelagii* has appeared in various forms. Augustine himself refers to it in *OS* 15 as *De Gestis Palaestinis*, and Prosper, *Against the Collator*, also describes it thus, while Possidius names it as *Contra Gesta Pelagii*. It is sometimes entitled *On the Activities of Pelagius* in modern works.

(b) Journals and works of reference:

AB	*Analecta Bollandiana*
AC	*Archaeologia Cambrensis*
ACant	*Archaeologia Cantiana*
AM	*Augustinus Magister*
AS	*Augustinian Studies*
AThA	*Année théologique augustinienne*
ATR	*Anglican Theological Review*
BA	*Bibliothèque Augustinienne, Oeuvres de Saint Augustin*
BTRL	*Bulletin of the John Rylands Library*
BSR	*Biblioteca di Scienze Religiose*
CC	*Corpus Christianorum, series Latina*
CMCS	*Cambridge Medieval Celtic Studies*
CPL	*Clavis Patrum Latinorum*
CQR	*Church Quarterly Review*
CR	*Clergy Review*
CRAI	*Comptes rendus de l'Académie des Inscriptions et Belles Lettres*
CSEL	*Corpus Scriptorum Ecclesiasticorum Latinorum*
CTJ	*Calvin Theological Journal*
DR	*The Dublin Review*
DTC	*Dictionnaire de Théologie Catholique*
EHR	*English Historical Review*
ET	*Expository Times*
HJ	*Hibbert Journal*
HTR	*Harvard Theological Review*
IER	*Irish Ecclesiastical Record*
IHS	*Irish Historical Studies*
JBAA	*Journal of the British Archaeological Association*
JEH	*Journal of Ecclesiastical History*
JRIC	*Journal of the Royal Institute of Cornwall*
JRS	*Journal of Roman Studies*
JRSAI	*Journal of the Royal Society of Antiquaries in Ireland*
JTS	*Journal of Theological Studies*
KTR	*King's Theological Review*
PAPS	*Proceedings of the American Philosophical Society*
PBA	*Proceedings of the British Academy*

PCA	*Proceedings of the Classical Association*
PG	*Patrologiae cursus completus, series Graeca*
PL	*Patrologiae cursus completus, series Latina*
PLS	*Patrologiae cursus completus, series Latina, supplementum*
RA	*Recherches augustiniennes*
RB	*Revue bénédictine*
RE	*Real-Encyclopädie der klassischen Altertumswissenschaft*
REA	*Revue des études augustiniennes*
REL	*Revue des études latines*
RHE	*Revue d'histoire ecclésiastique*
RPh	*Revue de philologie, de littérature et d'histoire anciennes*
RPThK	*Realencyclopädie für protestantische Theologie und Kirche*
RSR	*Recherches de science religieuse*
RThAM	*Recherches de théologie ancienne et mediévale*
SC	*Studia Celtica*
SH	*Studia Hibernica*
SP	*Studia Patristica*
STL	*Studia Theologica Lundensia*
TC	*The Churchman*
TCR	*The Contemporary Review*
ThL	*Theologische Literaturzeitung*
ThQ	*Theologische Quartalschrift*
THSC	*Transactions of the Honourable Society of Cymmrodorion*
UJA	*Ulster Journal of Archaeology*
VC	*Vigiliae Christianae*
WHR	*Welsh History Review*
ZCP	*Zeitschrift für Celtische Philologie*
ZKG	*Zeitschrift für Kirchengeschichte*

Bibliography

I cannot claim to have compiled a comprehensive list of works relating to Pelagius and the Pelagian controversy. This bibliography is no more than a hotchpotch consisting of books and articles which I have read or consulted in preparing this monograph, though I dare to hope that it may serve as a useful guide for any who may be interested enough to want to pursue their own enquiries into the subjects discussed. Where there are two or more editions of the same work, I have cited only those which I have consulted myself.

ADAM, K. 'Causa finita est', Festgabe Albert Erhard, ed., A. M. Köeniger, Bonn–Leipzig, 1922, 1–23.

ADAMS, R. 'Piers's Pardon and Langland's Semi-Pelagianism', Traditio 39, 1983, 367–418.

ALCOCK, L. A. Arthur's Britain: History and Archaeology, A.D. 367–634, London, 1971.

ALLEN, P. S. Selections from Erasmus², Oxford, 1918.

—— and H. M. Edd., Erasmi Epistolae I–XII, Oxford, 1906–58.

ALTANER, B. 'Der Liber de Fide, ein Werk des Pelagianers Rufinus des "Syrers"', ThQ 130, 1950, 422–49.

ANTIN, P. 'Rufin et Pélage dans Jérôme, Prologue I in Hieremiam, Latomus 22, 1963, 792–4.

ARMSTRONG, A. H. An Introduction to Ancient Philosophy, London, 1947.

—— Ed., The Cambridge History of Later Greek and Early Medieval Philosophy², Cambridge, 1970.

—— 'St Augustine and Christian Platonism' in MARKUS, R. A., ed., 1972, 3–37 (The Saint Augustine Lecture 1966, Villanova, 1967).

ARMSTRONG, C. B. 'St Augustine and Pelagius as religious types', CQR 162, 1961, 150–64 (summary in PCA 57, 1960, 27–8).

ARMSTRONG, K. The First Christian: St Paul's Impact on Christianity, London, 1983.

AUSTIN, A. W. 'Are religions enabling methods for survival?', Zygon 15, 1980, 193–201.

BABCOCK, W. S. 'Augustine's interpretation of Romans (A.D. 394–9)', AS 10, 1979, 55–74.

—— 'Augustine and Tyconius: a study in the Latin appropriation of Paul', SP 17, 1982, iii, 1209–16.

BADHAM, P. and L. Immortality or Extinction, London, 1982.

BAINTON, R. H.   *Here I Stand: a Life of Martin Luther*, New York/London, 1950.

—— *Erasmus of Christendom*, New York/London, 1977.

BARLEY, M. W. and HANSON, R. P. C.   Edd., *Christianity in Britain, 300–700*, Leicester, 1968.

BARNARD, L. W. 'Pelagius and early Syriac Christianity', *RThAM* 35, 1968, 193–6.

BARTHOLOMEW, D. J.   *God of Chance*, London, 1984.

BAUER, W.   *Orthodoxy and Heresy in Earliest Christianity*[2], London, 1972.

BEATRICE, P. F.   *Tradux Peccati*, Milan, 1978.

BENTLEY-TAYLOR, D.   *Augustine: Wayward Genius*, London, 1980.

BERGER, P. L.   *The Heretical Imperative: Contemporary Possibilities of Religious Affirmation*, London, 1980.

BETHELL, D. L. T.   'The originality of the Early Irish Church', *JRSAI* 110, 1981, 36–49.

BETHUNE-BAKER, J. F.   *An Introduction to the Early History of Christian Doctrine*[2], London, 1954.

BETTENSON, H.   *The Later Christian Fathers, Oxford, 1970.*

BEZZANT, J. S.   'Intellectual Objections' in VIDLER, A. R., ed., 1963, 79–111.

BIELER, L.   'The Mission of Palladius', *Traditio* 6, 1948, 1–32.

—— *The Life and Legend of St Patrick*, Dublin, 1949.

—— *Libri Epistolarum Sancti Patricii Episcopi*, Dublin, 1952.

—— *St Patrick and the Coming of Christianity*, Dublin, 1967.

—— 'St Patrick and the British Church' in BARLEY, M. W. and HANSON, R. P. C., edd., 1968, 123–30.

BINCHY, D. A.   'Patrick and his biographers, ancient and modern', *SH* 2, 1962, 7–173.

BLIC, J. de   'Le péché originel selon Saint Augustin', *RSR* 16, 1927, 512–31.

BOGAN, M. I.   Ed. and trans., *Retractationes*, Catholic University of America, 1968.

BOHLIN, T.   *Die Theologie des Pelagius und ihre Genesis*, Uppsala/Wiesbaden, 1957.

BONNER, G.   '*Libido* and *concupiscentia* in St Augustine', *SP* 6, iv, 1962, 303–14.

—— *St Augustine of Hippo: Life and Controversies*, London, 1963, repr. Norwich, 1986.

—— 'How Pelagian was Pelagius?: an examination of the contentions of Torgny Bohlin', *SP* 9, 1966, 350–8.

—— 'Les origines africaines de la doctrine augustinienne sur la chute et le péché originel', *Augustinus* 12, 1967, 97–111.

—— 'Rufinus of Syria and African Pelagianism', *AS* 1, 1970, 31–47.

—— *Augustine and Modern Research on Pelagianism* (The Saint Augustine Lecture, 1970), Villanova, 1972.

—— 'Augustine's Conception of Deification', *JTS* n.s. 37, 1986(a), 369–86.

—— 'Adam', *Augustinus-Lexicon* I, ed. C. Mayer, Basel/Stuttgart, 1986(b), 63–87.

BORIUS, R. Ed. and trans., *Constance de Lyon: Vie de saint d'Auxerre*, Paris, 1965.

BOURKE, V. J. *The Essential Augustine*[2], Indianapolis, Indiana, 1974.

BOUWMAN, G. *Des Julian von Aeclanum Kommentar zu den Propheten Osee, Joel und Amos: ein Beitrag zur Geschichte der Exegese (Analecta Biblica 9)*, Rome, 1958.

BOWEN, E. G. *The Settlements of the Celtic Saints in Wales*, Cardiff, 1956.

—— *Saints, Settlements and Seaways in the Celtic Lands*, Cardiff, 1969.

—— *The St David of History: Dewi Sant, our Founder Saint* (Address given to the Friends of St David's Cathedral, 1981), Aberystwyth, 1982.

—— *Dewi Sant: Saint David*, Cardiff, 1983.

BROOKS, E. C. 'The translation techniques of Rufinus of Aquileia (343–411)', *SP* 17, i, 1982, 357–64.

BROWN, P. R. L. 'Religious dissent in the Later Roman Empire: the case of North Africa', *History* 46, 1961, 83–101 (*Religion and Society in the Age of St Augustine*, London, 1972, 237–59).

—— 'Aspects of the Christianization of the Roman Aristocracy', *JRS* 61, 1961, 1–11 (*Religion and Society*, 161–82).

—— 'Religious coercion in the Later Roman Empire: the case of North Africa', *History* 48, 1963, 283–305 (*Religion and Society*, 301–31).

—— 'Saint Augustine', in Smalley, B., ed., *Trends in Medieval Political Thought*, 1963, 1–21 (*Religion and Society*, 25–45).

—— 'St Augustine's attitude to religious coercion', *JRS* 54, 1964, 107–16 (*Religion and Society*, 260–78).

—— *Augustine of Hippo: a Biography*, London, 1967.

—— 'Pelagius and his supporters', *JTS* n.s. 19, i, 1968, 93–114 (*Religion and Society*, 183–207).

—— 'The diffusion of Manichaeism in the Roman Empire', *JRS* 59, 1969, 92–103 (*Religion and Society*, 94–118).

—— 'The patrons of Pelagius', *JTS* n.s. 21, i, 1970, 56–72 (Religion and Society, 208–26).

—— *The World of Late Antiquity*, London, 1971.

—— *Religion and Society in the Age of St Augustine*, London, 1972.

—— 'Sexuality and Society in the Fifth Century A.D.: Augustine and Julian of Eclanum', in Garba, E., ed., *Tria Corda: scritti in onore di Arnaldo Momigliano*, Como, 1983(a), 50–69.

—— 'Augustine and Sexuality', in *Center for Hermeneutical Studies in Hellenistic and Modern Culture, Protocol Series of the Colloquies*, 1983(b), 1–13.

BRUCKNER, A. *Julian von Eclanum, sein Leben und seine Lehre*, Leipzig, 1897.

BU'LOCK, J. D. 'Early Christian Memorial Formulae', *AC* 105, 1956, 133–41.

—— *The Life of the Early Celtic Church*, Edinburgh, 1963.

BURKITT, F. C. *The Religion of the Manichees*, Cambridge, 1925.

BURNABY, J. *Amor Dei: a Study of the Religion of Saint Augustine* (The Hulsean Lectures for 1938), London, 1938.

—— 'The *Retractationes* of Saint Augustine: self-criticism or apologia?', *AM* 1, 1954, 85–92.

BURY, J. B. 'The origins of Pelagius', *Hermathena* 13, 1904, 26–35.

—— *The Life of St Patrick and His Place in History*, London, 1905.

—— *A History of the Later Roman Empire from the Death of Theodosius I to the Death of Justinian, A.D. 395 to A.D. 565*, London, 1923.

CAMERON, A. 'Celestial consulates: a note on the Pelagian letter *Humanae referunt*', *JTS* n.s. 19, 1968, 213–15.

CAMPBELL, D. T. 'The conflict between social and biological evolution and the concept of original sin', *Zygon* 10, 1975, 234–49.

—— 'On the conflict between biological and social evolution and between psychology and moral tradition', *Zygon* 11, 1976, 167–208.

CAPANAGA, V. *La teologia agustiniana de la gracia*, Madrid, 1933.

CAPPS, W. H. and WRIGHT, W. M. *Silent Fire*, New York, 1978.

CARNEY, J. *Studies in Irish Literature and History*, Dublin, 1955.

—— 'A new chronology of the Saint's life' in RYAN, J., ed., 1958, 24–37.

—— *The Problem of St Patrick*, Dublin, 1961, 1973.

CASEY, P. J. Ed., *The End of Roman Britain*, Oxford, 1979.

CASPARI, C. P. *Briefe, Abhandlungen und Predigten aus den zwei letzten Jahrhunderten des kirklichen Altertums und den Anfang des Mittelalters*, Brussels, 1964 (*Christiania*, 1890).

CAVALLERA, F. *Saint Jérôme: sa vie et son oeuvre*, Louvain/Paris, 1922.

CHADWICK, H. *Origen contra Celsum*, Cambridge, 1953.

—— *The Sentences of Sextus: a Contribution to the History of Early Christian Ethics* (Texts and Studies, n.s. V), Cambridge, 1959.

—— *Early Christian Thought and the Classical Tradition*, Oxford, 1966.

—— *The Early Church*, Harmondsworth, 1967.

—— *Priscillian of Avila: the Occult and the Charismatic in the Early Church*, Oxford, 1976.

—— 'New Letters of St Augustine', *JTS* n.s. 34, 1983, 425–52.

—— *Augustine*, Oxford, 1986.

CHADWICK, N. K. *Poetry and Letters in Early Christian Gaul*, London, 1955.

—— Ed., *Studies in the Early British Church*, Cambridge, 1958.

—— Ed., *Studies in Early British History*, Cambridge, 1959.

—— *The Age of Saints in the Early Celtic Church*, Oxford, 1961.

—— *Celtic Britain*, London, 1963.

CHADWICK, O. 'Euladius of Arles', *JTS* 46, 1945, 200–5.

—— *John Cassian*[2], Cambridge, 1968.

CHAPMAN, J. 'The Holy See and Pelagianism', *DR* 120, 1897, 88–111; 121, 1897, 99–124,

CHARLESWORTH, M. P. *The Lost Province or The Worth of Britain*, Cardiff, 1949.

CHÉNÉ, J. 'Les origines de la controverse semi-pélagienne', *AThA* 13, 1953, 56–109.

CLARK, M. T. *Augustine, Philosopher of Freedom*, New York, 1958.

COCHRANE, C. N. *Christianity and Classical Culture: a Study of Thought and Action from Augustus to Augustine*, New York, 1957.

COHEN, J. 'Original Sin as the Evil Inclination', *HTR* 72/3, 1979/80, 496–520.

COLLINGWOOD, R. G. and MYRES, J. N. L. *Roman Britain and the English Settlements²*, Oxford, 1937.

COOPER, T. 'On praying to God in English', *CR* 65, 2, 1980, 41–51.

COPLESTONE-CROW, B. 'The dual nature of the Irish colonization of Dyfed in the Dark Ages', *SC* 16/17, 1981/2, 1–24.

COURCELLE, P. 'Paulin de Nole et Saint Jérôme', *REL* 25, 1947, 250–80.

—— *Les Confessions de Saint Augustin dans la tradition littéraire, antécédents et postérité*, Paris, 1963.

—— *Recherches sur les Confessions de Saint Augustin*, Paris, 1968.

CROÍNÍN, D. Ó. 'New Heresies for Old: Pelagianism in Ireland and the Papal Letter of 640', *Speculum* 60, 1985, 505–16.

CROSS, F. L. Ed., *The Oxford Dictionary of the Christian Church²*, corr. repr. 1977.

CUPITT, D. *The Nature of Man*, London, 1979.

—— *Only Human*, London, 1985(a).

—— *Crisis of Moral Authority²*, London, 1985(b).

DANIÉLOU, J. *The Development of Christian Doctrine before the Council of Nicaea*, II, ed. and trans. J. A. Baker, London/Philadelphia, 1973.

—— and MARROU, H. I. *The Christian Centuries*, trans. V. Cronin, London, 1964.

D'ARCY, M. Ed., *St Augustine*, New York, 1957.

DAVIDS, J. A. *De Orosio et Sancto Augustino Priscillianistarum adversariis commentatio historica et philosophica*, Diss., The Hague, 1930.

DAVIES, W. *Wales in the Early Middle Ages: Studies in the Early History of Britain*, Leicester, 1982.

DAVIES, W. H. 'The Church in Wales' in BARLEY, M. W. and HANSON, R. P. C., edd., 1968, 131–50.

DAWKINS, R. M. *The Selfish Gene*, Oxford, 1976.

——'In defence of selfish genes', *Philosophy*, 1981, 556–73.

DEMPSEY, J. J. *Pelagius's Commentary on St Paul*, Rome, 1937.

DEVRESSE, R. *Essai sur Théodore de Mopsueste*, Studi e Testi 141, Rome, 1948.

DEWART, J. McW. 'The Influence of Theodore of Mopsuestia on Augustine's *Letter 187*', *AS* 10, 1979.

—— 'The Christology of the Pelagian Controversy', *SP* 17, iii, 1982, 1221–44.

DEWART, L. *The Future of Belief*, London, 1967.

DIDIER, J. C. 'Saint Augustin et la baptême des enfants', *REA* 2, 1956, 109–29.

DILLON, M. 'The Irish Settlements in Wales', *Celtica* 12, 1977, 1–11.

—— and CHADWICK, N. K. *The Celtic Realms*, London, 1967.

DINKLER, E. 'Pelagius' in *RE* 1937, 226–42.

DIVJAK, J. *Epistolae S. Aurelii Augustini*, CSEL 88, 1981, 32–8.

DIXON, N. *Troubled Waters*, London, 1979.

DODDS, E. R. 'Augustine's *Confessions*: a study of spiritual maladjustments', *HJ* 26, 1927/8, 459–73.

—— *Pagan and Christian in an Age of Anxiety*, Cambridge, 1965.

DUCHESNE, L. *Histoire ancienne de l'Eglise*, III, Paris, 1910.

DUMVILLE, D. N. 'Sub-Roman Britain: history and legend', *History* n.s. 62, 1977, 173–92.

—— 'The chronology of the *De Excidio Britanniae*, I' in LAPWIDGE, M. and DUMVILLE, D., edd., 1984, 61–84.

—— 'Late-seventh or eight-century evidence for the British transmission of Pelagius', *CMCS* 10, 1985, 39–52.

DUVAL, Y.-M. 'Julien d'Eclane et Rufin d'Aquilée: du concile de Rimini à la repression pélagienne', *REA* 24, 1978, 248–9.

—— 'Pélage est-il le censeur inconnu de l'*Adversus Iovinianum* à Rome en 393' *ou* 'Du "Portrait-Robot" de l'hérétique chez S. Jérôme', *RHE* 75, 1980, 525–57.

ELLIS, I. '*Essays and Reviews* reconsidered', *Theology* 74, 1971, 396–404.

ESPOSITO, M. 'The Patrician problem and a possible solution', *IHS* 10, 38, 1956/7, 131–55.

EVANS, D. S. *Stori Dewi Sant*, Llandybie, 1959.

—— Ed., *Buchedd Dewi*², Cardiff, 1965.

—— Ed., *Lives of the Welsh Saints by G. H. Doble*, Cardiff, 1971.

—— *Historia Gruffud vab Kenan*, Cardiff, 1977.

—— 'Ychwaneg am Ddewi Sant – ei fuchedd a'i fywyd', *THSC*, 1984, 9–29.

EVANS, G. R. *Augustine on Evil*, Cambridge, 1982.

EVANS, J. 'St Germanus in Britain', *ACant* 80, 1965, 175–85.

EVANS, R. F. 'Pelagius, Fastidius and the Pseudo-Augustinian *De Vita Christiana*, *JTS* n.s. 13, 1962, 72–98.

—— 'Pelagius's veracity at the Synod of Diospolis' in J. Sommerfeld, ed., *Studies in Medieval Culture*, Kalamazoo, Mich., 1964, 21–30.

—— *Pelagius: Inquiries and Reappraisals*, London, 1968(a).

—— *Four Letters of Pelagius*, London, 1968(b).

FAIRWEATHER, E. R. 'St Augustine's interpretation of infant baptism', *AS* 2, 1954.

FERGUSON, E. 'Inscriptions and the origin of infant baptism', *JTS* n.s. 30, 1979, 37–46.

FERGUSON, J. *Pelagius: a Historical and Theological Study*, Cambridge, 1956, repr. New York, 1978.

—— 'In defence of Pelagius', *Theology* 83, 1980, 114–19.

FERRARI, L. C. 'The Boyhood Beatings of Augustine', *AS* 5, 1974, 1–14.

FISHER, J. D. C. *Christian Initiation: Baptism in the Medieval West*, London, 1965.

FLOËRI, F. 'Le pape Zosime et la doctrine augustinienne du péché originel', *AM* 2, 1954, 755–61.

—— 'Remarques sur la doctrine augustinienne du péché originel', *SP* 9, iii, 1963, 416–21.

FOAKES-JACKSON, F. J. *History of the Christian Church from the Earliest Times to A.D. 461*, Cambridge, 1947.

FOSTER, I. L. and DANIEL, G. *Prehistory and Early Wales*, London, 1965.

FREDERIKSEN, P. 'Paul and Augustine: conversion narratives, orthodox traditions, and the retrospective self', *JTS* n.s. 37, 1986, 3–34.

FREEMAN, A. *The Benn Heresy*, London, 1982.

FREND, W. H. C. 'The Christianization of Roman Britain' in BARLEY, M. W. and HANSON, R. P. C., edd., 1968, 37–50.

—— *The Donatist Church: a Movement of Protest in Roman North Africa*, Oxford, 1971.

—— *The Early Church: from the Beginnings to 461*, London, 1982.

—— *The Rise of Christianity*, London, 1984.

—— *Saints and Sinners in the Early Church: Differing and Conflicting Traditions in the First Six Centuries*, London, 1985.

FRERE, S. S. *Britannia: a History of Roman Britain*, London, 1967.

GARCIA-ALLEN, C. A. *Pelagius and Christian Initiation: a Study in Historical Theology*, Washington, 1978.

—— 'Was Pelagius influenced by Chromatius of Aquileia?', *SP*, iii, 1982, 1251–7.

GAUDEL, A. 'Péché originel' in *DTC* 12/1, 275–624.

GILSON, E. *Introduction a l'étude de Saint Augustin*[3], Paris, 1949.

GLOUBOKOWSKY, N. N. 'The Greek Fathers' in WHITLEY, W. T., ed., 1932, c.II.

GOODWIN, R. P. Ed. and trans., *Selected Writings of St Thomas Aquinas*, Indianopolis, Indiana, 1965.

GREENE, D. 'Some linguistic evidence relating to the British Church' in BARLEY, M. W. and HANSON, R. P. C., edd., 1968, 75–86.

GRESHAKE, G. *Gnade als konkrete Freiheit: eine Untersuchung zur Gnadenlehre des Pelagius*, Mainz, 1972.

GRIMES, W. F. Ed., *Aspects of Archaeology in Britain and Beyond*, London, 1951.

GROSJEAN, P. 'Notes d'hagiographie celtique', *AB* 63, 1945, 65–130; 70, 1953, 312–26; 75, 1957, 158–226.

—— 'The Confession of St Patrick' in RYAN, J., ed., 1958, 81–94.

GROSSI, V. 'Il battesimo e la polemica pelagiana negli anni 411–413', *Augustinianum* 9, 1969, 30–61.

GUNTON, C. 'The theologian and the biologist', *Theology* 77, 1974, 526–8.

HAIGHT, R. *The Experience and Language of Grace*, Dublin, 1979.

HALL, S. 'Sub-Christian prayer: Pelagian didacticism in the Alternative Service Book 1980', *KTR* 4, 1, 1981, 1–7.

HAMMAN, A. 'Orosius de Braga et le pélagianisme' in *Bracara Augusta* 21, 1967, 346–55.

HAMMOND, C. P. 'The last ten years of Rufinus's life and the date of his move from south Aquileia', *JTS* n.s. 28, 1977, 327–429.

HANSON, R. P. C. *Origen's Doctrine of Tradition*, London, 1954.

—— *St Patrick, a British Missionary Bishop*, Nottingham, 1965.

—— *Saint Patrick: his Origins and Career*, Oxford, 1968.

—— *Mystery and Imagination*, London, 1976.

—— 'The Date of St Patrick', *BJRL* 61, 1978/9, 60–77.

—— and BLANC, C. *Saint Patrick: Confession et Lettre a Coroticus*, Paris, 1978.

—— *The Life and Writings of the Historical St Patrick*, New York, 1983.

HARDINGE, L. *The Celtic Church in Britain*, London, 1972.

HARDY, A. *The Living Stream* (Gifford Lectures, 1963/4), London, 1965.

—— *The Divine Flame* (Gifford Lectures, 1964/5), London, 1966.

—— *The Biology of God*, London, 1975.

—— *Darwinism and the Spirit of Man*, London, 1984.

HARNACK, A. von *History of Dogma*, trans. J. Millar, London, 1961.

HARRISON, K. 'Episodes in the history of Easter cycles in Ireland' in WHITELOCK, D., McKITTERICK, R. and DUMVILLE, D., edd., 1982, 307–19.

HEDDE, R. and AMANN, E. 'Pélagianisme' in *DTC* 12, 692ff.

HEFELE, C. J. *A History of the Christian Councils*, London, 1871–96.

HENRY, P. 'Why is contemporary scholarship so enamoured of ancient heretics?', *SP* 17, i, 1982, 123–6.

HICK, J. *Evil and the God of Love*, London/New York, 1966.

—— *Death and Eternal Life*, London, 1976.

—— *The Second Christianity*, London, 1983(a).

—— and M. GOULDER *Why Believe in God?*, London, 1983(b).

HODGSON, L. *The Grace of God in Faith and Philosophy*, London, 1936.

—— *For Faith and Freedom* (Gifford Lectures, 1954/6), London, 1968.

HUBER, K. C. *The Pelagian Heresy: observations on its social context*, Ann Arbor, 1984.

HUGHES, K. *The Church in Early Irish Society*, London, 1966.

—— *Early Christian Ireland: Introduction to the Sources*, London, 1972.

HUNT, E. D. *Holy Land Pilgrimages in the Later Roman Empire, A.D. 312–460*, Oxford, 1982.

JACKSON, K. H. 'Notes on the Ogam inscriptions of southern Britain' in Fox, C. F. and Dickins, B., edd., *Early Cultures of North-west Europe*, Cambridge, 1950, 197–213.

—— *Language and History in Early Britain*, Edinburgh, 1953.

JACKSON, M. 'Home cooking: British theology and the Universal Church', *Theology* 82, 1979, 244–51.

JACQUIN, M. 'Questions de prédestination aux Ve et VIe siecles', *RHE* 5, 1904, 266ff.

JAMES, E. 'Ireland and Western Gaul' in WHITELOCK, D., McKITTERICK, R. and DUMVILLE, D., edd., 1982, 362–86.

JAMES, J. W. *Rhigyfarch's Life of St David*, Cardiff, 1967.

JARRETT, M. G. 'Magnus Maximus and the end of Roman Britain', *THSC*, 1983, 22–35.

—— and DOBSON, B. edd., *Britain and Rome: Essays Presented to Eric Birley on his Sixtieth Birthday*, Kendal, 1965.

JOAD, C. E. M. *God and Evil*, London, 1942.

JOHNSON, S. *Later Roman Britain*, London, 1980.

JOLIVET, R. *Le problème du mal d'après saint Augustin²*, Paris, 1936.

JONES, A. H. M. 'Were ancient heresies national or social movements in disguise?', *JTS* n.s. 10, 1959, 280–98.

—— *The Later Roman Empire, 284–602: a Social, Economic and Administrative Survey*, Oxford, 1964.

—— 'The Western Church in the fifth and sixth centuries' in BARLEY, M. W. and HANSON, R. P. C., edd., 1968, 9–18.

JONES, O. W. *Rowland Williams, Trivium* Suppl., 1971.

JUNG, C. G. *Memories, Dreams and Reflections*, London, 1967.

KEE, A. *Constantine versus Christ: the Triumph of Ideology*, London, 1982.

KELLY, J. F. 'Pelagius, Pelagianism and the Early Christian Irish', *Mediaevalia* 4, 1978, 99ff.

KELLY, J. N. D. *Jerome: His Life, Writings and Controversies*, London, 1975.

—— *Early Christian Doctrines⁵*, New York, 1978.

KENNEY, J. F. *The Sources for the Early History of Ireland: I, Ecclesiastical*, New York, 1929.

KIDD, B. J. *History of the Christian Church to A.D. 461*, III, Oxford, 1922.

KIRBY, D. P. 'Bede's native sources for the *Historia Ecclesiastica*', *BJRL* 48, 1966, 341–71.

KOOPMANS, J. H. 'Augustine's first contact with Pelagius and the dating of the condemnation of Caelestius at Carthage', *VC* 8, 1954, 149–63.

KRUSCH, B. and LEVISON, W. Edd., *Vita Sancti Germani Episcopi Autissiodorensis* in *Passiones vitaeque sanctorum aevi merovingici*, VII, Hannover, 1919/20.

KÜNG, H. *Justification*, trans. T. Collins, E. E. Tolk and D. Grandskou, London, 1964.

—— *On Being a Christian*, trans. E. Quinn, London, 1977.

LACHOIX, B. *Orose et ses idées*, Montreal, 1965.

LAMBERT, M. D. *Medieval Heresy: Popular Movements from Bogomil to Hus*, London, 1977.

LAMPE, G. W. H. 'Salvation: traditions and reappraisals' in *Explorations in Theology* 8, London, 1981 (repr. from J. M. Turner, ed., *Queen's Essays*, Birmingham, 1980).

—— *God as Spirit* (Bampton Lectures, 1976), Oxford, 1977.

LAPIDGE, M. 'Gildas' education and the Latin culture of Sub-Roman Britain' in LAPIDGE, M. and DUMVILLE, D., edd., 1984, 27–50.

—— and DUMVILLE, D. edd., *Gildas: New Approaches*, Studies in Celtic History V, Woodbridge, 1984.

LEFF, G. A. *Bradwardine and the Pelagians*, Cambridge, 1957.

—— *Heresy in the Latin Medieval Age* I, Manchester, 1967.

LEVISON, W. 'Bischof Germanus von Auxerre und die Quellen zu seiner Geschichte', *Neues Archiv der Gesellschaft für ältere deutsche Geschichtskunde* 29, 1904, 95–175.

LEWIS, H. D. *Morals and the New Theology*, London, 1947.

LIEBESCHUETZ, W. 'Did the Pelagian movement have social aims?', *Historia* 12, 1963, 227–41.

—— 'Pelagian evidence on the last period of Roman Britain', *Latomus* 26, 1967, 436–47.

LIVINGSTONE, E. A.   Ed., *The Concise Oxford Dictionary of the Christian Church*, corr. repr., Oxford, 1980.

LLOYD, J. E.   *A History of Wales from the Earliest Times to the Edwardian Conquest³*, London, 1939.

LOOFS, F.   'Pelagius' in *RPThK*, 15, 1904³, 747–74; 24, 1913, 310–12.

LORENZ, R.   'Der Augustinismus Prospers von Aquitanien' *ZKG* 73, 1963, 217–52.

—— 'Gnade und Erkenntnis bei Augustinus', *ZKG* 75, 1964, 21–78.

LOT, F.   *La fin du monde antique et le début du Moyen Age*, Paris, 1927.

LOUTH, A.   'Messalianism and Pelagianism', *SP* 17, i, 1982, 127–35.

LOYER, O.   *Les Chrétientés Celtiques*, Paris, 1965.

LUBAC, H. de   *Augustinianism and Modern Theology*, London, 1969.

LUCAS, J. R.   *The Freedom of the Will*, Oxford, 1970.

—— 'Pelagius and St Augustine', *JTS* n.s. 22, 1971, 73–85.

—— *Freedom and Grace*, London, 1976.

LUMSDEN, C. J. and WILSON, E. O.   *Genes, Mind and Culture*, Harvard, 1981.

MACKIE, J. L.   'The Law of the jungle: moral principles and principles of evolution', *Philosophy*, 1978, 455–64.

—— 'Genes and egoism', *Philosophy*, 1981, 553–5.

MACMULLEN, R.   *Christianizing the Roman Empire*, Yale, 1984.

MACQUARRIE, J.   *Existentialism*, Harmondsworth, 1973.

—— *Thinking about God*, London, 1975.

—— *In Search of Humanity*, London, 1982.

MADEC, G.   'Connaissance de Dieu et action de grâces', *RA* 2, 1962, 273–309.

MANSON, T. W.   'Grace in the New Testament' in WHITLEY, W. T., ed., 1932, c.I.

MARKUS, R. A.   *Saeculum: History and Society in the Theology of St Augustine*, Cambridge, 1970.

—— Ed., *Augustine: a Collection of Critical Essays*, New York, 1972.

—— *Christianity in the Roman World*, London, 1974.

—— 'Pelagianism: Britain and the Continent', *JEH* 37, 2, 1986, 191–204.

MARROU, H. I.   *Saint Augustine and his Influence through the Ages*, New York, 1957.

—— *S. Augustin et la fin de la culture antique⁴*, Paris, 1958.

—— 'Les attaches orientales du Pélagianisme', *CRAI* 1969, 459–72.

—— (with A.-M. BONNARDIÈRE) *St Augustin et l'augustinisme*, Paris, 1980.

MARTINETTO, G.   'Les premières réactions antiaugustiniennes de Pélage', *REA* 17, 1971, 83–117.

MATTHEWS, J.   *Baptism, Eucharist and Ministry: Seven Studies*, London, 1982 (based on *Faith and Order Paper* No. 111, of the World Council of Churches).

MAUSBAEK, J. von *Die Ethik des heiligen Augustinus*, Freiburg, 1929.

MIDGELEY, M. 'Gene-juggling', *Philosophy*, 1979, 439–58.

—— *Evolution as a Religion: Strange Hopes and Stranger Fears*, London/New York, 1985.

MILLER, M. 'Bede's use of Gildas', *EHR* 90, 1975, 241–61.

—— 'The last British entry in the "Gallic Chronicles"', *Britannia* 9, 1978, 315–18.

MILLER, M. W. *Rufini Presbyteri liber de fide: a Critical Text with Introduction and Commentary*, Washington, 1964.

MOMIGLIANO, A. Ed., *The Conflict between Christianity and Paganism in the Fourth Century*, Oxford, 1963.

MOMMSEN, T. *Chronica Minora*, 3 vols., Berlin, 1891–8.

MONOD, J. *Chance and Necessity*, trans. A. Wainhouse, London, 1979.

MONTEFIORE, H. *The Probability of God*, London, 1985.

MOORE, D. Ed., *The Land of Dyfed in Early Times*, Cardiff, 1964.

MOORE, R. I. *The Birth of Popular Heresy: Documents of Medieval History 1*, London, 1975.

MORIN, G. 'Lettre inédite de l'évêque Evodius aux moines d'Adrumète sur la question de la grâce', *RB* 13, 1896, 481–5.

MORRIS, J. R. 'Pelagian Literature', *JTS* n.s. 16, 1965, 26–60.

—— 'Dark Age Dates' in JARRETT, M. G. and DOBSON, B., edd., 1965, 145–84.

—— 'The Dates of the Celtic Saints', *JTS* n.s. 17, 1966, 342–91.

—— 'The Literary Evidence' in BARLEY, M. W. and HANSON, R. P. C., edd., 1968, 55–73.

—— *The Age of Arthur: a History of the British Isles from 350 to 650*, London, 1973.

MOSS, H. St L. B. *The Birth of the Middle Ages*, London, 1947.

MOZLEY, J. B. *A Treatise on the Augustinian Doctrine of Predestination²*, London, 1878.

MUNZ, P. 'John Cassian', *JEH* 9, 1960, 1–22.

MURPHY, F. X. *Rufinus of Aquileia (345–411): his Life and Works*, Washington, 1945.

—— 'Melania the Elder: a biographical note', *Traditio* 5, 1947, 59–77.

MURRAY, J. C. *The Problem of God*, Yale, 1964.

MYRES, J. N. L. 'The *Adventus Saxonum*' in GRIMES, W. F., ed., 1951, 221–41.

—— 'Pelagius and the end of Roman rule in Britain', *JRS* 50, 1960, 21–36.

—— 'Introduction' to BARLEY, M. W. and HANSON, R. P. C., edd., 1968, 1–8.

NASH-WILLIAMS, V. E. *The Early Christian Monuments of Wales*, Cardiff, 1950.

NERNEY, D. S. 'A Study of St Patrick's sources, III', *IER*, 5th ser. ·72, 1949, 14–26, 97–110, 265–80.

NEWMAN, J. H. *Apologia pro Vita Sua*, London, 1949.

NOCK, A. D. *Conversion: the Old and the New in Religion from Alexander the Great to Augustine of Hippo*[3], 1961.

NORREGAARD, J. 'Grace in St Augustine' in WHITLEY, W. T., ed., 1932, c.IV.

NORRIS, R. A. *Manhood and Christ: a Study in the Christology of Theodore of Mopsuestia*, Oxford, 1963.

NUVOLONE, F. G. and SOLIGNAC, A. 'Pélage et Pélagianisme' in *Dictionnaire de spiritualité, ascetique, mystique, doctrine et histoire*, Vol. 12B, 1986, 2889–942.

NYGREN, G. 'Das Prädestationsproblem in der Theologie Augustins', *STL* 12, 1956.

OBERMAN, H. O. *Archbishop Thomas Bradwardine: a Fourteenth-Century Augustinian*, Utrecht, 1957.

O'MEARA, J. J. 'The Confession of St Patrick and the Confessions of St Augustine', *IER*, 5th ser., 85, 1956, 190–7.

—— *The Young Augustine: an Introduction to the Confessions of St Augustine*[2], London/New York, 1980.

O'RAHILLY, T. F. *Ireland and Wales: their Historical and Literary Relations*, London, 1924.

—— *The Two Patricks: a Lecture on the History of Christianity in Fifth-Century Ireland*, Dublin, 1942.

—— *The Two Patricks*, Dublin, 1957.

O'SULLIVAN, T. D. *The De Excidio of Gildas: its Authenticity and Date (Columbia Studies in the Classical Tradition vii)*, Leiden, 1978.

PANNENBERG, W. *Faith and Reality*, trans. J. Maxwell, London, 1977(a).

—— *Human Nature, Election and History*, Philadelphia, 1977(b).

PAPE, W. and BENSELER, G. *Wörterbuch der griechischen Eigennamen*, Graz, 1959.

PASSMORE, J. *The Perfectibility of Man*, London, 1970.

PATOUT BURNS, J. 'The interpretation of Romans in the Pelagian controversy', *AS* 10, 1979, 43–54(a).

—— 'Augustine's role in the imperial action against Pelagius', *JTS* n.s. 30, 1979, 67–83(b).

PATTERSON, L. *Theodore of Mopsuestia and Modern Thought*, London, 1926.

PELIKAN, J. *The Christian Tradition: a History of the Development of Doctrine* I, Chicago/London, 1971.

PETERS, E. Ed., *Heresy and Authority in Medieval Europe: Documents and Translations*, London, 1980.

PHIPPS, W. W. 'The Heresiarch: Pelagius or Augustine?', *ATR* 62, 1980, 124–33.

PIGANIOL, A. *L'Empire chrétien (Histoire romaine IV, 2)*, Paris, 1947.

PINCHERLE, A. *La formazione teologica di S. Agostino*, Rome, 1947.

PIRENNE, R. *La morale de Pélage*, Rome, 1961.

PITTENGER, N. *Picturing God*, London, 1982.

PLUMMER, C. *Venerabilis Baedae Opera Historica*, Oxford, 1896.

PLINVAL, G. de 'Recherches sur l'oeuvre littéraire de Pélage', *RPh* 60, 1934, 10–42.

—— 'La problème de Pélage sous son dernier état', *RHE* 35, 1939, 5–21.

—— *Pélage, ses écrits, sa vie et son reforme*, Lausanne, 1943.

—— *Essai sur le style et la langue de Pélage* (*Collectanea Friburgensia* 31), Fribourg, 1947.

—— 'Julien d'Éclane devant la Bible', *RSR* 47, 1959, 345–66.

—— *La crise pélagienne*, I. Introductions, traductions et notes par G. de Plinval et J. de la Tullaye, *BA* 21, Paris, 1966.

—— 'L'heure est-elle venue de redécouvrir Pélage?', *REA* 19, 1973, 158–62.

POPE, H. *St Augustine of Hippo*, London, 1937.

PORTALIÉ, E. 'Augustin, Saint' in *DTC²*, I, 1923, 2268–472.

—— *A Guide to the Thought of Saint Augustine²*, trans. R. J. Bastian, Westport, Conn., 1975.

POWELL, T. G. E. *The Celts*, London, 1958.

PRESTIGE, G. L. *Fathers and Heretics*, London, 1963.

PRETE, S. *Pelagio e il pelagianesimo* (*Biblioteca di Scienze Religiose* X, 5), Brescia, 1961.

PRICE, D. T. W. *A History of Saint David's University College*, I, Cardiff, 1977.

PUECH, H. C. *Le Manichéisme: son fondateur, sa doctrine*, Paris, 1949.

RADFORD, C. A. R. 'The earliest Irish Churches', *UJA* 40, 1977, 1–11.

REES, B. R. 'The conversion of Saint Augustine', *Trivium* 14, 1979, 1–17.

REFOULÉ, F. 'Datation du premier concile de Carthage contre les Pélagiens et du *Libellus Fidei* de Rufin', *REA* 9, 1963(a), 41–9.

—— 'La distinction "Royaume de Dieu-Vie éternelle" est-elle pélagienne?', *RSR* 51, 1963(b), 247–54.

—— 'Julien d'Éclane, théologien et philosophe', *RSR* 52, 1964, 42–84, 233–47.

—— 'Julien d'Éclane', *Catholicisme* 6, 26, 1966, 1236–9.

RICHARDS, M. 'The Irish settlements in South-West Wales: a topographical approach', *JRSAI* 90, 1960, 133–52.

RICHARDSON, A. Ed., *A Dictionary of Christian Theology*, London, 1969.

RIST, J. M. 'Augustine on free will and predestination', in MARKUS, R. A., ed., 1972, 218–52.

RIVIÈRE, J. 'Hétérodoxie des pélagiens en fait de rédemption?', *RHE* 41, 1946, 5–43.

ROBINSON, J. A. T. *The Roots of a Radical*, London, 1980.

RONDET, H. *Gratia Christi*, Paris, 1948.

—— *Le péché originel dans la tradition patristique et théologique*, Paris, 1967.

—— 'Rufin de Syrien et le *Liber de Fide*', *Augustiniana* 22, 1972, 531–9.

ROWE, W. L. 'Augustine on foreknowledge and free will' in MARKUS, R. A., ed., 1972, 209–17.

RYAN, J. Ed., *Saint Patrick* (Thomas Davis Lectures), Dublin, 1958.

SAGE, A. 'La prédestination chez S. Augustin d'après une thèse récente', *REA* 6, 1960, 37.

—— 'Faul-il anathématiser la doctrine augustinienne de la prédestination?', *REA* 8, 1962, 240.

—— 'Praeparatur voluntas a Domino', *REA* 10, 1964, 1–20.

—— 'Péché originel: naissance d'un dogma', *REA* 13, 1967, 211–48.

—— 'Le péché originel dans la pensée de Saint Augustin de 421–430', *REA* 15, 1969, 75–112.

SALWAY, P. *Roman Britain*, Oxford, 1981.

SAWYER, P. H. *From Roman Britain to Norman England*, London, 1978.

SCHLEIERMACHER, F. D. E. *The Christian Faith*, trans. H. R. Mackintosh and J. S. Stewart, London, 1928.

SCHNITZER, J. 'Orosio e Pelagio', *Religio* 8, 1937, 336–43.

SELL, A. P. F. 'Augustine versus Pelagius: a cautionary tale of perennial importance', *CTJ* 12, 1977, 117–43.

SHARPE, R. 'Gildas as a Father of the Church' in LAPWIDGE, M. and DUMVILLE, D., edd., 1984, 193–205.

SHAW, B. D. 'The Family in Late Antiquity: the experience of Augustine', *Past & Present*, 115, May 1987, 3–51.

SHELDON-WILLIAMS, I. P. 'The Cappadocians' in ARMSTRONG, A. H., ed., 1970, 432–56.

SIMONE, R. J. de 'Modern research on the sources of St Augustine's doctrine of original sin', *AS* 11, 1980, 205–27.

SIMS-WILLIAMS, P. 'The evidence for vernacular Irish influence on early medieval Welsh literature' in WHITELOCK, D., McKITTERICK, R. and DUMVILLE, D., edd., 1982, 235–57.

SINGER, P. *The Expanding Circle: Ethics and Sociology*, Oxford, 1981.

SMITH, A. J. 'The Latin sources of the Commentary of Pelagius on the Epistle of St Paul to the Romans', *JTS* 19, 1917/18, 162–230; 20, 1919, 55–65.

—— 'The Commentary of Pelagius on "Romans" compared with that of Origen–Rufinus', *JTS* 20, 1919, 127–77.

—— 'Pelagius and Augustine', *JTS* 31, 1929/30, 21–35.

SMITH, W. and WACE, H. Edd., *A Dictionary of Christian Biography, Literature, Sects and Doctrines*, London, 1877–87.

SMITH, W. T. *Augustine: His Life and Thought*, Atlanta, Georgia, 1980.

SONNTAG, F. 'Augustine's metaphysics and free will', *HTR* 60, 1967, 297–306.

SOUTER, A. 'The Commentary of Pelagius on the Epistles of Paul: the problem of its restoration', *PBA* 2, 1905/6, 409–39.

—— 'Another new fragment of Pelagius', *JTS* 12, 1910/11, 32–5.

—— 'Freiburg fragments of an MS of the Pelagian Commentary on the Epistles of St Paul', *JTS* 13, 1911/12, 515–19.

—— 'New Manuscripts of Pelagius', *ThL* 38, 1913, 442.

—— 'Pelagius and the Pauline text in the *Book of Armagh*', *JTS* 16, 1914/15, 105.

—— 'Pelagius' doctrine in relation to his early life', *Expositor* 1, 1915, 180–2.

—— 'The character and history of Pelagius' Commentary on the Epistles of St Paul', *PBA* 7, 1915/16, 261–96.

—— 'Pelagius' text of Romans v.12 with commentary', *ET* 28, 1916/17, 42–3.

—— 'The earliest surviving book of a British author', *TCR* 115, 1919, 76–82.

—— *Pelagius's Expositions of the Thirteen Epistles of St Paul* (*Texts and Studies* IX), Cambridge, 1922/31.

SPARROW-SIMPSON, W. J.   *The Letters of St Augustine*, London, 1919.

STEVENS, C. E.   'Gildas Sapiens', *EHR* 56, 1941, 353–73

STEVENSON, J.   Ed., *A New Eusebius: Documents Illustrative of the History of the Church to A.D. 337*, London, 1965.

—— Ed., *Creeds, Councils and Controversies: Documents Illustrative of the History of the Church, A.D. 337–461*, London, 1966.

STOKES, W.   Ed. and trans., *The Tripartite Life of St Patrick and Other Documents Relating to That Saint*, II, London, 1887.

TAYLOR, J. V.   *The Go-Between God*, London, 1972.

TENNANT, F. R.   *The Concept of Sin*, Cambridge, 1912.

TESELLE, E.   *Augustine the Theologian*, London, 1970.

—— 'Rufinus the Syrian, Caelestius, Pelagius: explorations in the pre-history of the Pelagian controversy', *AS* 3, 1972, 61–95.

THEISSEN, G.   *Biblical Faith: an Evolutionary Approach*, London, 1984.

THOMAS, A. C.   'The evidence from North Britain' in BARLEY, M. W. and HANSON, R. P. C., edd., 1968, 93–122.

—— *Britain and Ireland in Early Christian Times, A.D. 400–800*, London, 1971.

—— 'Irish colonies in post-Roman Western Britain: a survey of the evidence', *JRIC* n.s. 6, 1972, 251–74.

—— 'Saint Patrick and fifth-century Britain: an historical model explained' in CASEY, P. J., ed., 1979, 81–101.

—— *Christianity in Roman Britain to A.D. 500*, London, 1981.

THOMAS, J. F.   *Saint Augustin s'est-il trompé?: essai sur la prédestination*, Paris, 1959.

THOMPSON, E. A.   'Zosimus on the end of Roman Britain', *Antiquity* 30, 1956, 163–7.

—— 'A chronological note on St Germanus of Auxerre', *AB* 75, 1957, 135–8.

—— 'Britain A.D. 406–410', *Britannia* 8, 1977, 303–18.

—— 'Gildas and the history of Britain', *Britannia* 10, 1979, 203–26

—— *St Germanus of Auxerre and the End of Roman Britain* (*Studies in Celtic History* 6), Woodbridge, 1984.

—— *Who was St Patrick?*, Woodbridge, 1985.

THONNARD, F.-J.   'La prédestination augustinienne et l'interprétation de O. Rottmaner, *REA* 9, 1983, 259–87.

—— 'La prédestination augustinienne: sa place en philosophie augustinienne', *REA* 10, 1964, 97–123.

—— 'L'aristotélisme de Julien d'Éclane et saint Augustin', *REA* 11, 1965, 296–304.

—— 'La notion de "nature" chez saint Augustin: son progrès dans la polémique antipélagienne', *REA* 11, 1965, 239–65.

THORPE, W. H.   *Purpose in a World of Chance: A Biologist's View*, Oxford, 1978.

TODD, J. H. *St Patrick, Apostle of Ireland*, Dublin, 1864.

TOYNBEE, J. M. C. 'Christianity in Roman Britain', *JBAA*, 3rd ser., 16, 1953, 1–24.

TOYNBEE, P. *Towards the Holy Spirit*, London, 1982.

TRIGG, J. W. *Origen: the Bible and Philosophy in the Third-Century Church*, Atlanta, Georgia, 1983.

TRIGG, R. *The Shaping of Man: Philosophical Aspects of Sociology*, Oxford, 1982.

TURNER, C. H. 'Pelagius' Commentary on the Pauline Epistles and its history', *JTS* 4, 1902/3, 132–41.

—— 'Curiosities of the Latin interpretation of the Greek Testament', *JTS* 12, 1911, 273–5.

UNAMUNO, M. de *The Tragic Sense of Life*, trans. J. E. Crawford-Flitch, London, 1967.

VALERO, J. B. 'El estoicismo de Pelagio', *Estudios Eclesiasticos* 57, 1982, 39–63.

VAN DER MEER, F. *Augustine the Bishop: the Life and Work of a Father of the Church²*, trans. B. Battershaw and G. R. Lamb, London, 1978.

VANDERVELDE, G. *Original Sin: Two Major Trends in Contemporary Re-interpretation*, Amsterdam, 1975.

VIDLER, A. R. Ed., *Objections to Christian Belief*, London, 1963.

WADE-EVANS, A. W. *Life of St David*, London, 1923.

WALLACE-HADRILL, D. S. *Christian Antioch: a Study of Early Christian Thought in the East*, Cambridge, 1982.

WAND, J. W. C. *A History of the Early Church to A.D. 500*, London, 1963.

WARD, J. H. 'Vortigern and the end of Roman Britain', *Britannia* 3, 1972, 276–89.

WATSON, E. W. 'The Latin Fathers' in WHITLEY, W. T., ed., 1932, c.III.

WEBB, C. C. J. *Problems in the Relations of God and Man*, London, 1911.

WERMELINGER, O. *Röm und Pelagius: die theologische position der römischen Bischöfe im pelagianischen Streit in den Jahren 411–432 (Päpste und Papsttum VII)*, Stuttgart, 1975.

WEST, R. *St Augustine*, London/New York, 1933, repr. in *Rebecca West: a Celebration*, Harmondsworth, 1978, 157–236.

WHITELOCK, D., McKITTERICK, R. and DUMVILLE, D. Edd., *Ireland in Early Medieval Europe*, Cambridge, 1982.

WHITLEY, W. T. Ed., *The Doctrine of Grace*, London, 1932.

WIDENGREN, G. *Mani and Manichaeism*, trans. C. Kessler, London, 1965.

WILES, M. *The Remaking of Christian Doctrine*, London, 1974.

—— *Faith and the Mystery of God*, London, 1982.

WILKEN, R. L. *The Myth of Christian Beginnings*, London, 1979.

WILLIAMS, G. *The Welsh Church from Conquest to Reformation*, Cardiff, 1962.

WILLIAMS, G. A. *When was Wales?*, Harmondsworth, 1985.

WILLIAMS, H. Ed. and trans., Gildas, *De Excidio Britanniae*, London, 1899/1901.

—— 'Heinrich Zimmer on the history of the Celtic Church', *ZCP* 4, 1903, 527–74.

—— *Christianity in Early Britain*, Oxford, 1912.

WILLIAMS, H. A. 'Psychological Objections' in VIDLER, ed., 1963, 35–56.

—— *Some Day I'll Find You*, London, 1982.

WILLIAMS, N. P. *The Ideas of the Fall and of Original Sin* (Bampton Lectures, 1924), London, 1927.

—— *The Grace of God*, London, 1930.

WILLIS BUND, J. W. *The Celtic Church in Wales*, London, 1897.

WILSON, E. O. *Sociobiology: the New Synthesis*, Cambridge, Mass., 1975.

WILSON, P. A. 'Romano-British and Welsh Christianity: continuity or discontinuity?', *WHR* 3, 1966/7, 5–21, 103–20.

—— 'St Patrick and Irish Christian origins', *SC* 14/15, 1979/80, 344–80.

WINTERBOTTOM, M. Ed. and trans., *Gildas: the Ruin of Britain and Other Works* (Arthurian Sources 7), Phillimore/London/Chichester, 1978.

WOLFSON, H. A. 'Philosophical implications of the Pelagian controversy', *PAPS* 103, 1959, 554–62.

WOOD, I. 'The End of Roman Britain: continental evidence and parallels' in LAPWIDGE, M. and DUMVILLE, D., edd., 1984, 1–25.

WOODS, H. *Augustine and Evolution: a Study in the Saint's De genesi ad litteram and De Trinitate*, New York, 1924.

WRIGHT, D. F. 'Pelagius the Twice-Born', *TC* 82, 1972, 6–15.

YOUNG, D. 'Ethology and the evolution of human behaviour, 1: an introductory review', *Theology* 77, 1974(a), 394–404.

—— 'Ethology and the evolution of human behaviour, 2: suggestions for theology', *Theology* 77, 1974(b), 470–8.

YOUNG, F. M. 'Did Epiphanius know what he meant by Heresy?', *SP* 17, i, 1982, 199–205.

—— *Can These Dry Bones Live?*, London, 1982.

—— *From Nicaea to Chalcedon: a Guide to the Literature and its Background*, London, 1983.

ZIEGLER, K. and SONTHEIMER, W. Edd., *Der kleine Pauly: Lexicon der Antike*, Stuttgart, 1964.

ZIMMER, H. *Pelagius in Irland: Texte und Untersuchungen zur Patristischen Litteratur*, Berlin, 1901.

—— *The Celtic Church in Britain and Ireland*, trans. A. Meyer, London, 1912.

Index

169

170

2. Other Writers Cited

172

Pittenger, N. 47
Pius XII 75
Plinval, G. de xii, xiii, xiv, 1, 4, 78, 87, 89, 112, 114
Plummer, C. 120
Portalié, E. 30, 32, 42, 43, 44, 51
Powell, T. G. E. 116
Price, D. T. W. 81

Rahner, K. 126
Rees, B. R. 30
Refoulé, F. 9, 10, 13, 65, 91
Rhigyfarch (Ricemarch) 114
Richards, M. 118
Richardson, A. 95
Richardson, L. J. D. 117
Rist, J. M. 44, 45, 48, 49
Robinson, J. A. T. 22, 23
Rowe, W. L. 48

Sage, A. 44, 65
Salway, P. 112
Sartre, J.-P. 54
Schleiermacher, F. D. E. 24
Searle, J. 128
Sell, A. P. F. 132
Sheldon-Williams, I. P. 60
Simone, R. J. de 57
Singer, P. 74
Souter, A. xiii, 2, 76, 94, 122
Southey, R. 1
Spenser, E. 126
Spurgeon, C. H. 51
Stevenson, J. 108, 118, 119

Taylor, J. V. 73
Temple, W. 38
Tennant, F. R. x, 125
TeSelle, E. 42, 50, 59, 66
Theissen, G. 70, 71, 74
Thomas, A. C. 111, 113, 117, 118
Thompson, E. A. 108, 109, 110, 111, 113, 114, 118, 119, 120, 125
Thonnard, F.-J. 45
Thoreau, H. D. 82
Thorpe, W. H. 17, 67, 73
Tilby, A. 75
Tinsley, E. J. 95
Toynbee, P. 47, 53
Trigg, J. W. 8, 58
Trigg, R. 74
Turner, C. H. xiii, 122

Unamuno, M. de ix

Vidler, A. R. 52

Wallace-Hadrill, D. S. 86, 87
Ward, J. H. 112
Watson, E. W. 30
Webb, C. C. J. 66, 69

Wermelinger, O. xii, xiv, 1, 2, 3, 4, 6, 9, 11, 12, 32, 51, 64, 65, 67, 76, 91, 94, 98, 100, 107, 130
Whale, J. S. 129
Whitley, W. T. 28, 29, 30
Wiles, M. 46, 68
Wilken, R. L. 75, 126, 132
William of St. Thierry 132
Williams, G. 109
Williams, G. A. 110, 115
Williams, H. xiii, xiv, 76
Williams, H. A. 52, 53
Williams, N. P. 29, 30, 32, 39, 40, 44, 45, 50, 51, 55, 56, 57, 59, 62, 66, 70, 81, 84
Willis Bund, J. W. 121
Wilson, E. O. 74
Winterbottom, M. 114
Wittgenstein, L. 48
Wood, I. 110, 111

Young, D. 71, 72
Young, F. M. 87

Zimmer, H. xv, 121

3. General Index

Abelard, Peter ix
Adoptionism 24
adult baptism 12f., 77
Aetius 110
Agricola 108, 110, 112, 114, 123
Alaric the Goth 1f.
Alban, St 110
Albertus Magnus, St 124
Alexander of Hales ix
'Alleluia Victory' 109, 115
Alternative Service Book 1980 x
Alypius 6
Ambrose, Bp of Milan, St 20, 30, 59f., 62, 64, 66f., 87
Ambrose of Alexandria 41
'Ambrosiaster' 59f., 64, 77, 87
Anastasius, Pope 7, 9
Annianus of Celeda xii, 76
Anselm, Abp of Canterbury, St 115
apatheia 8, 86, 94
Apollinarianism 24, 26
Aquinas, Thomas, St ix, 56, 73, 80
Arianism x, 10, 23f., 26, 87, 110, 113f., 132
Arminius, Jacobus ix
Atticus, Patr. of Constantinople 63, 141
Augustine, Abp of Canterbury, St 115
Augustine, Bp of Hippo, St, conversion 30f.
  debate with Julian 98ff., 141f.
  earliest attacks on Pelagianism 11, 76, 140
  legacy to the Church 50, 69, 127
  letter to Pelagius 11f.
  on *adiutorium Dei* 40

173

175

Volume II

The Letters of Pelagius
and his Followers

To my good friends
Jean and Peter Walcot,
And my other, better half

Introduction

Who was Pelagius? Who were the Pelagians? What did they teach, and why was their teaching condemned as heretical in the early-fifth century AD? As in most fields of human enquiry the answers to such questions depend upon the evidence available and the way in which it is selected and used by the enquirer. The available evidence in the case of Pelagius and his 'followers' consists of the writings ascribed to them and the references to, and quotations from, those writings which can be found in the works of Jerome, Augustine and other contemporary writers, together with a handful of extracts taken from ecclesiastical and official documents of the period.[1] We have no *Life* of Pelagius or of his friends and associates, no fifth-century counterpart of Eusebius, no account of the Pelagian controversy from the pen of a disinterested historian of the time when the events took place, and very little comment from friendly sources or even neutral ones. In short, we have to rely almost entirely on the sparse information that we are able to glean from the extant works attributed to the early Pelagians themselves, supplemented or discredited by the comments of their leading opponents.[2] It is not difficult to see why Pelagius and the Pelagians have had such a poor press over the intervening years.

I. The Movement

In describing Pelagianism as a 'movement' I must add a word of caution: a modern dictionary may define the term as 'a group with a common ideology' or 'the organized action of such a group', but neither of these definitions is, strictly speaking, applicable to Pelagianism. Pelagianism was not a coherent theological statement, since the Pelagians held different opinions on the issues with which they were concerned and placed different emphases on them, and they certainly did not engage in a planned and uniform campaign of action. Thus, in the letters and tractates in this collection you will find a few references from time to time to

---

[1] For bibliographies of these writings see PLS 1,1101–69; 1679–83; Lapidge and Sharpe; Nuvolone and Solignac; and Rees, App.I.

[2] There are no grounds for believing that Jerome and Augustine at least could not be trusted to refrain from deliberately misquoting, as distinct from misinterpreting, their theological adversaries, however selective their quotations may have been. Marius Mercator and Orosius, on the other hand are less conscientious.

the Fall of Adam and its implications for his descendants, to freedom of will and its relation to grace, and to original sin; but you will very soon realize that the main emphasis of the teaching is not theoretical but practical – on the Christian life, on the need for baptism and conversion, and on the Last Judgement. Pelagius was above all else a moral reformer who became involved in a theological controversy through trying to defend the principles of his moral teaching.

Having received a sound education in his own country and left it as a young man to further his career in Rome,[3] he was almost certainly a Briton by birth. It is there that we first hear of him – that is, if we accept, as I think we should, that it was against him that Jerome was directing his abuse when, in a letter to a friend in 393 or 394, he described a critic of his scurrilous attack on Jovinian as 'a certain gossipy monk, a wanderer around the streets, the cross-roads and the highways, a pettifogger, a sly detractor, who with a beam in his eye strives to remove the mote from another's' and much more to that effect.[4] The saintly Jerome went on to cast aspersions at this 'monk's' sense of vocation, his notorious association with women, his refusal to join in open debate with the innocent object of his criticisms, and his pretentious but quite insupportable claims to excellence as a scholar, philosopher, teacher and biblical exegete: after all, he had only turned to religion when he had failed to make a career for himself in the law.[5]

But Pelagius was not a monk in the sense that he belonged to a religious community nor does Jerome's caricature chime with the high reputation which he had acquired in Christian circles in Rome since his arrival there – the very same circles once dominated by Jerome! In fact, it was just the right moment for him to arrive in Rome, where a new Christianized aristocracy had now grown up, pious, ascetically minded and dedicated to the study of the Bible: the place that Jerome had filled was vacant, and Pelagius was soon to gather around himself an influential band of supporters, among them members of the wealthiest families and even of the clergy, and it was to their recommendations that Augustine was referring when, as late as 411, he described him as 'a holy man, who, I am told, has made no small progress in the Christian life.'[6] Even in 413, when he had already written his first two anti-Pelagian works, he could address his future opponent as 'My lord greatly beloved and brother greatly longed for' in his reply to a letter received from Pelagius, now in Palestine.[7] Yet, by 415, the two men were engaged in open conflict which had taken them beyond the point where reconciliation might be possible. What had happened to bring about such a radical change in their attitude to each other?

---

[3] Souter, 1907, 423ff., suggested that he left as the result of a difference of opinion with his father.
[4] *Letters*, 50 (PL 22,512–16).
[5] Ibid.; Y.-M. Duval has argued that the unnamed 'monk' was not Pelagius but an identikit picture of the typical heretic.
[6] *On the Merits and Forgiveness of Sin and Infant Baptism*, I, i.1 (PL 44,185).
[7] *Letters*, 146,1 (PL 33,596).

The first sign of disagreement appears c.405 when, Augustine tells us,[8] Pelagius heard a bishop in Rome quoting the famous sentence from the *Confessions*, 'Give me what you command and command what you will.'[9] Pelagius was greatly annoyed, according to Augustine, and nearly went so far as to begin a legal action against the reader: he saw this interpretation of the nature of grace as totally unacceptable and, further, contradictory to the traditional doctrine. He made his own position abundantly clear in his *Commentary on the Pauline Epistles* and in his correspondence with his friends, not to speak of the circles in which he taught in Rome. And even after his departure from Rome c.409 and arrival in Palestine, where he met with hostile opposition from Jerome, he continued to state his opposition to what he regarded as Augustine's unorthodox opinion on grace, for example, in his *Letter to Demetrias* written in or around 413. In the meantime his younger friend, Celestius, who, unlike him, had stayed in Carthage en route to Palestine and had fallen foul of the African bishops there, was condemned for his heretical opinions on the subject of infant baptism and original sin in 411 and forced to leave Africa for the Middle East. Yet it was not until 415 that Augustine singled out Pelagius for special attention as the leader of the heretics, and it is also in that year that we find our first extant example of the use of the word *Pelagiani* to describe them – in a treatise written by Jerome.[10] Why *Pelagiani*? Well, at this stage there was no alternative: Rufinus of Syria, who, according to Marius Mercator, had sown the seeds of the heresy in Rome at the turn of the century and had made Pelagius his spokesman,[11] was presumably dead and Celestius was far away in Ephesus but Pelagius was still on the battlefield and, furthermore, was stirring up trouble in Palestine. In 415 Pelagius was arraigned before a diocesan synod at Jerusalem and, after that, the Synod of Diospolis, summoned by the primate of Palestine, Eulogius of Caesarea, and attended by thirteen bishops, and got away scot-free on both occasions. Encouraged, no doubt, by the outcome, he now wrote his lost treatise *In Defence of Free Will* and circulated his own account of his trial at Diospolis.

But Augustine rallied his forces, since he knew that Jerome and his *agent provocateur*, the Spanish priest Paul Orosius, sent to him by Augustine to warn him of the dangers of Pelagianism a few years before, had shot their bolt, and that his own reputation was at stake. Jerome's references to the Pelagians in his *Commentary on Jeremiah* and his more strident criticism in his *Letter to Ctesiphon* and *Dialogues against the Pelagians* had been no more successful than Augustine's treatises in 411 and 412[12] and the more recent one, *On Nature and Grace*, in 415. It was now time to mobilize the African bishops and enlist the support of

---

[8] *The Gift of Perseverance*, xx.53 (PL 45,1026). It has been suggested that Paulinus of Nola, a friend of Pelagius and correspondent of Augustine's, was the bishop concerned or at least, was present (Brown,1972,211; Courcelle,580).

[9] *Confessions*,X,xxix.40 (PL 32,796).

[10] *Dialogue against the Pelagians* (PL 23,495–590).

[11] *Book of Footnotes on Words of Julian*, pref.2 (PL 48,111).

[12] *On the Merits, etc*, sup. cit., and *On the Spirit and the Letter* (PL 44,201–46).

influential persons in Rome and elsewhere. This was a time when the African Church was better organized than that in Rome, which was still recovering from the shock of Alaric's attack on the city and, now that Ambrose was dead, lacked any comparable figure to lead it. It was not difficult for a skilled tactician like the Bishop of Hippo to put the right amount of pressure on the right people at the right moment. Letters were sent in all directions, usually backed up by Augustine's own account of the Synod of Diospolis, specifically directed at setting the record straight after Pelagius had allegedly distorted it in his. As a result of these measures and the impression created among the opposition by Pelagius' latest treatise, *On Nature*, both he and Celestius were condemned by Councils at Milevis and Carthage, and pressure put on Pope Innocent to excommunicate them. This he did after some delay with the reservation that Pelagius would be allowed to appear before him or justify his conduct by letter; Pelagius duly sent the Pope his *Letter of Justification* and *Confession of Faith*, supported by a letter of recommendation from Praylius, who had succeeded his former patron John as Bishop of Jerusalem. But the Pope died early in 417, and it was his successor, Zosimus, who received Pelagius' communications. In the same year, Celestius, who had been ordained priest at Ephesus in 415 but had been expelled from Constantinople subsequently, also appealed to the Pope of Rome by submitting his *Confession of Faith* and appearing before a tribunal at Rome as well. Pope Zosimus reserved his judgement for two months, so that the African bishops' representatives could appear before him, at the same time acquitting Pelagius for lack of firm evidence and warning the Africans that they should recognize the fact that so far neither he nor his friend Celestius had been expelled from the Church.

Pelagius seemed to have won another battle but he was soon to lose the war. Augustine returned to the attack, putting even more pressure on Zosimus to get him to reconsider a decision which was tantamount to reversing that of his predecessor, and the Emperor now intervened at the request of his officials at Rome – he was at Ravenna at the time – and issued an imperial rescript condemning all those who denied the Fall of Adam and banishing Pelagius and Celestius from Rome, where he apparently supposed them to be living. The Pelagian controversy had now become a political, as well as an ecclesiastical, issue, since stories had reached the Emperor of outbreaks of violence in the capital caused by Pelagian dissidents and of a physical attack on a retired official in the course of them. About the same time a Council of Carthage passed a series of nine canons against Pelagianism, and Zosimus at last gave in to the demands of the bishops and circulated an *Epistula Tractoria* which condemned Pelagius and Celestius and their supporters and excommunicated them, while ordering that all the bishops who supported them in Italy should also subscribe to the document. Pelagius was subsequently expelled from Palestine too after further intervention by Augustine and his friends. We do not know what happened to him after that or the date and place of his death but assume that it must have come about before 431, when the Council of Ephesus condemned the 'opinions' of Celestius without any mention of Pelagius, and that, quite possibly, he ended his days in Egypt, where a group of his remaining supporters still survived. We have no evidence to corroborate the suggestion that he spent some time in Antioch before retiring to Egypt.

The Council of Ephesus also confirmed the removal from office of four Italian bishops who were among those refusing to subscribe to Zosimus' *Epistula Tractoria* and had been expelled from Italy in consequence. One of these was Julian of Eclanum, the man who, with Augustine, dominated the final phase of the Pelagian controversy. Of noble stock and the son of a bishop, he himself became a bishop c.416, having made a considerable name for himself by virtue of his talents, his attachment to the simple life, his conscientiousness and Christian charity. But all this was of no avail when he joined, perhaps even led, his eighteen colleagues in refusing to accept the Pope's decision against Pelagius and Celestius. Deposed from his see and banished in 418, he retired to the Middle East and devoted most of the rest of his life to the harassment of Augustine. A formidable controversialist and natural dialectician, he was totally unscrupulous in pressing his attack on the ageing Bishop of Hippo, who must have hoped that he had now rid the Church and himself of the troublesome Pelagians, and in addition to reaffirming and refurbishing their case against his theology, also reopened the old sore of his alleged Manicheism.

Unfortunately Julian's two main works against Augustine[13] have been lost, and what we know of them is derived from Augustine's quotations from them; we also have fragments of five or, possibly, six letters of his and an abbreviated version of his *Commentary on the Book of Job*.[14] While it is true that he discovered and exploited new and effective lines of attack on Augustine, his criticisms were often so arrogant and offensive that they tend to obscure his undoubted ability and lessen our sympathy for him, and the account of the debate, insofar as it is possible to reconstruct it from Augustine's works, does little credit to either protagonist. At Ephesus in 431 his case, like that of his colleagues and of Celestius, was dealt with summarily, and their last hopes of some kind of rehabilitation disappointed. Julian retreated to the West this time and is said to have spend the rest of his life teaching Latin to the children of a Pelagian family in Sicily after a last, vain attempt to secure his reinstatement in the Church from Pope Sixtus III, whom he must have known well in earlier and happier days. Celestius too had appealed in 423 to Pope Boniface, Zosimus' successor, to pardon him but without success; he too was banished from Italy.

And so the last decade of Augustine's life brought him no respite from the Pelagians: in this period no fewer than ten of his anti-Pelagian treatises were written, some in response to Julian, others to reassure his friends and correspondents of the justice of Pelagius' condemnation and to answer queries on the subject of his own doctrine of grace which they had raised as a result of what they had heard or read of the controversy. For example, in 426 the monks of Hadrumetum in North Africa were divided into two warring factions after reading a copy of his letter to Sixtus, at this time a presbyter in Rome, which set out

[13] *To Turbantius* and *To Florus*.
[14] PLS 1,1573–679.

his case for predestination in its severest form; the beleaguered saint responded by sending the abbot and his monks two letters along with two treatises and a batch of copies of relevant documents to explain his point of view,[15] and even interviewed a few of them at his own home and kept them with him there for some time. We hear no more of the monks of Hadrumetum; but we do hear a great deal of the so-called 'Semi-Pelagians',[16] monks in Southern Gaul who had also been alarmed by what they had heard and read of the Pelagian controversy and, in particular, of Augustine's teaching on election and predestination, which seemed to them to be 'contrary to the opinion of the Fathers and the common view of the Church'.[17] Augustine defended his doctrine in two more treatises,[18] insisting that the theory of predestination was by no means a novel one but went back as far as Paul and that the only way for Christians to keep the faith and uphold the integrity of the Church was by persevering in obedience to the will of God as expressed in his commandments.

But the monks continued to protest that Augustine's teaching on predestination was revolutionary and a threat to their belief in grace as a partnership between God and man, which had never hitherto been challenged. They found a worthy champion and spokesman in John Cassian, a former pupil of John Chrysostom, whose standing in the Church was at that time above question and who was neither Pelagian nor Augustinian, since he rejected both the extreme view on free will held by Pelagius and Augustine's teaching on the Fall, concupiscence and predestination. He was supported by other highly respected leaders of the monks in Southern Gaul – Vincent of Lerins, for example, and, a little later, Faustus of Riez, but strongly opposed by Prosper of Aquitaine, whose efforts to win the support of Pope Sixtus III for his campaign against Cassian were notably unsuccessful and eventually petered out. Augustine's doctrine of predestination was rejected by the Council of Orange in 529 but his teaching on grace and free will came to be generally accepted by the Church, whereas Cassian's theory of the successive operation of will and grace – 'first the will acts, then the grace is given' – cost him his reputation as a theologian and the canonization which he surely deserved.[19] Pelagianism continued to worry the Church in Western Europe long after Augustine's death; even in the year before it took place Pope Celestine I found it necessary to send Germanus to Britain to quell an uprising by Pelagians there, and that warrior saint is believed by some to have had to make a second

15 Letters, 194 (PL 33,874ff.); 214, 215, 216,2,3 (PL 33,968ff.; 971ff.; 44,914,875ff.); On Grace and Free Will (PL 44,881–912); On Rebuke and Grace (PL 44,915–946).
16 Once defined by Harnack as 'popular Catholicism made more definite and profound by Augustine's doctrine'. It is a rather misleading term, as the last name that Cassian, for example, wished to have foisted on him would have been 'Semi-Pelagian'. It was first applied to the Molinists by their opponents.
17 See Augustine, Letters,225 (PL 33,1002–7; 44,947–54).
18 On the Predestination of the Saints and On the Gift of Perseverance (PL 44,959–92; 45,993–1034), originally contained in one work.
19 See O. Chadwick, 1968,114ff.

visit for the same purpose about twelve years later.[20] Despite that, the heresy may well have survived for centuries in one form or another in Britain, as it did in Gaul, Italy, Dalmatia and Ireland, where there is evidence of the popularity of the *Commentary* in the *Book of Armagh* and elsewhere in the Middle Ages. Nor is Pelagianism in the form of Semi-Pelagianism or Synergism without its supporters in the ranks of most denominations today.

II. *The Message*

At the heart of Pelagius' teaching was the belief that, when God created man in his own image, he endowed him with an innate capacity to choose between good and evil according to the prompting of his conscience, 'a kind of natural sanctity' which distinguishes between the two choices by following an 'inner law' and arousing the emotions appropriate to either, that is, shame and fear and guilt for evil, and joy, resolution and confidence for good. It is this innate capacity to make our own free choice between good and evil that we inherit from Adam, not the tainted legacy of original sin, and the sole effect of Adam's first sin upon us is that we habitually imitate him: it is not Adam's concupiscence (in the Augustinian sense)[21] but his example in disobeying God's command which turns us away from good to evil. Thus it is theoretically possible for a man to become perfect by avoiding sin, even if it is admitted that no one has yet been known to have succeeded in attaining that perfection; it will be easier to do so if one adopts an ascetic way of life, eschewing the pleasures of the flesh and the pursuit and enjoyment of wealth and any other worldly attraction which may tempt man to relax his efforts to lead a truly Christian life.

What assistance does God give to those who seek to become true Christians? His grace, available to all alike and not to certain chosen persons alone, consists of the grace of creation in the gift of free will and of the capacity to do good works, the grace of revelation in the divine law of the Old Testament and Jesus' teaching in the New, and the grace of atonement in the death and resurrection of Jesus and the remission of sins through baptism.[22] Pelagius and his followers have no doctrine of 'infused' or 'internal' grace; admittedly, when the heresiarch was pressed, he affirmed that God helps man by 'the manifold and ineffable gift of heavenly grace' but he never finds it possible – or necessary – to explain how this works in practice or to take a step further and 'make an unambiguous declaration of true internal assisting grace'.[23] Hence Augustine's oft-repeated criticism that 'he means by grace nothing else but law and teaching' seemed to be thoroughly justified in the light of one of the statements alleged to have been made by

---

[20] Prosper, *Against the Collator*, 21,2; *Chronicle*, year 429 (PL 51,271,594f.); Constantius, *Life of Germanus*, 12ff., 25ff.; see Thompson,1984,1ff.
[21] See Rees,61ff.
[22] See Bohlin, 46ff.; Evans,1968(a),100ff., and, especially, 111ff.
[23] Bonner,1966,356.

Celestius and cited at the Synod of Diospolis: 'God's grace and help are not given for single actions but consist in free will or in the law and teaching.'[24] Pelagius anathematized this statement, thus dissociating himself from it; but he never showed that he was capable of taking the leap of faith which would enable him to transcend it or even fully understood why Augustine and other non-Pelagians found his doctrine of grace to be deficient. For all their sincerity and commitment, Pelagius and his friends could not avoid giving the impression that for them the relationship between God and man was contractual rather than spiritual and that the essence of true Christianity was righteousness rather than love.

Who, then, are 'true Christians' in the Pelagian sense? They are men and women who are Christians not only in name but in deed. After baptism they strive to be perfect like their Church, which is 'without spot and wrinkle';[25] they study the divine law as set out in the scriptures and obey the commandments of Jesus in every particular, whether great or small; they are holy, innocent, undefiled, unstained, with no malice but only godliness and goodness in their hearts; they do not know how to harm or hurt anyone but only to help everyone; they do not know how to hate even their enemies but only to do good to their adversaries and pray for those who persecute them; they obey all God's commands, not just some of them; they do not swear oaths, they do not slander or flatter others or listen to flattery or slander of themselves; they love their neighbours, help the poor and needy, house the homeless, feed the hungry, sustain the widow and orphan, mourn with those who mourn, weep with those who weep, rejoice with those who rejoice and feel others' pains and share others' joys as if they were their own; they do not seek the praises of others or their possessions but rather the kingdom of heaven, which is their sole reward. And they do all these things in the name of Jesus because they are what he did as an example for them to follow. Great emphasis is put on the absolute necessity to do good works in order to merit the heavenly kingdom; but at the Last Judgement, when the good and the evil are separated like sheep and goats, no one can be sure of a place with God and his angels. The path to heaven is steep and narrow, and few can hope to climb it; but the prize which awaits those who do is infinitely superior to those which this world has to offer. The highest of all are reserved for the celibate, the Christian commandos, the elite of the Christian Church. Pelagianism began as an ascetic movement, following in the path of Christians in the East, in Egypt, for example, in Syria and in Palestine, and its adherents never allowed themselves and their converts to forget it: spiritual exercises in the form of prayer and scriptural reading and the reading or singing of psalms are urged upon converts but no instructions are given as to how to perform them and all three are a kind of meditation on the divine law, moral rather than spiritual in purpose. In fact, prayer is 'indisputably one of the weak points in the Pelagian

---

24 *On the Grace of Christ*,vii.8;x.11 (PL 44,337;365f.); *On the Activities of Pelagius*,xiv.30 (PL 44,337).
25 Ibid. xii.27.

programme',[26] and none of the texts in this collection gives more than a passing reference to it; though virgins and widows are encouraged to set a special time aside for private prayer and reading, these are but aids to the Christian life, which is concerned above all with obedience to the divine law and the performance of good works.

The aim of Pelagius and his followers was not to refine or revive the spirituality of the Church but to purge it of all the dross which it had accumulated over the centuries separating it from the purity and innocence of its infancy. Pelagianism was not intended to be a prop for the weary and faint-hearted but a school for would-be saints. It was 'the Christianity of discontinuity, the idea that conversion and initiation could make a total break in the personality',[27] and in proclaiming its necessity Pelagius was only maintaining an old tradition of the Church which, in his opinion, Augustine was trying to set aside. The heart of true Christianity for Pelagius was the moment when a man or woman was baptized and began a new life; this was what Augustine had also thought at one time but his own experience and his knowledge of human nature had brought him disenchantment: by the time he wrote Book X of his Confessions he had become convinced that neither conversion nor baptism and certainly not the use of the free will could overcome the habit of sinning and that only God's grace could prevail over the insidious, inner operations of inherited sin. When he wrote his treatise On Free Will against the Manichees in the years from 388 to 395 he could still speak of man's response to a divine call freely made by God and freely accepted by man in faith; but, in replying to questions put to him by his friend Simplicianus in 396–97, he wrote, 'I had tried to solve the question by upholding the freedom of the will; but it was God's grace that prevailed.'[28]

This was the message which caused the Pelagians to be condemned as heretics in the early-fifth century. In what sense was it 'heretical'? Surely not in the sense that there was an agreed doctrine throughout the Church on original sin, traducianism, predestination or even grace, a doctrine, that is, which was accepted 'semper, ubique et ab omnibus', 'always, everywhere and by everyone.'[29] But in the African Church there was such a doctrine, firmly held and deeply embedded in its teachings: it was Tertullian who introduced the idea of the seminal transmission of sin and had coined the term vitium originis to describe it;[30] it was Cyprian who had stressed that baptism was essential to counteract the contagion and that this cleansing process should be carried out as early as possible, something in which he disagreed with Tertullian, who argued that it should be delayed for as long as possible and did not favour infant baptism. What Augustine did was to build original sin and its transmission, infant baptism, grace and predestina-

---

[26] Nuvolone and Solignac, 2933.

[27] Brown,1972,200,n.2.

[28] Retractations,II,66 (PL 32,656).

[29] The famous 'Vincentian' triad containing the criteria for a dogma to satisfy before being accepted by the Christian Church.

[30] On the Soul,41 (PL I,2,764); in his earlier anti-Pelagian works Augustine uses the word delictum, but by 418 the term generally accepted in Africa was originale peccatum.

tion into a coherent theological system, while carrying the first and last of these to extremes hitherto inconceivable. In Africa Celestius had very little, if any, prospect of acquittal by the Council of Carthage in 411; in Palestine, on the other hand, at the Synod of Diospolis in 415 Pelagius had no difficulty in dissociating himself from the charges brought against his friend and, at the same time, evading those made against himself. Either Augustine was right in maintaining that the Synod was incapable of understanding what Pelagius was saying through an interpreter or its members were not greatly interested anyway. There was already a wide gulf between the doctrinal concerns of the Western and Eastern branches of the Church, and what the one regarded as an integral article of faith the other might dismiss as a matter of discretion, and vice versa.

Moreover, there was in the Western Church no coherent body of doctrine tried, tested and refined in the furnace of controversy and thus able to stand up to the Africans. There had been no heresy before this one, if one excludes Priscillianism which arose in the peripheral area of Spain and was, in many but by no means all respects, like Pelagianism, and there had been little open debate about matters of doctrine and belief in living memory except for that which had been engendered by Jerome during his lively stay in Rome. To form some impression of what the rest of the Western Church thought about Augustine's theory of original sin, free will and predestination we have only to recall the attitude of the monks of Hadrumetum and Marseilles: there can be no question that they were deeply shocked, and the episode at Hadrumetum gives us 'an exceptional opportunity of watching the immediate reaction of the humbler religious of St. Augustine's time to some of the more difficult of his writings'.[31] Living and working in a tradition derived from Egypt and Syria, they could see their simplicity of belief and life being undermined by these new-fangled and outlandish ideas. In Sicily, Britain and, probably, Spain as well there were signs of opposition to this seemingly novel theology emanating from Africa, and it may well be that, as far as Pelagius' fellow-countrymen and the other dissenters from Augustinian 'orthodoxy' were concerned, they regarded themselves as 'orthodox', because they wished to cling to their traditional beliefs, and the African bishops and their supporters as the 'heretics'.[32]

Nor did their superiors show any great enthusiasm for the African cause: Pope Innocent and his successor Zosimus delayed as long as possible before arriving at a decision in the case of Pelagius and Celestius and left a door open for them to appeal or recant; a decade or so later Celestine I showed himself lukewarm, to say the least, when Prosper appealed to him to discipline John Cassian. And the Emperor Honorius was obviously at sea when it was reported to him that there had been an outbreak of violence in Rome and that the Pelagians had caused it, and he showed his theological naivety when along with Pelagius and Celestius he also banished from Rome anyone 'who denied the Fall'. But in one of his

---

[31] N.K. Chadwick, 1955, 179.
[32] Cf. Markus, 1986, 198ff. He stresses the conjectural nature of his suggestion, and, I may have rather overstated its implications.

sentences he – that is, the imperial official who compiled the rescript – hit the nail on the head: 'this subtle heresy,' he comments, 'considers it a particular mark of low breeding to agree with other people and the balm of outstanding good sense to destroy what is generally approved.'[33] Their offence in his eyes was as much their arrogance and refusal to fall in with the views approved by the establishment as their denial of the doctrine of the Fall. As Bonner so aptly comments, 'With surprising perception the imperial chancery had taken the measure of Pelagianism and high-lighted its fundamental flaw: the self-confident superiority, derived from the aristocratic milieu in which it first grew and flourished and which it carried over into the Christian life.'[34]

On the surface the conflict between the Pelagians and the Augustinians must have seemed then, as it may seem now, to be about dogma and doctrine but beneath there ran a strong undercurrent of resentment and suspicion: the Pelagians deeply resented what they regarded as unwarranted attempts to stifle their teaching and interfere with their freedom to express their religious views, the Catholics were profoundly suspicious of what they saw as a threat to the very existence of their Church in its present form by the creation either inside or outside it of another minority 'church' composed of ascetics, celibates, virgins, widows and paupers and run by 'monks'.[35] Both sides were unreasonably inflexible in their views; both had exceeded the limits of true 'orthodoxy'; both made equally strident claims that they were defending the traditional doctrines of the Church. But, in fact, neither could be branded as truly 'heretical', neither could be called truly 'unorthodox'. In the heat of a controversy of this kind and magnitude it is almost impossible for the contemporary observer, let alone the active participant, to determine precisely what 'orthodoxy' is, not only because of regional differences but also because the final judgement awaits the emergence of a 'new orthodoxy'. In this case the judges were the ecclesiastical establishment and the political authority: the former were unlikely to commit institutional suicide in the interests of gaining a posthumous reputation for objectivity, the latter would avoid involvement for as long as possible and then intervene when further delay might endanger their own security.[36]

The match might well have ended in a draw; instead it went on to 'extra time', and at the end of that Augustine and his team won with the help of some

---

[33] I am indebted to Frend, 1985,135, for bringing this quotation from Honorius' Edict (PL 48,381) and also the following quotation to my attention.

[34] Bonner,1972,51.

[35] Cf. Jerome, Letters,133,12 (PL 22,1160): he claimed that such people preferred to be called 'Pelagians' rather than 'Christians'. Donatism was not easily to be forgotten.

[36] It has often been pointed out how political events influenced the course of the Pelagian controversy to the disadvantage of the Pelagians: Alaric's siege of Rome drove them out of Italy and exposed them to more critical eyes in Africa and Palestine; Honorius had much to thank Augustine for on account of his energetic and eventually victorious campaign against the Donatists, and this demonstration of Augustine's capacity for decisive action may well have influenced the Emperor when he received reports of what was going on in Rome and of Augustine's attempts to suppress the rebels.

questionable decisions made by the referees and touch-judges. And it was victory that counted, since it was the victors who received the cup and the kudos, gave the interviews and were established in the record books as the team of the year, whose style and tactics, stamped with success, would be used as models by future competitors. *Securus iudicat orbis terrarum*:[37] 'the referee's decision is final'!

III. *The Medium*

The Pelagian message was evangelical, salvationist and didactic; the medium by which it was transmitted was teaching – in personal contact, through treatises and in letters. Of the first of these we have only hearsay evidence derived from the criticism and gossip of the anti-Pelagians; very few of the treatises have survived except in fragments, and those which have are minor ones; but of letters and homilies in letter form enough are extant to enable us to become well acquainted with the opinions of the first generation of Pelagians. The range of topics discussed is very limited, consisting of advice or reprimand addressed to converts, penitents, virgins, celibates, widows and so on; but, though one has to put up with a good deal of repetition, inevitable in the circumstances, this in itself has the advantage of making it possible for the reader to compare and contrast the different treatments of the same theme by different writers.

Ever since the fifth century, when the letters and tracts contained in this collection were written, rash claims have been made from time to time as to the authorship of almost all of them and especially of the two groups in Part I and Part II. More recently, however, and certainly in the last two decades scholars seem to have begun to adopt a more cautious approach to problems of identification, and most of them would agree that only a few of our letters can be attributed to specific writers with complete or, as some might prefer to say, any certainty: only the letter *To Demetrias* and the *Confession of Faith* can be identified as the work of Pelagius on external evidence, subject to the reservation that he may have received assistance in writing them; the letter *To Celantia* and the tractate *On the Christian Life* both have their supporters. No one knows for certain who wrote the letters in Part II but we can be sure that it was *not* Pelagius himself but a man who held strong Pelagian views, that is, if we accept that it was one man who wrote them all. As for the texts in Part III, it would be a brave man who would venture to claim more than that most of them are Pelagian in the sense that they were written by Pelagians.

The main reason for all this uncertainty is to be found in the unusual circumstances in which the texts were written. Once Pelagianism had been declared a heresy, public debate on the rights and wrongs of its case was no longer possible except in regions far enough away from the ecclesiastical centres of the Western

---

[37] Augustine, *Against the Letter of Parmenian*,III,24 (PL43,101), 'the world's verdict is beyond dispute.'

and Eastern Empires to enable dissenters to express their views without fear of persecution. But such areas were few and far between: even Britain at the furthest extremity of the Western Empire would not be likely to escape attention any more than Sicily could be trusted not to harbour Augustine's informers.[38] Egypt might be a safe place of refuge but not Palestine or Syria after the Council of Ephesus in 431, and Pelagians in Italy would be forced to stay silent on pain of banishment or become part of an underground movement. All Pelagians were now officially branded as heretics within the boundaries of the Empire, and we must not forget that large tracts even of that had fallen into the hands of the barbarians by the middle of the fifth century or not long after. It would, therefore, be dangerous to admit to authorship of any document expressing the Pelagian viewpoint or to be caught in possession of a text written by Pelagius, Celestius or any other member of the group of Pelagians regarded as the leaders of the heresy.

An excellent illustration of what might, and did, happen to Pelagian works can be found in the history of the text of Pelagius' *Commentary*. Marius Mercator, a contemporary historian, referred to it as a work of Pelagius, and Augustine himself had seen it and dismissed it as 'some very brief, expository comments of Pelagius'.[39] But Gennadius, writing only about fifty years later,[40] cited as works written by Pelagius before his condemnation his treatise *On the Trinity* and his *Book of Extracts*, which suggests that he knew nothing of the existence of the *Commentary*, usually thought to have been written during the same period as the other two – unless, of course, his chronology of the Pelagian controversy was far from correct. Now, if there was such uncertainty about the authorship of the *Commentary* – or ignorance of its existence – in the fifth century, it will come as no surprise to learn that it did not begin to be recognized as a Pelagian work until the sixteenth and as a work by Pelagius until the turn of the seventeenth. It was not until the beginning of the twentieth century that the full importance of the *Commentary* for the study of Pelagius and Pelagianism became apparent, after Souter, stimulated by Zimmer and building on his pioneer efforts, applied himself to the mammoth task of restoring the text to something approaching the original and began to publish the first results of his research. Only two centuries before, Jean Garnier, one of the greatest authorities on the Pelagian heresy in his day, while noting that Ambrose had ceased to be regarded as the author of the *Commentary* since c.550, attributed it to 'the deacon Hilarius' instead.[41] If this could happen to one of the most important works of the heresiarch himself and 'the earliest extant work of a British author',[42] what sort of a fate could we expect for his treatises and letters and those of his followers?

Rufinus the Syrian was comparatively lucky: his *Book on the Faith* was dis-

---

[38] See my introductions to *On the Possibility of Not Sinning* and *On Riches* in Part II.
[39] *On the Merits*, etc., III,i.1 (PL 44,185).
[40] *On Famous Men*,43 (PL 58,83).
[41] But it was he too who first drew attention to a vital passage in Cassiodorus which everyone else had overlooked.
[42] M.R. James, *The Cambridge History of English Literature*,I,1908,65.

covered and published as long ago as 1650 and printed with annotations by Garnier in 1673; otherwise, only a much slighter *Confession of Faith*, also known as *Twelve Anathemata* and of disputed authorship, and a small extract from the Vulgate New Testament recently attributed to him have survived.[43] Celestius has been less fortunate in that, apart from his *Confession of Faith* as reconstructed by Garnier and others,[44] only a few fragments from his many writings are still extant. Representing the works of Annianus of Celeda, Pelagius' companion in Palestine and his amanuensis, sarcastically described by Orosius as his 'armour-bearer' and by Jerome as his 'voice' and 'shadow', we have versions of his Latin translations of sermons by John Chrysostom and the two Epistles of his own which have been prefixed to translations of the same writer's expositions of the Gospel of Matthew and Epistles of Paul.[45] Only a few fragments of Julian's works remain apart from his *Commentary on the Book of Job*, and, in any case, it is doubtful if we should describe him as a 'follower of Pelagius' rather than a 'follower of Celestius', since he seems to have had more in common with the latter than the former in theology, in ethos and in temperament. As for the lesser lights in the Pelagian firmament, most of them were doomed either to remain hidden in the appendices to the writings of others or to vanish for ever before the close of the fifth century; the brief letters which comprise our part III represent all that we can attribute to this anonymous group with any confidence.

But not long before Heinrich Zimmer's *Pelagius in Irland*, which laid the foundation for a reliable text of Pelagius' *Commentary*, and Souter's earliest papers announcing the discoveries which he had made in the course of his researches, Pelagian studies had entered upon a new and exciting phase when Caspari published a critical edition of the six letters which appear in Part II in translation. Other works or fragments also came to light as a result of the investigations of Morin and Martini and others, including a complete minor treatise *On the Hardening of Pharaoh's Heart*, the authorship of which is still in dispute,[46] and an abbreviated *Commentary on Job* generally believed to be the work of Julian, as we have already noted. And, all the while, scholars were involved in discussions of the authorship or authenticity of the small corpus which was becoming associated with Pelagius' name, combing the columns of Migne's *Patrologia Latina* for likely additions. In this field of exploration the most striking, if controversial, contribution was made by Georges de Plinval.

In an interim report on the progress of his investigations, published in 1934, Plinval attributed nineteen extant works to Pelagius, fragments apart, and added three more later when he published his biography of Pelagius in 1943, though he admitted four years later that seven of these works could no longer be regarded as certainly by Pelagius. Much has been achieved since then, and the application of more rigorous criteria has taken its toll of Plinval's selection: many of his attribu-

---

[43] See Nuvolone and Solignac,2890.
[44] PL 48,498–505.
[45] PL 48,626ff. There are resemblances in the first of these to the style of the letter *To Demetrias*.
[46] PLS 1,1506–39, not a letter or in letter form and so not included in this collection.

tions to Pelagius himself are now relegated to the second division reserved for his anonymous followers, and some have even dropped out altogether, being no longer regarded as Pelagian at all. After the *Commentary* and the *Confession of Faith* the most likely candidates for inclusion in a definitive canon of Pelagius' works are the letters in our Part I, but some doubt the authenticity of one or more of them. R.F. Evans began his investigation into the authorship of these at the point where Plinval had left off. After accepting the inadequacy of the latter's methodology, he went on to criticise the attacks made upon his work by Kirmer and Morris. Kirmer, writing almost immediately after Plinval's original article on the subject appeared, Morris nearly thirty years later, advanced arguments which would have carried greater weight if the evidence offered in their support had been stronger: the former applied a statistical analysis, which was palpably defective, to the style and language of the letters, the latter made assumptions about contemporary events in Roman Britain, on the one hand, and to the aims and essence of Pelagianism, on the other, which could not stand up to stringent examination.[47]

Kirmer's conclusion was that the author of all four letters was not Pelagius but Fastidius, and Morris agreed with him in ruling out Pelagius but thought it safer to place Fastidius inside quotation marks. This is not surprising when we recall that Fastidius owes his historical existence to one reference in Gennadius to 'Fastidius, Bishop of the Britons' and another in the emended heading of an eleventh/twelfth-century manuscript in which the name of Augustine has been erased and *fastidii epi*, 'of Bishop Fastidius', scratched over it.[48] On the strength of these two references however, Kirmer and others took the opportunity to put together a substantial corpus for Fastidius and at the same time to furnish him with a miniature biography linking him with the Agricola blamed for the Pelagian unrest in early-fifth-century Britain by Prosper of Aquitaine and with the Bishop Severian described in the same passage as his father. After exposing the flaws in the arguments of Kirmer and Morris, Evans refused to accept Fastidius as the author of the four letters and constructed a most convincing case for Pelagius based on a thorough examination of parallel themes and passages in them, the *Letter to Demetrias* and the *Commentary*, on the use of identical quotations from the scriptures in support of the same theme, and on similarity in style and vocabulary. Despite the fact that he sometimes permits his patent dedication to his case to affect his objectivity he has given us the best working hypothesis so far available. The chief objection to it is the obvious one, which he himself discusses, that the undoubted resemblances between the letters, the *Letter to Demetrias* and the *Commentary* just mentioned may be the result of imitation, not evidence of identical authorship.

The six Caspari letters have aroused just as much debate and controversy among scholars. Caspari himself wanted to ascribe all of them to Agricola, who depends for his existence on the one reference in Prosper cited above; we must

---

[47] Evans,1968,4ff.
[48] Caspari,353,n.3.

also remember that he was writing before the renaissance in Pelagian studies got under way. Baer, writing in 1902, and Morin, in 1904, assigned the letters to Fastidius, as did Kirmer in 1938, thus crediting his man with all the letters in our Part I and II with the exception of the one to Demetrias. And Haslehurst's translation of the Caspari corpus, which appeared in 1927 with Caspari's text alongside, was entitled *The Works of Fastidius*, the author claiming in his Preface that 'the work of a fellow-countryman of the fifth century surely merits transla-tion, however wrong-headed he may have been on some points',[49] a reference no doubt to his Pelagian opinions on free will, grace and sinlessness, which must have deeply offended his own theology of grace.

Four years before Kirmer's book appeared Plinval, not unexpectedly, had claimed the last five of the Caspari documents for his Pelagius, excluding the first as containing autobiographical information which was clearly inapplicable to him. Here Plinval's judgement was clearly at fault, since it is obvious to anyone who reads the Latin text – and perhaps even to those who use the English version – that the first letter belongs with the second and also with the incom-plete tractate *On the Possibility of Not Sinning*, and, very probably, the other three texts as well. The first letter cannot be detached from the other five texts in the corpus, and thus they are not the work of Pelagius either, not only because the autobiographical detail is inapplicable to him but also because the style and tone of these texts are quite different from those of the Evans letters in our Part I.

So, when John Morris arrived on the Pelagian scene in the early sixties, he was presented with three possible candidates for the authorship of the six letters, Agricola, Fastidius and Pelagius, all of them supported by reputable scholars. Very sensibly he jettisoned all three and, not so sensibly, replaced them with a dubious character of his own creation, a young radical, supposed to have fled from Britain in the early-fifth century for Sicily in the wake of the political and religious upheavals in his native country, the 'Sicilian Briton'. Now, in the first place, the author of the Caspari Corpus was certainly no Sicilian; secondly, he could just as well have come from Gaul or Italy; thirdly, the first Pelagians and their supporters were certainly not radical socialists but radical Christians, not political but moral reformers, not apparatchiks but ascetics. The 'Sicilian Briton' has now served his purpose and been given an honourable discharge, and his creator duly credited with provoking his fellow historians to think afresh about the nexus of problems from which that name emerged. The present writer would settle for 'The Pelagian Anonymous' or something similar in default of a better name but, as most of the early Pelagians are anonymous anyway, such a title might not be very helpful!

But there is still one more possible candidate to be considered, the man whose name appears in the titles which head no fewer than three of the Caspari texts, *On Riches*, *On Bad Teachers* and *On Chastity*, that is, 'the holy Sixtus, bishop and martyr'. It is inconceivable that this refers to the third-century Pope Xystus or Sixtus II, to whom the *Sentences of Sixtus*, translated into Latin by Rufinus of

49 Haslehurst, pref.,v.

Aquileia, were at one time wrongly attributed and whose life ended in martyrdom. But it might well be a reference to Pope Sixtus III, who, as a presbyter at Rome, had exerted considerable influence in ecclesiastical circles there at the time of the Pelagian controversy – Plinval describes him as *en quelque sort le porte-parole de l'aristocratie sacerdotale*[50]; he is known to have had Pelagian sympathies until his recantation in 418, mainly under pressure from the African bishops and Augustine and his friend Alypius in particular. It was to this Sixtus that Augustine wrote in that year to express his and Alypius' great joy on hearing the news that he had renounced 'that most fatal dogma (sc. Pelagianism) . . . which is diametrically opposed to the grace of God',[51] following this letter up with the long and elaborate epistle on predestination which so disturbed the monks of Hadrumetum.

Without entirely committing himself, Nuvolone appears to favour the possibility that Sixtus III was the author of the Caspari corpus, and it must be granted that the sketch of Sixtus' life and career which he provides could accommodate the writing of the letters and treatise contained in it: Sixtus' birth would be c.375, his marriage between 395 and 400, the birth of his daughter in the period immediately following that, then his adoption of an ascetic way of life under the influence of Pelagius and his circle, a stay in Sicily from 408 to 409, during which he wrote the first two letters, and, finally, his return to Rome and the composition of the remaining letters and treatise with the one entitled *On Bad Teachers* coming when the Pelagian controversy was well advanced.[52] There would also be time for him to be ordained priest c.415, to live down the memory of his Pelagian connexion and, eventually, after collaboration with Popes Boniface I and Celestine I, to become Pope himself in 432. It was he who refused Julian of Eclanum's request to be reinstated in 439 after his return to the West, and so, if he had written the Caspari corpus in his earlier days, he had indeed achieved a notable volte-face before his death in 440. Is it conceivable that the aggressive, outspoken author of those vehicles of extreme Pelagianism could have been capable of outgrowing and casting off his earlier opinions and beliefs to the extent that he then found it possible to condemn it and its adherents and turn his coat inside out to join the opposition? The answer is 'Probably, yes!': had not Paul done likewise long ago and joined forces with the erstwhile enemies whom he had persecuted, and had not Augustine in more recent times abandoned the Manichees after some nine years and established himself as a defender of the faith? History is strewn with examples of renegades who have found it possible to transfer their zeal for their old cause to the one that they have just acquired and even increase its intensity. More serious objections to replacing the 'Sicilian Briton' with Pope Sixtus III are the lack of biographical detail for the latter's career – as opposed to intelligent guesswork – and Pelagianism's unhappy record in attracting to itself plausible attributions which turn out not so long afterwards

---

[50] Plinval,1943,320.
[51] *Letters*,194 (PL 33,874ff.).
[52] See Nuvolone and Solignac,2916f.

to be unsustainable in the light of fresh discoveries and recommend the exercise of extreme caution.

But, whoever the author of the Caspari Corpus was, he was certainly a Pelagian whose views were more severe than those of Pelagius himself; he may have been under the influence of the Pelagian founding-fathers in Rome, if that was indeed the starting-point for his journey to Sicily, or he may have been won over by the arguments and example of the lady who became his spiritual mentor after he had arrived there. It has also been suggested that Pelagius and Celestius stayed for a time in Sicily on their way to Africa; as far as I know, there is no evidence that they did but the possibility cannot be ruled out.[53] In fact, R.F. Evans has taken it much farther: he believes that 'we now have concrete evidence that Pelagius did stop in Sicily' and that 'he gave to the man whom we are calling the "Sicilian Briton" copies of four of his works.' These, he claims, were his *Commentary*, *On the Christian Life*, *On Virginity* and *On the Divine Law*, all of which bear many resemblances in style and vocabulary to the Caspari letters which are too characteristic of Pelagius to be dismissed as mere coincidences.

Evans goes on to suggest that the 'Sicilian Briton' met and conversed with Pelagius – 'they were both, after all, Britons residing for the present in Sicily' (!) – and by this means acquired features of Pelagius' vocabulary and manner of expression. One is relieved to find Evans admitting that his suggestion 'may seem to be a bit unusual' and thus to some extent restoring his own credibility. It is, of course, possible that Pelagius and Celestius came to Sicily and stayed there for a while, long enough to enable them to sow the first seeds there and leave circles of supporters behind them; we know that they both stayed in Carthage, Pelagius for a short and Celestius for a longer period before they parted company. But it is just as possible that they did not visit Sicily at all but that Christians like the 'Sicilian Briton' and his lady teacher had already acquired copies of Pelagius' works for themselves and studied them in detail. We cannot even be sure that it was Pelagius and not Celestius who influenced the Caspari author, if they did visit Sicily, especially as the latter was more Pelagian than Pelagius! Indeed, Celestius himself would have been a strong candidate to replace the 'Sicilian Briton' if he were not ruled out by the clash between what little we know of his early life and the biographical details which are given in the letter to *An Older Friend*.[54]

We must now leave the lush fields of conjecture and return to our dull sheep and hard facts. Of one thing we can be sure: an absolutely essential feature of Pelagian teaching was its habitual use of biblical quotations. I have tried to list and index all that I have found in this collection of letters and minor treatises in letter form and to note differences between the Latin text employed by the

---

53 See Evans,1968,29; their stay would have been a short one anyway, as both were in Africa by 411 according to Augustine, *On the Activities of Pelagius*,xxiv.46 (PL 44,346). I suppose that one could stretch it from 409 to 411, if this fitted into one's theories.

54 Not only did he enter a monastery as a young man (Gennadius, *On Famous Men*,45) but he is also said by Marius Mercator (*Footnotes to the Words of Julian*,pref.; PL 48,111) to have been a eunuch from birth, which does not exactly qualify him to lecture on chastity to those who have known the opposite.

Pelagians and that of the Vulgate in the hope that others who are interested and qualified to do so will study them and perhaps form conclusions about possible patterns which may emerge. Lacking any qualifications in the field of biblical criticism, I shall content myself with making a few observations which may serve as a warning to the unwary, however obvious they may be to the majority of my readers. First and foremost, the Pelagians did not use biblical quotations to enliven a prosaic passage or to show off their own knowledge; they used them as proof-texts, that is, to validate an opinion or statement, just as Matthew used quotations from the Old Testament to authenticate important events in his narrative and, at the same time, to validate prophetic statements contained in them – and it is interesting to note at this point that he was easily the most popular source of scriptural quotations as far as the Pelagians were concerned. Secondly, it is not safe to set too much store by the textual differences, since Pelagius and his followers were using an Old-Latin text of the Bible for the most part, though parts of Jerome's translation of the gospels and parts of the Old Testament were becoming available by now and our earliest evidence of the revised text of the latter parts of the New Testament, which Jerome apparently did not translate, is said to appear in Pelagian works.[55] Thirdly, as Evans has rightly pointed out, very few of our Pelagian texts are available in a critical edition, and 'biblical texts were of all things the most subject to alteration.'[56] And, finally, where there are substantial differences, they may well be due to quoting from memory.[57]

In summing up his detailed study of Pelagius' style and language, Plinval concludes that his language, by and large, is classical, purer and more regular than that of very many of his contemporaries: he chooses his words and figures with great care, he avoids the popular terms, pseudo-archaisms and romantic expressions already spreading through biblical and Christian Latin texts, he is much more traditional than Jerome and Augustine and closer in his use of words to Lactantius and Cyprian than to writers of his own time, and his style recalls that of the last-named most of all.[58] But these conclusions are based on the assumption that Pelagius was the writer not only of the letters in our Part I but also of those in Part II with one exception, as well as of four letters in Part III.[59] One must, therefore, take them with a pinch of salt and offer in their place a few tentative comments of one's own derived from one's own reading – that is, until

---

[55] Livingstone,544, under 'Vulgate'.
[56] Evans,1968,34.
[57] The translations of the biblical quotations are those of the Revised Standard Version, amended, where necessary, to suit the Latin text where it differs from the Vulgate; but, as we have already noted, the quotations may well have been tampered with by editors and scribes before reaching us. I have also used the RSV abbreviations for the biblical titles.
[58] Plinval,1947, especially 116ff.
[59] In his introduction to this book Plinval stressed that the writings on which his conclusions were based were the same as the twenty-two which he had attributed to Pelagius in 1943 with the exception of two, not included in this selection, to which 'serious objections' had been raised; Plinval, 1947,11f.

someone undertakes the whole task of analysing Pelagius' style and language in
detail all over again but with different assumptions about authorship, perhaps
using the groundwork done by Evans and Kirmer as a starting-point. My comments would be that Pelagius does write, for the most part, clear and correct
Latin; he is at his best when expounding scripture, as in his *Commentary*, at his
worst when he is indulging in philosophical or psychological speculations. With
the exception of the letter *To Demetrias*,[60] however, his style is austere at times
and laboured: it is the style, I think, of a man who has devoted much care and
painful effort to mastering his second language without ever showing himself
capable of the fluency and spontaneity of a native.[61] This is not simply because
he has a penchant for writing in periods which would not have disgraced Cicero
or Livy: the 'Pelagian Anonymous' is just as fond of them, yet often succeeds in
enlivening them with an infusion of crispness and panache, as do one or two of
the writers in Part III also. '*Le style*', they say, '*est l'homme même*'; this may well
have been true of Pelagius: he wrote like the sober, earnest and correct man that
he was. But it is for his message and for its theological and historical importance
that we read him, not in order to be entertained by a display of pyrotechnics.

IV. *The Matrix*

The reader will not have failed to notice that cautious reservations have greatly
outnumbered firm conclusions in this Introduction. That is mainly because, by
the time the winners have written history, it is little more than 'a distillation of
rumour', as Carlyle once put it. In the case of Pelagius we owe the scattering of
hard facts about him that we do possess to a couple of official documents issued
by his enemies and references to him in their treatises and letters. In other words,
we still need much more information before we shall be in a position to form a
definitive judgement on him or, it follows, on the heresy which bears his name.
But there are two questions which must be put: 'Who *was* the founder of the
heresy which came to be known as Pelagianism?', and 'What was the matrix in
which it originated?' Jerome was the first to try to pinpoint the founder: it was
Pelagius, of course, and his heresy was an offshoot of Origenism. Having decided
that Pelagius was an Origenist, he had no difficulty in tracing his heretical
opinions to the influence of almost everyone else whom he considered to be
Origenist, working his way from his most recent antagonist, Rufinus of Aquileia,
through Palladius and Evagrius Ponticus to the Manichees and the Messalians.[62]
Marius Mercator, on the other hand, who was also a contemporary of Pelagius,

---

60 We have to allow for the possibility that this was not written without some assistance;
    see my introduction to the letter.
61 Jerome writes that 'his Latin is not bad for a provincial'. This is probably fair comment;
    I cannot enthuse about its 'elegance', as does Plinval.
62 *Letters*, 133 (PL 22,1150ff.).

took a different view: he identified Rufinus of Syria as the founder of the heresy and traced its origins to Theodore of Mopsuestia, who was later to give asylum to Julian of Eclanum: Rufinus, he said, had instructed Pelagius in his poisonous doctrine so that the latter might become his spokesman.[63] In the seventeenth century Jean Garnier, commenting on Mercator's statement, also identified Rufinus of Syria as the founder of Pelagianism and attributed Theodore's unorthodox views to Paul of Samosata, Bishop of Antioch, thus taking the heresy back to third-century origins; but, on occasions, when discussing the heresy, he refers to it as 'Celestianism'.[64] The word 'Pelagiani' appears for the first time in Jerome's Dialogue against the Pelagians in 415, and from that time Augustine also began to use it, having previously refrained from naming names in the hope that, as he claimed, they might have an opportunity to amend their ways.[65]

In any case, it was not the usual practice to use names of individuals at this time, unless it was absolutely necessary. By 415 it had become necessary: at first, in 411, Augustine had attacked Rufinus and Celestius for their views on infant baptism and original sin but now, in the third book of the same treatise, having just read Pelagius' Commentary, broadened his criticism to include him as well, while still speaking of him in complimentary terms. But he soon realized that conciliatory approaches were pointless, when he read Pelagius' Letter to Demetrias and his treatise On Nature; he now attacked him openly and seemed to have made up his mind that he was the heresiarch. In fact, as we have noted earlier, by now he had no alternative, as Rufinus was dead and Celestius was in the Near East; in any case, he now regarded the latter as Pelagius' pupil, although Orosius in Africa was claiming that both Pelagius and Celestius had 'sowed the heresy' there notwithstanding the fact that Pelagius had played no part at all in the controversy at Carthage.[66] The opponents of the Pelagians could be forgiven for finding the situation rather confusing, since the latters' leaders seemed to be putting up different targets to be fired at at different times: there was no coherent, uniform theology to attack, only a number of opinions, some of them stressed by one spokesman, others by another. Even Augustine took four years to identify Pelagianism as a heresy and Pelagius as its leader, though he himself later maintained in 417 that he had actually done this as early as 412 and was to repeat this claim in his Retractations, written in 426–27.

Granted, however, that he was right in assuming that Pelagius was the leader of the Pelagians in 415, which seems entirely reasonable, it is still arguable that he was not the founder of the heresy; indeed, it is possible to argue that there was no founder and that there could not have been one, if we take into account the unsystematic, almost casual way in which it came into being: as I have said elsewhere, it just 'growed and growed'. But let us admit that Pelagius was in at the beginning of the movement, to say the least, and then go on to address

---

[63] PL 48,258ff.
[64] Ibid. 257f.
[65] Retractations,II,33 (PL 32,644); cf. Letters,157 (PL 33,674–93).
[66] Book in Defence,3,4 (PL 31,1177).

ourselves to the second question posed above: 'What was the matrix in which it originated?' It would seem that the first seeds must have been sown when Rufinus the Syrian, Pelagius and Celestius came together in Rome at the turn of the fifth century. Rufinus arrived in Rome from Bethlehem on his way to Milan with documents entrusted to him by Jerome in 399 probably for use in his attack on Rufinus of Aquileia's translation of Origen's On First Principles and, according to Marius Mercator, he then wrote his own Book on the Faith, which was in the main an attack on Origen, in 399–402. Pelagius and Celestius came to know him while he was staying with Jerome's old friend Pammachius, and in 411 at the Council of Carthage Celestius referred to him as the priest whom he had heard questioning the transmission of sin.[67] There can be no doubt that Rufinus' Book on the Faith contained sections on original sin and infant baptism which must have made a great impression on both Pelagius and Celestius, since it seemed to reinforce some of the ideas which were forming in their own minds, and the latter responded quickly with his treatise Against Transmission of Sin.

Pelagius's reaction was perhaps not so immediate or obvious. Since his arrival in Rome in the eighties, presumably with little more than a basic knowledge of Christian doctrine and a wide reading of the scriptures, there had been ample opportunity to discuss the issues which interested him with members of the educated aristocracy with whom he soon became familiar. By now he would have become well-read in contemporary Latin theology and was able to quote from Ambrose, 'Ambrosiaster'[68] and also Jerome and Augustine in his Commentary; he had also acquired more than a smattering of Greek theology, mainly in translation, from Origen, John Chrysostom, Lactantius and, perhaps, Theodore of Mopsuestia, who was a contemporary of his. He would also have read Rufinus of Aquileia's version of The Sentences of Sextus – especially the verses in which Rufinus had distorted his Greek original, this providing Pelagius with a maxim to support his own view of free will with the authority of a much respected source[69] – and he would have followed Jerome's controversy with Rufinus and Jovinian with deep interest. From these theologians, both Greek and Latin, he had learned a great deal and had found in them a number of opinions similar to, or even corroborative of, his own. Torgny Bohlin, who made an exhaustive examination of Pelagius' theology, concluded that he made such good use of what he had found in earlier tradition that he was able to draw together hitherto unreconciled strands in Western and Eastern theology and knit them together into a unity.[70] The tension which he discovered was skilfully converted into a synthesis built around a grace of creation and a grace of redemption, thus making it possible for

---

67 On Original Sin,iii.3 (PL 44,387).
68 This name was coined by Erasmus, since Ambrosiaster's works had been ascribed to Ambrose for a long time; but Augustine referred to him as 'the late Hilarius', and many refer to him as Hilarius today.
69 See H. Chadwick,166; Evans,1968(a),64.
70 Plinval,1943,81 comments on Pelagius' 'disposition to assimilate from an author only what agreed with his own ideas'; Augustine would have agreed with him but would not have made the point quite so tactfully.

him to appeal to orthodox authorities at every point and so give the appearance of merely representing the Church's tradition. But to Augustine this *tour de force* seemed to be nothing else than a heresy which had resulted from the wrong use of orthodox traditions: in his response he was forced to seek new and more profound insights into the essence of Christianity and of man's freedom, and, as Bohlin points out, the resulting concept was so novel that centuries passed by before the Church properly understood what had happened.

All this, of course, is a product of hindsight. But, at the time when the gap between the Western and Eastern Churches was already beginning to widen, did the Roman Christians realize that their theologians were being bombarded by alien, oriental influences whenever they settled down to read in their studies or cells? Jerome, who should have been better placed to judge than most in his Palestinian retreat, thought that he could and gave an illustration of his superior knowledge by rattling off the names of the sources of Pelagius' heresy, all of them Greek Christians except Rufinus Tyrannius of Aquileia, and even he had spent half of his life in Alexandria and Jerusalem and founded a religious house for both sexes on the Mount of Olives. But Jerome himself must have had at least an inkling of the possibility that, as he once suggested jokingly in a letter to a friend, he had become 'half-barbarian, half-Greekling', 'a *farouche* expatriate' in the eyes of the newly Christianized aristocracy as it closed ranks and struggled to relate its Christianity to its cultural heritage from the pagan past.[72] Even those esoteric manuscripts which he persisted in sending to Italy – and the equally strange persons who brought them – constituted a threat to the fabric of Rome's regenerate society.

Asceticism too, a *sine qua non* of the Pelagian movement, had spread from the East and was now well established in the monasteries of the West. What the Antiochenes had done for the Pelagians' theology the Syrians and Egyptians had done for their way of life;[73] there were marked affinities between the Pelagians and Syriac Christianity – the same belief in a need to seek perfection, the crucial role of baptism in spiritual progress, and the resultant commitment to a moral confrontation with evil and a sustained assault on bad habits through the renunciation of physical pleasures and wealth. The Roman Christians saw ascetism and austere morality as ideals for their 'monks' to pursue in their cells; the Pelagians, like the early Syriac Church, saw them as essential ingredients of everyday life and the unremitting quest for perfection. They found their own concept of the Church as comprising only 'baptized ascetics'[74] confirmed by what they learned

---

[71] See Bohlin,109f. Not the least of Bohlin's services to Pelagian studies was to demonstrate Pelagius' total commitment to the eradication of Manicheism, which Augustine had brought to its knees after a tedious struggle with it throughout the earlier part of his episcopate. The Manichees were both dualists and determinists, for whom matter was evil, sin necessarily a component of human existence, and man's nature crippled from birth; they also completely rejected the Old Testament. There could be no compromise between them and the Pelagians.

[72] See Brown,1972,221.

[73] See Plinval,1943,133f.; Frend,124f.; Marrou,459ff.; Barnard,195f.

[74] Barnard,196.

about Syriac Christianity through the agency of middlemen like the two Rufinuses. In both settings, the Syrian and the Pelagian, asceticism and theology were mutually complementary. But whether Syriac Christianity actually sparked off certain tendencies and ideas in Pelagianism and, especially, in Pelagius and Celestius or merely reinforced them we cannot say.

What, you may ask, of Jerome's charge that, by claiming that it was possible 'for a man to be without sin if he so wished', as it was stated at the Synod of Diospolis, Pelagius was teaching Stoic, not Christian doctrine? Pelagius replied to the effect that he had indeed said that a man could be without sin, if he so wished, since this ability had been given to him by God, but he had not said that he knew of anyone who had been yet able to do this throughout his life, though it was possible after conversion by personal effort and with God's grace.[75] The second of Jerome's grounds for accusing Pelagius of Stoicism was that he taught the Stoic equality of sins; this Pelagius answered by explaining that what he taught was a difference in the gravity of sins but that it was just as important to avoid committing the smaller ones as the greater, since the first of these would lead to the second:[76] all the commandments had to be obeyed without distinction or exception.[77] Jerome also equated Pelagius' 'sinlessness', as he called it,[78] with Stoic *apatheia*, 'freedom from emotion', a misunderstanding of which so good a scholar should not have been guilty. Strict morality and respect for human nature and for the power of reason were certainly features of Stoicism and Pelagianism alike; but these similarities were superficial, and the metaphysics and epistemology underlying them were totally different. Furthermore, even Paul is said to have been influenced by Stoic language and, possibly, thought, the Christian Fathers were greatly affected by Stoicism and embodied some of its ideas in Christian moral philosophy, and, more recently, Ambrose had used Cicero's De Officiis as a model for his own De Officiis Ministrorum, through which the Stoic ethic of reason was transmitted to the Middle Ages. The name of 'The Christian Seneca' was a neat one for Pelagius' critics to give him but totally misleading and no more justifiable than Tertullian's description of Seneca as 'often one of us'.[79]

We can now address ourselves to the two questions which provoked this discussion of the religious and theological milieu in which Pelagianism was born and grew up. To the first we may fairly reply that, in the strict sense, there was no

---

[75] Augustine, On the Activities of Pelagius,vi.16 (PL 44,329); Jerome, Dialogue against the Pelagians,I,16,21 (PL 23,509,514).

[76] Confession of Faith,16 (PL 48,490,502); To Celantia,6 (PL 22,1207); On Virginity,7 (PL 30,167ff.); etc.

[77] This is perhaps the most common Pelagian theme to be found in this collection.

[78] See Rees,8,86,94. The word impeccantia (= 'sinlessness') does not occur in classical Latin, though the adjective impeccabilis does occur once – in the second century AD. Jerome uses it frequently in the present context, and it is possible that he invented it faute de mieux – or, should one say, faute de rien? Augustine does not appear to have used it at all; perhaps Jerome had read Seneca's warning in Letters,9,2 against using the literal alternative impatientia for fear of causing ambiguity!

[79] Long,236.

founder of Pelagianism: there were three men who were responsible for formulating and disseminating the main principles of its teaching in the early fifth century – Rufinus the Syrian, Pelagius and Celestius – and two of these were the main spokesmen of the movement in the early phase; by 415 at the latest one of these two, Pelagius, came to be identified as the leader of Pelagians, and it is on his writings that we depend in the main for our understanding of the theoretical basis and practical implications of the movement. As to the second question, the matrix or milieu in which the movement originated was the group of 'new' Christians which evolved and flourished in Rome in the late-fourth and early-fifth centuries and which provided a forum in which current theological views could be aired and examined, perhaps amended, in the light of novel ideas emanating from other regions of the Christian Church. This revisionary process might have gone on in peace for some time and Pelagianism might never have existed under that name, had it not been for the exodus caused by Alaric's invasion and the resultant exposure of Pelagian teaching to more intensive examination by Jerome, Augustine and their peers in North Africa and Palestine. Thereupon brains were racked, consciences searched, letters and treatises written and circulated around the Mediterranean and even beyond, synods and councils held, decisions pronounced, and, after this long and strenuous period of labour, a new orthodoxy sprung out of Augustine's head. 'Controversies emerge not only when people have new ideas, but also when they suddenly wake up to realize that they no longer have the old ones';[80] in this case both sides generated new ideas which they defended as old, and it was Augustine's grace that prevailed. At that time, yes, but not for ever, not everywhere, not in everyone's judgement: 'the doctrine of predestination with the related question of perseverance' were 'subjects felt to be so complex that eleven centuries later the Council of Trent wore kid gloves to deal with them and gave verdicts which removed none of the serious ambiguities'.[81] The Pelagians and Semi-Pelagians were justified in questioning their 'orthodoxy' in the fifth century.

---

[80] Brown,1972,220.
[81] H. Chadwick,1986,115.

PART I

THE EVANS LETTERS

1

To Demetrias[1]

In 413 Pelagius, now in Palestine, received an unexpected letter from the widow
Juliana, whom he had known in Rome and who had married into the Anician
family, at that time one of the most wealthy and influential houses in Roman
society; she had joined in the general exodus of aristocrats from Italy before and
during Alaric the Goth's final attack in 410 on Rome, which he had been
besieging since 408. But, unlike many other Christian aristocrats, the Anicians
had not headed via Africa for Palestine, the usual escape-route for the refugees;
instead, Juliana, accompanied by Anicia Faltonia Proba, now the doyenne of the
family as the widow of its former head, Sextus Petronius Probus, her young
daughter, Demetrias, and a sizeable entourage of other widows, younger women
and their servants, had settled in one of their many family estates in North
Africa.[2] A devout Christian, she had been welcomed on arrival by Bishop Aurelius of Carthage and the imperial commissioner, Count Marcellinus, and had also
been in touch with Augustine and his friend Alypius, Bishop of Thagaste, both
of whom had taken an interest in Demetrias' religious education.

An eligible fiancé had been found for Demetrias, now fourteen years of age,
and Jerome describes him as an exile, presumably from Italy, like her, at the same
time hinting that he may have been connected in some way with Count Hera-
clian, the military commander of the province, who had extracted large sums of
money from the Anician contingent as protection money and, not long afterwards, was executed for leading an uprising against the Emperor.[3] The wedding
arrangements were already well advanced when Demetrias suddenly announced

---

[1] *Epistula ad sacram Christi virginem Demetriadem*; PL 30,15– 45; 33,1099–1120. Neither
text is satisfactory, and some corrections to my version will therefore be necessary
when the critical edition promised by F.G. Nuvolone appears. The German translation
in Greshake and Geerlings, 1980, is said to be based on a new collation of the text but
this is not included in the copy of the book which I have been able to consult.

[2] On the Anician family or *gens Anicia* see Plinval, 1943,213ff. and Brown, 1972,
161–226, *passim*. Pelagius and Jerome both describe Proba as Demetrias' grandmother,
and most modern scholars have followed them; Brown, however, 1967, 340,456 and
462, refers to her as Demetrias' great-aunt. If he is right – and I suspect that he is –,
then Juliana would be the widow of Probus' nephew and not of one of his two sons; all
three men had been consuls.

[3] Jerome, *Letters*, 130 (PL 22,1107–24),5.

her intention of taking a vow of virginity; whether or not this decision was taken entirely on her own initiative we have no means of telling. Jerome thinks – or, rather, says – that it was; but then, 'he would, wouldn't he?' Juliana also said so, and so, of course, did Pelagius; but I must admit to a sneaking suspicion that, with Proba and Juliana, Augustine and Alypius at hand to advise her, the fourteen-year-old may well have been subjected to some degree of influence.

However that may be, Juliana and Proba declared themselves surprised but delighted at the news, and the former wrote to the most eminent theologians in the West at this time for advice for her daughter on the requirements of her chosen vocation – it was more like a royal command than a request, says Pelagius (section 1). Pelagius may well have been first choice in view of his close association with the ladies in the circles of the Christian aristocracy in Rome when he had been there; Jerome too was an obvious choice, since he too had been a spiritual counsellor to the same circles during his second, brief stay in Rome c.382–85 and now bestrode the Holy Land like a colossus. Augustine too was probably invited to write, since the Anician ladies had recently made his acquaintance and he had already advised Proba at her own request in the previous year:[4] Juliana's letter informing him of her daughter's consecration must surely have included such an invitation but if so, he did not refer to it in his reply, a letter to congratulate both Juliana and Proba but, for him, a brief one, in which he is mainly concerned to express his joy and his hope that other young women, especially those connected with the Anician household, would hasten to follow Demetrias' example and to seek a blessed state which neither of the two recipients of his letter had been fortunate enough to be able to enjoy![5] He also thanked them for the gift which had accompanied the letter from Juliana, an *apophoretum velationis* or memento of the veiling ceremony, and, in the following year, sent Juliana a minor treatise on widowhood.[6] Perhaps both Augustine and Juliana considered the letter and this treatise to be an adequate response to her original letter, especially as it included a number of references to the demands of chastity. We are also told that Pope Innocent I, who would have known Demetrias in Rome, wrote to give her his advice but I have been unable to find the evidence on which this suggestion is based.[7] Pope Leo I certainly wrote to her – a letter or tract on humility[8] – but that was many years later, after she had returned to Italy and was established on her own estate in the Via Latina, where, at Leo's persuasion, she founded a church dedicated to St Stephen.[9]

In his treatise *On the Good of Widowhood* Augustine thought it necessary to warn Juliana against listening to the 'tittle-tattle of certain men, enemies of

---

4   Augustine, *Letters*, 130,131 (PL 33,493–508).
5   Ibid.150 (PL 33,645).
6   *On the Good of Widowhood* (PL 40,429–50).
7   See PL 30,15; 55,422 for the suggestion, presented there as a fact.
8   PL 55,162–80 for the text and 413–24 for Quesnel's discussion of the authorship of the letter, which had previously been ascribed to Prosper Tiro of Aquitaine. Leo I was Pope from 440 until 461.
9   See Brown, 1972, 180.

grace, who try to defend the freedom of the human will'.[10] She does not appear to have taken kindly to the suggestion that the great house of the Anicii might be in danger of becoming tainted with heresy, and pointed out that it had never been involved in any heresy of real importance, distinguishing between such heresies, e.g. on the nature of the Trinity, and others concerned with trivia. Now this was something which Augustine could not afford to let go without comment, knowing, as he did, of Pelagius' earlier association with the Anicii and of the importance of keeping up the pressure on his potential supporters at a crucial time when the outcome of the Pelagian controversy was still so delicately balanced that the loss of a few influential patrons could make all the difference to either side. So he and Alypius returned the ball to Juliana's court in 417, replying that they were now able to explain the tenor of their earlier remarks, since they had been able to read for themselves 'a certain book' which had come into their possession and had been sent to Demetrias at the time of her consecration; what they had found in it, especially the opening sentence of section 11 but in many other places as well, clearly justified the fears which Augustine had expressed in his treatise of 414, since there was teaching here which was not only ambiguous but positively dangerous.

Had Demetrias received this book and read it? Who was its author? Could he and his friend have an assurance that she had not been persuaded by the sentiments expressed in it but would reject them as contrary to the true doctrine of grace? Devout believers like the Anicii could well be thoroughly orthodox on points of doctrine long decided and still fall into heresy over others which were causing fresh controversy. Finally, the two bishops admit that they now know the identity of the author from another letter written by the same man, Pelagius, in which he mentions his letter to Demetrias; they are also aware that that letter was sent by him in response to a request made by the holy virgin's mother! Was this letter really the same one which contained the offending passage on spiritual riches referred to and quoted in Augustine's treatise?[11] Juliana had by now, of course, returned to Italy, and so it was all the more necessary to undermine her support for Pelagius; in fact, there is good reason to believe that she, like most of Pelagius' earlier patrons amongst the Roman aristocracy, did distance herself from him in the final stages of the battle and after it had been won and lost.

So much for Augustine's attitude to Pelagius' *Letter to Demetrias*; it shows what a hornets' nest Juliana had stirred about Pelagius' head by her sincere and well-meaning attempt to involve him in the education of her daughter as a virgin. Nor was Jerome any more well disposed than Augustine to the idea of entrusting that education to a man with the heretical opinions of Pelagius. In his letter[12] he begins by giving a typically dramatic account of how, on the occasion of the consecration of Demetrias by Bishop Aurelius, there were spectacular celebrations in all the Anician estates in countries bordering on the

---

[10] *On the Good of Widowhood,* xvii.12.
[11] *Letters,* 188 (PL 33,849ff.).
[12] *Letters,* 130 (PL 22,1107–24).

Mediterranean and among Christians in exile generally: it was a *jour de fête* which was all the more welcome in the wake of the recent catastrophe in Rome – at this point he even rises to a quotation from Horace's *Odes* (III,3,7–8) – and the joy accompanying it was 'something to which the verbal skills of a Cicero or Demosthenes could not have done justice'. His own narrative with its customary flights of rhetoric left little to the imagination – 'somewhat romanticised' is how Plinval describes it with more than usual restraint[13] – but, the preliminaries complete, he got down to the job of directing Demetrias in more sober terms, urging her to dedicate herself to scriptural study, prayer, fasting and good works with special emphasis on the need to use her great riches wisely to help the poor and distressed. But he did not fail to seize this God-given opportunity to take a swipe *en passant* at Pelagius, with whom he was currently involved in controversy, by warning the virgin not to bother herself with theological problems, especially of the kind being raised by adherents of Origen, that is, the Pelagians. Rhetoric apart, this letter of Jerome's is an unexceptionable but quite unremarkable piece of moral instruction, which an old hand like its writer would be able to turn out on demand every day of the week, and I would rate it no higher than beta plus.

Pelagius' letter, on the other hand, is a real showpiece, much fuller and more detailed than that of his more illustrious opponent. It is also a highly important document, not only because it is the mature work of an experienced and respected spiritual counsellor but also because it contains, in the absence of all but a few fragments of his major works of moral theology, our most complete and coherent account of his views on the central Pelagian topics of 'the good of nature' and 'natural sanctity' and on how they relate to man's capacity to make a free choice between good and evil and thereby win merit in the eyes of God. His opening statement of the importance of getting to understand the full potential of one's nature before setting one's sights on the target of virtue is followed by a formidable regimen for the conduct of a Christian life – 'the message is simple and terrifying'[14] – specifically designed to match the Pelagian severity of its demands to the quality and aspirations of this very special novice. It provides a large-scale map of the route to moral excellence, annotated with warnings of the traps and pitfalls along the road and sharp reminders from time to time that the state of virginity, blessed though it undoubtedly is and far superior to that of the ordinary, run-of-the-mill Christian, will turn out to be no more than a mirage in life's wilderness, if the one who seeks to fulfil all its requirements fails to satisfy those of the Christian life as a whole. Many of the 'works of righteousness' mentioned are Pelagian commonplaces, and his frequent repetition of them marks Pelagius' impatience with what he regarded as the wishy-washy Christianity of too many of his contemporaries and highlights his passionate concern to make all Christians *integri*, 'authentic'.[15] It is to Demetrias', as well as to her

[13] 1943, 242.
[14] Brown, 1967,342.
[15] See Rees, 1988, 19 and cf. *To a Young Man*,3,2.

advisers', credit that she appears to have succeeded in keeping her vow to the end of her life despite all the manifold distractions and responsibilities of her social position.

How ironical it is that a work which must have given such great offence to Jerome should have for so long been attributed to him and tacked onto his own corpus of writings! Later, however, when scholars began to realize that its Pelagian character did not suit this ascription to Jerome, it was ascribed to followers of Pelagius like Celestius and Julian of Eclanum. Bede, for example, thought it was the work of the latter and made an interesting comment on the idea that it was Jerome's in his essay On the Song of Songs:[16] 'There are some who are so rash as to consider this book to be by Jerome, overlooking the fact that the charm and allure of its eloquence and the perversity of the misleading heresy it contains clearly prove that it is not Jerome's work.' One wonders what poor Jerome would have made of the first part of that statement of 'fact'! Bede also quotes several passages in the letter and concludes that the letter contains much excellent instruction but is marred by the author's failure to emphasize the need to rely on divine grace rather than free will and strength of mind.

But Augustine, as we have seen, knew it to be by Pelagius at least as early as 417 and probably much earlier and discussed it as a work by Pelagius in 418 in On the Grace of Christ.[17] Orosius also assigned it to Pelagius in 415, when he delivered a scathing attack on his use of the OT story of Joseph and Potiphar's wife (section 5) as 'inappropriate' and 'couched in obscene language', while at the same time admitting that he found it difficult to believe that Pelagius himself wrote the passage in question in view of its style, which was 'far above what one could expect from a man of such humble origins'; he concluded that Pelagius' friend and constant companion, Annianus of Celeda, must have done the actual writing, Pelagius supplying the opinions and arguments: Annianus played the part of 'armour-bearer' to Pelagius' Goliath, a role for which his great bulk and formidable appearance well suited him![18] There is no evidence at all about Pelagius' origins, except that he almost certainly hailed from Britain nor does his Commentary on Paul's Epistles bear out the suggestion that he was less than literate, since it shows many, unmistakable signs of a sound classical and philosophical education. Augustine often criticises his ambiguity but never his manner of writing, and Jerome, who refers to Annianus as Pelagius' 'voice' and 'shadow', admits that 'Pelagius' Latin is very good considering his provincial origins'.[19]

There is general agreement, then, among Pelagius' contemporaries that the Letter to Demetrias was his own work with Orosius lodging a caveat to the effect that Annianus played a part, possibly a considerable part, in its actual composition. The seventeenth-century scholar Jean Garnier, however, went farther even

---

[16] PL 91, 1073C–D.
[17] PL 44,359–86: xxii.23, xxvii.28, xxxvii.40–42, and xl.44, apropos of sections 25,1,3;17,8 and 9 in this letter respectively.
[18] Book in Defence against the Pelagians (PL 31,1174–1212), sections 29 and 2 respectively.
[19] Jerome, Letters,50 (PL 22,512–16).

than Orosius with the uncompromising statement that 'Annianus wrote all the works of Pelagius except his brief expository notes', the latter being a reference to the expository notes comprising his Pauline Commentary, which Augustine describes in the same way – 'brief', of course, means that the individual notes were brief, not the *Commentary*, which occupies no fewer that 265 columns in Migne's first supplement.[20] It is true that the *Commentary* uses ordinary words in many places to convey meanings expressed in the *Letter* in more recherché terms and that it is lacking in the many tricks of style employed in the *Letter*. But surely this is to be expected in view of the different purpose of the two: my own experience suggests that the style and vocabulary in the notes contained in two editions of Greek papyri which I once edited are noticeably different from those of reviews and articles of mine from the same period and, even more so, books written later. And the style of the *Letter to Demetrias* is in any case superior not only to that of the *Commentary* but to that of the fragments of the treatise *On the Trinity* and of other treatises and letters as well.

Without a shadow of doubt this letter is, as they say, 'something entirely different': the Latinity is more elegant than that of any other work attributed to Pelagius, and much greater use is made of metaphor, simile and other rhetorical devices. It was, after all, a very special occasion, when Pelagius had been given a chance to show what he could do in competition with others more distinguished than he; who can blame him for wanting to give the right impression to what would surely be a wide circle of influential readers, at a time when he and his cause needed all the support that they could muster, and for taking advantage of the expertise of Annianus to assist him in doing so? His friend was a fluent Latinist and sound Greek scholar; Pelagius was neither. But he *was* an original thinker, whereas the only other writings associated with Annianus' name were two epistles which he added under his own name to his Latin translation of the homilies of John Chrysostom, in one of which some of the phraseology bears a resemblance to that of the Demetrias letter.

Whatever we may think of Orosius on other grounds, he seems to have strayed far from the truth in his comment on the authorship of the *Letter to Demetrias*, but there is no great advantage to be gained from a last-ditch defence of the claim that Pelagius himself was the sole author; to what extent he had assistance from Annianus or someone else must be left an open question. But the teaching was undoubtedly his, and it is the teaching, not the way in which it is embellished, that provides the main justification for Plinval's description of the letter as 'one of the jewels of Christian literature',[21] even if the style certainly makes the medicine prescribed much easier to swallow. I do not know enough

---

[20] Augustine also refers to the *Commentary* as 'very brief notes' in his treatise *On the Merits and Forgiveness of Sins and Infant Baptism* (PL 44,109–200), III,i.1, the Latin word for 'notes' being *expositiones*, which is the Latin title of the *Commentary*. The statement by Garnier is in his Dissertation VI in PL 48,535–630, on p.626 and is followed by the text of the two letters – on Matthew and Paul – attached to Annianus' Latin version of John Chrysostom's homilies.

[21] 1943,245; see also Evans, 1962, 96f.

about those 'jewels' to enable me to evaluate the letter in comparison with them; but I do know that the finished product moves me, and I do not believe that it can have failed to move its recipient and to have had a profound influence upon her. What is most striking perhaps is Pelagius' sympathy, indeed empathy, with his young pupil, the delicacy and restraint with which he moderates his 'terrifying message', for example, the way in which he frequently urges her not to go to extremes of self-deprivation and excuses her from 'works of mercy', which he asks Juliana and Proba to undertake in her place so as to prevent her being overwhelmed by all her burdens.

Nor is there any sign of condescension or self-regard here, none of the slick showmanship of a Jerome or of the world-weary detachment of an Augustine. The impression which we get, and which Demetrias must have got, is that of an older, wiser friend, writing with deep feeling and sincerity from his own lifetime of experience and commending the values and obligations which he himself prizes above all else – in other words, of that same simple, devout Christian teacher whom she had once known as a child in Rome and heard expounding the mysteries of the scriptures to her elders, one whose judgement she could respect and trust, one who believed what he said and practised what he preached, one whose sole concern was to be about his Father's business. And as she read his advice, no doubt she would have in her mind's eye a picture of a rather eccentric, distinctly overweight, elderly gentleman, dressed in the simple habit of a monk, strict in his teaching and his behaviour, but capable of impressing the elite of Rome by his enthusiasm and example. Would she also be able to recall all that talk – over her head at the time perhaps – of the importance of making a free choice for oneself and then reflect that that was precisely what she had done? And would she remember how this same Pelagius had sat with her and explained in simple terms what Jesus meant when he said in his sermon on the mount, 'By their fruits you will know them', and how these fruits, when good, were products of human free will, aided by Jesus' example and teaching and God's grace?

Text

1, 1.   Even if I could claim to possess natural talent of a high quality and an equally high degree of artistic skill and believed myself for that reason to be capable of fulfilling with ease the obligation of writing, I would still not be able to enter upon this arduous task without considerable fear of the difficulties involved. It is to Demetrias that I have to write, that virgin of Christ who is both noble and rich and, which is more important, spurns both nobility and riches; assuredly it is as difficult for me to instruct her as it is easy for all to praise her out of admiration for her outstanding virtue. Who could possibly lack words to sing the praises of one who, though born in the highest station, brought up in the height of wealth and luxury, held fast by the strength and variety of this life's delights as if in the grip of the most tenacious of fetters, suddenly broke free and exchanged all her bodily goods simultaneously for goodness of the soul? Of one who cut off with the sword of faith, that is, her own free will, the very flower of a life still only just beginning and, by crucifying her flesh with Christ, dedicated it as a living and holy sacrifice to God and for love of virginity renounced the prospect of providing posterity for a very noble stock? An easy, simple way to make a speech is to let the very richness of the subject-matter speed it along its course; but we have to proceed along a very different road, since our purpose is to write a manual of instruction for the virgin, not an encomium, to portray not so much the virtues which she has already acquired as those which she has still to acquire, and to order the remainder of her life rather than to honour that part of it which is now in the past.

2. It is, however, very hard to deal with the character of one in whom there is such desire to learn, such eagerness for perfection that no teaching, however admirable, can really meet her needs: she rightly remembers what worldly wealth and honour she has rejected, what pleasures she has renounced, in a word, what attractions of this present life she has spurned, and for that reason she is dissatisfied with this common, mediocre kind of life of ours and, finding herself to be easily capable of being cheapened by mere association with the majority, seeks something new and unusual and looks for a special and singular quality of some kind in her life. She wants her conduct to become no less an object of wonder than her conversion has been: already noble in this world, she desires to be even nobler before God and seeks in her moral conduct values as precious as the objects which she spurned in this world. What outpouring of talent will ever satisfy a mind so enthusiastic and dedicated, so thirsty for a high degree of perfection? What power of speech, what fluency will ever be able to express in mere words all that this virgin is ready to fulfil by deeds? Yet we are entitled to crave indulgence when we offer a gift for the adornment of the Lord's temple which is only in proportion to our own powers, nor need we have any fear of exposing ourselves voluntarily to the malicious stings of envy by writing so rashly to such a noble virgin; we write at the request, nay, by the command of her venerable mother, who solicits it from us in a letter sent across the sea and revealing the remarkable force of her heartfelt desire. Thus she shows us with the greatest of ease the zeal and care with which she has planted the heavenly seed in her daughter and how she now desires it to be watered by others just as punctiliously. And so, free from any charge of rashness or of vain ambition, let us bend our energies to our appointed task and let us not lose confidence on the grounds of our moderate ability, since we do believe that it is being assisted both by the mother's faith and by the daughter's merit.

2, 1. Whenever I have to speak on the subject of moral instruction and the conduct of a holy life, it is my practice first to demonstrate the power and quality of human nature and to show what it is capable of achieving, and then to go on to encourage the mind of my listener to consider the idea of different kinds of virtues, in case it may be of little or no profit to him to be summoned to pursue ends which he has perhaps assumed hitherto to be beyond his reach; for we can never enter upon the path of virtue unless we have hope as our guide and companion and if every effort expended in seeking something is nullified in effect by despair of ever finding it. I also think that on this occasion, when the good in our nature calls for a fuller exposition commensurate with the greater perfection of life which has to be inculcated in the listener's mind, I have special grounds for adhering to the same sequence of exhortation as I have followed in my other minor works, in order that the mind may not become more negligent and sluggish in its pursuit of virtue as it comes to believe less in its ability to achieve it, supposing itself not to possess something simply because it is unaware that it is present within. When it is desirable for a man to put a certain capacity to use, it always has to be brought to his attention, and any good of which human nature is capable has to be revealed, since what is shown to be practicable must be put into practice. Let us then lay this down as the first basis for a holy and spiritual life: the virgin must recognize her own strengths, which she will be able to employ to the full only when she has learned that she possesses them. The best incentive for the mind consists in teaching it that it is possible to do anything which one really wants to do: in war, for example, the kind of exhortation which is most effective and carries most authority is the one which reminds the combatant of his own strengths.

2. First, then, you ought to measure the good of human nature by reference to its creator, I mean God, of course: if it is he who, as report goes, has made all the works of and within the world good, exceeding good, how much more excellent do you suppose that he has made man himself, on whose account he has clearly made everything else? And before actually making man, he determines to fashion him in his own image and likeness and shows what kind of creature he intends to make him. Next, since he has made all animals subject to man and set him as lord over creatures which have been made more powerful than men either by their bodily size and greater strength or by the weapons which they have in their teeth, he makes it abundantly clear how much more gloriously man himself has been fashioned and wants him to appreciate the dignity of his own nature by marvelling that strong animals have been made subject to him. For he did not leave man naked and defenceless nor did he expose him in his weakness to a variety of dangers; but, having made him seem unarmed outwardly, he provided him with a better armament inside, that is, with reason and wisdom, so that by means of his intelligence and mental vigour, in which he surpassed the other animals, man alone was able to recognize the maker of all things and to serve God by using those same faculties which enabled him to hold sway over the rest. Moreover, the Lord of Justice wished man to be free to act and not under compulsion; it was for this reason that 'he left him free to make his own decisions' (Sir.15.14)[22] and set before him life and death, good and evil,

___

[22] This is the translation in the 1985 edition of the New Jerusalem Bible, which is preferable in my view to the RSV here, because it makes the Pelagian sense of the text clearer to the ordinary reader. RSV brings in 'inclination' as the correct rendering of the key Greek word in this sentence, and it is only fair to add that this results in an

and he shall be given whatever pleases him (ibid.17). Hence we read in the Book Deuteronomy also: I have set before you life and death, blessing and curse; therefore choose life, that you may live (Dt.30.19).

3, 1. That is why we must now take precautions to prevent you from being embarrassed by something in which the ignorant majority is at fault for lack of proper consideration, and so from supposing, with them, that man has not been created truly good simply because he is able to do evil and is not obliged by the overpowering inclination of his own nature to do good on compulsion and without any possibility of variation. If you reconsider this matter carefully and force your mind to apply a more acute understanding to it, it will be revealed to you that man's status is better and higher for the very reason for which it is thought to be inferior: it is on this choice between two ways, on this freedom to choose either alternative, that the glory of the rational mind is based, it is in this that the whole honour of our nature consists, it is from this that its dignity is derived and all good men win others' praise and their own reward. Nor would there be any virtue at all in the good done by the man who perseveres, if he could not at any time cross over to the path of evil.[23]

2. It was because God wished to bestow on the rational creature the gift of doing good of his own free will and the capacity to exercise free choice, by implanting in man the possibility of choosing either alternative, that he made it his peculiar right to be what he wanted to be, so that with his capacity for good and evil he could do either quite naturally and then bend his will in the other direction too. He could not claim to possess the good of his own volition, unless he were the kind of creature that could also have possessed evil. Our most excellent creator wished us to be able to do either but actually to do only one, that is, good, which he also commanded, giving us the capacity to do evil only so that we might do his will by exercising our own. That being so, this very capacity to do evil is also good – good, I say, because it makes the good part better by making it voluntary and independent, not bound by necessity but free to decide for itself. We are certainly permitted to choose, oppose, approve, reject, and there is no ground for preferring the rational creature to the others except that, while all the others possess only the good derived from their own circumstances and necessity, it alone possesses the good of free will also.

3. But most of those who, from lack of faith as much as of knowledge, deplore the status of man, are – I am ashamed to admit it – criticising the Lord's work and asserting that man ought to have been so made that he could do no evil at all, and we are then in a position where what is moulded says to its moulder: Why have you made me thus (Rom.9.20)? And these most shameless of men,

absolutely literal and correct translation of the LXX version of Sir.15.14; the Hebrew word in question is *yeser*, a technical term, which does admit of a neutral translation in a minority of instances (see Rees, 1988, 54). The NJB version is also used for the next quotation, Sir.15.17.

23 A favourite Pelagian argument in favour of free choice; in Rees, 1988, 35 the concluding words have been incorrectly translated as '*from* the path of evil'.

while hiding the fact that they are managing quite well with what they have been made, would prefer to have been made otherwise; and so those who are unwilling to correct their own way of life appear to want to correct nature itself instead, the good of which has been so universally established in all that it sometimes reveals itself and brings itself to notice even in pagans who do not worship God. For how many of the pagan philosophers have we heard and read and even seen for ourselves to be chaste, tolerant, temperate, generous, abstinent and kindly, rejecters of the world's honours as well as its delights, lovers of justice no less than knowledge? Whence, I ask you, do these good qualities pleasing to God come to men who are strangers to him? Whence *can* these good qualities come to them, unless it be from the good of nature? And since we see the qualities of which I have spoken contained either all in one person or severally in several persons and since the nature of all is one and the same, by their example they show each other that all qualities which are found either all together in all or severally in each one are able to exist in all alike. But if even men without God can show what kind of creatures they were made by God, consider what Christians are able to do whose nature and life have been instructed for the better by Christ and who are assisted by the aid of divine grace as well.

4, 1. Come now, let us approach the secret places of our soul,[24] let everyone examine himself more attentively, let us ask what opinion our own personal thoughts have of this matter, let our conscience itself deliver its judgement on the good of nature, let us be instructed by the inner teaching of the mind, and let us learn about each of the good qualities of the mind from no other source but the mind itself. Why is it, I ask you, that we either blush or fear at every sin we commit, displaying our guilt for what we have done at one moment by the blush on our countenance, at another by its pallor, anxiously trying to avoid any witness even of our smallest offences and suffering pangs of conscience all the while? And why, on the other hand, are we happy, resolute, bold after every good deed we have done and, if this fact is hidden from sight, desire and wish it to be seen in broad daylight? Why else unless it is because nature itself is its own witness and discloses its own good by the very fact of its disapproval of evil and, by putting its trust only in a good deed, shows what alone benefits it? Hence it comes about that frequently, though a murderer's identity remains concealed, torments of conscience make furious attacks on the author of the crime, and the secret punishment of the mind takes vengeance on the guilty man in hiding;[25] nor is there any room for escape from punishment after the crime has been committed, since guilt is itself the penalty. That is why the innocent man, contrariwise, enjoys the peace of mind that comes from a good conscience even while undergoing torture and, though he fears punishment, still glories in his innocence.

---

[24] For the internal judgement of the conscience cf. *Cel.*14; *Life*,14,2; see also Rees, 1988,6,n.24, first sentence.
[25] For the phrase 'the guilty man in hiding' cf. *Cel.*14 again.

2. There is, I maintain, a sort of natural sanctity in our minds which, presiding as it were in the mind's citadel, administers judgement equally on the evil and the good and, just as it favours honourable and upright actions, so too condemns wrong deeds and, on the evidence of conscience, distinguishes the one side from the other by a kind of inner law; nor, in fine, does it seek to deceive by any display of cleverness or of counterfeit brilliance in argument but either denounces or defends us by our thoughts themselves, surely the most reliable and incorruptible of witnesses. This is the law which the apostle recalls when he writes to the Romans, testifying that it is implanted in all men and written as it were on the tablets of the heart: *For when gentiles who have not the law do by nature what the law requires, they are a law to themselves, even though they do not have the law. They show that what the law requires is written in their hearts, while their conscience also bears them witness and their conflicting thoughts accuse or perhaps excuse them* (Rom.2.15,16). It is this law that all have used whom scripture records as having lived in sanctity and having pleased God between the time of Adam and that of Moses: some of these must be set before you as examples, so that you may not find it difficult to understand how great is the good of nature, when once you have satisfied yourself that it has replaced the law in the task of teaching righteousness.

5, 1. Abel[26] was the first to follow this mistress and so served the Lord that, when he offered him a victim, his sacrifice was so gratefully received by God that it aroused the jealousy of his brother, and the Lord himself, recalling this righteous man in the Gospel, briefly set forth the grounds of his perfection (cf. Mt.23.35). For every form of virtue is contained under the name of righteousness: we read that the blessed Enoch so pleased God that he snatched him away from the midst of mortals and translated him from his earthly habitation, after reaching perfection in this world. Noah is said to have been 'a righteous man, blameless in his generation' (Gen.6.9), and his holiness is all the more to be admired in that he alone was found to be righteous, when literally the whole world was declining from righteousness, nor did he seek a model of holiness from another but supplied it himself. And for that reason, when the destruction of the whole world was imminent, he alone of all men was found worthy to hear the words: *Go into the ark, you and all your household, for I have seen that you are righteous before me in this generation* (Gen.7.1).

2. Before God, moreover, that man is esteemed righteous who is holy both in body and heart: Melchizedek is said to have been 'a priest of God' (Gen.14.18), and his merit can be easily understood from this fact, that he signified in advance the Lord's sacrament which was to come later and expressed the mystery of the body and the blood by the sacrifice of bread and wine and by the manner of this sacrifice of his prefigured the priesthood of Christ, to whom it is said by the Father: *Thou art a priest for ever, after the order of Melchizedek* (Heb.5.6; cf. Ps.110.4). Also, because he blesses Abraham, the first of the

---

[26] For this roll-call of the patriarchs, their forefathers and descendants cf. *Life*,7.

patriarchs, who is father of the Jews through the covenant of circumcision and father of the nations by his faith, he highlights most distinctly the example of him who by his faith has bestowed a blessing both on Jews and gentiles. Lot too, following the holy Noah in virtue, did not forsake righteousness, though living among examples of so many sinners, but, as the example of the whole world could not overcome the latter, so he too maintained his holiness against the vices of the multitude, when all the region in which he lived was sinning; and he, as the blessed Peter says, 'was righteous in his seeing and hearing' (2 Pet.2.8) and, set as he was among most evil men, shunned their evil deeds both with his eyes and with his ears and for that reason was snatched away from the fire, as Noah had been snatched away from the Flood.

3. What shall I say of Abraham, friend of God, what of Isaac and Jacob? How completely they fulfilled the will of the Lord we are able to determine even from this, that he wanted himself to be named *their* God as an intimate and special mark of distinction; I am, he said, the God of Abraham, the God of Isaac, and the God of Jacob (Mt.22.32); this is my name for ever, and thus I am to be remembered throughout all generations (Ex.3.15). Joseph, a faithful servant of the Lord from boyhood, is shown to be even more righteous and perfect through his tribulations: first he was sold into slavery to the Ishmaelites by his brothers and then sold again by those by whom he had seen himself worshipped in a dream; next, though handed over to an Egyptian master, yet he always retained the freeborn dignity of his soul and by his example taught slaves and free men alike that it is not a man's personal situation that tells against him when he sins but his mental attitude.

4. At this point, I beg you, virgin, pause for a moment or two and carefully consider the chaste attitude of Joseph's mind: as a young man he is desired by his master's wife but resists her attempts to make him desire her; she solicits, he rebuffs, and so the one who is accustomed to give the orders in all other matters is reduced to coaxing and begging in this one alone, since the lover of God cannot be vanquished by the love of a woman nor can his chaste mind be swayed by his adolescence or his lover's authority. Having been rebuffed several times, his mistress now sets her ambushes closer to his lines of defence: in secret and with no witnesses she lays hand upon him shamelessly and in even more wanton language urges him to commit the crime; yet not even thus is he overcome but returns deeds for deeds, as he has previously returned words for words and, having refused when asked, he now escapes when trapped and, before that word in the gospel was spoken: Every one who looks at a woman lustfully has already committed adultery with her in his heart (Mt.5.28); he, after having been seduced not only by the sight of her but almost by her very embrace, still does not lust after the woman.

5. You have marvelled at the strength of this man's chastity; now regard his benevolence. Before the prophet said: Let no man remember in his heart the ill will of his neighbour (Lev.19.18), *he* repaid hatred with love and, when he saw his brothers – nay rather, the enemies who were once his brothers – and wanted to be recognized by them, *he* bore witness that it was love, not resentment, that

he felt for them; *he* kissed each of them in turn and with the water of his tears, which he poured over the necks of his frightened brothers, washed away their hatred with tears of love and loved them always with true brotherly love both during his father's lifetime and after his death. Nor did he recall to mind the pit into which he was cast down to die or give a thought to the way in which his brotherhood had been sold for a price but, 'repaying good for evil' (Rom.12.17), he fulfilled the apostle's instruction when he was still subject only to the law of nature.

6, 1.   What shall I say of the blessed Job, that most renowned athlete of God, whose wealth was snatched from him, whose estate was utterly destroyed, whose sons and daughters died all together, and who, after all this, yet fought against the devil to the very end with his body? Everything that he possessed on the outside was taken from him, and his external possessions suddenly fell away, so that those more truly his own stood out clearly; he was as if stripped of absolutely all his outer garments and yet was able to stand triumphant in his nakedness, stronger and less encumbered, and, by bearing his own punishment, to overcome again the same enemy whom he had previously defeated by bearing his own losses. This is the testimony of the Lord himself upon him: Have you considered my servant Job? For there is none like him on the earth, a man against whom there is no complaint, a true worshipper of God, keeping himself away from all evil (Job.1.8; 2.3). Nor was this testimony undeserved, for, as he himself says, he always feared the Lord as the waves raging over him and was unable to bear the weight of his presence; at no time did he dare to scorn one whom he believed to be ever present with him but said: I am safe, for my heart does not reproach me for any of my days (Job 27.6).

   2.   Even before the time when the Lord enjoined that enemies should be loved, Job could say: If I have rejoiced at the troubles of my enemy, if I have said in my heart, 'It has been well done' (Job 31.29). When the Lord had not yet commanded in his gospel: Give to every one who begs from you (Lk.6.30), Job could already say: If I suffered a poor man to go out of my door with his purse empty (cf. Job 31.32). When he had not been able to read that word of the apostle: Masters, treat your servants justly and fairly (Col.4.1), Job could call confidently to the Lord: If I have harmed a manservant, if I have injured a maidservant, Lord, you know all (Job 31.13). Before the same apostle enjoined the rich 'not to be haughty, nor to set their hopes on uncertain riches' (1 Tim.6.17), he could possess his riches in such a way as to show himself to be rich in other respects: I put no trust in riches or in precious stones (cf. Job 31.24).

   3.   And he proved this not in words only but by deeds, since he did not grieve when he lost everything but could still say through it all: The Lord gave, and the Lord has taken away; as it pleased the Lord, so it has been done; blessed be the name of the Lord for ever. Naked I came from my mother's womb, and naked shall I return there (Job 1.21). When we lose something, we show with what affection we possess it, and the desire for enjoyment is betrayed by our grief at our loss; for how could a man experience desire for something when lost, if he had no desire for it when he possessed it? What a man Job was! A man of the gospel before the gospel was known, a man of the apostles before their commands were uttered! A disciple of the apostles who, by opening up the hidden wealth of nature and bringing it out into the open, revealed by his own behaviour what all of us are capable of and has taught us how great is that treasure in the soul which we possess but fail to use and, because we refuse to display it, believe that we do not possess it either.

7.   After the many things which we have said about nature we have also shown its good by the examples of holy men and have proved it. And lest, on the other hand, it should be thought to be nature's fault that some have been unrighteous, I shall use the evidence of the scriptures, which everywhere lay upon sinners the heavy weight of the charge of having used their own will and do not excuse them for having acted only under constraint of nature. In Genesis we read: The brothers Simeon and Levi have carried out their wickedness of their own free will (Gen.49.5,6). To Jerusalem the Lord said: Because they themselves have forsaken my way which I set before them, and have not obeyed my voice, but have followed the will of their own evil hearts (Jer.9.13,14). And again the same prophet: And you sinned against the Lord and did not obey his voice and refused to walk in his commands and in his laws and in his testimonies (Jer.44.23). He spoke also through the prophet Isaiah: If you are willing and obedient, you shall eat the good of the land; but if you refuse and rebel, you shall be devoured by the sword (Is.1.19,20). And again: All of you shall bow down in the slaughter; because, when I called, you did not obey, when I spoke, you did not listen, but you did evil before my eyes and chose what I did not delight in (Is.65.12). The Lord also says in the gospel: O Jerusalem, Jerusalem, killing the prophets and stoning those who are sent to you! How often would I have gathered your children together as a hen gathers her brood under her wings, and you would not (Mt.23.37)! When we see 'willing' and 'not willing', 'choosing' and 'rejecting', it is not the force of nature but the freedom of the will that is then understood to be at work. The books of both Testaments are full of evidence of this kind, wherein all good, as well as all evil, is described as voluntary, and we omit it now only for the sake of brevity, especially when we know that, dedicated as you are to sacred reading, you can drink more copious draughts direct from the fountain itself.

8, 1.   Yet we do not defend the good of nature to such an extent that we claim that it cannot do evil, since we undoubtedly declare also that it is capable of good and evil; we merely try to protect it from an unjust charge, so that we may not seem to be forced to do evil through a fault in our nature, when, in fact, we do neither good nor evil without the exercise of our will and always have the freedom to do one of the two, being always able to do either. For on what grounds are some to be judges, others to be judged, unless it is because the will works in different ways in one and the same nature and because, though all of us are able to do the same, we actually do different things? And so, in order that this essential fact may stand out more clearly, we must cite some examples. Adam is cast out of paradise, Enoch is snatched away from the world; in both the Lord shows freedom of choice at work, for, just as the one who sinned could have pleased the Lord, so the other, who did please him, could have sinned instead. Neither would the former have deserved to be punished nor the latter to be chosen by a just God, unless both had been able to choose either course of action. This is how we are to understand the matter of Cain and Abel and also of Jacob and Esau, the twin brothers, and we have to realize that, when merits differ in the same nature, it is will that is the sole cause of an action.

2. Noah in his righteousness rejected the world when it was destroyed by flood because of its sins, Lot in his holiness passed judgement on the crimes of the Sodomites; and the fact that those first men were without the rebukes of the law for the space of so many years gives us no small grounds for acknowledging the good of nature, not, assuredly, because God at any time did not care for his creatures but because he knew that he had made human nature such that it would suffice them in place of the law for the practice of righteousness. In a word, as long as a nature which was still comparatively fresh was in vigorous use and long habituation to sinning did not draw a dark veil, as it were, over human reason, nature was set free and left without law; but when it had now become buried beneath an excess of vices and as if tainted with the rust of ignorance, the Lord applied the file of the law to it, and so , thoroughly polished by its frequent admonishments, it was enabled to recover its former brilliance.

3. Nor is there any reason why it is made difficult for us to do good other than that long habit of doing wrong which has infected us from childhood and corrupted us little by little over many years and ever after holds us in bondage and slavery to itself, so that it seems somehow to have acquired the force of nature. We now find ourselves being resisted and opposed by all that long period in which we were carelessly instructed, that is, educated in evil, in which we even strove to be evil, since, to add to the other incentives to evil, innocence itself was held to be folly. That old habit now attacks our new-found freedom of will, and, as we languish in ignorance through our sloth and idleness, unaccustomed to doing good after having for so long learned to do only evil, we wonder why sanctity is also conferred on us as if from an outside source.

4. So much then by way of a cursory explanation of the good of nature, as it is also stated in another of my works:[27] it was something which we had to provide in order to pave your way to perfect righteousness and make it more level and easier for you to run along in the knowledge that there is nothing uneven or unapproachable confronting you. Even before the law was given to us, as we have said, and long before the arrival of our Lord and Saviour some are reported to have lived holy and righteous lives; how much more possible must we believe

---

[27] Pelagius' major treatise On Nature was not written until at least a year after this letter but Augustine makes a number of references to this dangerous concept of a natural grace conferred on man by giving him the capacity to choose freely between good and evil, insisting that it detracts from the power of divine grace (see Rees,1988, 91f.).

that to be after the light of his coming, now that we have been instructed by the grace of Christ and reborn as better men: purified and cleansed by his blood, encouraged by his example to pursue perfect righteousness, we ought surely to be better than those who lived before the time of the law, better even than those who lived under the law, since the apostle says: For sin will have no dominion over you, since you are not under law but under grace (Rom.6.14).

9, 1.　Since we have said enough on these matters in my opinion, let us now begin our instruction of a perfect virgin who by the purity of her moral life bears witness at one and the same time to the good of nature and the good of grace, since she has always drawn her inspiration from both of these sources. A virgin's first concern and first desire ought therefore to be to get to know the will of her Lord and to seek out diligently what pleases and what displeases him; in this way she may render to God, in the words of the apostle, her 'spiritual obedience' (Rom.12.1),[28] and may be enabled to direct the entire course of her life in accordance with his purpose. For it is impossible for anyone to please someone, if he does not know what it is that pleases him,[29] and he could well give offence even by his vow of obedience, if he has not learned in advance how to obey. And just as doing the will of the Lord is more important than knowing it, so knowing is prior to doing; the former takes precedence in order of time, the latter in order of merit, and it is for this reason that the prophet says: And you, Israel, be not ignorant (cf. Lev.4.; Num.15); and the blessed Paul: And if any one does not recognize this, he shall not be recognized (1 Cor.14.38), and likewise elsewhere: Therefore do not be foolish, but understand what the will of the Lord is (Eph.5.17). The beginning of obedience is wishing to know what is enjoined, and to have learned what you are to do is a part of your act of obedience.

2.　So you must realize that in the divine scriptures, which alone enable you to understand the complete will of God, certain things are forbidden, some are allowed, some are advised: evil things are forbidden, good things are enjoined; intermediate things are allowed, perfect things are advised; and all sin is contained in the two classes which are given pride of place, since God's command is involved in both, and the one who commands is entitled to forbid as well as to enjoin.[30] For righteousness is enjoined on everyone without exception, as the Saviour says, briefly but most comprehensively, in the gospel: Whatever you wish that men would do to you, do so to them also (Mt.7.12), that is, that we should inflict no evil upon others but offer them everything which is good, because we

---

[28] RSV has 'spiritual worship', NJB 'worship. . . as sensible people' or '[worship of] a spiritual kind', AV 'reasonable service', NEB 'the worship offered by mind and heart', and so on. LXX has 'reasonable service', and the Vulgate and our text *rationabile obsequium* = 'reasonable obedience/allegiance'. The sense of our text calls out for 'obedience', and, in my view, 'spiritual' renders Pelagius' meaning better than 'reasonable'. Paul is contrasting this kind of 'spiritual obedience/service' with the pagan use of animal sacrifices in worship; see Lampe, *Greek Patristic Lexicon*, fasc.3,793.

[29] Cf. *Law*,4,1.

[30] For the idea of a twofold commandment enjoined by righteousness cf. *Cel.*5 and *Virg.*6,1.

want both of these injunctions to be observed by others in their behaviour to us. This judgement binds everyone with just as much force as a commandment nor is it permitted to anyone at all to transgress what is imposed on everyone, and either to do what is forbidden or not to do what is enjoined is open contempt of God. The two classes which follow, however, one of which is allowed, the other advised, have been left under our control, so that we may either enjoy what is allowed and be satisfied with less honour as a result or reject even what is permitted for the sake of a greater reward.[31] Marriage is allowed, so is the use of meat and wine, but abstinence from all three is advised by more perfect counsel; freedom to marry has a bearing on the honour attached to virginity, and indulgence in meat highlights the virtue of abstinence.

3.   You, virgin, have disdained the marriage which you were permitted to make before you disdained it; burning with love for a greater reward, you have dedicated your virginity to God not because it was commanded but because it was praised, and you have translated the apostle's advice into a law for yourself; so having set foot on the wider field which you have chosen for the contest, you have thought not so much of the labours of the course as of the prize for victory.[32] You had read, I believe, that eulogy of perpetual chastity which is in the gospels, and the words of the Lord himself had excited you with the desire to preserve your virginity, when he praised the opinion of Peter on this matter on the grounds of the very magnitude and difficulty of the undertaking and, promising the kingdom of heaven to those who become eunuchs of their own choice, said: He who is able to receive this, let him receive it (Mt.19.12). And so, when an undertaking is so great, I do not command it, I do not impose it, but I offer it; nor do I compel anyone to undertake it but I challenge them to do so. Though it may appear to refer to men only, yet it is not addressed to men alone; rather, an equal reward for virginity is promised to both sexes, and the apostle says that he does not in fact have a commandment of the Lord concerning virgins but that he is merely giving advice;[33] he says, therefore: Do you desire proof that Christ is speaking in me (2 Cor.13.3)?

10, 1.   Having therefore followed the counsel of perfection, having set out to win the state of blessedness which attaches itself to a special intention, see to it that you keep the general commandment also. I have stated this before, and I now repeat it again, that in the matter of righteousness we all have one obligation: virgin, widow, wife, the highest, middle and lower stations in life, we are all without exception ordered to fulfil the commandments, nor is a man released from the law if he proposes to do more than it demands. Indeed, no one ought to avoid the things that are not permitted more than he who has rejected what was permitted nor does anyone give so firm a promise to fulfil the commandments as the man whose love of perfection has led him to ascend above their requirements

---

[31] Cf. Virg.6,1 again.
[32] For the higher reward awaiting the virgin cf. Virg.4,1.
[33] Cf. Virg.4,3; both passages quote 1 Cor.7.25, the one directly, the other indirectly.

and, while resolving to do more than has been commanded, shows that less has been demanded of him than he has been able to achieve. Next, if a man claims to be so obedient that he obeys with pleasure even the divine counsel, how can he escape the obligation to obey the divine commandment, since the former is a matter of choice, the latter of necessity? Of virginity it is said: He who is able to receive this, let him receive it (Mt.19.12); it is not said of righteousness: He who is able to do this, let him do it, but: Every tree that does not bear good fruit shall be cut down and thrown into the fire (Mt.3.10; Lk.3.9). Consider then, I beg you, the great difference between counsel and command: the former makes an exception for some, the latter embraces everyone without exception; the former offers a reward, the latter punishment; the former invites you to do something, the latter threatens you if you fail to do it.

2. So, distinguishing between these two by using your reason to the best of your ability, observe what you are offering and what you owe; or rather, now that you owe two debts, both your virginity, which you have voluntarily offered to God, and righteousness, which he himself has enjoined, pay both of these in full. The servant who pleases the Lord is the one who, while performing some piece of work voluntarily, yet carries out his orders as well, who does not do one thing in place of another but does both, and who does not alter the nature of his allegiance but adds to its scope. Do not let yourself be deceived by the examples of those women who, while applauding themselves on their chastity alone, reject the will of God and follow the dictates of their own wills. What they want to do is to offer the good of perpetual chastity not along with righteousness but in its place and to count the reward for their virginity as part of their compensation for sins; and in return for that prize they seek freedom from punishment or, in the grip of a folly which is even more shameless, consider that they should be given crowns in the kingdom of heaven and preference there over others, when they have closed up their own way of approach to it by transgression of the commandments given to them: Not every one who says to me, Lord, Lord, shall enter the kingdom of heaven, but he who does the will of my Father, who is in heaven, he shall enter the kingdom himself (Mt.7.21). And let them remember the foolish virgins who had to be driven away from the bridegroom's door and to whom it had to be said, 'I do not know you,' and let them be joined to those of whom the Lord himself says: On that day many will say to me, 'Lord, Lord, did we not cast out demons in your name, and do many mighty works in your name?' But I will declare to them, 'Truly I say to you, I do not know you; depart from me, all you evildoers' (Mt.7.22,23).

3. But the path that you have to tread is far different, you who have trampled under foot the love of this world and, by always considering the things which are of God, wish to show yourself a virgin of the apostles, you who await the Lord's coming as holy in spirit as you are in body and, continually pouring the oil of holy works into the lamp of your soul, are prepared to meet the bridegroom in the company of the wise virgins. You must avoid that broad path which is worn away by the thronging multitude on their way to their death and continue to follow the rough track of that narrow path to eternal life which few

find.[34] You have already laid down all the greatest encumbrances and in the very first moment of your conversion you have overcome everything which either delays you or recalls you from the journey of the spiritual life; you have spurned the pleasures of marriage, the concern for posterity, the attractions of luxury, the ostentation of the world, the desire for wealth, and you can say with Paul: The world has been crucified to me, and I to the world (Gal.6.14). What kind of completion is to be expected from one who has made such a beginning? Exert this same virtue of yours, this same sensibility, in what remains to be done and now, with that same strength of mind which enabled you to drive away the occasions of vice which presented themselves, reject the vices themselves; let your virginity be embellished with moral purity, let your perfect approach to life be followed by perfection in life itself.

4. Surely, if the life of the world had been to your taste, you would be taking pains to see that no one surpassed you in riches, in bodily adornments, in abundance of everything and in public esteem; as it is now, and since a different inclination calls for a different life, take care that no one surpasses you in the good life, no one excels you in moral purity, no one wins a place above you in the pursuit of virtue. And, in respect of those possessions which we mentioned first above, it was not your concern to ensure either that you surpassed everyone else or that no one else surpassed you, for all of them are sought from outside and whatever one hopes to receive from another source belongs to others, not oneself. The possessions mentioned afterwards, however, are under your control and are truly yours, since they do not come from outside but are produced in the heart itself. Not everyone who seeks the former finds them nor does he who has found them always keep them, since chance can snatch them away just as it can provide them; but everyone who seeks the latter finds them, and he who has found them need never fear that they may be snatched away from him, for the only good possessions are those which we neither find nor lose at any time save by the exercise of our own free choice.

11, 1. In this respect too, then, you have possessions which rightly entitle you to be set above others, indeed even more so; for everyone realizes that your nobility in the physical sense and your wealth belong to your family, not to you, but no one except you yourself will be able to endow you with spiritual riches, and it is for these that you are rightly to be praised, for these that you are deservedly set above others, and they are things which cannot be within you unless they come from you. Is this spiritual life to be the only one which does not strive after progress and in which each and every one is supposed to stay just as he was at the outset instead of striving to achieve greater things in his desire for growth? And when men can never be satisfied with the progress that they are making in all their worldly pursuits, is this to be the sole field of human endeavour in which it is considered sufficient to have done no more than make a start?

---

34 On the Two Ways cf. Cel.10, a very long passage, the content of which is compressed here into two short sentences.

In earthly things we burn with zeal but in heavenly we are as cold as ice; in small matters we show the greatest liveliness but when faced with those which are more important, we become paralysed.

2. It makes one ashamed when one thinks what enthusiasm there is in the world, with what solicitude men strive daily to attain greater perfection in all their individual enthusiasms. Enthusiasm for letters, for example, is quenched at absolutely no time of life; rather, to employ an aphorism of a secular author, it becomes more ardent with the very passage of time. Love of wealth is insatiable, desire for honour knows no fulfilment; possessions destined to meet with a speedy end are sought endlessly. But divine wisdom, heavenly riches, immortal honours we neglect in our indifference and sloth, and, as for spiritual riches, either we do not touch them at all or, if we get a slight taste of them, we at once suppose that we have had enough. The divine Wisdom invites us to its feasts in quite different terms: Those who eat me, she says, will hunger for more, and those who drink me will thirst for more (Sir.24.21). No one can have enough of such feasts or ever suffers from squeamishness because he has had too much: the more he drinks from that source the greater will be each man's capacity and eagerness for more. The Lord says in the gospel: Blessed are those who hunger and thirst for righteousness, for they shall be satisfied (Mt.5.6); for he wishes us always to be hungering and thirsting for righteousness here, in order that we may receive satisfaction from the repayment which we are given for our righteousness in the hereafter.

12. We must weigh well the sense of these words and, as a result, desire righteousness as strongly as we desire food and drink when hungry or thirsty, and to all without exception who desire the promise of eternal life we must say this. But your special task now is to consider how much you have to excel in magnanimity as one who has undertaken to do more than others are even obliged to do, prompted by your desire for a greater reward. In defining the nature of the virgin of Christ, the apostle set her far apart from the wife, distinguishing between the merit of the single state and that of matrimony by the different purposes underlying them: The unmarried woman and virgin is anxious about the affairs of the Lord, how to please God, to be holy in body and spirit; but the married woman is anxious about worldly affairs, how to please her husband (1 Cor.7.34). She who is holy in body and spirit does no wrong with her members or her mind;[35] but to do wrong is possible not only in the case of chastity but in any area of righteousness also, for if, though a virgin in body and in spirit, she nevertheless sins with her hands, eyes, ears or tongue, how can she be said to be holy in body? Secondly, if she has been corrupted by hatred, envy, greed or anger, how can she acquire holiness of spirit? And if the married woman, whose attachment to her marriage makes her think 'how she may please her husband' and how much she can leave for her children and who, in the grip of the manifold cares of this world, turns her

---

[35] Cf. Virg.9: both there and in this sentence 'mind' is the synonym for 'spirit' and 'members' for 'body'.

attention too infrequently to consideration of the will of God, yet is unable to excuse herself for sinning, what shall the virgin do, who has been released from all the impediments of this world and, free from other responsibilities, has entered a school, as it were, of chastity?

13.   If then you wish to make the extent of your intention equal to your morals and to be joined with God in everything, if you wish to make the light, agreeable yoke of Christ even lighter and more agreeable for you to bear, now especially devote your care to the blessed life, now apply yourself to ensuring that fresh zeal may always be kindling the glowing faith of your recent conversion and that the practice of holy conduct may the more easily grow in you at what is still a tender age. Whatever you implant in yourself at the outset will remain, and the rest of your life will run along on the course set by your beginning. At the very commencement the end has to be kept in mind: try even now to be the kind of person you want to be when you reach the last day. Habit is what nourishes both vices and virtues, and it is strongest in those with whom it has grown bit by bit from the start of their lives. The first five years are the best for moral training, for there is a flexible, yielding quality in them which can easily be shaped and directed according to the wishes of the instructor, and in almost all forms of life it is the tender one which is more quickly habituated. It is easy for small trees, while still young and with roots which can hardly be described as firm, to be moved in any direction as long as they are responsive to every guiding touch; since they are by nature curved for the most part, they are speedily corrected at the behest of the cultivator. Animals which are delicate and still in the earliest stages of their life are usually tamed without much trouble, and the more quickly they are weaned from the habit of indulging their feeling that they are free to wander, the more easily do their necks become used to the yoke or their teeth to the bit. Enthusiasm for literature is also better planted in tender minds, and that which first settles in the mind usually becomes more deeply rooted in the faculties. This same principle is most of all valid in the conduct of the good life: while the child's age is still flexible and its mind is easily led, the habit of doing good must be exercised and strengthened by the practice of constant meditation; only the best things must occupy the mind, and the practice of holy conduct must be implanted at a deeper level. Then indeed the mind climbs to the height of perfection and uses the advantage of long habit so as to acquire the ability to live well and, marvelling at its own qualities, will come to suppose that what it has learned was actually born with it or, in some measure, within it.

14, 1.   Consider, I beg you, how much holiness is looked for from you by your grandmother and mother, who, since they think of you as a new and brilliant light born to their family, have now transferred to you alone the whole concern of their minds and follow with a remarkable display of enthusiasm and approval the course which you intend to pursue. And, having shaped you for moral purity from the beginning of your life, they now desire to be surpassed by you, reckoning your victory to be to their credit. Their extraordinary faithfulness to God was most clearly revealed at the time when you declared your intention: then, although they had already prepared you for marriage, as soon as they learned of your changed wishes, they immediately encouraged you to pursue your new choice and gave a wonderfully prompt assent to it. With the authority of their will they gave added strength to a decision about which you were bound to be a little apprehensive in view of your age, made your vow the common vow of all three of you and, though they have seen many members of their family occupying the highest positions of honour, at no time rejoiced for any of them as they did for you, for they had never seen such a mark of greatness and distinction in anyone. Indeed, you alone have bestowed upon your house an honour which it has not previously possessed throughout its long history: the male members of it have produced memorable consulships, and the register of the most distinguished order in our state has frequently included names from your illustrious house, yet nothing has ever won greater distinction than this honour of yours, which has been inscribed not on a tablet made of earthly material but in the book of immortal memory.

2. *They* received tumultuous applause all over the world, and the common people expressed their pleasure by the remarkable unanimity shown in their acclaim of the well-earned honours which their consuls had gained; yet the glory attached to *your* honour is far greater, since it has given cause for joy in heaven and rejoicing to the angels. Through *your* action it is not courtesans who are enriched but virgins of Christ who are sustained, it is not the hunter and the charioteer who are made wealthy but Christ's poor who are supported. At *their* consulship divers provinces throughout the world to which your house's power extends sent exotic wild beasts and unknown animals to stain the soil of the cruel arena either with their own or with human blood; to *you*, however, chosen maidens are sent for you to present to God as most precious offerings and to challenge to follow your example by professing perpetual chastity – in service not to you but to God along with you. The glorious news of your act of public profession has spread abroad and become common talk among all men, and the whole world has become so exultant at your conversion[36] that people seem to have wanted all along for something to happen which, now that it has happened, they are still scarcely able to credit for all their great joy.

3. Kept in high suspense by the start which you have made and by this foretaste of the fame which is to be yours, all men and women are anxious to hear some wonderful news of you, and those who have appreciated the virtue shown by your initial declaration of intent now look forward to that which will appear in your future conduct. Consider now that the faces and eyes of all are turned upon you and that the entire world has settled down to watch the spectacle of your life. Take care not to disappoint so many, if they find in you less than they

---

[36] See the introduction to this letter for Jerome's description of the event and of the reaction to it; Pelagius is as guilty of hyperbole as is his opposite number but he does not go quite so far, even if he does get involved in a rather complicated piece of writing.

are looking for. But why am I talking with you about mere men and dragging their expectations into my encouragement of you? *Your* struggle is being witnessed by God himself, the ruler and Lord of all, with his army of angels; for *you*, as you strive with the devil, he prepares the crown of eternal life and makes a heavenly prize your spur to victory. See what spirit, what valour, you have to bring to this great spectacle, and measure the magnitude of the contest by the eminence of its spectators!

15. So, in this great struggle which you are about to undertake let your chief concern, the first object of all your preparation, be to win an overwhelming victory for virtue in this war of extermination, to swear fealty to all God's commands against the camp of the devil and not simply to shun the things that are forbidden but also to fulfil those which are commanded. For it is not enough for you to refrain from evil, if you refrain from good as well: the law of God is divided into two classes of orders and, while it forbids evil, it also enjoins good, and it prohibits neglect of itself on either count:[37] it is not only the servant who does what is forbidden who has neglected God but also the one who has not done what was commanded. We have already, a little earlier, quoted the judgement: Every tree that does not bear good fruit will be cut down and thrown into the fire (Mt.7.19). Do we then flatter ourselves on not being weighed down by evil fruit, when we are to be condemned for remaining unproductive of good? According to our understanding of this statement the Father will break off every branch which does not bear fruit in the Son, and he who hides in a napkin a talent which he has received is condemned by the Lord as a useless and good-for-nothing servant: it is culpable not only to have diminished that talent but also not to have increased it. Do not suppose that some commands are to be ignored simply because they are less burdensome, for both those that are very weighty and those that are very light have been commanded by God, and neglect of any commandment whatsoever is an affront to the one who gives it. Hence the blessed Paul addresses this instruction to us: Do everything without grumbling or questioning, that you may be blameless and innocent, as children of God without blemish in the midst of a crooked and perverse nation, among whom you shine as lights in this world (Phil.2.14,15).

16, 1. Let us pause for a little while at this point, virgin, and taking each of the words used by the apostle separately, examine those most precious pearls with which the bride of Christ must be adorned. What he says above is: 'Do everything'; so we are not to select some of God's commandments as if to suit our own fancy but to fulfil all of them without exception, nor to spurn some of his instructions as being mean and insignificant tasks but to have regard in all matters for the majesty of the one who gives them.[38] Surely no command from

---

37 The twofold commandment again; cf. *Cel.*5, in which 'two classes', 'forbids' and 'enjoins' all respectively translate the same Latin words.

38 A typical Pelagian point; cf. *Cel.*5 and 6, on which Pelagius enlarges here, and *Law*,5,1.

God can seem contemptible in our eyes, if we always bear in mind the identity of its author and respond 'without grumbling and questioning'. We see base and ignoble masters being openly ignored by their servants, who are accustomed to resist them to their face in response to all their demands, even the smallest. But this is not permitted nowadays in relation to noble persons: the more powerful the masters the more disposed to obey are the servants, who tend to obey even more willingly when ordered to perform more difficult tasks; indeed, at a king's command all are so ready for action, standing at their posts to obey, that they are even keen to be given their orders, and they not only believe that they will deserve well of their masters if they carry out those orders but consider the service which they give to be a sign of their master's favour in view of the dignity of the one who has given the orders, as if the fact that they have been given them at all is an indication that they have already deserved well of him.

2. It is God himself, however, that eternal, ineffable majesty and incalcul-able power, who sends us his holy scriptures and the writ of his own command-ments truly worthy of our worship, and yet we fail to receive them at once with joy and reverence nor do we consider the command of so mighty, so illustrious an authority as a great kindness, especially when it is not the advantage of the one giving the order which is being sought but the interest of the one who obeys it; on the contrary, with a proud and casual attitude of mind, in the manner of good-for-nothing and haughty servants, we cry out against the face of God and say, 'It is hard, it is difficult, we cannot do it, we are but men, we are encompassed by frail flesh.' What blind madness! what unholy foolhardiness! We accuse God of a twofold lack of knowledge, so that he appears not to know what he has done, and not to know what he has commanded; as if, forgetful of the human frailty of which he is himself the author, he has imposed on man commands which he cannot bear. And, at the same time, oh horror!, we ascribe iniquity to the righteous and cruelty to the holy, while complaining, first, that he has com-manded something impossible,[39] secondly, that man is to be damned by him for doing things which he was unable to avoid, so that God – and this is something which even to suspect is sacrilege – seems to have sought not so much our salvation as our punishment!

3. And so the apostle, knowing that nothing impossible has been com-manded by the God of justice and majesty, deprives us of this fault of ours of 'grumbling and questioning', which is wont to be found especially when com-mands are unjust or the standing of the one who gives them does not entitle him to do so. Why do we indulge in pointless evasions, advancing the frailty of our nature as an objection to the one who commands us? No one knows better the true measure of our strength than he who has given it to us nor does anyone understand better how much we are able to do than he who has given us this very capacity of ours to be able; nor has he who is just wished to command anything

---

[39] For human complaints at the severity of the divine law cf. *Cel.*15, where there are a number of close verbal parallels with this passage.

impossible or he who is good intended to condemn a man for doing what he could not avoid doing.[40]

17, 1.   The words which follow are: 'That you may be blameless and innocent' – that is, with reference to the fully perfect life. This one word 'blameless', which describes a qualification which God also orders to be investigated when electing a bishop, is quite sufficient; for how circumspect, how holy, is a life which incurs no blame! And who can be holier than the man who holds fast to the virtue of true innocence, never promising one thing in his heart and falsely declaring another with his lips? Again, 'As children of God without blemish': there is no more powerful exhortation than one in which divine scripture calls us to be children of God, for who would not blush and fear to do anything unworthy of so great a Father with the result that the man who is said to be a child of God is himself made a slave of vice? And that is why he adds: 'Without blemish', for it is not becoming that the stain of sin should be found in the children of God, because he himself is the fount of righteousness. 'In the midst of a crooked and perverse nation': that is to say, however vast the multitude of sinners that surrounds you, however countless the examples of vice, you ought still to be so mindful of your heavenly birth that, while living among evil men, you may yet overcome all evil. 'Among whom you shine as lights in this world': again we read in the gospel: Then the righteous will shine like the sun in the kingdom of their Father (Mt.13.43).

  2.   Life is compared to a reward, so that those who are to be given the brightness of the sun in the future shine forth here with a like splendour of righteousness and light up the blindness of unbelievers with works of holiness. That is the sense which is to be applied to this passage uttered by the same apostle in the course of a discussion with the Corinthians: There is one glory of the sun, and another glory of the moon, and another glory of the stars; for star differs from star in glory. So it is with the resurrection of the dead (1 Cor.15.41,42). In the kingdom of heaven there are different dwelling-places in accordance with the merits of individuals; for diversity in works makes for diversity of rewards, and a man will shine there in glory as much as he has shone here in holiness.

  3.   Now, therefore, direct your mind's attention to complete moral perfection and prepare yourself to lead a heavenly life for a heavenly reward: let a virgin's holiness shine forth for all to see in the manner of a star and reveal the magnitude of her future reward by the unusual quality of her behaviour. Your progress in good is easier because you are not held back by the habit of evil in the mind nor have we any fear that vices will slow down your progress in virtue and the harmful seeds sown by the devil kill off the growing crops of Christ. For if even those who by long habit of sinning have somehow buried the good of nature are able to be restored by repentance and, by changing their chosen way of life, to wipe out one habit by another and leave the ranks of the worst for those of the

[40]   See n.23 above.

best, how much more able are you to overcome evil habits which have never succeeded in overcoming you, since for you it is not so much a matter of driving vices out as of keeping them away! Without doubt there are pursuits which it is easier not to take up at all than to lay down again, once taken up.

18, 1.   Nor again is there such pleasure attached to these vices that we ought to prefer them to virtues because of it, since not all of them offer the inducement of delight and even those which seem the sweetest are rejected by the majority. Of all vices there are two which deceive men most with their own special pleasure, namely gluttony and lust, and these become progressively more difficult to give up as they become more pleasant to indulge in; yet these vices, so troublesome and so dangerous because of the delight taken in them, we have seen to be so spurned by many that virgins, for example, have persisted throughout their lives in total abstinence from them – to say nothing of those who, after a long period of indulgence in gastronomic delights and a long-standing enjoyment of lust, have dedicated themselves to self-control and chastity and exchanged both of these vices for virtues which are their exact opposites.

2.   There is, however, a very different consideration applying to other vices, which though they have no special charm about them, yet contain the causes of much bitterness, and, since they are much easier to avoid altogether, you will rarely come across people avoiding them. What pleasure, I ask you, does envy offer to the envious man, when envy itself tears him apart with the hidden claws of conscience and makes another's happiness the source of his own anguish? What reward does another receive from hatred except dread darkness in the soul and the horrors of a confused mind, as with grief on his face and in his heart he tortures himself with the very wish which makes him want to harm another? What benefit does his anger confer on the angry man, who, tormented by the savagest pricks of conscience, is so deprived by it of all judgement and reason that, while angry, he is believed to be out of his right mind? Run through all the sins in turn in like manner and you will find in them as many torments of the mind as there are vices which, to be sure, can be overcome more easily in that they have no pleasure with which to attract us. How much more difficult, how much harder it is – and I refrain from mentioning the labours of chastity – to abstain from wine and meat and even from olive-oil, and without benefit of these barely to exist on short commons sometimes for a period of two or three days, to disregard limbs enfeebled by fasts and vigils, to spurn the consolation of a warm bath, to deny the body its necessities and, so to speak, to do violence to one's nature! Show such greatness of spirit in all other respects and then consider what you are unable to achieve.

3.   But we, for shame!, because of a certain delight that we take in sin, exhibit some natural strength in some respects, while in others we become apathetic and, after spurning bodily pleasures out of love of virtue, once again give in to our evil ways to such an extent that we do not even spare a thought for the possibility that they can be got rid of. Where is the purpose in all this, where is the new way of life? I attack objectives which are difficult and call for great

effort without a thought of failure, while believing that tasks which are easier
cannot be performed. I overcome the most difficult obstacles only to be overcome myself by mere trifles. I surmount the heights and the steeps unwearied
only to faint when I reach the plains. I am happy to flee from what delights me
and yet unwilling to avoid what torments me. This is how it is with those who,
disregarding God's will, seek only what wins them praise more easily and quickly
results in fame but neglect the benefits of good moral conduct which are less
conspicuous. On the other hand, you, who have trodden underfoot the world and
its desires in order that, having done so, you make of them a step, as it were, on
which to climb to heaven, you must not seek this world's glory. Concentrate
rather on pleasing only the one who is often displeased with what pleases men
and who will one day judge the judgements of men themselves. Your abstinence
and fasting please God all the more because they are offered to him along with
moral sanctity, so that actions which others use as a mere facade to cover up their
vices become in you adornments of true virtue.

19, 1.   Consider, I beseech you, that high rank with which you have been
made glorious before God and through which you were reborn in baptism to
become a daughter of God and, again, by your consecration as a virgin began to
be a bride of Christ; let this honour conferred upon you remind you of the need
to devote care to your vocation on both these counts. There must be no room for
negligence when the prizes which have to be protected are so splendid: the
greater the value of a garment the greater the precaution which must be taken to
protect it from stain; a jewel procured with much gold is kept with greater care,
and, in general, all important possessions are guarded with greater vigilance.
Hence you too, if you wish to guard yourself adequately, ought always to consider
your own honour to be a precious possession, since everyone treats himself with
less caution the lower the opinion he has of himself. It is for this reason that we
are so often given the name 'children of God' in divine scripture, as it is said
through the prophet: And I will be your Father, and you shall be my children,
says the Lord Almighty (2 Sam.7.14), and the apostle says: Be imitators of God as
beloved children (Eph.5.1), and the blessed John says: Beloved, we are God's
children now; and it does not yet appear what we shall be, but we know that
when he appears we shall be like him, for we shall see him as he is. And every
one who thus hopes in him, let him purify himself as he is pure (1 Jn.3.2,3). He
wishes frequently to impress upon us the high worth of the heavenly teaching
given to us and to turn our sense of shame into a mark of honour.

    2.   That is why the Lord himself, when calling on us to practise benev-
olence, says: Love your enemies, do good to those who hate you (Lk.6.27), and:
Pray for those who persecute and slander you, so that you may be sons of your
Father who is in heaven (Mt.5.44,45); for it is not the case that God so makes
mankind capable of love that the gentleness of mind and kindliness which ought
to be so evident in the Christian are found in abundance in evil men also. But let
the Christian imitate the loving-kindness of God, who makes his sun rise on the
good and on the evil, and sends rain on the just and the unjust (ibid.45). So, let

us not find you, above all else, harming anyone even by word, so that you may apply yourself instead to helping everyone you can in every possible way and, as the apostle says, repay no one evil for evil but only evil with good. And let no word of disparagement escape the virgin's lips:[41] we have enough worthless people, people seeking to make a name for themselves by making others out to be worthless; they imagine that they can win themselves a high reputation by disparaging others and, being unable to find favour on their own merits, wish to find it by comparison with those who are still worse than they.

3. We have said too little about the need for you to refrain not only from disparagement yourself but even from at any time believing another's disparagement; this practice of disparagement is a very grave fault, because it makes another appear worthless, and you are to avoid defamation with the ears no less than the tongue. Be mindful of the scripture, when it says: Do not agree with those who disparage a neighbour, and you will not take a burden of sin on yourself on his account (Lev.19.16,17?), and elsewhere: See that you fence in your ears with thorns and listen to no evil tongue (Sir.28.24–6).[42] For the listener, who makes the detractor what he is, is the real accuser, and if he but avert his ears, tighten the muscles of his face and check the movement of his eyes by refusing to look, he can then prove the detractor to be guilty of slanderous talk, so that the latter learns not to be so ready to say what he has now found to be not readily listened to. Hence the saintly James asserts that 'he is a perfect man' who 'makes no mistakes in what he says' (Jas.3.2), and the scripture says: Death and life are in the power of the tongue. But let not your tongue know how to lie, slander and swear oaths, because a lying mouth kills the soul (cf. Wis.1.11); and according to the apostle: Revilers will not inherit the kingdom of God (1 Cor. 6.10).

4. And Christ himself forbade swearing, when he said: But I say to you, Do not swear at all; and again: Let what you say be simply 'Yes' or 'No'; anything more than this comes from evil (Mt.5.34,37). The apostle, briefly disposing of the vices of the mouth, says: Let no evil talk come out of your mouths but only such as is good for edifying faith, that it may impart grace to those who hear (Eph.4.29). And let a virgin's speech be discreet, unassuming and infrequent and esteemed not so much for its eloquence as for its modesty. Let all marvel at your modesty, while you stay silent, and at your discretion, when you speak; let your utterance be always gentle and calm; let it be adorned by sweetness mingled with dignity, by wisdom mixed with modesty; let it be firm and balanced, most acceptable as being appropriate to itself, and let there be due proportion of silence and

---

[41] For the sin of defaming others cf. Cel.16,1, in which there is very close verbal agreement with the passage immediately following this sentence.

[42] Cf. Cel.16,1 and Virg.10,2 and see my n.18 on the latter; in Sir.28.24 we have 'See that you fence in your *property* with thorns' – Pelagius seems to have altered this to suit his required sense here – and in 28.26, 'Beware lest you err with your tongue', which is also slightly different from the original text. The Leviticus citation is at best only a paraphrase.

talk. Nor should the virgin's mouth speak at all when it were better to have been silent; she should speak with great caution as one who must avoid not only evil speech but also speech which is superfluous.

20, 1.   Let it be a task for your highest knowledge and understanding to distinguish between vices and virtues which, though always contrary to each other, yet are linked in some cases by such resemblance that they can scarcely be distinguished at all. For how many reckon pride as liberty, adopt flattery as humility, embrace malice instead of prudence and confer the name of innocence on foolishness, and, deceived by a misleading and most dangerous likeness, take pride in vices instead of virtues? And though you ought to employ a very acute intelligence to distinguish all these and, by following all the virtues with their strict limits of demarcation, never to depart from them at all, yet you must be especially careful to avoid false humility and to follow that true humility which Christ taught us and in which pride is not included, for many pursue the shadow of this virtue, few its reality.[43] It is very easy to wear a modest garment, to give a more submissive greeting, to kiss the hands and knees with warm affection, to promise humility and gentleness with head bent to the ground and eyes downcast, to make subdued conversation in a low, faint voice, to sigh frequently and at every word to proclaim oneself a miserable sinner, then straightway to raise one's eyebrows, if offended by a frivolous speech, lift one's neck and suddenly exchange that refined tone of voice for a wild shout. It was another sort of humility that Christ taught us, encouraging us to follow his example when he said: Learn from me, for I am gentle and lowly in heart (Mt.11.29). When he was reviled, he did not revile in turn; when he suffered, he did not threaten (1 Pet.2.23); and this kind of humility is what the blessed Peter instils in us, saying: A tender heart and a humble mind, not returning evil for evil or reviling for reviling (1 Pet.3.9). Eschew verbal fictions at all times, dispense with feigned gestures and keep your conciliatory speeches for the proper occasions. Endurance of insult reveals the truly humble.

    2.   Therefore, let there be no room in your mind for any vice at any time: let there be no sign of pride, arrogance or haughtiness in you. Before God there is nothing more exalted than humility, and he himself speaks through the prophet: On whom shall I look, unless it be he that is humble and quiet and trembles at my word (Is.66.2)? And never let your spirit flare up in anger, since it is the nursery of hatred; let your mind be so full of the fear of God that you dare not be indignant at all but, rather, overcome your anger with fear. The blessed apostle, cleansing our soul and preparing it to become the dwelling-place of God, cries out and says: Let all bitterness and wrath and anger and clamour and slander be put away from you, with all malice (Eph.4.31).

---

[43] Cf. Cel.20, also on the subject of true Christian humility; in this sentence there is a very close verbal parallel with the corresponding passage in Cel.20.

21, 1.   Beware of flatterers as your enemies:[44] their speeches are smoother than olive-oil, but they themselves are like poisoned darts; they corrupt shallow souls with feigned praise and inflict their agreeable wounds on over-credulous minds. This vice has increased in our time and has now reached its furthest limit and so is incapable of being extended any farther. It is a subject and a study to which we have all devoted ourselves, so that we think it an obligation to play this game of mockery, and what we offer to others gladly as a kind of service we ourselves gladly accept from others in turn, praising in advance those by whom we wish to be praised in the hope of receiving praise ourselves. Often we put up a token resistance to the words of flatterers to their face but in the secret places of our mind we take delight in them and consider that we have received the greatest possible benefit if we are commended even with counterfeit praise, never giving a thought to what we really are instead of to what we may appear to others to be. So things have reached such a pretty pass that, blind to true merit, we care only for men's opinion of it and seek evidence for the quality of our life not from our conscience but from our reputation. Happy the mind that conquers this vice and neither flatters at any time nor believes flatterers, that neither deceives another nor is itself deceived, that neither does this great wrong at any time nor suffers it! Never let there be anything false or counterfeit in you; consider that your conscience, which assuredly is always exposed to God's eyes, occupies itself with a host of concerns; never hold fast to one thing in your heart while voicing another with your lips; let anything which is shameful to say be also shameful even to think.

2.   It is well known by now to everyone and has become common knowledge how useful and necessary to this vocation of yours is the virtue of fasting and abstinence, especially at your time of life when it is easier for the body to fall prey to the onset of passion, which is why refraining from eating meat and drinking wine has been praised in the apostle's utterance on the subject; love of chastity must avoid anything that has the power to inflame the body or supplies fuel to pleasure. Yet we do not want you to be so weighed down by the labour involved in this task of yours that you immediately collapse under its weight; for there are many who, through the excessive ardour of their mind, fail to calculate the extent of their own strength and, suddenly tumbling to the ground, have almost succumbed to weakness before achieving sanctity by their vocation. Moderation is best in everything and due sense of proportion is praiseworthy in all circumstances; the body has to be controlled, not broken. Therefore, let holiness be sought in moderation, and fastings, which so weaken the body, be practised in uncomplicated ways and with all humility of mind, lest they inflate the spirit and lest a matter calling for humility create pride instead and vices be born of virtue: But I – as he (sc. the psalmist) says – when they brought trouble on me, I wore sackcloth, I humbled my soul with fasting (Ps.35.13). Poor clothing, cheap food, wearisome fasts ought to quench pride, not nourish it. Who would turn a regimen for healing into a wound, damaging parts that are sound by the very

---

[44] The whole of this section has many similarities with Cel.17.

means by which the parts already damaged are to be cured? Or what hope of salvation will remain, if those spiritual remedies of yours turn out to be poisons?

22, 1. Let your works of mercy provide the justification for the labours of fasting, and your abstinence be made more acceptable because it helps to nourish the poor; the Lord says through the mouth of the prophet: I desire mercy and not sacrifice (Hos.6.6), and in the gospel of Christ we read the words: Blessed are the merciful, for they shall obtain mercy (Mt.5.7). But this responsibility I ask your grandmother and mother to undertake in your place: let them perform this role for you, let them raise your treasure on high to heaven, let it be their part to feed the hungry, clothe the naked, visit the sick, receive strangers into their home and invest money in the poor for Christ's sake and in hope of eternal reward, for it was he who said: As you did it to one of the least of these my brethren, you did it to me (Mt.25.40). And, especially while your spirit is maturing in its vocation, you should withdraw from all such occupations, devoting all your zeal and care to the ordering of your way of life; this should demand your time and occupy your mind to such an extent that you cease to feel yourself to be a rich woman or the mistress of a household and remember your noble birth only insofar as it leads you to compete with your family's distinction by your holy conduct, progress to greater nobility by adding spiritual virtue to noble birth, and pride yourself more on the kind of nobility which makes men sons of God and co-heirs with Christ. If you always have regard for this kind of nobility, believing that in it you possess a greater reason for joy, then you will cease to pride yourself on anything which gives you less.

2. Let all that dignity which you derive from your famous family and the illustrious honour of the Anician blood be transferred to your soul; let that man be counted famous, lofty and noble, let that man consider himself to be guarding his nobility and keeping it intact, who thinks it beneath him to become a slave to vices and to be overcome by them: For whatever overcomes a man, to that he is enslaved (2 Pet.2.19).[45] What can be more unworthy than servitude of the soul, what more base than that moment when either hatred masters it or envy rules over it, when either greed takes possession of it or anger holds it captive, or indeed any other vices claim it for themselves? It is impossible for anyone to flatter himself on his family's nobility, if he is a slave in more important respects; it is much more unworthy to be a slave in one's mind than with one's body. I do not think that I need warn you to keep your public appearances sparing and infrequent, since even consideration for worldly propriety will have taught you this much from your infancy and you should therefore have no difficulty in realizing that in this life you have to devote much greater care to the protection of something to which seclusion is more appropriate. I do advise you also to set a fixed limit on those visits which people have to pay to your bedchamber in order to tender their respects: do not allow them to become overfrequent or daily

---

[45] Cf. Cel.21 with this and the preceding sentence for this contrast between true Christian nobility and false pagan nobility based on birth and wealth.

events, lest they appear not so much to be performing a duty as to be giving you cause for restlessness.

23, 1. Though you are under an obligation to devote your whole lifetime to God's work and it is fitting that not a single hour be devoid of spiritual growth, since you must 'meditate on the law of the Lord day and night' (Ps.1.2), yet there should be a fixed and appointed number of hours when you are more completely free for God and are bound as if by statute to the most intense mental concentration. It is best therefore to assign a morning period to this work, that is, the best part of the day, and up to the third hour[46] to exercise your soul, so to speak, in this gymnasium in which it wrestles spiritually and daily engages in heavenly combat. During these hours each day pray in a more private part of the house with the door of your bedchamber shut (Mt.6.6). Even when you are in the city subject yourself to this discipline of solitude, remove yourself for a while from the company of men and join yourself more closely to God; then, when you return to the sight of your own family, show them the fruits of your reading and prayer. In that place of solitude you ought above all else to be feeding your soul on divine utterances and filling it with as much of this richer nutriment as may be able to satisfy it for the whole day.

2. Read the holy scriptures in such a way that you never forget that they are the words of God, who commands us that we should not only know his law but also fulfil it; for it is of no advantage to have learned what has to be done, if we then fail to do it. The divine text is put to best use if you hold it up to yourself like a mirror, so that your soul looks, as it were, at its own reflection in it and either corrects all the ugly blemishes or touches up the features which are attractive.[47] Reading should be frequently interspersed with prayer, and such a pleasing alternation in your holy task should arouse even more a soul continuously clinging to God: at one time, therefore, let the sequence of heavenly history instruct, at another a holy song of David delight, at another the Wisdom of Solomon inform, at another the rebukes of the prophets arouse, at another the perfection of the evangelists and apostles unite you with Christ in a life of complete sanctity.

3. Plant deep in your memory the things that must be kept in readiness for use and maintain them in good order by continually reflecting upon them; turn over frequently in your mind those which still have to mature, so that this persistence in divine study and spiritual training may embellish your conduct as a virgin and your sensibility and bestow holiness and wisdom upon you. That is why the scriptures say: Those who seek God shall find wisdom with righteousness (cf. Mt.6.33). But your reading must be done in moderation and a limit imposed upon it by prudence and not by fatigue; for just as immoderate fasting, overen-

---

[46] The Romans divided the period between sunrise and sunset into twelve hours, which, of course, varied throughout the year.

[47] *Cel.*15 employs the same image of the mirror, applying it to a specific text cited in 14 (Mt.7.12), whereas here it is applied to the reading of the scriptures in general.

thusiastic abstinence and vigils of extravagant and disproportionate length are seen as evidence of lack of restraint and bring it about by their excessive nature that it becomes impossible thereafter to perform such works even in a moderate way, so too intemperate enthusiasm for reading can come in for criticism, and thus a practice which is praiseworthy when kept within appropriate limits, is liable to be blameworthy if it exceeds them.

24, 1. It must be stated as a general principle, albeit briefly and summarily, that with good practices as well as bad whatever exceeds the bounds of moderation becomes a vice instead of a virtue. The ordering of the perfect life is a formidable matter, formidable, I say, and dependent for its success on a considerable degree of effort and study, and it calls for consummate wisdom to know what is the end which one is pursuing and how to pursue it and, by showing discretion in every act, to do nothing which is likely to make one regret having done it. Within the space of an hour one's conduct can undergo change, and fasting, abstinence, psalmody and keeping vigil demand a conscious act of will more than constant practice. The man who begins something as soon as he has willed it is perfect for this; or, to put it in another way, those who bring bodily strength fresh from the world to their vocation are able to follow it more easily. But to change one's moral life and to fashion in oneself special virtues of the mind and then to bring them to perfection is a matter which calls for intensive study and long practice. That is why so many of us grow old in the pursuit of this vocation and yet fail to gain the objectives for the sake of which we came to it in the first place.

2. But *your* conduct has to be something new, *your* moral seriousness, patience, compassion and godliness objects of wonder: whatever is holier and more perfect, whatever can commend you more highly to God and make you greater in heaven, that is what you must always pursue and embrace. The bride of Christ must be more splendidly adorned than anything else, since the greater the one whom one is seeking to please the greater the effort which is required in order to please him. The maidens of the secular world who prepare themselves for marriage and prefer to take advantage of the apostle's concession than to follow his advice and to accept the remedy for incontinence, that is, marriage, rather than the reward for continence, take pains to get themselves up with remarkable care and to make their natural physical beauty attractive by use of the cosmetic art so as to please their bridegrooms and excite them to greater love. This is their special concern day by day, colouring their faces with the appropriate paints, entwining their hair with gold, beautifying their heads with glittering gems and pearls, suspending a family fortune from their ears, decorating their arms and bosoms with bracelets and letting precious stones enclosed in gold hang down onto their breasts from their necks.

3. *Your* bridegroom requires no less adornment on your part, since he has made his universal Church to be without spot or wrinkle, has purified her by washing her with the water of salvation and desires her to become more beautiful day by day, so that, once cleansed of vices and sins, she may be for ever adorned with the splendour of virtues. If this is what he requires of his whole Church, which contains both widows and brides, how much more, do you think, will he expect of a virgin who seems to have been picked out from all his Church's most brilliant array of decorations like a flower, as it were, worthy of even greater honour?[48] So *you* must put on all the adornment which will enable you to please Christ, believe that, even if you have no desire to appear beautiful to men, your face is beautiful enough for God, and as a decoration for your head keep only what you acquired by the sacrament of unction, when a diadem of royal unguent was placed upon you as a token of the mystery of the kingdom of heaven.

4. As for the ears, their best ornaments are the words of God; it is for them alone that the hearing of the virgin should be prepared, they are what she should prefer to the most precious of stones. As for her limbs, all of them without exception must be adorned with works of holiness, and the whole beauty of her virginal soul, like a necklace made of jewels, must gleam with the multicoloured brilliance of her virtues.[49] Then will the King truly desire your beauty, saying to you: You are all fair, my love; there is no flaw in you (Song 4.7). These adornments of which I have spoken will also be your strongest protection, since the same qualities which are able to adorn you for God are also able to arm you against the devil, who sometimes enters the soul through some trivial vice or other and, if the bulwarks of our virtue do not resist him, drives us back from our post and straightway becomes our lord instead of our enemy. It is because of this that the scripture exhorts us and says: If the anger of the ruler rises against you, do not leave your place (Ec.10.4).

25, 1. From the very time when you were first consecrated to the Lord through your profession of virginity, our enemy's hatred of you grew, since, as one who counts another's gains as his own losses, he considers that, if there is anything which it pains him to find you about to possess, he has lost it himself. You need to employ a great deal of vigilance and attention, and the richer you have begun to be before God the more watchfully you must guard against the enemy: the traveller who is naked and goes empty-handed has no fear of the robber's ambush, and the poor man sleeps secure from nocturnal thieves, even if he does not make sure that his door is bolted; but the rich man's wealth makes him imagine a burglar's entry and robs him of his sleep at night through continuous worry. Hence your wealth too, your heavenly treasure, requires your care and protection: the richer you are the more vigilant you ought to be, for he who possesses more has good reason to be more afraid of losing it.

2. The creator of envy does not cease to envy, and he who was once cast out himself by God is tortured by envy which becomes so much the greater as he sees someone more greatly honoured before his eyes. He envied Eve her place in

---

[48] Virg.12 also contains an extended comparison between the secular and Christian bride-to-be; although there are considerable differences in detail, the general form of the discussion is very similar in both.

[49] Cf. Virg.10 for instructions on physical adornment – again with some differences in detail; for example, Virg.10 includes consideration of the kind of diet which the secular bride-to-be's fiance likes and dislikes.

paradise; how much more does he envy you yours in the kingdom of heaven! Even now he is prowling around everywhere, believe me, seeking to devour you, as the blessed Peter says (1 Pet.5.8); he stalks his prey like a roaring lion or like a cunning enemy with eyes everywhere, and he reconnoitres every possible way of approach to your soul to see if there is some point which is weak and less secure, through which he can creep in. Even now he is searching everywhere and probing every single point for a place to wound, and you must look out for ambushes with great care, so that, like Paul, you may not be ignorant of his designs (2 Cor.2.11): when he is describing the terrible powers and principalities of the devil, he yet urges us on to battle and reveals the forces of the enemy to us only in order to increase the vigilance of our soldiers, for he does not want us to be fearful but ready for the fray, he does not counsel flight but supplies us with weapons: Therefore, he says, take the whole armour of God, that you may be able to withstand in the evil day, and having done all, to stand (Eph.6.13). And straightway, handing us the separate items of equipment one by one, he added these words: Stand therefore, having girded your loins with truth, and having put on the breastplate of righteousness, and having shod your feet with the equipment of the gospel of peace, and at all times taking the shield of faith, with which you can quench all the flaming darts of the evil one. And take the helmet of salvation and the sword of the Spirit, which is the word of God, with all prayer and supplication (ibid.13–17).

3.   And since it is possible even for women to triumph in this war, take up these weapons of Paul's and look forward to certain victory with so great a leader to urge you on. For if you possess all these items of equipment, you will advance to the spiritual battle free from danger nor will you fear the devil with all his army: For a thousand will fall at your side, and ten thousand at your right hand; but they will not come near you (Ps.91.7). The blessed James too, that veteran soldier of Christ, promises us a victory in this war with no less authority: Submit yourselves therefore, he says, to God; but resist the devil and he will flee from you (Jas.4.7). He shows how we ought to resist the devil, if we are indeed in submission to God, and, by doing his will, to merit divine grace also and to resist the evil spirit more easily with the aid of the Holy Spirit. But the devil does not fight against us in the open order of battle or come to grips with us in the open face to face but overcomes us by trickery and deceit and uses our own will against us; our enemy acquires strength from our consent to his actions and, as it is often said, cuts our throat with our own sword.

4.   But an enemy who cannot overcome an opponent unless the latter is willing to be overcome is weak; so let us cast despair aside, let us put every vestige of fear of our adversaries far from our mind, let us not assist our enemies but defeat them. They indeed can give counsel but it is ours to choose or reject their suggestions, for they harm us not by compelling but by counselling, and they do not extort our consent from us but court it, which is why Ananias is asked: Why has Satan filled your heart to lie to the Holy Spirit (Acts 5.3)? Surely the apostle would never lay this as a charge against him if the devil had done it without the help of his own will. Eve too is herself condemned by the Lord precisely because

she was overcome by one whom she was able to overcome, for she who was overcome would not have deserved punishment for unrighteousness by the Lord, had she herself not been able to overcome.[50]

26, 1. The prime device of this most evil of all enemies, his most cunning statagem, is to employ notions as a means of wearing down souls inexperienced in coping with them and to assail minds newly embarked on their chosen vocation with that feeling of depression which sometimes results from their conduct itself, so that a mind may be easily deterred from making progress with a project as it begins to realize how harsh are the first steps involved. So it is his normal practice to implant in such a mind thoughts so base and so impious that the one who is tempted by them, believing the thought which has assailed him to be his own, comes to regard himself as having been made less effective in his vocation by his own unclean spirit and to reckon that his soul was much purer when he still loved the things of the world. For our enemy in his supreme cunning wishes to arouse in those whom he envies the dread of failure in their vocation that arises from despair of ever attaining holiness, in order that, even if he does not actually succeed in dissuading them from their purpose under pressure of despondency, he may surely be able to hold up their progress.

2. That is why you must above all lovingly study the holy scriptures, why your soul must be illuminated by divine utterances, why the dark shadows of the devil have to be dispersed by the flash of God's word; for the devil is quick to flee from the soul which is illuminated by divine speech, which is always occupied with heavenly thoughts, in which God's word, whose force the evil spirit is unable to endure, is constantly present. For that reason the blessed apostle compared it to a sword when listing the arms for use in the war of the spirit (Eph.6.17). It is perfectly safe, however, for the mind to become accustomed to differentiating between one thought and another – always subject, of course, to careful and watchful control – and, at the first stirring of the mind, either to approving or to disapproving of what it is thinking, so that it either nourishes good thoughts or immediately destroys bad ones. In this lie the source of good and the origin of sin, and thought is the beginning of every great offence in the heart, painting every single deed on the tablet of the heart, as it were, before doing it; for every deed and every word, whichever it may be, is laid out for inspection in advance and its future is decided by thoughtful consideration.

3. You can see what a brief moment sometimes separates a man's thinking each thought and his putting that thought into action, nor is anything at all done by the tongue or the hand or other limbs, unless thoughts have previously dictated it; hence the Lord also says in the gospel: Out of the heart of man come evil thoughts, adultery, fornication, murder, theft, false witness, greed, evil, trickery, unchastity, the evil eye, blasphemy, pride, folly. These are what defile men (Mt.15.19,20). Therefore, all your care and attention must be concentrated on

---

[50] Another argument supporting the use of free will in making a choice between good and evil.

keeping watch, and it is particularly necessary for you to guard against sin in the place where it usually begins, to resist temptation at once the very first time it appears and thus to eliminate the evil before it can grow and spread. When something has to be feared from its smallest beginnings and is the more easily overcome the more speedily it is resisted, one must not wait for it to grow; that is why divine scripture exclaims: *Keep your heart with all vigilance; for from it flow the springs of life* (Pr.4.23).

27, 1. One has to make a distinction, however, between those of one's thoughts which the will favours and embraces affectionately, those which are wont to flit past the mind like an insubstantial shadow and merely show a glimpse of themselves in passing – the Greeks call them *typoi*, 'impressions'[51] – and also those, to be sure, which offer promptings to a mind which is resistant and unwilling and as glad when they are expelled as it was sad when they were admitted in the first place. In those which show themselves only fleetingly to the mind and reveal themselves as if in flight, there is no underlying sin at all and no sign of fight; but with those which the soul struggles against for some time and which the will resists, we can expect an even contest. Either we consent to them and are conquered or we reject them and conquer them and win a victory in battle.

2. Thus sin exists only in the thought which has given the mind's consent to a suggestion, which flatters and fosters its own evil tendency and longs for it to erupt into action. This kind of thought, even if it is prevented from reaching any outcome and so fails to fulfil the wish that lies behind it, is nevertheless condemned as a criminal act by the Lord. We read this in the Gospel: *Everyone*, it says, *who looks at a woman lustfully has already committed adultery with her in his heart* (Mt.5.28); that is to say, before God, to whom everything is known even before it is done, the complete wish to act is reckoned as equivalent to the actual deed. You ought therefore – for I often repeat something which I want to be done invariably – you ought, I say, to meditate on holy scriptures without ceasing and fill your mind with them, to deprive evil thoughts of room to settle in by packing your soul with divine feelings and to show how much you love God by your love of his law. Hence the scripture says: *Those who fear the Lord will seek his approval, and those who love him will be filled with his law* (Sir.2.19). Then, realizing how much his wisdom helps you to love him, how much assistance there is in his divine law, you too will sing joyfully to the Lord with David: *I have laid up thy word in my heart, that I might not sin against thee* (Ps.119.11).

---

51 This is an unexpectedly recondite sense of the Greek word *typos* to find in Pelagius, and it suggests that Annianus may have unearthed it: Democritus and Epicurus used it to describe 'impressions' made on the air by bodies travelling through space, and Theophrastus used it in the same way, as did some of the Greek Fathers (see LSJ II,1b; cf. Lampe, op.cit., fasc.5,1418), while Plato (once) and the medical writers, Galen and Diocles (once each) use it to signify 'general indication'. The former sense seems the more appropriate here. (Incidentally, in Latin *typus* is normally a technical term in architecture and surveying.)

3. For the soul always needs to be aroused by spiritual spurs and to be revived daily with increased fervour;[52] application to prayer, illumination from reading, attention to vigils, these are its incentives by day and night. For nothing is worse in this vocation than idleness, which not only does not make new gains but also wastes those already won. It is the way of the holy life to delight in progress and gain strength as it takes place; in idleness it becomes lethargic and fails altogether. The mind must be renewed by fresh growth in virtue every day, and we must measure our journey through life not by what has been completed but by what remains to be done. As long as we are in this body, we should never believe that we have attained perfection, since, by refusing to believe that, we give ourselves a better chance of arriving at our goal; as long as we strive towards the objective ahead of us, we do not slip back, but when we begin to stand still, we take the downward path, and it is our lot not to advance but already to go backwards.

4. Let us make an end of all sloth and useless complacency based on the success of our labours in the past. If we do not want to go back, we must run on; the blessed apostle, living for God day by day, always paying attention not to what he has done before but to what he ought to be doing now, says: Brethren, I do not consider that I have made it my own; but one thing I do, forgetting what lies behind and straining forward to what lies ahead, I press on towards the goal for the prize of the upward call of God (Phil.3.13,14). If the blessed Paul, the vessel of election, who had been so clothed in Christ that he could say: It is no longer I who live but Christ who lives in me (Gal.2.20), yet still strains forward, still grows and progresses, what should we do whose only desire must be that at our end we may be compared with Paul at his beginning? Imitate therefore the one who said: Be imitators of me, as I too am of Christ (1 Cor.4,16). Forget all that is past and think that you are starting afresh each day, and do not reckon the past to be the present day, since it is on the present day that you must serve God. You will guard your gains best if you are always searching for more; if you cease to acquire more, your present store of acquisitions will suffer loss.

28. 'The labour is great,' you may perhaps say. True; but just think what we have been promised: all work tends to be lightened when the reward for it is considered, and it is hope of obtaining such a reward that consoles us for our labour.[53] This is why the hardy farmer rejoices in the fact that by the sheer strength of his plough he has broken into pieces a field long left unploughed with its fertile soil lying fallow, and in some strange way he is happy to measure his hope of getting a crop for his labours by the very difficulty of the work involved. So too the greedy trader despises the sea, when he dares to look on the foaming waves and the raging winds and, in the midst of all his toil and danger, thinks only of the gain which will result from it and forgets his weariness and fear at one

---

[52] For the whole of this passage on the need for renewal and persistence (down to the quotation of Phil.3.13,14) cf.Cel.32.
[53] On the magnitude of the virgin's task and the reward for performing it cf. Virg.2.

and the same time. Consider then, I beg you, the size of your reward, if something which is so immense can be considered at all. After the soul has departed, after the flesh has died, after the dust and the ashes, you, as a virgin, will be restored to a better state: the body that has been entrusted to the earth will be lifted up high to heaven, and your mortality exchanged for immortality. Thereafter you will be given the company of angels, will receive the kingdom of heaven and will abide with Christ for ever. What then will you give in repayment to the Lord for all that he has given you in repayment (Ps.116.12)? What will you consider difficult to do, when you have one who repays you with rewards so great? The answer is in the blessed apostle's words: None of the sufferings of the present time are worth comparing with the future glory that is to be revealed to us (Rom.8.18). What can we either do or suffer in this short life of ours that is worthy to be repaid with immortality?

29.   It is for this reason that the same apostle says: For this slight momentary affliction is preparing for us an eternal weight of glory beyond all comparison (2 Cor.4.17). Let honours be rejected, riches despised; let our life itself too be disdained for love of martyrdom, since these are all possessions which, if not surrendered in order to win the prize of eternity, would still perish at some time or other, for those who are always striving to possess something lose even that in the end.[54] How many we can recall seeing installed in possession of the greatest honours only to fall suddenly from the highest pinnacle of their earthly power, because they thought in their pride and elation that they were something other than mere mortals, only to reveal to us by their end what they really were! For in this world what is there that is lasting? What is there that is solid and real? What is there that is not brief, uncertain and subject to chance? What good is there in a thing which you are always in fear of losing, which you are afraid will be taken away from you or know will have to be left behind you? Even if it is not snatched from you by a calamity, it must surely be lost to you in death; even if our life were to be extended over a thousand years and we were to reach the last day of our whole life still in daily enjoyment of the pleasure given by luxuries, of what value, I ask, is that long stretch of time, if it is destroyed in the end? Of what profit is a pleasure which, as soon as it has ceased, will seem never to have existed at all? Come now, turn over in your mind the period of your life which is past. Will not all the past seem to you to have been like a shadow, all that you now see to be dim and uncertain like an insubstantial dream? An enfeebled old man can also experience this same feeling and can rightly say with the prophet: My days are like an evening shadow; I wither away like grass (Ps.102.11).

30, 1.   But if we can say as much even in this world, where our life, though short, is still highly valued because it is in the present, what are we likely to say in the future, when, with the greater knowledge of eternity, all that is past counts for nought? As you turn over these points carefully in your mind and despise the

---

[54] On the ephemeral nature of this world and its attractions cf. *Law*,8,2.

shortness of this life in contemplation of eternity, dismiss from it also with even greater determination the world which you have dismissed already and prepare yourself exclusively for that great day on which the world's glory must be brought to an end, that day, I say, which our Saviour compared to a flood (Mt.24.39) and which will catch out by its stealthy arrival many who have been lulled into a false sense of security (1 Thess.5.2). Describing it, the blessed Peter also says: But the day of the Lord will come like a thief, and then the heavens will pass away with a loud noise, and the elements will be dissolved with fire. Since all these things are thus to be dissolved, what sort of persons ought you to be in lives of holiness and godliness, waiting for and hastening the coming of the Lord God, because of which the heaven will be kindled and dissolved, and all the elements will melt with fire (2 Pet.3.10–12)? It came to pass recently, as you yourself have heard, when to the shrill sound of the war-trumpet and the shouts of the Goths Rome, the mistress of the world, trembled under the weight of a sad fear. Where stood our order of nobility then? Where were the occupiers of the fixed, distinct grades of their hierarchy? Everything was thrown into confusion and disorder by fear, in every home there was lamentation, and terror was spread through all alike.[55] Slave and noble were on the same footing: all saw the same image of death, except that those whose life was more pleasant feared it more.

2. If we are so afraid of the human hand of a mortal foe, what shall we do when the heavenly trumpet begins to thunder with a fearful blast and the whole world reverberates at the same time to that voice of the archangel which is louder than any war-trumpet? When it is not arms made by human hands that we see brandished over us but the very powers of the heavens in turmoil, as the prophet says: When the Lord comes to make the earth a desolation and to destroy its sinners from it (Is.13.9)? What terror, what darkness, what gloomy shadows will beset us then, when that day finds us, so often and so many times forewarned, yet still unprepared! Then, he says, will all the tribes of the earth mourn over themselves, and they will see the Son of Man coming on the clouds of heaven with much power and glory; then they will say to the mountains, Fall

---

[55] The Gothic assault on Rome left deep and painful marks on the Roman psyche, and this is especially true of its effect on the exiled aristocrats: after a thousand years of impregnability – not even Hannibal had entered it – its rape by Alaric was hard to credit, let alone endure. Brown, 1967, 289, describes Rome at this time as 'the symbol of a whole civilisation', 'a sort of pagan Vatican' and remarks: 'It was as if an army had been allowed to sack Westminster Abbey or the Louvre' or, we may perhaps add, 'the Temple at Jerusalem'. 'If Rome can perish, what can be safe?', asked Jerome. The pagans blamed the Christians for worshipping a false God and turning their backs on the old gods of Rome; and, in reply, Augustine began his massive defence of Christianity, *The City of God*, just about the time when this letter was sent to Demetrias or a little before (see his *Retractations* (PL 32,583–656),II,69). But Barrow, 1950,19 suggests that 'the extent of the destruction caused by Alaric should not be estimated too severely' and reminds us that 'Alaric himself was an Arian Christian and gave orders that life should be spared'. It is doubtful if much damage was done to Rome's public buildings and monuments, and there was certainly no general massacre.

on us, and to the hills, Cover us, and to the rocks, Open yourselves up for us (Mt.24.30; Lk.23.30).[56]

3. So be it with those who are preoccupied with the manifold cares of this world and give no thought to its end. But as for you, whose meditation day and night is of the coming of Christ, whose pure conscience longs for the presence of God, who can afford to await the end of the world as the time appointed for your reward, you will have cause for rejoicing from heaven, not for fear. Then, mingling with the choruses of the blessed and accompanied by holy virgins, you will fly upwards to meet your bridegroom and will say: I have found him whom my soul has sought (Song 3.4). Nor will you have any more to fear that you will be separated from him at any time, since you will be given once and for all the glory of immortality and the splendour of incorruption, and you will be with Christ always, as the apostle says: For the Lord himself will descend from heaven with a cry of command from the archangel and with the sound of God's trumpet. And the dead in Christ will rise first; then we who are alive, who are left, shall be caught up together with them in the clouds to meet the Lord in the air; and so we shall be always with the Lord (1 Thess.4.16,17). Let this then be your constant care and concern; let these be the thoughts that revolve continually in the virgin's heart; to them let your efforts be directed throughout the day, on them lay down your head to rest at night, for them let your soul awake again in the morning. No labour ought to seem too difficult, no time too long to wait, when the prize at stake is nothing less than everlasting glory.

---

[56] Both this chapter and *Law*,7,3 contain vivid accounts of the day of the Lord's coming, in which there are one or two verbal similarities like 'what shall we do?', and both quote Luke 23.30. If one were just a copy of the other, we would expect to find a closer and more obvious parallelism (Evans, 1968, 62).

2

On Virginity[1]

This letter has been attributed at different times to Athanasius, Hilary, Jerome and Sulpicius Severus and has appeared under three different titles – *Epistula ad Claudiam de virginitate, Ad Mauritii filiam laus virginitatis* and *Exhortatio ad sponsam Christi*. The editor of Migne, PL 18 included it in an appendix to Pope Innocent I's *Book of Rules* under the name of Athanasius, the editor of PL 30 in an appendix containing works wrongly attributed to Jerome, and the editor of PL 103 in one entitled 'Pseudo-Athanasius'. Johannes Clericus first placed it in an appendix to the minor works of Sulpicius Severus in 1709, and Halm – in his critical edition in CSEL 1 – also includes it in an appendix, though he rejects the attribution to Sulpicius on the grounds that the style of the letter, as of the other seven in the appendix, is far removed from that of the latter's authentic works. No doubt Gennadius is the authority for this incorrect ascription, since he states that Sulpicius 'wrote other letters to his sister Claudia' and showed Pelagian tendencies in later life.[2]

Plinval, Kirmer and R.F. Evans [3] have all demonstrated the Pelagian character of this letter: apart from a passage of about sixty words in section 8 which is 'in almost identical agreement' with one in the Pauline Commentary,[4] there are many other similarities in the use of themes, arguments and phraseology with passages from the commentary, the letter to Demetrias and even, in one instance, with a surviving extract from Pelagius' *Book of Testimonies*. Several of the scriptural quotations in the letter, about fifty in all, also appear in other letters attributed to Pelagius in this book of translations, and anyone who compares it with similar discussions of virginity in these letters may find it hard to resist the conclusion that all of them are the work of one author, Pelagius himself.

If this letter is by Pelagius, it may well have been written in the early part of the same period in which he was engaged in writing his Pauline Commentary, that is, soon after 404 and probably not later than 406, especially as a copyist of

---

[1]   PL 18, 77–90; 30, 163–75; 103, 671–84; CSEL 1, 225–50; CPL 741.
[2]   *On Famous Men*, 19 (PL 58, 1072).
[3]   Plinval, 1934, 24ff.; Kirmer, 140ff.; Evans, 1968, 20, 41ff.
[4]   *Comm.* 169, 5–11; Evans, 1968, 41.

the Codex Vindobonensis refers to Pope Innocent I's *Book of Rules* in the same MS as having been issued 'recently', meaning 404.[5]

Text

1.   Apart from the evidence supplied by the scriptures we are informed how great is the blessed state which holy virginity attains in heaven by the practice of the Church, from which we learn that a peculiar merit is attached to the recipients of this special form of consecration. For while the whole multitude of believers receives similar gifts of grace and all rejoice in the same blessings of the sacraments, those to whom you belong have something peculiar to themselves over and above what the rest possess:[6] they are chosen by the Holy Spirit out of the holy and spotless flock of the Church as holier and purer offerings on account of the merits given them for their choice of vocation and are presented at God's altar by his highest priest. The offering of so precious a creature is truly worthy to be considered a sacrifice to the Lord, and there is none who will please him more than a victim in his own image, for I believe that it was especially to such an offering that the apostle referred when he said: I appeal to you, therefore, brethren, by the mercy of God to present your bodies as a living sacrifice, holy and acceptable to God (Rom.12.1). Thus virginity possesses both what others have and what they do not have, since it obtains both common and special grace and also rejoices in the possession of the privilege of a consecration peculiar to itself. Ecclesiastical authority also permits us to call virgins the brides of Christ, since it veils those whom it consecrates to the Lord in the manner of brides, showing in this very special way that those who have shunned partnership of the flesh are destined to enjoy a marriage in the spirit. And, having spurned human marriage because of their love of God, they are deservedly united to him in spiritual union on the analogy of marriage. In them that saying of the apostle is especially fulfilled: But he who is united to the Lord becomes one spirit with him (1 Cor.6.17).

2.   It is a great thing,[7] imperishable and almost beyond the reach of bodily nature to lay luxury to rest and to extinguish by strength of mind the flame of concupiscence that is kindled by the torches of adolescence, to shut out by spiritual effort the forces of natural delight, to live contrary to the custom of the human race, to despise the comforts provided by marital partners, to reject the pleasure of having children and to reckon as nothing the possible advantages of

---

5   See Vallarsi in PL 30, 162; Rees, 1988, 2, n.4.
6   Cf. *Comm.* 190, 22ff. (on 1 Cor. 11.21) and 197, 17ff. with respect to the giving of the sacraments equally to all believers.
7   For the whole of this passage cf. *Dem.* 28.

our present life, when compared with the hope of a future state of blessedness. Great and wonderful is this virtue, as I have said, and destined for a deserved and remarkable reward commensurate with the extent of the labour involved in attaining it. I will give in my house and within my walls, says the Lord, a named place to the eunuchs which will be better than sons and daughters; I will give them an everlasting name which shall not be cut off (Is.56.5). And concerning such eunuchs the Lord repeats his promise in the gospel, saying: For there are eunuchs who have made themselves eunuchs for the sake of the kingdom of heaven (Mt.19.12). Great indeed is the labour of chastity but greater the reward, for the restraint demanded is temporal but the reward gained is eternal, since the blessed apostle John also says that 'they follow the Lamb wherever he goes' (Rev.14.4). I consider that this should be understood to this effect, that there is no place in the court of heaven which is to be closed to them and that all the dwelling-places in the divine mansions will be unlocked for them.

3.   But in order that the merit of virginity may shine forth with a brighter light and that it may be possible to understand more clearly how worthy it is of God, we must bear in mind that God, our Lord and Saviour, when he thought fit to take manhood upon himself for the sake of the salvation of the human race, chose no other womb than that of a virgin. And that he might show that virtue of this kind was most pleasing to him and reveal the good of chastity to both sexes, he had a virgin mother and was to remain a virgin for ever himself: he showed an example of virginity for men in himself and for women in his mother, so that it might be demonstrated that the blessed and perfect fullness of divinity was worthy to reside in either sex, since whatever resided in the son was also completely manifested in the mother. But why do I trouble to reveal the out-standing, sublime merit of chastity and to demonstrate the glorious good of virginity, when I am not unaware that many have discoursed on this subject and have proved its blessedness by the conclusive reasons that they have given and that no man of wisdom can possibly doubt that the task which involves greater labour is the one which also has the greater merit? Surely, whoever thinks chastity a matter for small reward or none at all is either ignorant of the labour involved or is unwilling to incur it. Hence it is that those men are always belittling chastity who either do not possess it or are forced to possess it against their will.

4, 1.   Now therefore, since we have set forth, albeit in few words, both the labour and the merit of chastity, we must take great care to ensure that a matter which consists of great virtue and is marked down for a vast reward cannot possibly fail to produce its own proper fruit. For the more valuable any kind of thing is, the more carefully it is guarded. But there are many things which fail to achieve their own excellence, unless they are aided in doing so by the assistance of others, as is the case with honey, which, unless it is preserved by being kept in wax and in the cells of the honeycombs and, to put it more precisely, is sustained by these aids, loses its natural agreeableness and cannot exist on its own, and as it is also the case with wine, which, unless the vessels containing it have a pleasant aroma and it is kept warm with pitch that is frequently renewed loses the potency of its natural sweetness. So too we must pay closer attention in advance to the possibility that virginity may need some things without which it may not by any means have sufficient strength to bear fruit, and that the great labour invested in it will profit it nothing, even while it is vainly believed to be of profit to it, simply because it is without the aids which are necessary for its success. For, unless I am greatly mistaken, the integrity of chastity is maintained for the sake of the reward of the heavenly kingdom, which it is quite certain no one is able to attain without meriting eternal life.

2.   But scripture testifies that eternal life cannot be merited save by complete observance of the divine commandments, when it says: If you wish to come to life, keep the commandments (Mt.19.17). Therefore no one has that life,[8] unless he has kept all the commandments of the law, and the man who does not have that life cannot be a possessor of the heavenly kingdom, in which it is the living, not the dead, who shall reign. Thus virginity, which hopes for the glory of the heavenly kingdom, will profit nothing on its own, unless it also possesses that to which everlasting life is promised, since it is through the possession of such life that the prize of the heavenly kingdom is gained. Those, then, who guard their chastity and purity and hope for reward from God's justice on account of it must, above all else, keep the precepts of the commandments, in order that the labour of a glorious chastity and abstinence may not be brought to naught.

3.   No one who is wise as a result of his study of the law is unaware of the fact that virginity is above commandment and precept, since the apostle says: Now concerning virgins I have no commandment of the Lord, but I give my opinion (1 Cor.7.25).[9] When, therefore, he gives advice on the need to possess virginity and does not lay down a rule on the subject, he has acknowledged that it is above commandment or rule. So those who keep their virginity are doing more than is prescribed; but it will profit you to have done more than is commanded only if you have also done what is commanded. For how can you boast of having done more, if in some respect you are doing less? If you want to fulfil the divine advice, then, above all else, keep the commandments: if you wish to attain the reward for chastity, you have to hold on to the things which will entitle you to merit life,[10] so that your chastity may be of the sort that can be rewarded. For just as observance of the commandments bestows life, so, on the other hand, transgression of them produces death, and the man who has been doomed to die because of his disobedience cannot hope for the crown awarded for virginity nor can he expect to be rewarded for chastity, when once his punishment has been settled.

---

[8]   On this and the following sentence cf. Dem. 9,3.
[9]   Cf. Dem.9,3, which does not include the quotation to support the reference to Paul.
[10] Dem.10,1 offers a striking parallel to this, almost identical in the grammatical structure of the Latin and certainly identical in meaning.

5.   There are three virtues which qualify one for entry into the kingdom of heaven: the first is chastity, the second rejection of the world and the third righteousness, and just as they offer a very great deal to those who possess them in conjunction with each other, so it is only with difficulty that they can be of benefit when separated, since each of them is required not for its own sake but for the sake of another. First of all, then, chastity is demanded so that rejection of the world may more easily follow, because those who are not held fast in the bonds of matrimony can more easily reject the world. Again, rejection of the world is demanded so that righteousness may be maintained, something which is difficult to fulfil for those who are involved in activities connected with worldly goods and mundane pleasures. Whoever, therefore, possesses the first qualifica-tion, that of chastity, but lacks the second, rejection of the world, possesses the first almost to no purpose, since he does not possess the second, for the sake of which the first is required. And if he possesses the first and second but lacks the third, that is, righteousness, he labours in vain, since the first two are especially required for the sake of the third. What does it profit him to possess chastity for the sake of rejection of the world and not to possess that for the sake of which he possesses it? Or why reject the things of the world, if you do not maintain righteousness, for the sake of which it befits you to possess chastity and rejection of the world? As the first qualification is necessary on account of the second, so the first and second are necessary on account of the third; and if the third is absent, neither the first nor the second will be of any benefit to you.

6, 1. But perhaps you say, 'Teach me then what righteousness is, so that, knowing it, I may be equipped to fulfil it more easily.' I shall tell you as briefly as I can, employing simple, ordinary language, since the subject with which we are dealing is such that it ought by no means to be made obscure by clever and eloquent expressions and since a matter which is necessary for the common good ought to be explained in the terms of common speech. Righteousness then is, quite simply, not to sin, and not to sin is to keep the commandments of the law. Keeping these commandments is ensured in two ways, by doing nothing which is forbidden and by striving to fulfil everything which is commanded;[11] this is what is meant by the saying: Depart from evil, and do good (Ps.34.14; 37.27). I do not wish you to suppose that righteousness consists simply in not doing evil, since not to do good is also evil, and in either case a transgression of the law is committed, and he who said, 'Depart from evil', also said, 'Do good.' If you depart from evil but fail to do good, you transgress the law, which is fulfilled not simply by abominating evil deeds but also by performing good works. Indeed, you are instructed not only not to strip one who is clothed of his garments but also to cover one who has been stripped of his garments with your own; nor only not to take bread away from one who has it but willingly to bestow your own on one who has none; nor only not to drive a poor man out of his lodging but also to

---

[11] For the twofold requirement of righteousness cf. *Dem.9,2* and *Cel.5.*

receive into your own one who has been driven out of his and has none as a result.

2. For it has been enjoined on us to: Weep with those who weep (Rom.12.15); but how can we weep with them, if we do not share at all in their needs nor give them any help in situations on account of which they are weeping? For God does not seek the useless moisture of our tears but, because tears are a sign of grief, he wants you to feel for another's needs as you do for your own and to help another as you would like help to be given to you if you were in such trouble, in accordance with the statement: Whatever you wish that men would do to you, do so to them (Mt.7.12). For to weep with one who weeps and, at the same time, to refuse to give to the one who weeps, though you are in a position to do so, is a mark of mockery, not godliness. In a word, our Saviour wept with Mary and Martha, Lazarus' sisters, thus showing by the witness of his tears his immense feeling of compassion for them, but the actions which were the signs of true godliness followed after, when Lazarus, for whom his tears were shed, was raised up and restored to his sisters. This was the way to weep in godliness with those who wept, that is, by removing the reason for their tears. But you will say, 'He acted as one who had the power to act.' But neither is anything beyond your powers being enjoined on you: he who has done what he could has done everything.

7, 1. But, as we began to remark, it is not enough for a Christian to abstain from evil, unless he has also fulfilled his obligations in the matter of good works. This is proved most of all by the testimony in which the Lord threatens that those who have not done all that is good shall be condemned to everlasting fire, though they have done no evil, when he says: Then the King will say to those at his left hand, Depart from me, you cursed, into the eternal fire which my Father has prepared for the devil and his angels; for I was hungry and you gave me no food, I was thirsty and you gave me no drink (Mt.25.41,42). He did not say: Depart from me, you cursed, because you have committed murder, adultery or theft; for they are condemned not for having done evil but for not having done good, not for committing forbidden acts but for not being willing to fulfil the commandments, and that is why they are also given up to the punishments of eternal hell. Hence we must give heed to the question of what hope they can have who are still doing something which is prohibited, when they are also condemned to the eternal fire for not having done the things which are commanded.

2. For I do not want you to flatter yourself on not having done some things simply because there are things which you *have* done, since it is written: Whoever keeps the whole law but fails in one point has become guilty of all of it (Jas.2.10). Adam sinned once and died; do you suppose that you can live, when you are frequently committing the very act which killed another, though he had perpetrated it only once? Or do you suppose that he had committed a great crime and that this is the reason why he was deservedly condemned to undergo a more severe punishment? Let us then see what it was that he really did: he ate of the

fruit of the tree contrary to the commandment given to him. What then? Did God sentence a man to death because of fruit from a tree? No, not because of fruit from a tree but because of rejection of a commandment. Therefore, it is not a question of the nature of the sin but of the fact of having disobeyed an order.

3. And he who told Adam not to eat of the fruit of the tree has himself ordered you not to slander, not to lie, not to detract, not to listen to the detractor, not to swear an oath at all, not to lust, not to envy, not to be lukewarm, not to be greedy, not to return evil for evil to anyone, to love your enemies, to bless those who curse you, to pray for false accusers and persecutors, to turn the other cheek to the man who strikes you, not to engage in a dispute in a secular court, to let your property go joyfully, if someone wants to take it from you,[12] to admit into your breast neither the evil of anger nor that of jealousy nor that of envy, to avoid the crime of greed, to beware of the evil of all pride and boasting, and to live, humble and gentle by the example of Christ, shunning the company of evil men to the extent that you do not even take any food with fornicators or the greedy or slanderers or the envious or detractors or drunkards or the grasping. If you reject him in any respect, then he will spare you also – *if* he spared Adam! Indeed there would have been greater reason for him to spare Adam, who was still ignorant and inexperienced and did not have the example of anyone who had previously sinned and died for his sin to deter him; but in your case, if you are willing to sin after receiving such lessons, after the law, after the prophets, after the gospels, I do not know how pardon can possibly be given to you.[13]

8, 1. Do you flatter yourself on the privileged state of virginity? Then remember that Adam and Eve were virgins when they sinned but, when they sinned, the perfect purity of their bodies did not profit them; a virgin who sins should be compared to Eve, not to Mary. We do not deny that there is a remedy of repentance available in the present life but we do urge you to hope for reward rather than pardon. For it is disgraceful that those who are looking forward to receiving the reward for virginity should request pardon for a crime and should do anything which is not permitted, when they have deprived themselves of the things which are permitted, since it is permitted to enter upon the partnership of marriage. And as those who have rejected the bond of marriage for love of Christ and for the glory of the kingdom of heaven are to be praised, so those who take advantage of the apostolic remedy because of the pleasure given by incontinence must be condemned, since they have already dedicated themselves to God. Therefore, as we have said, those who abandon marriage reject not what has been forbidden but what is permitted.

[12] Jerome quotes a sentence from *Extracts* in his *Dialogue against the Pelagians* I,29 (PL 23,522) which is identical with this one except that it refers to the third person: 'The Christian ought to be a man of such longsuffering that, if someone wants to take his property away, he lets it go joyfully.'

[13] The same argument is employed in *Comm.*182,12–17 (1 Cor.10.11), and many words used are common to both passages.

2. But if men and women of this kind swear oaths, if they slander, if they detract, if they allow themselves to listen to those who detract, if they return evil for evil, if they commit the crime of greed in dealing with the property of others or avarice in dealing with their own, if they give in to the poisons of jealousy and envy, if they either say or think anything improper against the teachings of the law and the apostles, if they display themselves in elegant and costly attire through desire to give sensual pleasure, if they do anything else which is not permitted in accordance with the common practice, what will it profit them to have rejected what has been permitted and to practise what is not? If you wish to derive benefit from having rejected the things that are permitted, then you must see to it that you do not do any of the things which are not permitted, since it is foolish to have feared what is less important and yet not to fear what is more. For the apostle says: The unmarried woman is anxious about the affairs of the Lord, how to please God, how to be holy in body and spirit; but the married woman is anxious about worldly affairs, how to please her husband (1 Cor.7.34). He thus claims that the married woman pleases her husband by being anxious about the affairs of the world but that the unmarried woman pleases God, because she is not anxious about the affairs of this world.[14]

3. Let him tell me then who it is that the woman who has no husband and yet is anxious about worldly affairs desires to please. Will not the married woman begin to be preferred to her in that case? Yes, because, by being anxious about worldly affairs, she is at least pleasing her husband; but that other is unable to please either a husband whom she does not have or God. But it is not fitting that we should pass over in silence this statement of the apostle either: The unmarried woman is anxious about the affairs of the Lord, how she may be holy in body and spirit. What then are the Lord's affairs? Let the apostle tell us himself; Whatever is holy, whatever is just, whatever is lovely, whatever is of good report, if there is any excellence, if there is any praise of discipline (Phil.4.8). These are the Lord's affairs which virgins who are holy and true in the apostolic sense think about and are anxious about day and night without intermission. The kingdom of heaven is the Lord's; the resurrection of the dead is the Lord's; immortality is the Lord's; incorruption is the Lord's; the splendour of the sun which is promised to the saints is the Lord's, as it is written in the gospel: Then the righteous will shine like the sun in the kingdom of their Father (Mt.13.43). The many dwelling-

---

14 Cf. *Comm.* 169,5–11, which discusses the same quotation from Paul in almost identical words. R.F. Evans, 1968, 41 comments: 'Two possibilities now suggest themselves: this (sc. *Virg.*) is a lost writing of Pelagius, or this is a writing of a Pelagian copying the master.' He favours the former, because his general comparison of the two works with each other has revealed so many similarities of diction and thought, and, of course, we know that *Comm.* was a work of Pelagius. But one must admit that the similarities, great though they are, could be the result of copying by a Pelagian extremely familiar with Pelagius' Pauline Commentary and even having a copy in front of him: after all, plagiarism was considered to be a tribute to the original author in the ancient world rather than an infringement of copyright. But Plinval, 1934,26 took the same view as Evans, and so, on balance, do I, since the internal resemblances between *Comm.*, *Dem.* and *Virg.* seem to me to be too strong to ignore.

places of the righteous in heaven are the Lord's; the thirtyfold, sixtyfold and hundredfold fruit is the Lord's. Those who are anxious about these things and about the works by which they may be able to attain them by merit are the ones who are anxious about the Lord's affairs. The law of the New and Old Testaments, in which the holy utterances of his lips shine forth, is also the Lord's, and any virgins who meditate upon these utterances without intermission are anxious about the Lord's affairs; and in them is fulfilled that saying of the prophet: The eternal foundations are on solid rock, and the commandments of the Lord are in the heart of a holy woman.

9.   Then there follow these words: 'How to please God' – God, I repeat, not man – and: 'How to be holy in body and spirit.'[15] He did not say, 'How to be holy in member or body only,' but 'How to be holy in body and spirit.' Now a member is only one part of the body but the body is a union of all its members. When therefore he says: How to be holy in body, he bears witness that she ought to be sanctified in all her members because sanctification of the rest of the members will not avail, if corruption is found even in one; also, she will not be holy in body, if she is contaminated by the defilement of even one, since the body consists of all its members. But in order that my meaning may be made clearer and plainer, let us suppose that there is a woman who is cleansed by the sanctification of all her other members and sins only with her tongue either through blasphemy or false witness; will all the other members absolve one, or will the others too be judged on account of one? If, then, not even the sanctification of all the other members will avail when only one is at fault, how much more likely it is that the perfect purity of one will not avail either, if all the other members are corrupted by the shame attached to a variety of sins!

10, 1.   That is why, virgin, I beseech you not to flatter yourself on chastity alone nor to put your trust in the purity of one member, but, in accordance with the apostle's words, maintain the holiness of your body throughout. Cleanse your head of all defilements,[16] since it is shameful for that which now shines with the brilliance of its heavenly adornment, having been sanctified with holy unction, to be soiled by paint or powder of saffron or any other pigment whatsoever or decked with gold or jewels or any other earthly ornament, and since preference for mundane and worldly adornment is a mighty affront to the divine grace. Cleanse your forehead, so that it blushes at human, not divine, actions and admit that feeling of shame which gives rise not to sin but to divine favour, as the scripture says: There is a shame which brings sin, and there is a shame which brings glory and favour (Sir.4.21). Cleanse your neck, so that it does not have to carry golden nets for your hair and hanging necklaces[17] but rather bear about it

[15] On the need for holiness in body and in spirit with the same supporting quotation cf. Dem. 12.
[16] On the cleansing of the bodily parts cf. Dem.24,2 and see also section 12 as compared with the same chapter of Dem.(n.19 below).
[17] Translated literally, the Latin text in CSEL 1,237 is as follows: 'Cleanse your neck, so

those ornaments of which the scripture says: Let not mercy and faithfulness forsake you, but hang them upon your heart as if upon your neck (Pr.3.3). Cleanse your eyes, withdrawing their gaze from all lust but never averting them from the sight of the poor and keeping them clean and free from all paints in the purity in which they were made by God. Cleanse your tongue from falsehood, since 'A lying mouth destroys the soul' (Wis.1.11). Cleanse it from disparagement, from swearing oaths, from flattery, from perjury. I do not wish you to think that the correct order has been inverted here by my saying that the tongue should be cleansed from swearing before it is cleansed from perjury: in fact, you will the more easily avoid perjury, if you do not swear an oath at all, and so the judgement will then be fulfilled in you: Keep your tongue from evil and your lips from speaking deceit (Ps.34.13). And be mindful of the apostle's saying: Bless and do not curse them (Rom.12.14). But remember this even more often: See that no one returns evil for evil to anyone or reviling for reviling; but, on the contrary, bless, for to this you have been called, so that you may obtain and inherit a blessing (1 Pet.3.9); and this: And if any one makes no mistakes in what he says, he is a perfect man (Jas.3.2). For it is shameful that those very lips with which you confess, request, bless and praise the Lord should be defiled by the filth of any sin. I do not know with what conscience anyone can make a request of God using the tongue with which he also lies or reviles or disparages; God listens to holy lips and speedily grants those prayers which an unstained tongue utters.

2. Cleanse your ears, that they may listen only to utterances which are holy and true, that they may never admit into them obscene or shameful or worldly words or listen to anyone disparaging another; it is on account of this that it is written: Hedge your ears with thorns and do not listen to an evil tongue (Sir.28.24),[18] so that you may be able to partake with him of whom it is said that: He was righteous in what he heard and saw (2 Pet.2.8.), that is, he sinned neither with his ears nor with his eyes. Cleanse your hands, that they be not 'extended to receive, but withdrawn when it is time to repay' (Sir.4.31) nor be ready to strike, but ready enough for all works of compassion and godliness. Cleanse your feet,

that your hair does not carry golden nets and hanging necklaces', and it has emerged from a number of emendations and variants. Either it is hopelessly corrupt, possibly with something omitted, or it is the result of a very simple error. I have assumed the latter to be the case and changed one letter – *capillis* for *capillus* – and this at least makes sense.

18 Pelagius is clearly fond of this quotation from Sirach, since he uses it also in *Dem.* 19,3 and *Cel.* 16,1 (see *Dem.* 19, n.42). He has altered one word – giving him 'ears' instead of 'property' – to suit himself or through a lapse of memory, if he had read the text of Ecclesiasticus (or Sirach) in an Old Latin version; he certainly used an Old Latin version of the Bible and, even if he had been able to get hold of a copy of Jerome's Vulgate, which was beginning to circulate at this time, it would have been an Old Latin version which he would have found in that too, since Jerome did not translate the Hebrew texts of some of the Books of the Apocrypha. The Septuagint (LXX), based on the Hebrew Bible, has 'property' but Ecclesiasticus (or Sirach) was not translated into Greek until the second half of the second century B.C. and was not a part of the Jewish canon. (The instruction as it stands in our text is so striking and novel that one hopes that it did appear in the original Hebrew!)

that they may not proceed along the broad and spacious road leading to the splendid and costly banquets of this world but tread the more arduous and narrow way extending to heaven, since it is written: Make a straight path for your feet (Heb.12.13). Recognize that your members were shaped by God the maker not for vice but for virtue, and when you have cleansed all your members from all the filth of sin and have been sanctified in your whole body, then you may understand that chastity will profit you and look forward with every confidence to receiving the palm of virginity.

11, 1. I think that I have now explained briefly but clearly what it means to be holy in body; now we ought to get to know what follows – that is, what it means to be holy in spirit also – in order that what it is wrong for one to do may not be right for one to think about either. The woman who sins neither in mind nor in body is holy in mind as well as in body, since she knows that God is the one who examines the heart also, and so she busies herself with the task of seeing that her mind as well as her body is in all respects free from sin; she knows that it is written: Keep your heart with all vigilance (Pr.4.23), and again: The Lord loves pure hearts, all those who are without blemish are acceptable to him (Pr.17.3; 11.20); and, elsewhere: Blessed are the pure in heart, for they shall see God (Mt. 5.8).

2. And I think that this statement is made concerning those whom their conscience convicts of no blame from sin, and I also believe that it is of them that John spoke in his epistle: If our heart does not condemn us, we have confidence before God; and we receive from him whatever we ask (1 Jn.3.21,22). I do not want you to suppose that you have avoided the charge of sinning if performance does not follow intention,[19] since it is written: Every one who looks at a woman lustfully has already committed adultery with her in his heart (Mt.5.28). Nor should you say, 'I have indeed thought of it but I have not carried it out', because it is a sin even to desire what it is a sin to do. Hence the blessed Peter instructed us to this effect: Having purified your souls (1 Pet.1.22); for if he had not been aware of such a thing as defilement of the soul, he would not have expressed a desire that it should be purified. And we ought to give more careful consideration to that passage which contains the following words: It is these who have not defiled themselves with women, for they have remained chaste, it is these who follow the Lamb wherever he goes (Rev.14.4); and we ought to reflect whether they are joined to the divine company and run to and fro over all the floors of heaven through the merit of their chastity alone, or whether there are other attributes whose assistance virginity requires in order to attain the glory of a state so blessed.

3. But how shall we be able to find this out? From the words which follow, unless I am mistaken, in which it is written: These have been redeemed from mankind as first fruits for God and the Lamb, and their mouth no lie was found,

---

[19] Cf. *Comm.*336,5f. (Gal.5.17), which has the identical formula, 'if performance does not follow intention'; for this use of Mt.5.28 cf. *Dem.*27,2.

for they were spotless (ibid.5). You see, therefore, that they are said to follow closely in the steps of the Lord not in respect of one member only but because they have passed their lives unspotted by the contagion of any sin quite apart from their virginity. It is for this reason above all that the virgin rejects marriage, that, while she is more secure in this respect, she may the more easily protect herself from all sin and fulfil all the law's commandments, something which is also sought of those who are married. For if she does not marry and nonetheless does things from which wives too are ordered to be free, what will it profit her not to have married? No Christian is permitted to sin,[20] and it befits all without exception who have been purified by the sanctification of the spiritual water to pass a spotless life and thus be allowed entry into the very heart of the Church, which is described as being 'without spot or wrinkle or anything of that kind' (Eph.5.27); but it is much more necessary that a virgin should fulfil this require-ment, since she is not prevented from carrying out the demands of divine scrip-ture to the full by having a husband or children or through any other family relationship nor, if she does sin, will she be able to defend herself by any kind of excuse.

12, 1. Virgin, maintain the intention which is destined to bring you a great reward. The virtue of virginity and chastity is glorious in God's sight as long as it is not undermined by other lapses into sin and evil. Recognize your status, recognize your position, recognize your intention. You are called a bride of Christ; see that you do nothing unworthy in the eyes of him to whom you are seen to be betrothed. He will quickly write your deed of divorce, if he sees even one act of adultery on your part. Any woman who is bound by the pledges of human betrothal[21] immediately begins to make careful and diligent enquiries of the members of her betrothed's household, his intimates and friends as to what the young man's habits are, what he especially likes, what he considers to be satisfactory, what is his accustomed way of life, how he regulates his everyday behaviour, what sort of banquets he enjoys, in what things he takes particular delight and pleasure. When she has found all this out, she so conducts herself in all respects that her own obedience, her own agreeableness, her own diligence, her whole way of life are in harmony with her husband's character.

2. And you, who have Christ as your betrothed, must also make enquiries about your betrothed's habits from his household and intimates and to enquire zealously and intelligently about the things in which he takes special pleasure, what kind of arrangement he likes in your dress, what kind of adornment he desires you to adopt. Let his most intimate associate Peter, who does not allow physical adornment even to married women, tell you in the words that he has

---

[20] The same association between membership of the Christian Church by baptism and the need to maintain the highest standards of morality in one's behaviour is to be found in Comm.363,3–6 (Eph.4.4) and 378,4f. (Eph.5.27) and is typical of Pelagius; see Rees, 1988,3,19f., and cf. also the letter On the Possibility of Not Sinning in Part II.

[21] For this long and detailed comparison of the bride of Christ and the young woman betrothed to a secular fiancé cf. Dem.24,2,3 and see section 11 and n.16 above.

written in his epistle: Likewise, let wives be submissive to their husbands, so that if there are some who do not obey the word, they may be won over without a word by the behaviour of their wives, when they see your reverent and chaste behaviour. Let not theirs be the outward adorning with braiding of the hair, decoration of gold or wearing of fine clothing, but let it be the hidden person of the heart with the imperishable jewel of a gentle and quiet spirit, which in God's sight is very precious (1 Pet.3.1–4). Let another blessed apostle also speak, who, when writing to Timothy, testifies in the same way on the matter of the discipline of wives who are believers: Likewise that women should adorn themselves modestly and sensibly in seemly apparel, not with braided hair or gold or pearls or costly attire but by good behaviour as befits women who profess chastity (1 Tim.2.9,10).

13.   But perhaps you say, 'Why did the same apostles not give those commands to virgins also?' Because they did not think it necessary, lest such a warning might seem in their case to be an insult rather than a means of correction. Nor, indeed, would they have believed that virgins would ever be so foolhardy as to take for granted that they could wear carnal and worldly ornaments which were not permitted even to married women. Of course the virgin ought to adorn and array herself; if she does not go forth suitably adorned and arrayed, how will she be able to please her betrothed? To be sure, she has to be adorned but let her array consist of inward ornaments, spiritual and not carnal, because it is grace of soul, not of body, that God desires of her. Therefore, you too, who desire your soul to be loved and dwelt in by God, must array it with all possible care and adorn it with spiritual clothing. Let nothing unseemly, nothing shameful be seen in it; let it shine with the gold of righteousness and gleam with the jewels of holiness and glitter with the most precious pearl of chastity;[22] let it be clothed in the tunic of compassion and goodness instead of in fine cloth and silk, as it is written: Put on then, as God's chosen ones, holy and beloved, compassion, kindness, meekness (Col.3.12). And let not the virgin seek the elegance due to ceruse or any other paint but let her rather possess the radiance of innocence and simplicity, the rosy colour of modesty and the purple glow of bashfulness and decency. Let her be washed with the nitre of heavenly teaching and cleansed with spiritual lotions; let no stain of evil or wickedness be left on her; and, that she may never give off the offensive odour of sin, let her be protected by the most agreeable of all ointments, namely, wisdom and knowledge.

14.   This is the kind of adornment that God seeks; this is the kind of array that he desires for the soul. Remember that you are called the daughter of God, as he says: Hear, O daughter, and consider (Ps.45.10). But you too must bear witness that you are the daughter of God, whenever you name God as your

---

[22] Cf. Dem.16,1, referring to 'the most precious pearls with which the bride of Christ must be adorned'.

Father. If then you are the daughter of God, see that you do nothing which is unsuitable in the eyes of God the Father and do everything as the daughter of God. Acquaint yourself with the way in which the daughters of the nobles of this world conduct themselves, with the manners which they usually show and with the exercise by means of which they train themselves. Some have such modesty, such seriousness, such discretion that they surpass the customary behaviour of other men and women in their regard for human nobility of character and, so as not to brand their honourable parents with any mark of disgrace through a lapse of theirs, apply themselves to the creation of a different nature by their conduct in human society.[23] So you too must have regard for *your* origin, consider *your* lineage, respect the honour of *your* noble stock. Acknowledge you are not only the daughter of a man but the daughter of God as well, graced with the nobility of divine birth. Present yourself in such a way that your heavenly birth may be visible in your person and your divine nobility shine clearly forth. In your person let there be a new dignity, an admirable probity, a wonderful modesty, a marvellous patience, a virginal gait and a bearing which indicates true purity, a speech that is always modest and uttered only at the proper time, so that whoever sees you will say with admiration in his voice, 'What am I to make of this readiness to submit to a new kind of human dignity? Of this show of respect for decency? Of this discreet display of nobility? Of this mature wisdom? This is not the product of mere human instruction, mere mortal teaching: it is some heavenly quality inside an earthly body that wafts its distinctive scent over me. I do believe that God lives in some human beings.' And when he gets to know that you are a handmaid of Christ, he will be even more amazed and will reflect what kind of master he must be who has such a handmaid.

15.   If you wish then to be with Christ and to share with Christ, you must live by the example of Christ, who was such a stranger to evil and wickedness that he did not retaliate even upon his enemies but rather prayed even for them. For I would not have you think those souls Christian who I do not say hate their brothers or sisters but who do not love their neighbours with all their heart and conscience before God as their witness, since all Christians are called to follow Christ's example by loving even their enemies. If you want to enjoy fellowship with the saints, cleanse your heart of all thought of evil and wickedness and let no one deceive you or seduce you with beguiling talk. The heavenly palace will admit none but the holy and the righteous, the simple and the innocent; evil has no place in God's presence, and he who desires to reign with Christ must be free from all forms of wickedness and deceit. To God nothing is so offensive, nothing so detestable as to hate anyone and to want to injure anyone; nothing is so commendable in his sight as to love everyone. The prophet knows this and bears witness to it when he teaches: You who love the Lord, hate evil (Ps.97.10).

---

[23] I have given what seems to be the meaning of this clause but the Latin text is extremely obscure as it stands.

16, 1. See that you do not love human glory in anyone, lest it become your portion to be reckoned among those to whom it is said: How can you believe, who receive glory from one another (Jn.5.44)? And of whom it is said through the prophet: Heap evils upon them, heap evils upon the proud of the earth (Dt.32.33); and elsewhere: You are confounded by your pride in your glory, by your dishonour in the sight of God (Is.23.9). I do not want you to have regard for those virgins who belong to this world and not to Christ, who, forgetful of their own intention and profession, rejoice in pleasure and delight in wealth and in their descent from nobility of a bodily kind. If they believed themselves to be truly daughters of God, they would never admire mere human nobility or pride themselves on having any distinguished father on earth after having known a divine birth; if they really felt that God was their Father, they would have no love for nobility of the flesh. Why do you flatter yourself, foolish woman, and take pleasure in the nobility of your family stock? In the beginning God created two human beings, and it is from them that the whole mass of the human race is descended; it was not the evenhandedness of nature that produced the nobility of this world but ambition inspired by greed.

2. Surely we are all made equal by the grace of the divine water, and there can be no distinction between those who have been created by a second birth, through which rich man as well as poor man, freeman as well as slave, the noble as well as the man of low birth is made a son of God; earthly nobility is put in the shade by the splendour of heavenly glory and can no longer match it in any respect at all, since those who in the past were unequal in worldly honours are now equally clothed in the glory of a heavenly and divine nobility. There is no longer any place for low birth nor is there anyone of lowly birth whom the majesty of divine birth adorns, except, that is, among those who do not think that heavenly honours are to be preferred to human; or if they do so think, how vain it is for them to prefer themselves in minor matters to those whom they know to be their equals in matters of greater import, and regard as their inferiors on earth those whom they believe to be their equals in heaven! But you, who are a virgin of Christ and not of the world, must avoid and shun all the glory that is attached to this present life, in order that you may attain that glory which is promised in the world to come.

17, 1. Avoid words of controversy and causes of animosity; shun also occasions for disagreement and dispute. For if, according to the apostle's teaching: The servant of the Lord must not be quarrelsome (2 Tim.2.24), how much more does this apply to the handmaid of God, whose mind ought to be more moderate as her sex is more modest? Keep your tongue from slander and place the bridle of the law on your mouth, so that, if perchance you have to speak, you do so only when it is a sin to keep silent. And take care not to say anything which lays you open to reprimand: a word once spoken is like a stone thrown, and, therefore, it should be pondered over long before it is uttered. Blessed indeed are the lips that never say anything which they would wish to recall! The speech of a chaste mind ought also to be chaste and of the kind that may always edify its hearers rather than drag them down, in accordance with the commandment of the apostle, when he says: Let no evil talk come out of your mouth but only such as is good for edifying, that it may impart grace to those who hear (Eph.4.29). Precious to God is the tongue which knows how to put words together only on divine matters, and holy is the mouth from which heavenly utterances come forth on all occasions.

2. Discourage on the authority of the scripture traducers of those who are absent as being mischief makers, since the prophet mentions this also as among the virtues of the perfect man, if a slanderer is brought to naught in the sight of the righteous for uttering charges which cannot be proved against his neighbour. You are not permitted to give a patient hearing to slander directed against another, since you certainly do not want others to do that when such slander is directed against you. Indeed, everything that goes against the gospel of Christ is unrighteous, as it is to tolerate the infliction upon another of something which you would find painful if it were done to you by another. Accustom your tongue to speak always of good persons and give a hearing to the praises of good men rather than the criticisms of the wicked.[24] See that you do all the good that you do for God's sake, knowing that you will receive a reward for it from God only insofar as you have done it out of regard for your fear and love of him. Take pains to be holy rather than to appear holy, since it profits you nothing to be valued for what you are not, and you lay yourself open to the charge of having committed a double sin – of not having what is credited to you and of pretending to have what you do not actually have at all.

18.   Take pleasure in fasts rather than feasts and remember the story of the widow who would not leave the temple, because she was engaged in serving God with fasting and supplication day and night. And if a widow, a Jewish widow at that, could do so much, what does it befit a virgin of Christ to do now? Give your love rather to the banquet provided by the reading of God's word and look for your satisfaction in spiritual feasts and the kinds of food which will refresh your spirit rather than your body. Avoid the varieties of flesh and wine which are on offer as being stimulants to passion and incitements to lust, and if by chance you do take a small quantity of wine, do so only when stomach-ache or excessive bodily infirmity compel you to do so. Conquer anger, check all feelings of animosity and avoid anything which brings remorse after the deed is done as being an abomination which is likely to lead to crime. The mind which desires to be the dwelling-place of God should be quite tranquil and peaceful and far removed from anger's furious rages, for God testifies to this, when he says through the prophet: On whom else shall I rest except the man who is humble and peaceful and trembles at my words (Is.66.2)? Believe that God watches all your deeds and thoughts and beware lest you do or think anything that is unworthy to

---

24 Or, possibly, 'good things. . . good things . . . wicked things': the Latin words concerned could be masculine or neuter, '*bonis . . . bonorum . . . malorum*'.

meet his divine gaze. When you desire to engage in prayer, present yourself in the right state of mind for one who is about to speak with the Lord.

19. When you repeat a psalm, consider whose words you are repeating and take pleasure in the contrition in your soul rather than in the sweetness of a trilling voice. For God gives his approval to the psalm-singer's tears rather than the charm of his voice, as the prophet says: Serve the Lord with fear and with fear rejoice in him (Ps.2.11). Where there are fear and trembling, it is shown not by the raising of the voice but by the lowering of the soul in lamentation and tears. In all your actions display carefulness, since it is written: Cursed is he who does the work of the Lord with slackness (Jer.48.10). Let grace increase in you with the years, let righteousness grow with the years, and let your faith appear the more perfect the older you become, for Jesus, who has left us an example of how to live, advanced not only in physical age but also in spiritual wisdom and grace and in favour with God and men. Reckon as wasted all the time in which you have failed to note an improvement in yourself. Maintain to the end that resolve to be a virgin which you have now taken, because it is the part of virtue not only to begin but to complete a good work, as the Lord says in the gospel; He who endures to the end shall be saved (Mt.24.13). Take care not to give any man occasion even to lust after you, since God is a jealous husband, and she who commits adultery against Christ is guiltier than one who does so only against her husband. Let your way of life be an example for all; surpass in your deeds too those whom you outstrip in the holiness of chastity.[25] Show yourself a virgin in all respects; let no suspicion of immoral behaviour be cast upon your person; let one whose body is perfect in its purity be also invulnerable in her conduct. And since, as we said in the introduction to this letter, you have become a sacrifice which belongs to God, and such a sacrifice undoubtedly imparts its sanctity to others as well, so that whoever worthily receives from it is also himself a sharer in that sanctity, so then let other virgins too be sanctified through you as if by means of a divine offering. Show yourself to be so holy in all respects in their company that all who come into contact with your life by hearing of it or by witnessing it may feel the full force of your holiness and realize that so much grace is being passed from your conduct to them that, through their very longing to follow your example, they too may become worthy to be a sacrifice devoted to God.

---

[25] The Latin text is again obscure but I think that I have given the correct sense.

3

On the Divine Law[1]

This minor treatise deals with a subject which was central to the Pelagian view of the true Christian life: endowed as we are with God's gracious gift of free choice, we shall only exercise that choice rightly if we seek baptism to cleanse ourselves of past sins and thereafter strive to resist the temptation to sin again by obeying the divine law revealed to us in the scriptures and by following the example and teaching of Jesus – a programme which Augustine dismissed again and again as 'nothing else but law and teaching'.[2] The treatise again takes the form of a letter, this time written to a friend of some standing in Roman society who has recently retired from official duties and has been baptized as a Christian convert. We have the name neither of the writer nor of the recipient of the letter, and, like the *Letter to Demetrias* and the treatise *On Virginity*, as well as an interpolated recension of Pelagius' commentary on the Pauline Epistles, it appears in a collection of pseudo-Jerome texts in Vol.30 of Migne, PL. But it is certainly not the work of Jerome, since it contains too many Pelagian features for that to be conceivable.

The editor of PL 30, Vallarsi, comments that the letter reads like a fifth-century work and could only have been written by a Pelagian; he attributes it to Faustus of Reji (Riez), whose life may well have spanned the greater part of the fifth century, on the grounds that the latter's friend, Gennadius of Marseilles, attributed it to him.[3] This attribution was rightly rejected by Caspari, who describes it as 'Semi-Pelagian' and leaves it at that; Plinval, however, attributes it to Pelagius himself, a possibility rejected by Morris for reasons based on his misunderstanding of three passages in the text.[4] Evans exposes this misunderstanding and has no hesitation in linking the letter with both the Pauline Commentary and the *Letter to Demetrias* on the grounds of a marked similarity in the themes developed in many passages and the use of the same biblical quotations.[5] In all there are fifty biblical quotations in this treatise, an average of five

---

1 *Epistula [ad amicum] de divina lege* or *Epistula [ad Thesiphontem] de scientia divinae legis*; PL 30, 106–16; CPL 740.
2 *On the Grace of Christ* x.11 (PL 44, 365f.).
3 See Vallarsi's preliminary note on the letter in PL 30, 104f. and Gennadius, *On Famous Men*, 85 (PL 58,1110).
4 Morris, 1965, 36f.
5 Evans, 1968, 23 and 59ff.

per section, but there is less similarity with those employed in the other minor treatises in our group. Nevertheless, the links with the Pauline Commentary and the Demetrias letter must be given considerable weight when we consider the question of its authorship, since those two works are unquestionably by Pelagius.

As to the date of the letter, Pelagius could well have written it some time in the second half of the first decade of the fifth century. There is a reference in section 9 to the imminent threat of a collapse of the temporal world, and the invasion by the Visigoths could be the threat which the writer had in mind; Vallarsi regarded this reference as an indication of a date towards the end of the century but this, of course, was in keeping with his attribution of the letter to Faustus. If, as we believe, Pelagius was the author of the letter, then a dating not long before the invasion of Rome by Alaric and his own flight to Palestine, that is, c.408–10, is quite likely and would have the added advantage of placing it in the same period of Pelagius' career as the two acknowledged works of his which it most resembles.

After a brief preface, couched in friendly and courteous terms and explaining that the author's main aim in writing the letter is to provide its newly baptized recipient with simple instruction in the requirements of the Christian code of law, based on the word of God and the teachings of Jesus as contained in holy scripture, a number of salient points are selected and discussed; for example, the purpose of baptism, the need to acquire true wisdom by close and constant study of the scriptures, the importance of keeping God's commandments, both positive and negative, both major and minor, the rewards of the future life as contrasted with the present life's attractions and the terrible consequences of failure to pass the ultimate test of the divine judgement, the responsibility of the Christian for the quality of his every action, and the need to persevere in righteousness and to press ahead without delay in the life of the spirit. The letter ends on a more personal note with a reference to certain rather impetuous and strongly worded questions which the recipient seems to have posed, two of them, for instance, asking whether a Christian had the right to retaliate and take an oath, both presumably arising from practical problems which he must have had to face very frequently in the course of his day-to-day work as a State official. Finally, it is suggested that the two men may meet to discuss such matters face-to-face, if the neophyte so desires.

Text

1, 1. I would now be attempting to excuse myself for my presumption in writing to you, were it not that the occasion itself, the reason and, at the same time, my affection for you give me defence enough, and that I do not at this moment want to impart my own words to you but God's. Added to all this is the fact that my essay in exhortation gains good faith from its honesty and strength from its truthfulness; it is not about uncleanness or error or deceit, but I give you plain warning in advance that you should not allow consideration of my moderate tone to mislead you into despising words of God offered in a spirit of tender affection to you, now an infant child of the Church, like milk to nourish you in your new state of infancy – as an interim measure, that is, until presently, when you have been educated either by your own efforts or by others to assume the role of a fully developed man, you can be given more solid fare to strengthen you. So I want now to enable you to know in full what I believe you already recognize in part, that it was for this purpose that our Lord, the Word of God, came down from heaven, namely, that through his assumption of our human nature the human race, left prostrate from the time of Adam, might be raised up in Christ, and the new man rewarded for his obedience with salvation as great as the perdition that once befell him through disobedience.

2. But since both these terms, obedience and disobedience, are incorporeal and not made of corporeal material, and because incorporeal things cannot be produced from corporeal, it is clear that incorporeal things are born from incorporeal; and if it may be assumed that incorporeal obedience, the antidote for disobedience, is produced by reason from an incorporeal soul, it is also clear that obedience results from a decision of the mind, not the substance of the body. From this reasoning we deduce that the call which we have received enjoys a standing in proportion to the dignity of the one who calls us but also rests upon the consent of our own will, so that the washing received by the believer's body may turn out to the greater benefit of his soul and bring the purification which consists in water and word to the essence of both body and soul through the service rendered by the mind.[6] But let me offer you some clear examples from the scriptures to back up with positive proof what I have just said. It is written in the apostle: As Christ loved the Church and gave himself up for her, that he might sanctify her, cleansing her by the washing of water with the word of life, that he might present her to himself glorious and without blemish (Eph.5.25–27). He said that the Church is cleansed by water and the word; and we undoubtedly are the Church, if we live without fault and blemish, as it is commanded. Bodily things are cleansed by bodily things, and spiritual by spiritual; the soul is seen to be washed by the word and water, the body by water only. As for the soul that continues to live on inside its former filth and desires, it must fear the judgement of the evangelist when he says: You blind Pharisee! First clean the inside of the cup, that the outside may be clean also (Mt.23.25). And indeed, if our bodies are vessels for our souls, then they will be truly clean only if they have clean and pure liquid inside them. On the other hand, though a cup be made of gold and be very

---

6   Pelagius never misses an opportunity to emphasize the important, indeed essential, part played by the free will of man in responding to God's call and obeying his commandments (see Rees, 1988, 31f.,60,88). Here, as in his introduction to the *Letter to Demetrias*, he supports his point with a quasi-philosophical argument of the kind that often obscures his meaning instead of clarifying it. He is more successful when he backs up his statements with scriptural examples, as in section 4, and lets them speak for him.

beautiful with its decoration of splendid jewels, if it contain poison, does not the deadly venom of the draught nullify the value of the precious metals, and will it not defile the sparkling brightness of the ornaments?

2, 1. But so as not to depart any further from the intention set out in my promise, I shall make good the statements contained in this little preface of mine by quoting the Lord's own words, in order that what I am saying may not be thought to have been invented by human understanding or contrived by an individual mind but be seen to have been built on a foundation of divine pronouncements. In the gospel of John the Lord says to his disciples: You are already made clean by the word which I have spoken to you (Jn.15.3). He did not say, 'Because you have been washed', and no more, but 'By the word which I have spoken to you and for that reason you are clean.' He knew that they had all been washed; but he proved that not all of them were clean inside, because Judas was among the others and he, after purification by water, became unclean again because of the evil in his mind. It is for this reason that, though he had earlier been washed along with the others, yet he is declared unclean by the Lord's pronouncement, and from his example it is clearly and plainly shown that he receives the grace of God who seeks it in that right order in which the scripture has taught that it should be sought. For if a man believes that he has been reborn by water as far as concerns the body and he has not been reborn in the spirit through the word, his hope of salvation is disappointed, because this is the reason for the transformation wrought by heaven, namely, that while the nature of the body remains unchanged, the old man may be changed and given a new disposition of mind. But as a dirty body, if not washed by water, will remain unclean, so the soul, if not cleansed by the divine word, will remain corrupted by filthy vices. If, therefore, by his own decision his body is washed with water, why does he reject what is greater if he already holds in his possession what is less?

2. It is folly for a man who has been wholly destroyed to desire to be partly saved, a man who, with his whole salvation in his power, is yet willing to be content with half measures and, contrary to the law of nature, believes that he has been saved in body alone, although it is more possible that the soul lives without a body before the day of resurrection than that the body continues without a soul. If a man suffers in two eyes and two feet and has available a medicine for both limbs but, when one foot or one eye has been cured, wishes to prevent the doctor from attending to the other, is he not to be condemned as insane both in the doctor's judgement and in the opinion of everyone else? 'But,' says someone, 'if we look for everything to come as the result of our own efforts, then there is nothing left for grace to provide.' Now I do not want anyone to make grace graceless heedlessly and on the pretext of ignorance, lest he turn his faith into a stumbling-block and the true cause of his salvation become the occasion for his death and destruction: if the reasoning behind this matter of grace is pursued in moderation, then and then only will it be an aid to life for a man instead of hurling him down to death, as it might perhaps have done because of his thoughtlessness.

3. Grace indeed freely discharges sins, but with the consent and choice of the believer, as Philip proves to the eunuch in the Acts of the Apostles, saying: If you believe with all your heart, you can (Acts 8.37).[7] By this testimony it is understood that there is no less danger if an unbeliever is baptized than if baptism is refused to a true believer. But that believer is close to the scriptures who believes with his whole heart, and if one must believe with the whole citadel of the heart, so that baptism may be given to faith on the merit of belief, then water is not sufficient for the baptized, since it does not reach the soul of the believer in his heart. And that the merit of the heart may not be placed at risk, we must receive the word by which the heart can be reached and cleansed, because if he who says that he believes is content with water, by which the limbs are cleansed from outside, and does not require the word, in which the soul glories, then he will be seen to have believed not from the heart, as he ought, but from the body, because by no means and for no reason can it be conceded to be possible that the body alone without the judgement of the mind is held to possess a special intelligence of its own.

3, 1. Confident therefore in your good sense, which, in accordance with its inborn goodness, would not allow anything untoward to be done even to another person, I ask you that for the completion of your instruction you give a more careful reading to the Lord's word, that is, the Gospel, from which you may receive a fuller knowledge of that light in which you have come to believe, so that you may be able to know in all matters what you are to do. For it is God's word, not mine, which will prove that without knowledge of divine law and discipline it is difficult for anyone to be able to be saved. The prophet Isaiah says: The man who will not learn the righteousness of God will not do his truth (Is.26.9,10). Likewise concerning this very same matter in the Book of Wisdom: And who will be perfect among the sons of men? If the wisdom of God is not with him, he will be regarded as nothing. For vain are all men who have not knowledge of the law of God (Wis.9.6). Hence the Lord replied in the Gospel to those who surmised that the truth is other than it actually is: You are wrong, because you do not know the scriptures (Mt.22.29), thus showing that in respect of the totality of salvation those who were unwilling to keep alight the lamp of the spirit, that is, knowledge of the divine wisdom, were made of mist and shadow. Some who reject that knowledge are themselves rejected by the Lord, speaking through the prophet, as it is written: Because you have rejected knowledge, I too reject you (Hos.4.6).[8]

2. Therefore let us by no means entrust ourselves at random to our own judgement, lest Isaiah cry out to us: Woe to those who are wise in their own eyes,

---

7   Pelagius' reference to possible criticism from the 'defenders of grace' is, of course, directed at Augustine and his supporters: again, his emphasis, as in the previous chapter, is on the importance of exercising free will in order to avoid sin, and the quotation from Acts is brief but to the point.

8   For the use of this quotation from Hosea to follow the symbolism of light/darkness, good/evil and knowledge/ignorance cf. Comm. 104, 15ff. (Rom.13.12).

and shrewd in their own sight (Is.5.21)! Hence Paul the apostle also says: If anyone thinks that he is wise in this age, let him become a fool that he may become wise (1 Cor. 3.18), for the wisdom of this world is foolishness before God. That is why it is said to the King of Tyre, vaunting himself on his human wisdom: For wise men shall not teach you (cf. Ezek.28.3, LXX), meaning, teaching is of heaven and wisdom of God. There is human wisdom too, we do not deny it; but one kind of wisdom urges a man to life, another drives him to death, because human wisdom, which is censured as folly, is described by the apostle, inspired by the Holy Spirit, as the gate of death (cf. Ps.9.13) and is shown to be the stuff of which everlasting death is made. As it is written in the prophet: The fool and the stupid alike will perish (Ps.49.10). The fool is one who has said in his heart, 'There is no God'; and the stupid man, though he confess God with his mouth in the actions of the present life, has not looked forward to eternity, as it is written: Better is a poor and wise youth than an old and foolish king who knows not how to look forward to the future (Ec.4.13).

3. It is indeed good for a man to be wise, if, in accordance with the scriptures, he is wise to the extent of looking to the future and considering the state of mortality with daily departures of men dying and the gradual destruction of the whole world as it sinks down through one loss after the other.[9] But if a man is led by consideration of the purpose he has adopted once and for all and wishes to be guided by his own judgement rather than God's and, disregarding the divine law, puts his own plans before those of God, let him fear the voice of the prophet, calling out: Woe to those who despise the law of the Lord (Am.2.4)! Fear, the pit and the snare are upon him. As heavy rain is useless, so are those who abandon the law and praise acts of ungodliness; but those who love the law surround themselves with a wall. Blessed is the man who meditates on the law of the Lord day and night (Ps.1.2), whose mind knows only how to examine again and again the utterances of God's word. The further he is from earthly thoughts the closer he is to God and heaven; to him the divine word also gives deserved praise and prefers to the rich the man who is truly richer, saying: Happy is the man who finds wisdom! For it is better to purchase it than treasures of gold and silver; it is more precious than precious stones (Pr.3.13–15). Likewise: All gold is a handful of sand in comparison with it, and silver will be regarded as mud compared to it (cf. Pr.8.19).

4, 1. But while we dally longer in our encouragement to wisdom, lest perchance someone may suppose that we prefer a teacher of the law to a doer of it

---

[9] The first of the two references in this letter – the second is in section 9 – to the topsy-turvy state of the world was taken by Vallarsi as a possible indication that the letter was written towards the end of the fifth century, when the imperial government was in a state of virtual collapse and the barbarians controlled most of the Western Empire; if he is right, then there would be support for his suggestion that Faustus of Riez was the author. But Rome had suffered enough in the first decade of the century to make this remark about the 'gradual destruction of the whole world' almost equally apposite to that period; see my n.55 on Dem.30.

contrary to the apostle's advice, we shall reply in the order laid down by him that we must get to know in advance what has been ordered or what forbidden, so that we may observe both with knowledge.[10] Besides, before one knows what the command is it is impossible to get to know what is to be done; it is thoughtless enough to imagine that the law imposed by our own will can suffice, when we read that even the apostle was beneath the law, since he himself says: To those who were without law I was as if without law, though I was not without the law of God but was under the law of Christ (1 Cor.9.21). And elsewhere: Bear one another's burdens, and so fulfil the law of Christ (Gal.6.2).

2.   Those who have been redeemed by Christ's passion through his dutifulness to his Father have been redeemed to this end that, by keeping the laws of their Redeemer, they may prepare themselves for the life laid up for them in heaven, and there they may in no way be said to arrive redeemed, unless they follow the commands laid upon those who seek to obey, as it is written: If you would enter life, keep the commandments (Mt.19.17); that is, draw away from every illicit act which you are forbidden to do and readily approach every good deed which you are ordered to perform, so that, by persevering in your old, wicked desires, you may not ruin the faith with which you believed by a continuing love for some old sin, and the knowledge of God, revealed to you by a new grace, may not be profaned by sins, as the prophet says: Falsehood and not faith has prevailed over the earth, because they have passed on from evils to evils and have not known me, says the Lord. Hence the blessed apostle John bears like testimony, saying: He who says, 'I know him', but disobeys his commandments is a liar, and the truth is not in him (1 Jn.2.4). And again: No one who sins has either seen Him or known Him (ibid.3.6). And sin exists not in one class of commandments only but in both: the man who disregards orders indeed sins but the man who does not observe prohibitions sins more.[11]

3.   Sacrifices and prayers will be rejected as offerings unless the mind of the one who makes the offering is pure and holy, and a stained heart makes an unstained victim unworthy, as the Lord says: If you are offering your gift at the altar, and there remember that your brother has something against you, etc. (Mt.5.23). Obedience to the commandments is more valuable than any offering and sacrifice, as the prophet says: Behold, to obey is better than sacrifice, and to hearken than the fat of rams (1 Sam.15.22). And elsewhere: The beginning of a right way is to carry out the commandments, which are more acceptable to God than to sacrifice victims (Pr.21.2,3). And elsewhere: Whosoever maintains the law multiplies his offering. It is a wholesome sacrifice to pay attention to commands and to depart from all iniquity and to offer sacrifice in atonement for an injustice.

4.   We ought not to flatter ourselves on carrying out commandments if we sin by infringing prohibitions, since the crime of transgression takes away the

---

10 Cf. *Dem.*9,2.
11 Righteousness is again defined as a twofold requirement and sinning as disobedience to either side of it; for this Pelagian commonplace cf. also *Virg.*6,1; 7,1; 8,1; *Law*,4,1.

merit gained by a deed well done; and this is proved not by an assertion based on my own understanding of the situation but by examples from both Testaments, where we find that even God's friends lost the credit won by their deeds of generosity in the past through one error arising from negligence. Thus Adam, after enjoying intimacy and discourse with God, recklessly trusted the devil when he led him astray and, as a result, overcome by desire for one apple, lost his place in Paradise along with many good things at the same time, because he ventured to try to gain possession of one good thing by a transgression.[12] Thus Lot's wife, after her earlier obedience of the angels, looked back contrary to their prohibition and was suddenly turned into a pillar of salt. Thus Sameias, on the very same day on which he had done wonderful things by the grace bestowed on him by a prophet, was thrown down and killed by a lion. Thus Judas, unhappiest of men, after the merit which won him his selection, after the glory of the signs revealed, after winning his status as an apostle, was deceived by his desire for a paltry payment of money and ended up by being caught in a noose, though he was one to whom a seat at the judgement in heaven was promised. And lest we should suppose that it is only through fraudulent use of another's property that danger threatens us, let us recall Ananias and Sapphira, condemned not because they had tried to get possession of their people's money but because they had laid out their own in such a diffident manner.

5.   After so many proofs and so many deaths I ask you whence comes this feeling of immunity from punishment for our sin which grows within us. What is this spirit of presumption which produces such audacity in our minds that, though we see holy men being punished even for trivial faults, we come to believe that we ourselves, sinning daily as we do in matters more numerous and of much greater importance than they, yet will be subject to only a moderate degree of damnation in eternity?

5, 1.   But it is never a light matter to despise God even in small things, since he pays regard not only to the nature of a sin but to the extent to which it brings contempt upon his person; and for this reason a man must attend not only to the nature of a command but to the greatness of the one who gives it.[13] At this point we can rule out that popular point of view which leads men who are devout in their own opinion and seem to themselves to be wise to say to me, 'It is sufficient for us not to commit major, criminal sins, since it is easy to omit minor offences.' Men like this, by occupying their minds with the wisdom common to all animate

---

[12] When Pelagius is writing about sinning and needs to quote examples to prove his point, he usually starts with Adam. But his Adam, unlike Augustine's, is no different from other sinners except insofar as he was the first of them and so set them an example to follow. Pelagius agrees with Augustine that Adam's Fall was the result of his patent disobedience of the divine command but he has no theory of original sin in the Augustinian sense, and concupiscence in the sense of sexual lust passed on by one generation to another *ad infinitum* has no place in his moral theology; on the nature of Adam's disobedience cf. *Virg*.7,2; *Law*,4,4.

[13] Cf. *Dem*.16,1.

creatures, ignore the need for spiritual intelligence and familiarity with the workings of the divine law, which frequently reveals a sin which does not seem to us to be a sin at all and which discovers godliness in an action in which we seek to expose an act of ungodliness. Saul and Jeoshaphat were kings of the people of Israel and, while they showed mercy to those whom God hated, incurred God's displeasure in a work of godliness. On the other hand, Phineas and the sons of Levi won the gratitude of God for human slaughter and the murder of their own relations. Do you see how greatly divine judgement differs from human sentiments because of our ignorance, so that sometimes to us, ignorant as we are of the way in which the heavenly judge dispenses judgement, acts seem to be unjust which are proved to have been done justly and rightly enough in the light of knowledge of the reasons which prompted them?

2. Again, deeds which are approved as good by our judgement are seen as for the most part base and disagreeable before God. What man today, willing to kill his own innocent son after the example of Abraham, would not be believed to be mad by human judgement? And, on the other hand, who, touching the Ark of the Covenant as did Ozam, would be damned in the opinion of men today? The bishop of the Ephesians who is called an angel in the Apocalypse and who held fast in his conscience the merits of many sufferings endured in the cause of the name of Christ, because he had allowed the initial heat of his behaviour at the time of the sufferings themselves to cool off, is recalled to repentance, as the scripture says: I know your works and your patient endurance, and how you cannot bear evil men; but I have a few things against you, that you have abandoned the love you had at first. Remember then from what you have fallen, and repent (Rev.2.2,4–5). Let us consider how great will be the fall of one who thoughtlessly despises the commandments, when such a downfall is said to occur in the event of their neglect by one who normally obeys them, or what condemnation we believe that the irreligious will receive, when the devout man receives such a reproof. Christ does not love a lukewarm disciple: He who would be my disciple, he says, let him deny himself and take up his cross and follow me (Mt.16.24); Through many tribulations you must enter the kingdom of heaven (Acts.14.22); Blessed are you when men revile you and persecute you and utter all kinds of evil against you; rejoice and be glad, for your reward is great in heaven (Mt.5.11,12).

6, 1. The glory of the future life must be compared to the disadvantages of the present one. The banners of the cross are sources of delight for Christians; the trophies of *our* life are borne not in ceremonial parades but in times of affliction; in *our* army brave men know how to bear abuse, not military fatigues; future blessedness is promised to poverty, not nobility. Shamefacedness indeed restrains the senator from following in the footsteps of the poor man Christ but let him hear Christ's words: For whoever is ashamed of me and my words in this adulterous and sinful generation, of him will the Son of man also be ashamed in the glory of his Father with the holy angels (Mk.8.38). Among parents, senators and scholars it is regarded as unseemly that a rhetorician should be content with simple words, voluntarily humbling himself for Christ's sake: he displeases his friends if, after previously cultivating ostentatious dress, he dons common and undistinguished garments in its place. But if I were still pleasing men, says the apostle, I should not be a servant of Christ (Gal.1.10); and the prophet in the psalm: For God scatters the bones of them that please men: they are put to shame, for God has rejected them (Ps.53.5). Offence to men which enables us to find how to serve Christ is as good as friendship with them which offers offence to God is dangerous, as it is written: Whoever wishes to be a friend of this world will be made an enemy of God (Jas.4,4).

2. Let each one of us state his own choice: I therefore for my part have decided in the meantime in accordance with my own humble understanding that it is better to be put to shame in the presence of sinners on earth than in the presence of angels in heaven or wherever the Lord may wish to reveal his judgement. Isaiah, a man of most noble rank among his own people who is said to have been the father-in-law of King Hezekiah, cast off his girdle at God's command and walked naked nor was he deterred from acceding to God's command by the shame brought upon him by such a difficult instruction, because he judged that there is nothing more honourable for a man than to obey his Creator. John the Baptist too, born noble both in flesh and spirit, chose a girdle as his dress from boyhood and locusts for food, a man drawn to the glory of this burden not by consciousness of sin nor by the need of poverty but by the blessedness of the world to come. Apostles are already hoping but fools and persons of no use and little faith are still being denounced: The sufferings of this present time are not worth comparing with the future glory which will be revealed in us (Rom.8.18); hence Paul, contemplating the future in his mind's eye, said: Who shall separate us from the love of Christ? Shall tribulation, or distress, or persecution, or famine, or peril, or sword? (ibid.35). *They*, the apostles, are not separated from their faith by perils but *we* are by pleasures; *they* bear the weight of chains in innocence, *we* carry around gold in guilt; *they* lie bound in prisons, *we* lie in luxury on our couches; *they* are put in fetters, praising God with a pure heart and unblemished thoughts, *we*, perhaps in church itself, ponder over legal actions; and though the grace of the law is given and hell or the kingdom of heaven promised to all equally, yet some meditate on riches, others on virtues.[14]

3. And when it is said to all in general: You shall worship the Lord your God and him only shall you serve (Mt.4.10), while others are serving God faithfully and without ceasing in innocence, compassion, chastity, fasting, *we* choose for ourselves adulterers whom *we* want to serve. If indeed, according to the judgement of the Gospel: Every one who commits sin is a slave to sin (Jn.8.34), and if, in fact, I am a lover of money, of glory, of pride, of ambition or pomp and ceremony, while I apply all the enthusiasm of my will to them, I am unable to serve the Lord, because it is written that no man can serve two masters. You are not your own, says the apostle, for you were bought with a great price. So

---

[14] For a similar comparison between the apostles' unremitting zeal in the face of suffering and persecution and our lack of it cf. Comm.392,13–393,1.

glorify God and carry him in your body (1 Cor.6.19,20). The Holy Spirit summons us with forbearance by our own law, knowing that this is protected by public usage among all men, so that the more the servant of the Lord is compared with a piece of private property the more careful he may be in performing God's work, and so that we may understand how active in God's work those who have been redeemed by the blood of Christ ought to be and how guilty those ought to be judged who, though they know that Christ's blood was given as the price of their salvation, offer their service rather to another who has provided nothing.

4. I ask you with what sense of decency will a man hope for reward in heaven for his obedience and toil, when all his anxiety has been centred on earth. The hireling of this world cannot receive the reward of Christ. Every soldier who has toiled bravely for his fellow-citizens in battle rightly expects rations in camp. The labourer is worthy of his hire (Lk.10.7), but it is also proper that he should receive the reward for his work from the source on which he has expended all his trouble and effort: No soldier on service gets entangled in civilian pursuits, since his aim is to satisfy the one who enlisted him (2 Tim.2.4), is what the apostle says. Hence I am fearful enough lest in that day of retribution on which each and every man is repaid according to his deeds before the tribunal of Christ those who have laboured more on earthly business than on heavenly may receive this response from their just judge: 'Go, if you are able, and seek payment for your services in that quarter in which you have rendered such devoted service.' Such a case is that of the five foolish virgins in the gospel who, while they occupied themselves with anxiety for the vanities of the world contrary to the rules of the order to which they had promised themselves, not having oil with which to kindle the true light, remained in darkness.

7, 1. But someone says, 'These examples of yours refer only to the few whom God has assigned to this special duty, since it is written: Many are called but few are chosen (Mt.22.14).' Now this is the question I wish to put to you first and to hear your answer, whoever you are who advance this argument: If the choice belongs to God himself, who is also responsible for the calling, why did he want to call more when he intended to choose only a few out of the many? Surely, out of two called you want that one to hold his place whom God has appointed by choice and the other, whom God does not protect by virtue of his choice, to fall. But if this is so, on this reasoning neither good nor bad actions belong to us, and the result will be that neither does guilt bring punishment nor are good deeds praised. But the apostle replies to this: If it is so, how could God judge this world? (Rom.3.6). Secondly, if you consider to be saints only the few whom you say are chosen and you are saying that those who are called are counterfeits, then how does the same apostle Paul summon those 'called to be saints' at the beginning of his epistles, as he does at the start of his book to the Romans, saying: To all God's beloved in Rome, called to be saints (Rom.1.7)?[15] If Christ suffered for a few, it

---

[15] Another bone of contention for Pelagius and Augustine is revealed in this passage: the

would be just that only those few should keep Christ's commandments; but if all of us who believe receive the sacrament of his passion through baptism without any discrimination, if all of us equally renounce the devil and the world, if the punishment of hell is promised to all of us who do not live in righteousness, then all of us ought to pay attention to the things which are forbidden and to fulfil the things which are commanded with the same diligence.

2. We know indeed that there are many dwelling-places with the Father in heaven but we also know that there are some dwelling-places which are more righteous than others and that they differ in the extent of their righteousness, just as one star is, in the words of the apostle, brighter than another (cf. 1 Cor. 15.41).[16] But he was comparing one star with another and not with a stone, because an earthly stone could not exist among the heavenly stars, just as neither could a sinner exist among the righteous in the kingdom of heaven; yet there are certain grades of glory among the righteous in heaven, as there are also grades of punishment among the sinners. And as there will be different forms of torture for the man who calls his brother a fool[17] and the one who merely calls him silly, so too in the kingdom of heaven there will be a different grade of glory awaiting the apostle Paul, who was made all things to all men so that he might save others, and the layman who has with difficulty been able to edify himself. I wish I could agree that there *are* a few who keep the commandments of God; actually I am afraid there are only a few who truly believe even in God's judgement.

3. Look! If from a sky suddenly overcast the brightness of the sun is denied to our sight, the clouds extend to our lowly place and rain threatens the earth, if, as usually happens when the elements have been aroused, thunder is violently shaken on the wheels of its chariot and then darts of lightning gleam terribly from it as they are thrown onto our eyes, then we are struck by terror and begin to tremble all over and, lying flat on the ground, lower our necks in submission with all our pride discarded. What then shall we unhappy creatures do when the heavens are overturned and the Lord arrives all afire in the company of all the power of his angels, when the stars fall down from on high and the sun is changed to darkness and the moon to blood, when the mountains melt like wax, the earth

---

latter's theory of predestination or, as some would have it, double predestination, which was closely linked and, in some respects, indispensable to his doctrine of grace, was anathema to Pelagius and his associates, and the resistance to it by the monks of Hadrumetum and, a little later, those of southern Gaul (the Semi-Pelagians) showed that Pelagius was right to question it. It was also to become the Achilles' heel of the Augustinian doctrine of grace in the Middle Ages; see Rees, 1988, 40ff.,50,101ff., 103ff.,128.

16 This clause consisting of five Latin words is difficult to translate but the sense is clear enough, that is, that in heaven there are dwelling-places which are graded to suit different grades of righteous persons. (The mind boggles at this suggestion of a 'Pelagian's Guide to Heaven'!) Cf. *Comm.*223,5–58 (1 Cor.15.41f.).

17 The Latin word in the text here, rendered 'fool', is the same as that in Mt.5.22, *racha* or *raca*, a transliteration of the Greek word in the NT, which is usually derived from Aramaic *raqa* (= 'empty one'); but that derivation has often been challenged (see Arndt and Gingrich, 741;LSJ, s.v.).

is ablaze and rivers dry up and seas are drained and, contrary to nature, fire produces dryness on the waters with all their moisture expended by divine influence, when sinners call to the mountains, 'Fall upon us,' and to the hills, 'Cover us' (Lk.23.30; cf. Hos.10.8)? When men call for death and it will not come when called, when crises turn into prayers and men desire what they have always hated, when the time is fulfilled which Jeremiah predicts in mournful mood, saying: I looked upon the earth, and lo! there were no lights. I saw the mountains, and lo! they were trembling, and all the hills were in confusion. I looked, and lo! there was no man to be seen, and all the birds in the sky were afraid. I saw, and lo! Carmel was deserted, and all the cities were alight with fire from the face of the Lord and from the angry face of his indignation; and all things were destroyed.[18]

8, 1. But in order to prevent the devil from persuading us by suggestion to believe these words for the fear they cause in us instead of the truth which is in them, let me remind you that future events are proved by past, since such events as took place in the Flood, at Sodom and in Egypt and Jerusalem are often said to have done so because of men's sins.[19] And the apostles, fit persons to foresee this terrible day which is to come upon the ungodly and the sinners, were humble men, arousing the dead from their sleep; we especially are the ones they awaken, for we daily kill ourselves by sinning and disregarding our lamentably weak nature, which is neither strong in adversity nor really secure at any time in prosperity. If food is taken without self-restraint or drink is imbibed without moderation and they arouse a light fever in the body, we become low in spirit, we are cast down, we heave sighs; no attention is then paid to the world around us or even to our own houses, no one thinks of the needs of his family estate or business, all prosecutions, all profits are laid to rest while the body is at risk. Off to the doctor we run, and rewards, gold and silver are promised to him in return for a remedy for our ailing flesh; sometimes even property rights and almost an entire inheritance are neglected or even given away in order to receive advice on how to save a life which is destined to perish at some time or other in any case.

2. But for everlasting salvation absolutely everyone is unconcerned, everyone is a miser, and all the spiritual income we have to bestow is strictly controlled by our niggardly minds, when a readier inclination and a more abundant spirit of generosity ought to be at work. And although the scripture says: Do not love the world or the things of the world (1 Jn.2.15), we so covet the things of the world, we so love them, that it is as if there were something which we brought with us into this world or were able to take away with us on departure. No one gives a thought to the shortness of our time here or the circumstances of our nature, no one considers or re-examines the fact that all things are vanity

---

[18] I have been unable to track down this quotation per se; it seems to be a conflation of a number of passages in Jeremiah.

[19] Cf. Comm.374,7ff. (Eph.5.6).

and are brought to a close by an appointed end.[20] Yet, if it so happens that among others visiting a sick man a cleric or priest or even a lay servant of God arrives, he is asked to pray, and one who had often been despised as of no consequence is besought in time of need to obtain by his prayers leave for the invalid to enjoy a longer life. So the cause of the crisis, which is feared when close-at-hand, while former objects of contempt are chosen and hitherto expensive possessions become worthless, is that very life which is pictured as a transformation after death,[21] when the pauper Lazarus is now received into his rest and the rich man, full of pomp and show in this life, is said to be tormented in his punishment.

3. But when the Lord, either moved by the utterances of the saints or as an act of kindness to his own creature or through the doctor's skill, restores his health in his abundant mercy, forgetfulness soon follows and everything changes over to its opposite: fear is turned into arrogance, gratitude into contempt, and as if we have never experienced any trouble at all or are unable to be recalled to such a state again, we rebel, we become puffed up and we neglect the period of life given us for repentance nor do we wash away our old sins with tears of regret but instead pile up sins unrepentant. Let us read the prophet Isaiah (Is.38.4ff.) and let us seek the example of Hezekiah as being requisite and suited to this case; for to him on his deathbed fifteen years are added to his former life through his own lamentations and the prophet's prayers, and then, having received the grace of such a gift, in humility and holiness, he devoted the period of life granted to him not to sins, not to pleasures, not to delights but to the Lord alone.

9, 1. But because in your case, respected and most beloved parent,[22] all cause for tears has been wiped away by a fresh act of grace, come, beware, run, hurry! Come, that you may advance in spirituality. Beware, lest, through lack of care and caution in guarding it, you lose the good that you have received. Run, that you may not be unheeding. Hurry, so that you may the more quickly understand, seeing that Paul, when already carrying around upon himself the chain set upon him by the Lord for the announcing of the Gospel, still said that he did not yet understand (cf. Phil.3.13),[23] though about to labour in the Lord's vineyard at the sixth hour, that is, in the middle life, as if by his labours as an eager and faithful

---

[20] Cf. Dem.29,1 on the ephemeral nature of this world and our neglect of eternal salvation through pre-occupation with its cares.

[21] The text is very odd here, and my translation assumes a grammatical error introduced by the copyist.

[22] The recipient of the letter is addressed as 'parent' or 'father' here and as 'son' at the end of the next chapter. 'Son' is, of course, an accepted form of address for a spiritual adviser to employ when writing to a pupil, and one assumes that the other term refers to the recipient's standing in his own private circle, since it can hardly be parens, meaning 'believer' or 'subject'.

[23] Cel.32 and Dem.27,4 both quote Phil.3.13,14 in urging Christians to try to renew themselves in virtue daily. Pelagius is alluding to the first of these two verses here but in a slightly different context, and Dem.27 also quotes Phil.3.13,14 in that same context of the need for a sense of urgency in the Christian life, if one is to make the necessary progress; cf. too Comm.408,4f.

workman he could overcome the long-standing doubts and sluggish lukewarm-
ness of others. While we have time, let us sow in the spirit, so that we may gather
in the harvest in spiritual deeds. And let us pay no attention to the chaff, which
the winnowing-fan of Christ will straightway separate from the wheat, until the
coming of the one who is to come. And according to the prediction of the
prophet let there be a separation between the righteous and the unrighteous,
between the one who serves God and the one who does not. As the Lord also
says elsewhere: Behold, my servants shall eat, but you shall be hungry; behold,
my servants shall rejoice, but you shall be put to shame (Is.65.13).

2. But let not the day of vengeance and retribution find us idle, that day
which is proved to be imminent and near-at-hand both by the ruins that clash
together on all sides[24] and by the witness of the scriptures. Let us consider that we
are sojourners in this world and live for the last days in the manner of foreigners:
For you are not of this world, we are told (Jn.15.19). Why then are we so busy, so
agitated in a strange land? No one elects to possess more in a foreign, inferior
country than in his own. We ought to have anxiety and care only about those
things which we can take with us; let the gentiles go around seeking the things of
the earth, since those which are in heaven are not due to them; let them covet
the things of the present, who put no trust in those of the future; but let the
divinity of Christ be the riches and inheritance of Christians, for they ought not
to be vexed on the grounds that they have less from others, when they have
received the Creator of everything. It remains for them to honour with their
obedience the God whom they have taken into their hearts, to worship him with
works, to confess him always in speech and in thought, so that when he arrives,
they may not be punished along with the stiff-necked and contemptuous but be
crowned along with the saints and those who fear God.

3. This, to be sure, I can ask of a man of your good sense that you should
not suppose that I have uttered these words under the influence of some superstition: I want you to be called a Christian, not a monk, and to possess the virtue of
your own personal claim to praise rather than a foreign name which is bestowed
to no purpose by Latins on men who stay in the common crowd, whereas it is
given legitimately by the Greeks to those who lead the solitary life.[25] Receive
then, my son, this discourse of ours in the spirit of honesty and truthfulness in
which we have spoken, because we do not seek the praise of men, as God is our
witness, nor do we speak to the end that we may win human friendship, lest by

---

[24] See n.9.
[25] Jerome, Augustine and Marius Mercator, all three of them contemporaries of Pelagius,
refer to him as a 'monk' but two other contemporaries, Paul Orosius and Pope Zosimus
speak of him as a layman, and he was never ordained. It is probable that he wore a
monk's habit as a mark of his ascetic way of life but there is no evidence that he
belonged to a religious community in the proper sense of the term. This passage shows
that he would want to restrict the use of the Greek word transliterated into Latin as
monachus to solitaries and to deny it to those who, as he says, 'stay in the common
crowd' like himself; see Rees, 1988, xiv and nn.23,25,26.

our words of flattery we deceive both ourselves and others, nor that we may seem to be somebody among men, but that men may merit great rewards before God.

10, 1. As for your questions, however, because you set them out in what may, by your leave, be described as a rather rebellious manner, I was unwilling to reply to them in plain, simple words, since I could not extend the right hand of peace to a militant – though it may seem inconsistent to withdraw somewhat from that position at the end of my letter. But since it is spiritual progress that is sought for among Christians, not procedural correctness, I have formed the opinion that I should add a few points which I think you will find it essential to have, until, that is, we can discuss person to person, if you so command, and without any semblance of tension and anger, the other matters which disturb you, as they usually do. For you said, unless I am mistaken, that you are justified in returning evil for evil and are under an obligation to take an oath with those that do so, on the grounds that our Lord sometimes took an oath or repaid evil with evil. In the first place, I am well aware that not everything which is becoming to our Lord is also becoming to us, his servants; but lest we may appear to be offering an insult to the Lord by using a comparison which places him on a level with his servants, let me perhaps begin my reply to you in another fashion. Why are we born of married women, not of virgins? Or why do our dead not rise again on the third day? The Lord, who forbade us to take an oath, often did so himself, I know, but that does not mean that we ought at once to blaspheme recklessly against him for forbidding others to do what he did himself, since it can be said to us that the Lord, whom no one forbade to swear, swore as Lord, but we, as servants, may not swear, being forbidden to swear by the law of the Lord. But let us not allow his example to become a stumbling-block for us: in fact, from the time when he forbade us to swear, he did not swear himself either.

2. And just as I have been able to give you satisfaction by my brief answer on the matter of taking an oath, so too, as you can foresee, this same way of understanding the problem can easily suffice to explain the question about exacting vengeance, since the present time of grace, in which the fullness of perfection has arrived,[26] is quite different from the time of the prophets, as the Lord says: You have heard that it was said to the men of old (Mt.5.21) that they should not kill, but I give you more perfect commandments,[27] and these the reader will find set forth in order in their appointed place in the Gospel. For from

---

[26] The idea that Pelagius and his contemporaries were living in a time when, through the grace of Christ bestowed in baptism, Christ's followers were able to achieve perfection is a commonplace of Pelagian teaching and attracted the hostile attention of Pelagius' critics. Jerome attacked it in his *Commentary on Jeremiah*, and Pelagius' accusers at the Synod of Diospolis in 415 again brought up the charge of preaching 'sinlessness' which had been dismissed by the diocesan synod at Jerusalem the year before (see Rees, 1988, 7f., 93ff.). The subject will be discussed further in connexion with the Pelagian tract *On the Possibility of Not Sinning* in Part II of this book.

[27] This is rather a muddle: the sentence starts with a *bona fide* quotation from Mt.5.21 and then changes 'You shall not kill' into 'that they should not kill', finishing with an

the time when the Son of God became the Son of Man; when the old heaven of the Jewish tradition became the new; when the Lamb is eaten not metaphorically but in truth; when according to the apostle, the old has passed away, and all things have become new (2 Cor.5.17); when it was commanded to set aside the image of the earthly man and to assume the form of the heavenly – since then, having died with him, we have risen again in Christ by his goodness.

apparent citation which is not in the gospels at all – that is to say, not in these words, although it does echo the references to 'a new commandment' in Jn.13.34, 1 Jn.2.7 and 2 Jn.5.

4

On the Christian Life[1]

In volume 40 of Migne, PL this letter appears in an appendix to the writings of Augustine, in volume 50 it is ascribed to Fastidius. It makes no sense at all to attribute it to Augustine, when he himself made it abundantly clear that he regarded it as a work of Pelagius and cited a passage from it against him, just as his accusers had done at the Synod of Diospolis in 415;[2] and the attribution to Fastidius depends upon the rather casual statement of Gennadius[3] that 'he (Fastidius) wrote a book *On The Christian Life* to a certain Fatalis', supported by the fact that a copy of it with Fastidius' name substituted for Augustine's in the margin by a would-be corrector was discovered in the seventeenth century in a MS from the eleventh or twelfth century at Monte Cassino. Gennadius of Marseilles (fl.470) is, as far as I know, the only contemporary or near-contemporary writer to mention Fastidius at all. It is he who places him between Theodotus of Ancyra and Cyril of Alexandria in his register, that is, in the first half of the fifth century, and the Abbot Trithemius (1462–1516) tells us no more than that Fastidius was known to have lived under the Emperor Honorius and at the time when Theodotus was Bishop of Antioch, that is, around 420–30, though the dates of the latter's bishopric are not certain.[4] If we add that we have only Gennadius' word for Fastidius' having been 'Bishop of the Britons' and that 'Fatalis' can hardly have been the recipient of the letter *On the Christian Life*, seeing that the author of it is addressing a widow – a *femme fatale?* –, we are left wondering how it is that some scholars have succeeded in attaching a small corpus of works to Fastidius' name.[5] Those who maintain that Fastidius wrote this letter also have to reconcile its Pelagianism with Gennadius' description of Fastidius' work as 'of sound and worthy doctrine', unless we accept that Gennadius became a Pelagian sympathiser late in life.

In recent times Morin, Caspari and Kirmer have attributed the letter to

---

[1] *Liber de Vita Christiana (Christianorum)*: PL 40,1031–46;50,383–402;CPL 730.
[2] Augustine, *On the Activities of Pelagius*, vi.16ff. (PL 44,329f.); cf. Jerome, *Dialogue against the Pelagians*, iii.14,16 (PL 23,586).
[3] *On Famous Men*, 56 (PL 58,1091); cf. Nos.12 and 13, introd.
[4] For these details see the editor's cautionary preface to the treatise in PL 40,1031.
[5] See, for example, Nuvolone, 2912ff.; Plinval, 1943,46 describes Fastidius as a *fantôme indécis!*

Fastidius, Morris to 'Fastidius' but Plinval and R.F. Evans to Pelagius himself.[6] There are certainly phrases and passages in it which are Pelagian, for example, with reference to the nature of Adam's sin in the fifteenth section and the suppliant's appeal for God's mercy on the grounds of merit in the eleventh – 'Pelagius' very words!', cried Augustine.[7] The only sound objection to Pelagius' authorship is the undoubted fact that he denied it when a passage from it was cited against him at Diospolis, the one from the eleventh section just mentioned; but such a denial, as has been shown by Evans,[8] would not be entirely out of keeping with his tactful use of 'economy with the truth' on that occasion. His contemporaries certainly thought that this letter was written by him, and there are many cross-references to his Pauline Commentary in it which suggest that it was written the same time as that work – or, if not by Pelagius, was heavily dependent upon it.[9] Pelagius is a much more likely author than the mysterious 'Fastidius', and he could well have written it either in the last years of his stay in Rome or, just possibly, his first years in Palestine; it had been in circulation for some time before it was cited against him at Diospolis in 415 and again by Augustine in 417.

After a modest disclaimer of his suitability to advise others on the Christian life, Pelagius examines the meaning and significance of the word 'Christian' and the status and responsibilities which it brings for one who is so described. There follow discussions of God's forbearance and restraint in administering punishment to sinners, his pleasure at being able to reward righteous conduct, his use of punishment as a form of instruction, and the kind of behaviour to be expected from God's people, such as, for example, neighbourly love at all times, the generous giving of alms and the doing of good works. The letter ends with a statement making clear who is truly a Christian and, in the present case, the kind of Christian a widow should be. There are ninety-one quotations from the scriptures, which is about average for Pelagius.

Text

Preface: The only reason which compels me, the greatest of sinners, more foolish than other men and more ignorant than all of them, to venture to advise you in a letter of some length to follow the path of holiness and righteousness is not confidence in my own righteousness, not expertise in wisdom, not reputation for knowledge, but my personal regard for you, which so encourages and challenges me, an ignorant sinner, to speak that, though I do not know how to speak, I cannot remain silent. And so I would prefer, if given a free choice, that you

---

6   For the bibliography relevant to this debate see Evans, 1968, 18ff. and 120ff., and Nuvolone, 2912ff.
7   *On the Activities of Pelagius*, vi.17.
8   1962, 1964.
9   See Evans, 1968, 36ff. for some notable parallels.

should gain your knowledge from those whose wisdom is richer, whose eloquence is greater than mine, whose knowledge is more abundant and whose conscience is freer from all infection by sin, so that they might properly instruct you by word and example. For, apart from the fact that the thick fog of folly and ignorance has so blinded our mind that it is incapable of feeling or saying anything divinely inspired, the realization of all our sins above all else prevails upon us to believe that this fog might conceal even any light that our mind could possibly possess; thus it comes about that, besides not having anything to say, we cannot offer with any confidence even what we have, if our conscience prevents us. However, until you can find someone better and more experienced, you must be content in the meantime with our rough-and-ready suggestions and make allowance for our affection for you, the function of which is not to examine carefully what it offers nor to seek what it does not have but gladly to impart all that it does have; and you must regard not so much the outward appearance of the service which we are offering as the intention of our mind, and note carefully what that intention has been able to deny you even when it has wanted to give you all that it possessed. It would have offered even what it did not possess if it could, but has been able to offer only all that it does. Thus the man who cannot be content in the meantime with water from a stream running down past him, until he can reach a more abundant, purer spring, is thirsty but not very thirsty; nor do I believe that the man who continues to wait for loaves that are fresh and white, though he has loaves of ordinary bread available, is really hungry enough. So you too, my most beloved sister, who, I am sure, hunger and thirst greatly for heavenly things, must in the meantime eat loaves of ordinary bread until you can find loaves made of white wheat, and drink from a little, muddy stream until you can drain the purer water of a more copious one. And let not the bread we offer be displeasing to you in the meantime, however coarse it may seem to you, for coarse bread may seem to be more uncultivated but it is also more robust, more quickly satisfies the hungry stomach and gives more strength to the weary than bread which is made of fine wheat and has a more refined appearance. So now I shall deliver my discourse to the best of my ability, and I shall explain as well as I can what is fitting for a Christian to do; nor can I discover a more appropriate beginning for this subject or a better point from which to start than by discussing the word 'Christian' itself and by explaining why someone is called 'a Christian'.

1, 1. No one among the wise and faithful does not know that *Christus* is translated as 'anointed'. But it is clear that only holy men and men sufficiently worthy of God have always been anointed nor have they been other than prophets or priests or kings. And so great was the mystery of this anointing itself that not all but only a very few were deemed worthy to receive it among the Jewish people, and this until the arrival of our Lord Jesus Christ, whom God has anointed with the oil of gladness – that is, with the Holy Spirit – above his fellows (Ps.45.7). From that time those who believe and are cleansed by the sanctification of his baptism – not some only, as had previously been the case under the law, but all – are anointed among the prophets and priests and kings.

And by the example of that anointing we are advised as to what sort of men we ought to be, so that in the case of those whose anointing is so holy their behaviour may be no less holy. For it is from the sacrament of this anointing both of Christ and of all Christians, that is, all who believe in Christ, that the designation and the name are derived, a name which he who by no means imitates Christ in vain tries to acquire: for what does it profit you to be called what you are not and to appropriate to yourself a name which belongs to others? But if it pleases you to be a Christian, then perform the works of Christ and adopt the name of Christian deservedly.

2. Or perhaps you want not to be a Christian but just to be called one? This is quite dishonourable and worthless, that you should want to be called what you are not; for no one transfers his allegiance to Christ in such a way that he is called a Christian without being one. He who is called a Christian openly declares that he has Christ as his Lord, and he truly has him only if he obeys and serves him in all respects; if not, then he is not a servant of Christ but a mocker and a scoffer who claims that he is the servant of one whom he merely pretends to serve. Hence a double judgement is reserved for him, both on account of his mockery of God, whom he has called Lord without due cause, and on account of the nature of his sin.

2, 1. But the long-suffering of a merciful God allows most of those who are unbelieving, shameless and treacherous to continue undisturbed in their sin, and so they suppose that God does not take vengeance for sin, merely because he does not wish to punish sinners immediately. Wretched and ungrateful creatures, careless of their own salvation, in that they even attribute to God the postponement of their destruction, not realizing that they are being saved by God for a double reason, both in order that by his long-suffering he may continue to make the human race the object of his concern and that he may not be judged impatient in wanting to condemn sinners! For were he not patient, the stock of the human race would have come to an end long ago, nor would we find sinners turning into righteous men if God were willing to punish sinners out of hand. For we know and have read of some who, before our time, deceived by their blind ignorance or through treachery or the fickleness of adolescence, were held in bondage to manifold sins of different kinds and yet were converted from their error later by the most merciful patience of a sustaining God and went on to perform works of righteousness even greater than the sins which they had previously committed.

2. God does not remit the penalty for sin but only delays its punishment nor does he free the persistent sinner from death but waits patiently, so that he may be converted, though late, and live, as the blessed apostle Peter says: The Lord is not slow about his promises but is forbearing on your account, not wishing that any should perish but that all should be converted to repentance (2 Pet.3.9).[10] Good, kind and merciful as he is, he does not strike you at once,

---

[10] Cf. Comm.20,8–16; 19,25–20,3 for the patience of God.

wanting you to recognize how great is his mercy and goodness towards you and preferring to await the repentance of the sinner and the ungodly and thus save a sinner when converted rather than punish him while still in sin: as the Lord himself says through the prophet, disclosing by the kindliness of his own utterance how much mercy and goodness he wishes to bestow on man: And if a wicked man turns away from all his sins which he has committed and keeps all my statutes and does what is lawful and right and merciful, he shall live and not die; all the transgressions which he has committed shall be forgotten; for the righteousness which he has done he shall live (Ezek.18.21,22). And: Have I any wish for the death of the unjust, says the Lord Adonai, and not rather that he should turn away from his evil way and I should make him to live (ibid.23)? And elsewhere: The wickedness of the wicked shall not harm him when he turns away from his wickedness (Ezek.23.12). And again: Turn, my sons that turn, and I will heal your contrition (Jer.3.22).

3. Behold how God warns you and challenges you to turn from your sins even late and thus to be able to be saved! Behold how he encourages the man already marked down for death to live instead, how gently, how mercifully he invites him not to deny our Father's goodness even to sinners, and how he still calls his sons those who have lost God their Father through sinning, just as he himself also bears witness with a tearful voice and an unhappy lament in another passage that he has lost sinners, saying: I have become without sons, I have lost my people on account of their sins (cf. Jer.15.7)! From this then know how God loves you, since he prefers you to live rather than to perish. And do you shun and despise him who loves you more than you love yourself? I do not wish for the death of sinners, says the Lord, but that they should turn and live (Ezek.18.32). You wanted to die through sinning, he wants you to live by turning. Foolish, irreverent, ungrateful man, that you do not agree with God even when he wants to pity you, when he prefers you to be saved by his goodness than to perish on account of your sin!

3, 1. Therefore let no one flatter himself, let no one deceive himself by foolish and vain distrust, let no one sin heedlessly and without restraint, since the wrath and judgement of God do not descend on the sinner at once, and so, when he is not at once destroyed, he forms the opinion that he has sinned with impunity; but let him realize this, that God delays rather than dissembles, that his wrath, though late, will come upon sinners suddenly and unexpectedly, as it is written: Do not say, 'I have sinned, and what harm happened to me?' For the Highest is patient in making his repayment (Sir.5.4). And elsewhere: Be not slow to turn to the Lord nor put off from day to day; for his wrath will come suddenly (ibid.7).[11] This warning is fulfilled in the case of most of those on whom, for their excessive sin, the wrath of God both descends in the present and is reserved for the future. But no one understands this, no one realizes it, nor does each man, when he receives adversity, reckon that it is being afflicted on him for his own

[11] Cf. *Comm*.19,22–25; 20,3–7 on the same subject.

evil deeds but thinks that what he has endured is a matter of everyday usage rather than the result of his crime.[12] And God does not seem to be punishing sinners in the present, because men do not realize when he is punishing them; for there are many whom no one notices but who are judged even now in the present before the day of judgement. Or would anyone claim that he has been able to see even in the present time a man living to a great age who is sacrilegious, bloodthirsty, greedy, a forger, murderer, thief, cheat, adulterer or guilty of other crimes? For we see examples of very many men which give us sufficient proof that the wicked and ungodly, when the end of their sins has been finally reached, are judged even in the present time and are denied their present no less than their future life.

2. But this can be more easily understood by the man who has at different times witnessed the demise of different judges as they conduct themselves in an ungodly and villainous manner; the higher their power the greater their audacity in sinning, since it believes that it is permitted to do everything which it is able to do, and so, not fearing another's judgement, they rush headlong into sin when judging others. Thus it happens that those who do not fear man's judgement when committing sin become aware of the fact that God is their judge and avenger. Others of them who had frequently shed the blood of guiltless souls were so conscious of the wrath and judgement of God that they themselves, having gladly shed another's blood, were afterwards constrained to shed their own. Others too who had perpetrated similar deeds, were so laid low by the wrath of God that they lay unburied and became food for the beasts of heaven. Others again who had unjustly exterminated a countless multitude of men were torn apart limb from limb and piece by piece, so that the number of their divided members was no smaller than the number of those whom they had punished and whom they had caused to be killed. And by their judgement many women were made widows when their husbands were unjustly put to death, many were left orphans by the killing of their fathers and, in addition to losing their parents, were reduced to beggary and nakedness, since they added to their impiety and cruelty what was so far missing by also despoiling the children of those whom they had caused to be put to death;[13] but now their own wives are widows, and their sons are orphans and daily seek their bread from others.

3. Does it not seem to you that that testimony of God uttered as a threat has been fulfilled in their case: You shall not afflict the widow and orphans; but if you do afflict them, and they cry out to me, I will hear their cry and will be angry at heart, and I will kill you with the sword, and your wives will become widows, and your children fatherless (Ex.22.22-24)? What an intolerable crime! What a villainous deed! What an excess of unbearable cruelty! Two most savage and atrocious crimes are being perpetrated at one and the same time: murder is

---

12 Cf. *Comm.*194,3-5 (1 Cor. 11.31) on the ignorance of those who fail to understand how God's judgement operates.
13 The sentence 'for. . . death' has been included here but the editor of PL 50 is probably right when he brackets it.

committed, so that plunder may follow it; husbands are killed, fathers too are killed, so that widows and orphans may be more easily robbed; and each one of these judges rejoices with the others in another's death as if he himself were not to die at some time. Therefore God is stirred with good cause by acts of cruelty and impiety of this kind; with good cause he reveals his judgement even before time in the case of certain men; with good cause such men are granted life neither in the present nor in the future. And by their example we are warned not to suppose that the wicked and impious can escape God's judgement even in the present.

4. Thus it is fitting for us to become more aware of this fact, that any individual is sustained by God's long-suffering only so long as he has not yet finally reached the limit and end of his sins; when that has been fulfilled, he is struck down at once nor is any indulgence reserved for him any longer.

4. It is made clear by the testimony of God himself that the limit and due measure of sins is fixed.[14] And the fact that each and every man, as he completes the allotted number of his sins, is judged either more quickly or more slowly, is most clearly shown when God speaks to Abraham of the destruction and burning of Sodom and Gomorrha's people, when they had now fulfilled the number of their sins, saying: The outcry against the people of Sodom and Gomorrha is complete, and their great sins are fully complete (Gen.18.20). And what does he say of the Amorites, who had not completed their sinning, who, as is well known, were destroyed many years after the aforementioned cities were burnt to the ground? The sins of the Amorites, he says, are not complete up to the present (Gen.15.16). By this example we are most clearly instructed and taught that each is allowed to complete his full number of sins and is sustained only so long as he has not done so, in order that he may turn and change. Let no one, I say, delude and deceive himself: God does not love the wicked, he does not love sinners, he does not love the unrighteous, the greedy, the cruel, the impious; but the good, the righteous, the pious, the humble, the guiltless, the gentle he does love, as it is written: For thou art not a God who delights in wickedness; the evil man shall not sojourn with thee nor shall the unrighteous stand before thy eyes. Thou hatest all evildoers, thou wilt destroy all who speak lies (Ps.5.4–6).[15]

5. 'But,' says someone, 'why is it that we see the good also dying along with the evil?' They are not dying but rather escaping, being set free from association with the evil and persecution at their hands and translated to a place of rest. To be sure, the ones who die and also pass away are those whom the punishment and the penalty of a greater judgement still await when they depart this world. The good are summoned before their time in order that they may no longer be

---

[14] Cf. Comm.76, 20–22 on the measure of sins granted to each individual: the people of Sodom and Gomorrha and the Amorites are referred to in both passages.

[15] For resemblances in phraseology cf. Comm.102,11 (Rom.13.4): 'Because God does not love the wicked but hates all evildoers.'

afflicted by hurtful men, but the evil and the unrighteous are taken away in order that they may no longer persecute the good. The righteous are called to their rest from oppression, tribulation and distress, the ungodly, on the other hand, are seized and carried off from luxury, wealth and pleasure to undergo their punishment. The former go to judge, the latter to be judged; the former to be avenged, the latter to have vengeance visited upon them,[16] as it is written: But the righteous man, though he die early, will be in a place of consolation (Wis.4.7). And again: While living among sinners, he was taken up (ibid.10). And again: For his soul was pleasing to God; therefore he took him quickly from the midst of wickedness (ibid.14). And again: While the journey of the unrighteous is to death, they (the righteous) are at peace (Wis.3.3). You see then that for the righteous and the worshippers of God this release from the body is rest, not punishment, and when they are released, they are set free rather than die. So the faithful are not afraid of release itself but rather desire and long for it to come, since they realize that through it rest, not punishment, is offered to them. But the unrighteous and the ungodly and all those who are conscious of their own crimes are rightly afraid of it because of their natural foresight, which makes them aware of being judged. Wherefore, when this account has been given and accepted, we ought not to sin at all, especially as we are not ignorant of the fact that judgement is both exacted of sinners in the present and reserved for them in the future.

6, 1. And let us not flatter ourselves merely on possessing the name and being *called* Christians but let us also believe that we are to be judged if we vainly claim for ourselves a name which belongs to others or if someone is so unbelieving, so unfaithful, so stubborn, so obstinate, so bold that he does not fear the anger and displeasure of God our Judge which is bound to come sometime, or is not put to shame by the habitual practice of men, or does not see how insensitive, how stupid, how foolish he is judged to be even by the very gentiles, if his vanity and madness are so great that he acquires for himself a name which belongs to others. For who is so vain and wretched as to dare to declare himself to be an advocate, when he is illiterate? Who is so mad and senseless as to declare himself to be a soldier, when he does not know how to wield arms? No one is assigned any name whatever without due cause: to be called a cobbler it is necessary to produce shoes; it is his skill in a craft that causes a man to be called an artificer or craftsman; for a man to be called a business man he sells at a higher price what he has bought more cheaply. For it is by examples of this kind that we recognize that there is no name without an act but that every name comes from an act.

2. How can you then be called a Christian, if there is no Christian act in you? Christian is the name for righteousness, goodness, integrity, forbearance, chastity, prudence, humility, kindness, blamelessness, godliness. How can you defend and appropriate that name, when not even a few of these many qualities abide in you? He is a Christian who is one not only in name but in deed, who

---

[16] Cf. *Comm.*467,4–6 (Col.3.13) for a similar use of the verb and noun in juxtaposition.

imitates and follows Christ in everything, who is holy, guiltless, undefiled, un-stained, in whose breast malice has no place, in whose breast only godliness and goodness reside, who does not know how to hurt or harm anyone but only how to help everyone. He is a Christian who does not know how to hate even his enemies but rather to do good to his adversaries and pray for his persecutors and enemies, following Christ's example; for anyone who is ready to hurt and harm someone else lies when he declares that he is a Christian. The Christian is one who is able to make the following claim with justification: I have harmed no man, I have lived righteously with all.

7.   But lest anyone think or believe that I am merely expressing my own personal opinion or suppose that he can afford to dismiss it lightly, because one speaks in accordance with one's own inclination rather than with the authority of the law, I shall now begin to offer examples of that law itself, both old and new, by whose precepts the entrance to life is opened up for us, and to show what God has commanded the human race to observe from the beginning of the foundation of the world and in what respects he has always been pleased or offended. For I maintain[17] that after Adam, who was the first man fashioned by God and of whose case there is no need to speak at present, there were twin brothers, Cain and Abel, at the beginning of the world, of whom the one pleased God, because he was blameless and righteous, but the other was not able to please God, because he was unrighteous and culpable. Next, with the passage of time, the scripture describes Enoch as having been sufficiently righteous and as one upon whom his righteousness bestowed so much that he knew not present death but was even snatched up from the midst of all mortal men in an unparalleled manner to gain immortality; and by his example it is shown that one righteous man is dearer to God than a very great number of sinners. Noah too was a righteous man, and we know what the merit of his righteousness brought for him, namely, that life was granted to him alone along with his family, after the whole world had been condemned by means of the Flood. Scripture bears witness to what Abraham gained by the merit of his faith and righteousness, in

---

[17] There follows a sequence of OT figures – Abel, Enoch, Noah, Abraham and Lot – which is almost identical with a similar sequence in *Dem.*5, except that that passage includes Melchisedek, Joseph and Job as well. The purposes of the two series are also different; see Evans, 1968, 35f., where he aptly notes the use of the word *iustus* ('righteous') in a comprehensive sense to cover obedience to *all* divine commandments without exception. In this way Pelagius seemed to his critics to be suggesting that some of the characters in the OT were able to achieve sinlessness before the coming of Christ and so by virtue of their own natural goodness; see Rees, 1988, 7f., 93ff. on the charge of teaching 'sinlessness' which was levelled against Pelagius, e.g., at the Synod of Diospolis in 415 (Augustine, *On the Activities of Pelagius*,vi.16) and, even earlier, in Jerome, *Dialogue against the Pelagians*,Pref.1 (PL 23,495ff.), and *Letters*,133,3 (PL 22,1152). Pelagius' main line of defence lay in arguing that, although it could not be proved that anyone had actually achieved sinlessness and had maintained it up to the end of his days, in theory it must be possible to do so; otherwise, Jesus would never have said in the Sermon on the Mount, 'Be ye therefore perfect . . .' (Mt.5.48).

that he alone at that time on the earth was God's friend, being the only man who had been found to be righteous. Again, what else was it but the merit of righteousness that enabled Lot to be set free from the fire, when all the rest of the people of Sodom perished? It would take a long time for us to go through the individual examples and review the merits of all concerned.

8,   1. As for the Jewish people, whom, being out of the seed of Abraham, God desired at first to belong to him above the other races, it is right and proper that we should know how he taught them and what he commanded them to do and what to observe. In the first place, his action in making them migrate to Egypt, when the region in which he had wanted them always to live had become derelict and their fatherland a desert, was in my view not without a good reason and by God's providence. And I think that the reason was this, that God, desiring to educate the people whom he had chosen as his own in works of mercy, godliness and righteousness as well as in the other good works, wished them to become strangers and captives in a foreign country, so that they might learn the misery of the condition of a captive in a strange land and of the toil accompanying it and thus find it easier thereafter to pity those who toil in a strange land, having themselves learned beforehand the sorrows involved in a state of alienage.[18] For no one would be so ready to pity the stranger and alien as one who knew the results of alienage, and no one brings in a stranger without a roof over his head to his own lodging as readily as does one who has himself previously stood in need of another's hospitality. No one is so ready to feed the hungry and give the thirsty drink as one who has suffered hunger and thirst; no one so readily clothes the naked in his own garments as one who has known the harm done to a man by nakedness and cold; no one so readily goes to the help of the man who is oppressed and wretched and in distress as one who has experienced the misfortunes of oppression and wretchedness and distress.
   2. Therefore it was with good reason that God, the master of mercy and godliness, who was later to issue a law by which to transmit to his people precepts governing mercy and godliness and all good works, wished them first to undergo all kinds of oppression and affliction and want in a foreign land, so that they might thereafter be able to pity those who suffer such things and to obey his commandments. As you would consider that man to have been a good farmer who, before casting the seed, spends a long time taming the soil with ploughs and rakes, in order that the seed which he is about to entrust to it may not be lost, so too God softens and tames his people long before he imparts to them the redeeming seed of his commandments. Finally, so that it may become more clear and manifest that they endured this lot for this reason, let us examine the commandments of the Lord himself, when he says: You shall not vex a stranger or oppress him, for you too were strangers in the land of Egypt (Ex.22.21). And again we read: The great God who is not partial and takes not rewards, executing

---

[18] One wonders what Pelagius would have made of the problem of the West Bank today!

judgement for the stranger, the fatherless and the widow. Love to give bread and clothing; for you too were in the land of Egypt (Dt.10.17–19).

3. And elsewhere he says: But if you have reaped the harvest in your field, and have forgotten a sheaf, you shall not go back to fetch it; it shall be for the sojourner, the fatherless, and the widow, that God may bless you in all the works of your hands: and you shall remember that you were a slave in the land of Egypt; therefore I give you this word as a command (Dt.24.19,22). From this it is easily perceived and discerned that it was for this reason that that people has been afflicted with all kinds of misery, namely, that they might be taught by their own example to pity another, as it is written: For through such works thou hast taught thy people that the righteous must be kind also (Wis.12.19). It is well known far and wide, I think, what sort of people he wishes his to be, and it is proved by numerous examples by what works they can win merit.

4. But lest it seem that what we have said is too little to make his will clear, let us add to it the precepts of the law and the prophets, and let us establish by the evidence of the old as well as the new law what pleases and has always pleased God and what he has commanded frequently to be done and observed: You shall love the Lord your God with all your heart, and with all your soul, and with all your mind, and with all your might (Dt.6.5), and: You shall love your neighbour as yourself (Lev.19.18). That the commandment of the law and the prophets is pre-eminent is established by the testimony of our Lord and Saviour, when he says: On these two commandments depend all the law and the prophets (Mt.22.40). And this fact cannot be rescinded or altered, that the whole instruction of the law as well as the prophets consists of those two commandments and that he who has been able to fulfil these has fulfilled the law, for there is nothing else required in the old law but that you should love God and your neighbour. And that man is truly a fulfiller and doer of the law who sins neither against God nor against his neighbour.

9, 1. But I ought not in the least to pass over and conceal what it means to love God and one's neighbour. He loves God who obeys his commandments in everything; he loves God who keeps his laws and precepts; he loves God who makes himself also holy just as God is holy, as it is written: You shall be holy; for I the Lord your God am also holy (Lev.19.2); he loves God who fulfils also that word of the prophet, when he says: You that love the Lord hate evil (Ps.97.10); he loves God who thinks only of heavenly and divine things, for God is a lover of holiness and righteousness and godliness only; and he loves God who performs no other deed than that which God is seen to love. For the teaching of our Lord and Saviour makes clear what it means to love God, when he says: He who hears my words and does them, he it is who loves me (Jn.14.21).

2. If therefore he loves God who does what God commands, then he who does not do it does not love God. On the contrary, everyone who does not love hates, and from this it is clear and manifest that God is hated by those who do not keep his commandments, of whom I think that the prophet was thinking when he said: Do I not hate them that hate thee, O Lord? and do I not loathe

them that rise up against thee? I hate them with perfect hatred; I count them my enemies (Ps.139.21,22). The righteous prophet hates sinners, adulterers and unrighteous men and those who scorn God's commandments, as he says in another place: I have looked with disgust at those who violate the covenant (Ps.119.158). And again: I hate unjust men but I love thy law (ibid.113). See then how righteous, how virtuous we ought to be who, besides not being permitted to behave badly ourselves, are not permitted to know those who do behave badly either! This the blessed apostle also makes abundantly clear by commanding that we must not even break bread with sinners, saying: If any one who bears the name of brother among you is guilty of immorality or greed, or is an idolater, reviler, drunkard, or robber – not even to eat with such a one (1 Cor.5.11).

3. God wanted his people to be holy and averse to all contamination by unrighteousness and iniquity. He wanted it to be such, so righteous, so godly, so pure, so unspotted, so sincere that the gentiles might find nothing in it which they could criticise but only what they could admire and say: Blessed is the nation whose God is the Lord and the people whom he has chosen as his heritage (Ps.33.12). It is fitting that the worshippers and servants of God should be such people – merciful, serious, prudent, godly, without reproach, untouched, unspotted – that whoever sees them is amazed and marvels at them and says, 'Truly these are men of God whose conduct is such.' A man of God ought to present himself and to act in such a way that there is no one who does not want to see him, who does not desire to hear him, no one who, having seen him, does not believe that he is a son of God, so that the word of the prophet may be fulfilled in him: His speech is so sweet, and he is altogether desirable (Song 5.16).[19] For if the Christian presents himself as such, if the servant of God shows himself as such, that he is made an equal in his behaviour of those who are enslaved to demons and idols, then through him God will begin to be blasphemed and they will begin to say, 'What a servant of God the Christian is, whose acts are so evil, whose works are so base, whose conduct is so bad, whose life is so ungodly, so rascally, so voluptuous, so despicable!' And he will be guilty under this prophecy: For the name of God is blasphemed among the Gentiles through you (Rom.2.24; cf. Is.52.5).[20] But woe unto those through whom the name of God is blasphemed! For God desires and requires of us nothing more than that through our acts his name may be magnified by all, as it is written: Offer to God the sacrifice of praise (Ps.50.14); for this is the sacrifice which God seeks and loves above all sacrificial victims, namely, that through the works of our righteousness his name should be everywhere praised and that he should be confirmed as the true God by the acts and works of his servants. Those truly love God who employ themselves in nothing but that through which his name may be glorified.

[19] Cf. the similar reference in the same general context in Comm.264,10f. (2 Cor.6.6).
[20] Evans, 1968, 99f. has a very interesting note on the use of the quotation from Isaiah here and in Comm.25,18ff.

10, 1. We have stated to the best of our ability how God ought to be loved; now, however, let us explain as well as we can what it means to love one's neighbour as oneself, though a statement of the topic itself is briefly presented in another passage, when it is said: What you do not wish to be done to you, do not to another (Tob. 4.15). Our Lord and Saviour also says: Whatever you wish that men would do to you, do so to them likewise (Mt.7.12); for there is no one who desires evil to be done to him by another. So he loves his neighbour as himself who wishes no evil to be done to him, because he does not wish it to be done to himself either; but he readily bestows on him anything good, just as he himself desires to get and obtain it from all, because the Christian is required not only to be free of evil but also to do good. For the man who, even if he has done no evil, does no good either is nevertheless not admitted to the prize of eternal life but is delivered up to the fires of hell, as we read that the Lord has said in the gospel about those who do no evil nor yet work any good; Depart from me, you cursed, into the eternal fire which my Father has prepared for the devil and his angels; for I was hungry and you gave me no food, I was thirsty and you gave me no drink, I was a stranger and you did not welcome me, naked and you did not clothe me, sick and you did not visit me, in prison and you did not come to me (Mt.25.41–43).[21] They are condemned, not because they have done evil but because they have not done good; for from this any prudent and wise man would recognize what hope those who are involved in evil deeds can have, when life is denied even to those who have done no evil, unless they have also done some good. For it is not only this that God asks of us, that we should not be evil, but also that we should be made good, since it is from their evil works that the evil are so called, and in the same way too, on the other hand, the good are named from their good works.

2. And there are two masters whom the good and evil respectively are seen to serve: the good God whom all serve who conduct themselves well, and, on the other hand, the evil devil of whom everyone who does evil is the servant. For it is demanded of us not only that we cease to be servants of the devil by not living badly but also that we be seen to serve God by living well. I do not know whose servant he is who is seen to be doing neither evil nor good, or how he can hope for everlasting life from God, if he has not earned it by good deeds. Let no one, I say, deceive and cheat himself by taking a personal view of the matter, let no one mislead himself by listening to idle opinion: whoever has not been good has not life; whoever has not performed works of righteousness and mercy cannot reign with Christ; whoever has not been kind, godly, hospitable, generous, merciful shall not escape hell's fire. God does not love the evil, he does not love sinners; whoever does evil is God's enemy; whoever is not without guile can have no part with Christ. For nothing more is asked of a Christian, nothing is more greatly desired of him, and nothing is more to be striven for with all his strength than that he should shut out ill will from his heart, than that he should not admit evil into the conscience that is in his breast, than that he should hold on to goodness,

[21] Cf. Comm.319,14ff. (Gal.3.10); 373,19–374,3 (Eph.5.5).

maintain righteousness and guard the purity of his mind. Be blameless, if you wish to live with God; be guileless, if you wish to reign with Christ. What does malice profit you, if it draws you along to death? what does evil, if it prevents you from reigning with Christ, if it destroys the man who possesses it? As it is written: An evil soul will destroy him who has it (Sir.6.4). If you wish to live, hear what the prophet says; if you love Christ's kingdom, hear how you may become worthy to gain it: What man, he says, is there who wishes to have life and desires to see good days? Keep your tongue from evil and your lips from speaking deceit. Depart from evil, and do good; seek peace, and pursue it (Ps.34.12–14). For God honours and loves the kind of men who do not know evil, who do not know how to lie, whose lips do not speak deceit, in whom only goodness and purity are seen.

3. Blamelessness is what commends us to God, guilelessness is what causes us to reign with Christ. It is made clear by many testimonies how God loves only the blameless and wishes them to be joined to him, as it is written in the psalms: The blameless and upright have clung to me (Ps.25.21). And elsewhere this commandment is uttered: Guard blamelessness and behold uprightness, for there is posterity for the man of peace (Ps.37.37). How much blamelessness bestows and confers on a man, even if it is observed late in life, is proved by the witness of the prophet David, who, though he had grievously sinned before, does not fear to be judged once he begins to know blamelessness, as he himself says: Judge me, God, for I have walked in my integrity (Ps.26.1). He knew therefore that he did not have to fear judgement any longer, because he had come to know blamelessness even late in life. And he says in another place: But thou hast upheld me because of my integrity (Ps.41.12). God upheld thereafter on account of his blamelessness one whom he had formerly rejected on account of his evil deeds. Indeed it is clear that the blameless are not confounded before God, when it is said: For as long as the blameless keep righteousness, they shall not be confounded (Pr.13.6). For nothing is worthier of God, nothing can be more dear to him, than that blamelessness should be maintained with all possible circumspection; though a man may appear devoted in his other works, if he has not blamelessness, it is in vain that he flatters himself on his devotion. If the Jews were enjoined to observe it, even when they continued to live under the old law and it was still allowed to them to hate an enemy, what is it fitting for you to do now as a Christian, when you are commanded to love your enemy? For when will you not be blameless or to whom will you be able to be evil, when you are commanded to be good to your enemies? But do you perhaps hate your neighbour also, when you are not allowed to hate even your enemy, and do you persecute your brother, when you are instructed to love your enemy, and do you believe that you are a Christian, when you keep the commandments neither of the New nor of the Old Testament?

4. And lest you should consider yourself a Christian without due reason and flatter yourself on possessing the name only, hear the apostle telling you what sort of person you must be: Let the thief no longer steal, but rather let him labour, doing honest work with his hands, so that he may be able to give to those in need. Let no evil talk come out of your mouths, but only such as is good for

edifying, that it may impart grace to those who hear. And do not grieve the Holy Spirit of God, in whom you were sealed for the day of redemption. Let all bitterness and wrath and anger and clamour and slander be put away from you, with all malice, and be kind to one another, tender-hearted, forgiving one another, as God too in Christ forgave you (Eph.4.28–32). And: Therefore be imitators of God, as beloved children. And walk in love, as Christ also loved us and gave himself up for us, a fragrant offering and sacrifice to God. But fornication and all impurity and covetousness must not even be named among you, as is fitting for saints, or filthiness, or silly talk, or levity, which is not fitting, but instead let there be thanksgiving. Be sure of this, that no fornicator or impure man or one that is covetous, that is, an idolater, will have any inheritance in the kingdom of Christ and of God (Eph.5.1–5). Let that man deservedly judge himself to be a Christian who keeps these commandments, who is holy, humble chaste and righteous, who spends his life in works of mercy and righteousness.

11, 1.   Do you consider him a Christian in whom there is no Christian act, in whom there is no righteous conduct, but evil, ungodliness and crime? Do you consider him a Christian who oppresses the wretched, who burdens the poor, who covets others' property, who makes several poor so that he may make himself rich, who rejoices in unjust gains, who feeds on others' tears, who enriches himself by the death of the wretched, whose mouth is constantly being defiled by lies, whose lips speak nothing but unworthy, foul, wicked and base words, who, when ordered to distribute his own possessions, seizes others' instead? And a man of this kind has the audacity to go to church and thoughtlessly and inappropriately stretches out his impious hands, stained as they are with illicit plunder and the blood of innocents, and from that defiled and profane mouth with which a little before he has been uttering either false or base words pours forth his prayers to the Lord as if conscious of no evil in himself. What are you doing, you shameless wretch? Why do you burden yourself with a greater load of sins? Why do you inflict on God an injury on top of your contempt? Why, as if to provoke his wrath more speedily and as evidence of the penalty which you deserve, do you hold out to God wicked hands for which he has no regard, having commanded that only holy and spotless hands be shown to him? Why do you put your requests to God with that very mouth with which a little before you have been speaking evil, the prayers of which, however multiplied, he abhors, as it is written: When you spread forth your hands, I will hide my face from you; and even though you make many prayers, I will not listen; for your hands are full of blood. Wash yourselves; make yourselves clean; remove your wicked deeds from your minds (Is.1.15,16).

2.   He who stretches out and offers his hands to God ought to be aware and certain of himself and confident of his blamelessness, since the apostle says: I desire then that in every place the men should pray, lifting pure hands (1 Tim.2.8). But he deservedly raises his hands, he pours forth his prayers with a good conscience, who is able to say, 'You know, Lord, how holy, how blameless, how free of all deceit and injury and plunder are the hands which I stretch out to you, how righteous, how unspotted and how free from all lying the lips with which I pour forth my prayers to you to ask you for your pity.' For such a man deserves to be heard speedily and, before he can pour forth his prayers in their entirety, is able to obtain the request which he is making.

3. For I know that there are those whom the deep fog of evil and greed has so blinded that, when it has turned out so successfully for them that they have been able to fasten their bonds on a poor man by means of their power over him or to overwhelm an innocent man with false witness or to overcome a weak man with their strength or commit theft or plunder, they give thanks to God, with whose help they believe that they have perpetrated such crimes, and judge God to be so unjust that they think him to have been their partner in crime.

12.   Fools and wretches are blinded by their iniquities to such an extent that they fail to understand that God cannot possibly be pleased with what he forbids and act as if one crime were not enough, unless another is also added to it by continuing to hold a wrong perception of God. Others again think that they are justified by making a small payment of alms from the property of the poor and by dispensing a very small bounty to one individual out of the amount which they have stolen from very many. One gets his food from money the loss of which makes several hungry, and from the spoils taken from many a mere handful are given a roof over their heads. These are not the sort of alms that God asks for nor does he desire one man to be treated to a show of conscientiousness at the expense of the cruelty shown to another; it is better for you not to give alms at all than to cause a great number to be despoiled of money from which you put a roof over the heads of a few, and to strip several of their clothes so as to clothe one. The alms of which God approves are those which are supplied as a result of righteous labours, as it is written: Honour God from your righteous labours and offer him a part of the fruits of your righteousness (Pr.3.9), for he abhors and rejects what is offered as a result of others' tears. For what does it benefit you, if one individual blesses you for a gift taken from something which causes many to curse you? Or what gain is bestowed on you by alms provided from another's property? Truly one has cause to fear that God does not have the wherewithal to feed his poor, unless you plunder another's goods.

13, 1.   Others again I have known whom their dark ignorance of their own folly and imprudence so cheats and deceives that they form the opinion that the faith which they pretend to have will profit them before God without works of righteousness; and through this kind of mistake they commit wicked crimes without fear of the consequences, believing that God is the avenger not of crimes but only of faithlessness. And they are not only content that they themselves should have perished in this way but they also strive to entangle in their snares those who do not possess the light of divine knowledge, and the saying of our Saviour is fulfilled in them when he says: If a blind man leads a blind man, both will fall into a pit (Mt.15.14). For if it is not crime but only faithlessness that is condemned, then we sin freely and without fear of punishment, and God has

given us his commandments of righteousness without reason, if faith alone and
without work of righteousness profits us. We cannot know the source from which
this error of ignorance, so ungodly, so wicked and so treacherous, crept in, unless
perchance it was from those who misled the people by misusing an example from
the old law and delivered them over with themselves to eternal death and
everlasting annihilation; and of them it is written: Do not listen to the words of
the prophets who prophesy to you, since they themselves are vain and speak
visions of their own minds and not from the mouth of the Lord. For they say to
those who reject the words of the Lord, 'It shall be well with you'; and to every
one who walks in his own will, to every one who walks in the error of his own
heart, 'No evil shall come upon you' (Jer.23.16,17).

2. We had indeed many testimonies, yes, testimonies taken from the whole
law, by which we were able to destroy and bury such a pernicious error; but so as
not to weary the reader for too long, let a few examples suffice out of very many,
and let the man who takes this to be the meaning of the law answer these
questions. Adam was created as the first man at the first foundation of the world;
was he condemned because of faithlessness or sin? I find that there was no
disbelief in him but only disobedience, which was the reason why he was condemned and why all are condemned for following his example.[22] Cain too was
condemned not by reason of faithlessness but because he had slain his brother.
Why say more? I read that the reason why this whole world perished in the Flood
was not faithlessness but crimes. I find no reason to blame disbelief for the
burning of Sodom and Gomorrha in a sudden fire but rather I attribute it to their
sins and crimes, as scripture most plainly shows when it says: The men of Sodom
were wicked and great sinners in the sight of God (Gen.13.13). Was it not their
sin that was responsible for the fact that the Jewish people were so often seen to
perish and be reproved?

3. But someone says, 'I do not accept the testimonies of the old law by
themselves, unless you offer me examples from the New Testament also.' Take
Ananias and Sapphira then, whom apostolic opinion condemned not for the
crime of faithlessness but because of theft and lies. Perhaps you are about to say
to me, 'Why then does the apostle say: For we hold that a man is justified by faith
apart from works of law (Rom.3.28).' I read that the very one who says this also
condemned a man in his absence, because he took his father's wife. The scripture
must be understood in the way that is seen to be acceptable by those who have
knowledge in all such matters and to be a matter of dispute only for those by
whom it is not at all understood. The apostle says that a man is justified by faith
apart from works of law, but not apart from those works of which I hear another
apostle say: Faith apart from works is barren (Jas.2.20). For the apostle Paul spoke
of the works of law, that is, of the circumcision of the flesh and the new moon
and the sabbath and other matters of this kind which the law had ordered to be

---

[22] I know of no more explicit refutation in Pelagius of Augustine's doctrine on the Fall
and Original Sin than this: Adam was condemned for disobedience and so are we ever
after for our imitation of his example.

done formerly but which were no longer necessary in the time of Christ; but the other speaks of the works of righteousness, meaning that he who has not done these is without life, though he may pretend that he has faith.[23]

4. But someone quotes the following saying of the apostle: For man believes with his heart and so is justified, and he confesses with his lips and so is saved (Rom.10.10). Foolish man! This is fulfilled at the time of baptism, when only confession and faith are desired of a man to enable him be baptized. For what does the washing of baptism profit us, if faith alone is sought without works? The faith of all holds that sins are washed away by baptism; but if there is to be sinning thereafter, what does it profit us to have washed it away? Listen to what the Lord says to a man once he has been made well: See, you are well! Sin no more, that nothing worse befall you (Jn.5.14). This the blessed apostle Peter also teaches most clearly, that a worse fate awaits the man who sins after he has come to know the way of righteousness, when he says: For if, after they have escaped the defilements of the world through the knowledge of our Lord and Saviour Jesus Christ, they are again entangled in them and overpowered, the last state has become worse for them than the first. For it would have been better for them never to have known the way of righteousness than after knowing it to turn back from the holy commandment delivered to them. For it has happened to them according to the true proverb, 'The dog turns back to his own vomit, and the sow is washed only to wallow in the mire' (2 Pet.2.20–22). This is also the teaching of the blessed apostle Paul when he says that the man who reverts to his former sin after receiving the sanctification of baptism is not saved without great repentance, saying: For it is impossible to restore again to repentance those who have once been enlightened, who have also tasted the heavenly gift, and have become partakers of the Holy Spirit, and have tasted the goodness of the word of God and the powers of the age to come, if they then commit apostasy, since they crucify the Son of God on their own account and hold him up to contempt (Heb.6.4–6).

5. The evangelist bears witness that a certain man came to the Saviour and asked what he should do to attain eternal life and that the Lord answered him thus: If you would have life, keep the commandments (Mt.19.17). He did not say, 'Keep faith alone.' For if faith alone is required, it is superfluous to order the commandments to be kept. But far be it from me to suggest that my Lord has given a commandment which is superfluous; yet this is what those who have now been made sons of destruction for their sins are saying, and this is what they take to be their sole comfort, namely, that they have been able to deliver others to everlasting death along with themselves. For if God does not punish the sinner, what becomes of that saying of the prophet: If the righteous man is scarcely saved, where will the impious and sinner appear (1 Pet.4.18; cf. Pr.11.31)? And elsewhere: For sinners shall perish (Ps.37.20); and again: Let sinners and the

---

[23] Cf. *Comm.*34,9ff.; 32,4ff. on the meaning of justification by faith and the correct understanding of Rom.3.28; on Pelagius' use of the phrase *sola fides* see Rees, 1988,77, citing Evans, 1968, 113 in n.99.

unrighteous be consumed from the earth, that they be no more (Ps.104.35); and again: As smoke is driven away, so drive them away; as wax melts before fire, so let sinners perish before the face of God (ibid.68.2). It is not the disbeliever and the faithless man that I hear condemned here as much as sinners.

6. And I read that our Saviour said in a certain passage: Not every one who says to me, Lord, Lord, shall enter the kingdom of heaven, but they who do the will of my Father who is in heaven (Mt.7.21). Without doubt those who called him Lord believed in Christ; but it is not for this reason – that they confess with their lips him whom they deny by their deeds – that the gate of the heavenly kingdom is opened to them. The apostle has also said that God is denied by deeds no less than by words: They profess to know God, but they deny him by their deeds (Ti.1.16). And in the gospel the Lord says: On that day many will say to me, 'Lord, Lord, did we not cast out demons in your name, and do many mighty works in your name?' And I will declare to them, 'I never knew you; depart from me, all you evildoers' (Mt.7.22,23).[24] They are said to have believed to the extent that they also performed good works in the name of the Lord, but their faith alone will not profit them, because they have not done works of righteousness. So, if faith only profits, why are those who are judged not for their faithfulness but for having done nothing that is good delivered along with Satan's angels to the fires of hell for ever, as it is written: And the King will say to those at his left hand, 'Depart from me, you cursed, into the eternal fire prepared for the devil and his angels; for I was hungry and you gave me no food' (Mt.25.41,42). Surely he did not say to them, 'Because you did not believe in me'; hence it is possible to understand that they are to be damned not because of unbelief but on account of their lack of good works.

14, 1. Let no one therefore deceive another or mislead him: unless a man has been righteous, he has not life; unless a man has kept Christ's commandments in all things, he cannot share with him; unless a man has despised worldly things, he shall not receive those which are divine; unless he has spurned human things, he cannot gain possession of those which are heavenly; and let no man judge himself to be Christian, unless he is one who both follows the teaching of Christ and imitates his example. Do you consider a man to be a Christian by whose bread no hungry man is ever filled, by whose drink no thirsty man is refreshed, whose table no one knows, beneath whose roof neither stranger nor traveller comes at any time, with whose clothes no naked man is covered, by whose help no poor man is sustained, whose good deed no one experiences, whose mercy no one knows, who imitates the good in no respect but rather mocks and insults them and does not cease to persecute the poor? Let such a thought be far from the minds of all Christians, let it be impossible that one who is such a man should be called a son of God.

---

[24] Cf. Comm.212,10 (1 Cor.14.37); 202,18 (1 Cor.13.2); see Evans, 1968, 129, nn.14,15 for additional comment.

2. *He* is a Christian who follows the way of Christ, who imitates Christ in all things, as it is written: He who says he abides in him ought to walk in the same way in which he walked (1 Jn.2.6). *He* is a Christian who shows compassion to all, who is not at all provoked by wrong done to him, who does not allow the poor to be oppressed in his presence, who helps the wretched, who succours the needy, who mourns with the mourners, who feels another's pain as if it were his own, who is moved to tears by the tears of others, whose house is common to all, whose door is closed to no one, whose table no poor man does not know, whose food is offered to all, whose goodness all know and at whose hands no one experiences injury, who serves God day and night, who ponders and meditates upon his commandments unceasingly, who is made poor in the eyes of the world so that he may become rich before God, who is held to be without fame among men so that he may appear renowned before God and his angels, who is seen to have no feigning or pretence in his heart, whose soul is open and unspotted, whose conscience is faithful and pure, whose whole mind is on God, whose whole hope is in Christ, who desires heavenly things rather than earthly, who spurns human possessions so that he may be able to possess those that are divine. Listen then to what is said to those who love this world and take pride and pleasure in the present time: Do you not know that friendship with this world is enmity with God? And whoever wishes to be a friend of this world makes himself an enemy of God (Jas.4.4).

15, 1. In these words, most dear sister, I have explained to you to the best of my ability what it is proper that a Christian should do. If, then, all without exception who are called Christians ought to be such persons, it is now the task of your prudence to assess what kind of widow you should show yourself to be, you who must be an example to all who conduct themselves aright. And I believe that you are not unaware that there are three kinds of widow. The one who is most perfect, destined for heavenly reward, is the one who, in the manner of that widow in the gospel, serves God in prayer and fasting night and day;[25] and the second, because she is said to have charge of children and a household, does not merit so great a reward but yet is not bound by sins; but the third is engaged in feasting and pleasure and is therefore reserved for everlasting death and punishment, as it is written: Honour widows who are real widows (1 Tim.5.3). First, then, come those who are also said to be *real* widows and are ordered to be honoured by so great a priest, that is, Timothy. Second are those to whom no honour is ordered to be given to them to possess, but to whom life is not denied; of whom it is said: But if any have children or grandchildren, let them first learn their religious duty to their own family and make due return to their parents (ibid.4). But those who make up the third class are the ones of whom it is written: Whereas the widow who is self-indulgent is dead even while she lives (ibid.6).

---

25 Cf. *Comm.* 494,25–494, 3 (1 Tim.5.5); in his commentary on the verse Pelagius names the 'widow in the gospel' as Anna, daughter of Phanuel, of the tribe of Asher.

2. Again, the apostle tells us what kind of a woman the widow of Christ ought to be: She who is a real widow has set her hope on the Lord and continues in prayers night and day (ibid.5). Nor do I want you to overlook the fact that when the apostle specifically mentions *real* widows, he shows that there are false ones also, that is, in deed, in mind, in conduct, if not in body; and elsewhere the same apostle describes the deeds and conduct of the real, chosen widow, when he says: Let a widow be enrolled if she is well attested for good deeds, if she has brought up children (which is understood as 'for God'),[26] if she has shown hospitality, if she has washed the feet of saints, if she has relieved the afflicted, if she has devoted herself to doing good in every way (ibid.9,10). This is the one he adjudged to be a *real* widow whose works are such as he describes. But how can a woman claim that she is a widow of Christ, if she has done no such thing at any time? Yet there are some who are rich, noble and powerful to whom perhaps it seems unbecoming either to educate their sons for God instead of for the world or to give hospitality to a stranger or to wash the tiresome, dirty and unkempt feet of saints and to touch them with their delicate, white hands. But neither will they be worthy in the future time to be the companions of saints whom they have so despised in the present, nor will they be able to share with Christ, whom they refused to sustain, the soles of whose feet they shrank from touching with their hands, since whosoever rejects his servants rejects Christ, as he himself says: He who rejects you rejects me (Lk.10.16). Mary had an abundance of tears with which to wash the feet of Christ but women of our time lack even the water to wash the feet of strangers.

3. So, most holy and prudent woman, do not imitate widows of the kind that feel ashamed to do good to others, though they have been bold enough in the doing of evil, who are disconcerted by the good life, though they are not disconcerted by sin, and who have offered themselves for death of their own free choice and do not return to life when invited to do so, who fear the laughter, mockery and gossip of men more than the judgement of God and find it dearer to their hearts to please wretched men than to please Christ. But be the kind of widow that God has ordered you to be, that the apostle commands you to show yourself to Christ; be a holy, humble and peaceable widow, and perform without ceasing works of compassion and righteousness. And whoever abuses you, who-

---

[26] Cf. *Comm.* 495, 1f. (1 Tim.5.10); in both instances the Latin word for 'has brought up' – *educavit* – is glossed in the same way but the verb used for 'understood' is different, which has led some scholars, e.g., Kirmer,26ff., to argue that this provides grounds for rejecting Pelagius' authorship of the treatise: 'People will want to use these parallel passages to support the thesis that Pelagius has composed both works. We think that this passage proves the opposite.' Needless to say, Evans strongly opposes this statement but he has to admit that this is the only time the Latin word used in this passage for 'is understood' – *subintelligitur* – is found in Pelagius' writings, the usual word being *subauditur*. But there is no reason why Pelagius should not use *subintelligo*: it was not a rare word at this time, and Ambrosiaster, Tertullian and Augustine all used it, as did Gregory the Great (see Evans, 1968,40 and 125, nn.21–25).

ever derides and mocks you, may you seek to please only God and do only the
works of Christ! Before all else, meditate on the commandments of your Lord
without ceasing, devote yourself earnestly to prayers and psalms, so that, if it is
possible, no one may discover you at any time otherwise engaged than in reading
and prayer. And when you have become such a person, remember us who love
you so much that we bestow on you in our absence what we are unable to bestow
by our presence.

5

To Celantia[1]

This minor treatise takes the form of a letter, written to a married lady of noble birth, on the subject of the way to live a godly life with special reference to the obligations of a Christian wife. Beginning with an exhortation to read and study the scriptures, it goes on to warn against pride in high birth and to insist that true nobility is by no means confined to the circles of the wealthy; on the contrary, riches may prove to be a handicap unless the responsibilities which they bring are understood and carried out. A great part of the letter is thus concerned with practical advice on how to conduct the household economy, how to behave to other members of the household, how to dress in a becoming manner and how to make suitable arrangements for prayer and personal devotions in the midst of the noise and bustle of a housewife's life. Towards the end special reference is made to a wife's obligations to her husband and, in this connexion, to Celantia's decision, taken some time ago but subsequently reversed, to abstain from sexual intercourse with her husband and that without mutual consent. The letter ends with the customary Pelagian warning against complacency: the pursuit of righteousness calls for the exercise of eternal vigilance and unremitting attention but it leads to rich rewards at the end of the road.

The question of the authorship of this letter has attracted even more than the usual amount of speculation expected in connexion with this group of Pelagian works. At first, it was attributed to Jerome – in 'seven of the ten manuscripts';[2] but two of these MSS give no ascription or title, and one (twelfth-century) has *apocipha* (sic) written in the margin by a later hand. Towards the end of the twelfth century the Abbot Guigo rejected it as a work of Jerome on stylistic grounds, and no one has assigned it to the latter since the time of Erasmus; he thought that Paulinus of Nola might be the author but Vallarsi suggested Sulpicius Severus on stylistic and other grounds.[3] More recently, Plinval has had no hesitation in attributing the letter to Pelagius, and other, more cautious scholars tend nowadays to agree with him: Evans endorses Kirmer's discussion of

---

[1] *Epistula ad Celantiam [matronam]*; PL 22,1204–29; 61,723–36; CSEL 29,436–59; 56,329–56; CPL 745.
[2] Evans, 1968,22.
[3] See his note (c) on PL 22,1204.

the many similarities between this letter and Pelagian teaching in general and, in particular, in the *Letter to Demetrias*, favouring a date for its composition c.414, that is, in the same period as the latter.[4] Once again there is a plethora of biblical quotations, seventy-eight in all, many of them also to be found in the Demetrias letter.

Text

1.   There is an old, well-known maxim in the scriptures to the effect that there is a shame in which glory and favour are found and that there is a shame again which is wont to bring sin (Sir.4.21). Though its own clarity makes its meaning apparent to everyone, I have come to understand its truth still better in the present case. For, having been challenged to write by your letters, which demanded this of me with their unusually strong entreaties, I long hesitated, I confess, before replying, my modesty urging me to stay silent; but this attitude was very strongly resisted by the persistent and forceful canvass of your prayers. The suppliant's humility fought keenly with my own hesitation and beat upon the gates of my mouth with the kind of violence that faith possesses in quantity, and when conflicting thoughts held my mind in the balance as it nodded in either direction in this manner, shame, that is, modesty, almost succeeded in shutting out duty. But that maxim of the sage quoted above armed me to drive away unprofitable modesty and to resolve this harmful silence, since I saw that the reason for writing was surely so honourable and so holy in itself that I quite believed that it would be a sin to hold my peace, reflecting within myself upon that word of scripture: A time to keep silence, and a time to speak (Ec.3.7); and again: And do not refrain from speaking at the time of salvation (Sir.4.23); and that saying of the blessed Peter: Always prepared to make a defence to any one who calls you to account (1 Pet.3.15).

2.   For you ask – and you ask in a manner which reveals both anxiety and caution – that we prescribe for you a fixed rule derived from holy scripture according to which you may direct the course of your life, in order that, by knowing the Lord's will, though surrounded by the world's esteem and the delights of wealth, you may yet come to prefer to possess moral resources and may be able, by holding firmly to your place in marriage, not only to please your husband but also him who allowed marriage itself. Not to satisfy a request so holy and a desire so pious – what else would that be but to refuse to take pleasure in observing another's progress? Therefore I shall obey your prayers and shall strive to encourage you, already prepared as you are to fulfil God's will, by the use of his own judgements. For the true Lord and master of all is the same one who

---

4   Plinval, 1934, 14ff.; Evans,1968,21f. The editor of PLS 1 (1103) also favours Pelagius, as does Nuvolone,2900.

commands us to please him and also teaches us how we may be able to do so. And so let *him* instruct you, let *him* teach you *himself* who, when the young man in the gospel asked him what he should do to merit eternal life, straightway set forth his divine commands, showing us that we must do the will of him from whom we also hope to receive rewards. That is why he bears witness in another passage: Not every one who says to me, 'Lord, Lord,' shall enter the kingdom of heaven; but he who does the will of my Father who is in heaven shall enter the kingdom of heaven (Mt.7.21). By this it is made manifestly clear that we do not merit a reward of such magnitude solely by confessing God, unless works of faith and righteousness are added.[5]

3.   For what kind of confession is it that combines belief in God with disregard of his commandment? Do we say, 'Lord, Lord,' either sincerely or truly, if we despise the commands of him whom we confess as God? That is why he himself says in the Gospel; But why do you call me, 'Lord, Lord,' and not do what I say (Lk.6.46)? And again: This people honours me with their lips, but their heart is far from me (Mt.15.8). And again he speaks through the prophet: A son honours his father, and a servant will fear his master. And if I am a father, where is my honour? And if I am a master, where is my fear (Mal.1.6). From which it is apparent that the Lord is neither honoured nor feared by those who do not carry out his commandments. And to David, who had committed a crime, it is said more explicitly: And you have despised God (2 Sam.12.9); and to Eli the Lord's utterance is: He that honours me I will honour, but those who despise me shall be brought to nothing (1 Sam.2.30).

4.   And are we of an untroubled and cheerful mind, we who with each single sin dishonour God, our most merciful and gentle Lord, and by provoking him to anger and spurning his command at the height of our pride, proceed to offend a majesty so great? For what can ever seem so proud, what so ungrateful, as to live contrary to the will of him from whom you have received life itself, as to despise the commandments of him who commands something in order that he may have good reason to reward it? For our God is not in need of our obedience but we *are* in need of his command: His commands are more to be desired than gold, even much fine gold, sweeter also than honey and the honeycomb, since in keeping them there is great reward (Ps.19.9–11). And the reason why he is angry with us, the reason why that divine immensity, that divine benevolence, is so deeply offended is that we show our contempt for it by accepting the loss of a prize so great: we reckon as nothing not only his commands but also his promises. Often therefore, nay, at all times we must turn over in our minds that judgement of the Lord: If you would enter life, keep the commandments (Mt.19.17); for this is the business which the whole law is conducting with us, this is the lesson which the prophets and apostles teach, this is what is demanded of us by both the

---

[5] For an extended discussion of the importance of works of righteousness see *Life*,13 with n.23.

voice and the blood of Christ, who for that reason died for all, that those who live might live no longer for themselves but for him who died for them (2 Cor.5.15). But to live for him means nothing else than to keep his commandments, which he entrusted to us to keep as a sure pledge of his love. If you love me, he said, keep my commandments (Jn.14.15), and: He who has my commandments and keeps them, he it is who loves me; and again: If a man loves me, he will keep my word, and my Father will love him, and we will come to him and make our home with him. He who does not love me does not keep my words (ibid.21,23,24). True love possesses great strength, and he who is perfectly loved claims for himself the entire will of the one who loves him, and there is nothing more demanding than love. If we truly love Christ, if we remember that we have been redeemed by his blood, there is nothing which we ought to be wishing for more, nothing at all that we ought to be more concerned to do, than what we know to be his will.

5.   There are, however, two kinds of commandments, which embrace the whole of righteousness: one is prohibitive, the other is jussive; for as evil deeds are forbidden, so good deeds are enjoined.[6] Under the former head hatred is commanded, under the latter zeal; by the former the mind is curbed, by the latter spurred on; under the former it is blameworthy to have acted, in the latter not to have acted. Hence the prophet says: What man is there who desires life and covets many days, that he may enjoy good? Keep your tongue from evil, and your lips from speaking deceit. Depart from evil, and do good (Ps.34.12–14). And the blessed apostle: Hate what is evil, hold fast to what is good (Rom.12.9). And so this twofold and contrary commandment, that is, prohibitive and imperative, has been imposed on all with equal force of law; the virgin, the widow, the wife are not exempt from this law: in any vocation whatever, in any station whatever, it is an equal sin either to commit deeds which are prohibited or to fail to do deeds which are commanded.[7] Do not let yourself be misled by the error of those who choose of their own volition what commandments of God above all to disdain or what to disregard as small and trivial and do not fear that, according to divine judgement, by despising small things, they will fail little by little (Sir.19.1).[8]

6.   It is indeed the way of the Stoics to dispense with differentiation between sins and to punish all transgressions alike, making no distinction between sin and error. But we, though we believe that there is a great difference between one sin and another, because that is what we read, yet say that it is quite helpful

---

6   Cf. *Dem*.9 for the doctrine of the twofold nature of commandments but applied to individuals in different circumstances.

7   For this definition of the twofold commandment and its application to all women of whatever status without exception cf. *Dem*.10,1 and 15.

8   Cf. *Dem*.16,1 for the inability of Christians to pick and choose which commandments to obey or disobey. In translating the Latin verb *contemnant* as 'disdain' I have followed the text given in CSEL 56 but it does seem to me that 'carry out' from the alternative reading *faciant* would give a better sense.

as a matter of precaution to fear even the smallest sins as if they were the greatest. For we abstain so much the more easily from any trangression whatsoever the more we fear its consequences, and the man who fears even small offences does not quickly proceed to commit the greater.[9] And I do not know, to be sure, whether we can describe as a trivial sin anything which is committed to the contempt of God; that man is the most prudent who bears in mind not so much *what* has been commanded as *who* has commanded it, and considers not the size of the command but the authority of the one who gives it.[10]

7.   And so, building as you are a spiritual home not on shallow sand but on solid rock, see to it first and foremost that you lay down foundations of blameless integrity on which you may be able the more easily to erect a high roof of righteousness. For the man who has harmed no one has fulfilled for the most part his obligations in the matter of righteousness, and blessed is he who can say with the saintly Job: I have harmed no man: I have lived righteously with all (cf. Job 27.6). Hence he said boldly and frankly to the Lord: Who will be judged with me (Job 13.19)? That is to say, 'Who can plead for your judgement against me, so that he can prove that he has been harmed by me?' It is a mark of a very clear conscience to be able to recite with an easy mind with the prophet the words: I walked with integrity of heart within my house (Ps.101.2). Hence he says the same elsewhere: God will not cheat out of good things those who walk uprightly (Ps.84.11). And so let the Christian soul drive away from itself all malice, hatred and envy, which are the greatest or even the sole seeds of harm; let it guard its innocence not by hand or tongue only but also in its heart; let it fear to do harm not by deed only but in wish also. For as far as the reckoning of sin is concerned, he who has planned to do harm has also done it. Many of our writers define an innocent man fully and correctly as one who harms no one even in a matter which ceases to benefit him. If this is true, you may rejoice in the blamelessness of your conscience only if you do not cease to help when you can; but if these two things are kept separate and distinct from each other and it is thought to be one thing not to harm because you are always able to do so but another to confer benefit when you can, one thing not to do evil and another to do good, then allow this thought to suggest itself to your mind again, namely, that it is not enough for a Christian to fulfil one function of righteousness when he is enjoined to fulfil both.

8.   Neither ought we to pay any attention to the examples of the crowd, which, following no moral discipline and observing no ordered way of life, is not so much led by reason as borne along by a violent impulse. Nor should we imitate those who lead a pagan life under a Christian name, bearing witness to one thing

---

[9]   This discussion of the relative weight given to different sins reminds one of the charge brought against Pelagius of teaching the Stoic doctrine of the equality of sins; see Rees, 1988,8 and 94 with the references in n.51, one of them to this passage, another to Virg.7,1 and the third to *Confession of Faith*,16.

[10] Cf. Virg.6.

by profession and another by conduct; as the apostle says: They profess to know God, but they deny him by their deeds (Ti.1.16).[11] Both faith and life ought also to distinguish between Christian and pagan and to reveal a different religion by different works. Do not, says the apostle, be mismated with unbelievers. For what partnership have righteousness and iniquity? Or what fellowship has light with darkness? What accord has Christ with Belial? Or what has a believer in common with an unbeliever? What agreement has the temple of God with idols (2 Cor.6.14–16)?

9.   Between us and them, then, let there be the greatest possible separation; let there be a fixed distinction between error and truth; let those who do not possess promises of heaven be content to understand the things of earth; let those who know not the things that are eternal involve themselves wholly in this brief life; let those who believe that they are immune from punishment for sins not fear to sin; let those who hope not for future rewards for virtue remain slaves of their vices. We, however, who confess with unconditional faith that every man must appear before the tribunal of Christ, so that each one may receive good or evil, according to what he has done in the body (2 Cor.5.10), we ought to be far removed from vices: And those who belong to Christ Jesus have crucified the flesh with its passions and desires (Gal.5.24). And let not those who confess themselves disciples of the truth follow in the footsteps of the erring crowd.

10.   The Saviour shows in the gospel that there are indeed two ways to conduct oneself and separate roads in life leading in different directions: 'How wide,' he says, 'is the way that leads to death, and those who enter by it are many,' and again, 'How narrow is the gate that leads to life, and those who find it are few' (Mt.7.13,14). See how great is the separation between these ways[12] and how great a distinction! The former leads to death, the latter to life; the former is crowded and trodden down by many, the latter is found with difficulty by a few; the former, sloping downwards, rendered softer by habitual vices and made attractive by the flowers of pleasure, easily draws to itself a multitude of travellers, the latter, made gloomier and rougher with its unaccustomed path of virtue, is chosen only by those who value not so much the charm of the route as the amenities offered by the place of lodging waiting at the end. The way of virtue has been made rough and unpleasant for us by earlier over-indulgence in the habit of vice; but if this is given another direction, it will find the smooth paths of righteousness (cf. Pr.2.20). Let us then make this the plan of our life, and let us learn from the evidence of our conscience which is the way along which we should walk in preference to all others. For everything that we do, everything that we say, is concerned either with the broad or with the narrow way. If we discover with a few the narrow way and the path which has, as it were, been

11 Cf. *Life*,1.
12 Cf. a shorter passage which agrees with this passage (to the end of the section) at many points in *Dem*.10.

cleared of obstructions, we move in the direction of life; but if, on the other hand, we follow the route taken by the many, according to the Lord's judgement we go to our death.

11.   If then we are possessed by hatred and envy, if we give way to greed and avarice, if we prefer the rewards of the present to those of the future, we walk along the broad way; for we have the multitude as our companions in seeking these rewards and we are surrounded on all sides by columns of people like ourselves. If we wish to satisfy our lust for anger to the full, if we wish to avenge insult, if we return curse for curse, if we keep a hostile mind against our enemy, we are borne along step by step with the majority. If we are either flattered ourselves or gladly listen to a flatterer, if we do not devote our attention to the truth and fear more to offend other men's minds than not to speak our own, we are likewise of the way of the many and have as many comrades as there are strangers to the truth. But, on the contrary, if we become strangers to all these vices, if we display a mind that is pure and free and treads all desire underfoot, and if we aim to be rich in virtue alone, then we press forward along the narrow way. For that way of life, which is the one you have chosen, belongs to few, and it is very rare and difficult to find suitable companions for the journey. Indeed, there are many who pretend that they are going by this way but by a variety of wrong turnings return to the way of the crowd, and it is for that reason that we have to fear that those whom we believe to be our leaders along the right way may turn out to be our companions in error instead.

12.   If, therefore, examples are found to lead us by this way to life and to keep to the right path of the gospel, they must be followed; but if they are either lacking or thought to be lacking, there is a pattern laid down for all by the apostles. God's chosen vessel[13] cries out to us and, as if calling us together to this narrow way, says: Be imitators of me, as I am of Christ (1 Cor.11.1). Surely the example of our Lord himself – and this is more important for all of us – shines out when he says in the gospel: Come to me, all who labour and are heavy laden, and I will give you rest. Take my yoke upon you, and learn from me; for I am gentle and lowly in heart (Mt.11.28,29). If it is dangerous to imitate those about whom you have reservations as to whether they should be imitated, surely it is safest to imitate him, and follow in the footsteps of him who said: I am the way, the truth and the life (Jn.14.6). For imitation which follows the truth never goes astray. Hence the saintly John says also: He who says he abides in Christ ought to walk in the same way in which he walked (1 Jn.2.6). The blessed Peter said: Christ suffered for us, leaving you an example, that you should follow in his steps. He committed no sin; no guile was found on his lips. When he was reviled, he did not revile in turn; when he suffered, he did not threaten; but he trusted to him

---

[13] Pelagius' favourite name for Paul, which originated in Acts 9,15 as a Greek translation of a Hebraistic expression (= 'chosen instrument'); see Arndt and Gingrich,242.

who judges unjustly (sic).[14] He himself bore our sins in his body on the tree, that we might die to sin and live to righteousness (1 Pet.2.21–24).

13.   Let us cease making excuses for our errors, let us desist from the shameful practice of trying to extenuate our misdeeds. It is no use at all trying to defend ourselves by citing precedents derived from the behaviour of the crowd and by making a habit of reckoning up the vices of others for our own consolation and maintaining that we lack people whom we ought to follow. We are despatched to seek the example of him whom we all confess that we must imitate. And for that reason let it be your special concern to know the divine law which enables us to think that we see the examples of the saints as if they were present now and to learn from its advice what has to be done and what has to be avoided. For the greatest aid to righteousness is to stock you mind with divine utterances and always to be pondering in your heart what you want to put into practice. When the people were still in a primitive state and men were unaccustomed to obedience, the Lord commanded them through Moses that, as a reminder to help them to recollect the Lord's commands, they should have borders at the extremities of their garments and should mark them with a flock of wool of the colour of hyacinth, so that, when glances are cast around here and there even casually, the recollection of the heavenly commands may spring to mind. But it is on the matter of these borders that the Pharisees are reproached by the Lord because they have begun to wear them in a perverse way not as an earnest reminder of God's commands but for their own self-display, presumably in order that they may be adjudged to be holy by the people for the diligence they show by demanding a greater degree of observance of the law.

14.   But in your case, keeping the precepts not of the letter but of the spirit, you must cultivate spiritually the memory of the divine commandments and should not so much recall God's precepts frequently as ponder them always. So let the divine scriptures be always in your hands and perpetually turned over in your mind. Nor should you suppose that it is enough to hold God's commandments in your memory, while forgetting them in your works; but become thoroughly acquainted with them, so that you may do what you have learned must be done. For it is not the hearers of the law who are righteous before God, but the doers of the law who will be justified (Rom.2.13). The law extends over a broad and vast field, which feeds and revives the mind of the reader with rare delights, blooming with various testimonies to the truth as if with heavenly blossoms. To be always recognizing all these witnesses and to be turning them over within yourself is a tremendous help in upholding righteousness; but for a brief passage which acts as an admonitory reminder you should pick out and inscribe over your heart that sentence of the gospel which is offered to us from the Lord's mouth as

---

[14] The Vulgate reading is *iniuste* but the Greek NT has the Greek word for 'justly' and modern English – and Welsh – translators follow suit.

an epitome of all righteousness: Whatever you wish that men would do to you, do so to them also; and, to express the full force of this precept, he adds the statement: For this is the law and the prophets (Mt.7.12).[15] For the kinds and categories of righteousness are infinite, and it is most difficult not only to take them down with the pen but also to grasp them in the thought; but *he* embraces all of them in one brief sentence and either acquits or condemns the hidden consciences of men by the secret judgement of the mind.[16]

15. With every act, therefore, with every word, even with every thought let this sentence be re-examined, since, like a mirror ready and always to hand, it reveals the nature of your will and also either exposes the wrong in the case of an unrighteous deed or shows cause for rejoicing in the case of a righteous one.[17] For whenever you have the kind of attitude to another that you wish another to maintain towards you, then you are keeping to the way of righteousness; but whenever you are the kind of person to another that you want no one to be to you, you have abandoned the way of righteousness. See how arduous, how difficult is this whole business of keeping the divine law! See what it is that makes us protest against the Lord for giving us hard commands and say that we are being overwhelmed either by the difficulty or by the impracticability of these commands! Nor does it suffice that we do not carry out the commands without also pronouncing the one who gives them unfair, while we complain that the author of righteousness himself has laid upon us instructions which are not only difficult and arduous but even quite impossible.[18] Whatever you wish, he says, that men would do to you, do so to them also. He wants love between us to be joined and fastened together by mutual acts of kindness, and all men to be united to one another by reciprocal love, so that, while each one provides for the other what all want provided for themselves, total righteousness, as in this command-ment of God, may be the common benefit of mankind. And – oh, the wonder of God's mercy! Oh, the ineffability of God's kindness! – he promises us a reward if we love each other, that is, if we give to each other those things of which each one of us has need in return. But we, with proud and also ungrateful spirit, resist his will, when even his command is an act of kindness.

16, 1. Never at any time run someone else down simply because you wish to gain credit for yourself by your disparagement of others, but learn rather to embellish your own life than to revile another's. And always be mindful of the saying of the scripture: Do not love disparagement, lest you be utterly destroyed

---

[15] For the same quotation referring to the meaning of righteousness cf. *Dem.*9,2.

[16] For an extended treatment of the internal judgements of conscience see *Dem.*4.

[17] Cf. *Dem.*23,2, also employing the mirror image and exhibiting a general and structural similarity, even if the content is not the same, the reference in one case being to a specific text, in the other to scripture reading in general.

[18] Cf. *Dem.*16, also depicting the way in which we complain at the severity of the law of God and using many identical phrases.

(Pr.20.13,LXX).[19] There are very few who renounce this vice, and rarely will you find a man who wishes to show his own life to be so far above criticism that he does not cheerfully set about criticising another's. And so great is the passion for this evil which has taken possession of men's minds that even those who have left other vices far behind them fall into this one as if it were the devil's last trap for them. But you must avoid this evil in such a way that you not only do not indulge in disparagement yourself but do not at any time even believe another who is engaged in it or bestow authority on a detractor by giving him your agreement and thus by your assent feeding his vice. Be not in agreement, says the scripture, with those who disparage your neighbour, and you will not take a sin upon yourself on his account; and elsewhere: Fence in your ears with thorns and do not listen to an evil tongue (cf. Sir.28.24).[20] Hence too the blessed David, enumerating the different kinds of guiltlessness and righteousness, was not silent about this virtue either, saying: Nor takes up a reproach against his neighbours (Ps.15.3), for the reason that thus he himself not only opposes but even harries the detractor. For he says: Him who slanders his neighbour secretly, I will destroy (Ps.101.5).

2. This vice is surely one which above all ought to be destroyed and utterly banished by those who wish to establish themselves in the holy life. For there is nothing which so disturbs the spirit, there is nothing which makes the mind so changeable and fickle as giving easy credence to everything and attending to the words of detractors with heedless agreement of the mind; for it is from this source that frequent disagreements and unrighteous hatreds arise. This is what often makes enemies even of the greatest friends, when a slanderer's tongue disjoins souls that are in harmony but are credulous. But, on the other hand, great is the mental peace and great the moral seriousness that come from not lightly hearkening to anything evil said about anyone, and blessed is he who has so armed himself against this vice that no one dares to criticise another in his presence! But if we had in us this concern not to believe detractors heedlessly, then all would be afraid of detracting, lest by detraction they make themselves and not others worthless. But it is because it is listened to with pleasure by almost everyone that this evil is so rife, this vice so rampant in many.

17.   Shun too the approbation of flatterers and the harmful compliments of deceit like plagues of the soul.[21] There is nothing that so easily corrupts men's minds, nothing that can inflict on the spirit a wound so sweet and gentle. Hence a wise man says: The words of flatterers are soft but they pierce the inner parts of the body (Pr.26.22). And the Lord says through the prophet: My people, those who bless you mislead you and confuse the paths of your feet (Is.3.12). This vice rules in many, especially at this time, and, which is most serious, it is put in the

---

19 This passage down to the end of the section contains many parallels with *Dem.* 19 and many instances of 'almost exact verbal agreement' (see Evans,1968,55f.).

20 Cf. *Dem.* 19,n.42 and *Virg.* 10,n.18.

21 Cf. this passage on the need to avoid flatterers and abstain from flattery oneself with *Dem.* 21,1.

place of humility and kindness. So it comes about that the man who does not know how to flatter is now thought to be either jealous or proud. And it is a great stratagem and one of considerable subtlety to praise another as a means of commending oneself and by deceit to bind the mind of the deceived to oneself, and the particular achievement of this vice usually consists in selling feigned praises at a fixed price. What, however, is this great fickleness of mind, what is this great vanity that leads one to abandon one's own conscience and follow another's opinion, an opinion which is false and counterfeit, to be snatched up by the wind of false praise, to rejoice in conniving at one's own deception and to accept an illusion as a kindness? So, if you desire to be truly worthy of praise, do not seek the praise of men but make your conscience ready for him who will bring to light the things now hidden in darkness and will disclose the purposes of the heart, and then you will receive your commendation from God (1 Cor.4.5).

18.   Let your mind then be attentive and watchful and always armed against sins; let your speech be in all matters modest and chaste and of the kind that makes it clear that it is prompted by the need to speak rather than the wish to do so; let your modesty adorn your common sense and, as has always been a special characteristic of women, let your sense of shame surpass all the other virtues that are in you. Consider well and long in advance what has to be said and, while still silent, take care in advance that there will be nothing for you to have to regret when you have said it; let your thought weigh your words and let the balance of your mind regulate the functioning of your tongue. Hence the scripture says: Melt down your silver and gold, make a balance for your words and a proper curb for your mouth and beware lest you err with your tongue (Sir.28.24–26). Let no curse ever pass your lips, since you are bidden to crown your kindness by blessing even those who curse you: Being, he says, of a tender heart and a humble mind, not returning evil for evil or reviling for reviling, but on the contrary blessing (1 Pet.3.8,9).

19.   But let your tongue know nothing of how to lie and to swear an oath, and let there be such love of the truth in you that you consider everything you say to have been said on oath. On this subject the Saviour says to his disciples: But I say to you, Do not swear at all. And, a little later: Let what you say be simply, 'Yes' or 'No'; anything more than this comes from evil (Mt.5.34,37).[22] Therefore in every deed and every word let your mind be kept quiet and calm, and let the presence of God always come to your thoughts; let your soul be humble and gentle and aroused only against vices; never let it be exalted with pride or twisted by greed or carried away by anger. For nothing should be quieter, nothing purer, nothing in a word more lovely than a mind which has to be made ready for the habitation of God, who delights not in temples gleaming with gold or altars picked out with jewels but in a soul adorned with virtues. That too is why the hearts of the holy are called the temple of God, on the testimony of the

[22] Cf. Dem.19,4, which uses the same verses in relation to lies and oaths.

apostle, who says: If anyone destroys God's temple, God will destroy him. For God's temple is holy, and that temple you are (1 Cor.3.17).

20.   Regard nothing as more excellent, nothing more desirable than humility; for this is the chief preserver and, as it were, warder of all the virtues, and there is nothing that can make us so pleasing both to men and to God as to be high in the merit list of life and lowest in humility, because the scripture says: The greater you are, the more you must humble yourself, and you will find favour in the sight of God (Sir.3.18). And God says through the prophet: On whom else shall I rest unless upon the humble and quiet man and him that trembles at my word (Is.66.2). Truly you must follow that humility, not the kind that is displayed and simulated by bodily gesture or by subduing the utterance of one's words but that which is expressed in the natural disposition of one's heart. For it is one thing to pursue the shadow of things, another the reality.[23] The pride which hides beneath outward signs of humility is made much more ugly thereby. For, by some means or other, vices are more unsightly when they are concealed behind an outward semblance of virtue.

21.   Never set yourself in front of someone else by reason of nobility of birth or think anyone who is more obscure and born in a lowlier station to be your inferior. Our religion knows nothing of the personal standing and material circumstances of individuals but examines their souls instead; it pronounces a man slave or noble on the basis of his morals. The only freedom before God is freedom not to be a slave to sin, the highest form of nobility before God is to be distinguished for virtue.[24] What can be nobler before God among men than Peter, who was a fisherman and poor? What more illustrious among women than the blessed Mary, who is described as a carpenter's bride? But to that poor fisherman are entrusted by Christ the keys of the heavenly kingdom, this carpenter's bride was thought worthy to be the mother of him by whom those very keys were given. For God has chosen the obscure things of this world and those that are despised, so that he may the more easily bring low the powerful and noble. And besides, it is in vain that a man congratulates himself on his high birth, when before God all are of like honour and of the same value, having been redeemed by the same blood of Christ, nor does it matter what are the circumstances of anyone's birth, when all of us without exception are reborn in Christ. For even if we forget that we are all descended from one man, at least we ought always to remember that it is through one that we are all reborn.

22.   Take care not to think yourself to be holy now if you begin to fast and abstain, for this virtue is an aid to holiness and not a sign of its perfection, and you should be all the more careful lest this contempt of yours for things which are

---

[23] For an almost identical sentence on true Christian humility see *Dem*.20,1.
[24] Cf. *Dem*.22,1 on the contrast between Christian nobility of character and the false nobility of the secular world.

allowed may create in you a certain heedlessness about those which are not allowed. Whatever is offered to God over and above the demands of righteousness ought not to hinder righteousness but to assist it. But what does it profit a man that his body be reduced by abstinence, if his spirit be swollen with pride? What praise shall we win for our pallor through fasting, if we are green with envy? What virtue is there in not drinking wine, if we are drunk with anger and hate? When the spirit is starved of vices, that, I say, is the time when abstinence is glorious, when the chastisement of the body is fine and magnificent. Indeed, those who possess the virtue of abstinence and exercise it fittingly and with understanding punish their flesh that they may break the pride of their spirit, so that they may descend, as it were, from the summit of their contempt and arrogance to fulfil the Lord's will, which is most likely to be carried out in humility. It is in order to employ the whole of their mind's strength in the desire for virtue that they withdraw it from the longing for a variety of different foods; and the flesh feels the labour of fasting and abstinence less strongly when the soul is feeding on righteousness. For the vessel of election too, when chastising and subduing his body, lest, while he preaches to others, he be himself rejected, does not do this only for the sake of chastity, as some ignorant folk believe; for abstinence does not help this virtue only but all virtues without exception. Nor does the great glory, or the whole glory, of that apostle consist solely in refraining from fornication, but rather he refrains from it so that his soul may be instructed by the chastisement of his body, and the more he refrains from desiring anything from pleasures the more able he is to think about virtues, so that the master of perfection may not display anything imperfect in himself, that the imitator of Christ may not do anything that falls outside the precept and will of Christ, that he may not teach less by example than by word and, after preaching to others, be himself rejected and, with the Pharisees, hear the words: For they preach and do not practise (Mt.23.3).

23.   But it is a part of apostolic precept and example that we should care not only for conscience but also for reputation. This teaching, given to us by the master of the gentiles, is not superfluous and unprofitable, since he wants strangers to the faith to make progress through the works of the faithful, so that the discipline of religion may commend religion itself. And for that reason he bids us shine like lamps in the world in the midst of a wicked and misguided people, in order that the disbelieving minds of those who stray from the path may dispel the shadows of their ignorance by the light given out by our deeds. Hence he himself says to the Romans: Taking thought for what is noble not only in the sight of God but in the sight of men (Rom.12.17). And elsewhere: Give no offence to Jews or to gentiles or to the church of God, just as I try to please all men in everything that I do, not seeking my own advantage, but that of many (1 Cor.10.32,33). Blessed is he who has ordered his life in such a holy and serious way that nothing evil can be even imagined about him, as long as the greatness of his merit fights against the wantonness of his detractors and no one has dared even to invent what no one else is likely to think credible. But if it turns out that

such a feat is too difficult and arduous to achieve, at least we must apply to our lives a degree of watchfulness sufficient to ensure that evil minds can find no occasion for disparagement and that we send out no spark to kindle unfavourable reports affecting our good name. Otherwise it is useless for us to be angry with our traducers, if we ourselves provide them with the material for traducing us. If, however, while we are watchful and careful to take every precaution in order to protect our reputation and in all our acts give precedence to our fear of God, they still go on raving against us, let us find consolation in our conscience, which is at its safest and most secure when it has given us not even the occasion to feel badly about ourselves. For to them it is said by the prophet: Woe to those who call good evil, who call light darkness, and call bitter what is sweet (Is.5.20). To us then the word of the Saviour will be applied: Blessed are you when men revile you falsely (Mt.5.11); and let our sole aim be that no one may be able to speak ill of us without lying.

24.   Let your home be the object of your concern in such a way that you can still allot a period of respite to your soul. Choose a convenient place, a little removed from the noise of the household, to which you can betake yourself as if to a harbour out of a great storm of cares and there, in the peace of inner seclusion, calm the turbulent waves of thoughts outside.[25] There let your study of divine readings be so constant, your alternations in prayers so frequent, your meditation on the future world so steadfast and deliberate, that you have no trouble in making up for all the employments of your remaining time by this spell of freedom from them. Nor do we say this with the purpose of detaching you from your family; rather our intention is that in that place you may learn and meditate as to what kind of person you ought to show yourself to your own kin.

25.   Control and cherish your household in such a way that you wish to be seen to be a mother of your family rather than a mistress and win their respect by kindness rather than strictness. Obedience is always more dependable and more acceptable when it is received from love than from fear. But, above all else, let the arrangement prescribed by apostolic rule be observed in a marriage that is respected and without stain.

26.   First and foremost, see that your husband's authority is upheld and that the entire household learns from your example the degree of respect due to him. Show by your obedience that he is the master and indicate his importance by your humility, since the more abundantly you honour him the more you will be honoured yourself. For, as the apostle says, the husband is the head of the wife (Eph.5.23), nor does the rest of the body derive its honour from any other source than the dignity of its head. Hence the same apostle says elsewhere: Wives, be subject to your husbands, as is fitting in the Lord (Col.3.18); and the blessed apostle also says: Likewise you wives, be submissive to your husbands, so that

[25] See Dem.23 for similar advice.

some, though they do not obey the word, may be won without a word by the behaviour of their wives (1 Pet.3.1). If, therefore, honour is due even to gentile husbands by the marriage law, how much more must it be rendered to Christians?

27. And in order to make known also the ornaments with which married women ought to decorate themselves, he says: Let not yours be the outward adorning with braiding of hair, decoration of gold or wearing of robes, but let it be the hidden person of the heart with the imperishable jewel of a gentle and quiet spirit, which is in God's sight very precious. For so once the holy women who hoped in God also used to adorn themselves and were submissive to their husbands, as Sarah obeyed Abraham, calling him lord (ibid.3–6). But in giving these instructions he is not ordering them to wear filthy clothes and to be covered with rough patches of cloth; rather he is forbidding extravagant apparel and sophisticated ornament and is commending simple adornment and dress. And on this subject the vessel of election also says: Also that women should adorn themselves modestly and sensibly in seemly apparel, not with braided hair or gold or pearls or costly attire but by good deeds, as befits women who profess chastity (1 Tim.2.9,10).

28, 1. I have discovered that several years ago now, fired by a remarkable fervour caused by faith, you resolved upon celibacy and dedicated the remainder of your life to chastity. It is the mark of a great soul and an indication of perfect virtue suddenly to renounce a pleasure already experienced, to shun the well-known allurements of the flesh and to quench with fervour the flames of a time of life still hot with passion. But I also learned at the same time something which causes me no slight anxiety and disquiet, namely, that you clearly began to observe this so great and good practice without the consent and agreement of your husband, although apostolic authority altogether forbids this, an authority which in such a case has not only subjected wife to husband but also husband to the power of wife. For the wife, he says, does not rule over her own body, but the husband does; likewise the husband does not rule over his own body, but the wife does (1 Cor.7.4). But you, as if forgetful of your marriage contract and of this agreement and law, vowed your chastity to the Lord without consulting your husband. And a promise is at risk, if it is still within the power of another to veto it, nor do I know how much pleasure is derived from a gift, if one is offering an object which belongs to two people.

2. We have already both heard of and seen many marriages broken through ignorance of this kind, and, as I am grieved to recall, adultery committed on the pretext of chastity: for while one party abstains even from acts which are permitted, the other lapses into acts which are not permitted at all. And in such a case I do not know who is to be accused more and who blamed more, whether it be the man who commits fornication after being repulsed by his wife or the woman who, by repulsing her husband, has in a manner exposed him to fornication. And, so that you may know what the truth is, I must set down a few points on the matter of divine authority. The rule of apostolic doctrine neither makes works of continence equal to those of marriage with Jovinian nor does it condemn marriage with the Manichaean.[26] So the vessel of election and master of the gentiles follows a moderate, middle path between either extreme, in this way conceding a remedy for incontinence and at the same time encouraging continence to seek its reward. The whole sense of his ruling in this matter is that either chastity be proposed only as the result of the decision of both parties or, at least, the obligation common to both be discharged by both.

29.   But now let us set down the apostle's very own words and reconsider this whole subject from its beginning. He says to the Corinthians: And now concerning the matters about which you wrote: It is well for a man not to touch a woman (1 Cor.7.1). And though he has praised chastity here, he yet adds, in order that he may not seem to be trying to prevent marriage: But because of the temptation to immorality, each man should have his own wife and each woman her own husband. The husband should give to his wife her conjugal rights, and likewise the wife to her husband. For the wife does not rule over her own body, but the husband does; and the husband not rule over his own body, but the wife does. Do not refuse one another (ibid.2–5). And again, lest he might seem to be excluding the possibility of chastity by saying so much from the standpoint of marriage, he follows it up with: Except perhaps by agreement for a season (ibid.5). And, immediately after, he almost protests against what he has just said, that is, 'for a season', lest he seem to be teaching not so much perpetual as temporary and brief continence. For he says: Through lack of self-control. But I say this by way of concession, not of command (ibid.5,6). Hence this phrase of his, 'for a season', teaches that there ought to be rehearsal of chastity, so that, when they have, as it were, explored the strength of their self-control for fixed intervals of time, both parties may safely give promise to each other of what both ought to be maintaining always. He states his full meaning quite clearly: But I wish that all were as I myself am (ibid.7), that is, in continuous and perpetual chastity.

30, 1. Do you see how carefully, how prudently the master has declared his judgement on chastity without providing any occasion for offence and not wishing so great a good to become insecure through the rashness of one of the two parties, when it should be confirmed and strengthened by the agreement of both?

---

[26] Pelagius later linked Jovinian and the Manichees again as advocates of extreme views in *Conf.*25, referring there to the charge of preaching 'sinlessness' which was brought against him by Jerome soon after his arrival in Palestine: 'Those who say with the Manichees that man cannot avoid sin err as much as those who assert with Jovinian that man cannot sin; for both remove the freedom of the will.' Jerome had attempted to depict Pelagius as a supporter of Jovinian's unorthodox view – for which the latter was condemned by synods of Rome and Milan in the latter part of the fourth century – because he, like many other members of the ecclesiastical circles in Rome, had criticised Jerome for the intemperate nature of his attack on Jovinian in his treatise *Against Jovinian*, written c.394 (see Rees,1988,4ff.; Plinval,1943,50ff.; R.F. Evans, 1968(a),31ff.).

And what, in all truth, is stronger and safer than that chastity which, having begun with the agreement of the two, is maintained by both for their common benefit, so that the one party may not set itself to persevere in virtue for both when, in fact, it is only concerned for itself. For this good, like others too, is to be praised in a person not only for having been begun but for having been completed. As you realize, for some time now our discourse has been engaged in traversing a rocky and difficult place nor does it dare to turn to one side or the other, fearing both equally as it does; but you should recognize your own peril from our difficulty, for we have preferred to depress you perhaps by speaking the truth than to deceive you with false flattery.

2. The evil, as you see, is twofold, a danger which is equally critical on both sides, and you are hemmed in by constraints on either side. To shun and despise your husband altogether is clearly contrary to the apostle's judgement; but to betray a chastity of such duration and not to render to God what you promised him is something to be feared and dreaded. As the common saying has it, you can easily turn a friend into an enemy, if you do not fulfil your promises to him. For this is what the scripture says: But when you make a vow to the Lord your God, you shall not be slack to it; for the Lord God will surely require it of you, and it would be a sin in you (Dt.23.21). That is why he (sc. Paul) tells you to render your husband the honour owed to him, so that both of you may be able to repay to the Lord the debt which you have vowed on both sides. In respect of his (sc. your husband's) conscience we do not lack confidence, if you had expected us to have only a little; nor is it that we are trying to hold you back from the good of chastity but, rather, that we are urging his spirit with all our strength towards the mercy-seat of chastity, so that he may offer a voluntary sacrifice to God as a fragrant offering, that his mind may be divested of all worldly bonds and bodily pleasures, and that thus you may *both* be able to adhere more completely to the Lord's commands. But – lest you should think that there is anything which we have said without due care – we have given you this instruction on the testimony of divine scripture, as the apostle also says: And two shall be one flesh (1 Cor.6.16); but now no longer one flesh (Mt.19.6), but one spirit (1 Cor.6.17).

31. This is a great and solemn obligation, and the way of chastity is an arduous one; but there are great rewards too, and the Lord summons us in the Gospel with these words: Come, O blessed of my Father, inherit the kingdom prepared for you from the beginning of the world (Mt.25.34). The same Lord says also: Come to me, all who labour and are heavy laden, and I will give you rest. Take my yoke upon you, and learn from me; for I am gentle and lowly in heart, and you will find rest for your souls. For my yoke is easy, and my burden is light (Mt.11.28–30). The same Lord says also to those at his left hand: Depart from me, you cursed, into the eternal fire which my Father has prepared for the devil and his angels (Mt.25.41): I know you not, workers of iniquity; there will be weeping and gnashing of teeth (Lk.13.27,28). Assuredly they will beat their breasts, they will mourn, they who so involve themselves in the cares of the present life that they forget the future one, they whom the Lord's coming will

find smothered in a sleep of ignorance and buried beneath the waves of a false security. Hence he himself says in the gospel; Take heed to yourselves, lest perchance your hearts be weighed down with dissipation and drunkenness and cares of this life, and that day come upon you suddenly like a snare; for it will come upon all who dwell upon the face of the whole earth (Lk.21.34,35). And again: Watch and pray; for you do not know when the time may come (Mt.25.13).

32.   Blessed are those who so wait and watch for that day that they prepare themselves for it daily, who do not flatter themselves on their past righteousness but, according to the apostle, are renewed in virtue every day (cf. 2 Cor.4.16). For the righteousness of the righteous man will not profit him from that day on which he ceases to be righteous, just as also his iniquity will not harm the iniquitous man from that day of his on which he turns away from iniquity (Ezek.18.21–24). Nor, therefore, ought the holy man to feel secure for as long as he remains in this life's struggle or the sinner to despair, since, according to the aforesaid judgement of the prophet, he is able to make himself righteous in one day; for you have the whole duration over which your life extends to enable you to achieve righteousness and not become more remiss because of your trust in your past righteousness. As the apostle says: Forgetting what lies behind and straining forward to what lies ahead, I press forward toward the prize of the high calling (Phil.3.13,14),[27] knowing that God has been designated as the examiner of the heart (Pr.24.12). And for that reason he busies himself so as to have a soul pure from sin, because it is written: Keep your heart with all vigilance (Pr.4.23), and again: The Lord loves pure hearts; for all those who are blameless are acceptable to him (cf. Mt.5.8; Pr.11.20). Therefore see that you order the rest of your life without offence, so that you can sing with the prophet: I walked with integrity of heart within my house (Ps.101.2). And again: I will go to the altar of God, to God of my exceeding joy (Ps.43.4), for it is not enough only to have begun, but to have finished is true righteousness.[28]

---

[27] Cf. *Dem.*27,3 on the need for daily renewal in virtue, citing the same verses and containing a marked parallelism in expression,
[28] This warning appears frequently in Pelagius and in other Pelagian writings.

PART II

THE CASPARI CORPUS

6

To an Older Friend[1]

This letter contains more autobiographical information from its writer than any other letter in this selection, in fact, more than the rest of them put together. The writer is a youngish man who has left his native country and, after a perilous journey by land and on sea, some, if not most, of it in the company of a man whom he describes as 'the holy Antiochus', has reached Sicily and settled there. He is replying to a letter from an older friend of some social standing who has written to rebuke him on various grounds – that his journey was an 'unreasonable' one because there was no need for him to seek God elsewhere, that he ought not to have associated with a man of ill repute like Antiochus and that it was unwise to risk being poor in a strange country.

The younger man certainly does not pull his punches in his reply, dealing with each of these criticisms in turn and ending with a few pieces of advice for the older man on how to lead the life of a true Christian. The tone of the letter is Pelagian: for example, we have the stock Pelagian argument that God would never have commanded men to be without sin if it were impossible to lead a sinless life – omitting any reference, of course, to the need of God's grace in order to avoid sin –[2] and the statements that sin is due to a fault of will, not of nature, and that Adam died because of his sin of disobedience;[3] as well as a criticism of

---

1   *Epistula 'Honorificentiae tuae'*: PLS 1, 1687–94; CPL 761; Caspari,4–13; Haslehurst, 1–17.

2   Cf., e.g., Dem.16 and see Rees,1988, 7f.,86,93ff. Pelagius had been accused of teaching 'sinlessness' at the Synod of Diospolis in 415 but his explanation was accepted by his judges (Augustine, *On the Activities of Pelagius*, vi.16)(PL 44,329f.). In any case, this charge became less and less important as other, graver accusations came to the front, for example, denial of original sin and of true grace.

3   Cf. Virg.7,2; Life,13,2; Law,4,4; and see n.16 below. Some Pelagians went even further, asserting that Adam would have died even if he had not sinned (Augustine, *On the Merits and Forgiveness of Sins and Infant Baptism*, I,ii.2)(PL 44,109f.); Pelagius' closest associate, Celestius, apparently did so, and the matter was raised by Pelagius' accusers at Diospolis among other alleged statements with which Celestius had been confronted by Bishop Aurelius at the Council of Carthage in 411 (Augustine, *On Original Sin*, iii-iv,3)(PL 44,386f.). Pelagius, however, dissociated himself from such statements and anathematised them (Augustine, *On the Activities of Pelagius*, xi.23,24 (PL 44,333f.) and *Incomplete Work against Julian*, II,93)(PL 45,1173); but Augustine, who was present neither at Diospolis nor at Carthage, continued to maintain that he had done this only

those who prefer to be *called* Christians rather than to *be* Christians and a brief
list of prerequisites for being a Christian, both of which are closely paralleled
elsewhere.[4] But the writer is not only a Pelagian; he is also a 'twice-born' Christian, whose new 'knowledge of the truth' has recently come to him in Sicily,
mainly through the religious instruction which he has been receiving from a
noble and highly respected lady who, *inter alia*, has dissuaded him from travelling
to the East. It is made abundantly clear that, although he promises to return to
his native land, bringing the Sicilian lady with him, he has rejected the pseudo-
Christianity of his former friends, having found a better way to follow his
Master's example.

There has been some disagreement as to the writer's place of origin: Caspari
thought that it was Britain and Morris agreed with him, suggesting that he
should be called 'The Sicilian Briton', a suggestion which Evans accepted;[5] but
Bonner has rightly pointed out that there is 'no justification for such an assumption' and prefers to call him 'The Sicilian Anonymous'.[6] In fact, his promise to
return to his native land is immediately followed by another that he proposes to
return to 'the city', which at this time might well refer to Rome itself. As for the
date of the letter, the only certainty is that it must have been before Francia was
converted to Christianity towards the end of the fifth century,[7] which is no help
to us in establishing it.

The authorship of this and the other Caspari documents is discussed in greater
detail in the Introduction.

Text ·

1, 1. I have read your letter, honourable sir, in which you adjudge my action
blameworthy and take a rather poor view of my dangerous expedition, criticising
it as unreasonable and asserting that God is everywhere and can be worshipped
in all places and that it is therefore superfluous to seek throughout other provinces one who can be found in their own homes by those who live godly lives and
desire to serve him with their whole hearts. Certainly it is well known that God

---

under pressure and to protect himself and, later, that the Pelagians in general shared
Celestius' opinion on Adam's death (op.cit.I,67; IV,43; *On Heresies*,88)(PL 45,185ff.,
1361f.; PL 42,48). Marius Mercator, another contemporary anti-Pelagian writer, also
claimed that Celestius had stated that Adam would have died even if he had not
sinned (*Memorandum on the Name of Celestius*,1)(PL 48,69) but not even he claimed
that Pelagius himself ever did so.

4 Cf. *Life*,1,6,11 and 14; YM,3,1 on the need to be an 'authentic' Christian.
5 Caspari,387; Morris,1965,37,40; Evans,1968,24ff. So far as I know, no one still argues
that 'Fastidius' wrote this letter, though the notion was once fashionable.
6 Bonner, 1972, 5ff.; he suggests that 'we avoid any guess as to his place of origin' (see
n.24 below).
7 Its date is discussed in the general context of the authorship of the Caspari corpus in
my Introduction.

is everywhere and that there is no part of his creation in which he does not dwell, as the prophet also bears witness: Whither shall I go from thy Spirit? O whither shall I flee from thy presence? If I ascend to heaven, thou art there! If I make my bed in Sheol, thou art there! If I take wing to the east and dwell in the uttermost parts of the sea, even there thy hand shall lead me, and thy right hand shall hold me (Ps.139.7–10). But it does not follow that, because he is everywhere, he can be worshipped in all places. For God is in Francia and in Saxony and in all foreign lands, yet there are no worshippers of God there; at the time when it was said: In Judah God is known (Ps.76.1), God was everywhere but he was known only in Judah.

2. So let your affection for me enable you to understand[8] that it is not enough for us to know that God is in all places and that we can serve him in every land but we ought also to try to find out *how* we have to serve him. It is easy to say, 'I know God, I believe in God, I love God, I fear God, I serve God', but the man does not know him who does not believe in him, does not believe in him who does not love him, does not love him who does not fear him, does not fear him who does not serve him, does not serve him who has belittled him in any way. But let us also demonstrate on the authority of the scriptures that the man who has despised his commandments does not know God or believe in him or love him or fear him. Listen to the words of the apostle: He who says, 'I know him' but disobeys his commandments is a liar and the truth is not in him (1 Jn.2.4). And elsewhere: No one who sins has either seen him or known him (1 Jn.3.6). And again, of the believer: He who believes in God gives heed to the commandments (Sir.32.24); from this we can understand that the man who does not give heed to God's commandments does not believe in him. And of the lover of God the Lord himself says in his gospel: Everyone who hears my words and does them, he it is who loves me (Mt.7.24; Jn.14.21). And the apostle says: For this is the love of God, that we keep his commandments (1 Jn.5.3). For it is superfluous to prove by the testimony of the law that he who has dared to despise him does not fear him, since it is possible to understand with the aid of natural wisdom that there is no fear where there is contempt and that, where there is no fear, service is inconceivable: where there is service, there is lordship, where there is lordship, there is fear, where there is fear, there is obedience, where there is obedience, there is righteousness.

3. From this you with your good sense must acknowledge that it is of no profit to confess God with one's lips and deny him by one's deeds; for the apostle is our witness to the fact that he is denied by our deeds, when he says: They profess to know God, but they deny him by their deeds (Ti.1.16). Nor should you any longer consider someone to be a Christian merely because he is called one, since something can be called what it is not.[9] Of certain men it is written: Those who say that they are Jews and are not (Rev.2.9); and elsewhere: Those who call themselves apostles but are not (ibid.2); and this shows that a thing is not

---

8 Haslehurst nodded here, translating *dilectio tua* as 'my dear lady'!
9 See n.4 above.

necessarily something because it is called it, but it can be called what it is not. For just as then men were called apostles who were not, so now men are called Christians who are not. Men are not Christians unless they follow the pattern and teaching of Christ, since the scripture says: He who says he abides in Christ ought to walk in the same way as he walked (1 Jn.2.6). A man is seriously mistaken if he supposes that he has already acquired something by simply obtaining the name of it, since the name belongs to the thing, not the thing to the name.

4. But, as the drift of my letter permits it, I shall briefly explain what it means to be a Christian.[10] A Christian is one who lives by Christ's example, of whom it is written: Because Christ suffered for you, leaving you an example, that you should follow in his steps (1 Pet.2.21). A Christian is one who never lies, never curses, who does not take any oath,[11] who does not return evil for evil but, on the contrary, good, who blesses those who curse him, who does good even to them who do evil to him, who loves his enemies, who prays for his traducers and persecutors, whose thoughts even are free from all malice and unchastity, who inflicts upon no one what he does not wish to be done to himself, but gladly imparts to all everything which he desires to be given to him and, in sum, who after the washing of baptism is free from sin. I say nothing of greater sins, since no one doubts that he to whom even lesser sins are not permitted is not allowed to commit greater crimes either.[12] For, knowing you to be a sensible person, I do not want you to answer me in the manner of the foolish, 'And who can be without sin?' For if a man could not be without sin, there would be no commandment to that effect; but it is common knowledge that there is such a commandment, and so we must either describe God as unjust or, since it is wicked to think thus of God, must believe that he has commanded what is possible.

5. In brief, if a man cannot be without sin, then something which is the result of that incapacity will no longer be a sin, because the incapacity is attributable to his nature; yet it is not to his nature but to his will that sin is to be ascribed, in order that the author of nature may not be adjudged to be to blame.[13] And see that you do not make the mistake of supposing that it is enough for you to keep some of all the commandments, when it does not profit a man enough to keep some of the law's commandments if he is manifestly transgressing others, since the scripture says: Whoever keeps the whole law but fails on one point has become guilty of all of it (Jas.2.10), which shows that a man who transgresses other commandments is liable to be impeached for those which he has kept.[14] To

---

[10] For the requirements of the true Christian cf., e.g., YM,4,2;5; Virg.7,3; 8,3; Life,6,2; 9,2; 10,4; 14,1,2; for those who call themselves Christians without being Christians cf., e.g., YM,3,1; Life,6,1; 10,4; Cel.8.

[11] Cf., e.g., YM,4,2; Cel.17; Dem.19,4.

[12] For greater and lesser sins cf. Virg.4,3; BT,13,1; 14,1,5; and see Rees,1988,94.

[13] The emphasis on the importance of free will is a clear indication of Pelagianism; the argument employed here is developed in NS; cf. YM,2,3, similarly worded.

[14] For the need to keep all commandments without exception cf. especially YM,3,1; Virg.4,2; 7,2; Dem.15; 16,1; 25.

give clearer proof that this is so, let us see which of all the commandments is the least important and what is accounted a suitable punishment for the sin which we have considered to be the least important, so that we may be able to assess the penalty for committing greater sins by comparison with the punishment given for breaking a minor commandment.

6. I suppose that there is nothing more trivial, no sin easier to commit, than that of calling one's brother a fool. But, says the Lord: Whoever says, 'You fool!' (to his brother), shall be liable to the hell of fire (Mt.5.22).[15] I beg you, give careful consideration to this question: what violation of a commandment will go scot-free when such a modest one has to be expiated by hell's fires? For Adam too transgressed once and died; not because he committed a great sin, since he had only tasted of the fruit of the tree, but because he had shown himself to be a transgressor.[16] Do we reckon ourselves Christians and feel confident that we can live, when we are overcome perhaps daily by some sin or other, whereas Adam sinned once and died? Will the one who did not spare Adam spare us? But God shows no partiality (Rom.2.11). No, it is he (sc.Adam) who should rather have been spared, since he was still ignorant, since he was not restrained by the prior example of any other man deservedly dying for his sin.[17] And yet he received no pardon as a special case. If then Adam, who had some grounds for pardon, was not pardoned, how are we to obtain pardon, when no special case for pardon is left to us?[18] You will quote to me that popular maxim: 'Then the whole world is perishing.' Whether the whole world is or is not involved in punishment by destruction, why should we wonder if what happened once happens again? Remember that the whole world perished in the time of Noah and only a few righteous persons were able to be saved.[19] And if God is the same now as he was then, why should we not believe what we have proved by experience to have already taken place?

7. Nor do I want you to accept the truth of that ungodly and blasphemous explanation which certain heathens offer, that God does not care for his own. If he had not cared for them, he would not have given them a law for living either nor would he have challenged them to progress in the good life through angels, prophets and all the saints nor would he have sent his son at last to show them the perfect life both by his teaching and by his example. For if he cared to create man as a rational being, we must believe that he cares just as much that he whom he created rational should not live irrationally. Let no one hoodwink your sincerity, let no one deceive you.[20] Unless a man is righteous, he cannot be saved,

---

[15] For the use of this quotation from Matthew cf. *Law*,7,3 and see n.17 there.

[16] See n.3 above and, for Eve's sin, *Dem*.25,4; cf. also Julian of Eclanum as quoted in Augustine's *Incomplete Work*,vi.23 (PL 45,1554ff.) for the same thought expressed differently.

[17] For Adam's 'ignorance' cf. *Virg*.7,3.

[18] The same passage contains an ironical reply to such a question: 'If you reject him in any respect, then, (I suppose) he will spare you also – *if* he spared Adam!'

[19] Cf. *Life*,7; *Dem*.5,2 on Noah's righteousness.

[20] Cf. *Virg*.15; *Life*,10,2; 13,1; 14,1; *Cel*.11; *Dem*.3,3; it is, of course, the main theme of BT.

but he will not be righteous unless he ceases to sin. As it is written: He who does right is righteous but he who commits sin is of the devil; for the devil has sinned from the beginning. The reason the son of God appeared was to destroy the works of the devil; whoever does not do right is not of God (1 Jn.3.7,8,10). I have summarized all these matters briefly so as to show that God cannot be easily worshipped everywhere, as some suppose in their ignorance, but only where knowledge of the way to worship him can be found. For how can a man worship God if he does not know how he ought to be worshipped?

2, 1. I too, when I lived in my own country, supposed myself to be worshipping God and congratulated myself on disdaining things that were permissible, while sometimes doing things that were forbidden.[21] For according to the apostle it is permitted even for the incontinent to marry; but to lie, to curse, to swear, to slander, to flatter, to accept persons for their rank, to take food with fornicators[22] or greedy men or drunkards or revilers, to hate one's enemy, to return evil for evil, to curse, to strike someone, and all those things which are included in the commandments of the law are both unlawful and prohibited. For what does it profit anyone to have disdained what is permitted and then to do what is not permitted? Doing the things that are commanded will help towards the accumulation of merits required for one's reward only if one does none of the things that are forbidden. So let not your love for me[23] take it ill that I have set out for foreign parts, since by taking this opportunity to go abroad I have discovered the knowledge of truth.

2. You should not let something which I regard as desirable become an object of regret for you or make my joy a reason for your sorrow. Now for the first time I am beginning to know the way to be a true Christian. I did indeed desire this before but my ignorance stood in the way of my prayers. Yet all-merciful God, who knows the things that are hidden from us, took care to bring to my notice what he knew that I wanted with all my heart's desire to achieve. For even if I have endured perils on my journey and perils by sea,[24] yet there are greater perils that I have avoided, namely, the chains of everlasting death and the flames of eternal fire; and though I remain a stranger to you for the time being, I have no regrets at present, lest I should be a wanderer for ever in the sight of God – although, in actual fact, a Christian can either be a wanderer nowhere, since all

[21] For this common distinction between things allowed and things not allowed – *licita* and *illicita* – see BT,n.23.

[22] Cf. Virg.7,3; Life,9,2.

[23] 'Dilectio tua', which I have again translated literally (see no.8 above). But perhaps we should take it in both passages as a typical Byzantine use of the abstract like *honorificentia tua* (= 'your honour') in this letter; cf. YM,1 and 7, and Chast.9,1, *parvitas*; NS,2,1, *pusillitas*; BT,1,4;3,1, *sanctitas*; 1,1, *eximietas*; Chast.10,4, *prudentia.*

[24] Cf. 5,1; it was partly on the basis of these two references to a long and perilous sea voyage that Morris,1965,37,40, gave the name 'Sicilian Briton' to our author, but Bonner,1972,5f. pointed out that a voyage from Gaul could have been equally dangerous. Might not one from Italy also have been difficult at this time, though, of course, much shorter!

the earth belongs to his Lord, or else a stranger among his own people, since the whole world is a place of exile when compared with the things to come.

3.   Do you regard me as blameworthy because the exigencies of the journey brought me into association with the holy Antiochus? I do not know your reason for intimating that his reputation is sullied,[25] for we may not believe of absent persons what we do not want to be believed of ourselves by men everywhere. The maxim, 'What you do not wish for yourself do not do to any one' (Tob.4.15), must be observed everywhere. I shall believe only what I have seen with my own eyes and what I have proved myself by my own efforts, because I know that saints are above all others the victims of envy and disparagement and the hatred that these arouse in this present world. I found no evil in him and cannot retain in my conscience anything but what I have discovered for myself.

4, 1. As for your comment to the effect that I should dread the thought of being poor in a foreign country and your declaration that it is in some measure better for us to give to others than to hope for what belongs to others, I ask you if by chance you have learned this among unbelievers and not among Christians, who know that the poorer they are the better they are. It is an opinion, it seems to me, not held by you alone but by all who try to excuse their own greed and disobedience and, to tell the whole truth, their lack of faith under the pretext of so-called reason, teaching what they do rather than what God's law instructs them. They prefer to understand the scriptures in this way according to their own actions rather than modify the nature of their own actions in accordance with the scriptures.[26] And because it is laborious and difficult for them to despise all their personal possessions according to the Lord's command in order to attain perfection, they commonly employ the maxim: It is better to give than to receive (Acts 20.35). But if you ask where that maxim which the apostle avers that the Lord uttered is written, or why it was uttered, they will be unable to reply; nevertheless, in defence of their own pleasures, they dare to cite it as evidence without knowing the occasion from which it is derived.

2.   But, to demonstrate briefly that it is not to be understood in the sense 'If it is better to give than to receive', we read that in one place the Lord said to a man who had the wherewithal to give: If you would be perfect, go, sell all your possessions (Mt.19.21; cf. Mk.10.21; Lk.18.22);[27] he who is commanded to sell all his possessions is allowed to possess nothing, and he who is to have nothing

---

[25] Nor do we know anything to the detriment of Antiochus' reputation – or, indeed, anything at all about him. But it does seem likely that he first awakened our author's interest in Pelagianism, possibly when the two men were at Rome together; see the introduction to this letter and the preceding note.

[26] A foretaste of our author's vehement and often bitter polemic against unsound doctrine in BT.

[27] Cf. YM,5, another foretaste, this time of Riches; the lady who had befriended him in Sicily had certainly obeyed Jesus' commandment to the rich young man in the gospels, as we see from 5,2.

ought to receive of others. So, if the Lord knew that it is better to give than to receive, he ought not only not to have urged a man who already occupied the higher position to choose the lower but also to have forbidden him when he wished to sell all of his own accord. But in teaching that this should preferably be done, he showed that it is better to do what he taught should be done. Or how can one not be perfect without selling all that one has, if 'it is better to give than to receive', when perfection is to be found in the better course of action? For we must believe that perfection lacks nothing.

3. Next, we read that the Lord himself and his apostles 'received'. If it is better to give than to receive, then those who gave must be reckoned as better than those who received from the givers. Finally, I have no reason to fear poverty if I follow the saying: Think not what you shall eat or what you shall drink or what you shall put on. Seek therefore first the kingdom of God and his righteousness, and all these things shall be given you (Mt.6.31,33). Nor need I be ashamed if I have to receive from another, but rather glory in it, if I see myself in this respect at least like my Lord and his disciples. Clearly it is better for me to give than to receive only so long as I am seen to possess anything.

5, 1. Now, as for the fact you are trying to persuade me to return to my own country, you are acting conscientiously and showing a clear indication of your affection for me, since, as it is a sign of men's hatred not to want ever to see those whom they do not love, so it is a sign of men's love to be distressed by the absence of those to whom they are joined by a firm bond of love and affection. But I must not leave in haste what I have only discovered slowly and with difficulty, for, after the labours of my great journey and countless dangers on the sea, he for fear and love of whom I have borne all this has revealed to my imagination a prize in the present for my toil, so that from present events I might gain some knowledge of what the future has in store for me.

2. In this land of Sicily I have found a woman of great nobility in men's eyes but much more noble in God's, who long ago, spurning and despising all her possessions, dedicated herself wholly to God. She has shown me the way of truth in all things. She too dissuaded me from going to the East, proving to me by reasoning as well as by the precedents of the law that God can be found everywhere by those who know him. When I had verified with greater certainty that her devotion, faith and knowledge were well known not only to the laity but also to many priests, I put myself entirely in her hands. Consider then, honourable sir, whether it is proper for me to abandon so completely the one who has enabled me to discover the knowledge of the truth and the way of eternal salvation. To her also I have offered my daughter,[28] although I am not unaware that you have a quite genuine affection for her. But no one can love a person more than do his or

---

[28] Meaning, of course, that he intended her to become a virgin under the lady's instructions; I cannot understand why Nuvolone,1986,2915 states that our author took the girl with him to Sicily.

her father and mother: I have always loved her more than you have, as is clear from the fact that while you have always wanted to bestow on her earthly possessions, I have attended to her heavenly needs, and it is the mark of a greater and better love to desire for, and confer on, its object greater and better things.

3. So I do not want you to try to stand in her way so soon, prompted by an overenthusiastic wish to show your natural affection for her. Think of her in the meantime as if she were a boy for whom it is necessary for the sake of his studies to be separated for a while from those who love him. But lest I seem to be totally disobedient to your behest, I promise to come to the city at a convenient time along with the most holy lady whom I mentioned above, by whose instruction I am desirous of being taught. For, as I have just promised you, I do indeed want to return to my native land but only after a period of time, when I have acquired some measure of divine knowledge. But I want my daughter to be a virgin in such a way as to understand how to preserve the good of virginity and what a virgin of God ought to do, in order that she may not come to resemble those in whom their love bears no fruit because of their ignorance, while they keep other commandments of lesser obligation, and whose chastity is often put at risk, while they lack the knowledge of how it ought to be protected.

6, 1. And you, most beloved parent,[29] must recall to mind the position which you have undertaken to uphold and remember that you are a Christian, taking care not to commit any of the things which are not fitting for a Christian to do. Maintain your blamelessness, maintain your righteousness, for without them no one can please God. Be holy, blameless, compassionate, chaste, hospitable and devout. Let your house be closed to no visitor; let no one, so far as is possible, be a stranger to your table; let the hungry and the needy be filled with your bread. Help the widows, defend orphans, protect the defenceless, succour the unhappy ones who labour, give assistance to all who are in want, so that you can say with the holy man: I have delivered the needy from the hand of the powerful, and I have helped the orphan who had no helper. The mouth of the widow has blessed me. For I was the eye of the blind, I was also the foot of the lame and the father of the weak (cf. Job 29.12,13,15,16). Above all, maintain your chastity and ensure that you keep at least the second good of continence, having lost the first, virginity.

2. Bring up your children for God; desire those whom you love faithfully to receive heavenly rather than earthly possessions. For there is no one who would not wish his children to possess what is better, and there can be no doubt that divine things are better than human. The man who desires his children to

---

[29] Cf. Law,9,1; but is it possible that our author's addressee is really his father, which would explain the latter's 'natural affection' for the girl? Probably *parens* ('parent') is intended only as a reminder of the addressee's obligations to his own children, referred to in 6,2, which he is now being asked to extend to the writer's 'poor little one' (*paupertatulam*) as well.

acquire earthly rather than heavenly possessions either does not love them or
does not believe in the things to come. To be sure, I pray you in your kindness to
show your accustomed shrewdness and care towards my poor little one, so that
she may feel my absence as little as possible. And you will receive due recompense for your services from him who commanded that good offices be rendered
to widows and orphans, as the scripture says: Be a merciful father to orphans, and
instead of a husband to their mother, and you will be like an obedient son of the
Most High (Sir.4.10).[30]

---

30 'Merciful' and 'obedient' are additions made by the author.

7

To a Young Man[1]

We have no good reason to doubt that this letter was written by the same man as the previous one, though some scholars have tried to prove that they were by different authors – mainly in order to bolster up their own theories as to the authorship of the whole Caspari corpus and of some of the Evans group as well.[2] The style and tone of the two letters in question are very similar, and they have the same central theme, that is, the criteria appropriate to the Christian life; they read like the work of a fairly recent convert anxious to enlist others to his new-found cause, and there is a freshness and zest about them which is rarely to be found in some of the documents in Part I.

In this case the addressee is a younger man who has – presumably fairly recently – completed his education in the pagan classics, has a tutor and counsellor named Martyrius, and might be said to have great expectations in the secular world. Clearly he too lives in Sicily, perhaps at Syracuse, since our author expresses the fervent hope at the end of his letter that they will be able to meet personally in the near future – though we have to admit that such an expression of hope is something of a cliché in Christian correspondence at this time.

After a preliminary thrust at any claims that secular literature might be thought to be superior to the Bible, our author goes on to encourage his addressee to get to know God's will for him and so equip himself to fulfil the divine commandments: ignorance of what is required and preoccupation with worldly concerns do not provide the sinner with an excuse for neglecting God. Nor is it sufficient to be called a Christian by others; to be a true Christian calls for knowledge, faith and obedience and for total commitment to God's commands. A brief summary of the requirements of a Christian follows, and a last word of kindly encouragement concludes the letter.

There are many echoes here, not only of the letter *To An Older Friend* but also of the Evans letters and tractates, especially *Law* and *Life*; indeed this letter might fairly be described as a very brief summary of the last two combined. The question of possible influence is discussed in my Introduction.

---

[1] [Epistula] ad Adolescentem or [Epistula] 'Humanae referunt litterae': PLS 1, 1375–80; CPL 732; Caspari,14–21; Haslehurst, 18–29.
[2] E.g.,Plinval,1943,37 (see Morris,1965, 31f.; Evans,1968, 13f.).

Text

1.   Secular literature recounts how a certain philosopher, speaking to a
young man whose silence used to conceal from others the fact that he was
present at all, prefaced his remarks thus: 'Speak, young man, so that we may
know you!' He wished to show that a man is appraised in the light of his
discourse; as long as he remains silent, he is unknown. But *our* philosopher,
endowed as he is with heavenly, not human, wisdom and inspired not by the
spirit of the world but by that of God – I refer to Solomon –, put the matter much
more clearly when he said: For a wise man is known by his speech, and perception and the sagacity that comes from knowledge by words of truth (Sir.4.24);[3]
and elsewhere: Do not praise a man before you hear him speak, for this is the test
of man (Sir.27.7).[4] We can well believe that human wisdom of a later period
appropriated this proverbial utterance for a subsequent writer so as to acquire a
quite unjustified reputation for it. Who could possibly be ignorant of the fact that
Solomon was a writer of an earlier date, unless, that is, he knows nothing of the
dates of different kingdoms and eras of history? But it makes no difference
whether a man utters his own words or appropriates those which are another's
property, as long as he is seen to be in agreement with a maxim which is of divine
origin, and it is established by human and divine testimony that a man is known
by his own words. Though I already believed this saying to be true in the past, I
can now admit that I have proved it for myself: for a long time I did not know
you personally, honourable sir,[5] but after hearing you speak, even if it was only a
few words, the invisible sounds revealed to me what your visible and physical
presence had long kept concealed from me. Your tutor, the holy Martyrius, had,
of course, long sung the praises of your piety to my humble self; but it is difficult
for human nature to trust another's witness as much as its own.

2, 1.   Therefore, since I have now found out for myself what I had long heard
from others, that you are Christian enough and wise enough not to scorn the
understanding that leads to truth, I am unwilling that you should make the same
mistake as those who suppose that they can sin with impunity because they are in
ignorance of the divine will – unhappy, miserable creatures indeed and utterly
ignorant of the truth, if they do not know that the ignorance which is born of
knowledge provides no one with an excuse! They do not know what they do not
know, because they know what they do not know; for they know that what they
do not know is good, and they do not know it because they do; and if they did
not know it, then perhaps they could have. What ignorance it is, then, that is

---

3   RSV: 'For wisdom is known through speech, and education through the words of the
    tongue.' Our author has used a version based on LXX, as also in the next quotation.
4   RSV has 'reason' for 'speak'. We shall find that our author has no qualms about
    inserting in his quotations words which he wants to use in his text.
5   Cf. OF,I,1 and see n.23 there as well as c.7 in this letter.

bred of knowledge! But someone may say, 'It is to my advantage to sin in ignorance rather than with knowledge.' But I maintain that, when a man knows what it is that he does not know, it is no longer a matter of true ignorance: perhaps ignorance is able to excuse a man who does not know even what he ought to know. But, to give you a more conclusive proof of the fact that this line of defence excuses no one, tell me what it is that God asks of his worshippers. Without any doubt it is that they do his will. What then does his will ask of them? Unless I am mistaken, everything that the commandments of his law specify should be done. Does God want that same law to be known or not? Without doubt, to be known. For how will his commandments be fulfilled, if the thing which he has commanded is unknown?

2. So the first demand made by God's will is that the things which he bids us know should be known, the second that, when they are known, they should be observed. If then his first wish is that we should know his commandments, how do you suppose that you can be excused by ignorance of the law when by that ignorance you become a transgressor of his first wish? For if I do not do what I know, I am a transgressor of his second wish but not his first, for I am doing the first thing that God has wished me to do; but *you*, having transgressed the first, how will you be able to fulfil the one which follows it? For it is possible both to fulfil his will and to neglect it, when you know it; but it is not possible to fulfil God's will, if you do not know it. For a man will find it easier not to do what he knows than to do what he does not know.

3. But, to make the proof even more conclusive, it is certain, as I said before, that God demands nothing of us except that we keep all his commandments, and this will be the sole ground on which he bases his judgement, if a man has preferred to disobey his commandment. Set two men who have despised his law to stand trial before the heavenly tribunal in God's court of judgement, the one having sinned in ignorance, the other with knowledge. To the latter the question put is, 'Why have you not fulfilled my commandments?' What will he say in reply? Nothing, I suppose. For he will not even be able to claim that God on some occasion gave him an impossible command, lest he seem to have blasphemed against him by charging him with injustice; and when he gives no reply, he will be sentenced to eternal fire, as we have been told. Then the second man, the one who sinned in ignorance, will be asked why he too did not do God's will. He will reply, I believe, 'Because I did not know it.' Next, he will be asked, 'Why did you not know it?' I do not know what he can answer to that question, unless perchance it be, 'Because I did not wish to', in which case he will be found guilty on two counts – of not doing and not knowing God's will. For God desires his commandments to be kept under any circumstances, and it makes no difference whether they are neglected knowingly or in ignorance. The following testimony, used by the blessed apostle, offers no excuse for ignorance when it says: For it is not the hearers of the law who are righteous before God, but the doers of the law who will be justified (Rom.2.13). How can a man be a doer unless he has first been a hearer? I do not see how a man can do something without knowing what he is doing. That is why the apostle does not blame the

hearer but desires him to be a doer, as it is written elsewhere: But be doers of the word and not hearers only, deceiving yourselves (Jas.1.22).

4. But so that you should not think that I am buttressing this position with my own personal proofs,[6] please accept an instance from the law to the effect that ignorance is of no help to sinners but rather an encumbrance. In the Books of the Kings[7] we read that Jonathan, the son of King Saul, in his ignorance broke the fast imposed on the people by tasting a little honey and, because he was guilty of this fault, provoked God to such anger that he would have punished him had not the people prevailed upon him by their prayers not to do so. And from this we are given to understand that even the sinner's ignorance is to be set down as his own fault. But, you will say, 'I have been preoccupied with worldly concerns.' Well, you had the spare time to read Virgil, Sallust, Terence and Cicero[8] and other foolish and pernicious writers, preaching not God but idols. But now you are hindered by various concerns and countless exigencies from reading the prophets and Christ and the apostles, the masters of divine wisdom and eternal life. So I do not wish you to stray any further from the path, since I have come to know that your devoutness is such that you are not unworthy of God's care.

3, 1. First, then, get to know God's will, as contained in his law, so that you may be able to do it, since you can be certain that you are a true Christian only when you have taken the trouble to keep all God's commandments.[9] I do not want you to pay any attention to the examples set by the majority, who claim the honour of belonging to this religion for themselves in name alone; for a prize so great belongs only to a few: How strait and narrow is the way that leads to life! And those who enter by it are few (Mt.7.14). It is not the name but the deed which makes a Christian; you will find it harder to discover the essence of something than its title. For those who think that they are Christians merely because they possess the name of 'Christian' are making a very serious mistake: they do not know that it is the name which belongs to the thing and not the thing to the name and that it is right to call a man what he is but foolish to call him what he is not.[10]

2. But perhaps you want to know what it means to be a Christian. A Christian is a man in whom can be found these three attributes which all Christians should possess: knowledge, faith, obedience; knowledge, by which we know God, faith, by which we believe in him whom we know, obedience, by which we render our allegiance and service to him in whom we believe. But each of those three is divided into two types: so, the two types of knowledge are (1) the knowledge by which we know God, (2) the knowledge by which we know his

6 Cf. *Life*,7, which begins with a similar sentiment.
7 Literally, 'Books of the Kingdom', of which there were four at this time, as in the Vulgate – 1 and 2 Sam. preceding 1 and 2 Kings as we now know them.
8 Our text actually has 'Tullius', Cicero's second name (*nomen*); 'Cicero', of course, is his third name (*cognomen*) and 'Marcus' his forename (*praenomen*).
9 Cf. OF,1,5; *Virg*.4,2; 7,2; *Dem*.15; 16,1; 25.
10 Cf. OF,1,3; *Life*,1,2; 6,1; 10,4; *Cel*.8.

will; the types of faith are (1) the faith by which we believe that God exists, (2) the faith by which we believe in him; it is one thing to believe that God exists and another thing to believe in him, for every man who believes in God believes also that he exists but not every man who believes that God exists believes in God. We believe that there is a God when we are assured of his existence but we believe in God only when we give faith to his promises. Obedience also takes two forms: (1) the obedience by which we are prevented from doing evil, (2) the obedience by which we are commanded to do good. A man with your good sense has to recognize that a Christian is one who has faith, that one who has faith is a righteous man and that a righteous man is none other than one who keeps God's commandments, but that the one who keeps God's commandments is the one who does no evil which God forbids and respects anything good which he orders to be done,[11] since the scripture says: Depart from evil, and do good (Ps.34.14; 37.27). For I do not want you to think that those who do some good things but also some bad are true Christians in any event, since the scripture says: Whoever keeps the whole law but fails in one point has become guilty of all of it (Jas.2.10).[12]

4, 1. Perhaps you say, 'State briefly for me the kinds of commandments that we have to keep.' There is nothing briefer than the definition given by the apostles of the charge of the Holy Spirit: What you do not want done to you, do not do to another (Tob.4.15);[13] and the Lord himself says: Whatever you wish that men would do to you, do so to them (Mt.7.12; cf. Lk.6.31). If a man properly understands and keeps these two aspects of the commandments, he will be able to keep clear of all sin; for the sum total of righteousness is contained in them – that a man should not do to another what he does not want done to himself, *and* that he not only should not do to another an evil which he resents being done to himself but also that he should show to another every good that he does not want another to deny to him. Such a man will not only repay another for a good which he does not want to be repaid to him but he will also repay an evil with a good which in like manner he does not want to be denied to him; and no one wants to receive retaliation for an injury inflicted on another. Thus the first aspect of the commandment is seen to correspond to the second in that what we wish men to do to us we too in like fashion should do to them. We want to be respected by all men, and so it will be proper for us to respect all men; we want no one to harm us, and so we likewise are to harm no one. But also, if we do harm another, we want some concession to be made to us, and so we ought to pardon those who have harmed us and to love even our enemies, because we take no pleasure in being the objects of their hatred either.

2. Need I say more? All possible forms of good are contained in these two testimonies, if one understands them correctly. A Christian may harm no one, if

[11] Cf. OF,2,1 and see n.21 there.
[12] A favourite Pelagian proof-text; cf. OF,1,5 and see n.14 there.
[13] RSV has 'What you hate, do not to any one', as does LXX too.

he is to fulfil this testimony and to be able to say, 'I have harmed no one, I have lived in righteousness with everyone.' It is not permitted to lie, to curse, to take an oath, to render evil for evil, to flatter, to accept persons for their rank, to hate an enemy whom one is commanded to love, as it is written: Love your enemies (Mt.5.44).[14] Thus a man of your good sense must understand whom it will be possible for him *not* to love when he is bidden to love even his enemies, and to whom he will be able to be evil when he is bidden to be good to those who hate him.

5.   It is not permitted to be covetous or have superfluous possessions[15] or to boast of earthly honours and riches, since in this present life it is poverty, not wealth, humiliation rather than nobility, that befits us, as the scripture says: The greater you are, humble yourself in all things, and you will find favour in the sight of God (Sir.3.18). Let every man who professes to be a Christian follow the example of his Teacher in all things, as it is written: He who says he abides in Christ ought to walk in the same way in which he walked (1 Jn. 2.6). For Christ claimed for himself neither high birth nor riches in this world, and the apostle states that we are God's children: Beloved, we are God's children now (1 Jn.3.2). It is therefore shameful for God's child to boast that he is a child of man[16] and to wish to be called rich in temporal things when he is promised eternal riches,[17] especially as he knows that the Lord has denied the kingdom of heaven to those who are rich in this life, since the Lord says in the gospel: It will be easier for a camel to enter through the eye of a needle than a rich man into the kingdom of heaven (Mt.19.24; Mk 10.25; Lk.18.25). You may be sure that the man who keeps those commandments is a great Christian but you must also understand that the man who spurns them is not a Christian and is called one in error.

6.   And since we are offered through Christ an example not only of godliness and righteousness but also of chastity, we must also follow the pattern of his example, so that we may prove that we are genuine disciples of him who chose to be a virgin himself and promised to virgins the reward of the kingdom of heaven, as he says in the gospel: For there are eunuchs who made themselves eunuchs for the sake of the kingdom of heaven (Mt.19.12).[18] There is nothing so dear to God as the good of chastity, in which we bear an especial likeness to him if after baptism we remain steadfastly uncorrupt and pure. For it is an infinite virtue to overcome the pleasures of the body, since he who has overcome an enemy has

---

14 Cf. OF,1,4 and n.10; *Virg.*7,3; and *passim*. It will be noted that the Pelagian list of requirements invariably includes the injunction 'not to take an oath'.
15 Cf. OF,4,2; *Virg.*7,3 and see n.12. Our author is now touching briefly on the main subject of *Riches*.
16 For the Christian practice on the continent during the fifth and sixth centuries of omitting the patronymic on memorials in deference to the command to 'call no man your father on earth' (Mt.23.9) see Rees, 1988, 116ff. and cf. BT,17,3.
17 Cf. the phrase 'eternal consulship' at the end of this letter; see n.20.
18 Cf., e.g., *Virg.*2.

become stronger than another but he who has subdued lust has become stronger than himself.

7. These remarks, honourable sir,[19] I believed that I should write in the meantime as far as a brief letter has permitted, though I desire to speak to you in your holy presence and to enlighten you on all the matters on which you have thought fit to consult me. I pray that you may ever live for God and rejoice in the honour of an eternal consulship.[20]

---

[19] See OF, n.23. Caspari, in a footnote to p.282, comments that 'the dictionaries do not know *honorificentia* as a form of address'; but that is certainly what it is here.

[20] Morris,1965,39 wrongly took this phrase in a literal sense but was corrected by Cameron,1968,213ff.; see also n.17 above.

8

On the Possibility of not Sinning[1]

This letter comes fifth in Caspari's edition, presumably because that is its place in his original manuscript; I have brought it forward, as it seems to fit in better with the letters *To An Older Friend* and *To A Young Man* than sandwiched between the much longer tractates *On Riches* and *On Bad Teachers*. It would seem fairly certain that the same man wrote all three letters 6–8, but this time we have no indication of the identity of his correspondent. After the usual introduction in his best courtly style, explaining his reasons for writing, our author goes on to develop the case for claiming that a man has the ability to be without sin, a theme already touched on in the two earlier letters; it might be argued that this letter is a natural sequel to the letter *To A Younger Man*, especially as the copyist has completed it by adding an almost identical version of the five concluding chapters of the latter.[2] Whether this was done deliberately or in error we have no means of saying but it would be strange if our author contented himself with the very brief statement of his case which we have been left with.

The letter is of considerable historical importance to us: in his account of the Synod of Diospolis in 415 Augustine includes a list of points of error alleged against Pelagius by 'some of our Catholic brethren in Sicily' and refers to his own correction of these errors as contained in his reply[3] to a letter from Hilary of Syracuse received in 414–415; one of these errors was the claim that a man can be without sin if he so wishes, included in Pelagius' indictment as the sixth item (cf. *OF*, n.2). To this item and to the repetition of the charge in the seventh Pelagius had replied that he *had* said that 'a man can be without sin and keep the commandments of God, if he wishes, for this ability has been given to him by God'; but he went on to add that he never claimed that 'any man can be found who has *never* sinned from his infancy up to his old age.'[4]

---

[1]   *[Epistula] de possibilitate non peccandi* or *[Epistula]* '*Qualiter*': PLS 1, 1457–62; CPL 735; Caspari,114–119; Haslehurst,190–199.

[2]   Thus the doublet begins 'For those who think. . .'.

[3]   *On the Activities of Pelagius*, xi.23 (PL 44,333f.); *Letters*,157 (PL 33, 674–93) – Hilary's letter is numbered 156; *On Original Sin*,xi.12 (PL 44,390f.).

[4]   *On the Activities of Pelagius*, vi.16 (PL 44,329f.).

In another work, also written in 415,[5] Augustine dealt with propositions said by 'brethren from Sicily' to have been advanced by Celestius, Pelagius' main collaborator, but to be held by many others as well. What all this adds up to is the likelihood that Pelagius or Celestius or both had spent some time in Sicily *en route* for Africa and that, as a result, a Pelagian circle had been established there. If this were correct, then the writer of the Caspari corpus would have been a member of this group and would have exerted himself to win over adherents to the cause by personal contact and correspondence, and this letter and the one written to a young man could be among several which he wrote with this end in view.[6]

Caspari's (1890) edition of this letter and the three following it in our collection was based on one ninth-century MS; it was corrected in 1902 by Julius Baer, using two earlier editions (1575, 1677) also based on Caspari's Vatican MS and adding conjectures of his own. In 1927 Germanus Morin discovered a twelfth-century MS containing our nos.9, 10 and 11 but in a different order and with the last part of *On Chastity* in a considerably more legible state than it was in the Vatican MS; this enabled him to make further suggestions for the improvement of the text. Haslehurst's (1927) text contains all four pieces as does Hamman's in PLS 1 (1959) but both are far from satisfactory. I was fortunate in being able to use Michael Winterbottom's admirably thorough collation of all the MSS and editions mentioned above which was published in 1987 and includes his own suggestions and which has put me, my readers and all other students of Pelagianism deeply in his debt. A more suitable tribute to John Morris' contribution to Pelagian studies would hardly have been possible.

Text

1, 1. How well we remember your piety and how deeply we respect it you will be able to understand from the fact that we could not entertain the possibility of not addressing, at least in a letter and even in his absence, one whom we were unable to see face to face; only loyalty and affection can ever arouse in us the urge to write such a letter, especially when it is a matter not so much of the writer's seeking his own advantage as of his fulfilling the obligations of a loving relationship. And though a Christian has to love everyone and is bidden to love even his enemies, yet he feels greater affection for those whose personal goodness demands that they should be cherished with all possible zeal and respect. For it is not so much the case that those who love such persons are doing so out of virtue

---

[5] *On Man's Perfection in Righteousness,* (PL 44,291–318).
[6] See Morris,1965,41; Evans,1968,29f. The possible implications are discussed in my Introduction.

as that those who fail to love them are liable to a charge of ill will; for it is not particularly praiseworthy to love those whom it would be blameworthy not to love. For this reason I, who am showing only the affection which is due to one of your character, feel that in this respect I am merely avoiding the risk of being blamed for harshness towards you rather than displaying any virtue myself. I call God as my witness when I say that, ever since I have been able to recognize it, I have admired your nobility of character, loved your good sense and the self-discipline revealed in your tolerance, and respected all the marks of seriousness in you which are so clearly manifested to all and sundry.

2. Therefore I have always found it hard to accept – and, just as if I had a grudge against this world, have lamented the fact – that a mind so fitted for the things of God should rather be hampered by the constraints of men and that one who ought to be seeking heavenly rewards should rather be pursuing earthly gains. Yet I have never despaired of believing that a soul so godly and so richly endowed and flavoured with all the refinements of good sense would one day come to despise corruptible and transitory things and want to transfer its allegiance rather to a preference for the things that are incorruptible and eternal. So it was with great elation that I rejoiced when knowledge of your increase in faith was brought to my humble attention not by rumour but by true report; undoubtedly this was because I am sure that a man is soon able to become weary of mortal pleasures when once some longing for immortality comes to him, and because it is common knowledge that a man who has been ambitious to progress in human affairs will be all the more anxious to advance in things divine once he has begun to hope for heavenly rewards with the same eagerness and self-confidence with which he seemed to be looking forward to those on earth. For of any two recognized goods there is no one who does not aspire to possess the better, and men always spurn the lesser once they have begun to hope for the greater.

2, 1. It has also reached my humble ears that you are heaping such praises on my insignificant person that you appear to think that there is nothing to be criticised in it except what is beyond criticism. That you should suppose this is typical of your inborn sense of kindness and your conscientiousness, and you can find no other or better way of praising one whom you love than by claiming that he is so faultless that the only fault which can be found in him is something with which no one can rightly find fault. But because I do know my own conscience, I realise that there are many things in me which merit criticism. So there is no call to hold me blameworthy in matters which are free from blame, since I can see for myself that I am open to criticism in matters for which I ought to be blamed.

2. It is quite different if, as often happens, actions which we know to have been done purposely and conscientiously are either censured in ignorance or misunderstood through lack of charity. For what can we believe to be so worthy of understanding, so consistent with godliness, as that God, the founder of righteousness and equity, cannot be seen to have done anything which ought

even to be suspected of being unfair and unrighteous? Consider how far removed from any suspicion of unrighteousness he should be who has no love for a man when there is any wickedness in him, but deprives him of his kingdom and delivers him up to the fires of hell if some mark of wickedness still remains in him. If then the one who has been created must be wholly righteous, what are we to expect of the one who created him? And if the one who is to be judged has to be wholly righteous, what are we to think of the one who judges? Surely it would be fitting for God to have given a command which it is impossible to fulfil, if such a thing is fitting for even a man to do; but if even human nature thinks it unfair to order anyone to do something impossible, how perverse it is to believe God to be capable of something which not even the nature of mortals would respect!

3. Is there anyone so thoughtless, so unrighteous, so totally ignorant of equity, as to dare to order a servant or any of his subjects to do what he knows to be beyond his capability? For instance, will any man instruct his servant to complete in one day a journey which takes four days or despatch him to swim across the waves of the wide sea rather than to sail over them or to climb impassable and inaccessible mountains with slippery peaks or to do anything else beyond his natural capabilities? If he presumed to give such an instruction, who would not think him not only unfair but mad as well, seeing him impose upon a man instructions which his own natural powers could by no means carry out? And if such a judgement can justifiably be made of a man of this kind, I leave it to your common sense to decide what men would think of a God whom they suppose to have given them an order which is beyond their natural capabilities.

4. So I beg you to set aside for a while any opinion which is based on a deep-rooted conviction, to rid yourself of any spirit of contention, to listen to my humble words with an open mind free from prejudice and to give your attention not to the opinions that are expressed in everyday intercourse but to the truth that is based on righteousness and reason. For I know that you are a man of understanding and that I am therefore able to proceed without undue concern, because I am defending a reasonable case before a reasonable judge.

3, 1. But someone will say, 'Is it then possible for a man not to sin?' Such a claim is indeed a hard one and a bitter pill for sinners to swallow; it pains the ears of all who desire to live unrighteously. Who will find it easy now to fulfil the demands of righteousness, when there are some who find it hard even to listen to them? Or how is a man to undertake with equanimity the works which are required, when the teaching underlying them sounds so unpleasant? Why do we any longer ask whether a thing is possible, when it is considered to be so unusual and contrary to nature that men cannot even listen to it? When will the blood-thirsty and cruel gladly accept such a claim? When will the greedy and lustful cease to be terrified by it? When will the extravagant and the mean bear it with equanimity? To sum all this up briefly: When will a man guilty of any crime or sin accept with a tranquil mind that his wickedness is a product of his own will, not of necessity, and allow what he now strives to attribute to nature to be ascribed to his own free choice?[7] It affords endless comfort to transgressors of the divine law if they are able to believe that their failure to do something is due to inability rather than disinclination, since they understand from their natural wisdom that no one can be judged for failing to do the impossible and that what is justifiable on grounds of impossibility is either a small sin or none at all. So the unhappy wretches rush headlong into various sins without any reflection and therefore maintain afterwards that they have not done things from which they claim that they were unable to abstain; and so it comes about that, under the plea that it is impossible not to sin, they are given a false sense of security in sinning.

2. Even if this were so, it should never be spoken of, since it would destroy those who hear it instead of edifying them. Anyone who hears that it is not possible for him to be without sin will not even try to be what he judges to be impossible, and the man who does not try to be without sin must perforce sin all the time, and all the more boldly because he enjoys the false security of believing that it is impossible for him not to sin. Such a man will never do penance appropriate to his misdeeds but will believe that God will lightly remit what rightly he ought not even to impute. But if he were to hear that he is able not to sin, then he would have to exert himself to fulfil what he now knows to be possible and when he is striving to fulfil it, to achieve his purpose for the most part, even if not entirely. Also, if he is prevented by some offence resulting from human frailty, at least his sins will undoubtedly be less frequent and more trivial. The man who labours and strives to be without any sin will humbly and submissively express his regret for the error of his ways, when he realizes that he has done what he could have avoided if he had but wanted to. Just as the former appreciation of the situation is prejudicial to those who listen to it in two ways, by giving them a false feeling of security when they sin and by leading them to conclude that penitence is not really a necessary means of redress, so the latter perception is understood to help in two ways, by encouraging them not to sin, because they have the capacity to avoid it, and by urging them more forcefully to repent and admit their voluntary transgression, if, as often happens, they have fallen into the error of committing a sin.

4, 1. If you object to this, saying, 'A man cannot by any means be without sin', then consider first whether that which is such that a man cannot be without it ought to be described as 'sin' at all; for everything which cannot be avoided is now put down to nature but it is impious to say that sin is inherent in nature, because in this way the author of nature is being judged at fault.[8] To say that a man cannot be without sin is like saying that a man cannot live without food or

---

[7] A forthright statement of the central tenet of Pelagianism; cf.4,1 below.

[8] On the dangers of such a challenge to divine authority cf. *BT*,13,1; *Virg.*6; *Cel.*6. Caspari inserted the Latin words *hoc si dicatur* (= 'if this were said') in this sentence, and

drink or sleep or other such things without which our human state cannot exist. But if that is what we must hold, how can it be proper to call sin by that name if, like other natural things, it cannot be avoided, since all sin is to be attributed to the free choice of the will, not the defects of nature?

2. But first we ought to understand the definition of sin itself, so that we may then be able to argue with greater cogency about the propositions that it is possible or impossible to avoid it. We have to find a definition of sin which covers two eventualities – failure to avoid things which are forbidden, and failure to do things which are commanded.[9] Now I want to ask the conscience of anyone with normal human feelings what are his views on the things which God has forbidden us to do – can they be avoided or not? If the former, he has rightly forbidden them; if the latter, I ask, first, on what reasonable grounds have they been forbidden, and, secondly, what is the justice in reckoning as a sin the commission of an act which cannot by any means be avoided; I also ask if the commands that have been given can be obeyed or not. If they can, then they have been reasonably and justly given; if they cannot, then they must be re-garded as pointless, nor can I see the justice of holding disobedience of orders which cannot possibly be implemented to be a sin. Again, if only things which could have been avoided have been forbidden and only things which could have been done have been commanded, how can we possibly refuse to accept that a man can be without sin, when we are ready to admit that nothing impossible has either been forbidden or been commanded – that is, if, as we have stated, all sin is included under the headings above?

3. But, to make the point still more plainly, you say that a man cannot be without sin. I ask first whether he was commanded to be without sin or was not so commanded. 'I believe that he was,' you reply. Why then was he so com-manded, if it was quite impossible for him to carry out the command? You have to accept one of these alternatives, either that the command was not given, seeing that it cannot be carried out, or that it *can* be carried out, because it *was* commanded, since, as we have said earlier, God would never have commanded the impossible. But, to make it absolutely clear that the command *was* given, let us make use of examples from the holy law. It is written: You shall be holy, for I, the Lord your God, am holy (Lev.19.2). And in the gospel our Saviour says: You must be perfect, as your heavenly Father is perfect (Mt.5.48). And the blessed apostle Paul says: Do all things without grumbling or questioning, that you may be blameless and innocent, as the children of God are without blemish (Phil.2.14,15). And elsewhere: And you, who once were estranged and hostile to his mind, doing evil deeds, but have now been reconciled to him in the body of his flesh by his death, present yourselves as holy and blameless and irreproach-

PLS 1 prints them in brackets; I see no need for them, and my own version makes perfectly good sense and is more faithful to the grammar without them.
9   Cf. YM, n.11 and OF, n.21.

able before him (Col.1.21,22).[10] And again, . . . you will be able to find . . . (This sentence is incomplete and is followed, no doubt through an error on the part of the copyist, by an almost identical version of cc.3–7 of the *Letter to a Young Man*, beginning at 'For those who think . . .'.)[11]

---

[10] Minor verbal alterations to the standard text are made here but the sense is the same.

[11] Nuvolone, 1986,2916, suggests that the letter was reduced to about a tenth of its original size by this loss and that the original text would probably have been developed at some length with the support of biblical quotations, themes such as the goodness and justice of God and the natural potential of man, examples of righteous men, the commandments of Jesus and rewards and punishments, ending with a personal word of encouragement to the addressee, whether real or imagined, followed by the usual concluding greetings. The letter must surely have been a substantial one, if it was considered by the anti-Pelagians in Sicily to be dangerous enough to merit the attention of Augustine (see the introduction to this letter).

9

On Riches[1]

This is the Pelagian tract which led John Morris to make his incisive but controversial comment that 'the crisp argumentation that wealth and property had
arisen in the past through "oppression"; that the existence of the rich, the fact
that society is divided into such "genera", is the cause of poverty, cruelty and
violence; and that society should be wholly reshaped, now and in this present
substance, by abolishing the rich and redistributing their property to the poor – is
by any textbook definition socialism. Further it is socialism of a coherence and
urgency that was hardly to be met again before the nineteenth century, or at
earliest the end of the eighteenth.'[2] Caspari had already commented that the
ideas of On Riches 'here and there remind us of socialism'[3] but this bare statement
did not do justice to the polemic contained in it in Morris' view. Taken in
conjunction with the letters To a Young Man and To An Older Friend and the
brief summary of the case against riches in On Bad Teachers 18,3, it provided the
main grounds on which he built his theory that the author of these pieces, whom
he supposed to have emigrated to Sicily from Britain under pressure from the
leaders of the Church there, was one of a group of young, Pelagian radicals living
in Britain at the turn of the fourth century and that it was their writings and
activities that prompted the political and ecclesiastical establishment to summon
Bishop Victricius of Rouen in the early years of the fifth.[4]

But, as we have already pointed out,[5] there is no reason to think that our
author came from Britain at all; indeed, it seems more probable that he was a
native of Italy or Gaul; and Pope Innocent's letter to Victricius in the Peterborough text of the Anglo-Saxon Chronicle is 'a Latin interpolation under the year
403' often linked with this visit but without any implication 'that it had any-

---

[1] [Epistula] [sancti Sixti episcopi et martyris] de divitiis (PLS 1,1380–1418; CPL 733; Caspari,25–67; Haslehurst,30–107).
[2] Morris,1965,50f.
[3] Ibid.: 'hier und da an die des Socialismus (sic) erinnern' – 'that seems to me an under-
statement' (Morris).
[4] For a summary of Morris' thesis and some of the objections to it see Rees,1988,111ff.
[5] In the general Introduction and the introduction to the letter To An Older Friend.

thing to do with Pelagianism in Britain'.[6] Others[7] have expressed strong opposition to the view that Pelagianism in Britain or anywhere else at this time can be seen as a deliberate attempt to undermine the structure of contemporary society by preaching 'socialism'. There is absolutely no evidence that Pelagius himself was at all interested in politics except insofar as involvement in it might prove a hindrance to the practice of a true Christian faith: his aim was to reform the Church, not to make a protest against the social policies and legislation of the imperial government, and his own criticism of riches was designed to promote right conduct by persuading Christians to espouse the ascetic way of life of their Master and his apostles, a programme to which not even his greatest opponents, Jerome and Augustine, could have raised any serious objection, even if the former was not altogether enamoured of monks.

A full discussion of the problem of the authorship of this tract and the other tracts and letters in Caspari's collection will be found in my Introduction. But, as far as *On Riches* is concerned, all that can be safely said is that we do not know to whom it was addressed or indeed whether it was addressed to anyone in particular, though it is possible that, like the letters in this batch of documents, its recipient was a Sicilian Christian known to its author. In the main it consists of a number of questions which might be put to its author with the intention of undermining his thesis on riches and of refuting arguments which he might wish to advance in support of it, and of his detailed replies to such questions. These replies are backed by biblical quotations, some of them and, in particular, Mt.19.21 and 24, Lk.6.24 and 14.33, Jn.19.27 and Acts 20.35, having to be explained at length in order to correct misinterpretations attributed to the author's Aunt Sally.

The style of the tract is highly rhetorical, and the arguments are presented with considerable subtlety, at times descending to casuistry, and will demand the closest attention of the reader; my own impression is that the writer may well have had the benefit of at least some degree of legal training but others may prefer to think that his Ciceronian style and his skill in marshalling his arguments are merely the products of a conventional training in the art of rhetoric. The tract is without doubt an impressive, comprehensive and powerful denunciation of riches as a stumbling-block to all who wish to attain Christian perfection, and Morris rightly comments on the freshness and liveliness of its language as well as on its unusual treatment of the origins and consequences of wealth, emphasizing the strong link between riches and political power, public eminence and an unchristian attitude to cruelty.[8] We might even go so far as to agree that many of the points made might easily find a place in a socialist manifesto today. But the motivation of its author was religious, not political, and it comes as no surprise that some of the leaders of the Sicilian Church were so alarmed that they

---

6 Thomas, 1981, 51; Victricius' visit to Britain is recorded in his *On the Praise of Saints*,1 (PL 20,443).
7 See Rees,1988,113, n.65.
8 Ibid.48f.

found it necessary to report the teaching of the Sicilian Pelagians to the person who seemed to them best qualified to counteract them and bring the culprits to book, that is, Augustine of Hippo, 'the defender of grace'.

It was Hilary of Syracuse who took it upon himself to write to Augustine probably c.414.[9] He warns Augustine that 'certain Christians in Sicily' are teaching heretical doctrines about the possibility of 'sinlessness' and the Christian rite of infant baptism and denouncing the acquisition and possession of wealth. The first of these topics could well be a reference to the incomplete tract *On the Possibility of Not Sinning*, in which there might also have been a discussion of the second, infant baptism, and the third is dealt with in both of the letters proper in this collection as well as in this tract. In his reply Augustine indicates that he is not unaware of the existence of a group of Christians who are disseminating false and dangerous views of this kind and that they are precisely the views associated with the name of Celestius, already branded as a heretic by a Council of Carthage held in 411.[10] Perhaps, he suggests, it is this man or his confederates who are spreading the same seeds of heresy in Sicily.

After dealing, fairly briefly for him, with 'sinlessness' and infant baptism in the general context of grace, he turns his attention to the outright and unqualified condemnation of riches, insisting that the case against them is not nearly as clear-cut as the followers of Celestius are trying to make it. He warns against their tendency to see everything in black and white: neither is wealth as such to be condemned nor poverty as such commended, and Jesus' injunction to the young man does not necessarily imply that all wealth must be disposed of but rather that every reasonable attempt should be made to use it for the benefit of the poor. He points out that there were two parts to the injunction: the first was an answer to the young man's question, 'What shall I do to obtain eternal life?', and it was *not* to sell all that he had but that he should keep the commandments; when the young man replied that he had done so and went on to ask, 'What do I still lack?', the second answer of Jesus was that if he would be *perfect*, he should sell all his possessions and give the proceeds to the poor. In other words, Jesus

---

[9] Augustine, *Letters*,156 (PL 33,673f.)(from Hilary) and 157 (PL 33,674ff.)(from Augustine).

[10] The association between Celestius and Pelagius began in Rome probably in the first decade of the fifth century and ended with their joint condemnation by the African bishops, the Pope and the Emperor in 418. After his first condemnation by the Council of Carthage in 411 Celestius left for the East, where he was ordained priest at Ephesus in 415 but was expelled from Constantinople by the Patriarch Atticus. He then appealed to Pope Zosimus against the decision of the latter's predecessor, Innocent I, in 416 that he and Pelagius be excommunicated; but after the final condemnation in 418 he returned to the East and his 'opinions' were finally rejected by the Council of Ephesus in 431. So far as our present evidence goes, we have none of his works, only quotations from them in Augustine, Jerome, Marius Mercator and other pillars of the establishment, though it is generally agreed that his theological views were more extreme than Pelagius', as a comparison of the two men's *Confessions of Faith* will show. It is clear that they must have collaborated in writing these but how and to what extent is hard to say.

drew a clear distinction between keeping the commandments and attaining perfection, and this is in complete agreement with Paul's instructions for rich people in 1 Tim.6.17–19.[11] No Christian, says Augustine, can possibly believe that Paul would contradict Jesus' injunction; it must be the Pelagians who have misinterpreted it. Let them follow the way of perfection, if they can; but let them not condemn those who choose rather to retain their possessions, while using them, like true Christians, for the benefit of others less fortunate.

It has been well said that 'Augustine's reply is a most remarkable testimony to his power of seeing the two elements on both sides of a moral question.'[12] But for the author of On Riches and his friends there was only one element, and nothing that even Augustine might say would persuade them to the contrary. By the time when he wrote his account of the trial of Pelagius by the Synod of Diospolis in 415,[13] he was able to record points of error of which the Pelagians were guilty and of which he had been informed by 'Catholic brethren in Sicily', a reference to the letter of Hilary. It is significant that errors which he had originally associated with Celestius were now considered by him to be sufficiently important to be also linked with the name of Pelagius, though the latter had little difficulty in convincing his judges, if not Augustine, that he had no responsibility for them. But they have, nevertheless, the authentic stamp of Pelagianism.

Text

1, 1. I would marvel that some men's minds are held captive and are possessed by their love and craving for earthly things to such an extent that they come to think that worldly wealth is a hindrance to no one, if I did not remember that all human beings suffer from the vice of thinking that what they love is better than anything else and of identifying deep down in their minds as the greatest good what they espouse with such love that they become totally incapable of being separated from it. This is also a characteristic of mankind that, when a man is held captive by any vice, he sees it as a great good in others, although the judgement of his own conscience tells him that it is in fact bad. For the power of a man's mind when it is perverted and corrupted by love of evil is so great that he gives assent neither to his own nor to other men's judgement but prefers to go against his own conscience – and everyone else's – rather than resist what he loves with such intense passion.

2. There are three sins which are swept along with such momentum and are inflamed by such fires of passion that it is almost impossible for them to be extinguished or subdued, and they are gluttony, avarice and lust. Anyone who becomes a slave to one of these is, as it were, hurled down headlong from the

---

[11] It is interesting to note that this is *not* a passage cited by the author of On Riches!

[12] Sparrow-Simpson,1919,145.

[13] On the Activities of Pelagius, and especially xi.23 (PL 44,333f.).

heights of life and light into death and darkness by his own instability and disquiet, so that he can hardly be recalled any longer by any of the curbs of instruction or bonds of teaching. And though all three of these are oppressive, they are so closely connected and bound to each other that it is almost impossible to tear them away from this mutual relationship and to separate them one from another; for it is very difficult for a man enslaved by the pleasures of gluttony to overcome avarice and lust, since the one gives him comfort and the other help; gluttony is as lonely without lust as lust is bereft without avarice, and avarice will appear somehow to hate itself, unless it is sustained by the help of gluttony, which persists only through avarice. So, as we have said, these three sins are essential to each other and thus can hardly be distinguished and separated from each other.

3. But lust and gluttony are more easily overcome than avarice, because in their case satiety arouses a certain feeling of repugnance, whereas avarice, since it is insatiable, is never wholly repugnant to those who love it; rather, the more it increases the more completely they love it, and, as it grows old with them, so it grows in strength also. Greed is like a fire that derives its kindling from the materials provided by worldly things. Add fuel to a fire and it will grow into an immense blaze; add to avarice what is not its own, and it will develop into an even greater fire of greed for more. Finally, in many men you will find gluttony and lust overthrown; but even those who censure avarice have great difficulty in entirely subduing it. From this we can observe how it keeps its hold on those who love it: even those who have already begun to hate it it strives to keep under its yoke. What wonder then if its worshippers continue to defend it quite shamelessly, when its power is so great that sometimes even those who have begun to denounce it remain to some extent under its sway!

2. But someone will say, 'Having begun to talk about riches, why do you bring up the question of avarice?', as if it were one thing to be avaricious and quite another to want to be rich. For just as a man possesses avarice because of riches – if, indeed, an avaricious man can be said to possess rather than to be possessed –, so he seeks riches because of avarice, and riches are able to continue in existence only so long as they are protected by their mother, as it were, that is, avarice. The avaricious man is not the one who makes generous donations to the needy from what he has himself; and the man who has already begun to distribute largesse will also begin to have nothing left over, while the man who has nothing left over will not be able any longer to be rich, since man is judged to be rich only because he has a great deal left over. Thus, as a man ceases to be avaricious, he also ceases to be rich.

3. 'But,' you will say, 'it is not the man who guards his own possessions that is avaricious but the man who plunders another's.' How many then of those who have property of their own have not previously coveted another's? It can be very hard for a man to become rich without having coveted another's goods at all. It is quite stupid to consider a man to be avaricious before he possesses property and

when is he only coveting it, and think him free from avarice when he has already begun to possess it. It is one thing to attribute lust to a man who desires to practise fornication before he actually does so, another to believe him to be free from lust if he has already begun to indulge in it. Just think: if the whole of a crime consists in what precedes the act, what does the crime itself consist of? I do not know how you would defend the performance of an act, if even the planning of it cannot be shown to be excusable, or how the fruit can be harmless in a tree whose flowers have grown from sin.

4, 1. But perhaps these arguments will not be acceptable unless they are supported by divine authority. Listen then to what the blessed apostle thinks of this matter and how he defines avarice. He says: Those who wish to be rich fall into temptation and into the snare of the devil and into many senseless and hurtful desires that plunge men into death and destruction. For avarice is the root of all evils (1 Tim.6.9,10).[14] By that one word 'wish', unless I am mistaken, he has defined avarice, a wish which we must believe to exist as much in those who are not yet rich but long to be so as it does in those who are rich and desire to remain so. For if you maintain that the desire for riches exists only in those who want to become rich instead of poor, then I ask you if those who are already rich do not wish to be so or have even begun to wish not to be so. If they wish to remain so, then there exists in them the desire for riches which comes from coveting them, and they too will be liable to the apostle's censure; and if they do not so wish, what necessity forces them to be what they do not wish to be?[15] Or why are they rich, if they do not wish to be? And if they really do not wish to be rich, why do they not make an effort to cease to be what they do not wish to be? For if they truly do not wish to have riches, why do they not cast them away or distribute them or strive by some means to be without them?

2. Or if someone wants to take their riches away from them, why do they try to prevent him, why do they resist, why do they even defend their riches by the authority of the tribunals of this world when, if they really did not wish to have them, they ought to be grateful if someone delivers them from something which they do not want, since the greatest blessing is to be without something which you possess against your will? If a man has a rotten member in his body through the fault of some weakness caused by disease, I think that he would gratefully accept its amputation and not be angry with a surgeon if he either cauterizes or cuts off the part which is of no benefit itself and makes other, sound limbs rotten by its proximity.[16] So too, those who do not wish to keep their riches ought to be grateful to those who take them away from them and not be angry with them; or, if they are angry and do not wish to be deprived of their riches,

[14] RSV has the traditional 'love of money'(= *cupiditas*, Vulgate); I have kept our author's *avaritia* but there is no clear distinction between *cupiditas* and *avaritia* except that the former has a wider range of meanings.

[15] The usual Pelagian emphasis on man's ability to choose.

[16] For analogies with medicine cf. 19,5,6; BT,3,1; 17,1; Chast.9,2; 10,3; Law 2,2; 8,1. Our author seems to be very well informed on the subject.

this manifest proof of their desire for them is confirmed by the angry defence of them which they put up; for everyone refuses to part with what he loves. This is a novel and quite unbelievable phenomenon that I now hear of, namely, that some men do not wish to be rich and yet are so, since it is much easier to meet a willing pauper then an unwilling rich man.

3. But perhaps you will say, 'It is one thing to want to become rich, another to want to remain rich.' What is the difference between wanting to become rich and wanting to remain rich? I suppose it is that the man who wants to become rich is not yet rich, whereas the man who wants to remain rich is rich already. Are we then to understand that the man who wants to become rich is culpable but that the man who is known to be rich already is not culpable, seeing that the sin consists only in coveting riches and not in possessing them? If that is so, then those who desire to be rich must make haste to be even sooner what they desire to be, because according to this interpretation they will be liable to punishment only so long as they are not what they desire to become. But as soon as they have begun to be what they desire to be, they begin to want no longer to become rich but to want to remain so, and since they have begun no longer to want to become rich but to remain so, they are exempt from the apostle's judgement, by which, according to some, those who want to become rich are held to be guilty only so long as they are not. And if assent is given to this interpretation, all who are taking away another's possessions have, as I have mentioned earlier, to hurry up in order to arrive at the sum total of their own riches in the sure knowledge that they will be culpable only so long as they have not become what they wish to become. If perchance this is the view that prevails among men, whose most frequent practice it is to substitute for the truth a profusion of words and deception tricked out in colourful arguments and in the allure of dialectic and who are persuaded that possession of wealth is harmless and that only the desire for it is sinful, then it is not a view which prevails with God: with him it is not subtlety in complicated argument that counts but plain, simple truth, and it is the authority of truth's judgement, arrived at by a divine decision, that will hold sway. And according to truth, if even those who have only the will to sin are to be punished, then those are much more liable to punishment who have also put into practice the evil that they have willed.

5, 1. 'Riches are evil then,' you will say. First, discover what riches are, and then work out their true value with all the skill of an accountant. Mankind is divided into three classes: the rich, the poor, and those who have enough, for every man must be accounted to be either rich or poor or self-sufficient. To be rich, so far as my meagre understanding is able to determine, is to have more than is necessary; to be poor is not to have enough; and to have enough, the mean between these two extremes, is to possess no more than is absolutely necessary.

2. But lest you should suppose that this is my definition and regard it as an opinion held by merely human intelligence and therefore to be despised, listen to what the Holy Spirit says when it speaks in the person of Wisdom: Give me

neither riches nor poverty but settle upon me a sufficiency of the things that are necessary (Pr.30.8).[17] Observe too that we have based the above definition not on the judgement of my own self-assurance but on the authority of the Holy Spirit: he who desired to be neither rich nor poor but asked only that a sufficiency of the things that are necessary be settled upon him showed quite plainly and clearly that whatever falls below or is in excess of sufficiency must be assigned either to poverty or to riches respectively. That being so, why do you hold it to be a good to have more than is sufficient – sufficient, I mean, not for the demands of avarice but for the needs of nature? For nothing can ever be sufficient for avarice, even if it possessed the whole world, so extravagant are its demands, and covetousness increases as the substance on which it feeds spreads by contagion. You have, I think, either read or perhaps heard read the saying: Anything more than this comes from evil (Mt.5.37). If you have either not read it or, having read it, suppose that it refers only to another context and is irrelevant here,[18] surely you can assess the true value of riches by the fact that a holy and wise man so completely rejects them that he goes so far as to ask that they be denied him. For you must consider what sort of good something can be if a sensible man can ask for it not to be given to him.

3. 'Yet he did not wish to be poor,' you will say, 'but asks rather that his poverty should be taken away from him. And for that reason, since you are trying to persuade me to live according to his wise example, you ought to deliver me too from poverty and need no less than from the greed for riches, and you should confine me only within those limits which you intimate that the man whose good sense you hold up as an example for me to follow asked for himself.' Clearly, in comparison with those who love riches and affluence and are not afraid to possess more than they need, though they can see many of their brethren in need, the man who distributes his surplus wealth to those in need and, in accordance with the teaching of the Old Testament, is content with what is enough is praiseworthy. But even more praiseworthy is the man who wishes to fulfil the commandments not only of the Old Testament but also of the New, especially when our Lord and Saviour has taught us this by word as well as by example – by word, in that he said: No man who does not renounce all his possessions can be my disciple (Lk.14.33; cf. Mt.19.21; Mk.10.21; Lk.14.26), by example, in that we read that after his assumption of the form of a man he was so poor that he did not possess even a place of his own where he might lay his head (cf. Mt.8.20; Lk.9.58). Of him the blessed apostle says: That, though he was rich, he became poor, so that by his poverty you might become rich (2 Cor.8.9), wishing to show that we are to be made rich with heavenly riches as soon as we despise earthly wealth following Christ's example, so that the saying of the

---

17 Our author's text contains a number of variations on the Vulgate here.
18 We might be prepared to agree with such a supposition, since the context of the quotation from Mt. is the importance of giving simple answers and not swearing oaths, 'this' being simply answering 'Yes' or 'No'!

blessed John may be fulfilled in all respects in us: He who says he abides in Christ ought to walk in the same way in which he walked (1 Jn.2.6).

6, 1. The comprehensive statement given above is not intended to be a vote of censure on wealth obtained without sin, expended on good works and not supplying its possessors with any need or occasion to sin, but on wealth derived from evil deeds, which provides those who enjoy it with frequent opportunities to do evil and yields no fruit in works of mercy, and which fawns upon its possessors with such pernicious flattery that they come to prefer to be rich in earthly resources than rejoice in the wealth of their heavenly inheritance. Note carefully, I beg you, what a great sign of arrogance and pride it is to want to be rich when we know that Christ was poor, and to take upon ourselves any of the power that comes with lordship, when he took on the outward form of a servant, as it is written: Have this in mind among yourselves, which is yours in Christ Jesus, who, though he was in the form of God, did not count equality with God a thing to be grasped, but emptied himself, taking the form of a servant (Phil.2.5–8). Surely everyone who is called a Christian professes that he is Christ's disciple, and Christ's disciple should follow his teacher's example in all things, so that in the deportment and conduct of the pupil his manner and doctrine may be in accord with that of his master.

2. What pattern of Christ is revealed in such a rich man? What likeness to him is shown in such a possessor of wealth? How can poverty be compared with affluence? What has humility in common with pride? What similarity is there between the man who has nothing and the man who has superfluous possessions? I shall say no more about material fortune; but let us see if the rich man's way of life has any similarity with that of Christ. There is none that I can see: the one is haughty, the other downcast; the one is proud, the other humble; the one is full of fury, the other of gentleness; the one is angry, the other long-suffering; the one is boastful, the other self-effacing; the one abhors the poor, the other embraces them, the one abuses them, the other extols them. The rich, with that vainglorious and proud spirit in which they covet for themselves the glory of this world, are sometimes accustomed to solicit earthly power and to take their seat upon that tribunal before which Christ stood and was heard. How intolerable is the presumption of human pride! You may see the servant sitting where the master stood, and judging where he was judged. What is this, Christian? What is this, disciple of Christ? This is not the pattern given by your teacher. He stood humbly before the tribunal; you sit on the tribunal, above those who stand before you, propped up by your pride, perhaps about to judge a poor man. You ask the questions, he was heard; you judge, he was subjected to the judge's decision; in your presumption you utter your judgement, in his innocence he received it, as if guilty; he said that his kingdom was not of this world, but to you the glory of a worldly kingdom is so desirable that you procure it at vast expense or acquire it with unworthy and wearisome servitude and flattery.

3. And all the time you convince yourself that it is from God that you receive what, in fact, you either procure with your ill-gotten gains or acquire at

the price of shameful sycophancy and oft-repeated acts of obeisance, bowing your head to the ground and addressing as 'Lord' one whom you scorn, while he, the trafficker in offices, also scorns you; and sometimes you glory in being called 'honourable', though the only true honour is that which is paid to moral character, not that acquired by money or shameful servitude. Before your eyes human bodies, of a like nature to yours, are battered with a scourge of lead or broken with cudgels or torn apart with claws[19] or burnt in the flames. Yet all this your holy eyes can bear to witness and your Christian disposition permits you to watch – and not only to watch but even to exercise the authority given you by your exalted rank and administer the torture yourself in the place of the executioner. I find the spectator quite loathsome enough; what am I now to say of the one who gives the orders? Reflect with me, earthly judge: does some hardening of the heart render you immune and exempt from the suffering endured by one who is of the same nature as yourself, or does the pain of his human body somehow fail to penetrate to the feelings of your human heart?

4. After something like this any Christian's heart remains in such a state of disquiet that he cannot even go to sleep unless he directs his pious concern to one who, on your instructions, has been torn to pieces by such a variety of punishments and such a multiplicity of cruel tortures, and he is stricken with a great fear of divine judgement, if he fails to show some compassion for him. And do *you* fear nothing, *you* on whose instructions he had to undergo all that suffering? Sometimes you give instructions for even an innocent man to be thrust into prison, urged on by motives like the need to do favours for others or to pay back injuries done to yourself, and then you appear to be important in your own eyes when you own personal grievance is redressed; yet Christians are overtaken not only by intense concern but by a considerable fear of divine anger if they do not try at once to discover such a man's whereabouts, while you enjoy complete peace of mind, *you* by whose instructions he was imprisoned. It is not enough to enumerate all the horrors, floggings, dungeons, darkness and unyielding bonds and chains; under a judge as many deaths from torture result as there are penalties inflicted. Thus great anxiety is aroused in Christians to perform acts of kindness and compassion, when they see themselves in the persons of their own kin torn to pieces and mangled by birds and wild beasts and in some cases denied burial; but you, the upholder of riches and trafficker in offices, after committing such acts, recline without a care in the world, resting on tapestries piled high beneath you as if you were enjoying the spoils of a triumph laid out at your feet, and entertain your guests with the tale of the man whom you savagely tortured and of the manner in which you brought about his death and cast him to the ground before the very eyes of the people; and lest anyone present at your feast should be struck with horror at the story, you go on to claim that, in doing this, you were beholden to the law, when, only a short while before, you were boasting

---

[19] The Latin word '*ungulae*' is used to describe instruments of torture. For this bitter attack on judges cf. *Life*,3,2, of which this lively passage may well have been a development.

that you lived by the law of Christ as one who not only hearkened to the gospel but even preached it according to popular report.

5. What is the reason, I beg you, for so great a discrepancy between persons who are called Christians by the same name and are bound by solemn obligation to the same religion that some of them engage in such unholy acts of cruelty that they are not afraid to oppress, rob, torture and, finally, kill, while others are so frightened by their feelings of compassion and sense of duty that they fear to be lacking in mercy to those whom the others have destroyed without any fear at all. It is worth giving careful consideration to what causes such diversity in men of the same faith. Has the same law of Christian conduct not been given to all who are called Christians? Or are they perhaps bound by two kinds of commandments different from each other, one by which some are by necessity bound to fulfil the obligations of compassion and sense of duty, the other by which others are given leave to perform acts of irresponsible cruelty? Or is a cooler fire made ready in hell for those whom it pleases to commit cruel acts and a hotter one for those who must practise godliness? We know that we are 'one body', in the words of the apostle (1 Cor.12.13); if we are truly one, then we should act as one. There is no room for such variety in the same people. Let us search the scriptures and weigh up with serious and careful thought which law we should adhere to and then choose one of these two alternatives, either to be compassionate or, shocking though it may be to hear, to live a life of professed cruelty, if that is what is expedient in our opinion.

7, 1. But notice, reader, why it is that the theme of my discourse has turned in this direction. We were speaking, unless I am mistaken, about the rich whom their cruel desires have immersed in excessive affluence and misled into performing all those ungodly and savage acts which we have mentioned earlier. Rightly, therefore, in almost all the scriptures God, who foresees all things,[20] censures and condemns the greed for riches which the fount of knowledge has truly revealed as the cause of human error.[21] As the good physician, who knows by the skill of his profession that melons, pumpkins, figs, apples and all kinds of fruit cause ill-health, censures them in the presence of his patient with all the vehemence at his command and endeavours to induce in him an aversion for them, knowing that he can be cured only if he rejects the causes of his illness above all else, so too the most skilful physician of our souls everywhere condemns the lust for riches which he knows to be the occasion of sin and would have us shudder at what is harmful, knowing that we are more easily detached from sin if its cause forsakes us.[22]

2. That is why he says in the Psalms: Put no confidence in extortion, set no vain hopes on robbery; if riches increase, set not your heart upon them (Ps.62.10). Someone will say, 'In this passage he appears not to have been

[20] On God's foresight cf., e.g.,11,3; BT,15,1.
[21] Cf. 1 Tim.6.10 and see n.14 above.
[22] See n.16: the reference to the dangers of eating fruit is interesting today!

warning us against riches in general but specifically against seeking after them.'
Yes, but what else is the chief source of riches but extortion and robbery? I can
give a most convincing proof of this fact by pointing out that we know that
nearly all those who were once poor and whom we can now see becoming rich
can become so only by extortion and robbery.

3. 'That,' you will say, 'may be true of those who were once poor and have
become rich; but what of those whom we know to have become rich as the result
of inheriting their parents' wealth and are properly described as 'born rich'? They
certainly appear to be able to possess riches acquired not by extortion but by just
inheritance; but I was talking not so much of the possession of riches as of their
source, since I think that they can hardly have been acquired without some
injustice.

4. 'How can you know the source of these riches,' you will say, 'when you
do not know when they started?' I know the present from the past, and I also
understand what I have not seen from what I see. If you were to ask me how men
or herds or flocks or all the manifold variety of living things were born a thousand years ago, I would reply that it was in every case by coition. And if you were
to say to me, 'How can you know that?', I would reply that I infer the past from
the present and that I am confident that every effect which I see to have a
certain cause now had the same cause then too, when I was unable to see it.

5. 'So riches are sinful?' Well, I do not say that they are sinful in themselves
but I do think that for the most part they are the result of sin. And if you are
willing to discuss the matter with me in a peaceable spirit and not in anger and to
cease to defend in a contentious manner the possessions with which you have
fallen in love, and, setting aside all inclinations to perverseness, to listen to the
voice of true reason in a calm and serene frame of mind, then perhaps I might be
able to prove to you that it is wicked to hang on to riches with too tight a hold.

8, 1. Does it seem just to you then that one man should have an abundance of
riches over and above his needs, while another does not have enough even to
supply his daily wants? That one man should relax in the enjoyment of his
wealth, while another wastes away in poverty? That one man should be full to
bursting-point with expensive and sumptuous banquets far in excess of nature's
habitual requirements, while another has not even enough cheap food to satisfy
him. That one man should possess a vast number of splendid houses adorned
with costly marble statues in keeping with the instincts of his vanity and pride,
while another has not even a tiny hovel to call his own and to protect him from
the cold or the heat? That one man should maintain countless possessions and
enormous expanses of land, while another cannot enjoy the possession even of a
small portion of turf on which to sit down? That one man should be rich in gold,
silver, precious stones and all kinds of material possessions, while another is
harassed by hunger, thirst, nakedness and all kinds of poverty? Add to this the
fact that we can see evil men abounding in excessive wealth and good men
struggling with need and destitution, which makes us even more suspicious of the
unfairness of this thing called riches.

2. 'What then?', you say, 'Do not riches come from God?' Whatever can be justly defended comes from God; but anything that is the result of injustice does not come from God, because whatever is bestowed on us by God as its origin ought to be free from all suspicion of having an unjust origin. So we must first prove that there is no injustice in riches and only then can we believe that they come from God. Surely we can agree that God is equitable and just, nay more, that he is the source of all equity and justice. First I ask what theory of justice, what principle of equity permits one man to enjoy the freedom of plenty and another to suffer the constraints of need. And if we know that some are rich by God's decree, while others are poor, how is it that we can sometimes see their positions reversed and very often undergoing a change to the opposite? How many poor men we know who were once rich, how many again who were once poor and are now rich! If these things had been so ordered at the beginning by God's decree, none of them could have changed to the opposite.

3. I beg you, therefore, to set aside all spirit of contention and to surrender and abandon your defence of the possessions that you love and reflect upon my words with a sincere and unprejudiced mind, examining the force of my remarks not as an advocate of your own cause but as a searcher after truth. If God had decreed that there should be inequality in all things, surely he would have made an unequal distribution of the gifts of his creation to all men and would not have allowed men whom he wished to be unequal in respect of his lesser gifts to be equal in respect of his greater gifts, and those who ought to be unequal in every respect would not be receiving to an equal degree the benefits of the sky, the earth or any element. Reflect then how those elements serve the needs of the human race which are distributed not according to men's judgement but by God's will, and you will then be able to infer a few truths from many and to understand lesser truths from greater. Observe whether the rich man enjoys the benefit of this air of ours more than the poor, whether he feels the sun's heat more or less, or, when rain is given to the land, whether larger drops descend on the rich man's soil than upon the poor man's, whether the glowing lights of the moon or the stars serve the rich man more than the poor. Do you not see then that we possess equally with others all the things which are not under our control but which we receive by God's dispensation, and on unjust and unequal terms only the things which are entrusted and subjected to our own rule for the sake of free choice and to test our righteousness?

4. But, to say no more on those matters, let us turn to the mysteries of the sacraments and consider if any inequality can be found in them which affects the situation of the human race.[23] Let us see if there is one law for the rich and another for the poor, if the former are reborn by one kind of baptism and the latter by another, if they do not obtain the same pardon for sin and the same sanctification of righteousness, if they are not all endowed with the one spirit, if they do not feed on the communion of the same altar and drink of the one holy

[23] For God's fair and equal distribution both of the gift of the sacraments and of worldly possessions cf. Comm. 190,col.1216,7ff.

draught. But if God the Dispenser's indulgence towards mankind is found to be equally distributed in things material and spiritual alike, it now begins to become clear that this inequality in the dispensation of riches must be ascribed not to divine favour but to human injustice. For why would God want men to be unequal in the lesser things, when he has made them equal in the greater? Is it not perhaps more fitting that he who receives the gifts of heaven without discrimination should also obtain the benefits of this world on equal terms with you? For I assume that the Holy Spirit should be preferred to all the honours and riches of this world. Do you suppose that he who is worthy to possess along with you that which is greater is unworthy to possess that which is less?

5. I ask you to answer this question too, you who think that riches are given by God: to whom do you suppose he gives them, the good or the bad? If to the good, why is it that the bad have them? If to the bad, why do the good have them? If both to the good and to the bad, why do the majority, whether good or bad, not have them? But if you say that riches are bestowed by God on the good but by the devil on the bad, I shall first ask why all good men do not rejoice in this gift of God's; secondly, I shall add that it is no great boon if God seems to bestow on the good what the devil can present to the bad.

9, 1. 'Do we then find that God has never bestowed riches on anyone at all?' you will ask. Sometimes surely but not always, not on all men perhaps and not from the beginning. Unless I am mistaken, we read that Abraham was the first to be made rich by God. If there was no rich man before Abraham, since he was the first to be made rich by God, then there can be no doubt that riches came from God at the beginning. But what if there was a very large number of rich men at that time and not just a handful? The scripture reminds us that there were kings and potentates from the outset. Well, in that case, riches did not come from God originally, since the man whom we know to have been the first to be made rich by God was not the first rich man.

2. So you say to me, 'What does it matter whether he was the first or the last, as long as it is quite clear that he was made rich by God?' Surely it matters, in that we must designate as a true good what originated with God, but what is reckoned to have begun not with an appraisal by God but through the pride of men cannot possibly be seen to be as good, even if some think that God took responsibility for it for various reasons after its validation by usage. For example, there was the King of Israel of whom we read that he was appointed not so much by God's will as through the perverseness of the people, although God's consent was added later, since he prefers to correct the sins that spring from human frailty with forbearance and gentleness than to punish them with the severity they deserve. There were also the sacrifices which the children of Israel had been accustomed to offer to idols in the land of Egypt but were afterwards ordered to sacrifice to God – not that God takes pleasure in the blood or flesh of animals, as he says elsewhere: Do I eat the flesh of bulls, or drink the blood of goats (Ps.50.13)? But, rather, in order to train gradually by principles derived from his own instruction a people which was weakened and degraded by a variety of

ungodly practices, he did not want them entirely to discard a custom which had long been in use and had been confirmed over a long period of time but to change it for the better in the interim, as he was to say later: What to me are the sheep of your whole burnt-offerings? For I have not made you to labour over frankincense or to buy me incense with silver nor I have desired the fat of your sacrifices (cf. Is.1.11; 43.23; Jer.6.20); for by then they were stronger and were able to absorb what they were unable to take in while still in a weak state of health. I think that we should understand that it was in a similar way that God gave riches to Abraham, his servant, whom he had found to be the only man on whom he could rely in the whole world, because men in their pride had already begun to enjoy their use and believed them to represent the highest good and in order that even so they might turn their minds and affections towards God, when they saw that he had bestowed on his worshipper so quickly and easily the very thing which they judged to be the best in the world.

3. I say nothing of the fact that at that time all things were done by way of an example, as the apostle says: For these things happened to them as an example for us (1 Cor.10.11). For now no man has to have his wife fashioned for him out of his rib in his sleep with God again acting as the fashioner simply because a rib of Adam was turned into a woman and in her was prefigured the church of Christ fashioned from the blood from his side in his sleep after his passion; nor must he be supplied with a concubine as well as a wife simply because Abraham had a concubine in addition to a wife and in them, as we know on the authority of the apostle,[24] this is an example of the two covenants; nor do we have to have four wives at the same time simply because it is said that Jacob had four wives at the same time and in them we have to understand either an example of the fourfold teaching of the gospel, which by its fruitfulness and its chaste lasciviousness brought about the spread of a countless progeny of the spirit through the efforts of the twelve patriarchs of the New Testament, or else of the four peoples, that is, Jews, Gentiles, Samaritans and Sadducees, joined to Christ by faith in spiritual wedlock.[25]

4. If these practices have ceased and are no longer to be employed now that the truth of the matter of which they were an example has overtaken them, though they were known to have existed at one time, why may we not believe that there was a mystical side to Abraham's riches and that, after serving its purpose by acting as a symbol of a future truth, the symbol must now make way for the truth which overtakes it? Finally, what does scripture testify on this? Observe what God says to Abraham: Go from your country and your kindred and your father's house to the land that I will tell you (Gen.12.1). It is after this that the scripture records that he was made rich, and so he was made rich by God after having been poor for God's sake. He had become poor by leaving his parents and country – and who can doubt that this was how it came about, unless he refuses

[24] Viz., Gal.4.22ff.
[25] On the mystical and symbolic interpretation of the OT cf.9,5; 18,11; Chast.3,4; Law,9,2; Dem.5.2. and passim.

to read the account of it as it is given? – and the purpose of this was to demonstrate that a man is able to obtain heavenly riches in the future at God's hands if he has consented to be poor and despise all his worldly possessions for God's sake in the present.

5. We must believe that what we have said of Abraham applies to others as well. For if you want to urge me to consider the instances of David and Solomon and of others whom we read of as having been rich at that time, then I too will urge you to consider other examples of behaviour which they offer and which it is not fitting for you to follow in all respects, now that it is necessary to adapt to a different situation and a new covenant, and so perhaps it will not be fitting to follow them in the matter of riches either. For if you suppose that you ought to seek riches because we know on the authority of the scripture that Abraham, David and Solomon were rich, then the same scripture witnesses to many other things relating to them. It says that they were circumcised in the flesh, that they observed the sabbath as a day of rest, that they also observed the feast of the new moon and the feast of the Tabernacle and other ceremonies of the law; and it tells us moreover that they had many wives and a great number of concubines, as we read in the story of Solomon. We ought therefore to practise all these things like them, if we have to seek riches following their example. Or if you believe that these things were designed to be symbols of the future in some mystical way and had to be practised only for so long as the truth of what they mystically symbolized had not yet been revealed, why should you not understand their riches in the same way, especially when you know that almost everything that was done in former times was intended to be a symbol?

6. Again, what reason is there for a man rather to follow the life and pattern of holy Abraham, David and others, when he is commanded to live by the example of Christ? I ask you, by whose death were you restored to life? By whose blood, by whose passion were you set free? Who was it that heard most unworthy revilings and abuse for your salvation? Who was it that bore your infirmities and removed the causes of your sickness and the wounds which were otherwise incurable? Who was the physician whom you employed when sick and already close to death? Whose was the head that was pierced with a crown of thorns which represented the brambles of your sins? Whose the face that was dishonoured with spittle? Whose the cheeks that were buffeted by Jewish palms? Who endured scourges that you should not be scourged eternally? Who drank gall and vinegar? Who was hanged upon a gibbet? Who endured curses upon the cross for the sake of your accursed and abominable life? By whose wounds were your wounds healed? Who brought you back from death to life? Who summoned you back from hell to heaven? Not a patriarch, not a prophet, not any other holy man at all, but Jesus Christ our Lord. He is our hope, he is our salvation, he is our redemption; it is he whom we have to imitate and follow; it is to him that we owe all our life; it is to him, as all know, that we belong.

7. It is quite unjust that we should despise and reject the one who bore all these things for our salvation and should prefer to imitate those who suffered nothing of this kind for our sakes, even if we know that in their time they pleased

God. The blessed apostle Peter says: Because Christ also suffered for you, leaving you an example, that you should follow in his steps (1 Pet.2.21). His steps, that is, and no one else's. When the Lord had taken the three disciples with him and ascended the mountain, and Moses and Elias, symbolically representing the law and the prophets, had suddenly appeared there, his Father's voice rang out like thunder from heaven, saying: This is my beloved Son; listen to him (Mk.9.7). That is: remember not the former things, nor consider the things of old; behold, I have now shown you new things, which I promised you before would come to pass in the future.[26] 'Him,' he says – no longer, that is, Moses or Elias, who preached the observance of the Jewish ceremonies which were to cease when Christ came, but 'him' whose coming the law and the prophets had promised, to whom men were now to 'listen' rather than to them and who came not to destroy the law but to fulfil it; for he fulfils the law by revealing it to be true, and he reveals it to be true by making to cease what the law had foretold would cease. And out of the old law he brought forth the new, and out of the old covenant he promulgated the new, so that he might make good the prophecies of the law and the prophets, including the statement: Out of Zion shall go forth the law, and the word of the law from Jerusalem (Is.2.3; Mic.4.2); and again elsewhere: I will give them a new covenant not like the covenant which I gave to their fathers (Jer.31.31,32). In all these matters we must now observe that we are not to imitate the men of old but Christ and that we are to keep not the commandments of the old covenant but those of the new.

10, 1. In what manner then are we to imitate Christ? In poverty, if I am not mistaken, not in riches; in humility, not in pride; not in worldly glory; by despising money, not by coveting it. And what are the commandments of the new covenant that we are to keep? First and foremost, those by which the occasion of sin is to be removed through contempt of riches. That is why you will find that the Lord gave no commandment to those who desire to follow him and to offer themselves as his disciples, which was of higher priority than to despise riches and the world, as he demonstrated to the man who offered himself on one occasion as his follower how he might follow him in the way he ought to follow, by saying: Foxes have holes, and the birds of the air have nests; but the Son of Man has nowhere to lay his head (Mt.8.20). That is to say: see whether you are able to be such a disciple that you can follow such a master; for it is easier for a poor man to follow a poor man, since the rich man rejects him, being ruled by his pride. Let there be an end to false allegory, now that we are furnished with the truth and now that it is not the approval of the reader that we are seeking but his improvement, it is not the ingenuity of the writer that is being presented to us but the truth of his subject matter that is being proclaimed.

2. Likewise elsewhere: If you would be perfect, go, sell all that you possess and give to the poor, and you shall have treasure in heaven; and come, follow me (Mt.19.21). You can see that not even this man is given permission to follow

[26] See Is.43.18,19; 48.3,6.

along the road to perfection until he has sold all that he has and distributed it to the poor. 'But,' you will say, 'it is his sins that he has to sell, not his property.' And where will he find a purchaser stupid enough to buy *them* – unless, perhaps, it be the person who understands the passage in such a sense? I do not know who is going to spend money in order to purchase something which is nothing but a nuisance even if you possess it free of charge. 'But,' you say, 'the devil will buy it.' I ask you, what price will the vendor get for it from *him*, and how will he distribute to the poor what he does get from him? 'Well then, it was a statement referring to the Jewish people as a whole, and the young man merely represented them symbolically.' Is the Jewish people the only one which is wealthy, the only one which riches can hinder, to which the kingdom of heaven opens its doors? 'He was rich,' you will say, 'in the commandments of the law, and therefore he is commanded to divide them up and sell them off separately.' Here too I ask who will buy them, or why he is bidden to sell at a price what he had received free of charge? This is how they discuss the passage quoted and argue about it and debate it, simply because they prefer to watch jealously over their riches than to keep Christ's commands, and love money more than the glory of the kingdom.

3. The Lord says the same thing again elsewhere: Unless a man renounce all that he has, he cannot be my disciple (Lk.14.33). What will you say in this instance? I suppose you will say that he is ordered to renounce his sins, not his property. But is a man able to strip off all his sins *before* becoming Christ's disciple? If so, what more has he to gain by taking Christ as his Master? Or in what respect will he be in need of Christ's teaching if he has already become righteous through his own efforts? But I ask you this, 'Are sins possessed, or do they possess us?' If *they* are possessed, it will be possible to understand this saying to refer to them: Every man who does not renounce all his possessions cannot be my disciple (Lk.14.33). But if, on the other hand, they possess *us*, no kind of reasoning permits us to interpret as referring to possessors what was actually said about possessions. To make it even clearer that our sins possess us rather than are possessed by us, listen to the Lord himself, when he says: Every one who commits sin is a slave to sin (Jn.8.34). A slave, as I see it, does not possess but is possessed. And if that is so, whether you want or do not want to be rich, you have to understand the passage as referring to worldly goods.

4. But when it has been established by clear reasoning that the statement refers not to sins but to worldly goods, they are in the habit of turning to another interpretation: they say, 'Of course these words have to be understood as referring to worldly resources but the command was given not to all men for all occasions but to certain men on certain occasions, that is, to the apostles, who had to follow their Lord in a variety of places and at that particular time when the Christian religion was putting forth its first shoots and believers were being continually harassed by the storms of persecution to such an extent that they were unable to remain in their own lands or retain their own possessions. Thus it was necessary for them to bow before the assaults of their persecutors and to distribute all their possessions, lest they lose all by being forced into flight. But now, when nearly all men are Christians through the Lord's graciousness and

even kings and potentates have to submit their necks to Christ's yoke, times are peaceful and calm and we are safe from all the troubles of persecution; so it is not necessary for anyone either to distribute or sell his property, since it was not so much the needs of his religion as the stress of persecution that demanded this of him.' How ingenious the greedy can be! They never want for a reply in order to prevent the loss of what they love! But, in fact, the light of plain reasoning will establish that such an interpretation is incorrect.

5. In answer to the first part of the interpretation which they now wish to adopt – namely, that the apostles alone were told to distribute all their possessions – I ask, 'When that young man approached the Lord and sought his advice as to what good he had to do in order to be able to earn the reward of eternal life, was the number of the apostles complete at the time when those words were spoken?' I think it was already complete. Why then did Christ also say to him: If you would be perfect, go, sell all that you possess and give to the poor, and you shall have treasure in heaven; and come, follow me (Mt.19.21), if only the apostles had to do this? And in the case of those who, in the Acts of the Apostles, undoubtedly sold all their possessions, some of them laying the price of what they sold at the apostles' feet, while others distributed them to the poor themselves, why were they willing to do this if they knew that only the apostles had to do it? Or if in their ignorance they supposed that an instruction given to particular individuals was really intended to be applied generally, then their inexperience ought to have derived enlightenment from the apostles' knowledge and an action resulting from ignorance to have been prevented on their authority from being done by those who came after them. But what if that act was not only not forbidden but laid down as approved and commended for posterity to imitate? If others were not supposed to do it, it ought to have been stopped right at the outset and no written record of it preserved for posterity to follow.

6. Why were Ananias and Sapphira punished by death for keeping back a part of the price of their property, if they were not required to surrender even the part which they had already handed over?[27] If they knew that only the apostles were required to act in this way, then they were under no obligation to offer that part either. 'They were punished,' you will say, 'simply because they had lied.' In that case, why was the apostle so anxious to be punctilious in dealing with a matter of no importance, and why did he condemn the falsehood by imposing such a serious penalty? For telling a lie about a matter which was beyond the call of duty ought no more to be thought contemptible than enforcement of the truth about it unjustifiable. It is preferable not to complete something when you ought not to have begun it at all.[28]

7. And if it was only the apostles who were obliged to keep this commandment, why do they afterwards exhort others to live by their example and in

---

[27] See Acts 5.1; for Ananias and Sapphira cf. *Law*,4,4; *Life*,13,3.
[28] The importance of finishing a task once undertaken is also emphasized in *Virg.*19; *Law*,4,4; *Cel.*30,1; 32.

nearly all of their epistles preach contempt not only for riches but also for the whole world, as we read that the blessed Paul wrote to the Corinthians: Be imitators of me, as I am of Christ (1 Cor.11.1), and again: I wish that all were as I myself am (1 Cor.7.7)? They would be doing this in vain, if they were quite unable to do it and not even obliged to do it anyway; for they were certainly not obliged to do it, if the command was laid on the apostles alone. And when he says: I want you to be free from anxieties (ibid.32), I think that he was preaching contempt for riches, the possessor of which cannot be free from great 'anxieties'. He then goes on to say: The unmarried man is anxious about worldly affairs of the Lord, how to please the Lord; but the married man is anxious about worldly affairs, how to please his wife (ibid.32,33).

8. Observe how free he desires you to be from the anxieties of this world, since he would have you give them not even a thought. This he also testifies in writing to the Philippians: Have no anxiety about anything, but in everything by prayer and supplication with thanksgiving let your requests be made known to God (Phil.4.6). I put it to the conscience of the rich whether they care nothing for their riches, whether they suffer from no anxiety on that score, whether they are never held back for the sake of riches from the performance of their duties to sing psalms, to pray, to read the scriptures or from any other divine works, whether they are free from the anxieties arising from lawsuits and litigation, whether they are never compelled to have recourse to secular courts contrary to the command of the Lord or his apostle, whether they are never stirred to action by cases concerned with rights of ownership or boundaries or any other cause of litigation which distract them from the works of the Lord and force them to transgress the commandments of God's law.

9. Therefore the blessed apostle John also says: Do not love the world or the things in the world. If any one loves the world, love for the Father is not in him. For all that is in the world is the lust of the flesh and of the eyes and pride in worldly possessions. And the world shall pass away, and the lust of it; but he who does the will of God abides for ever, as God also abides for ever (1 Jn.2.15–17). I pray you to weigh the force of these words carefully with all the sagacity and attention that your spirit and mind can command. 'Do not,' he says, 'love the world or the things in the world.' How can a man fail to love what he is so greedy to seek and possess? No one either clings with greed to what he does not love or seeks it for himself. 'If any one loves the world, love for the Father is not in him': what more could he say than that love for God is not in those who love the world?

10. Will you then say, 'Riches are not from God'? But who was it then that made gold and silver? Who placed precious stones in the earth which he had created? By whose decree was the earth founded? Or whose command was it that brought all things forth? Was it not God's? Who will deny this, unless he is either foolish or ungodly? Yet we should not think that all riches are from God merely because all those things are his which, when piled up in one heap, are called 'riches'. For, according to my earlier definition, I say that riches are not gold or silver or any other created thing but the superfluous wealth that is derived from

unnecessary possessions. Whether this wealth comes from God, who must be believed to be the source of equity and justice, I leave you to decide for yourself. For it is agreed that God created the things which we have just mentioned along with the rest of his creation, yet not in order that one man should become wealthy by the possession of unlimited affluence while another is tormented by excessive poverty, but that all should possess impartially and with equal rights what the source of all justice has granted them.

11. The blessed Peter also agrees with what has just been said: Who called us by his own glory and excellence, by which he has granted to us his precious and very great promises, that through these you may escape from the corruption that is in the world because of passion, and become partakers of the divine nature (2 Pet.1.3,4). From this, I think, it is quite obvious that it is not only the case that the apostles have to despise worldly wealth but that they also exhort and teach others to do likewise and to live by their example, being mindful of the Lord's injunction: Go therefore and make disciples of all nations, baptizing them in the name of the Father and of the Son and of the Holy Spirit, teaching them to observe all that I have commanded you (Mt.28.19,20). And elsewhere he says: What I say unto you I say unto all (Mk.13.37).

11, 1. Let the supporters of riches now reflect on these utterances, asking themselves whether riches alone have been overlooked by him who has impressed on others the need to observe whatever he had ordered the apostles to do. Perhaps you say: 'The command was given because of the critical circumstances of that time, in that men who had to avoid the unremitting attacks of persecution were unable to keep their possessions.' First I shall ask where have you read this, or what text of scripture has given you evidence to the effect that believers of this period distributed all their possessions as a result of flight or persecution. Or how did churches come to be founded in Jerusalem and throughout other cities, if all men had to forsake their property? It remains only for you to say that the churches were founded by foreigners and that the persecutors had more mercy on strangers than citizens!

2. Well, yes, I shall agree with you that fugitives would have to distribute estates, houses or anything else which could be regarded as immovable for the simple reason that they would be unable to carry them around with them through different countries. But were they unable to take money with them or carry it around? Or was it something of a hindrance to the fugitives, since a man would be more convinced of the need to flee or betake himself to foreign parts if the abundance of his resources enabled him to feel less anxious about meeting his expenses? If they sold their houses or lands or any other possessions which they disposed of for the sake of flight, why did they lay down the price of what they had sold at the apostles' feet, when they ought rather to have kept back enough to help them in their flight, having distributed all their possessions under that obligation?

3. But it is well that the Lord in his foresight anticipated that excessive love of avarice would produce such a clever misinterpretation and by the great

force of his divine utterance undermined its entire basis, when he denied entrance to the heavenly kingdom not only to those who had many possessions but to those who had money as well, by using an example which by comparison would illustrate the extreme difficulty involved. If he had said this with flight or persecution in mind, then he ought at least to have conceded the possession of money, with the assistance of which a fugitive could depart for foreign parts without anxiety.

4. But what kind of sense does it make if they want some of his disciples to have been rich, while maintaining that others could have had nothing owing to persecution? How can these two positions be consistent? Either some were rich and were now seen to be distributing all their possessions under no pretext of persecution, while others were allowed to keep their personal possessions, or, if all had to distribute their possessions by reason of persecution, how could any of them at all be rich? For one of these two interpretation must be accepted, since both cannot be appropriate at one and the same time: *either* they were rich and none of them was compelled to distribute his possessions, *or*, if he was so compelled, then they all were and none could have been rich.

5. 'And how is it then,' you will say, 'that we read that Zacchaeus the tax-gatherer and Joseph of Arimathea were rich?' You seem to be shifting your ground in claiming that it was not through allegiance to their religion but because of the difficulties of the time that it was necessary for all men to distribute all their possessions. For I deny that anyone among Christ's disciples was rich at that time; otherwise his statement which lays it down that only by despising their possessions could men become his disciples would appear to be untrue. And so I maintain that it was not through persecution but because of their religion that they dispersed and distributed their possessions. But on the matter of persecution I have already argued enough, proving conclusively that it was not for that reason that they sold their possessions, since they did not keep back for themselves the proceeds of the sale. Let us say something now of Joseph and Zacchaeus.

6. If you think that Joseph was rich after becoming a believer in Christ, because the scripture calls him 'rich', then Matthew will remain a tax-gatherer, because he was called 'the tax-gatherer' after he became an apostle. But we know that it was the custom in the scripture for some men to be called by their previous titles: it still entitles Abigail 'wife of Nabal the Carmelite' after her previous husband had died and she had become the wife of David, and it still entitles those gentiles who had come to believe in Christ 'gentiles' even after they had espoused the faith, and many others in the same way whom it would take too long to mention. Similarly, then, let us believe that Joseph was called rich, not because he was so at the time but because he had been, so that we may not seem to be disparaging a disciple of Christ by an incorrect understanding of the scripture.

7. 'But if he was not really rich,' you will say, 'where did he get the money to procure such a quantity of spice?' To say nothing of the fact that you do not read that it was he who procured it but Nicodemus, whom the scripture never

names as a disciple, the price of a hundred pounds of spice is indeed a great proof
of riches! A poor man, especially in that country, in which we can be certain that
it was sold more cheaply, could easily have possessed that amount of money; but I
do not understand this use of Zacchaeus as an example to be cited in support of
riches, when it is not only inconsistent with riches, in my view, but actually
contrary to it. For what has the scripture to say about him? That, having welcomed the Lord not only into his house but also into his faithful heart, he said of
his own accord and without prompting or teaching of any kind: Behold I give
half of my goods to the poor, and if I have defrauded anyone of anything, I restore
it fourfold (Lk.19.8). By this we understand that, after reasoning with himself, he
laid out half of his wealth in compensation for fraud and distributed the remaining half to the poor, so that he might share in that state of blessedness which was
promised to paupers in return for their sufferings.

8. As for the arguments in favour of riches that they usually advance, there
is one to the effect that, at the time of the Passion, when they had left the Lord,
the disciples returned to their own homes. This clumsy explanation gives no
satisfaction, since it not only fails to help their case but is even contrary to it, if
they, who were unable to follow the Lord without having disowned their possessions, are now unable to return to them without abandoning him. By this we
understand that rejection of their possessions denotes followers of Christ, desire
to return to them those who deserted him. Again it is written: The hour is
coming when you will be scattered, every man to his home, and will leave me
alone (Jn.16.32). If it is agreed that the disciples abandoned the Lord, let it also
be agreed that they are said, according to the way in which some understand it,
to have returned to their own homes. Hence we too should be afraid of abandoning the Lord, if we wish to return to our possessions. This I have said with the
reservation that, in fact, other apostles did not return to their own possessions –
which is the forced interpretation that some wish to give, doing violence to the
right sense – but were scattered to their places of refuge. For he did not say that
'you will return, every man to his home' but that 'you will be scattered'.

9. At that time, unless I am greatly mistaken, it was a case of taking flight,
not of some occasion for displaying greed or covetousness; it is quite absurd to
suppose that they returned to property which was no longer theirs, when we read
that before the Lord's resurrection they were shut up in one place because of their
fear rather than living separately in their homes or property. Indeed, if they had
wanted to recover their own possessions, there would not have been time in the
interval: for how much time was there between the Lord's passion and resurrection for us to believe that they were able to recover their own possessions or
return to their own properties? Especially when we know that their province was
almost a hundred and fifty miles away from the place where the Lord suffered –
Galilee, that is, of which it is certain that they were natives. For we read in the
Acts of the Apostles that the angel called them 'men of Galilee' (Acts 1.11); and
elsewhere: Are not these men of Galilee (Acts 2.7)?

10. They also use as an example the statement about the Lord's mother
which is contained in the gospel of the blessed John: And the disciple took her at

his command unto his own (Jn.19.27).[29] 'Into his own property,' *they* say. I ask first what property could a fisherman have in a strange province, since we have to believe that he did not have enough resources for a home even in his own region and even if he had renounced nothing. The words refer to the saintly John, son of Zebedee, who, according to the testimony of the scripture, left his father with the ship and the nets in the territory of Galilee in order to follow his Lord. Or, even if he had had a home before, how could he still have what he had already renounced? But how then are we to understand the words,'The disciple took her unto his own'? They must be taken as meaning 'took her as his own mother', not 'into his property', for he had been commanded by the Lord to respect her with the love due to a mother until he should rise again, so that she might be supported and comforted by him in place of her son. Finally, this is how it is written: He said to his mother, Behold, your son (ibid.26)! He did not say, 'Behold, your host!' And to the disciple he said, 'Behold, your mother!'; and 'that disciple took her unto his own' – that is to say, 'as his mother', not 'into his own property', since it was not a matter of her needing a place in which to live but the comfort of a son's love.

12, 1. Let us then turn to that notorious statement which lovers of this world believe that they can present as a reasonable argument, when they maintain, under the pretext of upholding godliness, that the counsels of perfection in the gospels ought by no means to be kept. For they say, 'If all men are willing to distribute their possessions and to keep nothing at all for themselves, where would we then find works of godliness and compassion to perform, when the supply of objects to which to direct them have been exhausted?' Or, 'How are the poor to be sustained, where are guests to be entertained, from what source are the hungry to be fed, the naked covered and the thirsty given drink, if worldly wealth is lacking?' Great indeed is their love of compassion and godliness, if they care more for the poor than for God! And I would that they really cared for the poor and not rather for riches, which they try to defend on the pretext of helping the poor and under the pretence of being obliged to practise godliness, not realizing that some are in need because others have more than they need. Get rid of the rich man, and you will not be able to find a poor one. Let no man have more than he really needs, and everyone will have as much as they need, since the few who are rich are the reason for the many who are poor.

2. But what sense is there in striving to achieve something which the 'perfect' were never bidden to do, while being unwilling to do what *was* bidden? We were told to possess nothing; but those who possess nothing were never given any command with regard to works of mercy. Observe then how wrongheaded

---

[29] RSV: 'And from that hour the disciple took her to his own home'; so too AV and NEB. The Vulgate has *in sua*, 'into (or to) his own [home]', and the Greek NT *eis ta idia*, which means the same; the words will not give the sense 'as his own mother', however much our author tries to extract it from them. But I have omitted 'home' from the quotation in order to enable him to argue the case for his own idiosyncratic interpretation, which would require at least *in suam*, if not *matrem*, 'mother', as well.

and inconsistent it is to neglect to do what we have been bidden to do for the sake of something which we have not been bidden to do, and so to seem to be afraid to implement an order which was not given merely to avoid doing what was! Thus you say, 'If I have become poor, how can I give alms?' – as if you were ever bidden to give alms when you have nothing or to possess superfluous riches so as to be able to be always giving them. The apostles too ought then to have given this reply to the Lord when he either called the poor 'blessed' or laid down that the rich could not possess the kingdom of heaven, had they not been thinking rather of Christ's command than of the riches which are defended only as a means of helping the poor.

3. You ask therefore, 'Who will there be any longer to do works of mercy, if all are striving to climb to the highest stage of perfection by renouncing their possessions?' But why do you not envisage the possibility that all men are able to attain to the highest stage both of fulfilling the obligations of compassion and of achieving perfection, especially as you know that it is only by degrees that each individual advances and makes progress in faith? Surely we can see that there are two classes of people in the Church, though all confess the same Lord – the catechumens and those who, after being catechumens, are cleansed and sancti-fied by the divine laver – and no one can be a candidate for baptism without first having been a catechumen. And though there must be these two classes, yet both are pressing on to the same end; for they either cannot or ought not to belong to the same class for the reason that it is quite clear that there were two classes from the beginning. Why then do you not hold the same opinion in the matter of compassion and perfection, that is, that we have first to attain to all the stages required by the obligations of compassion, yet nevertheless try to climb to the heights of perfection, and not abandon the highest stage of compassion because we are all striving to reach perfection, since, as I have said, the higher stage of perfection is reached only by degrees? To take an example from ordinary life, there are many classes in an orator's school but all are hastening to reach the highest. Yet the lower classes are not entirely empty because everyone is striving to reach the highest.

4. You are afraid that, if you renounce riches, if you renounce all the resources of this world, there will be no one to do works of compassion. Are you then the only possessor of property in the whole world, so that you fear that you can have no successor? I do not want you to defend your avarice on the pretext of compassion or with the excuse of helping the poor. Achieve your aim and climb from the lower class to the higher; your place will not be left empty: whenever a man has been baptized or becomes a catechumen, his place will be filled.

13, 1. Perhaps you say, 'And where shall I get food to enable me to live, if I have renounced all my possessions?' Ah, I can now see the reason why perhaps riches are boldly defended and the purpose served by the other arguments: it is, of course, our little faith, which we strive in vain to conceal under the pretext of compassion, while refusing to believe the Lord's promise when he says: Do not consider what you shall eat or what you shall drink or what you shall wear. For the gentiles seek these things; and your Father knows that you need them all. But seek first the kingdom of God and his righteousness, and all these things shall be set before you (Mt.6.31-33).[30] And he confounds our little faith by citing the example of the birds of the air and the lilies of the field. And lest with your customary perversity in interpretation you should judge that this was said for the benefit of the apostles alone, he added, 'For the gentiles seek these things' – not 'other Christians besides the apostles'.

2.   You surely believe all the promises made to you by the voice of God. You believe that, after you are dead and have been dissolved into dust and ashes, you are to be restored from the same bodily ashes through the grace of resurrection not only to your former state but to a better one, that of immortality and incorruption. And you also believe that, if you are willing to be worthy of it, you will be enriched by the glory of the heavenly kingdom and adorned with the splendour of the sun. Which is the greater gift? To provide all these things or to bestow the wealth of the present life? If the wealth of the present life is far inferior to even one of these gifts, why can you not believe that he bestows upon you the lesser gifts when you trust him to provide even the greater? If we do not believe that which is less, I do not know how we can prove that we believe that which is greater.

14, 1.   'But,' you will say, 'it will be a source of confusion, if the man who has been accustomed to give to others now receives from them.' If you were afraid of confusion, why were you so willing to give your allegiance to one whose mysteries are such a source of confusion to this world? For his birth and Passion and the whole course of his life after taking upon himself human form cause more than a modicum of confusion to unbelievers. But the Lord says of such things: Whoever shall confound me before men, I will also confound before my Father who is in heaven (Mt.10.33).[31] So you can see that we are ashamed to keep God's commandments not because of the obligation to do works of compassion but on account of men's confusion. We are too wise in matters of the flesh and are influenced by the understanding of the human mind more than by the force of the divine, and for this reason we make a serious and weighty mistake. We are ashamed of the whole way of life of Christ and his disciples, and yet we suppose that we belong to Christ; we are confused by their humility, poverty, shabby clothing and cheap and simple fare, by their mean treatment at the hands of this world, the abuse, the derision, the insults, by all those things, in fact, which we know to have been a cause for rejoicing not only to Christ himself but also to his apostles.

2.   On the other hand, we glory in pride, in riches, in splendid clothing, in agreeable food, in the nobility of this world, in the transitory praises of men. Anyone who has come to us poor after the pattern of Christ, of whom it is written that 'he had no comeliness or beauty, but his face was despised'

---

30   Our author has again departed from the accepted text even if in minor respects only.
31   The Vulgate has *negabo* (= RSV's 'deny') for our author's *confundam*, 'confound'.

(Is.53.2),[32] is provoked, mocked and ridiculed in the manner of the Jews and, like him whose form and likeness he bears, is judged to be a deceiver and a traitor. But if anyone, however unbelieving and encompassed by a variety of sins and wrongdoing, comes to us distinguished in appearance and clothed in splendid apparel befitting his rank, he is given pride of place over all the poor, however holy their lives, contrary to the apostle's command, and this world's style is preferred to the pattern of Christ (cf. Jas.2.1–3). But we believe that, by carrying on practices of this kind, we are following the mind and example of Christ, and we are 'confused', I suppose, in our attitude to all those things in which the example of Christ is portrayed, while glorying in all those which are appropriate to the honour of this world! We do firmly believe that our teachers, after Christ, are his apostles. Why then are we ashamed to live by the example of those whose disciples we profess to be?

15, 1. 'But it is better for me to live off my own resources rather than set my hopes on another's.' So far as human wisdom goes, it is indeed rated better; but by the standards of the divine wisdom I think that the apostles, who were sustained by others' wealth, were better than those who retained their own possessions. 'Then why,' you will say, 'does the apostle Paul say: Remember the word of Jesus, for he said, It is more blessed to give than to receive (Acts 20.35)?' But why is it then that we read that both he and his apostles received? Were those who gave more blessed than those who received? If it is more blessed to give than to receive, Paul received from the Macedonians, as he himself testifies, saying: For my needs were supplied by the brethren who came from Macedonia (2 Cor.11.9). And if it is more blessed to give than to receive, then we must accept that the Macedonians were more blessed than Paul, since we know that they gave to him. What do we have to say about that young man who is commanded to distribute all his possessions? Not only would our Lord not have given him such an order but he would even have prevented him from carrying it out of his own volition lest, after distributing all his resources, he would no longer have the means of giving, if, that is, it was always better to give than to receive; for it is not right for us even to suspect from Christ's teaching that he would have placed in a less blessed state those who could have attained a greater one. How can that young man be told: If you would be perfect, go, sell all that you possess (Mt.19.21), if it is more blessed to give than to receive, for the way of perfection is seen to lie where the greater state of blessing is to be found?

2. And the Lord says elsewhere: Unless a man renounce all that he has, he cannot be my disciple (Lk.14.33). And if it is more blessed to give than to receive, yet a man cannot be always giving, as some indeed wish to do, unless he has an abundance of wealth from his ownership of possessions, and the man who has an abundance of wealth does not renounce all his possessions, and the man who does not renounce his possessions in accordance with the Lord's injunction

---

[32] Yet another variation, inserting 'despised' from the following verse and 'his face' – for good measure.

cannot be his disciple. What then shall we say? That the man who is not Christ's disciple can be more blessed than the man who can be his disciple? If it is wrong to make such an inference, why then did he so lay down that, unless a man had renounced all his possessions, he could not be his disciple? Knowing that those who had the means to give were more blessed than those who had to receive, he would have driven the poor away from his discipleship rather than the rich, since it was proper that those who were able to attain the higher state of blessedness should rather be reckoned as Christ's disciples. But if, in fact, he chose the poor to be his disciples, then it is manifest that those who are chosen are more blessed than those who are rejected.

3. If that is so, how are we to understand the words: It is more blessed to give than to receive (Acts 20.35)? In my opinion the deed is better than the deed, not the person than the person, that is, the gift is better than the receipt of it, not the giver better than the receiver. But to clarify this statement of mine, I shall use an example: when a bishop or priest receives something from a layman, the gift of that layman ranks higher than its receipt by the bishop or priest, because the giver performs a work of righteousness when he gives, whereas the clergy must be considered to have done an act which is neither righteous nor unrighteous, when they receive; but the layman will not be more blessed than the bishop or the priest simply because his action seems to be more excellent than theirs.

16, 1. But if we are to believe that the man who gives always attains the highest blessedness and yet he will not always be able to give unless he remains rich, why does God so often criticise the rich and eulogize the poor, since the latter, being able to attain to a higher state of blessedness, are more worthy to be praised? 'But it is the *evil* rich that he blames,' you will say. Did you then read: Woe to you *evil* that are rich! (cf. Lk.6.24)? Or what need was there to add the label 'rich' at all, if he were not passing his judgement of condemnation upon them because of their riches? If he was rebuking the evil of men specifically, he would simply have said, 'Woe to you that are evil!' And if he is criticising not the rich in general but only the evil that are rich, he ought to have praised the rich that are good, if there are any such men to be found anywhere. And if you want his words, 'Woe to you that are rich!' to refer only to the evil rich, then he ought to say also of the good that are rich, 'Blessed are the rich'. He says quite clearly that there are men who are blessed but they are the poor (cf. Lk.6.20); if he had said, 'Blessed are the rich', then he would have been seen to be reducing to an even lower state the very class of men whom he pronounces blessed for being the opposite.

2. At this point I believe you will say, 'He praises the *good* poor'. Why then did he add the label 'poor', if he knew that no special mark of goodness was attached to poverty? For just as he would never have named riches in his statement of censure if he had not seen that they were worthy of censure, so too he would never have named poverty in his commendation of blessedness if he had felt that it was no aid to the attainment of goodness. I suppose that, in fact,

the Word of God had left out from his utterance words which, if added, would have led to the censure of the evil and commendation of the good! Omitting the names of those attributes which, in some men's judgement, can neither hinder nor help, he would have said, 'Woe to you that are murderers or adulterers or greedy for plunder or idolaters or slaves to any other kind of vice or sin!' Why does he leave out all other sins and misdeeds and name only riches as an object of censure, as one who knows that they are frequently the cause of all our faults? Again, why does he omit the names of all the other virtues in praising the beatitudes and name only poverty, if he did not know that it is the source of *all* our virtues? And if he is not specifically addressing his censure to riches and his commendation to poverty by extolling it, he ought somewhere to have praised the rich and censured the poor. Since, however, he both censures the rich in general and commends the poor in general, he plainly and clearly demonstrated that, by the authority of his judgement, he both condemned the greed for riches and extolled the name of poverty.

17, 1. I wish to add also something that no wise man will be able to dispute, namely, that it is difficult to acquire riches without committing every kind of evil. They are procured by calculated lies or clever theft or fraudulent deceit or robbery with violence or barefaced falsification. They are frequently accumulated by plunder of widows or oppression of orphans or bribery or, much more cruel still, by the shedding of innocent blood. If that is so, how can we imagine that something which is acquired by such a variety of crimes has the sanction of God? Far, far from our thoughts be a notion so ungodly! For God either forbids all the crimes mentioned above if they have not yet been committed, or condemns them when they have been perpetrated. So we can have no grounds whatsoever for regarding as conferred by God wealth which has been acquired by means which he forbids.

2. 'The wealth which I have amassed,' you will say, 'has accrued from legacies inherited from a variety of people.' This too can be most sinful if, by shutting out lawful heirs, you possess the goods of others which could have come to you only by employing deception or violent pressure. But let that pass, and let us suppose that nothing of the kind occurred and that they were bestowed on you freely and willingly: a just man always refuses to keep what has been given to him by an unjust will, and it is an unjust gift if it is bestowed on an heir who is no relation and poor parents are possibly excluded from inheriting.

3. Hence the Lord deservedly censures and condemns excessive wealth, since he saw greed for it to be the cause of sin. For what wise or sensible man would doubt that greed is the occasion of all evils, the root of crimes, the fuel of wrongdoing, the source of transgressions? Because of it no one can live in safety or travel without fear on land, sea or anywhere else for that matter. It is through greed that we have pirates on the ocean waves, highwaymen on the roads, burglars in towns and villages, and plunderers everywhere; it is greed that motivates fraudulent practices, pillage, falsehood, perjury, false witness, cheating, ungodly and cruel acts and every conceivable kind of misdeed. For its sake the

earth is daily stained with innocent blood, the poor man is stripped of his property, the wretched man is trodden underfoot and not even widows or orphans are spared. Greed drives men to spurn God's law almost every moment of the day and to outrage heaven's decrees by committing transgressions of all kinds one after the other; on account of it modesty is often assaulted, chastity overpowered, and shameless lust given free rein to revel in its forbidden pleasures; in order to satisfy it, parricide is often committed in thought or by deed, since a man will wish for his parents' death or even bring it about, when he is in haste to acquire riches and is driven to extremes by the force of his impatience and greed.

4. For the sake of wealth men also learn to commit accursed acts of unspeakable, unmentionable wickedness and ungodliness and rush into the study and practice of arts which are both disgraceful and criminal. In the search for riches morals are often ruined, souls are destroyed, and every good feature of human nature is profaned. In a word, how many rich men are free from pride, arrogance, haughtiness and disdain? What man is there, however gentle, humble, patient, kindly and moderate in his poverty, who does not become puffed up with haughtiness, swollen with pride, inflamed with anger and goaded into madness as his riches increase? When does a man of substance remember the frailty of his human condition? When does he not forget himself to such an extent that he imagines that he is not mortal? Or how can he ever realise what he is, when, from his proud and exalted position of eminence, he no longer deigns to know those who share his own human nature?

5. And so, in his wretchedness, in his desire to cease to be the man he is, the worse he becomes the better he thinks he is, and, overwhelmed by the sheer mass of his evil deeds, makes himself the slave of sins which are perhaps as great as the riches of which he is the master. He despises the needy man, who is maybe as much richer than himself in moral integrity as he is poorer in worldly wealth, and in his lowly state cannot find consolation even in the contemplation of his Lord. Listen to him saying, 'Just look at him, outcast, ragamuffin, and baseborn; and *he* is the one who dares to say anything in the presence of people in *our* position and, in his rags and tatters, to discuss *our* morals and conduct and to try to disturb *our* consciences and force them to recognize the truth by rational debate!' As if the rich alone were permitted to speak, and riches, rather than thought, had the right to reason out the truth!

18, 1. It is not in vain, then, that the Lord uses every opportunity to criticize and condemn riches, knowing, as he does, that greed for riches is the seedbed of all crimes. Nor was it without due cause that he as good as closed the entrance to the heavenly kingdom to rich men by his use of an analogy to illustrate the extreme difficulty which faced them, since he saw that they were entangled in all kinds of evil: It is easier for a camel to go through the eye of a needle than for a rich man to enter the kingdom of heaven (Mt.19.24), he said. What need have we to debate any further a passage whose meaning is absolutely clear – unless it is necessary to remind rich men to recognize that they will be able to possess the glory of heaven only if they find a needle large enough for a camel to pass through its eye, and a camel so small that it can go through the very narrow entrance provided by such a needle? Or if this proves to be something which is quite impossible, how will it ever be possible to accomplish something which is by definition still more impossible? Only, perhaps, if the rich man makes a proper distribution of his wealth so as either to become poor or to leave himself with just enough to live on, and then strives to enter where a man of substance cannot.

2. 'But,' you will say, 'the reference is not to a camel, which cannot possibly go through the eye of a needle, but to a ship's hawser!'[33] What an intolerable excess of ingenuity a man is forced to employ by his love of riches if he has to betake himself to names for ship's ropes in order to avoid being compelled to diminish his abundant supply of worldly resources! How blessed this ingenuity would be if only he could exercise such mental effort for the love of God! But a mind preoccupied with worldly attachments has no room for heavenly love. However that may be, this is a very inadequate argument and will never help the rich man's cause. As if it were any more possible for such a large rope to pass through the eye of a needle than it is for that very large animal, the camel! You have still failed to give enough thought to your examination of this matter, nor have you yet found an adequate form of defence which will enable you to live immune from punishment outside the heavenly abode. What help are you going to get from ships, whose gear is on such a huge scale? You will have to apply your ingenuity rather to a search through the weaver's stores to see if you can discover a thread there which is called 'a camel'! Such human folly must be subjected to at least a modicum of derision, however much one has to feel sorry for its wretchedness, so that men may realise that arguments which only succeed in provoking men to laughter will carry no weight with God.

3. 'But the difficulty involved in the definition given above,' you say, 'the Lord tempered, nay rather, removed entirely by a later reply when he said: What is impossible with men is possible with God (Lk.18.27).' Certainly it is 'possible' not only for rich men with all their paraphernalia and faults to be received into heaven but also camels as well! If we are dealing with what is 'possible with God', we shall find no man who is excluded from his kingdom, because nothing can be found which is impossible with God. But how can the earlier utterance stand,

---

[33] *Camelus* is a Latin translation of the Classical Greek word for 'camel', *kamelos*, found in Herodotus, Aeschylus, Aristophanes and others as well as in Mt.23.24 – 'straining at a gnat and swallowing a camel' – and elsewhere. The Greek word *kamilos*, on the other hand, appears only in the lexicographer Suidas (1967c) and in the scholiast's note on Aristophanes, *Birds*,1559 (lyric passage); LSJ notes that it is 'perhaps coined as an emendation' of *kamelos* in Mt.19.24 but also compares it with the Arabic word for 'ship's cable', *jummal*. Arndt-Gingrich, s.v., comments that in our quotation, as in Mk.10.25 and Lk.18.25, *kamilos* is the reading of several NT MSS and of several versions, e.g. the Armenian, and concludes that it may be a 'Byzantine invention' but that it 'has no place in the NT'. In my view, the parallel quoted above (Mt.23.24) seems conclusive proof that what is wanted here is a 'camel' as an example of a very large animal. The change from *kamelos* to *kamilos* would be the result of the normal process in NT and later Greek known as itacism or iotacism, whereby a number of vowels and diphthongs, including *i*, were pronounced as *ee*.

when either it ought not to have been delivered at all, if it was going to be
rescinded later by the exercise of God's power, or, if it had to be delivered, it
ought never to have been possible to render it meaningless?

4. It remains for us to try to interpret the meaning of the saying that what is
seen to be impossible with men is possible with God. When the Lord denied
admittance to the heavenly kingdom both to the man who was rich in possessions of every kind and to the man whose riches consisted of money only, on
hearing his words of judgement, the disciples were smitten with the grief that
comes with despair: they were not yet in possession of full and perfect knowledge,
since among them rich men were by Jewish custom considered to be of great
importance, because they were often seen to be performing works of compassion
in proportion to the excessive wealth which they owned; nor did they yet know
that a man who infringes even one commandment is held to be transgressing the
whole law in accordance with the Lord's utterance.[34]

5. So they reconsidered the matter amongst themselves and said, 'If so
difficult an illustration denies entry to the heavenly kingdom even to those who
find it possible to fulfil every obligation of godliness by using their abundance of
wealth in order to do so, what are we to think of the poor, who have not the
means to enable them to perform works of compassion?' Their reply shows that
this is what they thought. Thus they say, 'Who then can be saved?' (Mt.19.25;
Mk.10.26; Lk.18.26), as if no man can be saved if the rich could not or as if the
rich alone constituted the whole human race, though the poor are much more
numerous and scarcely one wealthy man can be found among a thousand who are
needy. That is why his reply to that young man is: What is impossible with men is
possible with God (Lk.18.27), that is, 'What seems to human thought to be
impossible, that anyone can be saved without an abundance of riches, is made
much more possible with God in his wisdom: a humble and holy poverty gives
him much greater pleasure than the proud and sinful ostentation of riches, and
even the good which is found in the possession of riches can be difficult to
achieve without the accompaniment of evil, since it is performed not so much for
the sake of deserving God's mercy as in order to acquire glory in the eyes of men.'

6. 'But,' you will say, 'God denied to the rich the kingdom of heaven, not
the attainment of eternal life, because the man who is denied possession of the
heavenly kingdom is not at once cut off from eternal life in consequence, since
life is possible with or without a kingdom: for every man who reigns lives but not
every man who lives also reigns.' My first question addressed to you is, 'Where do
you find mention of this life which you locate outside the kingdom?', and the
second, 'Can these men be saved who will have life without having the kingdom?' You say, 'I believe they can be saved.' Then why do the apostles say, 'Who
then can be saved?', if they know that only the kingdom was denied to the rich?
By this it is clearly and manifestly shown that where the kingdom is, there is life
also, and that where life is, there is salvation also, and that when there is no

[34] Cf. 19,2; *Chast.*8,2; 10,8; *Virg.*4,2; 7.2; *Dem.*15; 16,1; 25 – to take but a few examples of
this favourite Pelagian injunction, often supported by Jas.2.10.

salvation, there is also neither life nor kingdom, and those who are outside the limits of the kingdom cannot be saved.[35]

7. 'But the word "camel",' you will say, 'refers to the gentiles: for in their case, though corrupted by every kind of vice and devoid of all virtue, yet because, like camels, they have bowed down and surrendered themselves to Christ's faith, it is foretold that they will have an easier passage through the eye of the needle, meaning the path of the narrow way to the kingdom than will the rich man, that is, the Jewish people.' But I have already argued earlier that the rich man cannot possibly be identified as the Jewish people; so now let us see whether the gentiles can properly be described as the camel. I ask first what reason requires us to obscure such an important issue by introducing a different nomenclature, and what prevented the gentiles from being called by their own name, and what was the motive for calling them by another. You say that it is because, like the aforesaid animal, they were distorted by their various crimes and sinfulness. Then there was no wickedness in the Jews, I suppose; or, if there was, why are they too not designated by an illustration which employs the same comparison? Or, I would like to know, why is this comparison with a camel appropriate to men who are corrupted by sin and vice? 'Because its body is not straight,' you will say, as if there were any animal which can be drawn in a straight line without any curve or bend in its bodily outline, especially one which is supplied with a variety of differently shaped limbs. And although it has a multiplicity of curves and bends, yet it is straight in its nature, and if it has of its own nature what it does have, it is without fault. And if it is without fault, how can it possibly be compared with a man whose corruption is the result not of his nature but of his free will?[36]

8. 'Why then,' you say, 'does the Lord himself sometimes compare men to animals, for example, the Canaanites to dogs (Mt.25.26), Herod to a fox (Lk.13.22), the apostles to sheep (Mt.10.16), and evil men and false prophets to wolves (Mt.7.15)?' These comparisons refer not to bodily shape but to similarity of character, which even in animals themselves is controlled by a decision taken on a natural impulse. But you rightly call Herod a fox and the Canaanites dogs and the rest by the names by which they are called by the Lord; where, however, do you read that the gentiles are called camels, so that you have to call them by that same name too? But if it is nowhere so written, how dare you adopt for your own use something which lacks the sanction of any scriptural authority? From what text have you learned that the needle's eye has to be understood to mean 'the narrow way'? And if that is the true interpretation, how is the camel, that is, a people corrupted by all sorts of sin and wickedness, to tread it, when on the authority of the Lord's utterance it is ordained that it is for the few persons who are righteous? For either the gentiles in their wickedness and sinfulness will be the camel and, however long they remain so, will be unable to enter upon the narrow way or, if they rid themselves of all their errors of unbelief and wickedness

---

[35] For the distinction between the heavenly kingdom and (eternal) life which many tried to make cf. *Chast*.8,4 and n.2; *BT*,8 and n.15; *Virg*.4,1,2; *Life*,15,1.

[36] Another clear indication of our author's Pelagianism.

and become worthy to begin the journey along the track marked out for the straight way, then it will be no longer possible to call them 'the camel'.

9. Now that we have explained the interpretation by which, according to the way in which some people understand it, it was the gentiles who were designated by the name of the aforesaid animal, it will follow that in this passage, whether in literal truth or according to an allegorical device, a camel is unable to pass through the eye of a needle.

10. Again, what reason have we for believing that, when the narrow way and the kingdom of heaven have been conjoined and connected the one with the other, the Saviour then proceeded to separate them from one another?[37] For if the needle's eye is 'the narrow way', why does he then say, 'it is easier for a camel to go through the eye of a needle than for a rich man to enter the kingdom of heaven'? When he says that the one thing is 'easier' than the other, he is making a total distinction between them, and, if it is such a very great distinction, then it cannot be applied to the narrow way, since it is conjoined to the heavenly kingdom, not separated from it.

11. We must now consider the reason why those who are accustomed to discuss nearly all the Old Testament in allegorical and mystical terms[38] but to understand the precepts and actions in the New Testament in a more literal and simple sense, on the grounds that the actions of the Old Testament figures foreshadowed the truth of those which are depicted in the New, yet in the sole matter of riches either forget or change their previous practice by reversing the process and using things done under the law to defend riches and by interpreting them simply and without mystical imagery; and why at the same time they strive to conceal the precepts of the gospel under a cloak of allegorical obfuscation with no regard for the simple, literal truth, as if in this instance alone the New Testament were a figure containing allusions to the Old, when we know that the Old offers an image of the New in every respect. For they want the riches of Abraham and David and Solomon and the rest to be understood literally; but when they read something about contempt of riches in the gospel, they exert themselves to adulterate its meaning by employing a metaphorical treatment of it, although, as we have already stated, it is more fitting to allegorize the commandments of the law than those of grace[39] – unless, of course, they are trying by this means not so much to reinforce the scriptures as to defend the quality of their own way of life and, through false interpretation of the law and the use of every stratagem which their natural wit can devise, to protect what they love, not so much ordering their conduct according to the precepts of the gospel as modifying their understanding of the commandments of the gospel to suit their habitual actions. What they want is not so much to submit their way of life to the law as to subordinate the law to the way in which they conduct their own lives,

---

[37] For the 'narrow way' – either on its own or in contrast with the 'broad way' cf., e.g., YM,3,1; Chast.17,11,12; Virg.10,2; Cel.10,11; Dem.10,3.
[38] See n.25 above.
[39] Here too we have a Pelagian echo in the use of the word 'grace'.

not to live as they have been commanded to do but to adapt the commandments to the manner in which they live. Yet not only will such an interpretation not help its authors but we have to believe it to be a positive hindrance to them, since by it they are shown to be not only transgressing but also debasing the commands of heaven.

19, 1. But you say, 'First and foremost we must fulfil all the types of command-ments and purify our souls from the stains of all wickedness and misdeeds, and then distribute our worldly wealth.' An argument invented to defend both wealth and sin alike! When a man says that riches are to be rejected only when all precepts and commandments have been kept, and since it is very difficult for a rich man to fulfil all the commands of the law, it will follow that he will fail to fulfil the commandments in their entirety under the pressure of the needs and worries connected with riches and, while he is still looking forward to achieving this most difficult task, he will not at any time get round to rejecting his riches. Christ instructed his disciples differently: you will find that the first thing he taught them was that they should cast off all the encumbrances of this world in order that they might be able more easily to fulfil the commands of the gospel.

2. And this is especially shown in the passage where the Sower of the Heavenly Word introduces the parable in which riches are compared to thorns, choking the seed of the Word in the fields of our hearts with their cares and pleasures and rendering it unfruitful, just as thorns in the fields of the world render unfruitful all kinds of seeds or do not even allow them to germinate. If then our heart is likened to the soil and the Word compared to seeds but riches to thorns and brambles, who are we to regard as the cultivator of this piece of ground? The soul, unless I am mistaken. What then is the farmer's first job to be done on thorny soil? Should he first throw in the seeds and then, after they have put forth their fruit, root up the thorns? Or should he first clean the ground of everything that will hinder the seeds and then sow the grain which will produce good crops? And so we too, on this analogy, must first of all pull out the thorns of our riches to prevent them from hindering the growth of the good seed.

3. Perhaps you say, 'Why cannot I keep all the commandments of Christ and my riches also?' If you can, you must be sure that your riches do not hinder you. You have to be the first to know what the different types of commandment involve and subject them to a careful and searching examination to see if it is possible for even rich men to fulfil them. We are bidden not to lie or to slander or to commit perjury and not to swear an oath even in the cause of justice,[40] to render no man evil for good, to love our enemies, to pray earnestly for our persecutors and slanderers; we are not allowed to try to recover things taken away from us or to approach secular courts of law or to seek recompense from those who do wrong to us; we are forbidden to eat with fornicators, drunkards, slan-

---

[40] For this typically Pelagian injunction cf. OF,1,3; YM,4; Riches,19,2; BT,14,1; 22; Chast.10,9; Cel.19; Dem.19.4 – to take a few instance only; but I believe that this is the only time in this collection when the phrase 'even in the cause of justice' is added.

derers or plunderers; we are not permitted to allow a superfluous word to escape
our lips. What need have I to say anything about the greater sins, when no one
can possibly be in any doubt that those who are forbidden to commit even lesser
sins are not allowed to commit the greater ones either?[41]

4. I beg you to answer me according to the witness of your conscience
whether a man who is entangled in the bonds of riches can possibly fulfil all
these commands. For the more worldly wealth a man possesses, the greater the
burden of care and anxiety it brings with it. We know too that many who have
become poor for God's sake and, untroubled by all worldly possessions and all the
cares attached to them, are unimpeded by any of the obligations that go with
worldly possession and are as free of land as are immigrants, and yet they find it
difficult to keep the commandments in their entirety. If *they* have this difficulty,
what of those who are preoccupied with a tremendous weight of worry from their
riches and the immense responsibility associated with worldly possessions? And
lest anyone should suppose that it is sufficient to keep some of these commandments which we have mentioned above, even if not all of them are kept, it is
written in another place: Whosoever keeps the whole law but fails in one point
has become guilty of all of it (Jas.2.10).[42] And lest you think that this is to be
understood to apply only to the precepts of the Old Testament, I would have you
know that it was addressed to Christians, for whom it was already necessary to
fulfil the commandments of the new law, since they cannot enter the kingdom of
heaven without having first surpassed the upholders of the earlier document's
requirements by showing a greater commitment to righteousness. The blessed
apostle teaches us that the New Testament is also called 'the law', saying: To
those outside the law I became as one outside the law, not being without law
toward God but under the law of Christ (1 Cor.9.21); and elsewhere: Bear one
another's burdens, and so fulfil the law of Christ (Gal.6.2).

5. So, what are we saying? That riches are sin? Far from it! Not that they
are sin in themselves but that they offer an occasion of sin so long as they are
acquired by evil means or are possessed improperly, or the cares attached to them
give rise to neglect of the heavenly commandments or result in a need to commit
crimes more often. Therefore, the Holy Spirit testifies, saying: My son, do not
busy yourself with many matters; and if you become rich, you will not be free
from sin (Sir.11.10). So, as we have said earlier, riches provide the occasion of
sin, and excess of possessions causes error. The soul that is prudent and devout
and desirous of living a life free from stain and above criticism has to fear not
only sin but also any occasion of sin: Blessed is the man who fears all things for
the Lord's sake, says the scripture (Sir.34.15). Occasions of sin are like occasions
of ill-health:[43] as the man who is sick in body will find it difficult to recover his
former state of health, unless he first rids himself of all the occasions of bodily
weakness, so too the soul, when oppressed with the disease of sin and overheated

---

41 For this distinction between greater and lesser sins and commandments see OF,n.12.
42 See n.34 above.
43 See n.16 above.

with the fevers of wickedness, is able to grow strong again only with difficulty, unless it first excises all occasions of sin. And as a sensible invalid who wants to recover his health quickly weighs up for himself the causes and origins of his sickness, repelling and removing everything inimical to good health, however desirable, delightful and pleasant it may be, so the prudent and wise man who desires the good health of his better part, namely, his soul, has to come to understand all the occasions of sin and, after investigating them with all the attention at his command, to set them far out of reach of all the longings of his soul and no longer to want to love that which uses an agreeable taste to help it spread its deadly poison through his spiritual vitals, however sweet and pleasant it may be.

6. Now I do not wish you to say to me: 'But it was God himself who created this and that and the other thing for our enjoyment'; though it is true that the many different kinds of fruit, water from the coolest springs and the most agreeable varieties of wine are all God's creatures, it is also true that they are not for that reason given to the feverish, since they can cause even greater weakness. But why do I speak only of the sick, when it is not conducive to the health even of those who are sound in body to partake of such things without restraint and a sense of moderation? In the case of every kind of nutrient anything consumed beyond the needs of nature through excessive greed and pernicious gluttony is harmful.

7. But I shall grant you that it is possible for you to have riches – riches, of course, which have come to you by an inheritance from your parents honestly acquired – in such a way that their possession involves no infection by sin but rather supplies you with the means to do good works and not a cause of misdeeds. Let it be admitted that you may be a man of such virtue and goodness, such discernment and good sense, that you are the only, or almost the only, person or one of the very few persons able to turn to your own advantage the thing which is the cause of permanent damage to the salvation of others. How many are there who are as circumspect and prudent as you seem to be and so realize that they ought not to acquire wealth for themselves by evil means and, if it comes to them by honest means, try to use it in performing works of compassion and obligation? You have riches which have been honestly acquired and possess them in the right way; you perhaps have not obtained them unjustly but possess them justly. But others cannot see how you acquired them or how you possess them; they can only see that you have them, not how you got them or how you use them. And since they only want to imitate what they see, they will commence to seek riches by any means, fair or foul, and to commit many crimes in order to appear your equals or superiors in the extent of their possessions, and so your wealth will now become not so much an occasion of virtue as a cause of sin.

8. 'But for me,' you will say, 'it will be the means of doing good works.' A means of doing good works for you indeed but for very many a means of doing bad! And I no longer know if any good will come to you from something which is a cause of death for many. We can place little value on the goodness of something which kills many, while it is supposed to be profiting one. How much more

valuable will your action be, if, by distributing all your possessions, you perform a work which is good in three different ways! First, it will be a work of compassion because, when you have distributed all your possessions, you have to be considered as having reached perfection; secondly, by leaving nothing for yourself, you will not only be depriving all men of an occasion of sin but also be setting an example of virtue; thirdly, by distributing all your worldly resources, you are climbing the ladder of perfection.

9. What then am I saying? That, acting on our advice, you should hate the riches left you by godly parents, amassed by grandparents,[44] great-grandparents, great-great-great grandparents and great-great-great-great-grandparents and acquired with no sin incurred by themselves and no hurt or pain inflicted on others? Far from it! Nay rather, I encourage you to love such riches; for everything that a man loves faithfully he longs to keep as a permanent, not a temporary, possession. If you love your patrimony, then act in such a way that you may be able to retain it as an eternal inheritance. And if you really wish to do that, transfer it from earth to heaven while you have time, since whatever remains in this world must be destroyed when the world comes to an end. Therefore, whatever you transfer to heaven while you live you will, in fact, possess for ever; but whatever you leave here you have lost. Remember the maxim that says: Justify your soul before death; for there is no seeking of dainties in the grave (Sir.14.16);[45] and elsewhere: Before judgement, examine yourself (Sir.18.20). I count as noble and praiseworthy and to be preferred to all by virtue of his wisdom the man who so restrains himself by meditating on life and death that he sends all his possessions on before him and thus arranges for all his property to cease with himself. Of him, I think, it is written: The ransom of a man's life is his wealth (Pr.13.8). 'But how,' you will say, 'can earthly things be transferred to heavenly places?' By those, to be sure, of whom it is written: Go, sell all you possess and give to the poor, and you will have treasure in heaven (Mt.19.21).

10. We have to remember that we ought to live our lives in this world as strangers and pilgrims, as the blessed apostle says: As strangers and pilgrims abstain from the passions of the flesh (1 Pet.2.11), and another apostle says likewise: While we are at home in the body, we are away from the Lord (2 Cor.5.6). So, as we are strangers in this our earthly habitation, we ought to behave as strangers do: no one coming from India or Arabia or Egypt on business and intending to spend a short time at Rome or in any other place acquires houses or possessions there for himself or other property which seems immovable, but only gold or silver or merchandise of different kinds or anything which he is able to take back with him to his own country. Thus we too, in this time of

---

44 There is a slight difference here between Caspari's text and that in PLS 1, the latter preferring *abavis* for *ab avis*; but it is a matter of small importance, as all five words could be rendered 'ancestors' without discrimination. It will be noted that 'great-great-great-grandparents' are omitted in Caspari's version!

45 The striking difference between our author's 'Justify your soul' and RSV's 'beguile yourself' appears to be due to variant readings in the Greek MSS of the Apocrypha; the same citation occurs in BT,16,7.

pilgrimage, should desire, seek and accumulate with all toil and sweat and zeal only such things as we can take with us to the heavenly kingdom and in which we can find the joy that comes from wealth derived from an eternal inheritance.

20, 1. But I must not ignore either the excessively subtle and refined ingenuity of those who think themselves religious and are reckoned to be despisers of the world by themselves and by ignorant people, because they go about in more lowly attire, taking no pleasure in possessing ornaments or gold or silver or in display of more costly metal, and yet keep all their possessions hidden away in their treasuries and, motivated by sheer greed, retain possession of what they disdain to use in the eyes of men merely in order to enjoy a worthless reputation.

2. 'But I have sons,' you will say, 'for whom I want to keep all my possessions.' Why then do you feign contempt for something out of respect for religion when you are really protecting it out of consideration for your children? Or why do you applaud yourself and indulge in self-congratulation as if you were doing something original in making your sons heirs to all your possessions, when even unbelievers are in the habit of doing just the same? Perhaps you suppose that you are conferring some benefit on God by bestowing on your children rather earlier a gift which you were without doubt bound to leave them some day? What then are we saying? That you should completely disinherit your sons? Far from it! Rather, that you should leave them no more than their nature requires. For how can you be said to love them, if you are seen to confer on them something which will only harm them? What has been seen to be detrimental to your interests can be equally detrimental to theirs: for either it was not detrimental to you and you are vainly pretending to despise it, or, if it was detrimental to you, you ought not to confer it on them, since no one wishes those whom he loves to possess something which he knows to be detrimental to himself. And so, either you do not love your sons, if you want to give them things which are not in their interest, or, if you do love them, it is certain that you do not regard what you want to give those whom you love as not in their interest.

3. On the contrary, as we have said above, it is for the sake of winning glory among men that you pretend to despise as worthless what, deep down in your heart, you cherish as the supreme good. For, when our last hour overtakes us, we shall profit nothing from a famous progeny with numerous offspring or from the possession of substantial wealth derived from fertile land spreading far and wide through all the regions of the world or from the scores of houses which our excessive pride and arrogance have erected or from the manifold elegance and splendour of our costly garments or from the ostentatious display of our high offices and honours: to all of us, we know not when, that end will come when no man will receive for himself anything save the fruit of his works, be they good or bad. Gold, silver and the sparkling jewels of precious stones will profit us nothing when the day long ago fixed by God begins to glow and the very elements begin to crackle in the flames. Of that day the prophet bears witness, saying: The day of the Lord is great and dazzling, and who can endure it (Joel 2.11)? And the blessed apostle Peter: But the day of the Lord will come like a thief, and then the

heavens will pass away with a loud noise, and the elements will be dissolved with fire (2 Pet.3.10).

4. Since all these things are thus to be dissolved, what sort of persons ought you to be in lives of holiness and godliness, waiting for and hastening the coming of the day of the Lord, because of which the heavens will be kindled and dissolved and the elements will melt with fire (ibid.11,12). Likewise the blessed apostle Paul: A fearful prospect of judgement, and a fury of fire which will consume the adversaries (Heb.10.27); and its dreadful force the righteous man will escape but not the man who is rich, as the scripture testifies: Neither their silver nor their gold shall be able to deliver them on the day of the wrath of the Lord (Zeph.1.18; Ezek.7.19), and elsewhere: Treasures will not profit the wicked, but righteousness delivers them from death (Pr.10.2).

5. Let us hurry, therefore, while there is still time,[46] and, disregarding every excuse that our greed suggests, let us hasten on with all possible speed, lest that day discover us worthless and unfruitful. If we are truly faithful in the hope that we are to be rewarded with heavenly riches and enriched with the sublime gift of eternal possessions, let the earth be considered worthy only of contempt when compared with heaven, and all temporal and worldly possessions as foul as useless sweepings of dung when compared with that state of eternal blessedness. Let no man who would attain great things admire those that are small; since it is easy for us to despise our present state if we firmly believe in our future state. What point can there possibly be in our hankering and striving after possessions which even the worst of men are able to obtain? How many wealthy men are evildoers, how many are godless, wanton, defiled with unspeakable misdeeds and crimes! If we saw only the righteous, the wise, the chaste, the guiltless and the godly in possession of riches, every sensible man would be justified in desiring them with great eagerness, since they would be appropriate for the good alone. But since it is obvious that it is the wicked who have obtained them for the most part, I do not know why any wise man should wish to possess what he can see in the possession of fools and knaves.

6. 'But,' you will say, 'folly and knavery are to be found among the poor as well.' Yes, but no one covets poverty, and it is easier for the poor man to divest himself of such feelings than it is for the rich man, since poverty not only does not provide the raw materials for sin but in most cases renders it impossible, as the scripture says: A man may be prevented from sinning by his poverty (Sir.20.21). Observe then which is the better choice – what prevents sin, or what sometimes compels it. For we have demonstrated earlier on the authority of a divine utterance that a rich man can only with difficulty be a stranger to sin. Let us rather seek those riches in which we may be worthy to share with the assent of Christ and his angels.

7. Let us by all means be wealthy and rich but in good deeds and in holy and godly conduct; let us fill the treasury of our body with the gold of sanctity and the silver of righteousness. Let honesty be more precious in our eyes that any

---

46 Cf. Law,9,1; Dem.27.4.

ornament; let us adorn ourselves within, not without – that is to say, let us seek ornaments of the spirit, not the body. Let us adorn our soul, and let us paint it with all the colours of righteousness, in order that it may appear beautiful to God. For it will be adorned and embellished enough, if it has soberness of character, purity of conscience, the faith that comes from belief, the sobriety that comes from abstinence, the gentleness that is associated with long-suffering, the innocence of chastity, the godliness of compassion, lowliness of heart, the charity of love and that pure and inviolate innocence which preserves and nourishes all these virtues; no soul is as fair and beautiful in the sight of God as the one whose innocence outdoes a pearl in brilliance. Let us then seek with all the sagacity which we can command *these* riches, *this* wealth and *these* ornaments, in the knowledge that all who are not accompanied by a parade of *this* kind of opulence will be unworthy of the kingdom of heaven.

10

On Bad Teachers[1]

This letter contains several indications that it was written at a time when its author found it necessary to defend himself and others who held similar views against a charge of teaching heretical doctrine, for example, in his opening remarks (1,1) and in 17,2. We may therefore conclude that it was written when Pelagianism was being attacked not only by its opponents in Sicily but also by Jerome and Augustine, that is, in the period from 411 to 415, during which Augustine wrote his earliest anti-Pelagian treatises, *On the Merits and Forgiveness of Sins and Infant Baptism* (411), *On the Spirit and the Letter* (412), *On Nature and Grace* and *On the Perfection of Man's Righteousness* (415), and Jerome his *Commentary on Jeremiah, Letter to Ctesiphon* and *Dialogue against the Pelagians* (415); it was also in 415 that Orosius, who had initiated the attack on the Pelagians, wrote his *Book in Defence against the Pelagians*. We also recall that (c.414) Hilary of Syracuse took it upon himself to inform Augustine of the activities of 'certain Christians in Sicily' who were teaching heretical doctrines and that Augustine suggested that such teaching was probably connected with Celestius and his associates (see my introduction to *On Riches*); it is significant in this connexion that charges brought against Pelagius at the Synod of Diospolis in 415 were based on evidence supplied by 'Catholic brethren in Sicily'.

Even if we did not know all this, we would have enough internal evidence to show that the author of this letter is not only a Pelagian but also identical with the author of the tract *On Riches* and, in all probability, of the other documents in the collection first edited by Caspari: it is written in the same, rhetorical style, and there are many analogies both of vocabulary and content. These will be referred to in detail in my notes on the text but it may be useful to draw attention at this point to some of the general similarities to Pelagian teaching as it is found elsewhere.

The main theme of the letter is that too many Christians are being misled by unsound teaching on such fundamental subjects as the relation of works to faith, the need to fulfil *all* the commandments of the law of Christ, and the different grades of reward and punishment which will be assigned to the righteous and

---

[1] *Epistula [sancti Sixti episcopi et martyris] de malis doctoribus et operibus fidei et de iudicio futuro* PLS 1,1418–57; CPL 734; Caspari,67–113; Haslehurst,108–89.

unrighteous respectively on the Day of Judgement – hence the full title given to the letter in Migne, PLS 1 and elsewhere, namely, *On Bad Teachers, Works of Faith and Future Judgement*.[2] The author stresses the fact that faith by itself does not lead to salvation, that the true Christian must not select only some commandments to fulfil but carry out the lesser ones as well as the greater and that those who put their trust in unsound teachers can expect to be disappointed and rejected when they stand before the tribunal of judgement. Perhaps most significant of all the echoes of Pelagian teaching is the comprehensive statement of the intentions and expectations of Christ which the author suggests that he will make clear at the Last Judgement (18,2,3). For example, 'I had also formed the nature of your being so that it might be able both to understand and to do what it willed and thus you would be left with no excuse on grounds of ignorance or lack of ability,' 'The power of clear reasoning and understanding which I had bestowed on you would always enable you both to recognize and practise goodness and virtue for yourselves and to avoid with the greatest of ease such occasions of evil and vice as might occur', and again, 'In addition, I gave you a law and pronounced with my own lips the precepts and commandments which you were to keep and ordered them to be recorded and set down in writing in books, so that the knowledge which your inner nature already possessed might also be transmitted to you outwardly by your senses of sight and hearing and through this addition of the heavenly scriptures and the witness and admonitions of their writings to your feelings of conscience.' At this point Augustine would certainly have commented, as he invariably did when discussing what he regarded as Pelagius' denial of the importance of grace, 'He means only the law and teaching'.[3] To which Pelagius would undoubtedly have replied that he was not denying the need for 'the assistance of grace', that is, the grace of creation, the grace of atonement received through baptism and the grace to be won by 'righteousness through works performed in faith'.[4]

Other teachings in this letter which we can identify as 'Pelagian' are the author's interpretation of the Fall of Adam and Eve (13,1), his denunciation of riches (18,3), his condemnation of any kind of oath (14,1; 22) and his reference to the main arguments advanced in the unfinished letter *On the Possibility of Not Sinning* (2,2; 3; 4,1). And the vigour and extreme enthusiasm with which these teachings are expressed, the thoroughness and ruthlessness with which opposing

---

[2] This fuller title is a purely arbitrary description handed down to us by the early editors, as is its abbreviation to *On Works*, which is usually employed by modern scholars. A thorough reading of the letter reveals that its *leitmotiv* is the first of the three elements in the full title – 'bad teachers' – and that the other elements, 'works of faith' and the 'the future life', are subsidiary to the warning against relying upon contemporary teaching as a guide to righteousness. The theme of 'faith without works' appears briefly in *Life*,13,3 and several times in *Comm.*

[3] See, e.g., *On the Grace of Christ* vii.8 (PL 44,364); x.11 (PL 44,365f.); and iii.3 (PL 44,361), where Pelagius is said by Augustine to have condemned, when charged at the Synod of Diospolis, 'those who say that God's grace . . . consists of free will or law and teaching'; for a fuller account see Rees, 1988,33ff.

[4] See Rees,1988,91ff.

views are refuted and rejected, and the complete disregard of the possible consequences may well lead us to the conclusion that the author of this letter, as the
tract *On Riches* also suggests, is not only a Pelagian but a Pelagian who is
prepared to go to any extreme in order to present his case and to demolish the
contrary and, in his view, perverse opinions of his opponents. Pelagius himself
could never have written like this, indeed would not have dared to do so against
opponents of the calibre of Augustine and Jerome – although it must be added
that, on the small evidence that we possess, we might be justified in suggesting
that his associate Celestius could well have done so. But it must be remembered
that 'Pelagianism' is not, and never was, a theological system, and that even its
pioneers differed from each other in the emphasis which they placed on particular aspects of their teaching: rather, 'they were a mixed group, united by certain
theological principles which nevertheless left the individual free to develop his
own opinions upon particular topics.'[5]

Text

1, 1. You can judge the extent of my confidence in your honesty of purpose
and singlemindedness by this bold act of presumption on my part in venturing to
address to your excellency words culled from the crown of all literature and
worthy to be preserved for many a long year, since at the present time it is
scarcely safe to offer a discourse which is free and without restraint and which
quickly sends off its sparkle and remains unfettered by any of the bonds of
scripture. Two factors have encouraged me to be so bold – your Christian good
will,[6] in the presence of which I believed that there could be no danger in godly
discourse, and the generosity of your love, whose nature it is to find it easier to
disregard all warnings of danger than to deny to those whom it loves the chance
to say things which it thinks will be of advantage in the future. Added to this is
the fact I was so conscious of your godliness that I knew for certain that it wishes
and desires nothing more than to be constantly absorbing discussions of the holy
books, whether spoken or committed to writing, and to be the constant recipient
of preaching which you can recognize as worthy of being put into practice.
Though the eloquence of God's words may be savoured because of its natural
sweetness, yet to none is it so pleasant as to those who are striving to dedicate
themselves to his service as members of his household. It is an infinite source of
delight to the soul to realise that what is being preached to it is what it is actually
practising, and a soul that is holy can be as grieved to hear slipshod teaching as it
can rejoice in teaching which is grounded in true discipline. For the state of

---

5   Bonner,1970,31.
6   For this use of *christianitas* cf. *Riches*,6,3; *Chast*.6,1.

human nature is such that it is unwilling to listen to something other than that which it has decided to put into practice.

2. I also knew that you are so excited by your burning desire for the heavenly word that you count it a very great pleasure to have its comforts bestowed on you, whoever imparts it. You lack the leisure to choose individuals to provide you with something which you desire with such impatience to possess. A man who suffers from great thirst rejects the services of no man who gives him drink, and is happy to drink from any cup. And that is not because the flow of heavenly teaching is not abundant enough to satisfy your appetite for holiness but because your soul is so greedy to drink of it that, although richly supplied from its fountains, you do not refuse even little streams which exert themselves to produce tiny dewdrops slow to form. Men in the grip of unbridled greed and covetousness, though they possess all things in abundance and are already powerful enough through their possession of all manner of wealth, nevertheless, owing to their unbounded lust for acquiring even more, gladly accept anything offered to them by a poor man; so too you, overheated with that passionate fire of longing which was known to exist in the one to whom the reply of the Messenger was addressed because he was a man full of worldly desires, do not disdain to take in the words of your inferiors in the matter of true knowledge, even though you already possess a more abundant and richer supply of the treasures of heavenly doctrine. Not even the realization of my own misdeeds succeeds in deterring me, the chief of all sinners, from addressing you by letter and admonishing you despite the fact that you are my superior in every form of religious observance and piety: though I have a beam in my own eye, I would still wish to clear the vision of others who cannot be supposed to have even a mote in theirs, since I could not be unaware that you are so humble that not even the words of a greater sinner would arouse feelings of distaste in you, and that your hatred of sins is so great that not even a sinner's arguments are able to cause offence to you or make you reflect upon the person who is trying to undermine them, as long as eventually they come to an end.

3. I beg you therefore, if the bold manner which I have assumed in order to express myself with fluency should give you cause for offence to the susceptibilities of your holiness, to attribute this failing not so much to me personally as to the reasons already described earlier and, above all else, to the intense love which, while striving to show the grace of true affection, very often tends to overstep the bounds of humility. We can rest assured that boldness and presumption of this kind is supported by examples from the holy scriptures, for instance, that which contains the following words: Encourage one another and build one another up (1 Thess.5.11); and again: Let the word of Christ dwell in you in all wisdom, teaching and instruction of one another (Col.3.16); and again: I am satisfied about you, my brethren that you are full of goodness, filled with all knowledge and able to instruct one another (Rom.15.14). For in this passage, by putting goodness before both knowledge and instruction, he shows that the two last mentioned have their origin in the one which he named first, namely, love, that the true knowledge according to God is something which is given by love of

nothing but mutual instruction, and that goodness which labours in the use and study of doctrine for the benefit of others is as much to be praised as that commendable practical knowledge which seeks to perform offices of love.

2, 1. Doctrine which brings no progress in the soul is like medicine when the practice of it provides no cure for the sick. This is often the case with experienced physicians[7] who, trusting in their technical skill alone, take less care in investigating a disease in the light of the circumstances and time of its occurrence or in searching out the cause of the sickness or in observing the true nature of the ill-health. For in bodily diseases many and manifold infections are seen as the causes of physical weakness and different forms of sickness also arise with the change of seasons, and it is the duty of the experienced and skilful physician to weigh up, assess and compare all the symptoms with careful consideration, lest through squeamishness or in an attempt to avoid the painstaking labour involved he should kill the sick man by failure to apply sufficient care to a thorough investigation of all the symptoms and should bring discredit to his art by neglecting to examine all the hidden causes of the illness. So too, it is the business of the good teacher to examine, explore, understand and make known the causes of spiritual diseases and to observe the different occasions of their origin and only when he has come to understand all of them and has found out everything about them to apply the medicine of heavenly healing.

2. But, in supplying this analogy – indeed, in all my reasoning in this treatise –, I may seem to be adopting the role of a patient rather than a doctor, and a patient at that who, if he has an eye for the promotion of his own future health, ought to understand the causes of his sickness and so to avoid its recurrence. And if, as often happens, through cleverly concealed incompetence or downright ignorance and folly physicians are willing to give advice which is more likely to hinder than to assist the return to health, then let the wise patient doctor his own complaint. Having now become knowledgeable about his personal troubles, let him refuse and reject what he has come to recognize from his personal experience as harmful to himself. In the same way, we too, to speak of myself and others like me, should know both the causes and the remedies of our sins, which infect us and so produce our spiritual sickness, and should put our trust in our personal experience above all else; nor should we, like irrational invalids, assent to the deceit practised on us by certain men with their flattering and agreeable promises and so be willing to believe that we shall be able to profit from treatment which we know to have been of no help to others or venture to hope that we can escape unscathed from a situation which has brought other men to their destruction.

3, 1. For I believe that you clearly perceive the pestilence and the ruin which afflict our times by your innate good sense and powers of understanding – nay

---

[7] See *Riches*, n.16 and *Chast.*,n.38 for analogies with medicine in Parts I and II of this collection.

rather, through the revelation given to us by the Holy Spirit, whose grace we must suppose to be never wanting for those who live godly and holy lives – and that I should concentrate rather on examining the causes of others' sickness, since your own understanding and powers of discernment render you immune to it. Others' ailments are more easily understood by those who are free from them than by those who seem also to suffer from them, and we must not suppose that those who are seen to evade their attacks know nothing at all about them.

2. I have no doubt, therefore, that men as holy as you are realize that very many are suffering from an incurable disease of sin especially at the present time, because they think that *they* will not perish, because they possess the privilege of faith and confidence in their own belief, although they may not be keeping (for shame!) the great number of precepts contained in the heavenly commandments. And thus the very thing which confers eternal life on right-thinking persons, that is, faith, is turned into the cause of the death of unhappy men through the fault of their defective understanding, and that the very quality that divine mercy has provided as the occasion of salvation should become a source of death and destruction for ignorant mortals! The Lord did not offer a promise full of hope to believers so that they might be able to sin more freely and with greater impunity under the cover of faith but rather in order that those who had been granted forgiveness for their former offences through the remission gained by their new-found faith might sin no more. Faith is an aid in ridding us of sin, not in committing it more freely – that is to say, it releases us from sins already committed but does not grant pardon and immunity for those which we commit in future. So, if a man sins after gaining faith and receiving the holy laver, let him no longer hope for pardon through faith alone, as he did before baptism, but let him rather entreat it with weeping and wailing, with abstinence and fasting, even with sackcloth and ashes, and all manner of lamentation.

4, 1. But before all else we should seek to know the source of this error which has crept into men's minds and which has led them to suppose that faith in Christ came not so much to destroy as to defend sins, for defended they are and very much so, when they are nourished by a false sense of security. What greater security can there be than the belief that sins which before the time of grace[8] were severely punished can now be expiated with the aid of faith and with little or no punishment? If that were so, I cannot understand how the Lord Christ can be said to have come not to destroy the law but to fulfil it, if this means that through belief in him discipline has not been increased but diminished.[9] For, if all reason to fear is removed, then discipline is diminished, and reason to fear is

---

8 A typically Pelagian sense of the word 'grace'; cf. 10,1 and 14,5; *Chast.*9,2 and 12,2.
9 For the claim that a breach of the rules contained in the New Testament leads to a far greater punishment than transgression of commandments contained in the Old cf. 10,2,3; 14,5; *Riches*,9,5; 19,2; *Chast.*6,4; 9,1; 12,4.

removed if punishment is abolished, and punishment is abolished if it is circum-scribed by immunity from it and no satisfaction is sought through persistence.

   2. Where then are we to suppose that this wrong-headed understanding has originated if not in the minds of those who strive to justify actions which they do not fear to perpetrate and who prefer to try to convince themselves by any kind of conjecture that their impunity will bring them pardon instead of turning away from sins and misdeeds? For there are many men whom habits inculcated in them by bad instruction and long-established practice have so infected with bitter hatred, zealous emulation, passionate greed, malicious slander, raging anger, burning impatience, wanton pleasure, proud imitation, lying falsehood, savage abuse, or any other such vice that the thought of exchanging habits now of long standing for a new and wholesome way of life only arouses in them feelings of aversion. And if it happens that some of them chance to read the books of the divine scriptures, their only aim, whenever they discover precepts and teaching which enjoin greater perfection, is to employ the devious cunning of their intelligence and their skill in argument in order to distort them and modify their interpretation of them so as to justify their own way of life. This they do from a desire to appear not so much to despise the law as to be sinning on its authority, and to be refusing to do what they are told for the sole reason that the orders are to be understood in a different sense, though they are by no means unaware of the intrinsic significance of the truth and know full well that trickery and deception of this kind will not be to their advantage in God's sight but, on the contrary, have a disastrous effect, since the punishment which it brings both on them and on many others with less intelligence is to be the death of eternal destruction.

5, 1. But in their excessive desire for glory in the eyes of men they want to be considered holy and, at the same time, to be able to put off having to avoid disgraceful sins already of long standing, though they cannot be considered holy while these persist, and so they have devised a very clever and acute form of deception to befog the minds of simple folk in order to get a reputation for holiness with others despite the fact that in their own consciences they are sinners, and to encourage in others the illusion that they are still alive, whereas they are actually dead to themselves.

   2. They maintain that all those different kinds of sins into which men most often rush through defective habits and which only those who fear God greatly are known to avoid cannot in fact do any harm at all to holiness, employing most subtle and deceitful assertions and skilful proofs and arguments as a means of ensuring that by this stratagem they can keep their reputation for holiness without detriment to their customary passion for sinning. For the devil has used their greed for glory very cleverly in order to deceive them and has doubled their number of opportunities for sin by enabling them to defend their sins while still striving to acquire an undeserved reputation for holiness; thus they offend God in two ways, both by their defence of misdeeds which they ought to be avoiding rather than defending, and by their greed for a glory which they seek in vain:

they prefer an appearance of holiness to the real thing and to displease God rather than men. We ought not to wonder that such tactics are seen to be motivated only by an excessive desire for glory in the eyes of men, since the love of it is so strong that in most cases even the hope of heavenly and eternal blessedness cannot overthrow it nor can the fear of the endless horrors of hell weaken it.

3. This is why such men contend that an empty and barren faith without the support of any works of righteousness can be to their advantage, and teach that only ungodliness, that is, the impious perpetration of idolatry, is incurable. Thus they determine that these are the two principles which have to be observed, not from devotion to sound teaching but because they are easy to follow, since it is no trouble to preach a faith which is without works and requires absolutely no effort to abstain from the sin of idolatry. But I cannot understand how they can recommend the advantages of an easy belief to men who have been for so long enrolled in the faith and religion of Christ and cleansed by the same holy baptism, unless they think that men whose belief is beyond all doubt because they are proven Christians still persist in the faithlessness of pagans. For that reason it is the works of faith that should be preached to them and no longer a faith without which they would not be Christians at all. It would be a different matter if they regarded them as without faith because they fail to conduct their lives in accordance with the allegiance owed to that faith; but the reasoning which comes from perfect understanding proves that this is not the case, since they hold out to them the hope of eternal blessedness without works of holiness and they could never promise this if they denied them even the essence of an easy belief on the grounds that they live in error. But, as we have said above, they endeavour to put their whole emphasis on faith alone, because it is easier to commend faith by empty verbiage than to get works of righteousness done by people who are unwilling to do them. Even an unbeliever can make a false claim that he is faithful for the benefit of human ears, because faith is a thing which is beyond inspection and its reality can be tested only in the conscience of the man who professes it, not by the judgement of the man who hears such a profession; for it is very easy to make a false claim to something when there is no call to fear that the lie can be examined and exposed. But no one can find it so easy to feign righteousness, that is, the conduct of an innocent and spotless life, or to preach it to others, since the proof of it is before our eyes, and what can be revealed in action cannot normally be concealed by words. So a man finds it hard to dare to pretend when his pretence can be detected by the nature of his actions, or indeed to preach to others whom he knows to be well aware that he himself contravenes the doctrine which he preaches. That is why teaching is frequently offered on matters the truth of which is in dispute but on matters where the issue is not in question either little is said or there is complete silence.

4. Those who long for worldly glory and desire to enjoy the pleasures of human praise also show this characteristic, that they first examine the characters and lives of their audience and then modify the way in which they propound their doctrines so as to ensure that they cannot displease their minds, knowing

that instruction is held to be most successful if the discourse of the teacher is in complete harmony with the actions of their pupils and allows them that inestimable state of blessedness and immortality without demanding that they eradicate their pleasures; for those who aspire to universal popularity have first to act in such a way that they are loved by everyone, and this they will be unable to achieve unless they first find a way to satisfy the temperaments of those whose love and favour they seek. But it is hard to satisfy them without showing willingness in all matters to accommodate their teaching to the actions and practices of these same men, and so it comes about that through their excessive desire for fame they seek to be loved even by the wicked and justify their vices and sins, promising everlasting glory contrary to the true teaching of the law and the gospels to the very men whose praise they seem to be demanding rather than their salvation. And so they offer these same men the hope of eternity and immortality through the merit of an easy belief alone, because they know that faith, that is, profession of faith without righteousness, calls for no effort at all and that everyone will derive the greatest satisfaction from the kind of teaching that grants such a rich reward in return for no effort on their part.

5. But let fabrications and deceitful tricks of this kind which try to persuade us that an easy belief is possible without works and that faith alone can suffice for believers prevail, if it can, with those who do not know how to test invisible qualities by visible results and fail to understand that where there is no fruit of faith, there we must believe that there is no faith either. But what sensible man can doubt that where there is faith, there is fear also, and where there is fear, there is obedience also, and where there is obedience, there is righteousness also, while, on the other hand, where there is no righteousness, there is no obedience either or fear or faith? For these three are so conjoined and bound to one another that it is quite impracticable to separate them: men will only adjudge us to be right in ascribing merit to faith when we couple with it obedience to the commandments; otherwise it is to be feared that we shall be mistaken in flattering it if we claim that it alone and without the performance of good works is sufficient to merit eternal life.

6, 1. But lest we should seem to have been supporting this view by our own arguments alone, we must produce some examples from the divine law to prove the truth of our interpretation. The scripture says: He who believes in God gives heed to the commandments, and he who trusts in him will not suffer loss (Sir.32.24). If the scripture has said that the man who gives heed to the commandments believes in him, then it has undoubtedly exposed as an unbeliever the man who shows contempt for them by not giving heed to them. This the blessed apostle John also says: No one who abides in him sins; no one who sins has either seen or known him (1 Jn.3.6). We ought therefore to examine with greater care the question whether one who is reckoned to be ignorant of God by the apostle's definition can be considered to be 'faithful'. For who can doubt that where there is faith in a future life, there is both a desire for eternal blessedness and a fear of everlasting punishment? And wherever there are these two, it will be hard to find a reason to transgress, since either the love of imperishable blessings or the fear of unfailing tortures rules out such a possibility. And where sinning is easy, there is neither desire nor fear of what is to come.

2. Would that it were as easy to show signs of faith as it is to profess it! For this is what the holy apostle testifies, when he says: You have faith, and I have works. Show me your faith apart from your works, and I by my works will show you my faith (Jas.2.18), wishing to demonstrate that where faith cannot be shown it does not exist, because where it exists it is shown. For the works of faith are, as it were, its body, and as the operations of our incorporeal and invisible soul are expressed in the visible actions of our body, so the efficacy of an invisible faith is revealed in the practice of visible good works. The blessed apostle, however, would seem to have meant that works are the soul, so to speak, of faith rather than the body, by saying: For as the body apart from the spirit is dead, so faith apart from works is dead (ibid.26). He says this in order to show that faith, even if it exists, is futile unless it has the works of righteousness, as he testifies in an earlier verse, when he says: What will it profit, my brethren, if a man says that he has faith but has not works? Can faith alone save him? (ibid.14). And again: You believe that God is one; you do well. Even the demons believe – and shudder (ibid.19). Does it not seem to you that faith does not profit transgresors any more than it profits demons either? We must leave the quality of this interpretation to the reader's judgement but we ought not to overlook what the same apostle has said later on; what he says is: So you see that a man is justified by works and not by faith alone (ibid.24).

3. The judgement of the blessed apostle Peter can be seen to be in accord with these statements, when we find him saying: Make every effort to supplement your faith with virtue, and virtue with knowledge, and knowledge with self-control, and self-control with steadfastness, and steadfastness with godliness, and godliness with brotherly affection, and brotherly affection with love. For if these things are yours and abound, they keep you from being ineffective or unfruitful in the knowledge of your Lord Jesus Christ (2 Pet.1.5–7). From these passages I believe that it is now clear to everyone that profession of faith will be of profit for the glory of eternal life only to those who can show that they have faith by the practice of good works and by the witness of a holy life, but that it will not be sufficient to win the privilege of such a life for those who have defiled their lives by the shameful pollution of their sins and the disgraceful filth of their misdeeds.

7, 1. But you say to me, 'If faith without works profit not at all, why does the Lord say through his prophet: But my righteous one lives through faith (Hab.2.4; cf. Rom.1.17)?[10] This text gives us to understand that life can be granted to believers even on the profession of faith alone.' Undoubtedly it will be granted, but only to those to whom it is promised. To whom then is it promised? To the

---

[10] LXX, Hab.2.4, has 'my faith'; I have retained our author's 'my' in the translation, that is, 'my righteous one', whereas RSV has 'the righteous'.

righteous, unless I am mistaken. For he said, 'My righteous one lives through faith', not 'The sinner lives in faith, even if he persists in his life of sin'. Or, if what you read there is 'The man who persists in his sins lives through faith', or 'Faith alone justifies the sinner, even if he does not desist from sin,' it is only right that you should prove it. But my view is that the reward promised to the righteous alone is denied to those who persevere in their unrighteous acts. Remember that it is of baptized persons that we are speaking, not of catechumens. The Lord foresaw[11] that in these latter days there would be teachers who, under the cover of 'faith', would strive to undermine all strict discipline and righteousness by offering pleasant and persuasive forms of flattery, and that is why he erected in advance by his judgement a definition which would serve as an impregnable wall of righteousness that no battering-ram of false teaching would be able by any means to demolish. 'My righteous one lives through faith' – that is to say, 'Faith will profit for salvation only the man who is willing to be righteous by my standards.' It would not have been enough for him to say 'the righteous one' without adding the word 'my', lest it should be supposed that faith in any case conferred a great benefit on those who were righteous before men and not before God. As he says elsewhere: And you shall be righteous to me (Lev.20.26),[12] that is, not in men's sight, but in my sight, who examine even the hidden secrets of the heart.

2. Thus the words of the blessed apostle also confirm this interpretation of that most complete and true saying, when he says in the course of proclaiming the Lord's gospel: For in it the righteousness of God is revealed through faith for faith; as it is written, 'But my righteous one lives through faith' (Rom.1.17). Nor is it to be believed that God promised life without the works of righteousness, since he says elsewhere: Do not be deceived; neither the immoral, nor idolaters, nor adulterers, nor the effeminate, nor sexual perverts, nor thieves, nor the greedy, nor drunkards, nor revilers, nor robbers will inherit the kingdom of God (1 Cor.6.9,10).[13] He was speaking to Corinthians who were undoubtedly already believers and baptized and makes it perfectly clear that not only idolaters and the ungodly and perpetrators of any other more serious sins but also those who are entangled in even less grave sins are shut out from God's kingdom; so it is evident that the thief, the reviler, the drunkard and the greedy are excluded from inheriting it as much as the adulterer, the effeminate and the idolater. And to prevent us from supposing that he is not speaking of those who have committed *one* of the sins which he has enumerated but only of those who have committed *all* of them, he always prefixed his description of them with the words 'neither . . . nor', so that the truth might be made even more manifest that even the man who is guilty of any *one* of these sins and fails to give satisfaction by repentance will be excluded from the kingdom of God, being mindful of the saying which contains

11 Cf. 15,1; *Riches*,7,1; 11,3.
12 RSV: 'You shall be *holy* to me', as in the Vulgate.
13 My translation differs from RSV here in that I have retained 'the effeminate' as in our author's quotation and the Vulgate.

the following words: For the faith of the ungrateful man will melt like wintry frost, and flow away like waste water (Wis.16.29).[14] This he bears witness to in his letter to the Galatians also, when he says: Now the works of the flesh are plain: adultery, fornication, impurity, luxury, sorcery, idolatry, enmity, strife, rivalry, anger, quarrelling, party strife, heresy, envy, murder, drunkenness, carousing and the like sins, of which I warn you that those who do such things shall not inherit the kingdom of God (Gal.5.19,21). I think that here too, by prescription which is clear and plain enough for all to understand, it is decreed that the man guilty of any manner of sin cannot share in the kingdom of heaven. For, after enumerating the many sins included in the above list and since it would be a lengthy task for him to specify all the categories of sins, he employed a brief summary, so that he might be able to show that he bore them all in mind though he did not name them all, by saying: 'And the like sins, of which I warn you that those who do such things shall not inherit the kingdom of God.'

8, 1. 'But he denied admission to the kingdom,' you will say, 'and not life to sinners.' What then? Do you suppose that those who are outside the kingdom can have life? In what place are we to believe that life outside the boundaries of the kingdom is to be found? I find only two places in the scriptures, the kingdom and hell, that is, life and death.[15] If you have a third place where those neither in the kingdom nor in hell are located, it is only right that you should show it to me. Not that we deny that the righteous have different rewards which they have earned by their different labours, but they will all be in the same kingdom, where a rich reward is reserved for each of them in proportion to their righteous labour, either a hundredfold or sixtyfold or thirtyfold, and where the Son of Man, coming with his angels in the glory of the Father, will repay each man according to his works, where it shall be measured to every man with the measure with which he has measured, and where, according to the prediction of the prophet Zechariah, 'He that is feeble shall be like the house of David, and the house of

---

[14] The writer has substituted 'faith' for 'hope' (RSV;LXX) – to suit his own convenience or, more charitably, through a slip of memory?

[15] Cf. *Riches*,18,6; *Virg*.4,1,2; *Life*,15,1; but in *Chast*.8,2 a distinction is made between eunuchs, on the one hand, and married persons, on the other, claiming that the former would be rewarded with the kingdom of heaven but the latter only with 'life; if they have kept his commandments'. In his treatise *On the Merits and Forgiveness of Sins and Infant Baptism* I, xx.26 (PL 44,123) Augustine accused his adversaries, at that time Celestius and Rufinus the Syrian, of trying to distinguish between 'the kingdom of God' and 'the gift of salvation and eternal life', and he was to repeat this charge in his *Sermons*,294,2–3, *Unfinished Work against Julian* III,199 and *Against Julian* III, x.25 (see Plinval,1943,187). But this charge was made in connexion with their teaching on infant baptism, since they thought it necessary to make some distinction between the future state of infants who died unbaptized and that of those who died after being baptized, and it may be that the author of *On Chastity* felt it necessary to make a similar, special distinction between the married and the celibate, whereas here he is speaking in general terms. (I have omitted a sentence which immediately follows and seems to have been added by a later hand; Caspari and the editor of PLS 1 have placed it in brackets for that reason.)

David shall be like the house of God, like the angel of the Lord' (Zech.12.8), where 'there is one glory of the sun, and another glory of the moon, and another glory of the stars' (1 Cor.15.41), where 'he who sows sparingly will also reap sparingly' (2 Cor.9.6) – but yet he *will* reap – and where 'those who understand shall shine forth like the brightness of the firmament and the remainder of the righteous like stars' (Dan.12.3),[16] and there are many other texts like these which testify that the saints will have rewards of many kinds. We must take a similar view of sinners, namely, that each one suffers according to the deserts and punishment merited by his sin but in the same hell, and the difference between them is to be one of penalty rather than locality.

2. But to make it absolutely clear that there will be a separation into two dwelling-places only, one for the righteous and the other for the unrighteous, which they will receive in accordance with their conduct and deserts, let us use the example in the Lord's words: When the Son of man comes in his glory, and all the angels with him, then he will sit on his glorious throne. Before him will be gathered all the nations, and he will separate one from another as a shepherd separates the sheep from the goats, and he will place the sheep at his right hand, but the goats at the left. Then the King will say to those at his right hand. 'Come, O blessed of my Father, receive the kingdom, etc.' . . . Then he will say to those at his left hand, 'Depart from me, you cursed, into the eternal fire which my Father has prepared for the devil and his angels, etc.' (Mt.25.31–34,41), where he is seen to have indicated only two places, namely, one for those who are called to the kingdom and the other for those who are sentenced to the fires of hell. But if there were any third place which neither those who will reign nor those who will fall but those who will only live receive, the Lord would have indicated it too, and as he marks down some for the kingdom and others for hell, so he would have called others to life, if he had known that there was any dwelling-place for life outside the confines of the kingdom.

3. But it is very clearly stated that there are only two places in that testimony of the prophet in which are contained the words: And at that time your people shall be delivered, which is written in the book of life. And many of those who sleep in the dirt of the earth shall arise, some to everlasting life, and some to shame and everlasting contempt (Dan.12.1,2). But if there were any third place, he would doubtless have named that too. The blessed apostle also, when he denied possession of the one and only kingdom to idolaters as well, located life within the bounds of that same kingdom, for it is absurd to suppose that he left the ungodly any hope of living. But the utterance of the disciples, in which they despair of the salvation of the man to whom the Lord had denied only the kingdom, shows that anyone found outside the kingdom can by no means be

---

16 The text of Dan.12,3 is misquoted here: e.g., for 'the remainder of the righteous' RSV has 'those who turn many to righteousness' and the Vulgate 'those who educate men for righteousness'; our author may well have been using a Latin text of Daniel based on Theodotion's version but, if so, it does not correctly render that version's 'and (shall shine forth) from the midst of the many who are righteous like the stars, etc.'

saved and proves quite conclusively that there is no life elsewhere than in the kingdom; for it is wrong either to opine or to say that we are to believe that there can be life where there is no salvation. When the Lord had said: It will be hard for a rich man to enter the kingdom of heaven, and: It is easier for a camel to go through the eye of a needle than for a rich man to enter the kingom of heaven (Mt.19.23,24), the evangelist tells us that the apostles were saddened because of their anxiety for the salvation of men and said: Who then can be saved (ibid.25)? Consider then whether it is consistent with true reason to suppose that there can be any hope of life where there is no salvation.

9, 1. What are we to make of the statement that only the ungodly, defined as either idolaters or unbelievers, will perish? The result, of course, is that, as long as a privilege is promised in return for belief, the possibility of committing sin is encouraged and no one fears to sin when he is confident that death and the punishment of perdition await only the ungodly. Let such assertions carry weight, if perchance they can, with those who have no knowledge of the divine scriptures or, as I have often recalled, enjoy the comfort of a most evil and fatal sense of security which is given to them by the kind of teaching that smiles favourably on their lustfulness. But we who have some knowledge in us of the precepts of heaven, indeed can find no excuse at all in ignorance of the commands relating to the blessedness of a holy life, do not find our vision of the writings which are known to lead to the performance of good works obscured by any of the clouds that make them more difficult to understand, because the Lord by no means wished us to be hindered by any obstacle in understanding the teaching of righteousness and clearly granted us no opportunity to sin; for the scripture says: He has not allowed any one to be ungodly, and he has not given any one opportunity to sin (Sir.15.20). So it is quite impossible for them to mislead us with their subtle flattery and smooth persuasiveness into believing or hoping for anything other than that which has been established and settled by the divine law, especially if we are searching for religious knowledge with a pure and honest heart, if we are seeking not probable but certain truth, and if we desire both to know not what men say but what the whole law contains and also how to fulfil it. For it reveals plainly and in manifold ways that not only the ungodly and unbelievers but also sinners, if they persist in their sin, will be sentenced to perdition, as in this passage: Behold, the day of the Lord will come without consolation, in wrath and anger, to make the earth a desolation and to destroy its sinners from it (Is.13.9); and elsewhere: On the sinners he will rain snares, fires and brimstone, and a scorching wind shall be the portion of their cup (Ps.11.6); likewise elsewhere: The death of sinners shall be the worst (Ps.34.21)[18]; likewise elsewhere: Yet a little while, and the sinners shall be no more; though you look well at his place, he will not be there (Ps.37.10); and again: For the sinner shall

[17] Our text has *sine refrigerio*, which I have rendered as 'without consolation', instead of *crudelis* (= 'cruel') in the Vulgate (Greek, *aniatos*,LXX).
[18] RSV: 'Evil shall slay the wicked.'

perish (ibid.20); and again: His evils will take the unrighteous man to his death (Ps.140.11)[19]; and again: The righteous Lord will cut the necks[20] of sinners (Ps.129.4); and again: Salvation is far from sinners (Ps.119.155); likewise in Proverbs: Their evils will overtake sinners (Pr.13.21); and elsewhere: In an assembly of sinners a fire has been kindled (Sir.16.6); likewise in Ecclesiasticus: An assembly of sinners is like tow gathered together, and their end is a flame of fire (Sir.21.9); likewise elsewhere: The way of sinners is paved with stones, and at its end is darkness and punishments (ibid.10);[21] and many other texts which threaten not only unbelievers and the impious but also perpetrators of other sins with the punishment of destruction.

2. But it can be said on the other side, 'By "sinners" we are to understand the ungodly themselves, since we must suppose that the ungodly man is also a sinner.' If therefore, because the ungodly man can also be called a sinner, whatever has been said of sinners will be supposed to refer to the ungodly as well, then scripture will declare its threat to no sinner who lacks ungodliness, and men will now be able to sin without fear of punishment, since all fear is removed by the casuistry of such an argument. Yet we have to ask the man who wishes to reply in this way what is his definition of 'the ungodly'. I suppose it will be 'either unbelievers or men addicted to the superstition of profane idolatry'. We must then ask whom he judges to be sinners but not ungodly. Doubtless he will say, 'Those who claim that they have faith in God', even if they despise the commandments of his law. So unbelievers are to be considered ungodly and sinners, but believers sinners only; yet both the former and the latter are sinners, and though all of them are not ungodly, all of them, on the other hand, are sinners. What are we to make of the passage of scripture which says: All the sinners of my people shall die by the sword (Amos,9.10). Observe if anyone is excepted, when all are mentioned. And elsewhere: The Lord loves all who love him; but all sinners he will destroy (Ps.145.20); and also there is the passage which contains the words: Cursed be every one who does not abide by all things written in the book of the law to do them (Gal.3.10; cf. Deut.27.26). I think that he means that it is not only the man guilty of idolatry who will perish. It would be another matter if we are to suppose that the man who is under a curse can be saved. But let no one think that scripture now equates sinners with ungodly men because it declares that all will perish; the punishment will not always be the same for all because it is intimated that all will meet with the same destruction. But enough has been said above to prove this.

10, 1. Perhaps it will appear unnecessary to produce any evidence from the New Testament in order to give even more conclusive proof of the truth of this interpretation, when it is beyond all doubt that there is greater strictness with regard to almost all the obligations of righteousness and holiness under grace

---

[19] RSV: 'Let evil hunt down the violent men speedily!'
[20] RSV: 'cords'.
[21] RSV has 'its end is the pit of Hades'.

than under the law. Consequently it is wrong to suppose that, when a fuller and more complete measure of righteousness is demanded, a sense of security is given by the suggestion that a less severe warning indicates the possibility of a remission of sin. But for those who have less understanding of such matters we must offer at least a few instances and, in particular, cite the conclusion which the Lord arrives at in the judgement containing the words: Unless your righteousness exceeds that of the scribes and Pharisees, you will not enter the kingdom of heaven (Mt.5.20). From this we can see that we have to give more careful consideration to the question whether, after Christ's coming, the hope of future blessedness is denied to the ungodly only, when it is refused even to those who have fulfilled all the commandments of the law, unless they have also kept the additional commands of grace. For the righteousness of Christ's disciples will be able to stand out above that of the scribes and Pharisees, as long as they have fulfilled not only the precepts given to the scribes and Pharisees by Moses and the prophets but also the commandments given by Christ.

2. I am not unaware of the objections which those who entice men to sin and defend them are accustomed to make to this assertion: 'Our righteousness,' they say, 'has to exceed that of the scribes and Pharisees, not that of the law.' Now if he had prefixed his statement above by saying, 'I have come not to abolish the righteousness of the scribes and Pharisees but to fulfil it,' then the statement which followed it would seem to refer to the righteousness of his disciples. But when he said: I have come not to abolish them but to fulfil them (Mt.5.17), and added a little later: Unless your righteousness exceeds that of the scribes and Pharisees, you will not enter the kingdom of heaven (Mt.5.20), it is evident that he spoke of the righteousness of the law which he had said earlier that he had come to fulfil and which the scribes and Pharisees had upheld. What we now have to ask is whether the righteousness of the scribes and Pharisees is to be reckoned true or false; if it is true, then it was in accord with the law, and righteousness which is in accord with the law cannot be other than of the law; but if it is false, consider what a wicked blasphemy such an interpretation involves, since it maintains that the Lord commended to his disciples an obligation to exceed a righteousness which is false. For like must always be compared with like, and, if we are to suppose that the righteousness of the aforesaid scribes and Pharisees was false, then it was no longer righteousness at all but unrighteousness, and, if it was unrighteousness, why should it be called by the opposite name? We would have, to be sure, to assume that the Word of God was lacking in ability to give things their proper description, if he called a bad thing by a good name, and that he could not remember the earlier pronouncement which he had made through Isaiah: Woe to him who calls evil good and good evil (Is.5.20)! If then he was referring to the false righteousness of those whom he named, that is, the scribes and Pharisees, and not the true righteousness of the law, though it is a comparison of unequals, yet it would have been more appropriate for him to have said, 'Unless your righteousness exceeds the unrighteousness of the scribes and Pharisees, you will not enter the kingdom of heaven.' In fact, however, by keeping silent about unrighteousness and mentioning only righteousness, he

made it plain that he was speaking not of false righteousness but of true righteousness which, in this sense, was the righteousness of the scribes and Pharisees, because it had been proper for them to regulate the condition of their lives according to it, just as the righteousness which is known to us through the teaching of the New Testament is also called the righteousness of the apostles.

3. But why should we delay any longer on this matter, when the Lord shows us clearly in the words that follow what righteousness he means: You have heard that it was said to the men of old, 'You shall not kill, and whoever kills shall be liable to judgement.' But I say to you that every one who is angry with his brother without cause shall be liable to judgement (Mt.5.21,22). Now I ask what righteousness had forbidden men of old to commit an act of murder, that of the scribes and Pharisees or that of the law? If that of the scribes and Pharisees, then the Lord will appear to have been speaking of it when he said: Unless your righteousness exceeds that of the scribes and Pharisees, you will not enter the kingdom of heaven. But if it was that of the law, it is certain that he was speaking of that righteousness which he is seen to complete later by adding fuller commandments. For if he had begun with the unrighteousness of the scribes and Pharisees, not their righteousness, he would then have gone on to say 'You have heard that the scribes and Pharisees did this and that but your conduct must be different.' But by saying, 'You have heard that it was said . . .,' he compared saying with saying, not persons with persons. It is truly a matter of great credit to the apostles to have appeared to be better than the worst – even if the text can be understood in that sense! I am not so confident that I can defend the consciences of men[22] who strive to mislead the hearts of those of lesser understanding with such perverse and false teaching. While showing themselves unwilling to fulfil the commandments of the gospel and the apostles by doing more than the Old Testament has bidden them to do, they prefer to employ a trick of interpretation of their own devising and to expound a form of teaching which is different from that which true reason demands, lest they appear as exiles from the heavenly kingdom. Am I to suppose that it will be of any profit to me if I imagine that the opinion of the ignorant can confer upon me something which I know that I myself cannot obtain from my understanding of the truth, unless I have fulfilled all the obligations which will make me worthy to possess it? What is it that causes this kind of teaching but the fact that, as I have often said, we want to appear holy men, although we ourselves know full well that we are far removed from the rule of holiness? How shameless and heedless is the mind so habituated to daily vices and infected with ancient sins that it is not satisfied with living according to the law without also daring to corrupt the truth of the law itself by its false interpretation of it!

4. But it is good that the whole cycle of the gospel teaching reveals the strength and soundness of the judgement quoted earlier, which forbids not only killing but even anger and threatens the same punishment to the man who is angry without cause as the law had decreed for the killer. For it is written thus:

[22] For the appeal to conscience cf., e.g., *Riches*,10,7; 12,2; *Chast.*10,9.

You have heard that it was said to the men of old, 'You shall not kill; and whoever kills shall be liable to judgement.' But I say to you that every one who is angry with his brother without cause shall be liable to judgement (Mt.5.21,22). The reason why we take pleasure in perverting and adulterating this teaching by clever but wrong interpretation is that we are by no means willing to overcome the ingrained and deep-rooted savagery of our minds by adopting sounder principles of conduct, since its force is so powerful that it sometimes makes us liable to commit sins not only of anger but even of murder. For anyone who harms another as much as he can shows that he is willing to harm him even more, if he has the power to do so, and there are very many who inflict on others tortures far more cruel than death itself. Hence we should reflect whether those who are seen to have committed a wrong even more cruel than murder ought to be reckoned any more gentle than murderers. Of this the blessed John says: Any one who hates his brother is a murderer, and we know that no murderer – that is, any one who hates as much as the man who kills – has eternal life abiding in him (1 Jn.3.15). For John knew that wherever there is hatred, there remains the disposition to commit murder, since, though it is not as much the decrees of God as physical incapacity or the laws of the world that prevent the hands from murder, it is the will alone, which works within the man himself, that commits it. Finally, we enquire of the conscience of all who find it possible to hate others whether they want those whom they hate to survive at all, since it is very hard for them to do so. Thus, if they really desire their death, in what respect are they any different from murderers? Although their actions are not the same, yet their will is identical. The man who hates and the man who kills are in the same category, since both desire the death of one whom they do not want to live.

11, 1. Thus the commandments of the law, the prophets, the gospels and the apostles make heavy demands upon us, since they are contrary to our way of life and out of harmony with the will which controls our normal disposition. And that is why we maintain that such teachings corrupt and do violence to those commandments by the false sense in which they understand them, because it is easier to adulterate them by clever but perverse exegesis than to fulfil them faithfully. Hence we try to avoid the doctrine of righteousness and godliness and dash off to secure the support of an easy faith, because we are all full of unrighteousness and iniquity and find our only consolation in the claim that God does not place a solemn curse upon our actions, and in the belief that our transgression of his commandments will therefore go scot-free. In a word, we should instead consider our own actions and conduct with greater care and subject them to a penetrating examination and, if at all possible, arraign the invisible secrets of our minds before our visible deeds and actions and get to know the things that are hidden within us through the evidence of those that lie outside. Let us see how many of us are without hypocrisy, evil and deceit, how many are free from anger, immune to hatred and strangers to envy and malice. How many do not feign righteousness instead of practising it! How many do not rejoice at their neighbours' misfortune! How many do not long to disconcert another! How many are free from flattery, lying and respect of persons! How many, even when they perform a good action, do not perform it from desire for glory among men rather than out of obedience to the religion of God! We claim that we abstain from things lawful, yet at almost every moment we are doing things unlawful; we condemn acts which are not forbidden, yet commit acts which are.[23] Very many of us have rejected marriage, which, according to the apostle, Christians are allowed to contract, yet hate our brethren, which even the men of old were forbidden to do. We abstain from eating flesh but not from malice; it is easier not to eat what we may than not to hate someone else. We proclaim humility only by the utterances of our mouth, by our bodily bearing and by the apparel which we wear, yet within we are prouder even than kings. Hardly anywhere is there true humility, godliness or pure, unadulterated honesty. For the most part the seeds implanted in us by Christ have failed, and only those which the devil has sown are flourishing. One man slanders another and strives to defame his way of life. Everywhere are wars, battles and hateful disputes and hostile differences that arise from disagreement and litigation. Hardly anywhere is the bond of genuine peace and the firm foundation of harmony and love to be found. Everyone seeks his own personal reputation and longs to be honoured above another. No one allows his neighbour to be called higher or better than himself. Everyone is afraid that affection for another leads only to hatred of himself, imagines that praise of his neighbour means criticism of himself, and reckons that everything conferred on another has been stolen from himself. Hardly anyone speaks without carping at another; we suppose that we are commending our own way of life if we censure that of others, and we are confident that we have maintained the rule of righteousness if we scourge the righteousness of others as a mere fabrication. Truly the saying is fulfilled in us that: They all look after their own interests, not that of Jesus Christ (Phil.2.21), and: In the last days there will come times of stress. For men will be lovers of self, proud, lovers of money, arrogant, abusive, disobedient to their parents, ungrateful, unholy, slanderers, profligates, fierce, haters of good, treacherous, reckless, swollen with conceit, lovers of pleasure rather than lovers of God, holding the form of truth but denying the power of it (2 Tim.3.1–5).[24] Where now is the instruction originally given by Christ and handed down by his apostles? Where that holy love based on concord, by which all things were held in common by all men, no man counted anything he possessed as his own, and intellectual diversity was not an occasion for making invidious distinctions? For shame! At that time men had only recently begun to be Christians, and yet they shared houses without any discrimination; it makes me so unhappy when I think that no one yet called others his servants nor was there any distinction made between men and women, but even the least sophisticated of them then were better than our so-called 'perfect' members now! Where is the distinction which

---

[23] For the distinction between 'things lawful' and 'things unlawful' cf. 14,3; 25; YM,3,2; OF,2; Virg.6,1; 7,1; 8,1; Life,10,1; Law,4,2; 4,4; 7,2; Cel.5; 22; 28,2; Dem.9,2,3; 10,1; 15.

[24] There are some omissions here, and other words are not in the right order.

he introduced by naming his people 'lambs' and 'sheep'? For example: The good shepherd lays down his life for his sheep (Jn.10.11); and again: I have other sheep (ibid.16); and again: Behold I send you out as sheep in the midst of wolves (Mt.10.16). And to the blessed apostle he says: If you love me, feed my lambs (Jn.21.15,16)[25] But he also calls his people 'doves', saying in the Song of Songs: My fair one, my dove (Song,2.10,13), wishing, of course, that his people should copy by their simplicity the nature of those creatures whose names they bore. Now we are reversing all this by the perversity of our lives and are choosing other, unsuitable titles for ourselves, since we ought to be called wolves rather than sheep and kites rather than doves! How I wish that we could be satisfied with the ferocity of wolves and be content to possess the greed of kites! But our situation is much more serious, in that we have surpassed all the beasts and birds in savagery, since we do not spare even those of our own species, whereas they hunt only those of another.

2. What are we to make of the fact that, knowing ourselves to be full of iniquity and guile and almost always contemptuous of the heavenly commandments, we are still so deceived by our own ignorance or the tricks of the devil that we think ourselves to be most righteous, and so puffed up with feigned holiness that we reckon no one to be of any worth except ourselves? Why do you permit this to happen, you unhappy and miserable piece of flesh, soon to be eaten up by worms and reduced to dust and ashes? Why do you boast so? Why do you preen yourself so – as if you were entitled to some good reward for your evil way of life? The Lord says: When you have done all that I commanded you, say, 'We are unworthy servants; we have only done what was our duty' (Lk.17.10). Those who have 'only done all' are not allowed to boast, yet you congratulate yourself, when you are known to have done not even the least bit! Paul maintains that he is nothing, though the world had been 'crucified to him' (cf. Gal.6.14) and he no longer lived in himself but Christ lived in him, yet you think that you are something, when you live rather for vice than for virtue and do the will of the devil, not of God!

3. Then again, we feel aggrieved that we are not listened to, and so are in some measure displeased with God for not having answered our requests, as though we keep his commandments at all times and never despise his ordinances or remember that it is written that the Lord does not hear those who scorn him and despises those who disdain him, according to the faithful witness of scripture: As I spoke to them and they would not hear, so they will call and I will not hear, says almighty God (Zech.7.13). And this is made even clearer in the gospel, when it is said: We know that God does not listen to sinners (Jn.9.31).

4. What are we to make of the fact we strive to conceal our cruelty and savagery under the name of religion and commit the crime of ungodliness under the name of godliness? For when we wish to hurt one of our brethren or to weigh down his life with a heavy burden of infamy, we boast that we are doing this because of our zeal for righteousness and religion and faith, in order that we may

[25] This quotation consists of an abbreviated conflation of the two verses.

appear in the eyes of men to have done our unrighteous deeds in a righteous manner and be accounted holy in the sight of outsiders, when we are most wicked first in the sight of God and then in the judgement of our own conscience. The reverence and fear of God have failed in us to such an extent that it is not sufficient to sin but, on top of that, we find it necessary to defend our sins and to embellish our acts of ungodliness with the name of godliness, when, in fact, if we were to make it our object to excel in religion, we would be striving to correct one another in a spirit of gentleness and compassion rather than to bring one another into ill repute, and there would be no trace of hatred but only of respect, since we would be fulfilling the obligations of unadulterated love. For there is no man who can want to defame one whom he loves, even if he deserves to be defamed. From this it is perfectly obvious that, when our aim is not to correct the failings of one who is in error but to dishonour the life of one who does not merit such treatment, it is not the result of enthusiasm for religion but of sheer malice. We have proffered these considerations in order to demonstrate that we are defending vices nowadays and are placing all our hopes on an unsupported faith merely because it is easier for us to simulate faith than to avoid sin.

12, 1. But let us now return to our previous subject and produce conclusive evidence to prove that, according to the prescriptions of the New Testament also, it is not the sin of ungodliness alone but even apparently minimal faults that are condemned. But in order not to weary the reader's mind with a long sequence of selected examples and a numerous collection of proof-texts, we have to find a way to abridge our discussion by employing a handful of authoritative statements and citing only those which are held to be concerned with minimal sins; in this way, by observing how the least of sins are condemned, we can see clearly how the greatest will be punished. What then do we consider to be least of sins? I suppose that it is the one which is most committed by us out of sheer contempt for it, since it is despised for its very insignificance. What is it then? I cannot discover anything which we judge more lightly or commit more frequently than uttering superfluous words or calling some brother or other a fool; for these faults seem certainly to be unremarkable and insignificant enough. Let us then give more careful consideration now to the kind of punishment which is decreed for them, so that we can get to know the degree of punishment suitable for greater sins by examining what is merited by the lesser. I shall refer first to the case of the man who is guilty of making superfluous utterances: For every superfluous word that a man utters he will render account on the day of judgement (Mt.12.36)[26] When it is recorded that the offence of uttering a superfluous word will not go unpunished, I can find no fault at all which can escape examination at the time of judgement. Let us now hear what is decreed for the man who abuses his brother for being a fool: Whoever says to his brother, 'You fool!', shall be liable to the hell of fire (Mt.5.22). If, then, even the man who has called his brother a fool

---

[26] There are again changes in the words and word order here.

is liable to the hell of fire, I leave the reader to decide what sin *can* escape hell. Meanwhile, weighing the greater against the lesser and inferring the fate of the bigger from that of the smaller, I consider that no fault will go unpunished, when we find that not even those which are thought to be more trivial go unpunished. From this the clear and obvious conclusion is that either men are led on by the rashness of their minds, if they know this, or, if they do not, they are in the grip of blind ignorance, as long as they continue to assert in the face of such examples that it is only the unbelievers and ungodly who are to be subject to penal judgement.

2. But those statements made by the apostles indicate that not only unbelievers but also those guilty of other crimes will perish, and they also remind us, amongst other things, that he who does not love his brother abides in death (1 Jn.3.14); they bear witness too that the man who is seized with hatred of his brother is without doubt as good as a murderer (cf. 1 Jn.3.15), and they lay it down that the drunkard or greedy or angry or contentious or envious man or the man who through any kind of vice breaks away from the bonds of peace cannot share in the kingdom of God (cf. 1 Cor.6.9,10).

13, 1.   But lest we should suppose that this is a threat in words alone and hope that those words will not be converted into deeds because of God's exceeding mercy, let us set before our eyes examples from olden times, so that the past may at least help us to believe in the future. We ought to remember that those first humans were punished with death for transgressing one commandment, not because they desired to be as gods but because they ate of the fruit of the tree, for which they were afterwards rebuked by God. For no reason permits us to claim that they were charged only with a minor offence, if they had already committed a greater one. Next, let us consider well what is contained in the warning which preceded their transgression: In the day, he says, that you eat of it you shall die (Gen.2.17). He did not say, 'In the day that you desire to be as gods,' since it is not a question of the nature of the sin but of the transgression of a commandment.[27] Such a transgression, though it seemed in certain respects to be a lesser one, in this case can lead to a lighter punishment but not to immunity from punishment.[28]

2.   We know of many others who, by committing a single offence, offended God and forfeited his grace and were destroyed by different forms of death as a punishment. For example, we read how Onan, son of Judah, was smitten with divine chastisement for envying his brother's seed (cf. Gen.38.9,10); how Esau

[27] This statement with one small variation – 'it was not' for 'it is not' – is also to be found in Virg.6 (PL 30,167) and is attributed to *quidam nostrum* ('one of ours') in Gildas, *On the Ruin (and Conquest) of Britain* II, 38,2 (see Rees,1988,110f. and 111,n.58). The same sentiment, expressed in different words, will also be found in the letter OF,1. No doubt this section is a criticism of Augustine's contrary view in, e.g., *Expositions of the Psalms*,68,n.9,5 (PL 36,848): 'They wished to seize divinity and lost felicity.'

[28] For the distinction between greater and lesser sins and commandments cf., e.g., 14,1,5; *Riches*,19,2; *Virg*.4,3.

both lost his birthright and occasioned displeasure because of his greed for pottage (cf. Gen.25.29ff.,27.36ff.); how Miriam was covered with leprosy, because she had disparaged the holy man Moses, and would never had been cleansed of that infection, had not he, against whom she had sinned, interceded for her (cf. Num.12); how the sons of Aaron were consumed by fire from heaven, because they had offered fire which was unsuitable, and not even their priestly rank could take away the displeasure caused by this single crime (cf. Lev.10.1,2). The man who had gathered sticks on the sabbath was stoned to death for committing this crime (cf. Num.15.32–36); Eli the priest was condemned to punishment by death for his negligence and excessive leniency in correcting his sons (cf.1 Sam.2.22–25; 4.18); Jonathan, son of Saul, was exposed as guilty for tasting a small quantity of honey and would not have been excused either by the triviality of his offence or by his own ignorance, had not the whole people of Israel interceded for him (cf. 1 Sam.14.27,44ff.); Saul was deprived both of his kingdom and his salvation for having kept a part of the booty for himself (cf. 1 Sam.15.9,23,26–28), nor could the privilege of his office as king save him from the consequences of committing this one sin, since the case was dealt with at the tribunal of one with whom no man's person can excuse him; Uzzah was slain with a lethal blow for touching the ark, when he held it up reverently for fear that it would fall (cf. 2 Sam.6.6–8), and not even the fact that his transgression was prompted only by his religious feelings could excuse him for his sin. And I add also how the prophet and man of God was handed over to a lion's savage teeth on the very day on which he had foretold the future by the spirit of God and had given many marvellous signs of his excellence, because he took food with an unworthy man (cf. 1 Kings,13), and not even the merits of the good deeds which he had performed earlier could atone for one less culpable sin; and how Jehosha-phat, King of Judah, offended God by his friendship with the apostate King Ahab, and through the prophet it was said to him: You help the wicked and join with those who hate the Lord (2 Chron.19,2). It would take a long time to review all those whom we know to have merited the wrath of heaven by being responsible for one single act of transgression; but, profiting from their example, we too should dread to commit a transgression of *any* divine commandment.

14, 1. But someone will say, 'What sort of transgression is it to be angry without cause or to lie or to defame or to swear[29] or to return evil for evil or not to love an enemy and other such things which seem trivial in the judgement of men, because they are always being done and with a light heart?' That is how it comes about that greater crimes are also committed sometimes, when lesser ones are ignored.[30] But the man who despises such crimes as being insignificant ought to realize that to eat an apple, to gather sticks on the sabbath, to touch the ark, to take food with an unworthy person and other similar offences ought not to be

[29] Our author always puts great stress on the sin involved in swearing oaths of any kind: cf. 22; *Riches*,19,2; OF,2; CeL.17; *Dem.*19,4, etc.

[30] See n.28.

punished as weighty transgressions either; let him consider the act of transgression and not the transgression itself and pay attention not so much to the nature of the commandment as to the authority of the one who issued it. I want you to reflect upon the source of the commandment, not merely upon its content, and not concern yourself as to what *kind* of commandment it is that you judge worthy to be spurned as of no account, but *whose* it is, namely, almighty God's, who says that it is by men's estimate of his commandments that he is either honoured or held to be of no account; as he himself testifies, when he says: Those who honour me I will honour, and those who despise me shall be reduced to nothing (1 Sam.2.30).

2. And lest we should suppose that an empty and unsupported faith can suffice without keeping the commandments, we should remember that all those whom we enumerated above were men and women of 'faith' and were laid low not in consideration of any evidence of unbelief but on the grounds of transgression alone.

3. And lest we should believe that this happened only under the Old Testament and allow ourselves to be misled by unsound and perverse interpretation into thinking that the Old Testament was made complete by the new teaching of the gospel in the sense that it is now permissible to sin with greater freedom, it is fitting that we should recollect that Ananias and Sapphira were condemned to death on the judgement of the apostles for keeping back a part of their own money.[31] If a breach of a regulation which was, so to speak, their own went unpunished – for they themselves made the possession of such property unlawful by promising to God property which they would have been entitled lawfully to retain if they had not wanted to promise it to him –, what are we to think of those who are revealed as transgressors of any commandment? For if something was not allowed to go unpunished which was formerly lawful and could always have remained lawful but was afterwards made unlawful by their own free choice,[32] how can we believe that something is to go unpunished which was never lawful but was forbidden on the authority of divine censure? Let a man argue as much as he can and stretch the ingenuity of his mind as far as he likes in order to exaggerate the blame attached to such a sin; yet true reason will never permit the breach of a human ordinance to appear more serious than that of a heavenly commandment.

4. Nor are we dearer to God than all the persons mentioned above, so that we cannot suppose that we alone go unpunished if we commit sins like theirs which we know to have been so severely punished in their case. Nay rather, we ought to feel even greater fear when we consider that we are far worse than they were and when we understand quite unequivocally that the one who did not spare his acknowledged friends will not spare those whom he values less highly.

[31] On Ananias and Sapphira cf. 19,2; *Riches*,10,6; *Life*,13,3; *Law*,14,4.
[32] The reference to 'free choice' is another typically Pelagian feature, as is the phrase 'transgression of grace' in 14,5.

5. As we have often stated, the constraints of righteousness were increased, not diminished, by Christ's coming, since he came not to abolish the law but to perfect it. We must not suppose that the man who transgresses against the new covenant is liable to a lesser punishment than the man who transgressed against the old covenant, but rather to a greater penalty, since it is more serious to despise commands given through a son than commands given through a servant. But, in order to remove any possible doubts as to what we should believe on this matter, let us question the apostle. He himself says: A man who has violated the law of Moses dies without mercy on the testimony of two or three witnesses. How much worse punishment do you think will be deserved by the man who has spurned the Son of God, and profaned the blood of the covenant by which he was sanctified, and outraged the Spirit of grace? For we know him who said, 'Vengeance is mine, I will repay.' And again, 'The Lord will judge his people.' It is a fearful thing to fall into the hands of the living God (Heb.10.28–31). And again: For if they did not escape when they refused him who warned them on earth, how much less shall we escape if we reject him who warns from heaven (Heb.12.25). This shows that transgression of grace is even more to be feared than that of the law, and it is further strengthened by the authority of that utterance in which the Lord testified that not only those who do some evil but also those who do no good will be liable to everlasting fire, when he says: Depart from me, you cursed, into the eternal fire which my Father has prepared for the devil and his angels; for I was hungry and you gave me no food, I was thirsty and you gave me no drink, etc. (Mt.25.40,41). It is quite clear that he spoke not to unbelievers but to sinners, since he did not charge them with the ungodliness of unbelief, it being quite inappropriate, as has been said above, that men who have committed greater sins should be charged only with lesser, and since the wicked are not permitted to rise again at the judgement, as the scripture says: For the wicked shall not rise again at the judgement (Ps.1.5). And who but the ignorant would not know that unbelievers are wicked?

15. 'But it is the fire that is eternal,' you will say, 'its punishment is not everlasting.' It is a good thing that the Lord, who foresees all, anticipated this deceitful argument of men and, through the majesty of his divinity, foreknew that the desires of their own will would lead them to modify the interpretation of scripture.[33] That is why he says in what follows: Then will they go away into eternal punishment but the righteous into eternal life (Mt.25.46). It is not to be supposed that the wicked will suffer the punishment of everlasting fire, if any reasoning permits us to infer that there is any eternal punishment other than that in which it consists. Indeed we must also examine more carefully why it was that the Lord in this passage stressed not the length of the punishment but the fact that the fire was everlasting, as if he were concerned here not with the severity of the punishment but with the nature of the fire and desired to implant knowledge

---

[33] For the concept of God foreseeing excuses which might be offered by Christians cf. 7,1; *Riches*,7,1; 11,3. (N.B. also the reference to 'the desires of *their own will*'.)

rather than instil fear.[34] Or, if he spoke these words to instil fear and not to implant knowledge, being anxious by this means to recall the human race from their iniquities, we must then suppose that he was referring to the endlessness of the punishment and not to the interminability of a fire which would not relax its intensity, since there is no fear where there is no cause to know the perpetuity of something which you do not fear. For he says elsewhere too: If your hand causes you to sin, cut it off and cast it from you; it is better for you to enter life maimed than with two hands to be sent into the hell of fire, . . . where their worm will not die and their fire will not be quenched (Mk.9.43,48).[35] What are we to say here? That he desired us to know only that, if we have sinned, our worms will be immortal and the fire unquenchable, not that we have to fear the unceasing and unfailing punishment of immortal worms and unquenchable fire? The latter must be right, because the addition of the words 'their worm' and 'their fire' does not allow the other interpretation. For when the word 'their' is used, it clearly refers to the endlessness of the torment, and its endlessness must of necessity endure along with those who are condemned to it. If, on the other hand, they escape it at some time, we must suppose that it does not apply to them either, and that their devouring by worms will cease and their punishment by fire will come to an end; and so the saying 'their worm will not die and their fire will not be quenched' will be seen to be false, because we must interpret them as referring to the endlessness of the punishment. How then can there be an endless punishment, if the punishment itself ever ceases? 'But the nature of the fire,' you will say, 'and of the worms will persist only for the fire and the worms and not also for those to whom they were promised.' But it was for the latter that they were promised to persist. He did not say, 'The worm shall not die and the fire shall not be quenched, but 'their worm' and 'their fire'. These, that is, the worm and the fire, must be, so to speak, in the personal possession of the damned, and their punishment will be immortal and unquenchable.

16, 1.   'But these and many other similar statements,' you say, 'should be interpreted as having been made to cause terror, and yet we do not need to believe that they are statements of fact.' Then there will no longer be any fear, if belief in fear is lacking. For a man fears a dreadful experience only so long as what he fears is firmly believed in; but when once his belief in the cause of his fear fails, then the fear itself must cease also, since no one is so stupid as to suppose that he has to fear something which he knows to be unbelievable.

2.   But the question I wish to put is whether God wanted it to be known or not known that he said all this not so much in the interests of truth as to cause fear. I suppose it was the latter, for it is impossible that he wished you to know the

---

[34] Our text is confused, and there is evidence of some corruption of, or omission from, the original.

[35] This quotation is a conflation of two verses in Mark, the literal rendering of the Latin transliteration for the word translated 'causes you to sin' is 'causes you to stumble', and our author has added 'and cast it from you'.

reason for the deception which, as it is claimed, he had employed in order to cause fear, since this is something which you can fear only as long as you are not in a position to know that it is so. How then do you come to know what, according to you, God did not want to be known?

3. Here is something else for you to consider. Surely God wished this threat which he made in his statement to be feared for the sake of progress in a good and blessed life, and such progress would continue only for as long as ignorance of the truth prevailed in respect of the experience which he had decreed should be feared, for, when that ignorance came to an end, the fear would also come to an end. But when the fear is lacking, the unseen progress must of necessity also cease, since its cause was fear, just as ignorance was the cause of the fear. Anyone, therefore, who is willing to betray and to expose the beneficial ignorance of this matter, which ought to be kept secret and, for the sake of the spiritual progress of humanity, by no means revealed, must be supposed to have acted against the will of God as well as against the salvation of all mankind; he must be regarded as a rebel against God and as an enemy of human salvation, because he has both divulged a secret of the divine purpose and also made unprofitable to mankind something which, if it were to be of any profit to them, ought not to have been made public. And, to make my meaning clearer, I shall employ an analogy. Let us imagine a father who loves his son with a tender affection and for the sake of his spiritual progress often threatens him with terrible punishments, so that his young mind may be compelled to dread what the power of an excessive love does not permit its possessor to inflict. Now, if someone to whom the father's feelings for his son are perfectly clear interferes and says, 'You fear your father's threats and think that he is so cruel and stern that he would dare to inflict upon you what he is threatening? God forbid! I do not want you to be afraid. He says these things only to frighten you, and not because his father's love for you would ever dare to inflict on you punishments which he allows you to fear but not to endure as well.' Will we not judge that such a man, by depriving one who is expected to make spiritual progress both of his fear of, and respect for, his father and of his chances of making such progress at one and the same time, has harmed both father and son alike, since he has betrayed the former's plan and freed the latter's mind from the anxiety occasioned by a necessary fear? So too those who claim that these words were spoken only to cause fear and promote spiritual progress seem to me to oppose God as well as the interests of men: by disclosing the reason for these words, they cause God to be no longer feared and men no longer to make spiritual progress, since, as we have often said, progress is only made in this way as long as there is fear, and fear as long as there is ignorance, and when ignorance ceases, fear also ceases, and when there ceases to be fear any longer, progress also ceases. The betrayer of this secret must be considered to be an enemy of God, because he renders vain and useless what God is seen to have appointed as an aid to the spiritual progress of all men.

4. We must also ask through whom something which God wished not to be known came to be revealed to human knowledge; it is not right for it to be believed or said that it was by his own agency, even if it were so, or he would

seem to be working against himself. And if God could not do so, then there is no one else who could invent such a lie but the one who, at the very beginning of the world, took away their fear from the first two human beings by falsely declaring to them that he was able to reveal God's purpose to them – not that he was really privy to the divine secrets, but because he wanted to lead them astray by deceitful means while they were still dangerously callow and immature and thus delude them into concluding that they should put their trust in him rather than God. For what had God said? 'Of the tree which is in the midst of the garden you shall not eat, for in the day that you eat of it, you shall die' (Gen.2.17; 3.3).[36] On the contrary, the devil said: You will not die. For God knows that on the day on which you eat of it your eyes will be opened, and you will be like gods, knowing good and evil (Gen.3.4,5). How evil is men's wilfulness, always easily adapting the faith to suit their own wishes, and once it has been ascertained that it is in harmony with their wishes and desires, accustoming itself not even to consider the possibility that the very occasion of an easy belief which deceitfully favours its desires may be working against salvation and that the alternative choice which seems to be more difficult may, in fact, turn out to be more salutary! For men find it easier to believe the words even of the devil in order to gratify their bodily desires than to show faith in the divine decrees when these conflict with their own pleasures. There is nothing that a man can sooner believe than what he also longs to believe, and faith is never easier to find than when he is told that he ought to believe something which is condemned as soon as it is made known. That is why Eve readily believed in the serpent rather than God in order to satisfy her longing for a very desirable food, and Adam adapted his faith to his wife's persuasion rather than to the Lord's utterance.

5. But let us not suppose that this happened only to them, and let us not imagine that we are now immune to the stratagems of that tempter, especially when it is written: Be sober, be watchful. Your adversary the devil prowls around like a roaring lion, seeking some one to devour (1 Pet.5.8). We ought not therefore to give in to sleep and idleness or to allow ourselves to sink into a listless stupor. For the cunning of that serpent of old is still as strong as it ever was; the devil still prowls around his world; every soul that is like Eve's is still led astray, and Adam, uncertain as to how he should deal with woman's deceit, easily succumbs to agreement with it and is laid low through his delight in a lethal food. The devil is ever watchful, while *our* minds are at rest: I do not know what he may not do to men who are asleep, if he is so often able to creep up, cunningly concealed, even on men who are awake. For even in the claim that sinners are threatened with the punishment of everlasting fire not because it is true but in order to frighten them I reckon that the cunning of the old enemy is at work and identify his ancient craftiness and villainy, since this action too is just like what he did in the past. Consider if the very one who once led Eve astray in the form of a serpent is not now attempting to ensnare and destroy men with naive and guileless minds. Whenever I hear preaching of this kind, designed as it is to

---

[36] Another example of conflation of two verses.

emasculate a prescription given by God, I always recognize the hissing of that old serpent. For he who now says, 'You shall not be liable to eternal punishment, for God is merciful; he did indeed say this but only to frighten you, since he knew that you would find it difficult to sin as long as the fear of so grave a penalty still clung to your minds,' I realise is the same one who once said: You will not die. For God knows that on the day on which you eat of it, your eyes will be opened, and you will be like gods, knowing good and evil (Gen.3.4,5). Who would now dare to belittle God, if it were not one who has done so from the beginning? Who would dare to dishonour truth by calling it a lie, if not one who had already done so?

6. There is nothing that the devil has tried more to achieve than to give the impression that either he resembles God or God resembles him in some respect, as we detect him doing in this passage. Because he himself is a liar, he wishes to persuade men's minds that God is a liar too. But we who know that God is not only true but Truth itself and, because we know it, believe in him, we who have learned from the declaration in the Lord's own words that the devil was the only liar from the beginning (cf. Jn.8.44),[37] and know without any doubt that he has nothing in common with God, we, I say, must adapt our faith to God's utterances in every respect and believe that nothing will happen to us except what they promise, remembering that definition which says that God is Truth. For no lie can come forth from that which is by nature the truth, as the apostle also testifies: No lie is of the truth (1 Jn.2.21). It is a crime to refuse to have faith in God's proclamations and to think that there is any falsehood in the Father of Truth. God is indeed merciful: who but an impious man could ever doubt it? But he is also truthful. Believe that he is merciful then but also that he is truthful. Remember the text of scripture which proclaims that God is often merciful to sinners, in order that they should not wish to abuse the medicine of penitence by persisting in their present sin.[38] Again, lest you, trusting only in his kindness as a father, should presume on his forgiveness without ceasing to sin, that same text repeatedly proclaims that God is true; as in this passage: But thou, O Lord God, art merciful and gracious, slow to anger and abounding in compassion and truth (Ps.86.15).[39] If you believe that God is merciful, believe also that he is true: he is merciful, when he pardons those who do works of penance commensurate with their sins, true, in that he will deliver to those who persist in their sins and wickedness nothing other than what he has promised them.

7. But we, as I mentioned above also, are quick to believe only what seems to harmonize with our own wishes but find it hard to adapt our faith to what runs

---

[37] Our author has substituted 'liar' for 'murderer' (Vulgate and Greek NT); cf. n.14. But here the original text of Jn.44 gives him some justification, since it continues, 'and has nothing to do with the truth, because there is no truth in him'.

[38] This seems to me to make better sense of the text than the rendering strictly required by Caspari's punctuation as adopted by the editor of PLS 1.

[39] Our author has the text as given in the Vulgate and Greek NT and also in AV, namely, 'compassion and truth'; RSV translates 'steadfast love and faithfulness' and some modern versions prefer 'faithfulness and truth'.

contrary to our appetites and desires. On this matter the scripture testifies elsewhere, saying: My son, you have sinned; do so no more, but ask pardon for your former sins, that they may be forgiven you (Sir.21.1). And: Do not be so confident of atonement nor add sin to sin; and do not say, 'God's mercy is great, he will forgive the multitude of my sins'; for both mercy and wrath are with him, and his anger rests upon sinners (Sir.5.5,6). We must not suppose that God's mercy exists to enable us to sin with greater freedom and immunity but rather that we may repent and seek his pardon. For we sin even by holding wrong opinions about pardon itself, and we have to fear that we may fail to deserve it, if we abuse his protection by indulging in the comforts of sin instead of applying the remedies of penitence, and that the occasion of righteousness may be turned into an occasion of sin through the fault of our incorrect understanding. But lest anyone should hope to receive in the future what he had only pretended to obtain in the present life, divine scripture says: Do good to your friend before you die, and reach out and give to him as much as you can. Do not deprive yourself of a happy day; let not your share of desired good pass you by. Will you not leave the fruit of your labours to others, and what you have acquired by toil to be divided by lot? Give, and take, and justify your soul. Do works of righteousness before you die, for there is no seeking of dainties in the grave (Sir.14.13–17).[40] This is also testified to more plainly by the Lord through his prophet elsewhere, when he says: For those who are in the grave will not praise you nor will the dead bless you nor will those who are in the grave hope for your mercy (Is.38.18).[41]

17, 1. 'But,' it is argued, 'this teaching is too hard and difficult and rigorous and embitters the heart of most men.' As if the despair which by its very terror leaves us in possession of an assured hope is not preferable to a hope which by its deception causes us to lose the fruits of a true hope: a despair which offers us hope is much more to our advantage than a hope which leads to despair. I consider a physician who frightens sick men suffering from a mortal disease by telling them the truth in order to cure them is much more skilful and merciful than one who kills them with his excessive servility and false blandishments. We must pursue an assured hope, not a false one.

2. The reason why those whose teaching is so strict displease the majority, are also liked by a few but are loved only by those who manifestly uphold truth and righteousness is that they refuse to deceive anyone, do not venture to lie to anyone, are not respecters of persons, in the interests of truth spare no one, are seen not to be attempting to win the souls of their audience by false flattery, do not promise an uncertain hope in place of a certain one, prefer to be hated by all men for truth's sake than to be loved for a lie, refuse to pretend, do not spare even themselves, do not promise the kingdom of heaven without discrimination

---

[40] For 'justify your soul' see Riches,19,8,n.45. In addition to this divergence from the accepted text the Latin words for 'Do works of righteousness before you die' have also been inserted here.

[41] This quotation differs greatly from the accepted text.

to the wrathful, the envious, the cruel, the drunkards, the greedy, the grasping, the avaricious, the perjurers, the dishonest, the fornicators, the proud, the luxurious, the dishonourable, or any who are soiled with the filth of their vices. *They* do not use deceitful words to locate the Holy Spirit in the midst of such crimes, *they* maintain that those who are sanctuaries of sin are unworthy to become the dwelling-place of God and that the dwelling-place of a holy occupant must itself be holy, *they* say that members of Christ cannot be members of sin, *they* insist that only the holy, humble, chaste, sober, single-minded, innocent and godly will be with God, *they* declare that not all men without exception shall enter that heavenly and divine dwelling-place, the court of the everlasting King. Moses is prevented from treading on holy ground merely because his shoes are soiled, yet there are some who imagine that they can tread on heavenly ground with polluted hearts. So they acquire few friends but many enemies as a result of their teaching, since those who condemn sin and vice are bound to have as many foes as there are men who delight in practising wickedness. Hence it is too that they are harassed by wicked and ungodly cliques, are assailed with false charges, are besmeared with the dishonourable name of heretic, and almost all the talk of their enemies takes their disparagement as its subject.[42] But what wonder is it that the teaching of righteousness should seem heretical to men of shame? The secret of this heresy is apparent only to the enemies of those who preach it, whereas, if their words contained the true faith, it is their friends who would have been more likely to be able to understand it. Let them indeed be heretics, if even their enemies can find it credible that a man is able to hide his meaning from his closest friends and reveal it to absolute strangers, or prefer his foes to be privy to his secrets than friends who would conceal them. But, as we have already remarked a little earlier, they are defamed by charges of this kind because they say simply and clearly and without any trace of deception whatever truth is contained in the faith, relying upon the fact that at least some reward will be vouchsafed to them for never concealing the unadulterated teaching of righteousness through timidity; they realize that it is a very grave offence in God's sight to utter by word of mouth anything other than what conscience knows to be true, or to offer a sham imitation of the truth.

18, 1. But let these considerations carry what weight they can with men whose knowledge cannot extend beyond such information as their natural senses are able to acquire for them and who can be easily persuaded that a thing is what it is not, so long as they fail to discern what it really is. What shall we do then when the day arrives on which, with angels, archangels and other companies of the heavenly host standing together before the judgement seat of the Son of God, the secrets of our hearts are revealed, on which the full knowledge of every single act, not merely talk about it, will give witness, on which it will no longer be

---

[42] For this reference to attacks on the Pelagians as heretics see the introduction to this letter.

possible to conceal unrighteousness or feign holiness, on which it will be a matter not so much of a man betraying his deeds as of his deeds betraying him?

2. What shall we reply to him when he says to us, 'In the beginning I had fashioned you, the human race, from the slime of earth after my own likeness with immeasurable kindness and with one object – that you should follow me in all the ways pertaining to works of righteousness and should be in character like God, though manifestly unlike him in nature; I had also formed the nature of your being so that it might be able both to understand and to do what it willed and thus you would be left with no excuse on grounds of ignorance or lack of ability. And although the power of clear reasoning and understanding which I had bestowed on you would always enable you both to recognize and practise goodness and virtue for yourselves and to avoid with the greatest of ease such occasions of evil and vice as might occur, yet, in addition, I gave you a law and pronounced in the words of my own lips the precepts and commandments which you were to keep and ordered them to be recorded and set down in writing in books, so that the knowledge which your inner nature already possessed might also be transmitted to you outwardly by your senses of sight and hearing and through this addition of the heavenly scriptures and the witness and admonitions of their writings to your feelings of conscience. Nor were these means of instruction enough: I appointed prophets for you, men full of the grace of the Holy Spirit, from time to time to warn you by miraculous signs and good works and by divine predictions to keep and to guard the decrees which I had implanted in your natural conscience and laid down in the commandments of my law. But, not content even with that, in the end I came down myself and was pleased to take upon myself from a virgin's womb the human form of your race, so that I might witness in your natural form and show you that my commandments to you were quite capable of being put into effect.[43] I also suffered many things in the human form which I had taken upon myself for the sake of your safety and salvation. I endured most shameful abuse and insults and bore with patience and equanimity most cruel slights and wounds, being upbraided with the name of Beelzebub and charged with being possessed by devils. I was struck by the palms of men's hands, beaten with scourges, crowned with thorns, dishonoured by spittings and afflicted with other most shameful insults and injuries, mocked and, finally, hanged upon a gibbet. And so that my punishment might seem to lack no cruelty, while hanging on the cross I was given gall and vinegar to drink, which increased still further the extreme torments which I suffered. Despite all this I prayed for indulgence and pardon for all these so wicked, ungodly and cruel enemies, who did not cease to mock me even in the hour of my death, whose savage instincts not even the bitterest of punishments could satisfy.

3. All this I did in order to leave you an example of single-mindedness, innocence, godliness and clemency and, at the same time, demonstrate by actual

---

[43] Thus the reason for Jesus' incarnation was to teach men to obey the law – 'a merely Abelardian view of the atonement' (Haslehurst, xvif.), which makes Pelagian 'grace' 'no more than the law and teaching', as Augustine often asserted.

performance what I had enjoined in words. Where then is the effect of the teaching which I handed down to you? Where is the pattern of perfect and complete righteousness and goodness with which I supplied you? You have spurned nearly all my precepts and commandments and by the little value which you have set on all the sufferings which I bore for the sake of your safety and salvation you have behaved wantonly to one another and, with a degree of cruelty which exceeds that of the beasts and wild animals, have striven with one another in bitterest hatred and in contempt of the law. You, whom I taught by the teaching of my words as well as by the example of my works to love even your enemies, have not even spared your own brethren. I commanded you to shun riches so completely that I refused the wealthy entry to my kingdom by using an example to illustrate the infinite difficulty with which they were faced.[44] But, ignoring the rules which I have taught you and the example which I gave you by my way of life in revealing myself as poor for the sake of your spiritual progress, though, in fact, I own the whole world, you have so flattered the rich as to set all hope for the future on them most of all and inveighed with the deadliest hatred against anyone whom you perceived as wishing to defend the teaching contained in my commandments. I also forbade you to call any man 'father' on earth,[45] in order that no pride in earthly and worldly descent should remain in you after seeing an example of the pre-eminence of heavenly nobility, and that there should be no recollection of their fleshy and mortal birth in those whom the state of spiritual and eternal blessedness had already admitted into union with itself. But you have made such arrogant claims for the honour of your human ancestry that you despise others who lack the status of such a corruptible lineage as if they were base and ignoble, though you are not unaware that they have been ennobled by their descent from a heavenly seed. Some too, whom I had bidden to despise their own possessions, have defied my teaching and made inroads into other men's property, and though I had ordered them to be kind even to those who had done them wrong, they have persecuted men who have never troubled them and have waged wars among themselves with hatred and savage enmity, as if I had taught them dissension, quarrelling and contention, not peace and love and agreement with one another.'

19, 1. How shall we reply to this statement? What shall we answer? What shall we say? Perhaps we shall say that the reason for our negligence in obeying his commandments was that his own apostles afterwards only pretended to repeat his teaching, reckoning that there was little need to warn us by frequent and oft-repeated exhortations not to stray outside the doors of righteousness and holiness.

2. But if this is how we wish to reply, then that chief among the apostles, on the firm base of whose faith the spiritual fabric of the whole building was

---

44 For the author's teaching on wealth see especially *Riches*,9,4; 19,2; *Chast.*10,8; 17; the view expressed in the three letters is not identical but it is very similar in thought and word and generally more extreme than that of Pelagius himself. Possibly the influence of Celestius is again to be seen here.

45 See YM,n.16.

constructed and the foundations of the edifice of the Church were laid, who was found worthy to be the doorkeeper of the heavenly kingdom and whose judgements, delivered on earth, are ratified in heaven – he will instantly answer to the contrary and will say, 'I never kept silent where they were concerned; nay rather, I went so far as to repeat to them very often what you had said and to reprove them, and proclaimed what you had not said. I commanded them to put away all malice and guile and insincerity and envy and, like little babes, to long for the nutriment of a reasonable holiness and the nourishment of unadulterated food.[46] I instructed them not to think that bodily chastity was sufficient on its own but to purify their souls as well in loving obedience, in unfeigned brotherly love and in heartfelt affection.[47] I set before their eyes the nobility of their own birth, all the time showing them to be a chosen race, priestly and royal, a holy nation, God's own people.[48] I also taught them that they were partakers of the divine nature,[49] believing that they would be more ready to keep righteousness if they but knew the miraculous nature of their birth, since the realization that they were sprung from a stock which was not only honourable but holy would make them cleave to more honourable things. I often enjoined them to follow your example by being holy in all their conduct,[50] adding also the command which you had given long ago and which contains the words: You shall be holy, for I the Lord your God am holy (Lev.19.2). I earnestly exhorted them to be as citizens of heaven on earth, endowed with the strength of the spirit, and not to become estranged from it like aliens through the temptations of fleshly desires.[51] I also preached to them the glory of the righteous and the eternal punishment of sinners, so that either the longing for the state of blessedness which they desired might incline them or the fear of a terrible punishment impel them to lead a life of habitual holiness. And, that they might not suppose that the predictions for the future made by your unyielding righteousness were not true, I demonstrated their truth by proving them in this present life; for through the grace of your spirit I punished with death the husband and wife who had lied about a sum of money,[52] in order that those who had committed even lesser sins which had not been pardoned might realize the punishment awaiting greater offences. It is for them to answer themselves and tell us how these offences have disappeared or from what source they have obtained immunity from their sin.

20, 1. The apostle to the gentiles,[53] the chosen instrument,[54] one who, even while he remained on earth, shared the secrets of heaven, will also rise and cry

---

[46] Cf. 1 Pet.2.1,2.
[47] Ibid.1.22.
[48] Ibid.2.9.
[49] Cf. 2 Pet.1.4.
[50] Cf. 1 Pet.1.15.
[51] Ibid.2.11; Eph.2.19.
[52] Cf. Acts,5.1ff.
[53] Cf. Rom.11.13.
[54] RSV; electionis vas, literally, 'the vessel of election'; cf. Acts,9.15. But Pelagius omitted Hebrews from his Commentary.

out, saying 'In fourteen books containing letters I made known to them that they should not commit any act of unrighteousness or iniquity. I bade them to aim only to love single-mindedness, innocence, godliness and righteousness.[55] I urged them to live peaceably with all men.[56] I clearly enjoined them not to repay evil with evil but, on the contrary, with good.[57] I commanded them to reflect that you are their Father and to remember that they are your sons and so to continue to live in a state of reasonableness and free from any stain of sin.[58] I warned them to show themselves worthy to be the dwelling-place of your Spirit.[59] I often bore witness that they should recognize that they are members of your body.[60] I told them to let no evil talk come out of their mouths but always to speak of good things.[61] I commanded them openly and frequently to rid themselves of all bitterness and wrath and anger and clamour and slander with all malice.[62] I explained that those who did not have your spirit of gentleness and kindness were not your people, and I proclaimed with the clearest witness that only those belonged to you who had crucified their flesh with its vices and desires.[63] I also desired them to be free from jesting, foolish talk and deception and forewarned them against such faults,[64] and I commanded them not to fail in any matter which was worthy of God's praise, and did not want impurity and covetousness to be even named among them,[65] so that they might recognize how serious it is to commit an offence which it is unlawful to mention. Finally, how much I desired them to be free from sinners[66] of all kinds is perfectly clear from the fact that I did not want them even to keep company with sinners but to shun and avoid them so as not even to join and mingle with such men at a banquet.[67] I often warned them to show themselves as temples of God in all things[68] and as sons of God in all manner of holy living and to do works worthy of reward in the future. But, as far as I can see, they have not read my words, written in books under the inspiration of thy Holy Spirit, with the result that, instead of deciding that they were worthy of obedience, they judged them to be worthy of contempt. No wonder that they have despised my utterances, though inspired by you, when they have had no hesitation in transgressing and making nothing of the commandments of your lips, recorded as they are in the books of the gospels.'

[55] Cf. 1 Tim.6.11.
[56] Cf. Rom.12.18; 2 Cor.13.11; 2 Tim.2.22.
[57] Cf. Rom.12.17; 1 Thess.5.15.
[58] Cf. 1 Cor.6.17,18.
[59] Ibid.3.16,17; Rom.8.9.
[60] Cf. 1 Cor.6.15; Rom.12.5.
[61] Cf. Eph.4.29; Col.3.8.
[62] Cf. Eph.4.31.
[63] Cf. Gal.5.21–24.
[64] Cf. Eph.4.31.
[65] Ibid.5.3.
[66] Or 'sins'.
[67] Cf. Rom.16.17; 1 Cor.5.11; 2 Thess.3.6,14.
[68] Cf. 1 Cor.3.16,17; 6.19; 2 Cor.6.16; Eph.2.21; Rom.8.14.

21.   The disciple beloved of the Lord and especially distinguished for deserving the guerdon of such an honour and, by virtue of his great intimacy, given the privilege of reclining on the divine bosom, will also cry out, saying: I warned them in three letters to fulfil your precepts and commandments. I bore witness in all my words that the man who failed to carry out your statutes and commands neither loved you nor knew you.[69] I proclaimed that you were the true light, undimmed by any cloud of darkness, and that participation in your blessedness could not be possessed by anyone who did not rejoice in the gift of that light – that is, anyone who allowed the brightness of his way of life and conduct to be sullied by the darkness of pretence, hypocrisy or any sin at all.[70] I exhorted them to be mindful of their calling and, if they claimed to be your followers, to adhere to your actions and your way of life.[71] I taught them that the honour of being called the children of God has been conferred upon us.[72] I revealed to them that at the time of your coming the brilliance of your likeness would be bestowed on them,[73] and that every man who cherished hope in this faith belongs to you, and I warned them to purify themselves as you are pure.[74] I stated that no one who abides in you sins, and I testified to all that no one who sins has either seen you or known you.[75] I made it absolutely clear that only the righteous belonged to you and that all who committed sin were joined in partnership with the devil.[76] I showed them that no one born of God could sin, since they retain the recollection of their divine birth and cannot by any means sin as long as they retain the remembrance of their parentage.[77] To prevent them from flattering themselves on the possession of a mere name and title, I revealed to them the marks of the children of God as well as of the children of the devil, so that they might know that only the righteous are of divine lineage but that the unrighteous belong to the offspring of the devil.[78] I indicated that above all else they must love one another, and I warned them to love one another following your example, that is, to be willing to lay down their lives for one another.[79] I proclaimed quite clearly that anyone who hates his brother cannot have eternal life.[80] I taught them not to love in words only but to strive to reveal the purity of their love by true works.[81] I taught them with certainty that God would hear those who were free from the rebuke of their own conscience.[82] I disclosed that those who remain

---

[69] Cf. 1 Jn.23–5.
[70] Cf. Jn.1.9ff.; 1 Jn.1.5.
[71] Ibid.6,7; 2.9–11.
[72] Ibid.3.1.
[73] Ibid.2.
[74] Ibid.3.
[75] Ibid.6.
[76] Ibid.8.
[77] Ibid.9.
[78] Ibid.10.
[79] Ibid.11; 4.7; 2 Jn.5.
[80] Cf. 1 Jn.3.15.
[81] Ibid.18.
[82] Ibid.5.14ff.

holy in this world shall have confidence on the day of your judgement.[83] I taught
that no one who is perfect in the love of God need fear slander and abuse, or hurt
and injury, or any other kind of attack.[84] I bade them not to love the world or the
things that are in the world and proclaimed that anyone who loves the world
does not have God's love in him,[85] and I added that all the things of this world
that exceed the limits of our natural needs are not of the Father but have been
invented by the lust of the flesh and the lust of the eyes and the pride of this
world and the vainglory of this life,[86] and I bore witness that they ought not to
care for love of a world which we know will pass away in the fullness of time.[87] It
is for them to acknowledge themselves the extent to which they have despised
and shunned all these sayings of mine and plunged themselves into the depths of
malice, cruelty, hatred, wickedness, greed, deceit and every other kind of iniquity.'

22.   He too, who was chosen to be the third witness of the Lord's glory,[88]
whom the apostle describes as the second pillar of faith after Peter,[89] will spring
forward with words like these, 'I explained to them briefly but clearly in the text
of one letter what it was expedient for them to observe. To prevent them from
rushing into anger and hatred, I pointed out the evil attached to such anger, that
is, that it cannot fulfil God's righteousness.[90] Lest they should judge that your
heavenly and divine precepts were written merely to be read or heard, I enjoined
them to be doers of your word and not hearers only.[91] Lest they should try to
defend themselves by claiming the privilege of being 'religious', I testified that, if
they fell into the sin of having an unbridled tongue, their 'religion' is vain.[92] I did
not hesitate to employ a wide range of arguments to urge them not to respect
persons nor to show a perverse preference for those for whom you had prophesied
woe[93] – and to whom you had refused entry to the court of heaven by making use
of an analogy which indicated the great difficulty facing them[94] – over the poor
chosen in preference by you and described as 'rich in faith and heirs of your
kingdom';[95] nor to set before your companions in blessedness a man wearing
brilliant and expensive clothes and a glittering ring of great price.[96] Lest love of
worldly goods should shut out the love of your worship, I declared that friendship

---

[83] Ibid.4.17.
[84] Ibid.18.
[85] Ibid.2.15.
[86] Ibid.2.16.
[87] Ibid.17.
[88] Cf. Mt.17.1; Mk.9.2; Lk.9.28.
[89] Cf. Gal.2.9.
[90] Jas.1.20.
[91] Ibid.22.
[92] Ibid.1.26.
[93] Cf. Lk.6.24.
[94] Cf. Mt.19.23,24; Mk.10.23–25; Lk.18.24,25; see also n.44.
[95] Cf. Jas.2.5; Lk.6.20.
[96] Cf. Jas.2.1ff.

with the world is enmity with God.[97] Lest they should suppose that faith only is self-sufficient, I testified that the claim to possess faith would not profit them by itself and without works of righteousness.[98] Lest they should think that they possessed heavenly wisdom if bitter jealousy or persistent strife were in their hearts, I proved to them that this kind of wisdom was much more likely to come from the earth and the devil.[99] I pronounced that the wise man is to be recognized by a life of good works.[100] I gave them adequate, and more than adequate, warning not to speak evil of one another or to pass judgement on their brethren for an action for which the law had not condemned them or to appear to pass sentence not so much against a man's natural behaviour as against the commandments established by God or to boast of their superior wisdom by refuting actions which those commandments had decreed to be undeserving of the slightest criticism.[101] I bore witness in the strongest possible terms that they should not presume to swear by heaven or earth or with any other oath at all.[102] To prevent them from flattering themselves on keeping only those commandments which they had chosen to keep or from supposing that they were already righteous because they kept some of them while rejecting others, I explained that the man who had transgressed only one commandment was a transgressor of the whole law.[103] It is obvious from their own reply how far they have departed from the limits prescribed by such teaching and with what despair in their hearts they deceived not only themselves but others as well by presuming to interpret commandments so clear and palpable not by adherence to the truth but according to their own desires and pleasures, and by adulterating that truth with clever but false exposition.

23, 1. What, I ask, shall we reply to these charges? Shall we be able to claim either that such things were not written or that the sense of the things which were written were obscured for us because of the difficulty of understanding them, when they are all so clear and manifest that we know them to be completely free from any complication, concealment or obscurity? Perhaps we shall say,'We indeed acknowledge, Lord, all the charges laid against us, and we know for certain that we have no excuse to offer; but we should be given credit for having had faith, for having frequently called upon your holy name, for knowing you to be our only Lord and Creator, for having proclaimed the teaching of your law, for the fact that some of us have cast out demons in order to honour your most powerful name, have healed the sick and have performed other prodigies and miraculous works.' But his answer to us will be the same as that which he promised to give to such persons: Not everyone who says to me, 'Lord, Lord,'

---

97 Ibid.4.4.
98 Ibid.2.14ff.
99 Ibid.3.14ff.
100 Ibid.13.
101 Ibid.4,11,12.
102 Ibid.5.12; see also n.29.
103 Ibid.2.10; for the importance of keeping the whole law see Riches,n.34.

shall enter the kingdom of heaven, but he who does the will of my Father who is in heaven, he shall enter the kingdom of heaven. . . Depart from me, you evil-doers; I do not know you (Mt.7.21,23).[104]

2. What fear will then be the lot of us who are sinners, what sadness of heart, what groaning and lamentation, what weeping and tears, when we see the righteous rewarded with splendid gifts and ourselves accounted unworthy to receive that blessedness which has been assigned to men of like nature to us! What distress there is when you see what you have so greatly desired and, having seen it, are unable to keep it! When you marvel at it only in the possession of others, though you could have marvelled at it in your own, when you do not possess what you desire but have to endure what you loathe, when you see others being conducted by archangels and angels and the other divine attendants to the kingdom prepared for them with the pomp and dignity of heaven, while you are hurried off to the torments of hell by the ministers of punishment! How pitiable we shall then feel, with what shamefacedness we shall then stand before such glorious majesty, when we shall be found not to resemble in merit those whom we seemed to resemble in religion! With what sadness of heart and anguish of soul we shall be turned away from the face of God and the presence of all his saints and from those divine and immortal pleasures and have to depart to our appointed place with the devil and his angels! With what words and tears we shall bid farewell to the heavenly kingdom and those who possess it! It will be too late then to repent of having rejected sound teaching and of having refused to listen to the salutary warnings of the truth; too late then to express our dissatisfaction with those opinions which now satisfy the majority; too late to grieve over our neglect of the outcast and poor, at our assent to the words of men rather than those of God; too late to recognize the usefulness of that teaching whose severity once made us shudder; too late to deplore that hope which now makes a laughing-stock of most men; too late to feel sorry for having gazed with longing on human wealth and for having preferred to enjoy the honours of this temporal world rather than that of eternity. Some will attribute the cause of their death to their own lack of understanding, others to the instruction given by others; but the sorrow that comes from repentance will avail them no more, once the time for repentance has slipped from their grasp.

24, 1. And so, my most beloved, we must be always turning over these thoughts in our hearts and reflecting on them day and night. It is a great thing to be a son of God; it is infinitely great to attain to heaven after earth; possession of eternal life is abundance of riches; to shine forth with the brilliance of the sun is above all other splendour; to reign with God is more glorious than all other glory, more noble than all other nobility; our belief is beyond telling, our hope is beyond measure. What then is demanded of us in return for so great a gift? That we should live righteous and holy lives in the meantime. The life we lead is the price

104 Our author has inserted 'he shall enter the kingdom of heaven' and reversed the order of the last two clauses, also making some minor changes in the words used.

we pay for this state of blessedness, but only if it is worthy to obtain the reward of so great a prize: what we are seeking is no ordinary thing, and so our life ought not to be an ordinary one either; the conduct of the man who is looking for divine rewards must itself be divine. Men who live in a similar way cannot receive a dissimilar payment: it is folly to want to live like everyone else and yet to look forward to sharing a secret which has not been promised to everyone. Holy things are due to holy persons; heavenly kingdoms have been promised to heavenly people. What then do I mean by 'heavenly people'? Obviously, those who perform heavenly works, although they live on earth. On the other hand, everlasting punishment in torment is powerful and terrible, and the eternal fires of hell are greatly to be dreaded. If the things which we ought to desire do not attract us, the things that we ought to fear should at least deter us, and the motive of fear should at least supply what the desire for love ought to have bestowed upon us.

2. But let us suppose, as some men would have it, that we have no need to fear any future punishment in torment or to dread burning by any eternal fire and that we are to believe that such promises were made only to frighten us. Surely the discomfiture that awaits us ought to be enough to arouse our fear. What agonies of shame we shall feel when, before God's very eyes and in the sight of all the heavenly powers surrounding him in heaven, of the martyrs and the other saints standing by, the secrets of every one of us will be revealed, and all the sins which we have committed in thought and in deed will be exposed as if they were actually being done there on the spot and represented in the sight of all in their own image and likeness according to the testimony: I shall rebuke you, and lay the charge before you (Ps.50.21), when each man will drag along behind him like a rope the succession of sins which he has committed, giving rise to the saying: Woe to those who drag their sins behind them like a long rope (Is.5.18; LXX).

3. What feelings of shame and disgrace, I ask you, will then confound the hearts of those above all who were thought in men's judgement to be holier than the rest of mortals, when they are seen to be different from what they have appeared to men to be? What pangs of conscience will assail them when they hear this said of them in the assembly of saints: 'Are not these the men who in the world were said to be greater Christians than all the others? Was it not their fame that sped on the wings of common report throughout almost the whole world? How comes it that they have now been found to be different from what they were once thought to be? It is now apparent that they showed themselves to be righteous in the eyes of men rather than of God and deemed it sufficient for them to be held to be holy in the judgement of men, while showing not the slightest inclination to attain that holiness which is after God. What sorrow there will be, what lamentation, what groaning, when they hear such things being said of them! But those who were not honoured with any reputation for holiness will grieve less; for what wonder is it that the man who has always been held to be unrighteous is shown not to be righteous and is found to be what he was believed to be? The man who has never received any mark of esteem or honour does not find cause to feel greatly dishonoured but the man who was

once renowned and now sees himself stripped of all renown meets a fate which is heavier to bear than any punishment. To such a man his shame will seem endless, his discomfiture everlasting; so too, those who found it necessary to put their trust in a falsehood ought at least to have dreaded that, in consequence, they would be for ever subjected to dishonour and confusion.

25.   Let us make haste then, while there is still time,[105] and strive with all our might to overcome all our sinful habits and steep ourselves instead in works of righteousness and holiness, so that we may not have to endure unending torment and punishment, dishonour and discomfiture with the ungodly and the sinners but, rather, enjoy the glory of divine blessedness and everlasting brightness with the righteous and holy. Though it is entirely appropriate for me and those like me to make such an appeal, yet to you it may seem quite superfluous, since it is plain that you are so far from committing unlawful acts that you appear to have rejected even those which are lawful.[106] How can it be possible for men to venture to do what is forbidden, while fearing to do even what is permitted? But, as we said in our preface at the beginning of this letter, it is in the very nature of love that it should prefer to say something superfluous to those whom it loves than deliberately to keep silence.

[105] Cf., *Riches*,20,3; *Law*,9,1; *Dem.*27,4.
[106] See n.23 above.

11

On Chastity[1]

Once again the names of both writer and addressee are missing; but there are enough resemblances, verbal, stylistic and contextual, between this letter and the other documents in the Caspari collection to indicate that we are almost certainly dealing with the same writer as in the tractates *On Riches* and *On Bad Teachers*, and the recipient of the letter is clearly a rich young man, like the addressee of the first document in the collection, though there is not enough evidence to entitle us to identify him as the same person.

There are also several indications of the writer's Pelagianism: for example, in 3,5 it is claimed that 'no man is born corrupt', that is, corrupted by original sin; in 8,2 it is maintained that chastity is not a gift of grace but a natural possession (cf.8,4) and in 10,6 that virginity is not a gift of God but is 'present by man's own free will'; and in 8,4 a distinction is drawn between 'the glory of the kingdom', which is denied to married persons, and 'life', for which they are eligible 'if they are still able to keep all God's commandments in that (sc. the married) state', a distinction, however, which is denied on scriptural grounds in *On Riches*,18,6 and *On Bad Teachers*,8 (see n.15 there);[2] finally, we observe the usual, characteristically Pelagian warning not to swear any kind of oath 'even in a just cause' (10,9; cf., e.g., *Cel.*19, *Dem.*19,4).

In the introductory chapters chastity is described as 'the supreme good' and 'the foundation of holiness and righteousness',[3] defined as 'not to have intercourse of a carnal nature with either sex' and distinguished from incontinence in the matrimonial state. It is divided into two classes – virginity and widowhood –

---

[1] *Epistula [sancti Sixti episcopi et martyris] de castitate*: PLS 1,1464–1505; CPL 736; Caspari,122–67; Haslehurst,200–85.

[2] Caspari, followed by Haslehurst, thinks that the apparent discrepancy between this passage and *Riches* 18,6 can be easily explained on the grounds that, whereas the writer of *Riches* is discouraging the rich from supposing that, although their wealth might prevent them from entering the kingdom of heaven, they might still be eligible for the lower state of eternal life, and in BT,8 he is giving a similar warning to Christians who indulge in moral laxity; he finds, when dealing with married persons, that it is necessary to concede the possibility of a lower state in the future life for which they may be eligible if saved: 'he could not damn eternally all the married, much as he would have enjoyed doing so!' (Haslehurst, xxv); cf. also *Virg.*4,2; *Life*,15.1.

[3] Later, in the closing chapter, chastity is described as 'the mother of all virtues'.

with marital continence added to the latter. As in *On Riches* and *On Bad Teachers* the discussion then takes the form of suggesting various objections and difficulties which may be raised and of refuting them by a detailed examination of selected proof-texts. For example, the grounds for marriage are compared with its disadvantages and attendant dangers and with the great reward promised to all those who either remain chaste or decide to become chaste of their own volition. As in *On Riches* and *On Bad Teachers* much is made of the hypocrisy of those who seek to defend their own arguments, in this case for marriage, by citing examples from the Old Testament, while ignoring or misinterpreting the teaching of the New Testament which involves modification of the commandments contained in the Old Law. In this connexion the main proof-text is 1 Cor.7, which is analysed in great detail and at some length, and stress is laid on the imperative need to accept the authoritative rulings and counsel of Paul, 'the chosen vessel' and 'teacher of the gentiles', instead of relying on the mistaken exegeses of those whose main aim is not to discover his true meaning but to protect their own inclinations to licentiousness. Attention is also paid to the arguments that chastity is too difficult for all but a few, when, in fact, it is an easier way of life than licentiousness and less burdensome than marriage, and that, if universally adopted, it would lead to the end of the human race and of the world which it inhabits, when it is precisely for such an end and for the coming of the kingdom of God that Christians are accustomed to pray. Throughout the letter the writer returns again and again, like the Pelagian that he is, to the absolute necessity for all Christians to seek perfection by following at all times the example of Jesus, and it is with this that he concludes his letter in his eulogy of his addressee, which is to some extent reminiscent of Pelagius' commendation of the virgin Demetrias at the beginning of his letter to her.

Apart from the clear indications of its author's Pelagian sympathies there are no grounds to suppose that the contents of this letter would have been offensive even, say, to Jerome. On two occasions[4] we find the writer at pains to distance himself from the views which Jovinian had been expressing in Rome in the latter part of the fourth century and which Jerome had condemned in his treatise *Against Jovinian* in 393. When, in a letter to his friend Domnio, Jerome subsequently referred to 'a certain monk',[5] generally taken to have been Pelagius, in terms no less intemperate than those which characterize his polemic against Jovinian, challenging him to open debate and crying out, almost in despair, 'I do not condemn wedlock, I do not condemn marriage', the writer of *On Chastity* might well have echoed his words.[6] Nevertheless, there can be no doubt that Jerome, not for the first or last time in his long life, had gone over the top in his treatise *Against Jovinian* in his anxiety to chastise Jovinian for 'having placed married couples on the same level as consecrated virgins of the Church' when he

---

4 See 10,8; 16.
5 *Letters*,50,2 (PL 22,512); for arguments against identifying the 'monk' referred to as Pelagius see Duval,1980,530ff.
6 *Letters*,50,5 (PL 22,516).

went so far as to assert that 'even first marriages were regrettable, if pardonable, capitulations to the flesh' and that 'second marriages were only a step away from the brothel', that 'priests were holy only in so far as they possessed the purity of virgins' and that 'the married clergy were mere raw recruits in the army of the church, brought in because of a temporary shortage of battle-hardened veterans of lifelong celibacy' – 'a memorable statement of the ascetic viewpoint at its most unpleasant and impracticable'.[7]

The writer of this letter would not have gone to such extremes, even if he had been able to couch them in Jerome's inimitable prose. Indeed, Jerome himself was to find it necessary to clarify his position with regard to marriage in a letter to his friend Pammachius,[8] who had written to warn him of the controversy sparked off by the virulence of his attack on Jovinian and to tell him that his treatise had been withdrawn from circulation until tempers had cooled down. In his reply Jerome insisted that his earlier remarks should not have been taken to indicate that he condemned marriage for those who chose it because they felt unable to remain chaste. Our writer takes virtually the same view, while reserving the right to place chastity on a higher level than marriage, if only on the grounds that it had been promised the reward of the heavenly kingdom. But the more extreme views on the subject as expressed by Jerome in his treatise *Against Jovinian* did not lack supporters at Rome, and the controversy over marriage, chastity and clerical celibacy was to remain on the agenda for some time.[9]

As for Augustine, the treatment of chastity in this letter would not have been distasteful to him, however strongly he would certainly have opposed its Pelagian undertones. After making several uncompromising pronouncements on women in general and on marital intercourse in particular in the days before his baptism,[10] later, under the influence of his own spiritual development and his experience of pastoral duties as a Bishop, he was content to praise virginity and chastity in the highest possible terms and to accept that marital intercourse was permissible for the express purpose of producing offspring and thus avoiding extramarital intercourse.[11] And despite his personal contempt for physical pleasures and his approval of widowhood, which he eulogized in his minor treatise *On the Good of Widowhood*,[12] he remained a staunch defender of marriage, though his attitude to it tended to be idealistic, and wrote another minor treatise *On the Good of Marriage* as well as one *On Holy Virginity*, holding virginity to be the more perfect of the two states but, at the same time, warning virgins to beware of losing their humility.[13] Unlike Jerome, who could refer to 'the dirt of marriage',[14]

---

[7] Brown,1988,377.
[8] *Letters*,49,5 (PL 22,511ff.).
[9] On the controversy between Jerome and Jovinian and its possible consequences for Pelagius see Rees,1988,5ff.
[10] E.g., *Soliloquies*, 1,12 (PL 32,873f.).
[11] *Sermons*, 51,15,25 (PL 38,1842f.).
[12] PL 40,429–450, written for the benefit of Juliana, mother of Demetrias (see *Dem.*, introd.).
[13] *Sermons*,354,8 and 4 (PL 39,1567,1564f).
[14] In his treatise *Against Jovinian* I,26 (PL 33,247A).

Augustine maintained an enlightened and sympathetic attitude towards it, while rating martyrdom above virginity as 'the highest peak of human heroism',[15] and, like Ambrose, showed little interest in total clerical celibacy, which was becoming increasingly fashionable among his Italian contemporaries, while remaining completely committed to celibacy himself and an advocate of postmarital celibacy for all clergy.

Ambrose and Augustine would have agreed with our author in holding that in the scale of human perfection, virgins came first, widows second and married persons third; all three were above all else unyielding supporters of Paul's summary as contained in 1 Cor.7, even if they might have differed in interpretation in some particulars. But Pelagians, committed as they were to preaching the virtues of asceticism, were also committed to advocating poverty and chastity as prerequisites of the way of life followed by all true Christians as opposed to those who merely wanted the name but were either unable to unwilling to fulfil the obligations attached to it, and our author's characteristically Pelagian insistence on the evils of wealth and incontinence is developed to the full in *On Riches* and *On Chastity* respectively. It is true that he seems to reveal greater sympathy with married persons than with the moderately rich who try to compromise by disposing of a part of their wealth in favour of the poor. But both works maintain an equally sustained and unremitting polemic against their chosen targets, and *On Chastity* expresses much more severe views than *On Virginity*, which is 'comparatively eirenic' in tone (Evans,1968,123,n.72): the latter teaches that righteousness is the chief vocation of Christians with continence as an additional qualification for those who seek perfection, whereas the former insists that those who wish to become authentic followers of Christ must abstain entirely from sexual intercourse, whether married or single. For Pelagius the virgin's first concern must continue to be for 'spiritual obedience' (*Dem*.9,1,2), without which she will be unable to pursue the very special course which she has chosen as her lifelong vocation; for the author of *On Chastity*, on the other hand, chastity is 'the foundation of holiness and also righteousness' (2,1). He brings to his task of promoting chastity a fresh sense of urgency and a note of increased rigour and severity.

Text

1.   Although we know that your Christianity[16] is of such a kind that you possess the whole gift of holiness as if it were inborn in you and are rather able to teach others than to need teaching yourself, yet the excess of anxiety which springs from affection and which we are bound to show especially to the good leads us to fear that perhaps in the midst of the many considerations which are

[15] Brown,1988,397.
[16] For this use of the word *Christianitas* cf. *Riches*,6,3; BT,1,1 and n.6.

relevant to the subject there is one which may escape your notice. And so we have found it preferable to appear to be giving superfluous advice rather than to leave you in ignorance on any point of sound teaching, since we shall not lose anything if we pass on to you some information which you already possess, while profiting greatly if we also impart some item of knowledge which, as usually happens, you do not. For, as you are aware, it often happens that the item which is more necessary than everything else lies hidden among many other good things, and the others are placed at risk through ignorance of what is more important. It is also a trick played by our old and cunning enemy, who not unjustifiably makes a man the target for his hatred and envy as he tries to ascend by the merits of holiness to the very place from which *he* was expelled for his transgression,[17] and, on the pretext that it is something which is already permitted, removes from sight a good which it is necessary to acquire; by this means too he is often able to strip a man of all his good qualities, like a sly and ill-disposed craftsman who threatens the security of the entire fabric of a house by giving it a weak and inadequate foundation and sometimes causes the builder to lose the whole house through paying too little attention to that which holds it all together.[18]

2, 1. No one who has examined the examples available in God's law intently with his whole mind can doubt that chastity is the foundation of holiness and also righteousness; but if he begins to weaken in any respect, then it is to be feared that the whole fabric of his being is on the point of falling. But before I begin to say anything about the good of chastity, I can see that a definition of it is necessary, lest someone should perhaps think that we are dealing with the 'chastity' upon which the incontinent have bestowed that name; for they are now in the habit of defining it merely as abstention from adultery and incest, though their purity is dishonoured by the constant pollution of lust. And without doubt such persons will not unjustifiably applaud themselves on possessing the good of chastity if they compare themselves with adulterers, just as the latter will take some pride in their purity if tempted to commit the unnatural act of lust of the sodomites. Yet they are not reckoned as chaste for that reason, just as Sodom is not righteous either, although it is described as justified in comparison with Israel (cf.Mt.11.24). But I am dealing with true, not enforced, chastity, and that must be defined as a quality which is considered to be opposed to every form of sexual intercourse and concupiscence; nor should it be supposed to be genuine in the case of those who have violated it even in their thoughts, since the Lord says: Everyone who looks at a woman lustfully has already committed adultery with her in his heart (Mt.5.28). For in either sex true chastity is that which is polluted neither bodily nor in the mind.

[17] Cf. 17,2.
[18] Cf. 17,13 for a similar analogy; it is carried on here into the first sentence of the next section.

2. But I do not know how a man who is always incontinent even in his matrimonial state can be said to be chaste. It is a different matter if there is no distinction between chastity and incontinence; but if there is such a distinction, then the continent will not be chaste if the incontinent is chaste, or, if reason does not permit the continent to be deemed unchaste, that same reason will prevent the incontinent from being considered chaste. The distinction between continence and incontinence cannot be denied, for a distinction cannot derive its existence from the same source. A woman can indeed be called chaste if she keeps faith with her own man provided that he is her husband, but she will not be called chaste in respect of her husband unless she is continent in her relationship with him too. A man can also be called chaste in respect of an adulteress if he does not commit adultery, but not in respect of a woman unless he is continent in his relationship with his wife, since his wife is also presumed to be a woman. True chastity is not to have intercourse of a carnal nature with either sex.

3, 1. We divide chastity into two classes, one of virginity and the other of widowhood; to the latter we must add the continence of marriage in cases where one partner, though alive, is 'dead' from this point of view and, though he or she 'has' the other partner as wife or husband, in fact does not 'have' her or him in the sexual sense (cf. 1 Cor.7.29).[19]

2. Concerning then the first class of chastity, namely, virginity, I have some comments which have to be made; but I should first point out its good before its reward, because no one will doubt the value of something which he knows to be good, though he may have some qualms about it if he sees its price displayed before its merits are demonstrated.

3. Perhaps you say, 'What will you be able to say about the good of virginity or chastity, or what reason can you offer for preferring them to marriage when we know that marriages are of God? First I shall say that chastity is like God in this respect, that it continues steadfastly in the holiness of innocence; for you will not dare to say that the Divine Sovereignty does not possess a higher state of life. From this observe the first good of virginity, that our Divine Excellency possesses it, and what is worthy of God should be embraced by man. Secondly, we ought to know that this is the state of life of God's ministers also. I hear mention being made of angels, archangels, thrones, dominions and powers (cf. Rom.8.38; Col.1.16). Now we do not doubt that all of these are under the rule of singleness and chastity; nor would anything else be fitting but that chastity should minister to chastity. But if you maintain that this state of life has been conferred on them not so much by reason of their office as of their nature, since a spiritual substance cannot be joined in wedlock, I might indeed be able to reply that the reason for their office demanded that they be created such that their nature could by no

---

[19] The relevant text itself is cited in 9,13 but is used there for a different purpose, that is, to stress the shortness of the time available to mankind before the end of their lives; see n.65.

means be corrupted,[20] were I not to recall that the angels did at one time enter upon matrimonial unions, which proves that even angels possess chastity voluntarily; but it would take a long time to clarify this obscure passage (cf. Gen.6.1,2). Again, take an example from the human race, I mean priests, who are not permitted to stand by the altar and offer sacrifices to God unless they are continent; thus there can be no reason to doubt that incontinence cannot minister to God.

4. What am I to say about the whole of mankind, who are permitted to practise intercourse in marriage only for so long as they are seen to be in some way exiles from the Lord in the present time according to the apostle (cf. 2 Cor.5.6)? But when the day of resurrection has brought us into his presence and the saying of the blessed John has been fulfilled in us: We shall see him as he is (1 Jn.3.2), we shall no longer be permitted to marry, as the Lord says: For in the resurrection they neither marry nor are given in marriage, but shall be like angels in heaven (Mt.22.30). From this it is possible to infer that the state of matrimony has not been permitted to the angels because of their great intimacy with God, seeing that it is now refused to those to whom it was at one time allowed, once they have begun to be like angels in their proximity to God. Observe then how blessed it is for a man to display himself in such a form in his present life that he may be found both to resemble God and the ministers of God and to be already adopting the rule which will govern his future life.

5. Do you then consider it to be a small good that a man should maintain in his bodily innocence the likeness to God with which he was created from the beginning and to retain in perpetuity some resemblance to so great a majesty? The scripture says: And God created man in his own image and likeness (Gen.1.27). And justifiably so, for God had created him free from corruption, though he was later corrupted of his own free will but not without God's consent; we shall endeavour to give the reason for this later, as long as the present example can be taken as sufficient to show that he who was the first to be created in God's image was created uncorrupt. For our first nature ought to have possessed no attribute other than that which was first, and the first state of virginity and incorruption was consecrated in the person of the father of the human race himself, in whom it has already been shown figuratively that God cares more for virginity than for matrimony, since he created the former with his own hand but delegated the latter to men's free choice. Reflect carefully then, I beg you, on the good which is yours if you always remain such as God created man from the beginning and as he sent him forth thereafter, when he had brought him into the world. Observe what a blessing it is to be always in the state in which you were created and to preserve the features of your first birth. For no one is born corrupt nor is anyone stained by corruption before the lapse of an appointed period of time. Every man is seen to possess among his initial attributes what was there at the beginning, so that he has no excuse thereafter if he loses through his own negligence what he possessed by nature.

---

[20] Cf. 3,5 and see my introduction to this letter, para.2.

6. So choose now which is the better – that which nature gave at the outset or that which usage produced later. It is not right to say that it is burdensome to maintain chastity, when it is much more difficult to lose it than to keep it. And you must accept the truth of this statement; for there are many factors standing in the way of the man who wishes to be free to devote himself to licentiousness and desires to engage in endless pursuit of pleasure and lust: the earliest stages of boyhood, for example, in the course of which a man is unable to destroy the outward signs of his innocence,[21] be he never so anxious to do so, before a certain time; fevers and sundry diseases, which, while he is in their grip, preclude him not only from being able but even from wanting to indulge his lust; a wasted and enfeebled old age which is more concerned with drawing its last breath in the face of imminent death than turning its mind to wantonness; and, finally, nature itself, which does not suffer a man to indulge his passion unremittingly. From all these natural restraints chastity is free and immune, since nature fortifies it with defences so strong that there are times when it is preserved even against the will of its possessor: tender years do not hinder it, protracted age is not detrimental to it, neither natural forces nor diseases resist it; every stage of life is always able to protect it, every state of health constantly to maintain it; it is harder for a man to lose it unwillingly than to keep it of his own volition. What more need I say? No one will be able to practise licentiousness even for the space of one hour without ceasing but anyone who so wishes can retain his chastity permanently throughout his life. And who is not aware that God's foresight has so arranged things that it would be possible to guard with greater ease what he wishes to see displayed before his own eyes? Who then can now hesitate to preserve his chastity when the good attached to it is as easy to grasp as it is great in import-ance? Who would now want to prefer licentiousness when he cannot hope for it to be long-lasting or to offer a reward? Finally, let every sensible and wise man decide for himself which he would prefer to possess – that from which he can expect to receive no reward and which he can retain only with difficulty and for a short and limited period of time, or that which can be possessed in perpetuity and will bring him the compensation of a heavenly prize.

4, 1. But let me be silent for a little while on the subject of that future time when chastity is to be rewarded above all else, contenting myself with a discus-sion of conditions in this present, intervening period. I think that I can very easily persuade not only the religious, the faithful and those who hope for a reward for their chastity as promised by God but also the unbelievers and the impious that continence is to be preferred to matrimony and that the man who wishes to rejoice in the happiness which it brings will be blessed in the present life too.

---

[21] Cf. 5 above: 'nor is anyone stained by corruption before the lapse of an appointed time' – a reference, no doubt, to the physiological changes accompanying puberty. The Pelagians, of course, deny the possible existence in Adam's descendants of any trace of inborn sexual concupiscence, i.e. original sin.

2. But we do not recognize the good attached to anything until we have experienced its opposite, for before experiencing an illness even good health is held to be cheap. And so we must first set forth the troubles of wedlock and then discuss the desirable nature of the unmarried state, not, however, from a desire to condemn matrimony as the heretics do but in order to show more clearly the outstanding good of virginity. Yet even if we were to keep silent and utter no eulogies of the blessedness of chastity, anyone who has examined the misfortunes involved in marriage with all the attention of which his mind is capable would know what a great advantage there is in chastity.

3. I beg you who desire to put on the bonds of marriage to answer this question for me: on whose advice are you doing this? If it is on the advice of young people, well, youth is always changeable and unsteady, tumbling about this way and that on the different waves of thought that surround it without ever being able to form a mature decision. If it is on the advice of the masses, then what can possibly be more foolish than they, unless it be the man who considers them wise? If on the advice of relatives, not even their opinion is to be approved in all respects, since they are often in the habit of advising others to do not what they ought but what takes their fancy. 'On whose advice then,' you will say, 'am I to live my life, if that of myself, of ordinary folk and of my parents is useless?' Paul's, of course, and, to be more explicit, Christ's, who spoke in Paul and whose advice I shall reveal to you later on, when I come to deal with the evidence to be found in the sacred law. Now, in the meantime, let me argue from human experience and natural feelings, so that we may be all the more ashamed of ourselves if we as Christians are unwilling to acknowledge as a good what nature itself commends to us.

4. Well then, suppose I agree that you ought to marry. First I ask if you are able to be quite certain about the duration of your life, in case, as tends to happen to mere mortals, the last day carries you off before the hour of your wedding, when you are engaged in fulfilling your vows, and inflicts a double loss upon you, both that of your chastity, since you wished to marry, and that of your marriage, since you were prevented from entering upon it by death.

5. But I shall grant you the possibility that unpredictable things may happen. Let us then assume that your vows are given a favourable outcome and you enjoy a long life. I ask you in that case if you have made a sound judgement of the character of the woman whom you are about to marry; for you yourself are aware that such a good is difficult to find in women, as even secular literature testifies: Woman is ever a fickle and changeable thing.[22] A man may test the quality of anything before acquiring it except only his wife, whom no one can really know before he marries her. And this knowledge is born of great application, for even the trader in any spurious piece of merchandise fears a judgement based on careful scrutiny. It can happen that she is proud or quarrelsome, bad-tempered, impudent in her winebibbing, shamelessly loquacious, offensively unclean or to be feared for her charms, one who may either be coveted by other

---

[22] Virgil, Aen.4,569.

men or covet them herself. Nor do you know also whether she is likely to be sensible or foolish, and so in either case her condition gives you good reason to be afraid that she may be easily seduced, if she is foolish, or may conceal her sin under a clever disguise of folly, if she is wise. In this respect too a twofold disaster is to be feared: if her real nature is concealed, her wickedness will be endless, her sin incessant, and she will bring great shame upon her husband, at whom his wife's paramour will boastfully point a finger in scorn for the benefit of his companions and friends everywhere. It will also be his lot to suffer the more bitter misfortune of having to acknowledge another's children as his own or to love in his ignorance those whom he would hate if he but knew the truth, and to make an adulterer's children co-heirs with his own like the man who unwittingly confers such a favour on his own household servant. If, on the other hand, this kind of sin is detected, observe something even more disagreeable: such a disgrace will be made public, everyone will then begin to talk about it, and in such an event, shameful though it may be, there is not a scrap of pity for the victim. It is only the sin that merits both scorn and punishment, and perhaps the husband will be reckoned a man of dignity and wisdom in the conversation of fools, yet he will be an object for derision even for the man who is not worthy to be compared to his servants. And what additional troubles will beset him! He is compelled to accuse her whom he loves and unwillingly to wish for her death. His feelings of shame will struggle with his affection for her. Modesty will not permit him to pardon such a woman; his affection will not find it easy to condemn one whom he loves. Henceforth he will not know which gives him greater pain, loss of his wife or his disgrace. It will be shameful for him to grieve for one whom he himself has condemned; no one loses his wife in more unhappy circumstances than the man who is compelled to weep for one whom he has cast off. He is forced also to hate his children as long as he has doubts as to whether they are his, and so he will be an undutiful father as well as a cruel husband. And what are we to make of the tales which we read of some men killed by their wives with a lethal draught, others slain by their wives' paramours with the sword or a variety of ways of procuring their death? You need not fear any of these possibilities, if you are sure that they have never befallen any man; on the other hand, if you know that they have happened before, then you have to recognize the fact that you too are a man.

6. But let us suppose that the outcome of your marriage has been such a favourable one in all respects that there is no sign of characteristics of this kind in the woman you have married, though there are individual wives who are found to possess them all! It is certain that a man seeks marriage for the procreation of children; but how does he know that the wife whom he has married is not perhaps barren? If this happens, his chastity has been abandoned for no good reason nor will it be possible for him to seek another wife.

7. But in order to adjust our hopes to these uncertainties, let us suppose that she is not barren but fruitful. What are we to make of the accidents of childbirth or the countless risks of pregnancy? For it often happens that for one reason or another the embryo dies in the womb and the mother's life is endan-

gered at the same time. Such a critical situation arises that, to protect the life of the mother, the innocent infant is torn apart by the surgeons' lancets in the depths of the womb itself.

8. But let us still hope for better things and suppose that such human misfortunes cannot happen to us. Let us grant that there is a successful birth, which is of the utmost importance if the child or the mother or both are not to lose their lives; but surely it is not possible for the process to take place without some risk of death. What are we to make of the fact that a child is sometimes born a dwarf or with a squint or disabled in foot or hand or some other member? Sometimes too it is born with an 'evil spirit'.[23] But let us suppose that it is born unimpaired, strong and vigorous in all its members. There remains a hidden factor which breeds fear and suspicion in the parents, since they do not know how it will develop, whether it will be wise or foolish, intelligent or stupid. If it is clever, then there is bound to be the fear that it may not live long, if stupid, the sorrow that it has been born so.

9. But let us disregard all these possibilities and consider a child which has been successfully born and satisfactorily reared. Let us assume that he has an excellent memory, an outstanding intelligence and is endowed with the practical knowledge and seriousness which are associated with all the disciplines which can adorn the character. If it so happens that he is carried off by a sudden death as commonly occurs at any age, when he is full of the promise of a flowering youth, when his character and achievements are such that he is loved not only by relatives but even by strangers, all his parents' hopes will suddenly be brought to naught, all their care to no effect. Their joy is turned into grief, and now, when it is too late, they regret that they ever begot a child whom they were not permitted to keep for ever. Consider then how blessed and happy are those who are free from such misfortunes and are not alarmed even by the mere suspicion that such disasters may befall them.

10. We often find many too who are carried off by sudden death after only a few days of marriage, so that they seem to have married only to prevent them from eternally rejoicing in their chastity!

11. And what are we to make of the fact that nowadays everything has been so corrupted by the devil's influence that almost nothing can be done without practising idolatry, as the scripture says: They no longer keep their lives or their marriages pure (Wis.14.24), that is, from auguries and omens and everything else which is seen to be related to the promptings of idols. And, in order that you should not fail to recognize that this is what has to be understood from this passage, he ended his statement thus: For the worship of idols not to be named is the cause, beginning and end of all evil (ibid.27). It is idolatry which is practised in the taking of auspices for marriages, when a fixed day is singled out, when the actual hour of wedlock is indicated, when punctilious care is taken and attention

---

[23] Haslehurst suggests 'mentally deficient' for cum daemonio; I wonder if this slick but unpleasant modernism does justice to the complexity of the biblical expression? It is better to leave 'evil spirit' in quotation marks.

paid to ensure that no unhappy omen occurs. And though it is written: You shall not take omens or practise augury (Lev.19.26),[24] yet everything is arranged by means of augury and auspices. I say nothing of the disorderly crowd of revellers, of the obscene songs, of the bouts of drunkenness which can shock any respectable man, not to speak of a Christian, who is bidden to keep his ears and eyes free from the stain of all shameful and dishonourable behaviour, as the scripture says: Who stops his ears from hearing of the judgement of blood (Is.33.15),[25] and elsewhere: Turn my eyes from looking at vanities (Ps.119.37).

12. And, I ask you, what do you make of the fact that, with vices joining forces in this way, everything changes for the worse so that every provision is made for the satisfaction of greed and passion but the very rules of nature itself are overlooked? It is not enough for some people to be entangled in the sin of avarice, which the apostle goes so far as to declare to be idolatry and 'the root of all evil' (cf. 1 Tim.6.10), but they must needs add incest to their avarice. There are some who are not ashamed to enter upon matrimonial alliances with their mothers and even their sisters, inflamed not so much by sexual desire as by greed, in order that their family's wealth may not be dispersed or their patrimony divided up. A worthy partnership this indeed – of avarice and incestuous lust! For just as the former does not blush at the thought of seizing another's property so as to join it to itself, so the latter too is not ashamed to be coupled with its own flesh and blood. Rise up, holy Paul, rise up, apostle, you who severely censured the Corinthians because such fornication was being heard of amongst them as did not exist even among the gentiles (cf. 1 Cor.5.1)! Rebuke now the Christians of our own day as well, among whom marriages are being celebrated which are unworthy even of respectable gentiles, though you have already rebuked them enough by defining greed as the root of all evils, since if it were not so, these things would not happen either! You say to me, 'It was permitted to the holy Abraham' (cf. Gen.20.12). But 'the old has passed away, and all things have become new' (2 Cor.5.17). 'But,' you reply, 'the apostle nowhere forbade this.' See if he did not, and consider whether the one who advises a man to refrain even from lawful marriage has permitted him to have intercourse with his parents!

13. These are the proofs that I would cite to show the misfortunes which are attendant upon marriage but from which chastity is entirely immune and free. But let us set them all aside and believe that marriages are as free from assaults as they would be if they were wholly pleasing to God. What profit is there in loving what cannot always be possessed? What profit in seeking what is of uncertain

---

24 I have again translated the text as cited, especially as it seems to have given translators so many problems: for example, RSV has 'You shall not practise augury or witchcraft', AV 'Neither shall ye use enchantment, nor observe times (!)', the Vulgate 'You shall not practise augury or observe dreams', and so on. Our author's version seems to have been based on LXX.

25 LXX; translators omit the Greek word for 'judgement' presumably for textual reasons: RSV has 'hearing of bloodshed'.

tenure? But even if it could be held for the whole of this life of ours, everything has a brief tenure which comes to an end sooner or later.

5, 1. But you say to me, 'This is indeed sound reasoning, sanctioned by a considerable weight of experience, but it is not sufficient for me, unless you can confirm it by the authority of the scripture as well and demonstrate the esteemed good of chastity by evidence from that source.' Listen then to examples taken from the law.

2. When God wishes to descend upon Mount Sinai and bestow a vision of his majesty upon the whole people, he says to Moses: Go down, consecrate the people today and tomorrow . . ., for on the third day the Lord will come down upon Mount Sinai . . . . And Moses went down to the people and consecrated it . . . and said to them, 'Be ready in three days and do not go near the women' (Ex.19.10,11,14,15). This shows that chastity was necessary amongst other means of consecration, and we are given to understand that perfect holiness is impossible without it. And if continence even for a brief period profited them at that time to such an extent that they rejoiced in a vision of God's splendour, see what a great reward they will merit by their wish to preserve it intact for ever having received it as a part of their nature! They will not only be allowed to view God for a brief period but will also dwell with him throughout eternity, nor does true reason permit us to believe anything else but that perpetual chastity is recompensed with an eternal reward.

3. Listen to this too: when David avoided King Saul's anger by taking himself off in rapid flight and, along with his companions, had no bread to eat on the journey, since fear and hurry had prevented them from bringing any with them, he came to the temple of the Lord and asked the priest Abimelech for refreshment for his men, who were no less weary from hunger as from the labours of their journey. He answered him by saying: I have no store of common bread at hand but there is one loaf of holy bread; if the young men have kept themselves from a woman, they shall eat (1 Sam.21.4),[26] showing that it is easier for incontinent men to die of hunger than to receive consecrated bread. It is from this that I believe the well-known formula used by our priests before communion to have been derived, that is, 'Holy things for holy persons', in order that anyone who knew himself to be unconsecrated might understand that he ought not to partake of holy food. Again, the fact that, according to the law and the example of our Saviour himself (cf. Mt.12.4; Mk.2.26; Lk.6.4), it was not permitted at that time for any but the priests alone to touch bread which was held to be holy, shows that chastity was to some extent placed on a level with priesthood, since the chaste were allowed to eat what ought to be consumed only by priests.

4. And there is reference elsewhere in the scripture to the good of chastity, when the prople had perished grievously through incurring God's displeasure; for he says: And there was none left in Israel save the continent.[27] From this we

---

[26] Our author's version again favours LXX here.
[27] Like Haslehurst before me, I have been unable to track down this quotation.

undertand that out of deference to chastity other sins are sometimes treated lightly.

5. And if a chastity which was but temporary and imperfect so greatly benefited those who lived at that time, how much more shall one that is preserved in its entirety through eternity bestow upon us!

6, 1. So much for the Old Testament, where the high merit of chastity as yet radiated its splendour to a lesser degree in accordance with the nature of that time, which bade lustful persons to marry. Let us then pass on to the New Testament, whose complete light and perfect illumination no longer bid anyone to marry, and chastity sends forth the gleaming rays of its own brilliance and begins to shine with greater splendour because it both conceived and brought forth the Lord of all majesty.

2. There is no example which I can discover in it with a higher claim to be made known than that of our Lord himself, who by his coming and on his own authority consecrated the glory of chastity in both sexes – in his Virgin Mother and in himself – by showing himself to be willing both to be born of a virgin and to remain a virgin himself.[28] Chastity should begin to find favour with you, now that it is commended to you by such examples as these.[29] It is a fine thing that the Lord should want to possess in his flesh the good of incorruptibility which he already possessed in his spirit. What a good is that which the divine Majesty chose for itself! How great and glorious is the happiness of the man who has chosen to possess that renowned state which may enable him to be placed on the same level as God and the Son of God!

3. But I also think that we should not consider lightly what kind of a man was the prophet who went 'before the Lord to prepare his ways' (Lk.1.76), that is, the hearts of men – a virgin himself too, unless I am mistaken – and also the one who by the grace of the Spirit prophesied of him when first he was brought into the temple by his parents, namely, the righteous Symeon, of whom the scripture offers no evidence that he was married – for the divine law often appears to deny something about which it is silent – and Anna too, who remained a widow for eighty-four years. Again, after Christ began to teach, we find that all his disciples were either continent or virgins. I ask you to notice carefully how the New Testament begins with instances of virginity and widowhood which, unless I am mistaken, indicate that these should be the states of all of us who follow Christ.

4. We must also reflect whether we have an obligation to follow our lawgiver's example, for Christ is the lawgiver of Christians as Moses was of the Jews. Are Christians less obliged to imitate Christ than the Jews to imitate Moses? I think that we should also not fail to notice the name of the Testament itself, which, from our point of view, has undergone a change through the coming of Christ and the fulfilment of the law. The name I hear is 'New Testament', as the

[28] Cf., *Virg*.3, which is almost identical.
[29] Here it is Jesus' chastity which the addressee is urged to follow, in *Riches*,10,1 it is his poverty.

apostle says: Who has qualified us to be ministers of the new covenant (2 Cor.3.6). What new truth does it announce, if Christians are to live as did the Jews before them? To what profit did Christ come, if even after his coming we are still to follow the examples set us by the men of old?[30]

7, 1. Perhaps you will say, 'This is indeed powerful reasoning but it is supported by illustrations rather than by teaching; but I want authoritative teaching as well.' I could indeed reply that examples set by Christ ought to be followed in practice just as much as his words ought to be obeyed, as the scripture says: He who says he abides in him ought to walk in the same way in which he walked (1 Jn.2.6). But let us see if we can also discover the teaching of his words. In one place he says: If any man would come after me, let him deny himself to himself and take up his cross and follow me (Mt.16.24). How are we to interpret the words 'let him deny himself to himself', when a man cannot deny himself to himself, because his consciousness does not accept that he can either consider himself not to exist or be able to conceive of himself as other than the man he actually is? I suppose that this is denying himself, for instance, if someone says to him, 'You are Lucius,' and though he is Lucius, he were to answer that he is not, and this, though true perhaps of another man, is not true in his case. So how are we to understand 'let him deny himself *to himself*? Unless I am mistaken, in the sense that he is not to live for, or to, himself, that he is to reject every human desire, that he is to repel all fleshly and bodily pleasure, that he is to die completely to himself and to live wholly for him by whose death he was redeemed, as the apostle says: Christ died for all that those who live might live not for themselves but for him who for their sake died (2 Cor.5.15). This is to deny himself to himself, namely, to subject himself to the desires associated with no human pleasure; and if any thought comes to him from the direction of the outer man, let him respond to it by saying, 'Man, I know you not! As long as I was my own man, I even took pleasure in assenting to your suggestions, but now Christ has purchased me with the price of his own blood. I am not my own man any longer nor can I any longer do my own will but only his to whom I belong.'

2. I ask you, how can a man take pleasure in marriage or even think of it if he wants to fulfil the full force of this command? Surely a wife is acquired for a man's personal convenience, and if you marry, you are clearly not giving anything to God, who wishes you rather to remain unmarried. How then can you be said to have denied yourself to yourself when you still long to exercise your own will? And what follows the command of which we have been speaking? 'Let him take up his cross and follow me' (Mt.16.24) Believe me, men who are crucified take no pleasure in wantonness nor are they allowed to; and those who keep Christ's commandments take no pleasure in thinking of the flesh nor are they

---

[30] For Christ as the perfector of the law and the lawgiver of Christians cf. 9,1 and 12,4; Riches,9,7; 19,4; BT,4,1; 10,2,3; 14,5; this means that a far greater punishment will be the lot of those who break *his* commandments; it is *his* example that we are called to follow (cf. 7,1; 9,1; 17; Riches,6,1 and 9,7 again).

allowed to. That word of command can never be carried out in marital union. For as those who listen to Christ saying, 'If any man would come after me, let him deny himself to himself and take up his cross and follow me,' cannot possibly marry, so too those whose pleasure it is to display an excessive desire for matrimony, are listening, I think, to the voice of wantonness saying, 'If any man would come after me, let him claim himself all for himself and take up his pleasures and follow me.'

8, 1. But we should not pass over in silence that passage also in which the apostles, having discovered the difficulties involved in marriage, are reported as having said to the Lord: If such is the case of a man with his wife, it is not expedient to marry (Mt.19.10) – an answer sufficiently strict and uncompromising, and one which seems to have ruled out to some extent the possibility of following a line of action which it declares to be inexpedient. For who but a fool would want to do what is inexpedient? It is a different matter if the thing which is inexpedient cannot harm anyone in any respect either; in that case, if what is not expedient will not be able to harm him, then that which is expedient will not do him any good either. On the other hand, if we have to admit that what is expedient does good, then it will be impossible to deny that everything which is not expedient does harm.

2. But perhaps the Lord used his authority as a teacher to refute the disciples' naive and hasty attempt at a definition at a time when they were mere novices. Let us listen then to what he says and weigh up the force of his words with attentive minds: Not all men can receive this precept but only those to whom it is given (Mt.19.11). He confirmed their opinion, I think, by acknowledging the extent of the difficulty involved; if it had displeased him, it would have been more fitting for him to reply, 'Your definition is quite a harsh and unreasonable one. And how will the world be able to survive, if there is no cause of offspring?'[31] By saying, 'Not all men can receive this precept but only those to whom it is given,' we must understand him as having meant, 'Your definition is indeed sound but the greatness and sublimity of this saying is such that only those who examine it carefully receive it.' For I do not want you to understand the saying 'Not all men can receive this precept but only those to whom it is given' as meaning that only those can possess chastity on whom it has been conferred even against their will and by a fatal necessity, as men say;[32] otherwise you might infer that God confers favours,[33] deprive chastity of its due reward and render his exhortation null and void on both counts, if it is accepted not by those who receive it but by those to whom it is granted by divine favour. An exhortation to do something involuntarily will be as futile as the reward, for it will be

---

[31] Cf. 13,1,3,4 and *passim.*

[32] Cf. 10,6: virginity and continence are not regarded as gifts of grace but as a natural possession and a result of the exercise of free choice respectively. As Haslehurst points out (xviii), our author caricatures his opponent's view of grace, distorting the meaning of Mt.19.11 and 1 Cor.7.7, of which he omits the latter half.

[33] Cf.13,2; Riches,8,3.

unjust, and the man who does not possess a chastity which is denied him will merit censure less than the man who possesses it because it has been conferred on him will merit reward.

3. How then are we to understand the words, 'Not all men can receive this precept but only those to whom it is given'? Do not depart from the tone of the scripture and you will be unable to make a mistake. He said that the precept is given, not that chastity, which we cannot hope to receive from a source outside ourselves, is given, since, when we have it, we possess it naturally. For it is ours because it is born in us and is in us; and what is in us has to be preserved, not waited for. So this exhortation to preserve chastity is not received by all but only by those to whom it is given. To whom, then, is it given? To all Christ's disciples, who read both the gospel and the apostle[34] and realize from them that God desires nothing more than chastity. To whom, on the other hand, is it not given? To pagans, of course, and to Jews and to all who do not know the teaching of the New Testament, in which the good of chastity is most clearly revealed.

4. Then, to prevent anyone from supposing that every kind of chastity without exception merits the reward of the Lord, and to show what kind he intends to reward, that is, the kind which is preserved voluntarily and faithfully, not as the consequence of some accident at birth or a constraint imposed by human violence, he goes on to say: For there are eunuchs who have been so from birth in their mother's womb, and there are eunuchs who have been made eunuchs by men, and there are eunuchs who have made themselves eunuchs for the sake of the kingdom of heaven (Mt.19.10). Thus it is only the last of these three categories of eunuch who receive the kingdom of heaven, and that because they have made themselves eunuchs for its sake. But if others also receive it, then the act of castration will be wholly superfluous and so will the Lord's promise. For if those who have not made themselves eunuchs receive it, why are other men placed under a kind of obligation to undergo castration voluntarily? What then? Did the Lord condemn marriage? Far from it; what is generally held is that it was the glory of the kingdom that he denied to married persons, not life, that is, if they are still able to keep all his commandments.[35]

5. I leave it to your discretion to choose how you ought to interpret the passage in which the man who had married a wife was among others in excusing himself from attendance at his Lord's banquet, indeed went so far as to proclaim publicly that he would not come, and the Lord himself said that he should not taste of his supper. Let it suffice to have made these few statements about the gospel.

9, 1. Let us now turn to the letters of the blessed apostle and see what that teacher of the gentiles, the 'chosen vessel', has given as his ruling on matrimony. I observe that the Corinthians had written to the apostle and consulted him on this matter, requesting him to reply in letters telling them in his absence what

---

[34] Sc. Paul's *Epistles*.
[35] See the introduction to this letter, para.2 and n.2 above.

they should pay attention to in dealing with the married and the unmarried and virgins. But before coming to the apostle's statements, I must first ask why it was that the apostle was consulted about this matter, since no one doubted that marriage was permitted both by the testimony of nature and also by examples given under the law. For we know even from the promptings of nature that God created the different sexes for the procreation of human offspring, and we have a number of precedents in the scriptures which teach us that union in marriage was always permitted. Why then was it necessary for the Corinthians to make enquiries about a matter which was absolutely clear as if it were in doubt? Or had some new teaching reached their ears which had caused them to doubt that what had been permitted to men of old was still permitted to them? I think that this must be the case, since it would be quite pointless if they discovered for themselves that something which had formerly been regarded as a certainty was now open to question. What are we to believe then? I do not seek to deny that a modicum of understanding has been granted to your humble servant but I do this without prejudice to the claims of anyone else to whom God may have given a better revelation of the truth.[36] For I take the view that, in his first proclamation addressed to the Corinthians, the apostle preached no doctrine more forcefully than that of virginity and chastity and demanded that, above all else, the supporters of the new law should practise a novel kind of conduct, and believers in Christ should follow his example in all things according to Peter's saying: Christ suffered for you, leaving you an example, that you should follow in his steps (1 Pet.2.21).[37] And this was the reason why it became necessary for the Corinthians afterwards to consult the apostle, at a time when some were seen to be denying his teaching on chastity by displaying such passion in their incontinence. As I said above, if they had heard no new teaching, why did they need to question him on a matter which was quite clear?

2. But you say, 'Why did the apostle not foresee this possibility and qualify the manner in which he presented his teaching, so that no ambiguity would be left in it?' But even if he did foresee this, it has been the mark of a good teacher not so much to offer spontaneously some relaxation which the weak-minded are entitled to request as to allow it when asked. You should consider a consultant physician[38] to be sensible if he instructs a patient now convalescing to abstain

---

[36] For 'my humble self' (*parvitatis meae*) cf. YM,1; I have found only one example of this phrase in classical Latin – in Valerius Maximus' preface to his handbook of rhetorical illustrations dedicated to the Emperor Tiberius c.A.D.31. This suggests that our author may have met it in the course of his rhetorical training, to which he refers, also in the first chapter of YM, as 'secular literature'; but such phrases, combining an abstract noun with a personal pronoun, had become common by this time in epistolography (cf. 'honoured sir' or 'your honour' and 'a man of your common sense', *honorificentiae tuae* and *prudentiae tuae*, elsewhere in this collection, see OF,n.23) and became a common feature of Byzantine letters in Greek; see YM, n.23.

[37] See n.30 above and cf. OF,1,4.

[38] 'Physician-in-ordinary' (Haslehurst) is the usual rendering of the Latin word *archiatrus*, which is itself a transliteration of the Greek *archiatros*. I have permitted myself to use a modern equivalent here for the sake of clarity; for other comparisons with medicine cf.

from all fruit for his own good; but if that patient is unwilling to put up with such a restriction on his diet[39] as would require him to abstain from every kind of fruit, then the doctor will find it necessary to make minor concessions to prevent the patient from taking greater liberties; yet, for his own part, he still wants him to rejoice in the security offered by complete abstinence. So too the blessed apostle, as a lover of purity and chastity, desires first that all should reach the highest standard, but if anyone protests, he grants them lawful concessions and permits them albeit with reluctance, lest unlawful practices should develop. Had it been the highest good, he would not have granted concessions but rather issued his commands; nor would they have requested permission to attain a special standard of excellence, if they could have gained it before by their own choice. Finally, read, if you can, that the apostle willingly taught union in marriage without justifying it by the need to abstain from fornication, or considered marriage the highest good![40]

10, 1. But in order to make it clear on more obvious grounds that the apostle had no real desire to give people a licence to be incontinent, let us set out his own words: Now concerning the matters about which you wrote. It is good for a man not to touch a woman (1 Cor.7.1). First, he recorded in writing what he had already transmitted orally. And I think that it is impossible to doubt that his wishes were represented by what he stated in his first judgement and what he proclaimed to be 'good'. But of what woman are we to suppose that he was speaking? Of another's wife? I do not think so. Not even the Corinthians were so foolish as to ask the apostle whether they were permitted to dishonour others' marriages, something which nature itself condemned quite apart from the prohibition of such behaviour by the discipline involved in marriage. This I have said in order to refute those who strive to undermine the truths of scripture by their perverse interpretation of it simply to satisfy their own heated passion. If, then, reason does not allow us to suppose that he spoke of another's wife, it remains only for us to believe that he spoke of a man's own wife.

2. But, to make it easier for us to understand this passage, we must first realise that in it the blessed apostle began his discussion under three headings – married women, widows and virgins. Next, in the first part of his discussion he speaks as follows: Now concerning the matters about which you wrote: it is good for a man not to touch a woman; in the second: But to the unmarried women and widows I say (ibid.8); in the third: Now concerning virgins I have no commandment from the Lord (ibid.25). But I shall now return to the first section, in which it is plain that he was specifically writing to married women, not, as some foolishly suppose, to widows and virgins. This is what he says: It is good for a man

10,3; also Riches,4,2; 7,1; 19,5; BT,2,1; 3,1; 17,1; Law,2,2; 8,1; Dem.21,2; the closest parallel is Comm.159,13ff.
[39] There is a variant reading fragilitatis, 'state of weakness', but frugilitatis gives better sense.
[40] Cf. 1 Cor.7.2, where RSV renders fornicatio as 'immorality'. The implied sarcasm here is made clearer if we insert the words 'if you can' after 'me'.

not to touch a woman. He did not say: It is good for a man not to *marry* a woman, since he was discussing those who had already married. To what kind of 'touching', then, is it good for a man not to subject a woman? That public and ordinary kind of touching which we employ of necessity when we touch a book or tablets or anything like that? I do not think so but I believe it to be the kind of touching which is usual in marriage. Even Christ and his apostles and all of the saints have touched a woman with a pure and artless touch. What are you doing, apostle, lover of Christian chastity? Why are you reversing the normal order of speech? You are consulted about incontinence, and do you reply about chastity? Wantonness wants to hear about its good, not yours. Why do you labour in vain to establish what lust can afterwards overthrow by false interpretation? Again, when you say that it is good for a man not to touch his wife, by this you clearly prove that it is bad if he does touch her, since the only opposite to good is evil. Or is it to be assumed that it is bad in the sense that, although the incontinent man can be without sin, yet he holds an inferior rank? For it is bad for anybody not to be what is better. And if it is good for a man not to touch a woman whom he has already married, how much better it is not to know her at all! It will be easier for a man not even to think about what he has not got than to reject what he has, and no one placed near a fire escapes the heat.

3. Then he goes on to say: But because of the temptation to immorality, each man should have his own wife (ibid.2). 'Have,' he says, not 'marry', since he was speaking to men already married. And: Each woman her own husband (ibid.). Note carefully what he has said, I beg of you. 'Because of the temptation to immorality,' he says, 'each man should have his own wife.' He thus shows that, owing to the exigencies of the present, he has granted permission for something from which he previously wished men to abstain, that is, sexual intercourse, and in revealing the reason for his having allowed the institution of marriage, he clearly reveals also that it is not lawful except for the reason which permits it. In so far as he is perceived to have allowed marriage when a good reason occurs, he is held to have refused it in the absence of such a reason. The apostle, therefore, gave marriage as a medicine, so to speak, for the disease of immorality. So you must either confess that you are suffering from that same disease in order to make it necessary for you to use the medicine, or, if your conscience feels that you are in sound health, what reason have you for expecting to be given another's medicine, which, though apparently good for sick men because it rescues them from a lethal disease, yet is not free from that sting of remorse which the process of healing brings with it? For medicine will only give rise to unnecessary pain and distress in a healthy man.[41] No, do not let your body be weakened when careful attention is all it needs, not unnecessary treatment. It is clear that the apostle allowed marriage only to those whom he feared would fall into immorality if he did not exercise foresight. By saying, 'But because of the temptation to immorality, each man should have his own wife,' he showed us what he was taking precautions against for the future. So do not lay yourself open to needless slander.

[41] See n.38 for other analogies with medicine.

A continent man who arranges to get married is like a man of sound mind who is terrified by empty fears, supposes that he is possessed by the devil and desires to be exorcized at frequent intervals: such a man, apart from subjecting himself to unnecessary treatment, also incurs the disgrace of being a patient.

4. He goes on to say: The wife does not rule over her own body, but the husband does; likewise the husband does not rule over his own body, but the wife does. Do not refuse one another except perhaps by agreement for a season, that you may devote yourselves to prayer (ibid.4,5). What is meant by 'the wife does not rule over own body, but the husband does; likewise the husband does not rule over his own body, but the wife does,' except that, when either is provoking the other and bringing external pressure to bear by some means or other, neither is ever able to control the motions of the body in chastity and patience? And for as long as they fail to stay continent, their impulses are always cheating them of the prayer and communion with God which are to their mutual benefit, a benefit allowed especially to the continent to possess, as the same apostle says: Do not refuse one another except perhaps by agreement for a season, that you may devote yourselves to prayer, that is, – 'Be incontinent for a short time, so that you may be able to devote yourselves to prayer for a longer period.' 'And then come together again' – that is, he allowed them to return to married intercourse after continence in the period devoted to prayer, but only if the exigencies of incontinence demanded it. 'Lest Satan tempt you through lack of self-control' – here he gave his reason for making the concession which he had stated earlier, that is, to prevent the devil from offering them temptation by giving them occasion for incontinence. So a man of good sense like yourself[42] should observe what good there is in something which keeps you back from prayer and withdraws you temporarily from the body of Christ. For the fact that it is not fitting for the incontinent to communicate with God makes it very clear that even prayer is somehow forbidden to them, and it is plain that prayer is a lesser thing than communion, because not all who pray are permitted to communicate, whereas prayer is permitted even to those who do not communicate. Thus it is beyond doubt that it is not appropriate on any occasion for the incontinent to have access to that which is greater, when they are held to be prevented from participating in that which is less.

5. But this is made quite clear in the Old Testament, where it is written: All who are clean may eat flesh, but he who eats of the flesh of salvation that is the Lord's while uncleanness is upon him, that person shall be cut off from his people (Lev.7.19,20),[43] and many other things besides the flesh of animals, wherein the truth of the body of the Lord was prefigured, were not allowed to be touched by the incontinent. From this it can be perceived that those who suppose that the truth itself, whose image was so carefully protected in this way, can be treated

---

[42] See n.36 for this expresssion and cf. YM,4,2, where it is used with the same verb.

[43] The text is misquoted at one point: RSV has 'of the flesh of the sacrifice of the Lord's peace offerings', as does the Vulgate. Our author may have been quoting from memory; cf. n.90.

with less reverence are in the clutches of error as a result of their presumption and ignorance. 'But these words,' someone will say, 'are written in the Old Testament.' How great is the cunning of human depravity! When it is a question of contempt of riches and the good of virginity, which are especially commended in the New Testament, they take refuge in examples taken from the Old; but when we are dealing with intemperance in marriage as it is portrayed with great clarity in the old law, they resort to defending the New Testament! And the result is that they are seen to be without fear of either, whether the New or the Old. For why was it necessary for the New Testament to take such trouble with incontinence in this respect, though it did not wish all men to practise it? And it did not excuse it but rather increased its burden by not even allowing it to give itself to prayer with complete confidence! The law took away from incontinence only the right to sacrifice but grace refused it even the importunity of prayer, so that here too we may see the fulfilment of the saying: I have come not to abolish the law but to fulfil it (Mt.5.17). Perhaps you say, 'Things that were unclean under the law have been made clean by Christ.' Other things possibly, like various kinds of meat and everything mentioned in the New Testament as having been made clean through the Lord and his apostles, but not incontinence, which retains its old uncleanness to the extent that it even disqualifies a man from prayer and refuses him admission to priestly office. If it was made clean by Christ, why is it that it prevents prayer, or why must priests be continent? Clearly man is cleansed of all uncleanness through baptism, but only that he may thereafter persevere in the state in which he was when he was born of the Spirit.[44] On the other hand, he will be unclean whenever he is defiled with the filth of incontinence; this is clearly established by the testimony of the blessed John, when he says: It is these that have not defiled themselves with women (Rev.14.4). For if defilement is without uncleanness, even those whom the scripture describes as unclean will be able to appear clean, and lest you should suppose that this saying refers to adultery rather than marriage, he goes on to say: For they have remained chaste (ibid.). But if he had been concerned with adultery or fornication, he ought to have said, 'It is these that have not defiled themselves with harlots,' but he would not have deemed those who were continent in respect of so great a sin as worthy of praise. All this we have said without prejudice to the opinion of any man to whom something better has been revealed.

6. The apostle's judgement continues: I say this by way of concession, not of command (1 Cor.7.6); the apostle asserts that he is allowing the institution of marriage, not that he is commanding it, since they would not have expected him to *allow* them to attain to the highest good but to have *commanded* it confidently in this instance. Consider then what we ought to think of something which exists only by permission. He goes on: I wish that all were as I myself am (ibid.7); thus he indicates what he wishes and, at the same time, shows what he does not

---

[44] Cf. the definition of a true Christian in the letter OF,1: 'A Christian is one who. . . after the washing of baptism is free from sin.'

wish. Why then do you say, 'If he wished it, he permitted it only because it was necessary, not on account of genuine free will'? His words are: But each has his own special gift from God, one of one kind and one of another (ibid.). What are you doing, apostle? Do you mean by 'gift' something which you permit a man to possess only with difficulty? If the bond of marriage is a gift, then the pagans also rejoice in a gift of God! And if it is a gift of God, in what sense is it 'well for a man not to touch a woman'? Can it be 'well' for a man to lack a gift of God? Likewise, if virginity is conferred as a gift of God rather than preserved by man's own free will, then it lacks a reward, for no gift is deserving of a reward. Our eyes and hands and other members have been given to us by God but we shall be not presented with a reward for possessing them, unless, by the exercise of the freedom of will which has been granted to us, by our own movement and voluntary effort, we restrain them from all the practices of evil and dispose them to perform the offices of good works.[45] And if it is God's ordinance that arranges that some have the gift of virginity and others that of marriage, how can the apostle proclaim that he wishes anything else – namely, that all should be as he is himself – if this were quite impossible? For it would be impossible if different men had to possess different gifts. Or are we to believe that the apostle wished for anything which was contrary to God's ordering? Or why did he demand of all men something which depended on God's will? But if this interpretation cannot by any means stand, how then are we to understand the words, 'Each has his own special gift from God'? Obviously it is the gift of his own free will, in consequence of which he is given not only the state of marriage or of not marrying but also the choice of good or evil, death or life, as the scripture says: Before a man are good and evil, life and death, and whichever he chooses will be given to him (Sir.15.17).[46]

7. Later we find the following words: To the unmarried and widows I say that it is well for them to remain single as I do (1 Cor.7.8). Why does he say this to them, if it is not within their own choice to decide? Then, again, later: But if they cannot exercise self-control, they should marry (ibid.9). He did not say, 'If God has not given them this, they should marry,' which is what he ought to have said if he knew that it was not a matter of free will but of God's gift. And again: For it is better for them to marry than to be burned (ibid.).[47] So marriage is 'better' only because to be burned is bad; but there is something suspicious about a good which is rated 'better' than a grave punishment.

---

[45] Note the emphasis here upon the role of free will, not grace, in enabling a man to avoid evil and do good works.

[46] In again stressing the importance of free will here, our author attempts to strengthen his case by inserting 'good and evil' before 'life and death'!

[47] RSV renders the Latin word 'to be burned' as 'to be aflame with passion', NEB as 'to burn with desire', no doubt by analogy with 2 Cor.11.29. A Pelagian would surely have preferred the simpler translation, especially in view of the following sentences referring to a punishment. I find Brown's paraphrase of this sentence (1988,377) – '(Marriage was) suspiciously like an evil way of life' – untypically misleading.

8. Again: Now concerning the unmarried, I have no command of the Lord, but I give my opinion as one who by the Lord's mercy is trustworthy (ibid.25). Therefore you say to me, 'Look! The apostle proclaims that he has no "command" of the Lord concerning virgins.' But he testifies that he does not lack an 'opinion'. Surely you do not think it a light matter to despise God's 'opinion' in any event! For just as he did not give a 'command', because he did not have one to give, so too he would not have given his 'opinion' either, had he not received this from the Lord. Therefore, he gave what he had but did not give what he did not have, that is, he gave an 'opinion', not a 'command'. And in order that we might know for certain that the 'opinion' which he gave was no less God's than his own, he says later; But in my opinion she will be happier if she remains as she is. And I think that I have the spirit of God (ibid.40), showing by this means that his 'opinion' came not from his own conclusion but from the divine Spirit, for the divine Spirit is of God. 'Whatever you say,' you will argue, 'the apostle gave his "opinion" on not marrying but did not lay down a "command" ', because, in accordance with the interpretation of the heretic Jovinian of earlier times, you suppose that by this argument virginity is unnecessary.[48] If anyone were to ask you what manner of 'opinion' the apostle has given, you would have to admit that it is a sound one, since it was uttered under the influence of the Holy Spirit; for: The good man out of the good treasure of his heart brings forth good (Mt.12.35).[49] If he were to say to you again, 'What are we to make of the fact that in another passage we are forbidden to violate a sound opinion, since the scripture says: Do not despise any useful counsel (Tob.4.18),' he will force you either to deny that Paul gave a sound opinion – which no one in his senses could bear to hear – or to acknowledge that it is sinful not to put into effect what we are forbidden to despise. It makes no difference if it is not a 'command', as long as its resemblance to a command makes it as good as one.[50] It is for you to see for yourself how you can extricate yourself from questioning of this kind. Look! What I promised you long ago I have now revealed to you: whose opinion then will you follow – Paul's, or rather not Paul's only but the Lord's, who by his Spirit spoke through Paul, or one which satisfies you?[51] Happy are we to whom the Lord deigns to give advice on how to live, but unhappy if we despise such an adviser!

---

48 See the introduction to this letter for the controversy between Jerome and Jovinian; it was clearly very important to Pelagians to prevent their views from being identified with those of Jovinian, since Pelagius himself twice dissociates himself from him in his *Confession of Faith*, 24 and 25.

49 Our author has added 'of his heart', which is found also in Stephanus' third edition of the Greek NT and noted in the Oxford 1881 edition of the latter.

50 I have tried to make some sense of this sentence but the text is clearly unsound.

51 With Caspari's addition of *an tuae voluptatis* ('or one which satisfies you'), which is printed in square brackets in PLS 1 but which Haslehurst thinks unnecessary: 'the ellipse is far more effective'; I disagree.

52 The Latin word for 'advice' (*consilium*) is the same as that used again and again earlier in this chapter for 'opinion' or 'judgement' (Haslehurst). It would be possible to keep 'opinion' here too, if we were to translate the final clause '(unhappy) if we despise such a person when he gives his opinion', but this seems rather clumsy.

9. Again: I think that in view of the urgent – that is, the present – necessity this is good (1 Cor.7.26).[53] What then is this 'present necessity' because of which the apostle affirms that the state of virginity is good for us? Unless I am mistaken, he means that of the New Testament, since for us who wish to attain to the fuller glory which it promises the first necessity is to live by the example of Christ by persevering in innocence and then to obey his commandments more easily by ridding ourselves of the cares of all worldly business. For I believe that you are aware that a man cannot be saved if he transgresses even a single commandment, as the apostle says: Whoever keeps the whole law but fails in one point has become guilty of all of it (Jas.2.10).[54] Let us mention a few of these commandments, so that from these few we may understand the rest. We are commanded not to lie, not to curse, not to render evil for evil, not to swear even in a just cause;[55] we are bidden also to love our enemies and to do good to those who hate us and to pray for those who slander and persecute us; we are not permitted to approach secular courts of justice or to try to recover things which have been stolen from us or to seek recompense from those who inflict injury upon us, but rather we have to turn the other cheek to one who strikes us and to give up our cloak to one who takes away our coat; we are not permitted to eat with fornicators or greedy men or with those who curse or are drunkards or plunderers. I beg you to reply to me in accordance with the witness of your conscience[56] and tell me if you will be able to keep all these commandments when you are entangled in the exigencies of marriage. I am unmarried[57] and live free from and untroubled by the bonds of such a grievous burden, and yet I am scarcely able to keep these commandments in their entirety. What are we to do, if we are tied with the chains of such anxiety? Let no man continue to regard himself as a complete Christian just because the common people extol him and he appears to be better than the worst.[58] An old proverb tells us: 'Anything is counted good amongst

---

53 RSV has: 'I think that in view of the present distress it is well . . .', with a footnote to indicate that 'impending' is a possible alternative to 'present'; the Vulgate has *instantem*, 'pressing, urgent', the Greek NT *enestosan*, which has the same meaning but may also be rendered as 'present' here (Arndt-Gingrich). Our author explains 'urgent' as 'present', and it is clear that 'present' is required in the context in which he uses the word here.

54 For this Pelagian emphasis on the necessity of following Christ's example see my introduction to this letter and cf. the many instances in which it is stressed as well as *Riches*,18,4; 19,2; BT,22. For the keeping of the whole law cf. 8,2; 10,8; *Riches*,18,4; 19,2; *Virg.*4,2; 7,2; *Dem.*15; 16,1; 25.

55 For this characteristically Pelagian warning see my introduction to this letter (para.2) and cf. *Cel.*19 and *Dem.*19,4. For the requirements of a Christian cf. e.g., 12,3; OF,1,4; 2,1; YM,4,2,5; *Virg.*7,3; 8,3; *Life*,6,2; 9,2; 10,4.

56 For appeals to conscience couched in similar terms see BT, n.22.

57 In his letter *To An Older Friend* our author refers to his daughter (5,2 and 3) and commends her to his correspondent. We must assume that, when he describes himself as 'unmarried' here, he means that he no longer regards himself as married and that his earlier marriage has been annulled or that his wife is dead. In other words, he was 'free from a wife' (11; 1 Cor.7,27).

58 Cf. OF,1,3.

nothings'; but it is not held to be truly great if it is only the poverty of its barren situation that commends it. So too the man who is a little better than the wicked can go on to receive a smaller punishment[59] but not the reward of eternal life, which only the man whose conscience has borne witness that he is a Christian by virtue of having kept the commandments in their entirety will be able to possess.[60] We are bidden also to pray with ceasing, as the Lord says: Praying at all times (Lk.21.36);[61] and the apostle: Pray without ceasing (1 Thess.5.17).

10. How can an incontinent man fulfil these commands, when he is not allowed to pray unless he is continent? Rightly then did the apostle set the urgent, that is, the present, necessity before those whom he wished to persevere in their practice of the good of virginity, since he knew that they would have no difficulty in averting their thoughts from marriage once they had seen the greatness of virginity by contemplating it in their minds in this way. And after saying, 'I think that in view of the urgent necessity it is good,' he at once adds a second ruling to make good the ambiguity in the first, lest his expression of his thoughts might appear uncertain to anyone, by saying: It is well for a man to be as he is (1 Cor.7.26). The apostle maintains his position throughout and by no means alters the course of his judgement, declaring to virgins also what he had told widows and married women, that it is good to persevere in the practice of chastity, and saying, 'It is well for a man to be as he is.' I do not know how he wants the clause understood in respect to a man who, despising the 'opinion' of the apostle, nay rather, of the Holy Spirit, wishes not 'to be as he is'.

11. Again: Are you bound to a wife? Do not seek to be free. Are you free from a wife? Do not seek a wife (ibid.27). Let no one by a false interpretation mar our understanding of this clear statement or suppose that he has now avoided contempt of this passage by giving it a different sense from that which the truth demands. Nay more: he involves himself in greater guilt if he is not content to despise the divine utterance but goes on to falsify it. Nor will the sense which we extract from the Lord's scriptures be true merely because that is the sense which pleases us: the force of God's utterances furthers their own truth, not our inclination. In this connexion we must pay heed to the statement of the blessed Peter concerning all Paul's letters but especially concerning those who falsify this epistle, when he says: As also our beloved brother Paul wrote to you according to the wisdom given him, speaking of this as he does in all his letters. There are some things in them hard to understand, which the ignorant and unstable twist to suit their own wishes, as they do the other scriptures (2 Pet.3.15,16).[62] But not less to be feared also is that testimony which is offered as a threat to those who add anything to, or take it away from, the divine scriptures (cf.Rev.22.18,19); everything, therefore, is to be rendered as it is in its own context nor are some

---

[59] Cf. *Riches*,6,5.
[60] Cf. 14,6; 17,1; *Riches*,18,4; 19,4; *BT*,22.
[61] Vulg.; RSV has: 'Watch at all times, praying that . . .', i.e. with the comma placed differently.
[62] It is a little ironical that our author has himself altered the text here 'to suit his own wishes': he has replaced 'to their own destruction' with 'to suit their own wishes'!

things to be interpreted in the light of statements made outside the course of the discussion: it was with virgins, not marriage, that he was dealing in this passage. In short, this is how he began: Now concerning the unmarried I have no command of the Lord (1 Cor.7.25). Therefore, whatever he has said in this connexion must be taken as referring to an exhortation to virginity. So, when he says, 'Are you bound to a wife? Do not seek to be free. Are you free from a wife? Do not seek a wife,' this can only refer to the teaching of celibacy; for if a man bound in matrimony, whom faith has found in this state, is not allowed to be set free from her, how much more inappropriate will it be for a man who is already free to be bound? This is indeed a judgement with great force, which wishes the man who is free not to be bound as much as it does not permit the man who is bound to be set free. But of these two aspects of the same judgement we take one and, indeed, firmly uphold it, whereas we reject the other, reckoning it to be a sin for a man to leave his wife contrary to the apostle's prohibition; on the other hand, we think it a trivial matter if a man is joined in wedlock contrary to the parallel clause in the same ruling.

12. 'But,' you will say, 'the apostle changed his opinion in the words which follow: But if you marry, you have not sinned, and if a virgin marries, she has not sinned (ibid.28).' If you understand him correctly, he has not changed his opinion, nor is it right for us to suspect him of being fickle and changeable,[63] since we believe that his foundations were built on the solid base of divine wisdom. In the more obscure passages of scripture it is fitting that we should admit our own ignorance rather than explain something in an ungodly sense. In saying, 'Are you free from a wife? Do not seek a wife,' he is speaking specifically of those who were able to be continent. After further reflexion but still maintaining the same attitude to those who were complaining about incontinence, he says again, 'But if you marry, you have not sinned,' that is, you are incontinent, lest you should do worse, 'and if a virgin marries, she has not sinned.' For there is a boundless divide between not sinning and being what is worthy of praise. And: Yet those who marry will have troubles of the flesh (ibid.28).[64] I do not know what good any longer remains in marriage, when they have troubles in that state which seemed to be the only one in which they found happiness. And: For I spare you that (ibid). Consider what sort of state is that which we long to be spared!

13. Then: I mean, brethren, the appointed time has grown very short (ibid.29).[65] He set before them the shortness of time, so that by this means he might drive out the desire for marriage; for since our days according to the prophet are confined within the space of threescore years and ten[66] and the fruitfulness of marriage decreases almost from middle age, how foolish it is to sacrifice the glory of eternal virginity for such short-lived pleasure! I say nothing of the variety of accidents by which human life is often cut short: one man is

---

[63] An echo of the quotation from Virgil in 4,5.
[64] RSV: 'worldly troubles'.
[65] Paul means the time left before the end of this world and the Day of Judgement; our author takes it to refer to the shortness of human life; cf. 9,13.
[66] Ps.90.10.

crushed by a wall falling down, another dies of the heat of a fever, another is suddenly laid low by bursting a blood-vessel, another is killed in a shipwreck, another dies of madness, another perishes through being struck by lightning; others are struck down by robbers, others are murdered by the wiles and poisoned draughts of evil-doers, some are executed by command of the Emperor or the unjust sentence of someone in power. And in the midst of all the disasters, perils and deaths that befall the human race men find time to desire marriage and to think less of sudden death or, rather, of God's judgement than of their own desires! Or do you suppose that you cannot meet with any of these disasters which befall mankind? It is another matter if you deny that you are mortal. This then is why the apostle set before our eyes the shortness of time, that he might urge us too to seek the glory of virginity even by considering the fear of death.

14. And: From now on, let those who have wives live as though they had none (ibid.). I do not know how else this can be interpreted than that a man is very inconsiderate if, after hearing this statement, he desires to have a wife if he has not one already, when it is not expedient for those who have wives to possess them in the way which is customary in marriage. And lest any one should say, 'How then can the world continue to exist?',[67] he anticipates him with these words: For the form of this world is passing away (ibid.31), that is to say, 'Do not be concerned about that which is passing away.' And: I want you to be free of anxieties (ibid.32). We too ought to want what Paul wants.

15. And: The unmarried man is anxious about the affairs of the Lord, how to please the Lord; but the married man is anxious about worldly affairs, how to please his wife (ibid.32,33). I ask you, 'Whom would you rather please, your wife or God? If your wife, you will be seen to put wantonness before God; if God, how will you be able to have a wife when we know on the authority of the apostle that the man who has a wife cannot please God as a bachelor can? If you wish to please both your wife and God, you will be seen to have advanced a view which is foolish, difficult and contrary to the apostle's ruling and to have set yourself above the bachelor who pleases only God – if, that is, it is at all possible for you to please both God and your wife. Nor will it profit you not to have taken a wife, if taking one is no hindrance, and it cannot be a hindrance, if the married man pleases God as much as the bachelor. Again: There is a difference between a wife and a virgin (ibid.34).[68] 'In what respect?' you will ask. He replies: The unmarried woman is anxious about the affairs of the Lord, how to be holy in body and spirit; but the married woman is anxious about worldly affairs, how to please her husband (ibid.). To the unmarried woman, because of her anxiety about the affairs of God, he has granted holiness in both parts of her being, for he has testified that she is holy both in body and in spirit; to the married woman he has

---

[67] Cf. 13,1; cf. also the 'popular maxim' quoted in OF,1,6 in a different context – 'Then the whole world is perishing.'
[68] Cf. AV and the Greek NT; RSV and Vulg. omit this sentence, as do NEB and other modern translations, and RSV renders the same verb in the preceding verse as 'his interests are divided'.

allotted only anxiety for this world and the task of pleasing her husband, and he has said absolutely nothing of the holiness of both parts of her being. The apostle's silence seems to be a clever attempt to conceal his diffidence, for if the married woman is also to be considered holy, the apostle's ruling is meaningless. Thus, after seeing that such a severe distinction may give cause for displeasure to lovers of marriage, he went on to protect his earlier ruling with the following statement: But this I say for your own benefit, not to lay any restraint on you but in the interests of propriety (ibid.35).[69] But, apostle, not even this qualification of yours can be proffered without an implied criticism of marriage! For if this statement of yours is for their 'benefit' and if what you say is 'in the interests of propriety', how are we to understand its manifest contravention of your teaching?

16. Nor do I think that we should pass over in silence the fact that at that time the apostle is seen to have been preaching the need to maintain virginity and chastity with such steadfastness, though he was subject to heathen rulers and caught between two enemies of chastity, namely, the Jewish people and the gentiles. What would he have done, had he lived in our day? He would have curbed the shameless indulgence in wanton pleasures, I think, with even greater dedication.

17. As for that maxim which the ignorant are in the habit of citing: 'He who marries does well, but he who does not marry does better,' you will nowhere find that the apostle said it, nor was it possible that he could praise the married man elsewhere, when he had said in another passage that it was well for a man not to touch a woman. You will say that a father is clearly doing the right thing when he marries off a promiscuous daughter so as to prevent her from doing worse. The father then is praiseworthy when he provides for his incontinent daughter, just as the apostle's provision for the incontinent is praiseworthy; but those who have thrown away the chance of getting something better are not to be praised.

18. We must understand scripture in such a way that it may nowhere be seen as self-contradictory. You will nowhere find that the apostle allowed marriage of his own free will or without some cause or under some compulsion, and this is something which I could very easily prove if it were not a long business to go through all his epistles, in which he constantly repeats that at the present time we ought to be mortifying ourselves with Christ instead of looking forward to pleasures of the flesh; as we read in the epistle to the Romans: Do you not know that all of us who have been baptized in Christ were baptized into his death? We were buried therefore with him by baptism into death, so that as Christ was raised from the dead through the glory of the Father, we too may walk in newness of life (Rom.6.3,4). What will this 'newness of life' consist of, if even now we are to marry after the example of the old? Or how is a man seen to have mortified himself with Christ in baptism when his pleasure is not only in living in this present time but also in wanton behaviour? Again, we do not read that the practice of matrimony is reckoned among the kinds of behaviour which are the fruits of the spirit, something which is made very clear by the example of the

[69] RSV renders the Latin words *ad id quod honestum est* as 'to promote good order'.

passage in which the apostle describes the results of the works of the spirit, saying: But the fruit of the spirit is love, joy, peace, patience, kindness, goodness, gentleness, faithfulness, meekness, continence, chastity (Gal.5.22,23).[70] Since continence and chastity are named among other duties enjoined by the Spirit, the silence in connexion with marital relationship is doubtless due to the fact that it is found to be inconsistent with them, and I leave it to your intelligence to decide to what category something which is foreign to the things of the spirit must be assigned. Also: And those who belong to Christ have crucified their flesh along with its emotions and desires (ibid.24). Notice this carefully and observe that he has separated desire from emotions in order to show that those whom he marks off as belonging to Christ ought to crucify both sinful emotions and conjugal desire, which is to be attributed to uncleanness rather than to sin.

11, 1. We are not unaware of what Christians who are licentious and prefer promiscuity to Christ will reply to this: they say, 'It was in vain that God made male and female at the beginning of the world, if in some persons the production of offspring has ceased. It was in vain too that he uttered that sentence which without doubt applies to the origin of human propagation: Be fruitful and multiply and fill the earth (Gen.1.28); and again: Therefore a man will leave his father and mother and cleave to his wife, and they will become one flesh (Gen.2.24). And if marriage is the reason which hinders a man from pleasing God, how is it that we read that so many of the saints pleased God, when some of them are known to have had not only several wives but also numerous concubines, such as Abraham, Jacob, David and Solomon and others whom we find to have been so dear to God that they are numbered among the first patriarchs? And how is it that even virgins are to desire to go to the bosom of Abraham, a bigamist on account of his concubine?'[71]

2. I can see that according to this line of defence not only is the state of virginity undermined but all chastity as well as moderation in marriage is attacked, for if we are to follow the examples of olden times, it will be permissible not only to marry and have concubines but also to commit fornication as did Judah, Samson and others who are reported as having no more displeased God by their fornication than they pleased him by marrying. But if that is the case, how will the apostle's teaching stand when he forbids us even to partake of food in the company of fornicators?[72] The same apostle's exhortation will also be found to be superfluous and impossible to defend on any grounds whatsoever, when he lays such stress on his teaching about virginity that to it alone he attributes holiness

---

[70] Our author has the Vulgate text here, omitting only *longanimitas*, 'forbearance' after 'goodness'; RSV omits 'continence' and 'chastity' as well as 'forbearance'. But it is continence and chastity that are singled out for special emphasis in the next sentence of our text, and our author is not guilty of manipulation here.

[71] Haslehurst translates the end of this sentence as 'to the bosom of the bigamist Abraham, close to his concubine', which fails to observe the Latin word-order and does not give as good a sense.

[72] Cf. *Virg.*7,3; *Life*,9,2 for this typically Pelagian requirement based on 1 Cor.5.9.

in both parts of our being, both flesh and spirit, asserts that it is well for a man not to touch a woman, wishes married men to be as if they were unmarried, reminds us that a married man pleases both God and his wife, desires all to resemble him in chastity and does not mention the practices of marriage among the fruits of the spirit. We have to regard all these statemnts as unprofitable, unnecessary and groundless, if we are to follow the way of life of the ancients, since there is nothing so foolish as to forbid what is not hurtful or to teach what is not beneficial.

12, 1.   But before refuting these propositions in due order and showing by sound reasoning that they are no longer applicable to us, I want you to know first of all that those who suppose that Christians ought to live according to the old usage either are quite ignorant both of the law and of God's ordering or are, with great rashness and contrary to their own conscience, preaching what they like in order to be considered holy by men, even if they themselves hold a different view in their hearts.

2.   For we discover that there are three periods in which it is clear that different things were allowed to different persons – one before the law, another under it and a third, the present period, under grace. Before the law there was no practice of circumcision, no observance of the Sabbath, no instruction that anyone should fast; no one had heard of new moons, the feast of tabernacles and all the festivals of the law; no one abstained from the use of certain kinds of meat; no one yet observed the rites of sacrificing a lamb at annual intervals, celebrating the passover, avoiding unleavened bread, washing in different ways, and the other ceremonies of the law which we find required and maintained in the time of the law, when it was no longer permitted to live in the old way. Do not say to me, 'Abraham was circumcised when this was not a matter for the law,' since the apostle says: For if Abraham was justified by works of the law (Rom.4.2; cf. Jas.2.21).[73]

3.   As, then, we have shown that one thing was permitted before the time of law, so too we must believe that another thing is permitted to us and another way of life has to be followed after it, that is, in the time of grace; if we do not have to follow another way of life, grace will no longer be.[74] In sum, it is not now permitted to pluck out an eye for an eye or a tooth for a tooth or to render to anyone evil for evil or to hate one's enemy; furthermore, it is not permitted *not* to love either, or to swear at all or to practise circumcision of the flesh or to observe the Sabbath as a day of rest or to employ various kinds of washings or to offer fleshly sacrifices. Need I say more? It is now appropriate for the Christian to keep scarcely any of the observances required by the Old Testament, since we know that through Christ they have been either changed for the better or fulfilled – changed, as in the case of circumcision, the Sabbath and sacrifices, fulfilled as in

---

73   Neither of these texts makes specific reference to circumcision.
74   Cf. 10,6 for another example of Pelagian 'grace'.

the case of innocence, chastity or righteousness: innocence has been augmented to some extent in that not only murder but even anger is forbidden, chastity in that fornication is condemned even in the thoughts of the heart and mind and in that eunuchs are promised the reward of the heavenly kingdom, and righteousness in that we are not only forbidden to steal another's property but also taught to despise our own spontaneously.[75]

4. Therefore, if practices which were performed in token of the hidden secrets that truth might in future reveal have come to an end with the revelation of truth itself by Christ, and if the requirements for righteousness in a blessed life have been completed by the teaching of stricter disciplines, why do you still confront me with examples from the Old Testament? I do not have any longer to respect the semblance, when the substance and the truth have taken its place, but I do have to fulfil the demands of righteousness to greater perfection, as the Lord says: Unless your righteousness exceeds that of the scribes and Pharisees, you will never enter the kingdom of heaven (Mt.5.20). What will it profit me to observe a rite which can no longer enable me to possess the heavenly kingdom? The sole reason for our reading the Old Testament now is in order to marvel at the acts which God did in it, at the omnipotence of his works, at his mysterious plan, at wonders and signs, and to know the Christ promised in the last days and announced in that same Testament. But for the conduct of our lives we must pay special attention to the teaching of the New Testament.[76] You say to me, 'Did not he who made known the New Testament make known the Old also? Of course he did; but why do they have different names, if there is no difference in the works prescribed? If the Old was always to be observed, why did the New supersede it? Or if it had to be superseded, why is the Old to be observed now? Nevertheless, it is true that the Old is observed in the New, since what the Old announced in advance is still observed.

5. 'Well then,' you ask, 'did it not please God that marriages should be celebrated?' Of course it did, but he also wished circumcision, observance of the Sabbath and other things written in the law to be practised at that time; yet we do not have to argue that because something pleased him once it always pleased him. If it did, why have some things come to an end? So it is possible that marriages will not always please him, as we find that they once did. Or, if they always please him, they will never come to an end and, if they never come to an end, men will have to marry even after the resurrection. Or if they then come to an end, why can they not come to an end now for a reward, since they will have to end sometime of necessity?

13, 1. But perhaps you cite that favourite argument of the masses which all hypocrites who say one thing with their lips and keep another locked up in their

---

[75] Another example of our author's emphasis on free will.
[76] See n.30.

hearts offer in their defence: 'How will the world continue to exist,[77] how will the source of the human race survive, if the cause of propagation disappears?'

2. It has all been adequately provided for with forethought, reason and good sense! Am I to suppose then that Christ did not foresee this when, by promising the highest reward to all who voluntarily became eunuchs without exception, he doubtless wished all men to become eunuchs? For we cannot believe that he was partial[78] and a respecter of persons to the extent that he did not wish all men to be worthy of a reward of which he wished only some to be worthy. But perhaps, being preoccupied with an excessive fondness for chastity, he forgot the circumstances of the world and of his own creation! If only he had had such advisers then as he has now, what do you suppose that he would have done? He would, I suppose, have reformed his teaching and promised to the married what he promised to eunuchs! How immoderate and unbearable is the boldness of human folly when it causes you to erupt to the point of judging yourself to be wiser than God! Even if he had wished marriages to cease without any reward, as he will do at some future time, man who is made of earth and clay would, I suppose, judge that this should not be so. Or if a man judges himself to be more rational than God, why does he worship him when he supposes himself to be wiser than he is? Perhaps there is some reason that God did not want you to know. Rather, you do not wish to know, since you care more to devote yourself to worldly pleasures and wantonness than to probe the Lord's hidden secrets. What fools men are not to prefer to observe wholeheartedly what they know rather than to try to prove what they do not!

3. Again, why are you so anxious about a world in which you are bidden to live the life of a stranger and pilgrim? If you are truly a Christian, you should live in hatred of the world, as the Lord says: If you were of this world, the world would love its own; but because you are not of this world, but I chose you out of the world, therefore the world hates you (Jn.15.19). For how can you be not of the world if you are anxious about it? Or how can it hate you as a stranger if you are its keeper? The world must love the man who loves it, and the man whom the world loves is of the world, since hatred rather than love of the world is appropriate to a Christian. The Lord says likewise elsewhere: You will be hated by all men for my name's sake (Lk.21.17). By what kind of men? By the worldly and the

---

[77] Cf. 10,14 and see n.67 above.

[78] Cf. 8,2 and *Riches*,8,3 for *gratiosus* and *gratiositas* used to describe God a one who gives favours to some and denies them to others. Myres,1960, suggested that this sense of *gratia* as 'favouritism' was 'the key word in the (Pelagian) controversy', which is frequently attacked in the Theodosian Code, mainly in the period 360–419; he quotes passages from this letter and the letter *On Bad Teachers* as evidence for his thesis that it was the demand for elementary social justice that underlay Pelagian teaching against the Augustinian doctrine of grace, and applying this idea in particular to the resurgence of Pelagianism in Britain. Morris,1965, also saw Pelagianism as an attack on social corruption; see my introduction to the tractate *On Riches*. But Pelagius was a moral, not a social, reformer and thought of himself not as 'an enemy of grace', as Augustine did, but as a defender of *true* grace; for a discussion of the theses of Myres and Morris see Rees,1988,111ff.

fleshly, unless I am mistaken, who hate us because we are seen to despise what they love. If then the world, that is, according to this definition, the men of the world, clearly hate the Christian, why are you anxious about that which does not love you? The scripture says again: Do not love the world or the things of the world (1 Jn.2.15). How can a man not love the world if he has such anxiety about it that he prefers to forfeit the reward of virginity rather than have the world cease to exist? The scripture also says elsewhere: Do you not know that friendship with the world is enmity with God? Whoever wishes to be a friend of this world will make himself an enemy of God (Jas.4.4). How can a man not be a friend of the world if he cares more about it than about God's teaching?

4. So you say, 'How will the world continue to exist?' as if you have read that it is everlasting or suppose that it was so fashioned by God as to continue for ever. If, on the other hand, you are certain that it can come to an end some time or other, why are you anxious about its permanence? Lest you should doubt that it has to come to an end, listen to what the scripture says: Since you laid the foundations of the earth, and the heavens are the work of your hands, they will perish, but you endure (Ps.102.25,26; cf. Heb.1.10,11). And the Lord says in the gospel: Heaven and earth will pass away, but my words will not pass away (Mt.24.35), because he wants us to be more anxious about his words than about the continued existence of a transitory world. And the apostle: For the form of this world is passing away (1 Cor.7.31). And John, who did not wish us to love the world, because he knew that its end was nigh, after first saying: Do not love the world or the things of the world (1 Jn.2.15), followed this up with: And the world shall pass away, and the lust for it (ibid.17).

5. But even if you were certain that the world must endure for ever, yet you ought still to have done the Lord's will and to believe that by some means both the world could continue in existence and you could keep God's commandments, like the blessed Abraham, who was made a friend of God because he obeyed his will in all matters wholeheartedly and without any resistance. For though God had promised that he would bless his seed in Isaac, his son, he afterwards commanded him to offer him as a sacrifice. He did not hesitate to fulfil the command without wavering nor did he reflect why God was ordering the killing of the very one in whom he had promised that his seed would be blessed in the future, and his faith was so genuine that he believed that for God all things were possible, even the fulfilment of his promise after Isaac had been slain. His care for his only son did not prevent him from carrying out God's will without questioning it; but we are too consumed with anxiety and concern for the existence of the world and, though God promises that it will end, we want to bestow everlasting life upon it and are clearly more anxious about it than about its Creator.

6. 'But,' you will say, 'the world is to come to an end only when God wills it.' So, whenever he does will it, your anxiety will be of no avail, and, whether you marry or do not marry, the world cannot be brought to an end without God willing it or continue to exist for longer than he wishes. Why then do you induce a state of anxiety in yourself about something which depends on God's will?

7. And how does it come about that you ask in your prayers that the kingdom of God should come more speedily when it cannot come before the end of the world, as the Lord says: My kingdom is not of this world (Jn.18.36)? Why then do you ask in your prayers for the consummation of something for whose existence you are so anxious in the case of marriage? From this we can infer that either your prayers are without faith or your anxiety is groundless. You have to choose between two alternatives and either cease to ask for the end of something about whose existence you are anxious or cease to be anxious about the existence of something for whose end you ask. If we are anxious about the world, we are keeping God's commandments in a perverse way, as if we ought to love it all the more because his commandments tell us to refrain from loving it!

8. But the blessed apostle, when he says: I wish that all were as I myself am (1 Cor.7.7), undoubtedly did not think about the existence of the world, since, if he had known that something could intervene to make his wish impracticable, he would never have wished for an impossibility. For when he wishes all men to be as he himself is, he made no exception and, by making no exception, he showed that all men not only ought to be but are able to be such as he wished them to be, for, as we have said, he would never have wished for something which either ought not to, or could not, happen.

9. But even if I grant you that it is necessary and consistent with the will of God that there should be some part of the people through which the succession of the human race may be increased, surely Jews and pagans, not to mention heretics, whose chastity is no more to be approved than their faith is to be accepted, and also all incontinent Christians have not been lacking to maintain the cause of human propagation, if only to prevent this necessity from falling to the lot of true Christians, for whom it is appropriate that they should live according to the example of Christ and his apostles.

10. But, even assuming that owing to an excess of chastity and continence the world comes to an end, why are you for this reason so anxious? Or do you fear lest, if the world ceases to exist before its time, you alone among the other virgins who possess the kingdom of heaven as a reward for continence and chastity and are worthy of eternal glory may be called to account at the time of the resurrection for not having have married?

14, 1. But we have said enough on this topic. Let us now return to the question which we left off discussing earlier; though we may have answered it satisfactorily by showing that examples from olden times cannot be altogether applicable to Christians, it will become still clearer if we resolve it by taking each possible objection in turn.

2. In the first place, someone may say that male and female were created with the sole object of begetting offspring. I ask if this applies to all or only some. If it applies to all, then those whom we read were unmarried were born in vain, such as Elijah, Elisha, John, the holy Mary, our Lord himself and his apostles, all of whom we are to believe to have acted contrary to God's ordering; if it applies to all, then we must believe that difference in sex was established for no other

reason than that of fertility. Or, if it does not apply to all, we can be seen to be like them.

3. Next you may say, 'At the time of the resurrection will this difference in sex be left undisturbed or not?' I think it will, and yet, according to the Lord's ruling, fertility will no longer be relevant there. Why then may we not suppose that in accordance with his will it can now be in the present as it will be in the future?

4. Who were told to: Be faithful and multiply and fill the earth (Gen.1.28)? Adam and Eve, unless I am mistaken, who were in sole possession of a world untilled and uninhabited and needed companionship no less than people to cultivate the soil with them. So it was right to tell them to multiply and be fruitful and fill the earth, since the earth was still an empty desert. How can this utterance possibly apply to us, when the earth can barely support us any longer and only by great effort can we obtain an adequate supply, so to speak, of the basic elements of life?

5. Again, he who told Adam and Eve at the beginning to be fruitful and multiply himself in the end handed down an example for those who did not want to marry, himself too promised the heavenly kingdom to eunuchs, himself says through his apostle that it is well for a man not to touch a woman, that he wishes all to be even as he himself was, that he who has a wife should be as if he did not, and that it is well for a person to remain as he is. Let him who has given his assent to the first utterance give it also to the second, nay to the second rather than the first, since a subsequent order always overrules an earlier one.

6. Again, many things have been done of necessity which do not always have to be done in the same way: the first man was made of earth, afterwards men were not; the first married couple were brother and sister, later couples were no longer even close relations. For if you want me to abide by the utterance made at that time, I for my part shall tie you down to its obligations in their entirety, so that either you follow it completely, if that is what is expedient, or you realize that you have to adopt a different way of life, since: The old has passed away, the new has come (2 Cor.5.17). Those who were told in the beginning to 'be fruitful and multiply' were, I note, as brother and sister. Give your assent then to the marriages of that time, if the utterance wins your assent. But you say, 'Brother-and-sister marriages are later forbidden but marriage is not.' You may say that; but not everyone is allowed to marry, since, when those who are allowed to do so are described, it is quite clear that those who are not mentioned are not allowed. For who can possibly doubt that when he named one of two parties as being allowed to marry, he did not allow the one whom he did not name? And if something is not allowed to a person, I take it that it is forbidden. When he said: If a man cannot exercise self-control, let him marry (1 Cor.7.9), how else did he want this to be understood except as meaning that the man who *can* exercise self-control should *not* marry? But he who advised men to persevere in virginity also, I think, refrained from advising marriage, and I do not want you to think it a trivial matter to count as nothing the advice of the Holy Spirit speaking through the apostle.

15, 1. You say, 'Abraham had a wife and yet pleased God and was the first to merit the name of patriarch.' Although it may seem that we have given a satisfactory answer to such arguments by showing on several occasions that old precedents cannot be prejudicial to our position, yet there are still a few additional remarks which we may make to meet all points.

2. You say that Abraham had a wife and was more pleasing to God than all other men even with a wife. Now you should be aware above all else of the fact that at that time there was a fourfold reason for marriage. The first reason was that, according to the apostle, everything was still being done mystically and symbolically,[79] as he says: All these things that happened to them were symbolic (ibid.10.11; NEB).[80] For something ought to be done symbolically only as long as the reality which it symbolizes has not taken place, and when the reality has been revealed, the foreshadowing of it in the symbol ceases to exist, since it was regarded as a messenger of the reality which was to follow. And in order that you may know for certain that at that time marriages also were celebrated symbolically, listen to the apostle's symbolic explanation of the marriage even of the parents of the human race themselves, when he uses this testimony: Therefore a man will leave his father and mother and cleave to his wife, and they will become one flesh (Gen.2.24). And lest anyone should suppose that this commandment is to be observed carnally by everyone under the new covenant as well, he goes on to say immediately: This mystery is a profound one, and I am saying that it refers to Christ and the church (Eph.6.31,32). Yet who but the ignorant can doubt that there was some sacramental significance in Abraham's wife and his concubine, particularly when the same apostle has called Hagar 'Mount Sinai' and is seen to compare Sara to 'the Jerusalem above' (cf. Gal.4.25,26)? The second reason is that, as we have already said, the world was still an empty desert. The third is that men at that time were not burdened with such a quantity of commandments and precepts that they were scarcely able to keep them if married. The fourth is that they could not be influenced by the consideration that they had not been dissuaded from marriage either by advice or by example but rather had been commanded to marry; the men of that period would have been despising the commandment if they had not married as much as we are despising it now if we are continent and yet wish to seek marriage. Consider whether any of these reasons which we have mentioned makes it expedient for us to marry – that is, if there is any truth which your marriage symbolizes, or if there is land which is still uninhabited, or if the burden of commandments laid upon you is so light that you can easily fulfil them even as a husband, or, and this must be considered before all else, if you have been given neither the example nor the teaching of chastity to induce you to seek its reward.

3. 'Whatever you may say,' you will reply, 'Abraham pleased God as a married man.' This, I suppose, is the only fact about him that you retain in your

---

[79] Cf. *Riches*,9,4; *Law*,9,2; *Dem*.5,2.
[80] RSV: 'as a warning', AV: 'as ensamples'; but Vulg. has *in figura*, and the Greek NT *typicos*.

memory; the rest you have forgotten. Why did he please God? Was it because he had a wife? I do not think so, since he was already married before he was justified. 'But he did not displease God,' you will say. Then it remains for us to try to understand how he pleased God if, by being married, he could neither displease nor please him. It was by his obedience, I think, in that in those days he manifestly did not oppose God's will in any respect. He is told: Go from your country and your kindred and your father's house (Gen.12.1); he departed without any hesitation and kept the gospel's commandments before the time of the gospel by not hesitating to leave his parents or his home or his native land in order to please God. Later he is commanded to inflict the wound of circumcision on a member of his own body and gladly consents to do so and to accept the pain it caused. He is bidden to renounce his son, of his own seed, though begotten of a handmaid, along with his mother, and he does not refuse to do so. Lastly, he is commanded to offer Isaac to God as a sacrifice and thus kill one whom he loved according to the testimony of the scripture, and without any delay he obeys. This then is how Abraham pleased God, and in his time he was found to be disobedient and rebellious to not one of God's commands. And now at last you must consider yourself to be like Abraham if you too in your day obey God's will in all respects without the slightest hesitation as you know that he did in his day; for he would have obeyed joyfully if he had been told, as you are now told, that is, before he married: It is well for a person to remain as he is (1 Cor.7.26), and again: Are you free from a wife? Do not seek marriage (ibid.27), or, after he had married: It is well for a man not to touch a woman (ibid.1), and: Let a man who has a wife be as though he had none (ibid.29).[81] For it would have been easy for him to make light of marriage, when he was able to make light of the fruit of marriage, and easier to protect the innocence of his body, after having inflicted a wound on it; also, he could easily make light of a son not yet begotten when he did not hesitate to slay the one whom he had already reared. What would you do if you were bidden to give up children already begotten, when you hesitate to make light of those of whom you are not certain whether you can beget them at all?

4. I ought also to draw your attention to other examples which he set, since, if they seem to you to be appropriate, then marriage may also seem to be appropriate; but if not, neither ought marriage to seem appropriate. You say, 'Abraham had a wife and yet pleased God.' Then you ought not to have been baptized either. Abraham was circumcised in the flesh; then you ought to have been circumcised in the same way. Abraham never fasted; then you ought not to fast even on appointed days, though it has been pronounced a sin for you to disregard a fast. Abraham offered animal flesh in sacrifice to God; then you too ought to offer similar sacrifices. 'God forbid!' you will say, 'It is now a different time.' Oh! So it is a different time when it is a matter of baptism, circumcision, fasting and sacrifices but not when it is a matter of marriage! For he who taught you to be circumcised in the spirit, to fast often, to be baptized once, to offer a

---

[81] The plural has been changed into the singular in this quotation.

different kind of sacrifice, himself exhorted you also to seek the glory of virginity by his advice as well as his example, in that he promises the heavenly kingdom to eunuchs and in that the apostle who testified that Christ is speaking through him said: Now concerning the unmarried I have no command of the Lord, but I give my opinion (ibid.25), and, by his example, in that he himself did not marry.

16. But there is one utterance of the blessed apostle that I ought not to overlook: he delivered it when he wanted to show up not those who exhorted chastity but those who despised it in the manner of heretics. This utterance, which contains the words: Who forbid marriage and enjoin abstinence from foods (1 Tim.4.3), heretics take in another sense and are seen to be invoking it in defence of wantonness; it is also the utterance which Jovinian and his supporters advanced as the main front for their blasphemous teachings.[82] But if the apostle is to be understood as wrongly censuring teachers of chastity and virginity in this utterance of his, then he forgot himself and will be shown to be in opposition to no one more than to himself, since, as we have demonstrated earlier, he preached chastity with such steadfastness that he wished all men to be like himself. We must therefore understand that he was speaking of those who condemn marriage as a sin and believe that it was not established by God and do not permit marriage to those to whom the apostle permitted it, namely, the Manichees and the Marcionites, who believe that there is one God of marriage and another of virginity.[83] But we acknowledge that there is one and the same God of both; we do not condemn marriage or forbid the incontinent to marry but, following the apostle's example, both recommend the good of purity and chastity to the incontinent and, if they say that they are incontinent, do not deny them the remedy of marriage as permitted by that same apostle.

17, 1. I have given, I think, adequate and conclusive proof that it is no longer appropriate for us to follow the pattern in every particular. We ought not, then, to be always practising what it was possible to practise at some time or other for various reasons, especially when the scripture sets a definite and proper time for

---

[82] Cf. 10,8; 16, and see my introduction to this letter and n.9.

[83] Pelagius and his supporters were especially severe in their opposition to Manicheism and to its teaching of the inevitability of sin and claimed that even Augustine had not been able to dissociate himself entirely from the Manichean idea of evil which had influenced him in his youth. Jerome, on the other hand, saw the Pelagians as Manichees, including them in his long list of precursors of Pelagianism (*Letters*, 133; PL 22,1150ff.), only to be charged by them in turn with possessing Manichean tendencies himself. After the condemnation of Pelagius and Celestius as heretics the last of the early Pelagians, Julian of Eclanum, returned to the attack on Augustine's 'Manicheism' and engaged in bitter controversy with him on the subject until his death; on the significance of Manicheism for the Pelagian controversy see Rees,1988,14ff., 24f. and 86ff., and for Pelagius' condemnation of their views his *Confession of Faith*, sections 22 and 25. Marcion had been excommunicated by the Church at Rome in 144; he rejected the OT as concerned only with the law, while holding that the Christian gospel, a gospel of love, was represented by Paul's Epistles or rather the ten which he accepted as canonical and which did not include the Pastoral Epistles.

almost everything: A time to weep, and a time to laugh; a time to be born, and a time to die; a time to mourn, and a time to dance; a time to embrace, and a time to refrain from embracing (Ec.3.2,4,5).[84] Let him who made no spot in your body find no spot in it. Behold two lovers who are competing for your form and beauty, that is, chastity and wantonness: the former says, 'I do not forsake my own', the latter, on the other hand, 'But it is my custom always to steal another's'; the former, in order to win your agreement, promises the glory of the heavenly kingdom, the friendship of God and the fellowship of the angels, the latter is seen to be offering you the transitory wealth of this world and human riches. Be a just judge: choose at once the one to whom you belong by nature and law, whose gifts are known to be superior. For we are not unaware of the stratagems which the enemy in his envy of chastity and perfection is always using at this time to attack you, sometimes by the suggestions of others, at other times by your own thoughts. For he is so cunning and rascally that, apart from wanting to deprive the wedded of the reward of their innocence, he also makes them persist in unlawful acts often on the pretext that they are lawful, since he knows full well that it is difficult to keep the commandments in their entirety when married. These are the kind of suggestions that he often makes to you: 'Are you not going to marry then? Are you going to remain childless? To whom are you going to leave such wealth, so great an estate? Is it not sufficient that your sisters have chosen this way of life? If you follow their examples, through whom will your family be renewed? Does it then seem to you to be a good thing that the whole source of your stock may dry up?'

2. It is by means of advice of this kind that the devil cheats and deceives[85] simple and ignorant minds, so that, while they are worrying about the future increase of the human family, they deprive themselves of the protection of that other family to which they belong, the heavenly, and while they are seeking to provide themselves with heirs to their earthly resources, they themselves are unable to become heirs of God. But when such thoughts come to your mind as a result either of your own reasoning or of another's words, remember that the kind of heirs that are more appropriate for a Christian are surely those of whom it is said: Go, sell what you possess and give to the poor, and come, follow me (Mt.19.21; Mk.10.21; Lk.18.22). He who has heirs such as these makes God his heir too, as the scripture says: He who is kind to the poor lends to the Lord (Pr.19.17). For it is quite foolish to prefer uncertainties to certainties and to place your hopes upon descendants to succeed you when you do not know if you are able to have them. Let God be your posterity, hand over your property to him, put your estate in his keeping, so that for the future *you* may own *him*.

3. Have you quite forgotten the saying which maintains that it is so hard for a rich man to be able to be saved that it is admitted to be easier for impossibilities to take place, like a camel passing through the eye of a needle, than for a rich man to be able to climb into the kingdom of heaven. We can

---

84 Our author has selected four of the fourteen contrasting pairs given in the text quoted.
85 Cf. OF,1,7 for a similar warning using the same verbs; see also *Dem.*25;26.

already see the truth of this saying being fulfilled at the present time, in that nearly all the rich lack the good of virginity for which the heavenly kingdom is especially promised as a reward. It is mere folly for a Christian to wish to leave heirs in this world, when he is bidden to lose his inheritance of the whole world thereby, and to worry about a posterity which is in the future and is uncertain as well, when he is forbidden to have thought for the morrow. Listen to the promise which God makes to eunuchs and the great reward which he offers us in compensation for the loss of the joy of possessing children, which is in any case short-lived and never free from sorrow: I will give them, he says, in my house and within my walls a named place that is better than sons and daughters (Is.56.5)[86] Notice carefully what he says: 'better than sons or daughters', which means, 'I will give them a place which is better than they would have had if they had chosen to have sons and daughters.'

4. There is scarcely a wise man alive who would not undoubtedly choose the better of two options. Yet, if you still want to have children and cannot endure to be barren, then have them by all means; but beget children born of Mother Wisdom and of spiritual seed through God's word, not of this world. Be the kind of father that Paul was, who said: I became your father through the gospel (1 Cor.4.15).[87] Let this utterance be fulfilled in you: 'Blessed is the man whose seed is in Sion, not in the senate, and whose household is in Jerusalem, not in the city of Rome, which is compared to Babylon for its crimes!' For you must beware lest in your longing for children of the flesh you become incapable of being yourself a son of God, since it is written: Every one who has left father or mother or wife or children or lands or house for the gospel's sake will receive a hundredfold in this world and in the world to come eternal life (Mt.19.29; cf. Lk.18.29,30).[88] So you, bidden as you are for the Lord's sake not to have regard for children already reared, have to ask yourself if you ought to prefer children not yet born at all to obeying his higher will. How can you ever prefer God's reward to certainties, if you prefer even uncertainties to it? A thing is not the object of a full and perfect love if something else is preferred to it. But if you take pleasure in observing the happy and agreeable married lives of some, even if they are short-lived and never without their attendant griefs, then consider also the unceasing wrangles, contentious divorces and manifold disasters which beset others; if you are attracted by the lot of those who rejoice in the fact that they have begotten a number of worthy children, then let the thought of those who lament their cruel loss of children through sad and premature death deter you.

5. It is much easier not to beget children at all than to lose them when begotten. Those who refrain from begetting children after the flesh do not, of course, have their love to give them pleasure but neither do they have their sorrows to bring them grief: they miss the joy of having begotten them but they

---

86 AV and Vulg.: 'a place and a name'; RSV has 'a monument and a name'.
87 The citation omits 'in Christ Jesus' after 'father'.
88 Our author gives us a mixture of these two texts with some alterations: he has 'for the gospel's sake' in place of 'for my name's sake' (Mt.) and 'for the sake of the kingdom of God' (Lk.), and has changed the order of words in the first part of the sentence.

never have to endure the tortures of grief that attend their loss. Or are you afraid that the source of your family may dry up? Then remember that our duty is to desire a family that is in heaven, not on earth. What a terrible loss it is indeed to see the end of a process of procreation which is bound to stop at some time or other! Why do you wish for the existence of the very ones who will perhaps make it barely possible for you yourself to exist? I advise you to prefer that kind of family which would without a shadow of doubt be able to live on for ever by your side in the heavenly places. For there are many considerations to deter a wise man from thinking such vain thoughts: let him first reflect that he might not have been born, secondly, that he might have been born and then met with a premature death, and thirdly that he does not know how long he has to live and that it is quite uncertain whether he is able to beget children. Why then should not a man reject of his own free choice what he may possibly have to go without of necessity?

6. 'I fear,' you will say, 'to offend my parents, whose dearest wish is that our family stock should be replenished through me.' You are not markedly loyal or steadfast in fearing to offend your parents for God's sake, yet for your parents' sake you are not afraid of losing the reward of a higher state of blessedness, though that means preferring your parents' wishes to God's will and giving human beings priority over his love. What kind of parents are they if they do not want you to be that which is better?? Such parents either do not love their son or do not have implicit trust in the future. There is no one who does not want his children to reach what he knows to be a more perfect state, unless it be one who either is doubtful about perfection itself or grudges his children's good, which is unbelievable;[89] people of this sort are to be accounted enemies rather than parents, and it was of them, I think, that the Lord said: A man's foes will be those of his own household (Mt.10.36; Mic.7.6). And again: He who says to his father or mother, 'I regard you not', or disowns his brothers and ignores his children has observed your righteousness and kept your covenant (Dt.33.9). And again: He who does not hate his father or mother is not worthy of me (Mt.10.37; cf. Lk.14.26).[90] We ought not to place our parents before him who placed neither his parents nor indeed himself before us and who, when he was teaching his disciples and was interrupted by a message to the effect that his mother and brothers were standing at the door and wanted to see him, answered saying: Who is my mother, and who are my brothers? Whoever does the will of my father in heaven is my brother and mother and sister (Mt.12.48–50; Mk.3.33–35; cf. Lk.8.21) – not that he scorned his holy mother but to teach us by his own example who are the parents whom we ought rather to regard as such and to show us that we, to whom he did not prefer even his good parents, ought at least to prefer him to bad parents.

---

[89] For the Christian parent's obligation to consider the spiritual well-being of his children cf. OF,6,2.

[90] Our author again combines the words in the two texts and is probably quoting from memory; cf. n.43.

7. It is indeed wicked of you to wish to prefer anyone to him who did not prefer himself to you and did not refuse even to die for you, and you are preferring a great deal to him when you reject what he wanted you to esteem highly, and choose rather what he wanted you to esteem less. For the apostle says: Who shall separate us from the love of Christ? Shall tribulation, or distress, or persecution, or famine, or nakedness, or peril, or sword (Rom.8.35)? Whoever is separated from the things that Christ loves is severed from his even greater love; a man does not perfectly love another if he does not want to possess what he knows the one whom he loves to care for greatly. It is a very sad matter if marriage or parents hold us back from perfect love of him, when not even death or the sword should separate us from it.

8. 'But this,' you will say, 'is something which is to be observed only in times of persecution.' You are wrong if you suppose that a Christian can ever enjoy peace in this life: we suffer persecution whenever we are compelled to abandon any obligation which is attached to holiness; but it is much more serious if we are persuaded to do so and if pleasures demand of us what not even punishment ought to be able to wrest from us by force. Whenever we overcome in matters of this kind, we win the crown of victory, but whenever we are overcome, we feel the loss of the hope of a higher reward. Or are you afraid that perhaps your parents may disinherit you if you disdain them? An inheritance is not to be greatly desired when it takes away the reward of inheriting the heavenly kingdom; such property ought not only not to be coveted but also to be rejected when it is offered, for we who have learned to despise our own possessions are easily able to refuse also what our parents offer us.

9. Of what value is a human and earthly inheritance to us, when we are promised one that is heavenly and divine? Let us spurn all such wealth and say with the prophet: I have not desired the day of man (Jer.17.16),[91] and elsewhere: The Lord is my chosen portion and my cup; thou hast restored my inheritance to me (Ps.16.5; LXX and Vulg.).[92] But *he* loved God with his soul and mind and wholeheartedly trusted in God's promises, whereas *we*, I fear, shall be seen to love him only superficially and in the eyes of men but to love the world more in our hearts; for that which is without doubt preferred to something else is loved more than it. And it is an even more serious matter to barter for an earthly inheritance and human riches the virginity which Christ promises to reward with the heavenly kingdom. What an excess of passion for wantonness you show in purchasing at such a low cost what God buys at the far higher price of eternal glory! For we read that the kingdom of heaven is virtually denied to the rich, as the scripture says: It will be hard for a rich man to enter the kingdom of heaven (Mt.19.23; cf. Mk.10.23; Lk.18.24); yet it is promised to eunuchs and the continent: there are eunuchs, he says, who have made themselves eunuchs for the sake of the kingdom of heaven (Mt.19.12). I do not know how a man can hope for the reward of the heavenly kingdom when he chooses rather that to which it is

91 Vulg. and LXX; RSV: 'the day of disaster'; AV: 'the woeful day'.
92 RSV: 'thou holdest my lot.'

refused and sacrifices that to which it is promised for the sake of that to which it is denied.

10. Well then, you who bring glory to Christians, go on and finish what you have begun, treading underfoot all bodily pleasures with all the strength of mind that you can summon and devoting yourself only to spiritual activities. Do not allow yourself to be outdone by women, who, though members of the weaker sex, have conquered great sins by their virginity; just as the sex into which you were born has made you their superior in physical strength, so let your way of life make you at least their equal. How long, after all, is this life of ours, even if we are able to reach the appointed limit which has been set to it? Add to this the fact that we have to fear an unforeseeable death at any time, since a man can die from the moment he even begins to live.[93] Let us then use this brief term to win something which we can possess for ever. How else are you to account for the fact that you may both hear of and learn about and, if you wish, see many Christians who are afraid of God's judgement and so smitten with fear at the prospect of his coming that, although no blame for having sinned can be attached to them, they do not cease to afflict their bodies with abstinence, prayer and fastings and even wallow in sackcloth and ashes, when they recall that it is written: For the day of the Lord is great, and who can endure it (Joel 2.11; cf., Jer.30.7)?[94] And elsewhere: If the righteous man is scarcely saved, where will the sinner and the impious appear (1 Pet.4.18)? And the words of the apostle: I pummel my body and subdue it (1 Cor.9.27). While others, then, weaken their bodies with abstinence and fasting, consider whether it is appropriate for you to nourish yours with feasts and choice banquets. While they often pass their nights in sober vigil following Christ's example, your soft bed does not even permit you, bloated as you are with food, to watch even when you wish to do so. While they spread sackcloth and ashes about their limbs, pallid and afflicted with all kinds of mortification, you strut around bedecked with ornaments, radiant and joyful. While they spend nearly all their time in tearful prayer, you take delight in laughter and wantonness. While they wear themselves out in an unremitting struggle with the devil, you take pleasure in occupying yourself with the delights of the flesh, Is there not one God for all? Do not all Christians await the coming of the same Judge? Or does a gentler fire await some perhaps and a harsher fire others, so that some are so anxious and others so unconcerned?[95] Believe me, they too would wish to be free from concern if they but realized that this is what would be to their advantage!

11. 'But,' you will say, 'this is the lot of the few.' Yes indeed, and the narrow way by which we enter the kingdom of heaven is for the few alone,[96] and so is that supreme reward for innocence which is promised to virgins only, and you should be among those few if it is your wish to possess what is promised to the few. Marriage, on the other hand, is the lot of almost all men, including the

---

[93] Cf. 17,5.
[94] Omits 'and very terrible'; cf. nn.43 and 90.
[95] Cf. *Riches*,6,5.
[96] Cf. YM,3,1, citing Jas.1.22; see also *Virg*.10,2; *Cel*.10; 11; *Dem*.10,3.

wicked and foolish; it is no great matter to want to do what all men do and to possess what even the worst men seek to attain. But, to say nothing of human beings, wild animals also indulge in wantonness, cattles and birds also marry, and it is no great achievement to possess something in common with pigs and dogs. But it is a fine thing to strive rather after the state and rule of God and his angels; it is a fine thing for you to imitate in your present life those in whose company you are to believe that you will always be in the life to come. Acknowledge how great is the good of chastity from the fact that the incontinent man can neither read nor pray in faith but either presumes in his ignorance to offer sacrifices and to touch the Lord's body or fears to do so because he knows what it is that he is doing. The chaste and temperate man, on the other hand, cherishes the faith given him by his conscience and, supported by the authority of his chastity, does all these things with complete confidence. When *he* prays, he speaks as if he were in the presence of God, nay rather as one friend to another, as the scripture says: But I have called you friends (Jn.15.15); when *he* reads the scriptures, no confusion of mind holds him back, and *he* is able to offer sacrifice to God with assurance as well as to receive the Eucharist in faith when it is celebrated.

12. What then, my most beloved one? If you love Christ, love what is good in his sight; if you love God, preserve what God takes special pleasure in having preserved: preserve purity, preserve chastity, retain your inner continence and, if perchance you lapse in this respect, obtain forgiveness by his approval of your prayers. We have already demonstrated earlier that to some extent chastity is placed on an equal footing with the priesthood. If you persevere in the innocence of virginity, you will be treated as an angel by God and as a god by men; but if you reject his good gift, which I do not believe to be possible, you will retain the glory of virginity neither with men nor before God. Let no man deceive or seduce you with empty words;[97] it is difficult for a Christian to be able to be perfect, unless he perseveres in the single life and in the holiness of chastity.[98] I confess my wonder at the outstanding goodness of your soul at such a youthful age and at the maturity of your mind in so young a body. Nor am I alone in this: all those who have been able to make your acquaintance love, admire, respect and honour you. And this novel feeling of wonder and admiration moves them to alarm at the thought that someone of your age should prefer the steep and narrow path[99] to that broader way along which we see even some older men walking, and that a mind so young has been found to follow Christ, especially when it comes from the ranks of the rich, for whom salvation is difficult.[100]

---

[97] See n.85; cf. also *Virg.*15; *Life*,10,2; 13,1; 14,1.

[98] Cf. 10,9, and, for a similar warning with regard to the need for complete poverty, see *Riches*,12,3.

[99] Cf. 11 and n.96.

[100] Cf. 10,8; 17,9; *BT*,18,3; *Riches*,9,4; 19,2, and *passim*; *OF*,4,1; *YM*,4,1. Although the teaching on riches differs slightly in the five works and is particularly severe in the tractate On Riches, as is only to be expected, it is broadly the same in all of them – often with strong verbal resemblances.

13. In these times, when to many men righteousness is almost an unknown quantity, your praises are sung on everyone's lips, and there is no one who does not marvel at the way of life that you are following at such an early age. You must never lose a good which is so great or be willing to mar the noble and perfect structure that you are building by spoiling even one corner of it.[101] Do not allow the world to deprive you of one jot of the future glory which will be yours; guard this one possession with great care, so that you may the more easily possess everything. For chastity is the mother of all virtues, and it is often the case that when it is lost or retained, it is lost or retained along with all its offspring. But you have already surpassed older men in character and have outdone the long-lived in maturity of spirit. What more can I say? In these times, if you do not allow licentiousness, which is a breeding-ground for vices of all kinds, to get the better of you, you stand almost alone.[102]

---

[101] In other words, it is essential to keep all the commandments, not one only, as is often stressed not only in this letter (see n.54) and the other documents in the Caspari collection but also throughout the works in Part I of this book; cf. e.g., Virg.4,2; 7,2; Dem.15; 16,1; 25.

[102] The concluding sections of this letter beginning at 'Well then, you who bring glory to Christians' at the commencement of section 10 have been supplied from the edition of Morin (see PLS 1,1503,n.(a) and the last paragraph in my introduction to No.8).

PART III

MISCELLANEA

12

To a Widow[1]

We have had occasion more than once before to refer to a quotation from the late-fifth-century writer Gennadius which runs as follows: 'Fastidius, a British bishop, wrote to a certain Fatalis one book *On the Christian Life* and another *On Preserving Widowhood* of sound doctrine, worthy of God.'[2] It has also been noted that one of the oldest MSS of Gennadius has Britto ('Briton') in place of 'a British bishop' or 'a bishop of Britons' with the episcopal title added later; in addition, in order to avoid the embarrassment of the addressee of a letter *On the Christian Life* being, as the text reveals, not 'a certain Fatalis' but a widow, some scholars have seen fit to point out that, if we insert commas before and after 'and another *On Preserving Widowhood*', the second letter need no longer be connected with Fatalis. The view expressed in the introduction to *On the Christian Life* in our Part I is that that letter was probably written by Pelagius and that, consequently, if Fastidius did write 'a book *On the Christian Life* to a certain Fatalis', it was not the one which is in Part I.

As for Fastidius' alleged work *On Preserving Widowhood* it is not surprising that its authorship has also been the subject of much discussion. Morin, who, as we have seen, attributed the Caspari corpus to Fastidius, attributed this text *On Preserving Widowhood* to him as well, having discovered it in PL 67, where it was ascribed to Caesarius, Archbishop of Arles. Haslehurst,[3] who followed Morin and ascribed all the Caspari corpus to Fastidius, suggested that the resemblances of this letter to the sixth in Caspari's corpus are strong enough to justify attributing both to the same author: thus our *Letter to An Older Friend* would become Gennadius' *On the Christian Life* and this letter his *On Preserving Widowhood* – provided, of course, that commas are inserted before and after '*Widowhood*'. He admits, however, that 'verbal similarities are few' and 'it is impossible to place any passage in VII (our letter) in a parallel column with any similar passage in I to VI (the Caspari letters)'; but he discovers enough similarities of other kinds to permit him to conclude that 'to anyone with a literary instinct the similarities

---

[1] *De viduitate servanda* ('On Preserving Widowhood'); PL 67,1094–98; CPL 1019a; Haslehurst,286–91.
[2] *On Famous Men*,56 (PL 58,1091).
[3] *The Works of Fastidius*,viif., xlixff.

between VI and VII' – *On Chastity* and *On Preserving Widowhood* – 'are remarkable.' He has the good sense to leave the matter 'to the decision of the reader',
and the present writer is content to do the same, while reminding his readers
that, if we do not accept Fastidius as the author of the Caspari letters I–VI – and
there seems no good reason why we should –, there is no argument in favour of
attributing this letter to him either. Nor have we grounds for attributing it to
Caesarius of Arles: Morin, who was something of an authority on the latter, said
that there was not a single phrase in the letter which suggested that it should be
attributed to him. If it was the work of the Archbishop of Arles, then it has no
place in this collection, since he was strongly opposed both to Pelagianism and
Semi-Pelagianism.

Admittedly, this letter is not markedly Pelagian in its teaching: for example,
that blessed word *arbitrium*, 'will', occurs only once, in a general sense (1,1). On
the other hand, it is a very brief letter and hardly lends itself to doctrinal
statements, and there are occasions when it recalls passages in *On Chastity* as well
as possessing an ethos which is just as strict and ascetic as anything in the
Caspari corpus and a style which is as rhetorical as that of the 'Pelagian Anonymous'. But after reading Parts I and II we may decide that the resemblances are
not so much characteristic of Pelagian teaching as commonplaces of contemporary writing on morality, and that the fact that the arguments for bachelordom in
On Chastity are similar to those for widowhood in this letter, that the rhetorical
comparisons of the states of marriage and widowhood in both works also contain
resemblances and that this letter has the usual plethora of biblical quotations and
examples is not enough to prove that *On Chastity* and *To A Widow* are by the
same author. Probably not; but the latter is almost certainly Pelagian.

The letter begins and ends with a comparison between marriage and widowhood, interspersed with exhortations to humility, modesty and sobriety, to chastity and continence, to prayer and fasting, to almsgiving and other good works,
and supported by a number of citations of widows and other women whose
actions were approved of by the Lord and rewarded accordingly. But of sympathy
to the bereaved woman there is not a word, and the references to the 'yoke', the
'shackles' and the 'servitude' which she had to endure under her husband can
hardly be described as tactful or indicative of the caring, loving relationship
which might be expected to be the distinguishing feature of a good, Christian
marriage. He says (section 3) that he is under an obligation to visit the widow
himself. Let us hope that, if he visited this one, he found it possible to overcome
his 'Pelagian' principles in the interests of common humanity and Christian
charity: *neque semper arcum tendit Apollo!*[4]

---

4   Horace, *Odes*, II,10,19ff.

Text

1.   Listen to me, bereaved daughter: though you have lost the comfort that comes from love and your husband's yoke has been removed from your neck, you will be happier if you stay as you are. Do not let vain thoughts deceive you with the suggestion, 'Who will provide me with food at the time when it is needed or who will protect my fatherless children?' You have better reason to rejoice now than when you were bound by a husband's shackles. Behold, you have been released from a husband's law, which held you back, and you are now under the direction of your own will. Do not sigh because you have lost your hope in this world; remember, my daughter, that the Lord is 'the hope of all the ends of the earth (Ps.65.5).' Do not be anxious that you have been left alone; remember the Lord, who 'upholds the widow and the fatherless (Ps.146.9).' Pray to the Lord, as the apostle says: She who is a real widow and is left all alone continues in prayers and supplications day and night; whereas she who is self-indulgent is dead even while she lives. If any widow has parents or grandchildren, let her learn first to rule her own household well and to make some return to her parents, for this is pleasing and acceptable before God (1 Tim.5.5,6,4).[5]

2.   Be humble, modest and sober in all things, lest perchance you appear to be offensive, as it is written: Refuse to enrol younger widows, for when they grow wanton against Christ, they desire to marry, and so they incur condemnation for having violated their first pledge and learn to be idlers, gadding about other women's houses, and not only idlers but also gossips and busybodies, saying what they should not say (ibid.11–13).[6] Be continually in your own house, praying tearfully that God may give you chastity and bodily continence. Unhappy and wretched though you may be, what an awful reproach you bear if you are not continent! What mental turmoil you undergo if you do not curb your flesh! Labour always in God's work. Look at the good widow who is the wife of one man, 'if she has brought up sons, shown hospitality, washed the feet of the saints, relieved the afflicted (ibid.9,10).' You will be happy if you do all this; for there are many widows who have had two or three husbands but do not have the benefit of the commandment to be honoured by all men, as does the woman who has had only one husband: 'there were many widows in the day of Elijah, and he was sent to none of them but only to Zarephath, in the land of Sidon (Lk.4.25,26).'[7] Note that none of those were rewarded save only she who gave

---

[5] This 'quotation', which is also used by Augustine, On the Good of Widowhood,18 (PL 40,444), omits a phrase after 'alone' and changes 'let her continue' to 'continues'; v.4 is moved from the beginning to the end of the quotation.
[6] The changes here are only minor; the text and the Vulgate have in Christo, which makes little sense unless the preposition is forced to mean what it cannot, and I have retained the rendering of RSV (and AV), though my own preference would be for, e.g., 'whose passions have turned them away from Christ' (cf. NEB).
[7] The greater part of v.25 and the last clause in v.26 are omitted.

him hospitality at the time of need, when there was a mighty famine and, on the arrival of the holy Elijah, she prepared a table for him; like that widow whose substance consisted of two copper coins only, yet offered these to the Lord, hoping in the simplicity of her heart that she would receive a hundredfold;[8] and like the widow called Judith who did not leave the roof of her house, serving the Lord day and night with fastings and prayers, and whom the Lord protected from the hand of Holofernes, lest she be polluted by sinful deeds.[9]

3.   Happy widow, in that she brought such joy to her fellow-citizens and deserved to have such confidence in herself that she freed her people from the edge of the sword! See what the widow's chastity achieved, and how, because of it, she became famous over the whole earth, both praised by the Lord and renowned among all men! How happy you are, widow whom the Lord remembers! Like that widow whose only son had died and won the Lord's pity, so that he was restored to life;[10] like that widow in the Acts of the Apostles, Dorcas by name, who did many acts of charity, so that, when Peter arrived, all the widows showed the garments which she had made while she still lived, and Peter saw the works of the widow woman and prayed and restored her to life;[11] like that widow who daily cast herself down before the feet of a certain rich man, so that she might be avenged upon her enemy, and the rich man, seeing her tears, said: Even if I neither fear God nor regard man, yet because this widow bothers me, I will avenge her (Lk.18.4,5). See how a widow is avenged if she maintains her chastity and humility; and I myself am bidden to visit her, since the apostle says: Visit the orphans and widows in their affliction (Jas.1.27).

4.   How happy you are, widow, in that you are so commended by the Lord in all things! But he who does not pity you is judged by the Lord, for he himself says: If you do not judge the causes of widows and do not pity orphans, I will judge you, says the Lord.[12] Blessed are you, widow, in that you have the Lord himself as your judge and defender. Weep for no one now, my daughter, since you are in a better situation than you were before: before you put your hope on a man, but now you put it in the Lord Jesus Christ; before you thought as man thinks, but now you think as God does; before you delighted in the lust of the flesh and the dangers of dress but now you think above all else of the pleasure of obeying the law and maintaining chastity; before you were the servant of your husband but now you are the free woman of Christ. How good it is for you to be free of anxiety rather than endure servitude to a husband! It is good to lie alone in bed and rise up clean rather than to lie conscious of your lust and uncleanness of the flesh.

---

8   Cf. Mk.12.42.
8   Cf. Jud.8.5.
10 Cf. Lk.7.12–15.
11 Cf. Acts 9.36–41.
12 I have not been successful in my search for the source of this quotation; Ps.68.5 and, possibly, Is.1.7?

Before you were bent beneath the heavy yoke of a husband; but now you stand erect, bearing the sweet yoke of Christ.

5.   Rejoice, my daughter, that you were once up for sale to be the servant of a husband but now have earned your liberty at the hands of God. Remember, my daughter, the Canaanite woman who by her importunity became worthy to receive a kindness from our Saviour;[13] but also that woman who washed the Lord's feet with her tears and wiped them with her hair;[14] that woman who brought the precious ointment and poured it upon the Lord as he sat at table;[15] that woman who touched the Lord's garments, and instantly the flow of her blood was dried up;[16] and that woman who sat at the Lord's feet to hear how she might be able to flee from the wrath to come.[17] Consider, my daughter, the path of humiliation along which these very women trod in order that they might merit a blessing on this account. Be like them in obedience, in humility, in almsgiving, in receiving strangers, in watchings, in fastings, in all sobriety. These are the things that pleased Christ. Labour, my daughter, day and night in the Lord's work, so that you may be bound to the Lord now that you have been set free from man, that you who were to receive fruit thirtyfold may now be worthy to receive it sixtyfold through him who lives for ever and ever. Amen.

---

13 Cf. Mt.15.22–28.
14 Cf. Lk.7.37,38.
15 Cf. Mt.26.6–13; Mk.14.3–9.
16 Cf. Mk.9.20–22.
17 Cf. Lk.10.39.

13

To Fatalis (?)[1]

This incomplete homily in the form of a letter was discovered by Dom Morin in the eighth-century Codex Augiensis[2] and identified by him as the 'book on the Christian life' written by Fastidius to a certain Fatalis according to Gennadius (see the introduction to the previous letter).[3] He had previously identified a homiletic text found in a Vatican MS of roughly the same period[4] as Fastidius' letter to Fatalis but changed his opinion when he saw that his new discovery contained several phrases and some sentences which had clearly been 'lifted' by the Vatican text. The present letter, he now decided, was the work of Fastidius on the Christian life just as the letter *To a Widow* was the second. His cup was full! In fact, the main interest of the present letter may well be that the homiletic piece in the Vatican MS which repeats so many of its phrases and sentences has more recently been identified as the twentieth homily of Caesarius of Arles, and we have already noticed in the introduction to our last letter that it too was once attributed to the same Caesarius. If the present letter is Pelagian and also Caesarius', then we have here an excellent example of a 'gamekeeper turned poacher' instead of the other way round.

Though in itself a lively enough piece, full of Pelagian echoes, especially of *On Riches* and *On Chastity*, our letter is, as Plinval was not slow to point out, of small literary value, a conflation of edifying comments slung together without any great attempt to produce a cohesive result. One notable difference from the Pelagian works in Parts I and II is that this text is composed of short, aphoristic sentences in place of the much longer, periodic sentences of Pelagius and the 'Pelagian Anonymous'. But there is an abundance of Pelagian themes: the need to imitate Christ, the superiority of the apostles over latter-day Christians, the folly of acquiring worldly possessions, the vital importance of being a Christian,

[1] *Epistula sancto Fatali de vita christiana* or *Admonitio Augiensis*; PLS 1,1699–1704; CPL 763.
[2] Codex Augiensis 221; hence the alternative title usually given to it nowadays.
[3] Morin,46,1934,3–17,esp.3f.
[4] Vat.Pal.Lat.216; the text is there entitled *Excarpsum de epistola sancto Fatali de vita christiana*, 'Excerpt from the letter to the holy Fatalis on the Christian life'; it was first edited by Morin in *Rev.Ben.*13,1898,484–87 and again in his article quoted in n.3 above and CCL 103, 1953,91–94.

not just being called one, the two Ways, the hypocrisy of many churchgoers, the dangers of putting off total commitment to Christianity in favour of the illusory pleasures of the world, the merits and advantages of celibacy as compared with marriage, the spurious attractions of wealth and property, the crucial part played by the conscience in regulating behaviour, and so on.

No doubt there would have been many more of these Pelagian common-places,[5] if the homily were complete; as it is, the text breaks off suddenly while the author is still in full spate.

Text

1.   I warn you to think more carefully about the salvation of your soul, fearing what has been written, namely, 'The encumbrances of the world have made them wretched.'[6] Cast away, I beg you, everything that is adverse to it, before the whip is turned into a sword. Let the king enter his bedchamber, that is to say, let Christ enter your heart. Let the way lie open for the bridegroom to go in to meet his bride, so that, after spiritual union and after the embrace of an eternal cousin, the soul may sing out in joy, 'Lo! we conceived and went into labour and brought forth the breath of salvation (cf. Is.26.18).' Behold, Jesus walks up and down before the door seeking a habitation; let us receive him into the bedchamber of our heart, so that he may receive us into the blessedness of his kingdom. Let us beware in our dealings with any of the poor lest they suffer the indignity of beating upon our door for a long time and say to us: I was a stranger and you did not take me in (Mt.25.43). The chief apostles of our religion invite us to follow them and imitate them, calling upon us to reign in heaven with them, on condition that we suffer with them on earth. *They* were not separated from Christ by torture; but *we* are separated from him by idle talk and slander. The punishments inflicted on *them* by their persecutors did not change them; *we* are discouraged by our confusion alone. *They* did not yield to dangers; *we* are overcome by pleasures. *They* spurned all their possessions in order to begin to follow Christ; *we* do not spurn others' property and so do not follow him. *They* are generous in handling their property, we are greedy in handling others', though it is certain that whatever is desired in this world is alien to Christ and foreign to the faith.[7]

2.   But how can something be said to be mine which was acquired by another's labour before it was mine, and, after it has begun to be mine, is

---

[5] Plinval,1943,30, dismisses this letter along with the letter *To a New Penitent* (*Magnum cumulatur*) as 'rapsodies inhabiles', which is possibly a little harsh.

[6] This is not a biblical quotation but is very popular with Caesarius of Arles; see Haslehurst,293, where he states that the latter quoted it fourteen times in his homilies, and the footnote (1) in PLS 1,1699, which refers us to the *Vision of Paul*.

[7] Cf. a similar passage in *Law*,6,1.

transferred to another at some time or other? Before it was mine, it belonged to another; after being mine, it will belong to another and be separated from me, as I from it. Therefore it is not mine, unless it can be with me always. Let us then give up the things which are alien, hostile and adverse and separate us from God, and follow those which are our own. Let us not be reluctant to abandon weakness and seek after virtue. Let it not be tiresome for us to listen to what is to our advantage. With good advice I can bear the loss of something which could have destroyed me if I had retained it. It is not imprudent to turn aside from a path which bandits have blocked and besieged.[8] If we live in the spirit, we cling to the footprints of Christ; if we follow Christ, it ought to be apparent from our actions. Every tree is recognized by its fruit. Therefore, if we perform the actions of the spirit, we please Christ; but if we seek the pleasure of the flesh, we cannot please God. I do not want you to deceive yourself, my brother; I do not want you to pride yourself upon the false name of Christianity, I do not want you to be seduced by a faith that is fictitious or by a righteousness that is not true: the kingdom of God does not reside in a name but in goodness. A great prize cannot be won without labour, since what the psalmist says is true: By the words of your lips I have avoided the ways of the violent (Ps.17.4).[9]

3.   If what we are seeking is not conventional, then the way in which we live should also be out of the ordinary. Two ways are described in the gospel: the one is broad and leads many to death, the other is narrow and confined, and along it a few enter upon life.[10] On one of them Christ holds sway, on the other the devil: each path has its own leader. Let everyone now look to the path along which he walks, the footway which he traverses. I do not know how anyone can reach Christ who is in heaven, when he follows rather a leader who has been cast out of heaven. I ask you, 'What is this madness of yours that makes you want death and refuse life, follow your enemy and desert your king, flee from your redeemer and love your destroyer?' Surely, Christian, you renounced the world and the devil in baptism in order that you might cross over wholeheartedly to your redeemer; why then do you forget your promise, having one thing on your lips but doing another in your works? For when we ourselves and all that we have belong to Christ, why do we not serve him in such a way that we serve the devil in nothing? If Christ were not a sufficient reward for me, it would be correct for me to accept a greater one or adapt myself to the service of another. Is it impossible for one who has given us life also to give us sustenance in the present, not to speak of the future? Or cannot the one who made our body provide us with a tunic? Or will not the one who gave the soul to our body before it had done

---

8   PLS marks a lacuna after *Non est*, 'It is not', into which I have inserted 'imprudent', which seems to me to make sense.
9   This is not the Vulgate text, which has 'the hard ways', as does LXX; AV has 'ways of the destroyer'.
10 We have frequently met 'The Two Ways' in these Pelagian texts but always in the opposite sense with the narrow and difficult way leading to heaven and the broad, easy one to hell.

anything to merit it restore the body to the soul after merit has been gained? While unbelieving races enjoy the use of the creation every day, shall God deny to the righteous what is not denied to unbelievers? Are *we* failing him in obedience rather than *he* us in his favours? He has more to censure in me than I have to complain at in him; in going against his word I believe something to be possible which he judged impossible: I believe that I can serve two masters, which I could not do even if I shared myself equally between them.

4.   But, as it is, I frequently enter a church and wish that, having entered, I were really present there: they move their lips in prayer but their wavering mind is absent; the body comes to God's house but the mind has stayed in the council-chamber or in the lawcourts or among soothsayers of ill repute; the reader recites, the priest proclaims, the deacon calls for an orderly silence but we whisper about slanders and lawsuits.[11] And if ever through the importunity of the teacher the mind is reawakened to attend to his warnings, the breast is beaten with the fists, and the guilt of the whole man is punished in one member by unmerited blows, so that the mind may remain undisturbed in its unrighteousness but not in the church. What does it profit you that you beat your breast, if you do not cast out the sins shut up within it? It is of no profit that someone is chastised for his sins, if he returns to his sins immediately. You utter a few complacent words inside but when you get back outside again, you fail in respect of every virtue. That is why the Holy Spirit rightly proclaims through Isaiah: This people honours me with their lips, while their heart is far from me (Is.29.13). I ask you, 'If we always perform actions which belong to men, when shall we perform those which are of God? And if our speech and thought and acts are deployed for the benefit of the flesh, for gains to satisfy our greed, for the state, for the payment of tribute, when will our soul sigh for heavenly things?' And we shall say with the Jews: We have no king but Caesar (Jn.19.15).

5.   And what wonder is it that there are those who falsely employ the name of religion in our time, when even in that of the apostles men who were not apostles were called apostles? They were the men whom the apostle reproved in the Apocalypse. For there are many – and this is worse – who rejoice in the names of righteous men and Christians but are not righteous in the sight of the Lord. There are many who are called holy out of favour or love or in comparison with those who are worse; yet no one will immediately become what he is called by man, if it is not approved by God or perceived in the conscience. How many turn their gaze upon concupiscence but are believed by men to be chaste, when before the Lord they are judged adulterers? How many appear to be innocent of stealing the goods of others not because they do not wish to do so but because they are not able to? Yet a man is not innocent before the Lord unless he be pure in heart also; before him no man is righteous unless he fulfils his commandments and not only loves his neighbour but loves his enemy also with his whole heart,

---

[11] Cf. a similar passage in *Life*,11,1.

unless he not only does not do or speak any evil but does not return evil when he has suffered it. God wishes to find total innocence in man both inside and outside; but complete innocence is not found in the man who, though he is not guilty of doing evil, is guilty of wishing it. He is not innocent of doing harm, because he even harms himself; rather, he is certainly guilty of doing harm, because he does not spare even himself; and if a man does not spare himself, who else is there whom he would have spared if he could? Come to your Lord with your heart, come also with your body. Let your goodness call you to serve before anger hurries you away to be punished.

6.   But someone says, 'I am a young man; I have a lifetime before me; when I have reached the years of maturity, then I must think of fearing my Lord, since it is certainly my intention to return to my Lord at some time.' See, I have you by your own words: you are a voluntary follower of your own enemy. Where are you going, you who say that you will return some time? If the things that you are striving for are not evil or dangerous, why do you admit that you have to escape them after a while? Or if they are things that you have to abandon after a while, have to condemn because of your wish to repent, why do you pass over from a sure path to ways that are unsure? Why follow rough paths and desert the smooth? Why do I excuse myself on the grounds of my tender age from the need to undertake that journey which I could have and ought to have undertaken when I was even younger? I give pledges for the future, when I am uncertain even about tomorrow. In the view of our ancestors there was a blessing upon the fields; with us it is found in our souls. Their happiness was clearly on earth; ours is just as clearly in heaven. In their time those who had wives but no sons were thought by the people to be under a curse; in ours those are considered blessed 'who have wives as if they do not have them (1 Cor.7.29).' When Adam had as yet no wife, he was told: It is not good that the man should be alone (Gen.2.18); now, on the contrary, it is said: It is well for a man to remain as he is (1 Cor.7.26). There is one time and there is another time, says the Preacher, a time to embrace and a time to refrain from embracing (Eccles.3.1,5).[12] The ancients left father and mother to cleave to their wives; now Christians leave their parents to cleave to Christ. Then 'they were two in one flesh (Gen.2.24)'; now they are two in one spirit. 'If this is what we do,' they say, 'to what advantage has it been to have learned to read and write? Who will inherit that estate which he hopes for? Who will comfort a bereaved mother? Who will rule the household? Who will defend his dependants? Who, finally, will be able to put up with the rebukes of friends and fellow-citizens?'

7.   These are the chief of the false attractions which are set against the true life; this is the serpent who seduces with his guile so that he may deceive. He

---

[12] Our author – or a scribe – has substituted for the well-known words *omnia tempus habent*, 'everything has a time', the enigmatic and almost untranslatable *tempus et tempus*, which I have ventured to interpret for him.

burdens a man with the care of a mother and a family inheritance, so that he may become separated from his eternal inheritance and the family of God: but if we but arm ourselves, that is, with the scriptures and if we think more about the eternal than the transitory life, we shall crush his fiery darts underfoot with reason and truth. First, without doubt I would conform to this world, if I could be confident of remaining in it; I would adapt to a wife, if I did not perceive the hazards involved in marriage.[13] How many betrothed of both sexes have departed this world before the day appointed for their marriage? Should they squander their chastity by taking marriage vows merely to have no temporal pleasure either? How many men marry to have sons only for their wives to remain barren? How many men have cruelly lost sons whom they have educated to fulfil their expectations, so that you might suppose that they begot them and reared them merely in order to mourn them? The grief that stays with them after their sons' burial is greater than the joy after their birth. How many have come to hate after marriage the wives whom they loved before? How many are there who by their gold and money have acquired for themselves only boredom and weariness? How many who have given jewels only to receive poison in return?

8.   But, to omit the rest of my arguments, which are infinite, out of a desire to curtail the discussion, I shall suggest one point only, which is relevant to my case, that chastity is safe from all these evils. For in the midst of the wreckage caused by troubles and disasters chastity enjoys a peaceful and unsullied security. It does not have the ephemeral pleasures of the body, which the apostle still called tribulation, but it does have an everlasting habitation in the heavenly places. It does not have what death can take away in the end but it does have what eternal life can protect. It does not rejoice with men in this world but it will rejoice with the angels at the resurrection. It does not make merry at the birth of sons but neither does it grieve at the loss of those of whom it has been deprived. It does not see fit to possess an earthly inheritance, because it rejoices in the sure and certain hope of possessing paradise. It has no country house but neither does it pay tax. It lacks property but it is not plagued with the trouble of looking after it.

9.   The man who devotes the whole of himself to his Creator has nothing to give to Caesar. My life is not my own: the life which I had received I threw away; the life that I now have was acquired for me by the blood of my Lord. Bought as I was at a great price, I cannot do my own will:[14] the servant is not greater than his master (Mt.10.24). Can I ever be a happy property-owner in a world in which my master went in need, or expect the services of slaves where he himself served? He

---

[13] There is a similar passage in *Chast.*4,7,8.

[14] I have considered the possibility that *meam facere voluntatem* in our text means 'make my own will', since *voluntas* often has this sense in classical writers, e.g. Cicero, Tacitus and Pliny. But 'do my own will' is much more appropriate here in the sense of 'do what I want'; cf. 'do the will of God' in the scriptures.

washed the feet of the holy apostles; do I demand the services of my betters? He who deserved all had not where to lay his head; am I to desire all when nothing is owed to me? How can a soldier become wealthy in the area in which his general was a pauper? Let no one incite me to possess riches whose possession breeds slavery, whose pleasures, while they delight, also kill. It is the pomp and ceremony that the eyes see; but it is the care and stress which will torment the mind. Obligations connected with matters which expect to make profit from a source from which they procure only sins are evil, and while a man gains something to leave to his descendants, he condemns himself to eternal pauperdom. What will it profit a man, says the Lord, to gain the whole world and forfeit his life? Or what can a man give in return for his life (Mk.8.36,37)? With what impudence and with what a conscience does he search for something that he can give to defend himself in his hour of danger, when he has been unable to take anything away with him? From what source will he clothe himself when naked, redeem himself when a prisoner, see light when he is blind, if he will not equip himself beforehand by giving alms to the poor? Many in common with the five foolish virgins will long to provide themselves with what have now become necessities – but too late; and when they approach the merchants to buy light, they will remain in darkness.

10.   And pay attention to this, dearest brother, that just as we want to apply a remedy without any delay when our body falls ill, so we ought to devote care to our soul when it is sick, the soul upon which the Holy Spirit imprinted for a second time the impression of its own form in the holy laver[15] of the font. Let us look to the actions of our soul, which in this life receives the instruction needed to maintain our integrity: let it be its own witness, its own judge, and if it feels that anything has been done contrary to the teaching which it has received, let it condemn itself by its own judgement before the uncertain end of this world, lest it perish with it. Let it also pay attention to the limbs which it has unwisely raised up against itself as instruments of its own destruction, and when one of them has been defiled, let it be cleansed by the same means. Let its laughter be turned into lamentation, and its inebriation dissipated by fasting; and if its audacity has broken out into the commission of major crimes, even the deeds which are permitted must be rejected, so that those which are not permitted may be redeemed. It is much harder to be chastised by physical punishment than by one's own will, but it is better to be tormented by the fire of one's own conscience than by the flames of hell.[16] The flesh which has committed a deadly crime ought not to be freed from tears, or the soul which has lost its entitlement to life be relieved of grief. No man rejoices at the loss of a head of cattle; how much more should a man pour forth the whole burden of his grief at the death of a soul wrought in the image of God?

15 PLS has *lavacro* which, strictly speaking, is synonymous with *fontis*, as 'laver' is with 'font'.
16 The emphasis on 'will' and 'conscience' is typically Pelagian.

11.   Let us look also at those who lose their neighbours or friends or relatives, how they mourn, how they weep, how they refrain from laughing or feasting and how they give themselves over entirely to sorrow and lamentation at the loss of another. At such a time they show no concern for matters of state, they take no pleasure in banquets, they seek no relaxation in conversation . . .(The text breaks off at this point.)

14

To a Sister in Christ[1]

The title usually given to this letter, solely on the strength of Gennadius' comment quoted in the introduction to the letter *On Virginity*, is 'Letter of the Holy Presbyter Severus to his Sister Claudia concerning the Last Judgement'. But there is no mention of a Claudia in the letter itself, the addressee being addressed as 'sister' or 'dearest sister', nor, as Halm has pointed out, does it seem likely that Sulpicius Severus, an historian and hagiographer and friend of Paulinus of Nola and Martin of Tours who is said by Gennadius to have leaned towards Pelagianism in the latter part of his life, wrote it. Halm therefore places this letter, along with *On Virginity* and six others, in an Appendix to his critical edition of the letters of Sulpicius Severus (CSEL 1) under the heading of 'Letters of Dubious Ascription'.[2] References to an addressee as 'sister', 'brother', 'son' or 'father' are no more than Christian familiar titles normally used in contemporary epistolography.

The letter itself is one of a series of exhortations sent by her spiritual father to a young woman dedicated to the Christian faith and life at her own request and in the hope that they will compensate to some extent for his failure to visit her in person. On this occasion, he tells her, he will abandon his customary practice of urging her to avoid sin and indulgence and, instead, content himself with a final warning to her to persevere in her efforts without relaxation and a brief description of the fate which awaits sinners in the day of their judgement. After suggesting the kind of defence which they will offer for their conduct, he introduces the Patriarchs, Jesus and John the Evangelist to confront those who complain that they have not been given sufficient warning of their future punishment, thus confirming his statement that ignorance will not be accepted as an excuse for failure to comply with God's commandments.

Much of this is reminiscent of the documents in the Caspari corpus, and the style of the letter is more like that employed by the 'Pelagian Anonymous' of Part II than that of Pelagius himself in Part I. Plinval saw no reason to doubt its authenticity as a letter of the heresiarch but it is very unlikely that he did write

---

[1] *Epistula sancti Severi presbyteri ad Claudiam sororem suam de ultimo iudicio*; PL 20,223–27; CSEL 1,219–23; CPL 746.
[2] He also comments that the style of the letter is not that of Sulpicius.

it: true, there is a touch of Pelagianism here and there, and its eschatology and general tone entitle it to a place in this collection. But it is not patently Pelagian, more the work of a sympathiser who was thoroughly familiar with Latin literature of the classical period and obviously skilled in the arts of communication. The text, by the way, despite Halm's efforts to improve it, remains unreliable in several places.

Text

1.   After reading your letter, my feelings were so deeply affected that I was unable to hold back my tears. On the one hand, I wept with joy, because I could see from the very words of your letters that you are living in accordance with the commandments of our Lord God, while, on the other, I could not help grieving for lack of your company, because I was separated from you through no fault of my own and would have been so even more if you had not written to me. Was I, then, never to enjoy the company of such a sister? I bear witness by your hope of salvation[3] that I have often wanted to visit you, only to be prevented up to now by the one who is wont to prevent us.[4] I was impatient to satisfy my longing by seeing you, and it seemed that at the same time we would be doing our Lord's work, since, one comforting the other, we would be able to live with this world's burden trampled beneath our feet. But, as things are, I have given up any longer fixing a day and a time for a visit, since, whenever I have done so, I have found it impossible to carry out my purpose. So I shall wait upon the Lord's will in the hope that by my prayers and your supplications he may enable us to reap the fruits of our perseverance.[5]

2.   But because you have desired me to give you in all the letters which I sent to you precepts to guide your life and faith, I have now used up all my words by writing so often and am therefore quite unable to write anything fresh to you which I have not written before; actually, by God's favour you have no need of further admonition, since, by perfecting your faith at the very commencement, you reveal a devoted love in Christ. Yet there is one warning which I can give you – not to seek again the things that you have already transcended, not to long for the things which you have rejected, not to turn around and look back again once you have set your hand to the plough;[6] undoubtedly, if you do turn back and yield to this fault, your furrow must perforce lose its straightness, and the cultivator[7] will surely fail to receive his reward. Moreover, he does not receive even a

---

3   Or 'I call your salvation to witness'.
4   Cf. this passage with Rom.1.9–12, of which it may well be an imitation.
5   I have kept the old reading instead of Halm's *praesentia* ('presence').
6   Cf. Lk.9.62; cf. *To a New Penitent*,2.
7   As usual in those days long before the rise of feminism the masculine form is used even though it is inappropriate to the context and there is a feminine equivalent.

part of it if he has failed in part, for, as we have to flee from sin to righteousness, so the man who has once entered upon the path of righteousness must still beware not to lay himself open to sin; for it is written that 'his righteousness shall not profit the righteous on the day on which he has gone astray' (Ezek.33.12; LXX).[8] And so it is on this that we must take our stand, in this we must labour, in order that, once having escaped from sin, we may not lose the rewards prepared for us. Our enemy stands ready against us, hoping speedily to strike the man stripped of his shield of faith. So, let us not cast our shield aside, lest our flank be exposed; let us not put away our sword, lest the enemy begin to lose his fear of us; when he sees an armed man, he will go away. Nor are we ignorant of the fact that it is hard and difficult to struggle daily against the flesh and the world; but if you think of eternity, if you consider the kingdom of heaven which the Lord will undoubtedly deign to bestow on us even if we are sinners, what suffering is worthy, I ask you, to make us deserve such rewards? Besides, our struggle in this world is of short duration: even if death does not overtake us, old age will; the years slip by, time glides past, and, as I hope, the Lord Jesus will speedily call us to himself as persons whom he has greatly longed for.

3.   O, how happy will be that departure of ours, when Christ receives us in his own abode, purged from sin's stain by living a better life.[9] Martyrs and prophets will come up to us, apostles will join us,[10] angels will rejoice, archangels will be glad, and Satan, being conquered, will turn pale despite his bloodstained lips, since he will lose what he had prepared for himself in us.[11] He will see glory granted to us through pardon and merits honoured by glory; we shall triumph over our conquered enemy. Where shall the wise men of this world be seen then? Where shall the greedy man, the adulterer, the ungodly, the drunkard, the slanderer be recognized? What shall these wretches say in their own defence? 'We did not know you, Lord, we did not see that you were in the world; you did not send the prophets, you did not give the law to this world; we did not see the patriarchs, we did not read the examples of the saints. Your Christ was not on earth, Peter was silent, Paul refused to preach, the evangelist did not teach. There were no martyrs whose examples we might follow, no one foretold your future judgement, no one instructed us to clothe the poor, no one enjoined us to prohibit lust, no one persuaded us to fight against greed; we fell through ignorance, not knowing what we did!'

---

[8] Cf. Ezek.18.24, of which this 'quotation' is a paraphrase.
[9] Cf. *Law*,2.1; this is a typically Pelagian emphasis on a deliberate choice of behaviour in order to obtain remission of sins.
[10] Reading *iungentur*; the variant is *tangentur* ('will be touched'). Presumably our choice will depend on whether we take this clause with the previous one or those which follow immediately after it.
[11] Viz. the pleasure which he hoped to feel at the sight of their sins and subsequent rejection by God; cf. *To a New Penitent*,1.

4.   Against these the righteous Noah[12] will be the very first to proclaim from the band of saints on the other side, 'I, Lord, foretold that a flood would come upon us on account of men's sins, and after the Flood I offered myself as an example to good men, since I did not perish with the wicked who perished, that they might know both the salvation in store for the innocent and the punishment awaiting the sinners.' After him the faithful Abraham will confront them and say, 'I, Lord, laid the foundations of the faith by which the human race was to believe in you in the middle age of that world;[13] I did not hesitate, Lord, to offer up Isaac to you as a victim when he was still young, that those men might realize that there is nothing which ought not to be presented to the Lord, once they understood that I myself did not spare even my only son; I, Lord, at your command left my country and my kin, that this should be an example to encourage them to abandon the world's wickedness and the age's sin; I, Lord, was the first to recognize you, albeit in bodily form, nor did I hesitate to believe in the one whom I saw, though you seemed to me to be of a substance other than my own in order that man might understand how to judge not by the flesh but by the spirit.' And the blessed Moses will support him, saying, 'I, Lord, at your behest handed over the law to all of them, so that a spoken law might at least restrain those whom a free faith could not check;[14] I said, 'You shall not commit adultery (Ex.20.14),' that I might prevent licentiousness and fornication; I said, 'You shall love your neighbour (Lev.19.18),' that love might abound; I said, 'You shall worship the Lord alone,' that they might not sacrifice to idols or allow temples for them to exist;[15] I commanded that false witness should not be spoken, that I might shut their lips against all lies;[16] I explained the things which had been done and the words which had been said from the beginning of the world through the spirit of your goodness working in me, that the knowledge of the past might impart to them the teaching of the future; I prophesied your coming, Lord Jesus, that it might not come as a surprise to them to be able to acknowledge him whose future coming I had predicted earlier.'

5.   After him David, worthy to bear the seed of his Lord, will stand up and say, 'I, Lord, proclaimed you by every means possible; I declared that your name alone was to be served; I said, "Blessed is the man who fears the Lord (Ps.112.1)," 'I said, "The saints shall exult in glory (Ps.149.5)," I said, "The desire of sinners shall come to naught (Ps.112.10)," that these men might acknowledge you and

---

[12] For this series of statements about their efforts to warn the ungodly of the need to repent and change their ways cf. the similar passage in *BT*,19–22, in which the apostles defend themselves against a charge of failing to instruct Christians how to live in accordance with the divine commandments and teaching of Jesus.

[13] If we assume that the writer believed that Abraham lived c.2000 BC and that the world began c.4000 BC, this claim would be about right.

[14] A reference to God's introduction of the 'file of the law' to correct man's habitual tendency to sin through incorrect use of the freedom to choose which God had given him; see *Dem*.8 for a full account of this central Pelagian idea (Rees,1988,35).

[15] Cf. Dt.6.13; Ex.20.4.

[16] Ibid.16.

cease to sin; I, when I had been invested with royal power, yet lay down covered
with sackcloth, with ashes laid beneath me and all the emblems of my splendour
cast aside,[17] that these men might be given an example of gentleness and humility; I spared the enemies who desired to kill me, that these men might
approve of my compassion as something to be imitated.' After him Isaiah, worthy
of the Spirit of God, will not remain silent either but will say, 'I, Lord, when you
were speaking through my lips, gave this warning, "Woe to those who join house
to house (Is.5.8)," that I might set a limit to their greed; I bore witness that your
anger fell upon sinners, that, if hope of reward did not restrain them from
committing misdeeds, at least fear of punishment might do so.'

6.   After them and several others who have discharged their duty to instruct
us the Son of God himself will speak as follows, 'Assuredly, uplifted on my seat
aloft, holding heaven in the palm of my hand and earth within my fist, spread
wide within and without, being on the inside of everything that is brought forth
and on the outside of everything that moves, incalculable, infinite in natural
power,[18] to the sight invisible, to the touch inaccessible, I deigned to be born in
the flesh in order that I might live among you as the least of your number so as to
be able to subdue the hardness of your hearts and to mitigate the faithlessness
with which you treat the teachings of salvation, and, having laid aside the glory
of God, I put on the form and attire of a servant that, sharing with you your
bodily weakness, I might admit you in return to share in my glory by obeying the
precepts of salvation. I restored health to all the sick and infirm, hearing to the
deaf, sight to the blind, speech to the dumb, use of the feet to the lame, that I
might prevail on you by heavenly signs the more easily to believe in me and in
the things which I had proclaimed; I promised you the kingdom of heaven; I also
found a place in Paradise for the robber who acknowledged me just before the
moment of his death, that you might follow even the faith of him who had
merited remission of sins. And that, by my example offered on your behalf, you
too might be able to suffer, I suffered for you, lest man should hesitate to suffer for
himself what God had endured for man;[19] after my resurrection I revealed myself
that your faith might not be confounded; I issued a warning to the Jews in the
person of Peter, I preached to the gentiles in the person of Paul; nor do I regret
what I have done, since the results of it are good. Good men have understood my
work, faithful men have brought it to perfection, righteous men have completed
it, merciful men have consummated it, and there is a goodly number of martyrs
and saints. The men who made the objection we have just heard were surely in
the same body, in the same world as you. Why then can I find no good work in
you, your descendants of vipers? You have done no penance for your evil deeds
even up to the last day before your end. Of what importance is it that you

17 Halm suggested that the word *vestimentis* in the Latin text at the end of this clause is a
    gloss, and I have omitted it from my translation.
18 Or, with different punctuation, 'incalculable in nature, infinite in power'.
19 Cf. Acts 20.28, where there is doubt as to whether we should read 'with his own blood'
    or 'with the blood of his own Son'. The first verges on the heretical.

worship me with your lips, if you deny me with your deeds and works? Where are your riches now, where are your honours, your power, your pleasures? Upon you I pronounce a new sentence; you are subject to the judgement of which I gave warning before.'

7.   Then the evangelist will recite this judgement to those unhappy men, 'Go into outer darkness, where men will weep and gnash their teeth (Mt.22.13; 25.30).' Wretched are those who are not moved by these words! They will witness their own punishment and the glory of others. Let them make use of this world, provided that they do not enjoy the eternity prepared for the holy; let them abound in riches, let them recline on gold here, provided that they are poor in eternity, for of them it is written: The rich suffer want and hunger (Ps.34.10).[20] But, in respect of the good, scripture has added the following words: But those who seek the Lord shall lack no good thing (ibid.). Therefore, my sister, though these men mock us, though they declare us to be foolish and miserable, let us rejoice all the more at their abuse, for by it glory is heaped on us but punishment on them. But let us not laugh at their folly; let us rather grieve for their unhappiness, because there is among them a great number of our own people, and if we can but win them over, then our glory is increased. Yet let them do as they please, let them be to us as gentiles and publicans; but let us keep ourselves safe and sound. If now they rejoice while we grieve, we shall rejoice later while they grieve in turn. Farewell, dearest sister, most beloved in Christ.

---

[20] Vulgate and LXX.

15

To Pammachius and Oceanus[1]

The above title[2] appears to have been given to this letter for no better reason than that it was at one time assumed to have been written by Jerome and that Pammachius and Oceanus are known to have been friends of his.[3] But, as Erasmus pointed out as long ago as the fifteenth century, there does not seem to be anything in the letter which is at all relevant to Pammachius or Oceanus, unless Jerome had had occasion to change his mind about them: elsewhere he always proclaims their piety and other good qualities, here they are upbraided for their failings![4] The only indication that the author of the letter was writing to more than one person is in his use on two occasions of *fratres*, 'my brothers', in addressing them – Erasmus nodded here, by the way, since he suggested that there was nothing to show that the letter was sent to two persons rather than one; rather, we might say that there is nothing to show that it was sent to two persons and not several. And now that Jerome is no longer believed to have written the letter, we might justifiably maintain that there is no longer good reason to suppose that Pammachius and Oceanus *were* the recipients.

But there is still just a possibility that they were, if the letter was written by Pelagius or one of his followers, who might well find Pammachius and Oceanus to be very appropriate targets for a brief homily of this kind especially in view of the obvious respect in which they were held by Pelagius' old enemy, Jerome.[5] There can be no doubt that the letter is Pelagian in tone and content: there is the reference to will and the ability to use it in section 1, and there are also common Pelagian themes in the succeeding sections, for example, disobedience

---

1. *Epistula ad Pammachium et Oceanum de renuntiatione saeculi* or *Epistula Fastidii ad Fatalem*; PL 30, 239–42; CPL 633,32=742.
2. The alternative is derived from a title attached to a manuscript edited by J.B. Pitra which reads *Epistula Fatavi ad Fautalem* and was corrected by him. Poor old Fatalis! How overcome he would have been if he had received all the letters apparently sent to him by his friend Fastidius!
3. See PL 30,1034 and 1039 in the Index to Jerome's works for his references to them.
4. For Erasmus' comment those who can read Latin may like to consult Vallarsi's note in PL 30,239.
5. We find another letter allegedly addressed to an Oceanus in PL 30,282–88 (also pseudo-Jerome).

to God's commandments, hypocrisy, flattery, lack of spiritual growth, the insatiate appetite of greed, the inevitability of eternal judgement and, to sum all this up, the failure to renounce the world and all its pleasures in the name of Jesus. In fact, Plinval originally attributed this letter to Pelagius himself, though he was to modify this claim later;[6] perhaps he realized that Pelagius could never have written it, since the writer's style is quite the opposite to his. It has something of the fire and aggressiveness of the 'Pelagian Anonymous' of Part II; but *he* could never have crammed so much into such a small space.

Despite, or perhaps by reason of, its brevity this little homily is a pleasure to read: it is concise and to the point and at times resembles the Roman historian Tacitus; like Tacitus' Latin its terse phrases and compact sentences are often not at all easy to translate, and the present translator has to admit that there are one or two places where he cannot be certain that he has been able to convey the sense which the writer intended.

Text

1.   A man who invites an Ethiopian to use his private bath, even if he does not succeed in removing his black pigmentation for him, surely accepts payment from him and even rejoices in the profit of the market, though unable to be joyful at the other's whiteness. In the same way, without a doubt, a man who cautions a disobedient Christian in words that come from God, though unable to remove the recusant's sins, yet receives a reward for ministering in a spirit of true charity. But do I say this because I despise you? Do I speak thus because I do not love you greatly? I reply in the words of the apostle: God is my witness (Phil.1.8): I shall continue to do what I am doing but I do not reject you; I do grieve, however, to see evidence of unfaithfulness, not faith, appearing in my friends, because the testimonies which you hold are Jewish, not Christian. Seeing, you do not see, and hearing, you do not hear. I shall put it in strong terms: I am disturbed on two counts, in that I fear to offend those who hear me but I fear more those who reject the commandments, since those who pretend not to hear God's word are considered to be in a worse state than idols. They have ears but not the will to use them; they do not hear, they do not touch with their hands, they do not grasp with them.

2.   Hence, in comparison with evil men, they are better, because they do not covet with their eyes or run off along paths which are contrary and hostile to the will of God; but objects which are naturally deaf are rightly judged to be better than men who are disobedient. Let the prophet speak, if I am lying; let

---

6   See Plinval, 1943,44; 1947,9; nevertheless, he approved of this letter to the extent that he described it as 'interesting'.

David speak who did not deny that men of this sort are to be compared to serpents: Like the deaf adder that stops its ears, so that it does not hear the voice of the charmer (Ps.58.5). And let them consider whether it be not right to compare them to serpents who conceal with all their skill and cunning the fact that nature has not granted them the gift of hearing. Can men be called Christians when they surrender the name which was given to the first human beings? Jeremiah says: Behold, their ears are closed and they cannot hear this (Jer.6.10).[7] Yet not because they cannot but because their will has introduced a factor of impossibility by acting in opposition to nature, since for a long time their innate morals have been corrupted through habitual evil-doing as they have gone on doing the opposite and have been brought down by evil works. In the same way, vessels full of mud cannot receive and contain pure liquid, and a field choked with thorns cannot feed the seeds cast upon it but merely suffocates them, unless the thorns are first rooted out by the labours of the farmer; so too a mind filled with the attractions of worldly concerns cannot sustain the divine word, unless it first cuts down within itself with the scythe of the gospel all the cares of this world and the sources of all its crimes. Perhaps I seem to some to sin less, because God passes it over for the time being; but the day will come when our deeds have to be displayed as if they were painted on a tablet.[8]

3, 1. How many there are for whom it would have been better on that day if they had been without the sensations in their limbs and the strength in their vitals! And how many who are mute and speechless will be happier then than those who can speak! And how many shepherds will then be preferred to philosophers, how many country bumpkins to orators, how many whose dull wits will be preferred to Cicero's subtleties! Job, a holy man, concerned for his good name even in his time of trial, called out thus in his grief and pain: What does light profit in time of torture? To what end were my knees joined to me? To what end did I suck the breasts? Why did I not die in the womb and perish as soon as I came out of the womb (cf. Job 3.11,12).[9] If God's friend said this while still in the light of day, what will his enemies say when they are in the darkness? If he groans when fever burns him, what will the man do whom hell consumes? If he, a man whose feet have always run in the love of God, grieves that his knees have been

---

[7]   RSV; AV has 'uncircumcised' instead of 'closed', as do the Vulgate, LXX and the Hebrew text.
[8]   Or, possibly, 'as if they were recorded in an account book'.
[9]   The two verses have been placed in a different order from that generally accepted, and our author has either misquoted or misunderstood the second question: 'Why were my knees joined to me?' surely makes little or no sense. But he is not alone in finding the clause difficult, since there are many variants in editions and translations. The Vulgate has *'quare exceptus genibus?'*, 'why was I received by (her) knees?', which would presumably refer to the mother's squatting in order to give birth, as she may well have done at that time in an Eastern Mediterranean country, and thus receiving the baby on her knees. But I should not venture into the sacred precincts of the biblical scholars and exegetes.

joined to him, what will the man say whose feet have never stood in the truth? One who led a good life regrets that he lived after his birth from the womb, because a worm which would itself have to die was eating him: what will those who lead wicked lives do, when the eternal fire and a worm which will never die await them? This is a hard saying; who can listen to it (Jn.6.60): that is what those disciples said who ceased to follow in Christ's footsteps in the gospel and, having taken offence at the divine word, chose to love this world rather than God; those whose stomach is their God refuse to listen to instructions to cultivate the practice of fasting.

2. Recommendations of chastity are an offence to the dissolute; as the prophet says: A straight way is an abomination to the unrighteous.[10] Already in days of old it was said by Isaiah that Christ would be a stumbling-block for infidels.[11] I cannot flatter lest I should deceive my brother, and the words of Solomon strike me, when he says: The words of flatterers are sweet to the taste but they strike down to the innermost parts of the stomach (Pr.18.8).[12] The doctor who allows a wound to heal before the festering has subsided is not trustworthy; we cannot always be giving you milk, but neither ought you to keep on behaving as infants.

4. You say to me, 'How many years have passed since we were born again in Christ?' Let anyone consider how far he has progressed in the heavenly age since that time. I do not know how pleasing to their parents are infants who are only five or ten years of age, if they persist in keeping the tiny stature with which they were born. What then can be said of us if calculation of the time which has passed finds us to be not just tiny but abortive. 'They will go from virtue to virtue,' it has been written of good Christians. Let us see if we *are* Christians: what virtue has been added to our stature since our rebirth in Christ, what humility in prosperity, what patience in adversity, what capacity to rejoice in time of tribulation, to be happy in time of loss, to display indulgence when offended or chastity when we have an opportunity to be wanton? Others move on daily from virtue to virtue, we from weakness to weakness; others become better from one moment to another, we are often made only worse, as if we do not expect to face the same judge as the others. We are fools if we have assented to the one Saviour of all those who believe and yet do not believe that there will be one Judge. 'One faith, one baptism, one Church, one God', says the apostle (cf. Eph.4.5,6).[13]

---

[10] I have not been able to trace this quotation to its source; in fact, the editor of PL 30 does not even print it as a quotation.
[11] Literally, 'a block for stumbling over'; cf. *Law*,10,1, where the word used is *skandalon*, a transliteration of the Greek word which is frequently found in the NT (See Arndt/Gingrich, s.v. *skandalon*,760. The usual Latin expression is *lapis offensionis*, 'a stone for stumbling over'.)
[12] The first clause is closer than the Vulgate and LXX to our modern translations.
[13] It is interesting to find the phrase 'one Church' inserted in the text here.

5.   The man, then, who is evil today will be worse tomorrow, the man who is greedy today will be greedier tomorrow: a year ago one country house was enough to satisfy my greed; now, this year, perhaps even a fifth is not sufficient. Formerly my mind was stretched to the limit to provide me with ten *solidi*,[14] now a hundred have begun to be of little value to me; and when true Christians, true sons of God who go on from virtue to virtue, rejoice at being given an opportunity to display virtue if they lose something, I am unable to eat my breakfast free from anxiety unless I am acquiring other people's money. What are you doing, blind greed? Why are you so cruel in dealing with an infant? Why so savage in dealing with another man's son? Are you turning upside down the ordering of nature and religion? You have now set at the bottom what ought to have been at the top, and senseless gold rules over all alike. And what is it or what kind of thing is it, I ask, that turns us away from God? What is this brilliance, and how great is that on account of which the brilliance of the true sun is lost to me? Gold and silver are only yellow clay obtained from sand and ore, and, as the prophet says, 'Gold is the word which causes us to stumble,' since, when the mind's judgement has been overturned, it is sold to lust by means of gold: a man acquires a *solidus* by employing the same cunning which loses him his soul, he gains a painted likeness of the emperor and loses the true likeness of Christ. Do you want to know how dangerous are the love of possessions and the urge to acquire money? It was through this that Judas betrayed the Saviour, and surely, when it is heard or read of, so great a crime causes us all to shudder; we condemn the impious disciple with all our might, yet in our ignorance we stab ourselves with our own dagger.

6.   How many Judases among us condemn Judas? How many of them, when they betray their own souls by their greed and hand them over to eternal torment, become both traitors and also dead men? Do we suppose, my brothers, that the prophets are joking when they preach, the apostles laughing when they speak, and Christ threatening judgement to no avail? But jokes are not jokes when punishments interrupt them; let them be believed to have spoken in jest but only if they suffered in jest! Isaiah is cut by a saw; Daniel is cast to the lions; Paul is maimed by a sword; Peter is hanged on a cross after the example of our Lord – and all this so that they might call us back from our sins by their teaching. But I fear that the gift of these divine acts of kindness has the opposite effect upon the disobedient, and what was given to us in this world for our salvation leads only to punishment at the judgement; I fear that our faith is more of a joking matter than their faith and their words; I fear that we shall not be able to save ourselves with our jokes, and as we enter the church with laughter on our lips, so he too will laugh at us, as it is written: He who dwells in the heavens will laugh them to scorn (Ps.2.4). There are many things which could be said but the end of my sheet of parchment also brings to a conclusion both the distaste

---

[14]   A golden coin introduced by Constantine: our '£.s.d' stands for *librae, solidi, denarii.*

aroused in you by my rough and unpolished style of writing and also my own labours. I have only one point which I am still anxious to make, that Christians ought to love heaven and not earth, to obey God's word rather than the devil's and to fear eternal judgement more than that of men.[15]

---

[15] Cf. the almost identical summary in *To a New Penitent*,8.

16

To a New Penitent[1]

Here we have a brief homily addressed to a man who has recently become a 'penitent' by taking a vow to follow an ascetic way of life in token of his repentance of his former behaviour and involving the wearing of mean apparel and the distribution of his worldly wealth.[2] It is not particularly Pelagian, indeed quite the contrary if we accept Caspari's view that the sentence 'Let us act courageously and, imploring his help, apply ourselves to keeping his commandments as far as we are able' (section 6) is "quite unpelagian";[3] but, in fact, there is nothing especially unpelagian in the sentence quoted, and the warnings given to the new penitent are very like those which appear in Pelagian documents of a similar nature. Pelagians were dedicated to the leading of an ascetic life and thus setting an example to fellow-Christians not by entering a monastery but by remaining in the world, though not of it; it was by adopting this kind of vocation that Pelagius began to be called a 'monk', a title which he himself did not seek or commend to his followers: 'I want you to be called a Christian, not a monk.'[4] A better reason for not identifying the writer as a Pelagian might be his tendency to quote Jerome, for example, in section 5, where he cites the latter's deprecation of the practice of 'throwing a cheap cloak over our shoulders but keeping a full purse hidden in it'.[5]

Nevertheless, despite his suspicion that the author of the letter may not be a Pelagian, Caspari still attributed it to Agricola, as one might expect, and others have since followed him. He is particularly struck by three passages in it: 'Let us run to him with a glowing, not a lukewarm spirit . . . disciple' and 'Everyone may say . . . to me' (both in section 6) and 'Blessed is the man . . . precious stones'

---

1   *Humelia de penetentibus* or *Homilia de paenitentibus*, usually referred to by its opening words, *Magnum cumulatur*; PLS 1,1694–98; CPL 762; Caspari,171–78.

2   See especially section 5; a developed system of public Penance had emerged by the third century, involving enrolment in the order of penitents with the consent of the bishop, exclusion from Communion for the time being and commitment to prayer, fasting and almsgiving until sufficient penance had been done and the penitent was considered fit to rejoin his congregation, though bound to continence for the rest of his life (see Livingstone, under 'Penance').

3   Caspari, 397,n.2.

4   *Law*,9,3; see Rees,1988,xiv and n.26.

5   I have not been able to locate this quotation.

(section 7), since they are almost identical with passages in *Law*,5,2; 6,2; and 3,3 respectively.[6] He does not share Vallarsi's view that they were written by the same man, however, but suggests that the author of *Law* was the copier; if we believe Pelagius to have been the author of *Law*, the reverse is more likely to be true. Morin thought that Fastidius was the author of this letter, which is no surprise either; Plinval is not really interested in it, since it is clearly not Pelagius' work, and consigns it on the grounds of its lack of literary value to the same category of *'rapsodies inhabiles'* as the letter said to have been addressed to Fatalis.[7]

The letter consists mainly of bits of advice or encouragement, supported by the usual scriptural quotations, which often follow the Septuagint more closely than the Vulgate and give one a distinct impression that they are quoted from memory or liberally adapted to suit the author's purposes. He is certainly further from the Vulgate than the authors of the documents contained in Parts I and II, and if he is quoting from a contemporary Latin Bible, it is unlikely to have been the same version as those used by Pelagius and the 'Pelagian Anonymous'.

Text

1.   The soul's cup of joy is full when it has acquired the remedy which its Creator supplies or has been carried into the harbour of true salvation from the dangerous hurricanes of this world and has climbed to the top of the rock of safety from the muddy depths of the time in which it lives. So, dearest brother, I found myself full of joy and gladness when I saw that you had entered upon such a state of conversion and heard that you were having recourse to the medicines of repentance. The Lord, who stung my heart to love, will also give me the speech with which to express myself. First, I should like to praise your intention; but praise of a famous labour does not admit of the use of the language of flattery. It is indeed quite inadequate that as wretched a man as I should proclaim and eulogize on earth what the angels honour in heaven, seeing that the angels, in the opinion of the gospel, rejoice more over one penitent than over ninety-nine righteous persons who need no repentance (cf. Lk.15.7). Therefore, since what truth says is true and what has the approval of truth is worthy of our faith, we must believe that the angels rejoice at the conversion of a penitent. But because angels rejoice, demons are sad: the angels rejoice because a man is going to ascend to heaven, the demons are sad because a man is going to ascend there out of their presence; the former are glad because their number is increased, the latter are sorrowful because they have lost one of their company.[8]

---

6   Caspari,392f.
7   Plinval,1943,30; see also the introduction to the letter *To Fatalis* (?),No.13.
8   Cf. *To a Sister in Christ*,3.

2.   Rejoice then and be glad, most beloved brother, and give thanks to
Christ without ceasing, since, in offering an example to others, the Lord has seen
fit to receive you into the band of the righteous because of your conversion to a
better life. For no one comes to the Lord unless he has reached out his hand to
him according to what he himself says in the gospel: No one comes to me unless
the Father, who sent me, draws him (Jn.6.44). So we must take every possible
precaution to prevent that old serpent, whose habit it has been right from the
beginning to set his hidden snares, from throwing over us any of those nets of
concupiscence which we could well do without, since it is written in the words of
the apostle that he has a thousand names and a thousand devices for harming us.
And if we have learned or are able to discover only a few things out of so many
and that with difficulty, what are we to do except ask for God's help against his
attacks; for it has never been his custom to prepare his traps in the open but in
secret, since he can see that there is no point in rushing at Christ's defences in a
fiery mood, and so he draws back a little to do battle with us at a later stage.[9] This
is the reason for the debates that start up within us, so that what once pleased us
begins to arouse dissatisfaction in our minds and what was once the object of our
prayers begins to be rejected: likewise the mind begins to love once again what it
had previously repelled, that so many, putting their hands to the plough and then
looking back again,[10] are prevented from entering the kingdom of God. (cf.
Lk.9.62), while they begin to love again what they know that in reality they
reject.

3.   Let us then give this question our most careful attention and recollect
what the most blessed Paul says: Forgetting what lies behind and straining to
what lies before, I press on toward the prize of the upward call of Christ
(Phil.3.13,14).[11] Let us speed on then with all our strength,[12] in order that after
many struggles have been completed, after insults, after abuse from evil men we
may be able to say confidently with the apostle: I have fought the good fight, I
have finished the race, I have kept the faith (2 Tim.4.7). If we wish to proclaim
these words with a clear conscience, let us labour among the strangers and the
poor here, so that later we may be rewarded in our fatherland there, let us sow in
tears here, so that we may reap in joy there according to the saying of the
prophet: May those who sow in tears reap in joy (Ps.12.5). Let us cut out greed
from our hearts as far as we are able, let us pluck out pride, let us root out envy,
and instead let us plant humility and sow love in them, and let true affection bear
its fruit.[13]

---

[9]   Ibid.2.
[10] Ibid. and see n.6.
[11] The same quotation appears in *Dem.*27,4 and *Cel.*32, where the word used for 'prize' in
      the Vulgate is *bravium* (from Greek *brabeion*), found also in 1 Cor.9.24, and as *brabeum*
      in late Latin writers, for example, Prudentius and Tertullian.
[12] For the need for speed cf. e.g., *Law,*9,1; *Dem.*27,4; *Riches,*20,5, etc.
[13] Another familiar instruction; cf. e.g. *Riches,*19,2 and *To Pammachius and Oceanus,*15,2.

4.   Let us hearken to the testimony given by John in his Epistle, when he says: Do not love the world or the things in the world. If any one loves the world, love for the Father is not in him. For all that is in the world, the lust of the flesh and the lust of the eyes and the pride of human life, is not of the Father but is of the world. And the world will pass away, and the lust of it; but he who does the will of God abides for ever (1 Jn.2.15–17). And the apostle James says: Do you not know that friendship with the world is enmity with God (Jas.4.4)? For this means that if anyone wishes to be a friend of the world, he is an enemy of God. And the apostle Paul teaches us thus, when he says: If then you have been raised with Christ, seek the things that are above, where Christ is, seated at the right hand of God. Set your minds on the things that are above, not on things that are on earth. For you have died, and your life is hid with Christ in God. But when Christ who is your life appears, then you also will appear with him in glory (Col.3.1–4). As it seems to me, the holy apostles have given us these instructions in order that we may not love those who are lovers of this world and mockers of God's ministers but those who are known to be lovers of Christ and his saints in accordance with the warning given by the Lord in the gospel, when he says: A new commandment I give to you, that you love one another. By this all men will know that you are my disciples, if you have love for one another (Jn.13.34,35). As in another passage the evangelist relates of our Lord himself: And when he had entered the temple and was in the midst of the crowds, some one came to him and told him that his mother and his brothers were standing outside, asking for him. And stretching out his hand to his disciples, he said, 'Here are my brothers! For whoever does the will of my Father in heaven is my mother and brother and sister (Mt.12.46,47,49,50).'[14]

5.   Let us give our serious attention and consideration to the way the Lord himself invites us to his kingdom. This is what he ways: Come to me, all who labour and are heavy laden, and I will give you rest (Mt.11.28). Let not our eyes turn downwards to the earth again, when now they are raised so high to heaven with God's inspiration. Let the earth keep what belongs to it; let them collect thorns and thistles who desire to bear the likeness of men; for us, however, it is good to cleave to heaven. So let us find friends for ourselves far away from the mammon of unrighteousness, friends who will receive us into our eternal place of habitation. It is not enough to have put away your splendid garments and to have assumed indifferent ones, to have put on a humble face before men, if your heart burns with greed before God. As for the future, as the holy Jerome says, it is not important or useful to us to throw a cheap cloak over our shoulders but keep a full purse hidden in it. If we cannot hear the Lord saying: Do not be anxious about the morrow (Mt.6.34), let us listen to the apostle: If we have food and clothing, let us be content with them (1 Tim.6.8); if we cannot hear the Lord with his apostles, let us listen to the servant with the soldiers: The ransom of a

---

[14] The alterations and omissions here are extensive and support the idea that the writer is quoting from memory.

man's soul is his personal wealth (Pr.13.8)[15] It is inappropriate for us to enrich with gifts men for whom the Christian religion seems to be an object of abuse, with whom chastity is judged to be detestable, humility to be evil, fasting to be hateful and poverty entered into voluntarily for Christ's sake to be madness. These are the people who gladly revile God's servants, belittle them in their own banquets and put them to sit opposite the sons of their own mother in order to cause offence; they are also the ones whom the Lord condemns in the gospel, when he says: It will be better for him to have a great millstone fastened round his neck and to be drowned in the sea (Mt.18.6). Therefore the day of examination will come, when they will say to one another with a groan, as the holy scripture testifies: These are the men whom we once held in derision and made a byword of reproach – we fools! We thought that their lives were madness and that their end was without honour. Why have they been numbered among the sons of God? And why is their lot among the saints (Wis.5.4,5)?

6.   Woe to those who act thus, whose speech crawls along like a crab, who prefer to give their love to this world rather than to God! For the psalmist pronounces sentence on them, saying: Some glory in chariots and others in horses, but we shall glory in the name of our Lord; they are ensnared and fall, but we have risen and stand upright (Ps.20.7,8). Let us lift up the eyes of our heart to him who lives in heaven, and 'as the eyes of servants look to the hands of their masters, or as the eyes of a maid to the hands of her mistress, so let our eyes look to the Lord our God, till he have mercy upon us (Ps.123.1,2)'; and when he has taken pity on us, let us not depart from him or be separated from the one who said: Lo, I am with you always to the close of the world (Mt.28.20); but, rather, let us act courageously and, imploring his help, apply ourselves to keeping his commandments insofar as we are able.[16] Let us pay no attention to the vanity and empty follies and love of this world, which we know to be fleeting, temporary and ephemeral, not permanent. Let not tribulation separate us from the love of Christ but, groaning and pouring tears from our hearts, let us humble ourselves in the sight of the Lord and 'let us kneel before the Lord our Maker, let us come into his presence with thanksgiving and call upon him in songs of praise (Ps.95.6,2)'. Let us run to him with a glowing, not a lukewarm spirit, since Christ does not love a lukewarm disciple. Everyone may say what he wishes; but meanwhile I formed my own judgement, based on my consciousness of my own insignificance, that it is better for me to be put out of countenance before sinners on earth than before holy angels in heaven or wherever it may please him to reveal his judgement to me.

7.   And though the apostle instructs us to pray without ceasing, yet, while we appear to have some time at our disposal for managing the tasks entrusted to

---

[15] Here the quotation is from LXX: idios ploutos in LXX becomes propriae divitiae in the quotation but that is not in the Vulgate; I have rendered it as 'personal'.
[16] See the introduction to this letter.

us, let us not cease to pray to the Lord at the appointed hours too, as the authority of the Church teaches us,[17] and implore his mercy, since the man who is instructed in the law of the Lord is indeed blessed: Blessed is the man who meditates on his law day and night (Ps.1.2), whose mind and words are always going over God's utterances again and again. Such a man is not undeservedly praised in the words of God uttered through Solomon, when he says: Happy is the man who finds wisdom; for it is better for him to gain it than treasures of gold and silver, more precious than precious stones (Pr.3.13–15; LXX). If therefore, dearest one, we are conscious in ourselves of any temptations – since an enemy is in the habit of imposing them upon us frequently –, let us not be discomforted or grow sad but rather, as we have said, beseech Christ's help to enable us to repel the devil's temptations, because 'the sufferings of this present time are not worth comparing with the glory which is to be revealed to us in the future. But creation waits with eager longing for the revealing of the sons of God (Rom.8.18,19).' And in another passage: Blessed is the man who endures trial, for, when he has stood the test, he will receive the crown of life, which God has promised to those who love him (Jas.1.12).

8.   But since I must take care not to become loquacious, I ought now to bring my homily to an end. My Lord and dearest one, my friend always longed for in Christ, please see fit to receive this communication from my humble self with a kindly and well-disposed heart. Pardon me, if perchance anything that I have said has been clumsily worded, since love knows not fear and 'wounds inflicted by a friend are more trustworthy than the kisses of an enemy given spontaneously (Pr.27.6; LXX).' I have only one point which I am still anxious to make, that, being Christians, we ought to love heaven, not earth, and to obey the will of God rather than that of this world, and to fear eternal judgement more than the judgement of men.[18] Pray for me and act in such a way that my writing and your reading of this letter may bring only credit to us both.

---

[17] A characteristic of Penance was the 'prayer of the hours'.
[18] Cf. *To Pammachius and Oceanus,5,* for an almost identical summary of the Christian's obligations.

To a Lapsed Penitent[1]

This brief letter was at one time attributed to Pelagius himself by Plinval,[2] though it is difficult to see why: for one thing the style is nothing like that of Pelagius, and at the same time there is very little which is reminiscent of Pelagianism to be found in it except the severe terms in which its rebuke is framed and the uncompromising picture of the true penitent which it paints. It is addressed to a man whose pride in having taken the vows of a penitent deceives him into relaxing the rules which those vows oblige him to obey; it is the same old story that we hear again and again in Pelagian letters and treatises: too many Christians, virgins, penitents, widows congratulate themselves on their titles without upholding the obligations which those titles bring with them. In this case it is clearly imperative that the addressee should be faithful to his promises through a renewal of his repentance in true humility. The parable of the Prodigal Son points out to him the way ahead, and the examples of the Good Shepherd and the woman who lost her drachma in the dirt assure him that Jesus will come to his rescue and return him to his proper place in the ranks of the righteous. The only alternative to such a course is eternal damnation.

One of the most interesting features of this letter is its very strong resemblance to a sermon wrongly attributed to Ambrose for no obvious reason,[3] so strong that there can be no doubt that one was copied from the other, though the phrasing is often markedly different, as is the general style. The pseudo-Ambrose omits some of the quotations given by this letter, notably, all the lamentations which follow the words, 'turn not away from thy servant in anger' in section 4, while this letter omits the first paragraph referring to the Pharisees and the concluding words of the pseudo-Ambrose 'to which the Lord leads us, he who lives and reigns with the Father and the Holy Spirit world without end, Amen.' This kind of inaccuracy *inter alia* tempts me to suggest that it is our writer who

---

[1] *De homine paenitente et adhuc in saeculo commorante* or *Epistula de vera paenitentia*; PL 30,242–45; CPL 633,33–743.

[2] 1943,44.

[3] PL 17,657–60; the editor, the great Migne himself, comments: 'How unjustifiably this letter was ascribed to Ambrose no one could fail to detect even from a first reading.'

was the copyist but it is impossible to be certain and the matter is not of vital importance. The pseudo-Ambrose is certainly the more polished piece of writing, since our letter is no more than mediocre as an example of Latinity. Did our man take the pseudo-Ambrose and rewrite it, adding extra citations from the Bible, including a long series of quotations and semi-quotations at the end of section 4, culled perhaps from a contemporary missal for penitents, and recasting it in his own words, a practice not unknown among undergraduates and, sometimes, their teacher, or did the preacher who composed the pseudo-Ambrose come across some excellent ideas rather roughly expressed and rephrase them in language more suitable for the pulpit, something which harassed clergy have been known to do at times? Or were both borrowing from the same original text?[4] The Latin text of our letter, by the way, is often unreliable.

Text

1.   I rise to attack you, whom I know to be faithful.[5] My rebuke hurries towards you, whom I believe to be proud. You maintain that you are repentant, when your entire life is spent in this world; you maintain that you are repentant, when you are taking up again habits that you once discarded; you maintain that you are repentant, when you overlook God in your pursuit of the devil's works. I do not know in what your repentance consists. You maintain that, while enveloped in God's righteousness, you have added pride to it; you maintain that, while seeking to enjoy another's flesh, you become as weary as a dog returning to its vomit, as a hungry dog or a pig worn out by the heat and lying prostrate on the muddy soil. I cannot discover where your penitence is; I have walked to the place of penitence, and I have not found your penitence there: you who had deserted the world can be found only there again. You who laid down the pride of the flesh now bend your shoulder to carry it again; you who had turned your back on greed are now turning back to meet it again; you who had rejected vanity now return to its favour; you who had fled the pomp of the world have now fallen into its hands again. Yet you walk about proudly and with your head erect, not

---

4   For a similar, though by no means parallel, example of plagiarism, cf. the introduction to No.12. Is there any significance in the fact that the copyist was certainly the preacher in that instance? And that his citations are so much more accurate?

5   This does not sound very convincing: how can a man who has failed to fulfil his vows be described as 'faithful'. Possibly my translation of the Latin word *surgo* is too vigorous and it would be better to say something like: 'I rise to address you whom I know to be one of the faithful'? But with a writer like this we can never be certain; indeed, with such a text, we cannot even be sure that the last word was not *infidelem*, 'unfaithful'. This would certainly be more consistent with the use of *fidelis* in the first sentence of section 2 and would give us a contrast between the penitent's condition now and at his baptism.

knowing that it is written: What has our arrogance profited us? And what good has our boasted reputation[6] brought us (Wis.5.8)? And again that it has been said: All those things have vanished like a shadow (ibid.9).

2.   You recall that you *were* faithful when you had been renewed by the water of baptism, as it is written: Wash yourselves; make yourselves clean; remove the evil of your doings from your minds (Is.1.16).[7] He exhorts them to be washed; but you, though you had been washed, became dirty again. You cannot now be washed all over again, as Peter says to the Lord: Lord, not my feet only but wash also my hands and my head, wash me all over. He who has bathed once does not need to be washed again (Jn.13.9,10).[8] But if you want to be cleansed again, give alms, and, lo!, all of you is clean, because it is alms that cleanses all dirt. Humble yourself in all things, and you will find grace before God. Be subject to him and beseech him, lest you strive to do evil; for those who do evil will be wiped out (Ps.37.9). Pray to the Lord with tears every day to see if perchance your sins may be absolved, 'since God opposes the proud but gives grace to the humble (Jas.4.6; cf. 1 Pet.5.5)'. Remember the son who went to live in a far-off country and squandered his substance among harlots by riotous living but later, having been humbled, came again to himself and said: How many of my father's hired servants have bread enough and to spare, and I perish here with hunger? I will arise then and go to my father, and I will say unto him, 'Father, I have sinned against heaven and before you, I am no longer worthy to be called your son; treat me as one of your hired servants (Lk.15.17–19)'. But the father, when he saw his son's humility and that he was worn out through lack of means, was moved by pity and ordered a fatted calf to be killed for his humble son. Remember therefore, my son, that Christ died for you, the Christ who had formerly been the fatted calf. But the man's elder son became sorrowful: why was Christ, who had been the fatted calf, killed? His father, however, reproached him, saying: Son, you are always with me, and all that is mine is yours. It is fitting for you to make merry and be glad, for this my son was dead, and is alive again; he was lost, and is found (ibid.31,32). Blessed are the people for whom Christ died! What joy their Father shows, when that which has died comes to life again, and that which has been lost is found!

3.   See, you have now been made whole! Do not sin, that nothing worse may befall you (Jn.5.14); look then at the place from which you have fallen, and beat your breast and perform acts of penitence. If you do anything less, the Lord will come to you and remove your candle from its place, unless you do penance. Remember, my son, that Christ left the ninety-nine righteous men and sought

---

[6]   All the texts and translations I have been able to consult give us 'arrogance', not 'reputation'.
[7]   The same applies here, where we have 'minds' instead of the usual 'eyes'.
[8]   This is a very rough rendering of the text as given in the Vulgate and elsewhere.

the one man who was a sinner and, having found him in a pathless place, brought him back upon his shoulders. Or the woman, that is to say, the Church of sinners, who had lost one drachma (cf. Lk.15.8–10) and lit a lamp, that is to say, Christ, who is the light of righteousness, and when she found the coin in the dirt, called together her friends and neighbours, which means that the Church rejoiced over one sinner who had been found and, having raised him up from the dirt, placed him among the chief men of his people, that is, with the apostles and prophets (cf. Ps.113.7,8). See what a sinner's repentance can do, when the man who lay in the dirt is found with the chief men! The man I call 'penitent' is the one who groans day and night and redeems his sins by works of mercy; the man I call 'penitent' is the one who beats his breast because he has done wrong and asks the Lord to prevent him from doing again what he has admitted;[9] the man I call 'penitent' is the one who does not rush after his desires and prevents himself from following his own wishes; the man I call 'penitent' is the one who loves what he has previously neglected and forgets what he has done. Let the things that are good stay fast in you, and those that are evil be wiped out. If you do not observe penitence, you will fall into the hands of the Lord and be punished in accordance with his greatness:[10] Depart from evil and do good; seek peace, and pursue it (Ps.34.15); as it is written: I have ceased from evil and sought good things. Produce worthy fruits, then, of your penitence, and you shall not say, 'I have sinned, and what sorrow has come to me!'

4.   Do not add sin to sin, saying, 'God's pity is great', but be sure that pity *and* anger come from him. Turn again to the Lord and beat on your breast, saying: Against thee only have I sinned, and done that which is evil in thy sight (Ps.51.4); Remember not the sins of my youth and of my ignorance, O Lord (Ps.25.7); Hide not thy face from me, and turn not away from thy servant in anger, thou who hast been my help; cast me not off, forsake me not, O God of my salvation (Ps.27.9); Cast me not away from my presence, and take not thy Holy Spirit from me (Ps.51.11). Heal my soul, for I have sinned against thee, and turn my eyes that they see not vanity. Make thy face to shine over thy servant, and make me safe in thy mercy. I have cleaved to thy testimonies, O Lord; do not confound me. Deliver me not into the hands of those who oppress me. Guard me, O Lord, like the pupil of thine eye, protect me under the shadow of thy wings. I have made known my sin to you and have not concealed my acts of unrighteousness. I shall confess to you, O Lord, with all my heart. Lord, hear my prayer, and let my cry come unto thee. Turn not thy face away from me in the day of my tribulation, incline thine ear unto me. On the day when I call upon thee hearken unto me speedily. Make a sign with me for good, so that those who hate me may

---

9   Or, possibly, 'committed (already)'?
10 Pseudo-Ambrose has 'the severity of his judgement', which sounds better and gives better sense.

see it and be confounded. Grant me, O Lord, that I may be refreshed, before I go away and shall be no more.

5.   Behold the repentance of one who humiliates himself; how can one who laments in such terms fail to receive pardon? Who cannot hear him and be moved,[11] for 'every one who exalts himself will be humbled, and he who humbles himself shall be exalted (Lk.14.11)'. Why do you glory in your evil-doing, you whose power is in your unrighteousness (Ps.52.1)? It is better for you not to promise and then to pay than to promise and then not pay (Ec.5.5). You say that you are repentant, and yet delight in fleshly lust. Your sins do not cease to walk abroad, and you say that they are inactive. But to the sinner God has said: What right have you to recite my statutes, or to take my covenant upon your lips? For you hate discipline, and you cast my words behind you. If you see a thief, you are a friend of his; and you keep company with adulterers. You give your mouth free rein for evil, and your tongue frames deceit. You sit and speak against your brother; you slander your own mother's son. These things you have done and I have been silent. You thought unjustly that I would be one like yourself. But now I shall rebuke you and lay the charge before you. Mark this then, you who forgot the Lord, lest I rend and there be none to deliver! He who brings thanksgiving as his sacrifice honours me; to him who orders his way aright I will show the salvation of God (Ps.49.16–23).[12]

6.   Behold what a threat the Lord makes against the sinner. As for you who say and maintain that you are repentant, where is your repentance? It has been shut out by pride and contempt: you have failed to follow God. Listen, my son, and draw back your foot from the world which you have renounced. Repent then of all the pomp of your unrighteousness. Lay hold on the faith which you have previously lost through your desire to give your assent to the devil and darkness, leaving behind you the Lord who is light. Remember, my son, the meaning of this: I desire mercy and not sacrifice (Hos.6.7). The Lord will have mercy upon you, if you do these things when you read them and follow the path of penitence in obedience. Truly, if you do penance with your whole heart, if you have the Lord before your eyes, if you abandon the gluttony of the wine cup and its poison and accept the chalice of salvation, if you meditate on the law of the Lord day and night, if you lavish all your care upon him, then you will rejoice and exult in the Lord, having overcome wickedness. Then you will receive your abundant reward in heaven, because you have laboured in this way in the Lord's work; then the Lord will be your helper in the day of judgement; then you will stand full of confidence at the right hand of the Lord with his saints, and he will say to you: Come, O blessed of my Father, inherit the kingdom prepared for you, the king-

---

11   Again pseudo-Ambrose's Latin reads better: 'Who can hear him and not be moved?'
12   This is RSV's version in full and without alteration; but I do not greatly like it.

dom which my Father who is in heaven has prepared for you (Mt.25.34).[13] But to the unrighteous he will say: Depart from me, you cursed, into the eternal fire which my Father has prepared for the devil and his angels, where their fire will not be quenched, and their worm will not die. Then the righteous will go away into eternal life but the sinners into the eternal fire (ibid.41,46; Mk.9.48).[14]

[13] Another example of carelessness in quotation, and once again pseudo-Ambrose differs from our writer; but this time he misquotes too, giving *perpetuum* for *paratum*.

[14] The quotation is a mixture of Matthew and Mark; 'their worm will not die', which is out of Mark's version, echoes 'when the eternal fire and a worm which will never die await them' in 15,3. But no doubt this is a commonplace in writing of this kind, and the style of that letter is much more attractive than that of this one, which discourages me from suggesting that the author may be the same man as the author of this.

18

To a Professed Virgin[1]

This letter, addressed to a young woman who has taken her vows as a virgin but has recently given some evidence that she is beginning to stray from the strait and narrow path by seeking the company of worldly friends, was originally attributed to Ambrose and by Plinval to Pelagius. Both attributions were clearly wrong: it is a piece of small literary merit and has little else to commend it, being mainly made up of commonplace warnings, repetitions and inaccurate, sometimes irrelevant, quotations. The only grounds for including it in this collection are, first, that it is a typical example of the attitude of contemporary ascetics both to the representatives of that evil world which they themselves have rejected and abandoned and to those who have joined their own ranks only to slip back again into their old, bad habits, and, secondly, that it is therefore in the same category as No.17 in this collection, *To a Lapsed Penitent*. At some points there are clear resemblances between the two letters but this is inevitable when their purposes are identical – to recall the Prodigal Son or the Lost Sheep before it is too late – and there is nothing to suggest that both were the works of the same 'spiritual father'.

We are never actually told what the 'unhappy woman' has done wrong or is accused of having done wrong, which makes the letter even less interesting. The main criticism seems to be that she has begun to keep the wrong kind of company, and she is therefore warned of the dangers to which she is exposing herself and reminded of the virtues which she is putting at risk by venturing back into a world which can only lead to eternal damnation: there is no possibility of compromise with the people or the ways of the world; for the true follower of Christ it is a case of all or nothing, life or death. The letter ends with a blessing – an encouragement which the addressee would surely be in need of by the time she had read it.

Unless especially interested in the aberrations of our Pelagians in quoting from the Bible, the reader is advised to ignore the footnotes here, as they are wholly concerned with such mysteries, of which this letter contains far more than any other in our collection.

---

1   *Epistula ad virginem devotam*; PL 17, 579–84; CPL 747.

Text

1, 1. Listen, my daughter, and consider, and incline your ear; forget your people and your father's house, since the king will desire your beauty. Since he is your Lord God, they too will worship him (Ps.45.10,11).[2] It is to be *his* bride that you have dedicated yourself; you are said to be dedicated to God. What have you to do with the people of this world, and what dealings have you with them? What knowledge do you wish to acquire in their company? Is it the knowledge of how to destroy oneself, which is the kind that they pursue? If you desire chastity, they do not have it; if you seek faith, who among them is a faithful companion for you? And if you seek Christ, he is not among them. I do not know what you are looking for, what kind of friendships and what sort of conversations you can have with them. You have dedicated yourself to the destruction of all the things of this world: how then can you seek a world which you have renounced? You wish to return to your own vomit like a dog or like a sow that has been washed to its wallowing in the mire (cf. 2 Pet.2.22),[3] as it is written in the apostle's words: If I build up again those things which I tore down, then I prove myself a transgressor of the law (Gal.2.18). And this same idea is found again in the following words: All that is in the world is the lust of the flesh and the lust of the eyes and is not of the Father but of this world (1 Jn.2.16).[4] And elsewhere it is said again: Whosoever wishes to be a friend of this world will become an enemy of God (Jas.4.4). What have you to say, you who who have been dedicated to God? Why do you want to please men? What do you wish for? What are you seeking? If you seek God, he is with you; but if you seek man, this is not what you dedicated yourself to.

2. What are men? They are men of this world: And the world passes away, and the lust of it; but he who does the things that are written abides for ever (1 Jn.2.17).[5] I do not know what you want. If it is gold or silver, if it is life or splendid clothes, then this is not what enabled you to find favour with God, this is not what God admires but it is 'a broken and a contrite heart (Ps.51.17).' Why do you seek the men of this world, on whom the holy apostle Paul delivers judgement, saying: Whose god is their belly, and they glory in their shame, with minds set on earthly things. But our commonwealth is in heaven (Phil.3.19,20).

---

[2] The Vulgate has the same text as does LXX but the Hebrew version has the imperative instead of the future indicative (third plural), and most translators translate as either 'bow to him' (RSV) or 'worship (thou) him' (AV). The Roman edition of this letter has transferred 'the daughters of Tyre' at the beginning of the next verse to the last clause in this one, giving 'and the daughters of Tyre shall worship him'.

[3] Cf. *Life*,13,4 with special reference to sinning after baptism.

[4] Our writer omits 'and the pride of life' after 'eyes'; he also inserts 'and' after the first 'world'.

[5] 'The things that are written' takes the place of 'the will of God' in the established text; the reader can already see that this man is quoting from memory.

If we have a commonwealth in heaven, we ought to seek the things that are above, where Christ is, not the things that are on earth (Col.3.1,2).[6] I ask you, my sister, who are the men of this world? It is not men who are your spiritual brothers that you are following, you are following men of the flesh, and if they are not satisfied, they will grumble. You have cast your pearls before swine, who will trample them under foot and turn to attack you (Mt.7.6). Have you not heard the words: Look out for the dogs, look out for the evil-workers (Phil.3.2)? The men of this world are those who do not follow in Christ's footsteps. I ask you, what do they reveal to you? Tell me, is it chastity, which they do not have? Well, is it faith, which they do not discover? Or teaching, which they do not follow either, unless it be the devilish wisdom of this world? Or fasting, which they hate? Or abstinence, which they condemn? Or humility, which they oppress? Or sobriety, which they neglect? Or an honest mind, unless by that we mean a false and deceitful one? Or modesty, which they cast from them? I do not know what it is that you want to pursue in their company.

2, 1. But what is it that you say? 'I am bringing them over to my side.' But if they come over to your side, it is of no profit to you. What does the wolf seek with the lamb? Or what does a dog seek except bread? Why does a lion growl except for his prey (cf. Is.31.4)? Keep yourself chaste, if you can. What is it that you wish to learn which you are not doing already yourself? As the apostle says: Do not believe every spirit but test the spirits to see whether they are of God (1 Jn.4.1). And if you accept *their* teaching, they will teach you what *they* are doing and what *they* are following – concupiscence, fornication, lust, greed, cheating, uncleanness, immodesty, extravagance, drunkenness, dishonesty, obscene speech, foolishness, crimes, anger, quarrelling, and every kind of evil. What have you to say, unhappy one, or what excuse do you give? You have dedicated your soul, so that you might withdraw from these kinds of men; but what are you looking for now? I ask you not to become confused when they make up stories about you for their own use, saying, 'Look at this woman dedicated to God, who is following us; for she has abandoned her own path and strayed over the boundaries of her land and has failed to find the way back to her own residence. Come, let us take her over and lead her to our way.' Unhappy girl, you have fallen upon the broad and spacious way that leads to death! The way that is evil seems to you to be good: you follow them in your madness and without realizing that you are falling straight into their trap. Do you not remember that the way that leads to life is strait and narrow (cf. Mt.7.14)? The way that is good appears to you to be laborious; have you forgotten that it was said that: Through many

6 RSV and Vulgate have 'If then you have been raised with Christ'; our writer either deliberately or by a slip of the memory has repeated 'commonwealth' from the previous quotation – I would prefer 'place of residence' to RSV's 'commonwealth' myself. He has also omitted 'seated at the right hand of God. Set your minds on things that are above,' between 'Christ is' and 'not the things'.

tribulations we must enter the kingdom of heaven (Acts 14.22)? But now your wish is to follow your own will; have you not read Solomon's words: From the beginning good things were created for good people, just as evil things were for sinners (Sir.39.25). And again, in the same man's words: The beginning of man's life will be worked out spiritually (ibid.26?). And again: The spiritual man judges all things, but is himself judged by no one (1 Cor.2.15).

2.   What do you seek with them? What has a believer in common with an unbeliever (2 Cor.6.15)? Or what does a holy person have to do with the flesh? You can be a virgin in body but not with a corrupt mind. Your eyes have been blinded by the great heat and passion of the flesh, because they have a beam lying within them; your ears are filled with all the dirt that is associated with men; your feet are swift and not slow to make their way to the door that leads to the outside world. Where is your sense of holiness? Where your modesty, sobriety, seriousness, chastity, moderation, faith, continence, pureness of mind? Where are all those qualities in front of which you had placed the faith which you lost? It would have been better that you should not have vowed and acted than that you should have vowed and not acted (Ec.5.5).[7] You cannot serve two masters, God and mammon (Mt.6.24); with the crooked you show yourself perverse (Ps.18.26); it is not possible to join an old piece of cloth with a new, for it takes away its strength, and a worse tear is made (Mt.9.16).[8] The birds that fly join with those which are like them, and truth will return to those who practise it. Far be it that you should be said to be my sister, when you mix with such people! Either make the tree good and its fruit good, or make the tree bad and its fruit bad, for every tree is known by its fruit (Mt.12.33); and a man clings to one like himself (Sir.13.16). A dove released from a man's hand immediately returned to him to the Ark (cf. Gen.8.8,9); but a crow sent out followed the flesh, which is what you wish to follow too, so that you do not return to Christ's door. You behave like the beasts of the field and the birds in the heaven: like the crow, you do not remember the Lord, who freed you from the flood; you do not seek your own shaded and comfortable bed, where you have enjoyed a temporary rest. You do not keep the storm before your eyes; you have forgotten Christ's love and cling to the love of the people of this world instead, people who have no love in them except that of the devil; they seek another's meat and do not cease to do so until they die. Leave these men, unhappy one, lest they eat your chosen meat, and strip off the bones that belong to you, and you are left naked and deprived of what is yours as in a cucumber-field.[9]

---

7   Here we have the Latin *facere* ('do', 'act') for the Vulgate's *reddere* ('pay', 'render'); the complete version of the sentence in the Vulgate is 'It is much better not to vow than not to pay what you have promised after vowing'. Another lapse of memory?

8   RSV: 'And no one puts a piece of unshrunk cloth on an old garment, for the patch tears away from the garment, and a worse tear is made.'

9   After the cucumbers have been picked, I imagine; but I am no horticulturalist. The use of *caro* ('flesh' and 'meat') is difficult here; I have translated it as 'meat' in this context but I accept that it may be a *double entendre* – if the writer is capable of such subtlety.

3. Now what will you do, when you are naked and deprived? You will go to
your neighbours, whom you formerly hated, asking them for a covering for your
shame; but they refuse to give it to you, saying, 'Where are your splendid clothes
which you used to wear before?' What do you say in reply to the woman whom
the cold has caught in its grasp? They rejoice at the misfortunes which have
come to you. Then you will beat your breast and say, 'Unhappy am I, to whom
such a fate has come! What profit did that captivity which made me a prisoner,
wretched and unhappy, bring to me? Whither shall I go from thy Spirit? Or
whither shall I flee from thy presence? If I ascend to heaven, thou art there! If I
descend into hell, thou art present! If I take my wings in the morning and dwell
in the uttermost parts of the sun, even there thy hand shall lead me, and thy right
hand shall hold me (Ps.139.7–10).' Then you will say, 'I will go and return to my
first husband, for it was better then than now (Hos.2.7); it was he who used to
give me my clothing and my oil when it was meet to do so. But now what am I to
do?' Then you return weeping to your own house, from which you had gone out
rejoicing. You will sit in a corner in your house mournful and sad, lamenting day
and night, seeking someone to join you in your sorrow but there will be no one,
and people to console you but you will find none. And those whom you hated
before will give you alms, and they will shake their heads over you, saying, 'Look,
here is the woman who was dedicated to God but has now become like dung
upon the road and like a State which is overcome. Where is her chastity? Where
are all those things which followed her? They have deserted her, because chastity
was their leader, and she has lost her chastity, and so they have all fled.'

4. Now what will you do, unhappy one? Where are those whom you followed after? Let them redeem you, if they can. But what can you give in exchange for your soul, which you disposed of deceitfully by your disobedience, in
that you did not listen to your brothers and sisters when they remonstrated with
you not to join yourself to men of this world? What can we do for you now, what
can we say to you, we whom you refused to listen to, unless it be to lament over
you and to say, 'Spare her, O Lord, spare her.' And perhaps he will see fit to listen
to our weeping and wailing and to give you the inclination to turn to him once
again, reminding you of your sins with these words: How many of my father's
hired servants have bread enough and to spare, but I perish here of hunger! I will
arise therefore and go to my father, and I will say to him, 'Father, I have sinned
against heaven and before you; I am no longer worthy to be called your daughter;
treat me as one of your handmaidens, that I may live (Lk.15.17–19).'[10] What if
he should perchance kill that fatted calf for you? For I am filled with zeal for you:
I betrothed you to Christ to present you as a pure bride to her one husband. Now
I am afraid that as the serpent deceived Eve by his cunning, your thoughts will be
led astray and be deprived of the love which is in Christ Jesus (2 Cor.11.2,3).

---

[10] Here he is being unnecessarily subtle when he changes masculines into feminines in
the quotation to suit his addressee: the verses quoted are not meant to be spoken by her
but by her Lord.

3, 1. Pay attention then and beware of men of that kind, so that you may be called my sister and my lady. Go into your room and close the door and pray to your Father (Mt.6.6) to give you a sound mind and understanding, so that you may know whom you ought to follow and whom to avoid; for there are many who pretend that they are what they are not, but they lie, and you do not realize that it is your soul that is at stake. Do not let them lead you away captive like an ox which is led to the slaughter or a dog to be tethered. Do not hasten like a bird into a snare. Listen to me: direct your feet away from them, sit industriously in your home, employ your hands in doing what is good, so that you may have the wherewithal to share with those who support you. Pray without ceasing and do not be too ready to appear in the streets.[11] Fight the good fight, run more quickly, and strive to make your own that in which Christ has made you his own (cf.Phil.3.12). Let men hear you and rejoice in your good purpose and in the intention with which you live: Give alms, and behold, everything will be clean for you (Lk.11.41). Do not let it irk you to visit the sick, for by them you will be strengthened in love. You shall not swear at all neither in truth nor lying: but let what you say be 'Yes' or 'No', for anything more than this comes from evil (Mt.5.34,37).[12] Be angry and do not sin (Eph.4.26) with men who do evil by finding excuses when sinning.[13] Humble yourself, my daughter, before the Lord, for God opposes the proud but gives grace to the humble (1 Pet.5.5,6; Jas.4.6). Come to him that he may make your radiant, and you will not be ashamed in his sight (cf. Ps.34.5). Leave behind you the pleasures of this world and clothe yourself with the constancy of virtue. Set aside the clothing of this world and put on the tunic of everlasting life. Abandon the fare of this world and receive the holy nourishment of the saints.[14]

2. Remember how Shadrach, Meshach, Abednego and Daniel refused the meat and wine of the gentiles and accepted only vegetables and beans (cf. Dan.1.8–16). Remember how the Maccabean woman suffered because of swine's flesh and her sons were fried and boiled in oil (cf. 2 Macc.7.1–5). Walk, my daughter, with a holy bearing, modest, sober and serious. Cast off lies, speak the truth with your neighbour. Pray, my daughter, without ceasing; fast often and give alms, since charity delivers from death and keeps you from entering the darkness (Tob.4.11). The giving of alms is a good gift which cleanses all dirt and filth. You will be blessed if you do all these things when you read them. Be zealous for what is good, so that you may forget what is evil. May the Father and the Son and the Holy Spirit bless you with the blessing with which he saw fit to bless our fathers, Abraham, Isaac and Jacob. Pray for me, my daughter, because I am concerned for you, as it is written: Pray for one another (Jas.5.16); likewise, 'a

---

[11] Cf. Dem.22,2.

[12] 'In truth' and 'in lying' replace 'by heaven' and 'by earth' presumably.

[13] Another eccentric quotation: 'Be angry and do not sin' is Eph.4.26 but I cannot trace the rest of the sentence; perhaps it is not meant to be a part of the quotation.

[14] Our text in PL 17 gives 'the holy things of the saints', whereas the Roman edition has 'the food of the saints'; I have compromised.

brother that helps his brother shall be exalted."[15] The Lord will exalt you to holiness and love, as it is written: He who loves his neighbour has fulfilled the law (Rom.13.8). May the Lord fulfil all your petitions (Ps.20.5)! May God the Father grant you this through Jesus Christ, his son, our Lord and God, our King, Judge, Saviour and Redeemer, who was blessed with the Holy Spirit for ever and ever, Amen.

---

[15] I cannot find this 'quotation'. It is sometimes difficult to tell whether our author is quoting or paraphrasing.

Select Bibliography

The following list of publications includes only those which I have had occasion to consult in writing this book or to refer to in my Introduction and footnotes together with a few others which readers may find useful. A fuller bibliography on the Pelagian controversy will be found in my Pelagius: a Reluctant Heretic, 151–67, and a comprehensive one in Nuvolone and Solignac, 2936–42.

1. Books

Barrow, R.H., Introduction to St.Augustine, The City of God, London, 1950

Bohlin, T., Die Theologie des Pelagius und ihre Genesis, Uppsala/Wiesbaden, 1957

Bonner, G., St. Augustine of Hippo: Life and Controversies, London, 1963, repr. Norwich, 1986

————, Augustine and Modern Research on Pelagianism, Villanova, 1972

Brown, P.R.L., Augustine of Hippo: a Biography, London, 1967

————, Religion and Society in the Age of St. Augustine, London, 1972

————, The Body and Society, New York, 1988/London, 1989

Caspari, C.P., Briefe, Abhandlungen und Predigten, Brussels, 1964

Chadwick, H., The Sentences of Sextus, Cambridge, 1959

————, Augustine, Oxford, 1986

Chadwick, N.K., Poetry and Letters in Early Christian Gaul, London, 1955

Chadwick, O., John Cassian², Cambridge, 1968

Courcelle, P., Les Confessions de Saint Augustine dans la tradition littéraire, antécédents et postérité, Paris, 1963

Evans, R.F., Four Letters of Pelagius, London, 1968

————, Pelagius: Inquiries and Reappraisals, 1968(a)

Ferguson, J., Pelagius: a Historical and Theological Study, Cambridge, 1956, repr. New York, 1978

Frend, W.H.C., Saints and Sinners in the Early Church, London, 1985

Greshake, G. and Gcerlings,W., Quellen geistlichen Lebens: Die Zeit der Väter, Mayence, 1980

Haslehurst, R.S.T., The Works of Fastidius, London, 1927

Kelly, J.N.D., Jerome: His Life, Writings and Controversies, London, 1975

Kirmer, I., Das Eigentum des Fastidius im pelagianischen Schriftum, St. Ottilien Oberbayern, 1937

Lapidge, M. and Sharpe, R., A Bibliography of Celtic Latin Literature 400–1200, Dublin, 1985

Long, A.A., Hellenistic Philosophy, London, 1974

Plinval, G. de, Pélage, ses écrits, sa vie et son reforme, Lausanne, 1943

————, Essai sur le style et la langue de Pélage, Fribourg, 1947

Rees, B.R., Pelagius: a Reluctant Heretic, Woodbridge, 1988

Souter, A., Pelagius's Expositions of the Thirteen Epistles of St. Paul, Cambridge, 1922/31

Sparrow-Simpson, W.J., The Letters of St. Augustine, London, 1919

Thomas, A.C., Christianity in Roman Britain to A.D. 500, London, 1981

Thompson, E.A., St. Germanus of Auxerre and the End of Roman Britain, Woodbridge, 1984

Zimmer, H., Pelagius in Irland, Berlin, 1901

2. Articles, Lexica, etc.

Arndt, W.F. and Gingrich, F.W., edd., A Greek-English Lexicon of the New Testament[4], Chicago, Illinois/Cambridge, 1952

Barnard, L.W., 'Pelagius and early Syriac Christianity', Recherches de théologie ancienne et mediévale 35, 1968, 193–6

Bonner, G., 'How Pelagian was Pelagius?', Studia Patristica 9, 1966,350–8

————, 'Rufinus of Syria and African Pelagianism', Augustinian Studies 1, 1970, 31–47

Bury, J.B., 'The Origins of Pelagius', Hermathena 13, 1904, 26–35

Cameron, A., 'Celestial consulates: a note on the Pelagian letter Humanae referunt', Journal of Theological Studies n.s. 19,1968, 213–15

Duval, Y.-M., 'Pélage est-il le censeur inconnu de l'Adversus Iovinianum à Rome en 393?', Revue d'histoire ecclesiastique 75, 1980, 525–57

Evans, R.F., 'Pelagius, Fastidius and the Pseudo-Augustinian De Vita Christiana', Journal of Theological Studies n.s. 13,1962,72–98

————, 'Pelagius's Veracity at the Synod of Diospolis' in J. Sommerfeld, ed., Studies in Medieval Culture, Kalamazoo, Mich., 1964, 21–30

Lampe, G.W.H., ed., A Patristic Lexicon, Oxford, 1961–68

Liebeschuetz, W., 'Did the Pelagian Movement have social aims?', Historia 12, 1963, 227–41

————, 'Pelagian evidence on the last period of Roman Britain', Latomus 26, 1967,436–47

Livingstone, E.A., ed., The Concise Oxford Dictionary of the Christian Church, corr.repr., Oxford, 1980

Lucas, J.R., 'Pelagius and St. Augustine', Journal of Theological Studies n.s.22, 1971,73–85

Markus, R.A., 'Pelagianism: Britain and the Continent', Journal of Ecclesiastical History 37, 2, 1986, 191–204

Marrou, H.I., 'Les attaches orientales du pélagianisme', Comptes rendus de l'Académie des Inscriptions et Belles Lettres 1969,459–72

Morin, G., 'Le De Vita Christiana de l'évêque breton Fastidius et le livre de Pélage Ad Viduam', Revue Bénedictine 15, 1898, 481–93

————, 'Pélage ou Fastidius?', Revue d'histoire ecclesiastique 5, 1904, 258–64

————, 'Fastidius ad Fatalem', Revue Bénedictine 46, 1934, 3–17

Morris, J.R., 'Pelagian Literature', Journal of Theological Studies n.s.16, 1965, 26–60

Myres, J.N.L., 'Pelagius and the end of Roman rule in Britain', Journal of Roman Studies 50, 1960, 21–36

Nuvolone, F.G. and Solignac, A., 'Pélage et pélagianisme', Dictionnaire de spiritualité, ascetique, mystique, doctrine et histoire, 12B, 1986, 2889–942

Phipps, W.W., 'The Heresiarch: Pelagius or Augustine?', Anglican Theological Review 62, 1980, 124–33

Plinval, G. de, 'Recherches sur l'oeuvre littéraire de Pélage', Revue de Philologie 60, 1934, 9–42

Sell, A.P.F., 'Augustine versus Pelagius', Calvin Theological Journal 12, 1977, 117–43

Smith, A.J., 'Pelagius and Augustine', Journal of Theological Studies 31, 1929/30, 21–35

Souter, A., 'Pelagius' doctrine in relation to his early life', Expositor 1, 1915, 180–2

Teselle, E., 'Rufinus the Syrian, Caelestius, Pelagius: explorations in the prehistory of the Pelagian controversy', Augustinian Studies 3, 1972, 61–95

Winterbottom, M. 'Pelagiana', Journal of Theological Studies n.s. 38, 1987, 106–19

Wright, D.F., 'Pelagius the twice-born', The Churchman 82, 1972, 6–15

3. Original Texts

(a) These can be found in:
- CSEL Corpus Scriptorum Ecclesiasticorum Latinorum
- PL Patrologia Latina
- PLS Patrologiae Latinae Supplementum

(b) There is a register of them in:
- CPL Clavis Patrum Latinorum

Index of Biblical Citations

Lightning Source UK Ltd.
Milton Keynes UK
UKOW05f0840020317
295703UK00001B/6/P